HANDBOOK OF WISE INTERVENTIONS

Handbook of
Wise Interventions

HOW SOCIAL PSYCHOLOGY
CAN HELP PEOPLE CHANGE

edited by
Gregory M. Walton
Alia J. Crum

THE GUILFORD PRESS
New York   London

Library of Congress Cataloging-in-Publication Data

Names: Walton, Gregory M. (Gregory Mariotti), editor. | Crum, Alia, editor.
Title: Handbook of wise interventions : how social psychology can help people change / editors, Gregory M. Walton, Alia J. Crum.
Description: New York : The Guilford Press, [2021] | Includes bibliographical references and index.
Identifiers: LCCN 2020030933 | ISBN 9781462543830 (hardcover ; alk. paper)
Subjects: LCSH: Social psychology. | Social problems. | Operant behavior. | Change (Psychology) | Psychology, Applied.
Classification: LCC HM1033 .H3727 2020 | DDC 302—dc23
LC record available at *https://lccn.loc.gov/2020030933*

About the Editors

Gregory M. Walton, PhD, is Associate Professor of Psychology and the Michael Forman University Fellow in Undergraduate Education at Stanford University. His research focuses on how basic social-psychological processes contribute to major social problems, such as how negative stereotypes and stigma change school settings for minority group members in ways that can undermine these students' feelings of belonging and achievement. Dr. Walton develops novel psychological interventions to address these processes, including to increase student motivation, improve academic achievement, and reduce achievement gaps between groups. He is a recipient of many awards for his research, including the Cialdini Prize and the Wegner Theoretical Innovation Prize from the Society for Personality and Social Psychology.

Alia J. Crum, PhD, is Assistant Professor of Psychology at Stanford University and Primary Investigator of the Stanford Mind and Body Lab. Her research focuses on mindsets; how they affect important outcomes in such domains as exercise, diet, and stress; and how they can be consciously and deliberately changed through intervention to increase physiological and psychological well-being. Dr. Crum is a recipient of awards including the Director's New Innovator Award from the National Institutes of Health and the Rising Star Award from the Association for Psychological Science. She has worked as a clinical psychologist for the VA health care system and has developed interventions focused on mindset change for organizations, including LinkedIn, UBS, Stanford Health Care, and the U.S. Navy.

Contributors

Shannon T. Brady,PhD, Department of Psychology, Wake Forest University, Winston-Salem, North Carolina

Christopher J. Bryan, PhD, McCombs School of Business, University of Texas at Austin, Austin, Texas

Patricia Chen, PhD, Department of Psychology, National University of Singapore, Singapore

Robert B. Cialdini, PhD, Department of Psychology, Arizona State University, Tempe, Arizona

Geoffrey L. Cohen, PhD, Department of Psychology, Graduate School of Education, and (by courtesy) Graduate School of Business, Stanford University, Stanford, California

Alia J. Crum, PhD, Department of Psychology, Stanford University, Stanford, California

Mesmin Destin, PhD, Department of Psychology, School of Education and Social Policy, Institute for Policy Research, Northwestern University, Chicago, Illinois

Carol S. Dweck, PhD, Department of Psychology, Stanford University, Stanford, California

Amit Goldenberg, PhD, Negotiation, Organizations and Markets Unit, Harvard Business School, Boston, Massachusetts

Noah J. Goldstein, PhD, Anderson School of Management, University of California, Los Angeles, Los Angeles, California

James J. Gross, PhD, Department of Psychology, Stanford University, Stanford, California

Eran Halperin, PhD, Department of Psychology, Hebrew University of Jerusalem, Jerusalem, Israel

MarYam G. Hamedani, PhD, Center for Social Psychological Answers to Real World Questions, Stanford University, Stanford, California

Isaac J. Handley-Miner, BA, Department of Psychology, Boston College,
Chestnut Hill, Massachusetts

Emily J. Hangen, PhD, Department of Psychology, Harvard University,
Cambridge, Massachusetts

Judith M. Harackiewicz, PhD, Department of Psychology, University of Wisconsin–
Madison, Madison, Wisconsin

Ivan A. Hernandez, MS, Department of Psychology, Northwestern University,
Chicago, Illinois

Chris S. Hulleman, PhD, Curry School of Education and Frank Batten School of Leadership
and Public Policy, University of Virginia, Charlottesville, Virginia

Jeremy P. Jamieson, PhD, Department of Psychology, University of Rochester,
Rochester, New York

Kristin Layous, PhD, Department of Psychology, California State University, East Bay,
Hayward, California

Hae Yeon Lee, PhD, Department of Psychology, Stanford University, Stanford, California

Mohini Lokhande, DPhil, Expert Council of German Foundations on Integration
and Migration, Berlin, Germany

Laura B. Luchies, PhD, Center for Social Research, Calvin University,
Grand Rapids, Michigan

Denise C. Marigold, PhD, Social Development Studies, Renison University College
at the University of Waterloo, Waterloo, Ontario, Canada

Tim Müller, DPhil, Berlin Institute for Integration and Migration Research,
Humboldt University, Berlin, Germany

Jessica M. Nolan, PhD, Department of Psychology, University of Scranton,
Scranton, Pennsylvania

Jason Anthony Okonofua, PhD, Department of Psychology, University of California,
Berkeley, Berkeley, California

Michael Ruiz, BA, Department of Psychology, University of California, Berkeley,
Berkeley, California

P. Wesley Schultz, PhD, Department of Psychology, California State University San Marcos,
San Marcos, California

David K. Sherman, PhD, Department of Psychological and Brain Sciences, University
of California, Santa Barbara, Santa Barbara, California

Erica B. Slotter, PhD, Department of Psychology, Villanova University,
Villanova, Pennsylvania

Eric N. Smith, PhD, Department of Psychology, University of Texas at Austin, Austin, Texas

Gregg Sparkman, PhD, Andlinger Center for Energy and the Environment,
Princeton University, Princeton, New Jersey

Nicole M. Stephens, PhD, Kellogg School of Management, Northwestern University, Evanston, Illinois

Sarah S. M. Townsend, PhD, Marshall School of Business, University of Southern California, Los Angeles, California

Bradley P. Turnwald, PhD, Department of Psychology, Stanford University, Stanford, California

Gregory M. Walton, PhD, Department of Psychology, Stanford University, Stanford, California

David S. Yeager, PhD, Department of Psychology, University of Texas at Austin, Austin, Texas

Contents

PART II. **Health and Well-Being**

PART III. **Conflict and Relationships**

PART IV. Sustainability

Introduction

Gregory M. Walton and Alia J. Crum

The interventions shared in this volume address some of the hardest problems we face in our personal lives and as a society. Long-standing educational inequalities lead to lost potential, social conflict, and worse health and economic prospects. Too many people are unhappy in their marriages and stressed in their jobs. Rates of obesity, diabetes, and cardiovascular disease continue to creep upward, but even simple remedies, like motivating healthy eating, remain notoriously difficult. Conflicts between cultures and groups appear intractable. Climate change is upon us, yet reversing widely practiced unsustainable behaviors can feel like a lost cause.

You might wonder: What in the world are such diverse problems all doing in the same book? The answer is that we can make progress on each using a "psychologically wise" intervention (Walton & Wilson, 2018). Each chapter describes the everyday *interpretations* that feed into a problem and, in turn, shows how helping people to new ways of thinking that are authentic, appropriate, and adaptive for their context can make a difference, sometimes profound.

The "wise intervention" approach is distinct from other traditions and social reforms because it does not rely on improving the objective qualities of situations, such as to hire more tutors or to rearrange a cafeteria to make healthy options more accessible, or of people, such as to increase students' IQ. Instead, the power of wise interventions comes from the rich intersection between psychological interpretations and the contexts in which they arise. Wise interventions recognize that how we make sense of ourselves, other people, and our circumstances does not exist in a vacuum but is a product of the cultural and social contexts in which we live. They then rely on a simple observation: that altering a maladaptive or pejorative interpretation, especially at a key time or in an important context, can change how a person engages with the contexts and settings they inhabit.

An enormous benefit of this approach is that, in the right circumstances, an initial change in interpretation can become self-confirming. Then, even a brief exercise can transform people's lives. For example, the intervention discussed by Slotter and Luchies (Chapter 16) used three 7-minute exercises to help couples take a third-party perspective on conflict in their marriage. This strengthened marital relationships over a year. Walton and Brady (Chapter 2) discuss a social-belonging intervention, delivered in an hour-long session in the first year of college. It improved grades over 3 years and life and career satisfaction 7–11 years later.

How is that possible? How do these interventions work? What do they tell us about people and social problems and efforts at reform?

To showcase this work, we invited the leading researchers who originally developed diverse wise interventions to share their work. We gave each author a detailed 12-point outline and asked them to address specific questions in a common order. Some chapters present well-established interventions. For example, values affirmation (Sherman, Lokhande, Müller, & Cohen, Chapter 3) and social norms interventions (Nolan, Schultz, Cialdini, & Goldstein, Chapter 18) have been tested and replicated in numerous contexts for more than a decade. Others share hot-off-the-press approaches that have only recently been tested in real-world situations (e.g., Sparkman's dynamic-norm approach, Chapter 19; Turnwald & Crum's taste-focused labeling intervention, Chapter 12).

The 12 questions we asked authors are ones we believe are important for any intervention to address—even (especially) if the answers are still being worked out. They are as follows:

First, we asked for *background*: "What is the intellectual history, research tradition, and theorizing from which the intervention draws?" For instance, Sherman and colleagues (Chapter 3) describe basic research on people's need for self-integrity, the need to see oneself as adequate, moral, and competent; how defensiveness and poor functioning can result when this need is threatened; and how this insight led to value-affirmation interventions that bolster a sense of self-integrity to help students who face negative stereotypes in school perform better, shrinking inequalities.

Second, we asked about *psychological process*: "Describe how past studies shed light on a critical psychological process—the subjective meanings the intervention will aim to affect." Wise interventions address an array of fundamental interpretations:

- *Is something good or bad?* Are stress and arousal helpful or harmful (Crum, Handley-Miner, & Smith, Chapter 9; Jamieson & Hangen, Chapter 10)? Are vegetable dishes appealing or unappealing (Turnwald & Crum, Chapter 12)?
- *Can things change?* Can challenges improve or are they fixed and permanent, such as academic struggles (Dweck & Yeager, Chapter 1), feelings of nonbelonging in school (Stephens, Hamedani, & Townsend, Chapter 5; Walton & Brady, Chapter 2), experiences of bullying (Yeager & Lee, Chapter 13), or groups in conflict (Goldenberg, Gross, & Halperin, Chapter 15)?
- *Who am I and what can I become?* Am I a good and decent person (Sherman et al., Chapter 3)? What are my values and how can they be expressed in my behavior (Bryan, Chapter 11)? Is schoolwork useful to me and relevant in my life (Hulleman & Harackiewicz, Chapter 4)? How can I act efficiently to achieve my goals (Chen, Chapter 7)? What am I grateful for (Layous, Chapter 8)? What kind of person could I become if I work hard in school (Destin & Hernandez, Chapter 6)?
- *How should I understand people and relationships?* When my partner compliments me, does that mean he or she loves me (Marigold, Chapter 17)? How should

I interpret conflicts with a spouse (Slotter & Luchies, Chapter 16) or a student who misbehaves in class (Okonofua & Ruiz, Chapter 14)? Can bullies change, or will I always be a victim (Yeager & Lee, Chapter 13)? Can my relationship with a place improve (Stephens et al., Chapter 5; Walton & Brady, Chapter 2)?

Third, we asked about *evidence*: "What is the evidence of the effectiveness of the intervention in improving personally and/or socially important outcomes?" Each chapter presents evidence from at least one randomized controlled trial that shows how an intervention can improve important outcomes in a real-world setting, such as reducing suspensions for middle school students (Okonofua & Ruiz, Chapter 14), improving attitudes and behavior between Israelis and Palestinians (Goldenberg et al., Chapter 15), increasing healthy eating (Bryan, Chapter 11; Turnwald & Crum, Chapter 12), or raising academic performance over time (Dweck & Yeager, Chapter 1; Walton & Brady, Chapter 2; Sherman et al., Chapter 3; Stephens et al., Chapter 5; Destin & Hernandez, Chapter 6; Chen, Chapter 7; Jamieson & Hangen, Chapter 10; Yeager & Lee, Chapter 13).

Fourth, we asked about *mechanisms*: "Describe evidence for how the intervention achieves these effects." For instance, Crum and colleagues (Chapter 9) show how an intervention that represents stress as enhancing (as opposed to debilitating) can improve health and work performance by changing what people pay attention to, what emotions they experience, what they are motivated to do, and what their bodies are prepared to do, as evidenced by their physiology.

Fifth, we asked about *effects over time*: "Does the intervention produce lasting benefits? Why, how, and when?" For instance, Walton and Brady (Chapter 2) show that the social-belonging intervention improves school performance and life success over years by helping students engage more in the school social community (e.g., e-mailing professors, joining student groups) in ways that build peer and mentor relationships of lasting benefit.

Sixth, we asked about *heterogeneity*: "In what kinds of social contexts and with whom is the intervention more and less likely to be effective and why?" For instance, Dweck and Yeager (Chapter 1) discuss how growth mindset of intelligence interventions are more effective in high schools where peer norms support growth-oriented behaviors—and less effective in schools where acting on a growth mindset might be uncool. Value-affirmation interventions are more effective with people whose identities are under threat in a context, such as negatively stereotyped racial-minority students, but less effective for people not under threat (Sherman et al., Chapter 3).

Seventh, we asked about *cousins*: "What other interventions is this intervention most closely related to? How is it similar and how is it different?" For instance, Jamieson and Hangen (Chapter 10) and Crum and colleagues (Chapter 9) both aim to help people see stress as an asset and not a negative. But they use distinct approaches that make one more suitable for motivated performance contexts and the other for cases where the specific stressor is not easily identified or is more chronic and diffuse.

Eighth, we asked about *content and implementation*: "Describe the intervention content or exercise in concrete terms and provide specific examples. Consider including and annotating specific intervention materials." Many chapters provide detailed resources for implementing the intervention. For instance, Turnwald and Crum (Chapter 12) share a toolkit that teaches practitioners how to label foods more indulgently (*https://sparqtools.org/edgyveggies*). Walton and Brady (Chapter 2) include annotated materials and share reflections from practitioners who implemented the social-belonging intervention at diverse institutions through the College Transition Collaborative at Stanford University.

Ninth, we asked about *nuances and misconceptions*: "What are one to two nuances people might miss about the intervention that are critical to its effectiveness? What do these nuances tell us about the nature of the intervention and the psychological process it targets?" Stephens and colleagues (Chapter 5) caution against ways a different education intervention could be misunderstood or misused to perpetuate stereotypes.

Tenth, we asked about *implications for practice*: "Discuss how this intervention can be implemented effectively in field settings to make a difference for people's lives and/ or institutional goals." For instance, Turnwald and Crum's (Chapter 12) taste-focused labeling approach flies in the face of the typical strategy for promoting healthy foods— highlighting their healthy attributes—which can inadvertently make them *less* appealing.

Eleventh, we asked about *implications for theory*: "What does this intervention tell us about who we are, about people, and psychological processes? What does this intervention tell us about a given social problem?" Sparkman's (Chapter 19) dynamic norms approach shows that people conform to salient *change* in norms, even when this behavior would violate current norms—that is, to behaviors that are not yet but are becoming normative. And Yeager and Lee's (Chapter 13) intervention to teach students an incremental theory of personality highlights the important role played by implicit perceptions of fixedness ("I'll always be a victim; you'll always be a bully") in retaliatory processes that contribute to school bullying.

Twelfth, we asked about *future directions*: "What are the high-priority next steps for this intervention for research?" Many of our authors offer suggestions for testing particular theoretical questions, including for scaling interventions and for moving to new contexts. For instance, Destin and Hernandez (Chapter 6) discuss how their pathways intervention could be extended to peers and teachers to instill systemic change.

While all sections of each chapter will be of value to readers, some may be more relevant for some readers than others. If you are a practitioner looking for a solution in a specific area, you may be most interested in the "Content and Implementation" section, which provides direction for applying a particular intervention; but we also encourage you to be mindful of the "Nuances and Misconceptions," as well as the "Heterogeneity" sections, which will help you apply the intervention skillfully and thoughtfully and avoid misunderstandings. If you are a social psychologist conducting similar research, you might be particularly interested in the "Psychological Process," "Mechanisms," and "Effects over Time" sections. We encourage all readers to compare and contrast across chapters, as noting the similarities and differences across approaches will help engender a deeper and more integrated understanding of what wise interventions are, how they work, and how they move outcomes that matter.

How are the chapters organized? Somewhat artificially, by the primary outcome of interest investigated in a line of research to date. However, important outcomes are often deeply interrelated, as are academic motivation and achievement, health, well-being, and personal relationships. Thus, many powerful psychological interventions affect multiple kinds of outcomes, or could do so as explored in future work, even as a primary focus has been in one area to date.

Together, these interventions illustrate the truth that every social problem is, in part, a psychological problem (Walton & Dweck, 2009). Yet no social problem is only a psychological problem. Nor are wise interventions a silver bullet. The problems we face are beastly, complex, and stubborn. And beastly, complex, and stubborn problems require solutions from all angles, including a careful consideration of resources, incentives, nudges, and the capacities of individuals for change. Wise interventions offer an additional tool.

In some ways, this volume represents a back to the future for social psychology. The field was forged out of the need in the mid-20th-century to understand the intergroup animosities and conflicts that defined World War II. Then followed a "cognitive revolution" and an intense focus on controlled laboratory experimentation and deep understanding of psychological processes. As the new century dawned, researchers began to fuse these methodological and theoretical insights with a renewed commitment to real-world, ecologically valid contexts—a focus that has since exploded. It's back to the future, but with a new level of empirical sophistication and vigor for using social-psychological insights to understand and address the pressing problems of today.

What wisdom you have in your hands! The interventions presented in this volume were not easy or simple to construct. They are founded on *hard-won psychological insights,* typically cultivated over years of research in the laboratory and the field, with an intense commitment to understanding how interpretations play out in the real world and how altering them might help people achieve their goals. Yet all of the interventions you will read about are under construction and that construction is ongoing (Dweck, 2017). In each case, there are important questions outstanding about why, how, for whom, and in what contexts an intervention works or does not work. There is much we have yet to learn. Above all else, we invite you to a journey of discovery about the role of psychology in our everyday lives and how we can build this understanding to improve our lives, the lives of others, and our societies.

Welcome!

REFERENCES

Dweck, C. (2017). Growth mindset is on a firm foundation, but we're still building the house. *Mindset Scholars Network Blog.* Retrieved from *https://mindsetscholarsnetwork.org/ growth-mindset-firm-foundation-still-building-house.*

Walton, G. M., & Dweck, C. S. (2009). Solving social problems like a psychologist. *Perspectives on Psychological Science, 4,* 101–102.

Walton, G. M., & Wilson, T. D. (2018). Wise interventions: Psychological remedies for social and personal problems. *Psychological Review, 125,* 617–655.

PART I

EDUCATION

CHAPTER 1

A Growth Mindset about Intelligence

Carol S. Dweck and David S. Yeager

> Wise interventions can create a world of new meanings for people, and growth-mindset interventions portray a world in which human abilities are not fixed but can be developed. Growth-mindset-of-intelligence programs are grounded in decades of foundational work and have undergone years of development and testing. These programs not only vividly convey the idea of malleable ability to students but also make students eager to adopt the idea and able to apply it in their schoolwork and in their lives. In this chapter, we discuss the roots and the evolution of growth-mindset-of-intelligence interventions, recent large-scale experiments that shed light on how and when they work best, and our vision for the future of these interventions.

Wise interventions create a psychological world and invite people to enter it. It is often a world that equips them to face potentially threatening challenges and to face them with greater confidence and effectiveness because they have a new way to think about those challenges. As a result, they are more likely to behave in ways that can bring better results, be they emotional, social, or academic/professional results.

A growth mindset about intelligence is the belief that intellectual abilities are not fixed but rather can be developed, for example, through hard work, good strategies, and help and mentoring from others. In contrast, a fixed mindset is the belief that intellectual abilities are fixed and cannot be improved. In this chapter, we show how growth-mindset interventions have been developed and refined with the aim of creating a world of meanings—one that encourages students to take on challenges, interpret setbacks or struggles in adaptive ways, and persist in the face of failure (e.g., Aronson, Fried, & Good, 2002; Blackwell, Trzesniewski, & Dweck, 2007; Paunesku et al., 2015; Yeager, Romero, et al., 2016; Yeager et al., 2019; see Dweck & Yeager, 2019, for a review). Ultimately, this can result in greater growth and achievement, potentially decreasing long-standing grade disparities.

Yeager and Lee (Chapter 13, this volume) show how a growth mindset about personality can create a similar psychological world in the social domain and how growth-mindset-of-personality interventions can, in this way, have an impact on depression, anxiety, and social behavior, such as aggression.

Because a growth-mindset intervention seeks to create a world of new meanings, an important theme of this chapter is that it is not sufficient to simply "teach the facts" of a growth mindset and then expect students to change. The intervention must be sensitive, resonant, and compelling in the way it introduces the concept, explains it, helps people understand how to apply it to their lives, and motivates them to do so (see Dweck & Yeager, 2019; Yeager, Romero, et al., 2016). Moreover, the environment a person is in must support this new understanding and the actions it motivates.

BACKGROUND

Mindset research grew out of two lines of previous research: learned helplessness (Seligman & Maier, 1967) and attribution theory (Weiner & Kukla, 1970). The research on learned helplessness showed that animals exposed to uncontrollable negative events eventually stopped trying to prevent those events or escape from them. They remained passive even when the environment later changed and would have rewarded their efforts. We saw this behavior as perhaps similar to that of students who give up in the face of difficulty when in fact they have the ability to learn and do well.

Attribution theory, particularly the groundbreaking work of Weiner and colleagues (e.g., Weiner, 1985; Weiner & Kukla, 1970), revealed the importance of studying people's perceptions and interpretations—in this case, how people understood the causes of their successes and failures (i.e., the "attributions" they made for their successes and failures). In doing so, it provided a way to begin to understand the psychology of persistence versus helplessness in humans—that is, it gave us a way to understand why, among people who are equal in ability, some respond to challenging, threatening, or negative events (such as failure) with persistence and some do not. The research growing out of attribution theory suggested, for example, that viewing your failure as resulting from your lack of effort was more likely to motivate persistence than viewing it as coming from your lack of ability, since the latter is often seen as more stable and less controllable (see Weiner, 1985; Weiner & Kukla, 1970).

Attribution theory's great gift to the world was a well-defined variable (attributions) that could be precisely manipulated and could change behavior. The whole idea that motivation could be based on interpretations was tremendously exciting, especially since the field was emerging from the long behaviorist era in which ascribing any thinking to any organism, even humans, was seen as unscientific. However, whereas attribution theorists viewed ability as stable and uncontrollable (Weiner, 1985), mindset research took people's interpretations a step further by proposing that people could view ability itself as something that is fixed or, instead, as something that can be developed. Moreover, these different mindsets about ability could set the stage for the different attributions when a failure or setback occurred. This idea spawned a new research program to understand the ramifications of these different perspectives on ability (see Dweck & Leggett, 1988).

Mindsets can be seen as beliefs about the nature and workings of human attributes (or attributes of the world): What is this attribute, what are its properties, how does it work? In the case of mindsets about intelligence, the mindset is a belief about whether intellectual abilities are fixed or can be developed; it is a belief about whether people can develop their abilities through their own agency in the context of the necessary guidance, mentoring, and support from others. The research has shown that these mindsets—the belief in ability as fixed or as malleable—are related to a host of meaningful variables and it has established the effects of mindsets on academic outcomes. More specifically, mindsets have been found to be at the center of a web of variables, which we have called a "meaning system" (Blackwell et al., 2007; Dweck & Yeager, 2019; Robins & Pals, 2002). This means that the mindsets, when activated, may trigger and act through a host of other psychological variables.

Generally speaking, a fixed-mindset meaning system is organized around people's concerns about their (fixed) abilities and how these abilities will appear or be judged. Holding a fixed mindset has predicted people's adoption or display of *negative effort beliefs* (the belief that the need for high effort implies low ability or that effort will be ineffective for those with low ability; Blackwell et al., 2007; Leggett, 1986; Miele & Molden, 2010; Miele, Son, & Metcalfe, 2013); their *performance goals* or *performance-avoidance goals* (the desire to validate or protect one's ability, often by avoiding challenges that might reveal inadequacies; e.g., Hong, Chiu, Dweck, Lin, & Wan, 1999; Robins & Pals, 2002; see also Blackwell et al., 2007); their *helpless attributions* (the belief that setbacks imply low ability; Blackwell et al., 2007; Dweck & Yeager, 2019; Hong et al., 1999; Robins & Pals, 2002); and, as a result, *fewer positive strategies* in the face of setbacks (persistence, remediating deficiencies, appropriate help seeking; Blackwell et al., 2007; Moser, Schroder, Heeter, Moran, & Lee, 2011; Nussbaum & Dweck, 2008; Robins & Pals, 2002), which can lead to less than optimal learning or performance.

In contrast, the growth-mindset-meaning system tends to be organized around learning and developing one's abilities. Holding a growth mindset has predicted people's adoption or display of more *positive effort beliefs* (the idea that hard work can build abilities), *learning goals* (the desire to improve one's ability by approaching challenging learning tasks), resilient *attributions* (the belief that setbacks do not signify a lack of ability but signify a need to change strategy), and, as a result, more positive, *"mastery-oriented" strategies* in the face of setbacks (sticking with challenging assignments rather than falling back to easier ones), which can lead to enhanced learning or performance.

These mindsets have particular resonance in a society that has been divided in its beliefs about the nature of intelligence. On the one hand, there has been a belief, stemming from the writings of Galton (*Hereditary Genius*; 1892), Terman (*Genetic Studies of Genius*; 1926), and Jensen (*The g Factor*; 1998), that intelligence is hereditary and unchangeable—and that it determines what people are capable of accomplishing. One of us (Dweck) had a sixth-grade teacher who was so enamored with this view that she seated the class around the room in IQ order and treated students accordingly.

However, there has also been a forceful opposing view, which was well articulated by Alfred Binet, the co-inventor of the original IQ test. Binet (1909/1975) expressed his alarm at the increasing use of his test by people who asserted that they were measuring what they considered to be fixed intelligence. Binet did not see it that way at all: "A few modern philosophers . . . assert that an individual's intelligence is a fixed quantity, a quantity which cannot be increased. We must protest and react against this brute pessimism. . . . With practice, training, and above all, method, we manage to increase our attention, our memory, our judgment and literally to become more intelligent than we were before" (1909/1975, pp. 106–107). (See, e.g., Diamond, Barnett, Thomas, &

Munro, 2007; Ramsden et al., 2011; Rueda, Posner, & Rothbart, 2005, for research on the malleability of intellectual abilities and executive function; see Sauce & Matzel, 2018, for a thoughtful perspective on the role of environment and experience in the development of intellectual abilities). This view of intellectual ability as something that can grow with experience and learning is in harmony with the strand of American culture that reflects a can-do attitude and the idea that, no matter who they are, people can develop themselves with the necessary support and opportunities. Our research on mindsets has examined the impact of people's *own* beliefs about intelligence and has asked: What is the impact on people's motivation and achievement of taking one view or the other?

The relationships between the fixed or growth mindsets and the variables that are allied with them and give them their power have been studied in several ways. These include moderate- to large-sample correlational studies in which mindsets predict the other variables in the meaning system, which then go on to predict academic or social–emotional outcomes (Blackwell et al., 2007, Study 1; Dweck & Yeager, 2019; Robins & Pals, 2002; see Figure 1.1). They have also been investigated by demonstrating a correlation between mindsets and specific variables in a given setting and then, in a separate study, manipulating the mindsets to produce that effect experimentally to demonstrate the causal effects of mindsets (e.g., Hong et al., 1999).

As an example, Hong et al. (1999, Study 1) initially showed that participants who held more of a growth (vs. fixed) mindset were more likely to attribute their failure on a laboratory task to effort, a factor that is typically considered highly controllable. They

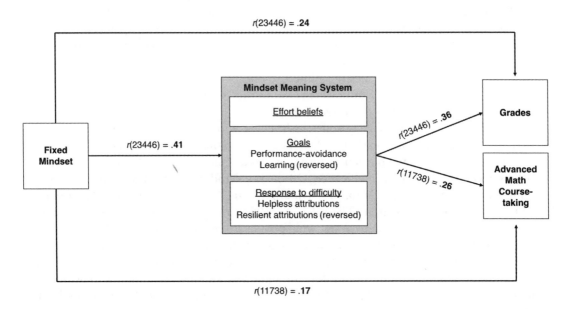

FIGURE 1.1. The links between mindsets, the mindset meaning system, and academic outcomes in three large studies. The mindset meaning system index is a composite of five items representing the meaning system constructs. Mindset was measured with three fixed mindset-framed items. Statistics are zero-order correlations estimated by meta-analytically aggregating three datasets: The U.S. National Study of Learning Mindsets (NSLM) pilot (N = 3,306; Yeager, Romero, et al., 2016); the U.S. NSLM (N = 14,894; Yeager et al, 2019); and the Norway *U-say* experiment (N = 5,246; Rege et al., in press). All p's < .001.

also showed, in a field study (Study 2), that those holding more of a growth mindset were more likely to take remedial action in the face of a deficiency—in line with their greater emphasis on effort attributions. But were the mindsets a causal factor in the effort attributions and remedial action?

To provide some background, in Study 2, freshmen at the University of Hong Kong were offered the possibility of taking a remedial English course. Among those who were deficient in English, this would be an excellent idea since all academic work and materials were in English. Yet among the students who were deficient, those with more of a growth mindset were the ones who showed far more enthusiasm for taking the course. It looked as though those with a fixed mindset might possibly put their college performance in jeopardy rather than admit to needing a remedial course.

Then, in an experimental study (Hong et al., 1999, Study 3), students were *temporarily* taught a growth or fixed mindset (by means of a persuasive article) and then experienced a failure on a task taken from an intelligence test. How did they understand their failure and were they willing to take a tutorial that could improve their performance on the test? After their poor performance, those in the growth-mindset group were more likely than those in the fixed-mindset condition to attribute their poor performance to a lack of effort, and were also far more likely to opt for the remedial tutorial. Finally, follow-up analyses suggested that the difference in effort attributions mediated the difference in the tendency to take remedial action. In short, this experiment showed that the mindsets can directly cause a difference in attributions and, in turn, a difference in the willingness to address one's deficiencies. (It is important to note that all students were thoroughly debriefed at the end of the study.) A series of experiments by Nussbaum and Dweck (2008) lent further support to the finding that a growth mindset can cause more constructive, remedial actions in the face of failures than a fixed mindset.

We are often asked how mindset theory is related to attribution theory. As suggested above, the answer is twofold. Mindsets grew out of attribution theory and mindsets can set the stage for students to orient toward different attributions, as shown in our experimental studies. When students are thinking in terms of fixed traits versus malleable qualities, different reasons for their failures come to mind.

PSYCHOLOGICAL PROCESSES

We just spelled out the meaning systems that have been revealed by research on fixed and growth mindsets. Here, we focus on how it all works when students are experiencing those meanings.

When students enter challenging or uncertain academic situations—as they do when they go to a new school or take a difficult class—they often worry whether their intellectual abilities are up to the task. In a fixed mindset, where those intellectual abilities are viewed as limited and unchangeable, they may wonder whether they will look and feel dumb. As a result, a cascade of processes (the fixed-mindset-meaning system, Figure 1.1) can be triggered. Students may then be afraid of the looming challenges, become reluctant to exert effort (or become anxious when they do), see setbacks as confirming their worst fears—and so on in a continuing cycle. We have seen firsthand that even students who make it into the top universities in the United States can be caught in this fixed-mindset cycle, worrying about saying something stupid, making a mistake, or getting a disappointing grade, and thereby revealing what they perceive to be their "permanently deficient" intellectual capacity.

For one project we sought to understand what the fixed mindset sounded like in students' own voices. This project (sponsored by the Carnegie Foundation for the Advancement of Teaching) focused on community college students who had failed a placement test and were required to take developmental (remedial) math courses, an abyss from which many never emerge. After failing the placement test, there was palpable despair in many, expressed in fixed-mindset language, such as "I am embarrassed by how stupid I am and suddenly feeling very discouraged . . . I can't even tell which fraction is bigger than another, or where they should fall on the number line. I feel like crying."

Such fixed-ability attributions for their placement in remedial math were common: "I don't think I'm a math person"; "Me and math are like oil and water"; "When I got to this [math] class, it was pretty much like a brick wall . . . I'm just not that kind of person"; and "My whole family [was] never good at math. . . ." They also spontaneously expressed negative effort beliefs. Here is a student talking about how other students—those who did not place into remedial math—do not need to apply effort to learn: "They're the ones who really catch on quickly—they can really advance their skills."

The task of a growth-mindset intervention is to break this cycle and to shift students into a growth-mindset-meaning system. In a growth mindset, students may, of course, still be anxious when they enter a new school with as yet unknown standards and requirements, but they may also be excited about being exposed to new subjects and about what they will learn. And even if they have a disappointing initial experience, they may be more likely to remain ready to exert effort, give more positive attributions for setbacks, and continue to exhibit constructive strategies to make this learning happen— particularly if they are in supportive environments.

EMPIRICAL EVIDENCE

Initial Interventions

Three early-stage randomized trials evaluated growth-mindset interventions in face-to-face settings with relatively modest samples (Aronson et al., 2002; Blackwell et al., 2007; Good, Aronson, & Inzlicht, 2003). Although the interventions varied in the format for conveying a growth mindset, in the growth-mindset materials, and in the populations of students who participated in the evaluation studies, they produced similar results. Students who received the growth-mindset intervention tended to show greater academic performance relative to controls, as measured by grades or achievement test scores.

More specifically, in their seminal study, Aronson et al. (2002) asked university students to mentor younger students and to write "pen pal" letters to them over the course of several sessions. This was the first use of the "saying-is-believing" exercise for growth-mindset interventions—that is, the mentoring of the younger students was intended to help instill the growth-mindset messages in the university students themselves. In this exercise, the participants encouraged the younger students to adopt a growth mindset by explaining to them that the "brain is like a muscle," and that connections in the brain grow stronger in response to rigorous learning experiences (messages that are now core to the growth-mindset intervention). Over the next semester, the African American college students in the growth-mindset group earned higher grades (grade-point averages [GPAs]) overall compared to two control groups that received either no treatment or information about multiple intelligences, as well as showing higher enjoyment and valuing of academics. A second study, conducted by Good et al. (2003; N = 138 across four conditions), found that an in-person growth-mindset program had a significant overall effect on the achievement test scores of middle school students and was effective at narrowing the gender gaps in achievement.

In another seminal study, Blackwell et al. (2007) implemented a growth-mindset intervention via eight in-person workshops. The study was conducted with seventh-grade students (N = 91 across two conditions) who attended a relatively low-achieving junior high school where students' math grades were declining over the seventh-grade school year. Blackwell and colleagues embedded several sessions of training in growth mindset within a larger eight-session workshop on study skills and compared the effects to a group that received eight sessions of study skills alone. The growth-mindset content began with scientific content, or "news you can use." (See Figure 1.2.) As in the Aronson et al. (2002) and Good et al. (2003) interventions, the Blackwell et al. intervention led students to envision themselves growing stronger connections in their brains as they

You Can Grow Your Intelligence
New Research Shows the Brain Can Be Developed Like a Muscle

Many people think of the brain as a mystery. They don't know much about intelligence and how it works. When they do think about what intelligence is, many people believe that a person is born either smart, average, or dumb—and stays that way for life.

But new research shows that the brain is more like a muscle—it changes and gets stronger when you use it. And scientists have been able to show just how the brain grows and gets stronger when you learn.

Everyone knows that when you lift weights, your muscles get bigger and you get stronger. A person who can't lift 20 pounds when they start exercising can get strong enough to lift 100 pounds after working out for a long time. That's because the muscles become larger and stronger with exercise. And when you stop exercising, the muscles shrink and you get weaker. That's why people say "Use it or lose it!"

But most people don't know that when they practice and learn new things, parts of their brain change and get larger a lot like muscles do when they exercise.

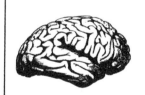

Inside the cortex of the brain are billions of tiny nerve cells, called neurons. The nerve cells have branches connecting them to other cells in a complicated network. Communication between these brain cells is what allows us to think and solve problems.

FIGURE 1.2. The first page of the scientific article that was used in the Blackwell, Trzesniewski, and Dweck (2007) intervention and that served as the starting point for many subsequent revised interventions. Reprinted with permission from L. S. Blackwell.

learned from new and challenging content. This was followed by activities to illustrate how learning can make you smarter.

Blackwell and colleagues (2007) found a significant effect of the experimental condition on change in grades following the intervention. Specifically, students in the study-skills control group continued to show declines in their math grades. However, for students in the growth-mindset condition, the decline in grades was halted. The everyday behaviors of students in the treatment group showed that they were more motivated and engaged, as well—that is, math teachers, blind to students' experimental condition assignments, were more likely to nominate students for showing improvements in challenge seeking and hard work when they had been in the growth-mindset condition. Thus, when students learned that the brain's abilities can be developed over time, they seemed more willing to seek out challenges and to stay engaged in their math classes, despite the difficulty.

Preparing to Scale Up

These early studies, although small in scale, raised an intriguing question: Could the growth-mindset message be communicated even more efficiently, in a way that could be scaled up? If so, then it would be possible to replicate these growth-mindset intervention effects in larger and more generalizable samples, and to begin to conduct studies that shed light on mechanisms that explain the sustained effects from a short treatment.

Starting in the 2010s, a number of randomized trials did just that. Using a newly created online platform, Paunesku and colleagues (2015) administered abbreviated versions of the scientific content about the brain's malleability from the Blackwell et al. (2007) study, along with a "write a letter to a future student" exercise that drew on the Aronson et al. (2002) method. These short, self-administered, but still compelling, growth-mindset sessions were delivered via a web survey, which made it easier to reach larger samples and to randomly assign students to condition. Students' grades were obtained from school records several months after they completed the intervention.

The first time this shorter intervention was evaluated in a randomized trial was in a pilot study with community college students taking developmental math—a population with striking fixed mindsets, as suggested previously. In this pilot study (see Yeager & Dweck, 2012, for a description), we learned that the growth mindset intervention significantly reduced the rate at which students dropped out of their developmental math course (from 20% to 9%).

It may seem surprising that we saw such promising results from a short online treatment. But the vivid and emotionally persuasive message that your brain can grow when you work hard on hard tasks and that you no longer had to feel "dumb at math" because schoolwork was hard resonated with students deeply and, they told us, felt liberating. The letters students wrote "to a struggling friend" suggest how much they related to the growth–mindset message:

> "Friend, I know you have been struggling in school for a little while and are becoming discouraged, but there's something I'd like to share with you. I read this interesting article recently and it explained how we can grow our brains. They did studies on animals and it showed that learning new skills to work your brain could help

us become smarter and better at any subject. We can use better strategies to learn things and practice, practice, practice. So maybe we can be study buddies and learn new skills to work and grow our brains to make new and bigger and better connections. I hope this encourages you because you are not 'dumb' and could just use a little help, and maybe we could do it together."

Or this from a focus group several months after the intervention:

"I thought I'd never do well and I felt so confused. . . . It was hard to see it at the time, but all that confusion really paid off. It's like something I read about the brain—when you don't understand something, that's when your brain can grow the most. I really believe that now. . . . After a lifetime of thinking 'I can't do math,' I finally feel like I can be good at this!!!"

The initial evidence, both the data and the testimonials, convinced us that even time-limited exposures to the growth-mindset idea, when done well, could be inspiring and actionable for students who needed to hear it.

The next crucial step involved randomized evaluation studies in grade 9–12 settings, and across multiple schools. Paunesku and colleagues (2015; $N = 1,594$ students, $K = 13$ schools) evaluated the shorter intervention, somewhat revised for high school students. They found that the growth-mindset intervention improved GPAs in "core" classes (math, science, English, and social studies) for students who, prior to the intervention, were earning lower grades than their peers.

Scaling Up Further

Yeager and colleagues next tested whether this "scalable" intervention could be improved, adapted, and scaled up further, and whether doing so could improve outcomes for an entire population of students. In a first case, the population was the entire incoming class at a large, public 4-year university. Yeager, Walton, and colleagues (2016, Experiment 2; $N = 7,335$ students) took the previous Paunesku et al. (2015) intervention and added testimonies from more advanced students in which they described how they used a growth mindset to make sense of the difficulties that accompanied the transition to college. This updated growth-mindset intervention significantly improved full-time enrollment rates among students who face disadvantages on the basis of their race or social class, thereby potentially narrowing the achievement gap. Later, a different team of investigators replicated the study and found treatment effects on first-year grades among Hispanic/Latinx students at a different large, public 4-year college (Broda et al., 2018; $N = 7,686$).

In the next case (Yeager, Romero, et al., 2016), the population of interest for the growth-mindset intervention was ninth-grade students making the transition to U.S. public high schools. This study served as a pilot study for a larger intervention with a nationally representative sample of ninth graders, discussed below. In this pilot study, the intervention was put through an iterative design process to tailor the message for this population. The result was a version that sharpened the elements that had been added over the years: compelling scientific information, engaging writing exercises, and testimonies from older students. This intervention was evaluated in a preregistered randomized trial (N = 3,676 students, K = 10 schools). As predicted and as found in the Paunesku et al. (2015) trial, the intervention improved the grades of ninth-grade students who had had relatively lower grades beforehand (Yeager, Romero, et al., 2016).

These studies, however, were all conducted with samples of convenience—that is, samples that were relatively easy to recruit. The kinds of sites that are typically eager to opt into experimental interventions may yield biased effect sizes (Allcott, 2015; Tipton, 2013). Because of this, the evidence obtained from the experiments we have presented so far show only that growth-mindset interventions *can* have effects in some places and for some students, but it cannot tell us where, how, and under what conditions the intervention would be effective.

To find this out, building on the foundation of the prior studies, we launched the National Study of Learning Mindsets, which was a longitudinal evaluation of a growth-mindset intervention in a nationally representative sample of U.S. public high schools (Yeager et al., 2019; see also Dweck & Yeager, 2019). Conducting randomized trials in a nationally representative sample is rare, but it was important for taking the next big steps in our research program. This study used an expert third-party research firm to recruit the representative sample and collect and process the data. With a representative sample, we could now locate schools that showed stronger and weaker effects and we could use measures of schools' and students' characteristics to gain new insights into mechanisms that sustained or curtailed the effects of growth-mindset programs.

We also further upgraded the material, making it more attractive and compelling, as well as adding new exercises, including an exercise in which students wrote about how they could use their stronger brains to achieve the goals they valued in life. (The reason for this is that we did not assume that all students would want stronger academic skills for their own sake but might need to reflect on a personal reason to "grow their brains.") As in previous studies and in line with our preregistered prediction, the growth-mindset intervention improved overall GPAs for ninth-grade students who, prior to the intervention, were earning lower grades in their schools relative to their peers (students below the median in GPA in their schools; Yeager et al., 2019).

We are excited to report that researchers are now beginning to take our materials and evaluate scaled-up growth-mindset intervention materials in other nations. One group of economists, working with the World Bank, showed effects of a growth-mindset intervention among adolescents in high-poverty areas of Peru (Outes, Sánchez, & Vakis, 2017). Another group, led by economists, replicated the growth-mindset intervention effects among high school students in Norway (Bettinger, Ludvigsen, Rege, Solli, & Yeager, 2018; Rege et al., in press).

Heterogeneity

Interestingly, although a growth-mindset intervention tends to influence mindsets and the choice of challenge tasks (such as the choice of hard vs. easy problems) for students across the achievement spectrum (Rege et al., in press; Yeager, Romero, et al., 2016; Yeager et al. 2019), it has translated into higher grades chiefly among those students who are not already earning high grades. It is possible that higher-achieving students may show benefits on other outcomes, such as opting into more challenging courses over time, and we have evidence from the National Study of Learning Mindsets (Yeager et al., 2019) and a replication in Norway (Rege et al., in press) that this is the case. Thus, heterogeneity of intervention outcomes may depend on where the student has room to move—up the grade ladder or into more challenging courses.

One important way to learn about what leads to heterogeneity in intervention effects is to conduct your experiment in settings that have high and low levels of a factor. In the National Study of Learning Mindsets we focused on the extent to which the peer and teacher factors would influence the growth-mindset effect, and found that the growth-mindset intervention was more effective at changing grades when the school or classroom context was supportive of the growth-mindset message—that is, stronger effects on grades appeared when peer norms favored challenge-seeking behaviors (Yeager et al., 2019), or when the teacher held more of a growth mindset (Yeager et al., 2020). We examine these findings in more detail below as we turn next to how intervention effects are sustained over time.

In sum, it appears that a growth-mindset intervention is most effective among students (1) who are facing ongoing academic challenges, and (2) who are in school or classroom contexts that support the maintenance of growth-mindset beliefs and behaviors.

Effects over Time

What happens after a growth-mindset intervention? The previous section identified some of the factors that can facilitate long-term growth mindset effects, but here we delve a bit more deeply into the proposed sequence of processes that may unfold over time to bring about those effects. This is a topic that has, of course, been of great interest to us.

We assume that after a growth-mindset intervention, students may try out growth-mindset beliefs and behaviors, such as greater challenge seeking and harder work in the classroom, and if this yields positive results—such as greater learning, higher grades, approval from teachers, or support from peers—the greater challenge seeking and hard work will continue and even increase.

We mentioned above that in the National Study of Learning Mindsets (Yeager et al., 2019), the mindsets of students' math teachers made a difference. Specifically, the teachers who themselves held more of a growth mindset had students who showed larger sustained effects of the growth-mindset treatment (Yeager et al., 2020). This could well be because teachers with more of a growth mindset are more likely to notice changes in students' challenge seeking and effort, to believe that these changes can make a difference in learning, and therefore to support these changes.

There were early hints of this in the Blackwell et al. (2007) intervention that an environment that is supportive of growth-mindset behaviors could play a role. In that study, as noted earlier, their seventh-grade math teacher did not know which students had received a growth-mindset versus control (study-skills) intervention. Nonetheless, the teachers singled out more of the students in the growth-mindset group as showing changes in academic effort, in perseverance, in the seeking of challenges, and in requesting mentoring. Noting the changes, these perceptive teachers may have rewarded, supported, and helped sustain the students' increased dedication to their work.

Another factor we mentioned earlier that made a difference in the longevity of the mindset effects was peer norms (Yeager et al., 2019). Did peers in a student's school show a strong norm of seeking to work on challenging tasks? We found that when they did, the overall advantage of the growth-mindset group over the control group was larger than average (in fact, about double). However, when the peer norm of challenge seeking was weak, the students showed little or no effect over time of having received a growth-mindset treatment—even though the intervention changed their mindsets and led them to choose a challenging task within the intervention session to the same degree as students in the schools with strong peer norms. This finding suggests that when students considered putting their growth mindset into practice in their classrooms, perhaps they felt reluctant to go up against established peer norms and risk disapproval, or they may have actually tried out new behaviors in the classroom and were not met with support or approval. Future research could study this process as it unfolds, as well as systematically investigate ways to influence peer norms to allow and support growth mindset behavior.

Finally, a new growth-mindset intervention performed in Norway (Rege et al., in press) showed how school policies could allow or prevent the effects of a growth-mindset intervention. Some of the schools in the study required students to choose the level of their math course before the school year began. Other schools, however, allowed students to make their choice a couple of months later, after the start of the new school year. Since the growth-mindset intervention was administered after the start of the new year, it was chiefly students in the latter schools who were able to profit from the intervention in terms of being motivated to choose advanced math courses at an appreciably higher rate than the control group.

Clearly, there is still much more to learn about student, peer, teacher, and school factors that can help sustain growth-mindset effects over time and, in particular, about the processes through which they do so. This learning will help make future interventions more effective for more students and will inform educators how best to create cultures and policies that are more conducive to challenge seeking, persistence, and achievement in their students.

Effect Sizes

What effect sizes would be considered noteworthy for a growth-mindset intervention (or any educational interventions)? Experts in evaluation studies (e.g., Cheung & Slavin, 2016; see also Hill, Bloom, Black, & Lipsey, 2008; Kraft, 2018) have argued that evaluating effect sizes requires choosing the appropriate benchmarks. In the current case, this means asking: What effects are typical for rigorous, high-quality educational interventions, ones that seek to improve meaningful educational outcomes, such as grades? In other words, what effect sizes are typical for large-sample interventions (be they ones involving changes in curriculum, instruction, school organization, or student motivation) that use randomized trials and choose important, objective student outcomes as the dependent variable?

Prominent educational economist Susan Dynarski (2017), addressing educational outcomes, concluded that "a fifth of a standard deviation [0.20 SD] is a large effect." This statement is based on the "best-evidence synthesis" movement, which uses evidence from large, rigorous evaluation studies to determine the effects of interventions that seek to raise grades or test scores (Cheung & Slavin, 2016). It was recently confirmed by a report on a large number of the newest randomized trials in education funded by the U.S. federal government (Boulay et al., 2018). Among these promising interventions, the ones that ended up having significant effects tended to top out at around 0.20 SD.

To give a better feel for the magnitude of this effect, around 0.20 SD is the effect of a year of schooling for adolescents, a year with an excellent versus average teacher, or a smaller class size for adolescents (see Yeager et al., 2019, for a review). Given the many variables affecting outcomes in educational settings, this effect is an achievement, even for multifaceted, labor-intensive, and costly programs.[1]

There is a larger point, however. The point is that even a seemingly modest effect propagated over large numbers of students, particularly at a very low cost, can produce meaningful changes in the education and economic trajectories for many, many students. The growth-mindset intervention with its online platform and very low cost per student is capable of scaling to large populations, leading more students to enjoy challenges, pass courses they might have failed, take harder courses than they would have, and contribute to society in ways they might not have otherwise.

It is noteworthy, then, that growth-mindset interventions have shown much of what is considered a "large" effect size in real-world educational experiments. Not surprisingly, early studies that involved multiple sessions conducted by highly trained professionals showed larger effect sizes. However, these procedures were time-consuming and costly, and therefore not really scalable.

One should not expect the same effect sizes for studies that delivered much more minimal (under an hour) self-administered, online growth-mindset materials. Nonetheless, the effect size on core course GPA for lower-achieving students several months postintervention for studies that delivered these more minimal growth-mindset programs was 0.10 SD–0.14 SD across three replication studies (Paunesku et al., 2015; Yeager, Romero, et al., 2016; Yeager, Walton, et al., 2016; see also Yeager et al., 2019), and the National Study of Learning Mindsets as well—that is, growth-mindset interventions can provide roughly half of the largest effects typically seen for much more extensive and expensive adolescent interventions.

Considerably larger effects were found in the National Study of Learning Mindsets for schools that had peer norms that supported a growth mindset (and that were not already among the highest achieving 25% of schools). Low- or medium-achieving schools with supportive norms approached or exceeded treatment effects of 0.20 SD (Yeager et al., 2019). Moreover, as we learn more about the factors that sustain the treatments and turn them into higher grades and more advanced course taking, we hope to enhance the effectiveness of the growth-mindset programs and obtain even higher effect sizes.

In sum, the effects of our growth-mindset interventions are noteworthy compared to many of the most successful large and comprehensive educational interventions and are found under the most rigorous of conditions. These effects are especially meaningful given the very low per-person cost of the intervention, the ease of access, and the short time involved in its administration.

COUSINS

Growth-mindset-of-intelligence interventions have many offspring and many cousins. But before we turn to these relatives, we mention again some of the siblings, such as the

---

[1] Larger effects have sometimes been obtained when interventions are not rigorously evaluated (e.g., did not use randomized controlled designs with large samples) or when researchers control the tests that students take as the postintervention measure (so the intervention could "teach to their test"; Boulay et al., 2018; see also Cheung & Slavin, 2016).

international large-sample replications that have used our materials, such as Bettinger et al. (2018) in Norway, and Outes et al.'s (2017) World Bank project in Peru. We also wish to mention an intervention with parents (Andersen & Nielsen, 2016) and intervention-relevant (although not yet intervention-based) findings with teachers (Canning, Muenks, Green, & Murphy, 2019; Fuesting et al., 2019; see also Rattan, Good, & Dweck, 2012). In the research by Canning et al. with 150 college science, technology, engineering, and math (STEM) professors, those professors who held a more fixed mindset had double the achievement gap among their students—that is, double the achievement gap between White/Asian students and students from underrepresented minority groups. On average, everyone did better with the growth-mindset professors but especially those from under-represented groups. Further, students reported that the growth-mindset professors used pedagogical practices that put more emphasis on learning and development, and this was a mediator of the enhanced performance. These findings provide a foundation for future interventions with teachers, and we continue to discuss this in "Future Directions" below.

Another line of work that is paving the way for future mindset interventions is a program of research on organizational mindsets, spearheaded by Canning, Murphy, and colleagues (2020). In a series of studies, spanning data from major business organizations to data from laboratory experiments, people's perceptions of an organization's fixed or growth mindsets about talent predicted such important things as their own commitment to the organization, their report of immoral practices within the workplace, and their perceptions of true support for innovation even when it might not succeed.

The growth-mindset-of-intelligence interventions have already given birth to a program of research on growth-mindset-of-personality interventions noted earlier, spear-headed by David Yeager (see Yeager & Lee, Chapter 13, this volume), in which students were taught that personality was not simply fixed but consisted of qualities that could be developed over time. Among other things, these interventions have led to meaningful improvements in adolescents' aggression (Yeager, Trzesniewski, & Dweck, 2013) and stress responses (Yeager, Lee, & Jamieson, 2016), and decreases in the onset of symptoms of clinical depression in students in their first year of high school (Miu & Yeager, 2015; see also Schleider & Weisz, 2016).

Scholars have also taken growth-mindset interventions into the real world of conflict resolution (Halperin, Russell, Trzesniewski, Gross, & Dweck, 2011; Goldenberg et al., 2018; Goldenberg, Gross, & Halperin, Chapter 15, this volume), showing, for example, that teaching the parties in the Middle East conflict that groups do not have fixed, inher-ent qualities (are not inherently evil or aggressive) can lead to increases in hope for prog-ress and in support for real concessions, increases that endured over a 6-month period of unrest.

Mindset research has also begun to address issues of health (Burnette, Forsyth, Des-marais, & Hoyt, 2019; Mueller, Rowe, & Zuckerman, 2017; Thomas, Burnette, & Hoyt, 2019). Moreover, growth mindset interventions in the area of health (beliefs about the nature and causes of health and disease) pioneered by Alia Crum and her colleagues (Crum, Leibowitz, & Verghese, 2017) have yielded many landmark findings, including findings that illuminate the workings of placebo effects (see also Crum, Handley-Miner, & Smith, Chapter 9, this volume).

Growth-mindset interventions that enhance empathy are also beginning to emerge (Weisz, 2018; see Schumann, Zaki, & Dweck, 2014), as well as interventions that teach a growth mindset about emotions (the idea that people can modulate and improve their emotions; Smith et al., 2018). There are also other lines of research that could easily spawn interventions in the future, such as research on growth mindsets about prejudice (beliefs about whether prejudice is fixed or malleable; Carr, Dweck, & Pauker, 2012; Neel & Shapiro, 2012; see also Rattan & Dweck, 2010, on the confronting of bias) and research on mindsets or theories about willpower (beliefs about whether the capacity for willpower is fixed or malleable and limited or abundant; e.g., Job, Walton, Bernecker, & Dweck, 2015; Mukhopadhyay & Yeung, 2010).

As we have seen, growth-mindset interventions address the issue of whether a human attribute, such as intelligence or personality, can be developed—that is, whether it is controllable through personal agency and environmental support or not. However, these are not the only possible kinds of mindsets. Other mindsets can address beliefs about different aspects of the nature and workings of attributes of humans or the world. For example, in a fascinating line of work, Crum, Salovey, and Achor (2013; see also Crum, Handley-Miner, & Smith, Chapter 9, this volume) have studied whether people believe stress is good (facilitating) or bad (debilitating), the consequences of these beliefs, and the benefits of an intervention offering people a view of the potential benefits of stress. Following this lead, Haimovitz and Dweck (2016) have examined beliefs about whether failure is facilitating or debilitating, finding that parents who believe failure is debilitating seem to be transmitting more of a fixed mindset of intelligence to their children. These are just some of the relatives in the large and growing growth-mindset family.

INTERVENTION CONTENT AND IMPLEMENTATION

As an overview, growth-mindset interventions teach students that their intellectual abilities are not fixed, but can be developed with effort, good strategies, and lots of input, advice, and support from others. They are taught that they can build a stronger brain, and this is backed by compelling scientific research on how the brain changes with learning.

But this is not enough. This is just the first, informational, part. The rest of the intervention has to resonate with students' experiences. It has to place students' school experiences within the growth-mindset-meaning system. Growth-mindset interventions convey, for example, that feelings of effort or difficulty in school are signs that you are growing your abilities, not signs that you lack ability. The intervention also helps students to understand how they can put a growth mindset into practice in their schoolwork and to see how a growth mindset can help them personally in their life goals. It has to take them into the world of growth mindset and make them want to and be able to live there.

The Intervention Basics

The growth-mindset intervention has evolved over the years as it has been evaluated in new studies and in different contexts (see Dweck & Yeager, 2019). Throughout its life, the intervention has usually involved three elements. The first is scientific credibility. The growth-mindset intervention conveys the new and emerging neuroscience of the brain's amazing potential to change and develop, and it explains that it is through intensive learning that denser and stronger neuronal connections are formed. The intervention goes on to explain that, therefore, struggling to master something new or experiencing setbacks are not signs of inability, but rather are the means through which people strengthen the connections in their brains and get smarter.

The second element is a sticky or memorable metaphor: that the brain is like a muscle (Aronson et al., 2002). Intervention participants learn that the way that academic experiences strengthen the brain's connections can be seen as analogous to how strenuous exercise strengthens our muscles. The goal of this framing is, again, to undermine negative effort beliefs and fixed-ability attributions and instead evoke the value of effort and difficulty in a growth-mindset-meaning system.

The third critical element involves features that help bring these ideas to life. These include testimonies from older students who were exposed to and used growth-mindset messages to improve their learning in school. In more recent interventions, we have added testimony from one or more admired figures who used a growth mindset and its principles to achieve their goals in life.

There are also writing assignments for the participant. One of the most commonly implemented exercises in the growth-mindset intervention, as we mentioned earlier, is a "letter to a future student" writing assignment (originated by Aronson et al., 2002). Students imagine a future student their age who is having a hard time in school and does not yet know the growth-mindset message. They are then asked to write a compelling and encouraging letter to the future student, using the ideas they just learned about a growth mindset. These ideas are listed for them as a reminder of what they can include. Not only might this exercise lead the participants to elaborate on the growth-mindset ideas more fully (resulting in improved memory of the intervention messages), but it can also encourage internalization of the message through the "saying-is-believing" effect (Aronson, 1999) discussed above—an effect that can enhance the likelihood that students will apply the learning to their own schoolwork in the future.

Finally, in recent iterations, we have included an exercise to help students understand why it's important to have a stronger brain. Through the work of others (e.g., Fryberg, Covarrubias, & Burack, 2018), we realized that not all groups of students may believe that increasing their intellectual abilities is a valuable pursuit for its own sake. For this reason, we now include an exercise that asks students what they hope to achieve in their lives and then asks them to write about how a stronger brain could help them achieve it.

Despite all these elements, an intervention can easily be derailed if it does not convey respect for the participants. This is particularly important with adolescents. Thus, we begin the program by inviting students not only to participate in the program but also to contribute to its development, since they are the experts on school and student life. In this way, they are not simply research participants but are potential shapers of the future program. In other words, we enlist them as collaborators who have important information to offer, and we request this information throughout the intervention.

As suggested above, every growth-mindset-of-intelligence intervention must be tailored to the target population in terms of, for example, age, school transition, and culture or subgroup. In our own interventions, we have spent considerable time molding the program to the psychology of the particular participants in that study. This is why in our national study of the transition to high school we helped students understand why a strong brain is important—we realized, as noted above, that this value is not universally understood or shared. This means that researchers or practitioners must address the issues, needs, values, and norms of their population in tailoring a new growth-mindset intervention.

It is also worth clarifying what the growth-mindset intervention *does not* do. The intervention does not promise students that they will reach any particular level of ability in the future or that they will achieve any specific goal. Rather, the intervention emphasizes the capacity for continued development and improvement over time.

Current interventions also avoid focusing on effort alone as the vehicle for intellectual growth, since sheer effort may be useless if a student does not have good strategies or effective mentoring from others. For this reason, the intervention does not simply exhort students to "try hard." Moreover, effort exhortations alone are unlikely to be effective even for promoting effort. Adults are always nagging students to try harder, with little effect. But perhaps even more importantly, high effort has negative implications in a fixed-mindset-meaning system: If you have to try hard, it means you are not smart (see, e.g., Blackwell et al., 2007; see also Meyer, 1982). Thus, continual effort exhortations could be insulting or threatening to students.

In summary, growth-mindset interventions begin by providing basic information about the malleability of intellectual abilities—about the brain and its capacity for growth. This is done in a compelling way, first scientifically and then in a personally meaningful way—that is, in light of the scientific evidence, students are led to reinterpret the meaning of effort and setbacks, not as negative things, but as vehicles for growth. Along the way, they are given opportunities to internalize the growth mindset and they are led to think about how a stronger brain could help them in their important future endeavors.

NUANCES AND MISCONCEPTIONS

The concept of a growth mindset may seem quite simple: It is the belief that abilities (or other personal attributes) can be developed. However, we have found that it can easily be equated with other concepts that people are familiar with (such as being open-minded) or with isolated aspects of the meaning system (such as effort).

Many educators have succeeded amazingly well in communicating and implementing a growth mindset in their classrooms and schools (Berger, Woodfin, & Vilen, 2016; Crow & Dabars, 2015). An elementary school principal whose school implemented growth-mindset concepts reported:

> "By embracing the productive struggle and helping our students understand that through doing hard things they have the opportunity to grow their brains, we have unleashed a wave that has contributed to our student growth landing in the top ten percent of our state."

And yet, there are many nuances to a growth mindset and its implementation that must be kept in mind for implementations to be effective. Here are questions we have been asked, along with our answers and their implications for interventions or educational practice.

  • *If a person has a growth (or fixed) mindset about intelligence, does he or she have the same mindset about other human qualities, such as personality or athletic ability?* There is only a very modest correlation among mindsets about different abilities or qualities, so people can most definitely have different mindsets about different attributes. We have also observed that people can have different mindsets about themselves and others. They may think, for example, that their own intelligence is more fixed than other people's, but their personality is more malleable than others'.

• *Within a domain, like intelligence, do people have just one mindset and not the other?* In the past few years, we have come to understand that while people can have predominantly a fixed or predominantly a growth mindset about intelligence, everyone is a mixture. For example, a person may be in a growth mindset most of the time, but certain events, such as challenges, criticism, or failure, can trigger a fixed mindset. Indeed, any event that makes people feel that their intelligence is being judged (by themselves or others) can trigger a fixed mindset in them. This suggests that future interventions, rather than just teaching a growth mindset, might also teach students how to recognize their "fixed-mindset triggers" and how to work their way back to a growth mindset in the face of triggering events (e.g., Orosz et al., 2020). Indeed, interventions in general can more deliberately teach people strategies to maintain intervention effects over time.

• *Is a growth mindset all about effort?* As we noted, perhaps the most common misconception is that a growth mindset is strictly about effort—that all a student needs to do is to apply effort and all will be well. However, sheer effort, without good strategies, resources, support, and mentorship, is often insufficient. And, if students are led to believe that sheer effort should be sufficient, they may feel particularly inept when they fail. Again, putting the onus entirely on the students and their effort denies the critical importance of environmental support and resources in fostering success. Another practice that can result from putting an exclusive emphasis on effort is the offering of lavish praise for students' effort while neglecting their poor learning progress. This kind of praise is meant to make students feel good even if they are failing to make strides in their learning. This is ironic because implementing a growth mindset is precisely about helping students make progress in developing their abilities, not about hiding their deficiencies behind a veil of praise.

The bottom line is that educators or intervenors who simply focus on effort are most likely not creating a full growth-mindset-meaning system or building an environment that supports it, and their age-old exhortations to try hard (or their frequent praise for effort) could end up being ineffective or undermining.

• *Does a growth mindset mean that everyone is the same; that there are no differences in talent or ability; that anyone can achieve anything?* While a growth mindset is the belief in everyone's potential to continually develop and improve, it does not mean that everyone is the same at any given time, and it does not guarantee that even with great effort everyone can end up at the same place. Although we believe that people's potential is typically great—and usually cannot be known in advance of good mentoring, good strategy use, opportunities, and devotion to learning over long periods of time—educators may mistakenly believe they are instilling a growth mindset when they tell their students, "You can do or be anything!" However inspiring this may sound, it may often be unhelpful, particularly when the educator is not paving the way by giving students knowledge about the routes they must travel, a head start on the many skills and strategies they must learn, and perhaps preliminary access to resources required to start them on their path. In fact, students may later blame themselves when they fail to achieve their goals.

• *Are lectures on growth mindset enough?* In this context, we might also mention that some educators provide a lecture or two on growth mindset, show some TED Talks, or put a growth-mindset chart on the walls, but do not change their practices or classroom culture in ways that would really make students believe that they should take on challenges, not worry about mistakes, ask for help, or take pride in their progress. Good implementation requires that these growth-mindset supports be baked into teachers' policies and practices. The key point is that those designing a growth-mindset intervention need to develop a deep, nuanced understanding of the concepts it rests on and then design the intervention to expertly convey the concepts, why they are important, and how to apply them. Even with our decades of research on mindsets and our experience with mindset interventions, it still took us 2 years to develop the intervention materials we delivered in the National Study of Learning Mindsets (see Table 1.1). In designing a classroom or school to support a growth mindset, educators also need to think through how their practices foster and reward taking on challenges, sticking to them, using strategies, interpreting failures, and, perhaps above all, valuing progress.

IMPLICATIONS FOR PRACTICE

There is growing evidence that educators' mindsets play a role in students' motivation and achievement. Above we cited research by Canning, Muenks, and colleagues (Canning et al., 2020) demonstrating that college students, especially those from underrepresented groups, earned lower grades in the STEM classes of fixed-mindset professors and reported less motivation in those classes. Research is also beginning to document the things educators do in their classes that have these effects, such as focusing on

TABLE 1.1. The R&D Process Used to Develop a Scalable Growth-Mindset Intervention

Phase	Years	References	Step
1	2010–2012	Paunesku et al. (2015); Yeager, Walton, et al. (2016)	1.1. Test the "base" versions, adapted from in-person interventions
2	2013–2014	Yeager, Romero, et al. (2016)	2.1. Attempts to rewrite 2.2. A/B tests ($N \approx 3,000$) 2.3. User testing ($N \approx 300$) 2.4. Extensive rewriting to finalize "new" version
3	2014–2015	Yeager, Walton, et al. (2016)	3.1. Head-to-head test of "base" versus "new" with proxy outcome ($N \approx 7,500$) 3.2. Preregistered evaluation of "new" versus control, GPA outcome, convenience sample ($N \approx 3,600$)
4	2015–2016	Yeager et al. (2019)	4.1. Extensive rewriting to finalize "newer" version 4.2. Preregistered evaluation of "newer" versus control, GPA and course-taking outcomes, national sample

Note. R&D, research and development; GPA, grade-point average. Adapted from Dweck and Yeager (2019). Adapted with permission from Sage Publications, Inc.

and rewarding improvement or giving students chances to revise their work, as well as resources for improving their work (Canning et al., 2019; Sun, 2015; see also Rattan et al., 2012). And, as we noted above, similar findings are beginning to emerge from the National Study of Learning Mindsets, which included data from math teachers and their students.

These findings are important. It is our view that the full potential of growth-mindset interventions to enhance students' motivation and achievement will not be realized until we can supplement direct-to-student interventions with teacher interventions and perhaps with school reform (since it may be difficult to create growth-mindset climates when teacher are themselves evaluated on their students' short-term test scores). As we saw earlier, many educators may not have learned the nuances of a growth mindset and, even if they have, there are still many factors that may discourage teachers and school administrators from experimenting with new school or classroom learning and reward structures: (1) educators may not know how to turn their knowledge into classroom practices that communicate and support growth mindsets in their students and (2) the incentive systems embedded in schools and institutions—such as teacher accountability or school rankings based on test scores—may discourage teachers from experimenting with new practices and (3) cultural models (Markus & Kitayama, 2010) of how teaching and learning are supposed to proceed may not be optimal for many students (teachers lecturing rather than students collaborating and mentoring one another; relatively permanent ability groupings; grading strictly on outcomes and not factoring in improvement; short-term classroom units rather than longer multifaceted projects that may involve work in the community).

Prominent educators have grappled with many of these issues. For example, using a growth-mindset perspective, Boaler (2015) has rethought mathematics teaching; Berger and colleagues (2016), in the Expeditionary Learning (EL) schools, have rethought elementary school structure and curriculum; and Michael Crow, the president of Arizona State University, has completely overhauled the conception, purpose, structure, curriculum, and practices of his institution to provide a model for the modern U.S. university (see Crow & Dabars, 2015). In each of these cases, students engage in more self-initiated, deeper, more intrinsically motivated learning—the kind of learning that sustains a growth mindset and the kind of learning that will help students think and thrive in the modern world. It would be exciting to study these programs directly to determine whether growth mindsets are indeed fostered and sustained in these settings and to examine the role that the mindsets might play in enhancing the benefits of these programs.

One impediment to improving practice is that teachers do not have good ways to gauge which of the teaching practices they try are working and which are not. For example, if a teacher tries some growth-mindset practices meant to enhance student engagement with challenging material, how can they tell whether they have succeeded? In an exciting new undertaking, Dave Paunesku and Sarah Gripshover (research scientists at the Project for Educational Research that Scales [PERTS]), and their colleagues (*www.perts.net/engage*) have devised and are testing methods for quickly and anonymously surveying students on a weekly basis to see whether there are changes in their reported engagement that follow their teachers' introduction of new methods.

Finally, in a major new initiative, Stephanie Fryberg and Mary Murphy (professors at the University of Michigan and Indiana University, respectively), working with teachers in the Seattle, Washington, public school system, have been developing a new curriculum to teach educators a more deeply nuanced growth mindset and how to implement it in their classrooms. Once it is completed and rigorously tested, it will be made available to educators online at no cost. At the same time, C. Y. Chiu (professor and Dean of Social Science at the Chinese University of Hong Kong) and his colleagues, working with educators in Hong Kong, are developing and testing online programs for teachers and administrators. It will be interesting in the future to understand cultural differences in how growth-mindset interventions are best designed and implemented.

In closing this section, we call attention to what a daunting task it is to create growth-mindset programs that all teachers can use successfully. Some of the most skilled psychologists, researchers, and educators are dedicated to this task, but it will surely take considerable time before the task is complete. Indeed, we think that changing classroom culture is the next "Mt. Everest" that the mindset research community will need to climb together.

IMPLICATIONS FOR PSYCHOLOGICAL THEORY

Mindset research and interventions support the idea that people build powerful beliefs about themselves, and that these beliefs can affect their motivation and ultimately their accomplishments (Dweck, 2017; Walton & Wilson, 2018). In the case of fixed and growth mindsets, based on their experiences in their settings and the messages embedded in their culture, people develop beliefs about whether their attributes, such as intelligence, are fixed at a certain level or can be developed. As we have seen, these mindsets—by signaling to people what they can or cannot accomplish in a given environment—can have cascading effects, influencing their goals, effort, reactions to setbacks, and longer-term performance.

This viewpoint has important implications for understanding how people work—that is, what makes them tick. It locates beliefs at the core of motivation and what is so important is that beliefs can be changed (Dweck, 2017; Walton & Wilson, 2018). Thus, mindsets (and the other key psychological variables explored in this volume) give psychologists and practitioners a target for interventions. It does not mean that it is easy for people to see things in a new way, but with helpful input they can often get there. When beliefs that play important roles in people's lives are targeted, the results can be greater than one might expect, and this, we believe, is why short interventions done properly can be effective. The emphasis on beliefs also leads us to try to understand the environments people are in, how those environments support different beliefs, and how we might alter those environments to support more fruitful ways of thinking—that is, ways of thinking that help people reach their goals.

Mindset interventions show us that social problems often have a psychological component (Walton & Dweck, 2009). Whether we are talking about recycling, energy consumption, healthy eating, or school dropout, we are often trying to get people to change their behavior by changing their minds. Yet, many or most interventions in the "real world" are based on the idea that change, such as educational change, comes only from large, costly restructuring of schools or curricula. Of course, structural change will always be highly important, and mindset changes and structural changes can work well together. Nonetheless, when structural changes are not yet forthcoming, "sufficient" structural factors may be in place to make a change in "psychology" take root. In the

National Study of Learning Mindsets, meaningful change took place among students in lower-achieving schools. Many schools may not have been well resourced but there were still opportunities for learning that could be better capitalized upon.

What other social problems can benefit from addressing beliefs to bring about behavior change? The other chapters in this volume provide many compelling examples.

FUTURE DIRECTIONS

We have already shown the potential of growth-mindset interventions to improve students' outcomes on a large scale, as in the National Study of Learning Mindsets. Throughout the chapter we also discussed the high-priority next steps, such as understanding more about the school contexts that support and sustain growth-mindset effects or understanding how to help educators to implement a growth mindset more effectively. Another direction is to understand more about which effects—GPA, advanced course taking, maintaining full course loads, school persistence, and college entrance—should be expected for which students in which contexts. We noted that different metrics are affected in different settings and with different students, but we are eager to understand this better.

Yet another direction is to understand how to move education toward a focus on students' more joyful, more self-directed, more meaningful learning and away from such a strong focus on achievement test scores. The former, in the context of a growth-mindset environment, will prepare students for today's challenging world; the latter will not. Thinking about today's world, we would love to understand more about how to make work environments embody more of a growth mindset to enhance employees' challenge seeking, persistence, teamwork, innovation, and development, and we and others have been conducting research in this area (Canning et al., 2020).

Many, many institutions could become places of growth. Even prisons could potentially become places of greater growth and not just places of retribution. In 2008, I (Dweck) received a letter from a man who, as a juvenile, had been sentenced to life imprisonment. He asked me if I really believed he could change and he requested a copy of my book *Mindset*. In early April of 2019, I received the following e-mail from him, entitled "I'm Home":

"Dear Professor Dweck,

"Over a decade ago, I read an article about a book that you wrote titled 'The Psychology of Success.' I was imprisoned at that time, serving a life sentence that I incurred as a juvenile under the age of 18. I wrote you a letter about the book and you responded by sending me a handwritten note with an autographed copy of the book.

"I just wanted to inform you that I was instrumental in civically engaging with the DC City Council and the Mayor to change its laws for juvenile lifers. Through the enactment of the Incarceration Reduction Amendment Act of 2016, I was released on March 21, 2019, 15 days ago.

"I just wanted to contact you to let you know that I am home, I have published eleven books, and I am doing the work in society for people to humanize and love one another. . . . I have accomplished many things . . . thanks to the Psychology of Success that you taught me in your book. Thank you for seeing me as human while I was still inside of a cage!"

Overall, we would love to see more growth-mindset philosophies embedded in the world we live in. What if people's Facebook postings were not just about their successes and highlights but also about the challenges they are taking on, the goals they value and are struggling to reach, or the admirable ways they are reacting to setbacks? What if others provided helpful suggestions and support (and likes!) for these postings?

What if more books, television shows, and movies were less about creepy, dystopian cultures or creatures from the abyss and more about people in interesting and challenging situations working together to create self-improvement and change, however difficult? And what if political leaders could be helped to focus us more on how we could grow as citizens and contribute to the common good rather than on who is competent or worthy and who is not?

We see no more important issue today than supporting human potential, and we hope to see growth-mindset programs and practices play a key part in potential and its fulfillment.

ACKNOWLEDGMENTS

Preparation of this chapter was supported in part by the William T. Grant Foundation, the Yidan Prize Foundation/Optimus Foundation, the National Science Foundation (Grant No. HRD 1761179), and the National Institute of Child Health and Human Development (Grant No. 10.13039/100000071 R01HD084772-01 and Grant No. P2C-HD042849 to the Population Research Center at the University of Texas at Austin). The content is solely the responsibility of the authors and does not necessarily represent the official views of the National Institutes of Health and the National Science Foundation.

REFERENCES

Allcott, H. (2015). Site selection bias in program evaluation. *Quarterly Journal of Economics, 130*(3), 1117–1165.

Andersen, S. C., & Nielsen, H. S. (2016). Reading intervention with a growth mindset approach improves children's skills. *Proceedings of the National Academy of Sciences of the USA, 113*(43), 12111–12113.

Aronson, E. (1999). The power of self-persuasion. *American Psychologist, 54*(11), 875–884.

Aronson, J. M., Fried, C. B., & Good, C. (2002). Reducing the effects of stereotype threat on African American college students by shaping theories of intelligence. *Journal of Experimental Social Psychology, 38*(2), 113–125.

Berger, R., Woodfin, L., & Vilen, A. (2016). *Learning that lasts: Challenging, engaging, and empowering students with deeper instruction.* San Francisco: Jossey-Bass.

Bettinger, E. P., Ludvigsen, S., Rege, M., Solli, I. F., & Yeager, D. S. (2018). Increasing perseverance in math: Evidence from a field experiment in Norway. *Journal of Economic Behavior and Organization, 146,* 1–15.

Binet, A. (1975). *Modern ideas about children.* (S. Heisler, Trans.). Menlo Park, CA: Suzanne Heisler. (Original work published 1909)

Blackwell, L. S., Trzesniewski, K. H., & Dweck, C. S. (2007). Implicit theories of intelligence predict achievement across an adolescent transition: A longitudinal study and an intervention. *Child Development, 78*(1), 246–263.

Boaler, J. (2015). *Mathematical mindsets: Unleashing students' potential through creative math, inspiring messages and innovative teaching.* San Francisco: Jossey-Bass.

Boulay, B., Goodson, B., Olsen, R., McCormick, R., Darrow, C., Frye, M., . . . Sarna, M. (2018). The Investing in Innovation Fund: Summary of 67 evaluations (No. NCEE 2018-4013). Retrieved from National Center for Education Evaluation and Regional Assistance, Institute of Education Sciences, U.S. Department of Education: *https://ies.ed.gov/ncee/pubs/20184013.*

Broda, M., Yun, J., Schneider, B., Yeager, D. S., Walton, G. M., & Diemer, M. (2018). Reducing inequality in academic success for incoming college students: A randomized trial of growth mindset and belonging interventions. *Journal of Research on Educational Effectiveness, 11*(3), 317–338.

Burnette, J. L., Forsyth, R. B., Desmarais, S. L., & Hoyt, C. L. (2019). Mindsets of addiction: Implications for treatment intentions. *Journal of Social and Clinical Psychology, 38*(5), 367–394.

Canning, E. A., Muenks, K., Green, D. J., & Murphy, M. C. (2019). STEM faculty who believe ability is fixed have larger racial achievement gaps and inspire less student motivation in their classes. *Science Advances, 5*(2), eaau4734.

Canning, E. A., Murphy, M. C., Emerson, K. T. U., Chatman, J. A., Dweck, C. S., & Kray, L. J. (2020). Culture of genius at work: Organizational mindsets predict cultural norms, trust, and commitment. *Personality and Social Psychology Bulletin, 46*(4), 626–642.

Carr, P. B., Dweck, C. S., & Pauker, K. (2012). "Prejudiced" behavior without prejudice?: Beliefs about the malleability of prejudice affect interracial interactions. *Journal of Personality and Social Psychology, 103*(3), 452–471.

Cheung, A. C. K., & Slavin, R. E. (2016). How methodological features affect effect sizes in education. *Educational Researcher, 45*(5), 283–292.

Crow, M. M., & Dabars, W. B. (2015). *Designing the new American university.* Baltimore: John Hopkins University Press.

Crum, A. J., Leibowitz, K. A., & Verghese, A. (2017). Making mindset matter. *British Medical Journal, 356,* j674.

Crum, A. J., Salovey, P., & Achor, S. (2013). Rethinking stress: The role of mindsets in determining the stress response. *Journal of Personality and Social Psychology, 104*(4), 716–733.

Diamond, A., Barnett, W. S., Thomas, J., & Munro, S. (2007). Preschool program improves cognitive control. *Science, 318*(5855), 1387.

Dweck, C. S. (2017). From needs to goals and representations: Foundations for a unified theory of motivation, personality, and development. *Psychological Review, 124*(6), 689–719.

Dweck, C. S., & Leggett, E. L. (1988). A social–cognitive approach to motivation and personality. *Psychological Review, 95*(2), 256–273.

Dweck, C. S., & Yeager, D. S. (2019). Mindsets: A view from two eras. *Perspectives on Psychological Science, 13*(3), 481–496.

Dynarski, S. M. (2017). For better learning in college lectures, lay down the laptop and pick up a pen. Retrieved from *www.brookings.edu/research/for-better-learning-in-college-lectures-lay-down-the-laptop-and-pick-up-a-pen.*

Fryberg, S. A., Covarrubias, R., & Burack, J. A. (2018). The ongoing psychological colonization of North American indigenous people: Using social psychological theories to promote social justice. In P. L. Hammack (Ed.), *The Oxford handbook of social psychology and social justice.* New York: Oxford University Press.

Fuesting, M. A., Diekman, A. B., Boucher, K. L., Murphy, M. C., Manson, D. L., & Safer, B. L. (2019). Growing STEM: Perceived faculty mindset as an indicator of communal affordances in STEM. *Journal of Personality and Social Psychology, 117*(2), 260–281.

Galton, F. (1892). *Hereditary genius: An inquiry into its laws and consequences.* London: Macmillan.

Goldenberg, A., Cohen-Chen, A., Goyer, J. P., Dweck, C. S., Gross, J. J., & Halperin, E. (2018). Testing the impact and durability of a group malleability intervention in the context of the Israeli–Palestinian conflict. *Proceedings of the National Academy of Sciences of the USA, 115*(4) 696–701.

Good, C., Aronson, J., & Inzlicht, M. (2003). Improving adolescents' standardized test performance: An intervention to reduce the effects of stereotype threat. *Journal of Applied Developmental Psychology, 24*(6), 645–662.

Haimovitz, K., & Dweck, C. S. (2016). What predicts children's fixed and growth intelligence mind-sets?: Not their parents' views of intelligence but their parents' views of failure. *Psychological Science, 27*(6), 859–869.

Halperin, E., Russell, A. G., Trzesniewski, K. H., Gross, J. J., & Dweck, C. S. (2011). Promoting the Middle East peace process by changing beliefs about group malleability. *Science, 333*(6050), 1767–1769.

Hill, C. J., Bloom, H. S., Black, A. R., & Lipsey, M. W. (2008). Empirical benchmarks for interpreting effect sizes in research. *Child Development Perspectives, 2*(3), 172–177.

Hong, Y., Chiu, C., Dweck, C. S., Lin, D. M.-S., & Wan, W. (1999). Implicit theories, attributions, and coping: A meaning system approach. *Journal of Personality and Social Psychology, 77*(3), 588–599.

Jensen, A. R. (1998). *The g factor: The science of mental ability.* Westport, CT: Praeger.

Job, V., Walton, G. M., Bernecker, K., & Dweck, C. S. (2015). Implicit theories about willpower predict self-regulation and grades in everyday life. *Journal of Personality and Social Psychology, 108*(4), 637–647.

Kraft, M. A. (2018). Interpreting effect sizes of education interventions. Retrieved from Brown University: *https://scholar.harvard.edu/files/mkraft/files/kraft_2018_interpreting_effect_sizes.pdf.*

Leggett, E. L. (1986). Individual differences in effort/ability inference rules and goals: Implications for causal judgments. *Dissertation Abstracts International, 47*(6-B), 2662.

Markus, H. R., & Kitayama, S. (2010). Cultures and selves: A cycle of mutual constitution. *Perspectives on Psychological Science, 5*(4), 420–430.

Meyer, W. U. (1982). Indirect communications about perceived ability estimates. *Journal of Educational Psychology, 74,* 888–897.

Miele, D. B., & Molden, D. C. (2010). Naive theories of intelligence and the role of processing fluency in perceived comprehension. *Journal of Experimental Psychology: General, 139*(3), 535–557.

Miele, D. B., Son, L. K., & Metcalfe, J. (2013). Children's naive theories of intelligence influence their metacognitive judgments. *Child Development, 84*(6), 1879–1886.

Miu, A. S., & Yeager, D. S. (2015). Preventing symptoms of depression by teaching adolescents that people can change: Effects of a brief incremental theory of personality intervention at 9-month follow-up. *Clinical Psychological Science, 3*(5), 726–743.

Moser, J. S., Schroder, H. S., Heeter, C., Moran, T. P., & Lee, Y.-H. (2011). Mind your errors: Evidence for a neural mechanism linking growth mind-set to adaptive posterror adjustments. *Psychological Science, 22*(12), 1484–1489.

Mueller, C., Rowe, M. L., & Zuckerman, B. (2017). Mindset matters for parents and adolescents. *JAMA Pediatrics, 171*(5), 415–416.

Mukhopadhyay, A., & Yeung, C. W. M. (2010). Building character: Effects of lay theories of self-control on the selection of products for children. *Journal of Marketing Research, 47,* 240–250.

Neel, R., & Shapiro, J. R. (2012). Is racial bias malleable?: Whites' lay theories of racial bias predict divergent strategies for interracial interactions. *Journal of Personality and Social Psychology, 103*(1), 101–120.

Nussbaum, A. D., & Dweck, C. S. (2008). Defensiveness versus remediation: Self-theories and modes of self-esteem maintenance. *Personality and Social Psychology Bulletin, 34*(5), 599–612.

Orosz, G., Walton, G. M., Böthe, B., Tóth-Király, I., Henderson, A., & Dweck, C. S. (2020). *Can mindfulness help people implement a growth mindset?: Two field experiments in Hungary.* Unpublished manuscript, Stanford University, Stanford, CA.

Outes, I., Sánchez, A., & Vakis, R. (2017). Cambiando la mentalidad de los estudiantes: Evaluación de impacto de ¡Expande tu Mente! Sobre el rendimiento académico en tres regiones del Perú, *83*, 1–106. Retrieved from *www.grade.org.pe/wp-content/uploads/ddt83.pdf.*

Paunesku, D., Walton, G. M., Romero, C., Smith, E. N., Yeager, D. S., & Dweck, C. S. (2015). Mind-set interventions are a scalable treatment for academic underachievement. *Psychological Science, 26*(6), 784–793.

Ramsden, S., Richardson, F. M., Josse, G., Thomas, M. S. C., Ellis, C., Shakeshaft, C., . . . Price, C. J. (2011). Verbal and non-verbal intelligence changes in the teenage brain. *Nature, 479*(7371), 113–116.

Rattan, A., & Dweck, C. S. (2010). Who confronts prejudice?: The role of implicit theories in the motivation to confront prejudice. *Psychological Science, 21*(7), 952–959.

Rattan, A., Good, C., & Dweck, C. S. (2012). "It's ok—not everyone can be good at math": Instructors with an entity theory comfort (and demotivate) students. *Journal of Experimental Social Psychology, 48*(3), 731–737.

Rege, M., Hanselman, P., Solli, I. F., Dweck, C. S., Ludvigsen, S., Bettinger, E., . . . Yeager, D. S. (in press). How can we inspire nations of learners?: An investigation of growth mindset and challenge-seeking in two countries. *American Psychologist.*

Robins, R. W., & Pals, J. L. (2002). Implicit self-theories in the academic domain: Implications for goal orientation, attributions, affect, and self-esteem change. *Self and Identity, 1*(4), 313–336.

Rueda, M. R., Posner, M. I., & Rothbart, M. K. (2005). The development of executive attention: Contributions to the emergence of self-regulation. *Developmental Neuropsychology, 28*(2), 573–594.

Sauce, B., & Matzel, L. D. (2018). The paradox of intelligence: Heritability and malleability coexist in hidden gene–environment interplay. *Psychological Bulletin, 144*(1), 26–47.

Schleider, J. L., & Weisz, J. R. (2016). Reducing risk for anxiety and depression in adolescents: Effects of a single-session intervention teaching that personality can change. *Behaviour Research and Therapy, 87*, 170–181.

Schumann, K., Zaki, J., & Dweck, C. S. (2014). Addressing the empathy deficit: Beliefs about the malleability of empathy predict effortful responses when empathy is challenging. *Journal of Personality and Social Psychology, 107*(3), 475–493.

Seligman, M. E., & Maier, S. F. (1967). Failure to escape traumatic shock. *Journal of Experimental Psychology, 74*(1), 1–9.

Smith, E. N., Romero, C., Donovan, B., Herter, R., Paunesku, D., Cohen, G. L., . . . Gross, J. J. (2018). Emotion theories and adolescent well-being: Results of an online intervention. *Emotion, 18*(6), 781–788.

Sun, K. L. (2015). *There's no limit: Mathematics teaching for a growth mindset.* Doctoral dissertation, Stanford University, Stanford, CA. Retrieved from *https://searchworks.stanford.edu/view/11059824.*

Terman, L. M. (1926). *Genetic studies of genius* (Vol. 1). Stanford, CA: Stanford University Press.

Thomas, F. N., Burnette, J. L., & Hoyt, C. L. (2019). Mindsets of health and healthy eating intentions. *Journal of Applied Social Psychology, 49*(6), 372–380.

Tipton, E. (2013). Improving generalizations from experiments using propensity score subclassification: Assumptions, properties, and contexts. *Journal of Educational and Behavioral Statistics, 38*(3), 239–266.

Walton, G. M., & Dweck, C. S. (2009). Solving social problems like a psychologist. *Perspectives on Psychological Science, 4*(1), 101–102.

Walton, G. M., & Wilson, T. D. (2018). Wise interventions: Psychological remedies for social and personal problems. *Psychological Review, 125*(5), 617–655.

Weiner, B. (1985). An attributional theory of emotion and motivation. *Psychological Review, 92*(4), 548–573.

Weiner, B., & Kukla, A. (1970). An attributional analysis of achievement motivation. *Journal of Personality and Social Psychology, 15*(1), 1–20.

Weisz, E. (2018). *Building empathy through psychological interventions.* Stanford, CA: Stanford University Press.

Yeager, D. S., Carroll, J. M., Buontempo, J., Cimpian, A., Woody, S., Crosnoe, R., . . . Dweck, C. S. (2020). *Teacher mindsets help explain where a growth mindset intervention does and doesn't work.* Unpublished manuscript, University of Texas at Austin.

Yeager, D. S., & Dweck, C. S. (2012). Mindsets that promote resilience: When students believe that personal characteristics can be developed. *Educational Psychologist, 47*(4), 302–314.

Yeager, D. S., Hanselman, P., Walton, G. M., Murray, J. S., Crosnoe, R., Muller, C., . . . Dweck, C. S. (2019). A national experiment reveals where a growth mindset improves achievement. *Nature, 573*(7774), 364–369.

Yeager, D. S., Lee, H. Y., & Jamieson, J. P. (2016). How to improve adolescent stress responses: Insights from integrating implicit theories of personality and biopsychosocial models. *Psychological Science, 27*(8), 1078–1091.

Yeager, D. S., Romero, C., Paunesku, D., Hulleman, C. S., Schneider, B., Hinojosa, C., . . . Dweck, C. S. (2016). Using design thinking to improve psychological interventions: The case of the growth mindset during the transition to high school. *Journal of Educational Psychology, 108*(3), 374–391.

Yeager, D. S., Trzesniewski, K. H., & Dweck, C. S. (2013). An implicit theories of personality intervention reduces adolescent aggression in response to victimization and exclusion. *Child Development, 84*(3), 970–988.

Yeager, D. S., Walton, G. M., Brady, S. T., Akcinar, E. N., Paunesku, D., Keane, L., . . . Dweck, C. S. (2016). Teaching a lay theory before college narrows achievement gaps at scale. *Proceedings of the National Academy of Sciences of the USA, 113*(24), E3341–E3348.

CHAPTER 2

The Social-Belonging Intervention

Gregory M. Walton and Shannon T. Brady

All students travel a social distance in coming to school. They leave behind families and communities to enter new social spaces where they strive to build new friendships and relationships with instructors while taking on challenging learning and achievement tasks. In entering a new social space, people can readily wonder whether they will belong, but particularly so when their social group is negatively stereotyped or underrepresented in that space. In this state of *belonging uncertainty,* everyday challenges can seem to threaten one's belonging in the setting as a whole. To protect this sense of belonging, the social-belonging intervention represents the general truth that common challenges and worries about belonging are normal in an academic transition and improve with time. Across a dozen randomized field trials, the intervention, delivered as an interactive exercise lasting an hour or less, has improved students' integration into secondary and postsecondary school communities and raised academic performance years into the future. Typically the greatest benefits are observed for students from groups that are negatively stereotyped or under-represented in the context. Here we review the origins of the social-belonging intervention in basic research; discuss its relationship to other psychologically "wise" interventions; review outcome effects; discuss heterogeneity and processes over time; share materials to promote effective use; and discuss implications for psychological theory, education, and policy.

BACKGROUND

The roots of the social-belonging intervention lie in both the sociocultural history of the United States and the intellectual tradition of social psychology, especially research on the experience of students who contend with negative stereotypes in school.

For African Americans, other people of color, and people from lower social class backgrounds, too often the history of the United States has been a fight for acceptance.

In school, this battle has been waged in court battles for desegregation (e.g., *Brown v. Board of Education*), in national law (e.g., the Civil Rights Act of 1964), in school district (e.g., school busing) and university policy (e.g., affirmative action), in civil protests, and in individual students' and families' lives (see Figure 2.1).

Simultaneously, students of color have had to contend with stereotypes that allege the intellectual inferiority of their group. The early psychologist Lewis Terman (1916), a prominent eugenicist, introduced IQ to America as a fixed constraint that justified the exclusion of children from mainstream education: "Children of [low IQ] should be segregated in special classes and be given instruction which is concrete and practical. They cannot master, but they can often be made efficient workers, able to look out for themselves" (p. 92). Moreover, Terman identified this inability with race: "It is interesting to note that M. P. and C. P. [children with low IQ scores] represent the level of intelligence which is very, very common among Spanish-Indian and Mexican families of the Southwest and also among negroes. Their dullness seems to be racial, or at least inherent in the family stocks from which they come. . . . These boys are uneducable beyond the merest rudiments of training" (p. 91).

As legal, social, and political pressure to integrate schools mounted, the formal rejection of children of color has, to some extent, receded. Yet the legacy of exclusion and negative stereotypes remains (e.g., Herrnstein & Murray, 1994). What is it like to enter a school setting in which your group has been excluded, is stereotyped as less able and less worthy, and may still be underrepresented? Could concerns about belonging that arise from this circumstance contribute to educational inequality today? By understanding the psychological consequences wrought by this legacy of injustice, can we develop theory-based ways to mitigate inequality and better support today's diverse students?

FIGURE 2.1. The 1957 desegregation of Little Rock Central High School. Reprinted from the Will Counts Collection, Indiana University Archives.

PSYCHOLOGICAL PROCESSES

Stereotype Threat

An important early observation in the development of the belonging intervention was that inequalities in school achievement do not simply reflect differences in ability. Instead, inequality reproduces at successive levels of education, even among students with the same preparation (Steele, 1997; see also Walton & Spencer, 2009). For instance, even with identical SAT scores and high school grades, Black college students earn worse grades on average than White students, and women earn worse grades in math and science than men. This "underperformance" is so common as to be termed "lawful" (Steele, 1997, p. 615). What in the college environment prevents equally well-prepared Black students and women from achieving at the same rates as Whites and men?

Claude Steele and colleagues (Steele, Spencer, & Aronson, 2002; Steele, 1997, 2010) pointed to a psychological burden imposed by negative stereotypes. Specifically, Steele and colleagues theorized that when a negative stereotype is on the table people can worry that others could view them through the lens of that stereotype: "If I do poorly, people could think the stereotype is true." For a student invested in school, this extra pressure, termed *stereotype threat,* can cause distraction and anxiety that undermines performance, ironically seeming to confirm the stereotype. In seminal studies, high-performing Black college students scored worse than Whites on a test composed of items from the Graduate Record Exam (GRE). But when the same items were represented as a laboratory puzzle-solving exercise—and thus as nonevaluative and irrelevant to racial stereotypes—Black students did as well as Whites, controlling for baseline SAT scores (Steele & Aronson, 1995). Similar patterns emerged among women in math (Spencer, Steele, & Quinn, 1999), and in hundreds of studies (Steele, 2010). Moreover, research has identified key mechanisms of this process, including distraction and a drain on executive functioning and cognitive resources, which lowers performance (Schmader, Johns, & Forbes, 2008).

Belonging Uncertainty

The fear in a testing situation that one could be seen in light of a negative stereotype may be the tip of the iceberg. Students who face negative stereotypes or underrepresentation may harbor a broader concern: "Can people like me belong here?" (Walton & Cohen, 2007; see also Goffman, 1963; Mendoza-Denton, Downey, Purdie, Davis, & Pietrzak, 2002). It is this broader concern that is addressed by the social-belonging intervention.

Worries about belonging in school are evident in stories told by many racial-minority and first-generation college students. Former first lady Michelle Obama wrote in her senior thesis, "I sometimes feel like a visitor on campus; as if I really don't belong. . . . It often seems as if . . . I will always be Black first and a student second" (Robinson, 1985, p. 2). Supreme Court Justice Sonia Sotomayor said she felt like "a visitor landing in an alien country [in college] . . . I have spent my years since, while at law school, and in my various professional jobs, not feeling completely a part of the worlds I inhabit" (in Ludden & Weeks, 2009).

We define a sense of belonging as a person's perception of the quality of his or her relationship with a valued school, work, or community context as a whole. This relationship goes beyond personal ties to individuals in the setting. Instead, it is fundamentally symbolic. It arises from events and experiences that represent to the person his or her relationship with the setting itself (Walton & Brady, 2017).

Belonging uncertainty is distinct from a person's level of belonging. A student can generally believe that he or she belongs at his or her school yet still question this belonging—that is, still worry or feel unsettled about it (Walton & Cohen, 2007; see also Mallett et al., 2011). The student may agree with both "I belong in my school" (belonging) and "When something bad happens, I feel that maybe I don't belong at [school name]" (belonging uncertainty).

Uncertainty about belonging itself, often informed by an awareness of negative stereotypes and underrepresentation, creates an important form of disadvantage: It shapes the perspective from which people make sense of everyday experiences in a setting. When people question their belonging, daily adversities can seem to mean that they, or people like them, do not belong in general in the setting (Walton & Cohen, 2007).

The idea that uncertainty about belonging might shape the interpretation of social events draws on classic research on hypothesis-confirming processes, which finds that evidence consistent with a person's expectations stands out in perception to shape judgments (Darley & Gross, 1983). Consistent with this theorizing, an early laboratory study exposed Black and White college students to a subtle social cue: difficulty listing friends who would fit in well in a field of study, in this case computer science. For White students this experience had little effect. But it caused Black students' sense of belonging and potential in the field to drop precipitously (Walton & Cohen, 2007, Experiment 1). Moreover, the event carried a racial meaning. When asked to advise peers interested in pursuing computer science or another field, difficulty listing friends led Black students to discourage a Black peer, but not White peers, from pursuing computer science. It was as if they had inferred that "people like me" might not belong there.

Pointing to a similar conclusion, daily diary studies show that everyday challenges can give rise to feelings of nonbelonging more so for Black than for White students at predominately White colleges (Walton & Cohen, 2007, 2011; see also Aronson & Inzlicht, 2004; Mendoza-Denton et al., 2002; Murphy et al., 2020) and more so for women than for men in male-dominated quantitative fields (Walton, Logel, Peach, Spencer, & Zanna, 2015). Thus, if a first-year college student from a socially disadvantaged background fails a midterm, fights with a roommate, feels homesick, or has her work criticized, she may risk inferring that she does not belong in college in general. Crucially, the events that signify a lack of belonging need not appear significant to a third party. In 2014, Michelle Obama recalled her experience coming to college:

> When I first arrived at school as a first-generation college student, I didn't know anyone on campus except my brother. I didn't know how to pick the right classes or find the right buildings. I didn't even bring the right size sheets for my dorm room bed. I didn't realize those beds were so long. So I was a little overwhelmed and a little isolated.

Despite decades of professional success, Obama still recalls her reaction to bringing the wrong sheets to college. To her at that time, they were more than just ill-fitting sheets, an inconvenience to be remedied with a trip to the store. The event implied that the answer to the implicit question she held—"Does a person like me belong here?"—might be "no."

The need to belong is fundamental (Baumeister & Leary, 1995) and closely linked to health, well-being, achievement, and identity (Walton & Brady, 2017). If a student infers that he or she does not belong in school, it can be exceedingly difficult to stay motivated and engaged and build relationships in school. Thus, inferences of nonbelonging can become self-fulfilling. They can deprive students of the supports needed to succeed in a challenging academic environment. When doubts about belonging arise from disadvantage, this process can perpetuate inequality.

How the Social-Belonging Intervention Bolsters Belonging

One way to remedy inequality, then, is to provide students a legitimate and nonpejorative narrative for understanding common adversities and challenges to belonging. Drawing on classic attributional retraining interventions (Wilson, Damiani, & Shelton, 2002), the social-belonging intervention uses carefully written stories from diverse older students to convey the truth that worries about belonging in a new school are normal or common at first for students from all backgrounds and that these worries generally lessen with time as students reach out to others and come to feel at home. That lens can forestall global, threatening interpretations of negative experiences.

Typically, these stories are shared in written form. To drive home the key message, the intervention uses powerful persuasive techniques. First, it leverages social norms: Challenges and feelings of nonbelonging are represented as typical and as typically improving. Second, it uses social proof: Students are exposed to individual exemplars who illustrate the treatment message through personal experience. Third, the exercise is interactive. Students are asked to complete a *saying-is-believing* exercise in which they describe how the process of change portrayed has played out in their own experience so far and how they anticipate it will play out going forward (Aronson, 1999). For instance, they might write a letter to help future students with their transition. That way participating students (1) actively engage with the ideas about belonging presented, deepening learning; (2) apply abstract ideas to their own experience, increasing relevance; (3) advocate for these ideas to others, a powerful means of persuasion; and (4) understand themselves as helping others, not as receiving help, taking on an empowering rather than a potentially stigmatizing role.

As a whole, the intervention aims to help students appreciate belonging as a *process* that develops over time, in which challenges are normal and to be expected, and one they can facilitate, rather than as a quality that a person simply has or does not have.

EMPIRICAL EVIDENCE

Outcomes

The social-belonging intervention has been evaluated in at least a dozen rigorous, randomized controlled field experiments testing effects on core academic outcomes. Improvements are observed most often for students who face negative stereotypes and underrepresentation in a school setting.

The seminal study delivered the intervention or active control materials to a small sample of Black and White students in the first year at a selective, predominately White university ($N = 92$). Delivery took place in hour-long one-on-one sessions. The intervention raised Black students' grades over 3 years, through senior year, with no change for White students, halving the racial achievement gap over this period. It also improved Black students' confidence in their belonging, well-being, and self-reported health at the end of college (Walton & Cohen, 2007, 2011).

A second study adapted the intervention for women in engineering. Students in the first semester of a selective engineering program (N = 228) took part in 45- to 60-minute small-group sessions. In majors with a critical mass of female students, which averaged 33% women, there was no gender inequality in first-year grades and no treatment effect. But in male-dominated majors, which averaged just 10% women, the belonging intervention raised women's first-year grades, eliminating a large gender inequality. It also improved women's reported experience and confidence in their prospects of success over the first year (Walton et al., 2015).

Later studies have examined ways to reach larger populations, including online through college and university systems that incoming students complete before beginning college. Yeager and colleagues (2016) created intervention modules, lasting ≅30-minute each, and tested these in three different institutionwide samples (i.e., ≥90% of each population). In the first, students graduating from urban charter school networks (N = 584)—almost all Black and the first in their families to attend college—completed online materials in May of their senior year of high school. The social-belonging intervention, adapted for this population, raised the percentage of students who stayed full-time enrolled in college over the next year from 32 to 43%. In the second, students entering a large public university (N = 7,418) completed online social-belonging, growth-mindset, or control materials in the summer before matriculation. Receiving either intervention increased the percentage of negatively stereotyped minority and first-generation college students who completed the first year full-time enrolled from 69 to 73%, reducing the gap with nonminority, continuing-generation students by 40%. In the third, students entering a selective private university (N = 1,596) completed either the social-belonging intervention, an intervention focused on critical feedback (see Yeager et al., 2014), one focused on cultural fit, or control materials in the summer before matriculation. Receiving any of the interventions raised first-year grades among negatively stereotyped minority students and first-generation White students, reducing the achievement gap with more advantaged students by 31%. (In the latter two cases, the various treatments were equally effective.) Not all trials have been effective, however, as another online, prematriculation trial did not affect first-year academic outcomes (Broda et al., 2018).

The belonging intervention has also been scaled through first-year classes. Murphy and colleagues (2020) adapted the intervention for a highly diverse urban broad-access institution and implemented it as a personal reading-and-writing exercise in an hour-long session in first-year writing classes (N = 1,063). The intervention raised the percentage of negatively stereotyped minority and first-generation students who stayed enrolled over the next 2 years from 64 to 73%. Binning and colleagues (2020), having observed gender disparities in an introductory physics course and racial disparities in a biology course, adapted the intervention for these classes and implemented it in class through story sharing, personal reflection, and small-group conversation. The intervention eliminated each disparity, raising course grades for women in physics and for non-White students in biology.

Another study adapted the intervention for the transition to middle school and delivered it to Black and White students early in sixth grade over two 30-minute class sessions (N = 137; Goyer et al., 2019, Experiment 2). The intervention reduced disciplinary citations among Black boys through the end of high school by 65%, reducing the disparity with White boys by 75%, and supported higher levels of belonging and fewer worries about negative stereotypes through middle school. Another study tested the same materials with diverse sixth-grade students in 11 public middle schools across a district (N = 1,304). Here all students benefited in sixth grade, including reductions in disciplinary referrals, higher grades, reduced absences, and improved school attitudes (Borman, Rozek, Pyne, & Hanselman, 2019). A third study adapted the intervention for the transition to high school and found improvements in attendance, course passage rates, and reduced discipline citations, especially for racial-minoritized students (Williams, Hirschi, Sublett, Hulleman, & Wilson, 2020). A final study, conducted in a German university, found improvements in first-semester grades for students with a migration background (Marksteiner, Janke, & Dickhäuser, 2019).

Mechanisms

How does the belonging intervention foster lasting gains? Figure 2.2 depicts a process model. Most proximally, the intervention aims to forestall global inferences of nonbelonging due to commonplace, everyday experiences in school (see Figure 2.2B). Consistent with this, an early study found that, in the first week after delivery, the intervention did not alter the kinds of challenges students reported on a daily basis. But it seemed to prevent Black students from inferring on the basis of daily challenges that they did not belong in school in general, thereby sustaining students' sense of belonging on more adverse days (Walton & Cohen, 2007). To illustrate, one day a Black student reported,

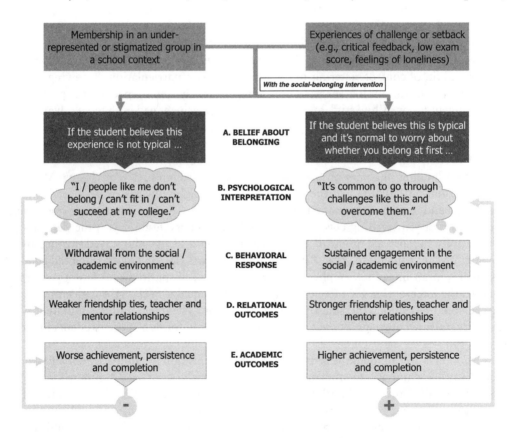

FIGURE 2.2. How beliefs about belonging can affect students' behavior and academic outcomes in the transition to college. Adapted from Yeager et al. (2016) with permission from the authors.

"Everyone is going out without me, and they didn't consider me when making their plans. At times like this I feel like I don't belong here and that I'm alienated." The intervention did not prevent adversities (the first sentence) but it mitigated the global inference (the second sentence). Over this week-long period, a tight relationship was found in the control condition between how much adversity Black students reported each day (how good or bad their day was) and their level of belonging that night and the next afternoon: Following worse days Black students reported lower levels of belonging. That relationship was not present for White students. And it was severed for Black students by the intervention. This change in the construal of daily events statistically mediated the gain in grades for Black students over the next 3 years, through graduation (Walton & Cohen, 2011; see also Murphy et al., 2020; Walton et al., 2015).

Effects over Time

By protecting students' sense of belonging in the face of adversity, the intervention helps students stay engaged in school (see Figure 2.2C). Over the first week following treatment in the original study, the intervention increased students' reports of the extent to which they e-mailed professors, attended office hours, met with study groups, participated in class, and studied (Walton & Cohen, 2007). Later studies found the intervention increased students' likelihood to live on campus and seek out academic support services during their first year of college (Yeager et al., 2016, Experiments 1 and 3). These behaviors help students integrate into the campus community (see Figure 2.2D). Indeed, the intervention has been shown to help students develop close friendships on campus, to become more involved in student groups, and to develop mentor relationships (Walton et al., 2015; Yeager et al., 2016, Experiment 3). Similarly, in middle school, it can improve cycles of interaction between Black boys and their classroom teachers (Goyer et al., 2019).

A follow-up of the original belonging intervention illustrates the lasting benefits that mentor relationships can confer to students. As noted earlier, students received the intervention in the first year of college with no subsequent treatment. Seven to 11 years later, at an average age of 27, Black participants who had received the intervention reported greater life and career satisfaction (Brady, Cohen, Jarvis, & Walton, 2020). Statistically, these effects were mediated by reports of greater mentorship during and after college. Consider this report (Black, treatment condition):

> "The first semester of my freshman year was very difficult for me. I was struggling academically, didn't feel like I fit in, and was unhappy with my major. . . . I began to spend more time speaking with my freshman counselor. We really bonded, and she helped me to realize that I did belong at [school]. Thanks to her, I was able to connect better with my peers and perform better academically. We've kept in touch ever since."

These results are consistent with a model in which the intervention mitigated early worries about belonging to help students reach out and build mentor relationships, which then empowered adult success (cf. Leitner, Ayduk, Boykin, & Mendoza-Denton, 2018). Thus, the intervention unlocks the potential of both students and school contexts.

Notably, this role of the intervention can be opaque to recipients. In the same sample, participants could not recall at the end of college what they had learned in the intervention and credited none of their success in college to it (Walton & Cohen, 2011). The intervention does not work through the salience of its central message. Instead, it helps students make sense of their ongoing stream of social experience in more productive ways, helping students build relationships of lasting benefit.

Heterogeneity

The social-belonging intervention addresses a specific circumstance: People who want to belong in a setting but who worry that they might not. The intervention is not designed to promote a sense of belonging in general, for instance among people who have no desire to belong in a setting. It will not help an artist with no interest in investment banking feel that she fits in on Wall Street.

However, most people care about the school and work settings that define their lives at least to some degree and want to belong and succeed in them. In such settings, the intervention is generally most effective for people who face group disadvantage, such as negative stereotypes or underrepresentation (e.g., Walton & Cohen, 2007, 2011; Yeager et al., 2016; cf. Borman et al., 2019). Benefits may also be greatest in specific circumstances that give rise to greater levels of group-based threat, such as science, technology, engineering, and math (STEM) settings in which women are grossly underrepresented (Walton et al., 2015) or where performance disparities are large (Binning et al., 2020).

To achieve lasting gains, the intervention further depends on affordance of the school environment in which it is delivered, especially the degree to which the environment affords genuine opportunities for belonging (Walton & Yeager, 2020). If, instead, group-based threats make belonging unrealistic (see Figure 2.1), the intervention may be ineffective and inappropriate. Further, if students do not have access to adequate learning opportunities, financial aid, or other objective supports, no psychological exercise is likely to improve long-term outcomes.

Thus, the intervention should be most effective for students who have reason to question their belonging in a setting they care about but which nonetheless offers opportunities for belonging for them, including opportunities to develop positive relationships that support lasting gains. Additionally, the intervention will be effective only when its central message is not already present in the setting in impactful, genuine ways.

COUSINS

The belonging intervention is related to a number of other psychologically "wise" interventions, each of which addresses how students make sense of important aspects of the school environment to improve relevant education outcomes.

First, it draws directly on classic *attributional retraining interventions* (Perry & Hamm, 2017; Wilson et al., 2002), which likewise aim to change students' attributions for the causes of setbacks in academic transitions. Yet such interventions have focused on academic struggles, discouraging stable, internal attributions (e.g., "I'm dumb") in favor of unstable, external ones (e.g., "It takes time to learn how to study in college"). These interventions can raise achievement, especially for struggling students, but they focus less on the belonging-related doubts that arise from stereotypes and a history of disadvantage and thus on mitigating group-based inequality.

Growth-mindset-of-intelligence interventions also provide a hopeful narrative in the face of setbacks. They communicate to students that intelligence is not fixed but can grow with hard work, good strategies, and the help of others (Dweck & Yeager, Chapter 1, this volume), thus implying that, if you fail a math test, you are not "dumb at math" but can improve with effort and a new approach. Like attributional retraining interventions, growth-mindset interventions focus less on social-relational worries that arise from negative stereotypes and thus on this source of group-based inequality.

Like belonging interventions, *theory-of-personality interventions* focus on students' social experience in school and the possibility of improvement in the face of challenges. However, they emphasize not belonging but the potential for individuals to change and, in particular, the idea that bullies need not always be bullies and victims need not always be victims (Yeager & Lee, Chapter 13, this volume). Among adolescents, this can reduce aggression and increase prosocial behavior following ostracism, improve mental and physical health, and raise academic achievement.

Value-affirmation interventions share a common origin with belonging interventions in research on stereotype threat. But rather than providing an adaptive narrative for understanding adversities, affirmation interventions aim to protect people's sense of inherent worth and value to help them cope (Sherman, Lokhande, Müller, & Cohen, Chapter 3, this volume; see also Garcia & Cohen, 2013). They do so by asking students to reflect on values of enduring personal importance, which serve as unconditional sources of worth and helps people confront threats more effectively. The processes initiated by affirmation interventions can be both similar to and different from those initiated by belonging interventions (see Cook, Purdie-Vaughns, Garcia, & Cohen, 2012; Sherman et al., 2013; Walton & Brady, 2017). In the only direct empirical comparison, both the belonging intervention and an affirmation-training intervention (inspired by classic affirmation interventions) improved women's psychological response to daily events (e.g., confidence in handling daily adversities) and raised first-year grades in male-dominated engineering fields (Walton et al., 2015). Yet other processes differed. Whereas the belonging intervention helped women develop greater friendships with male peers, affirmation increased women's identification with their gender group and promoted friendships with other women. It was as though the former helped women experience a warmer climate in engineering while the latter helped women develop personal resources to weather a chilly climate.

Difference-education interventions also address social challenges faced by students from marginalized backgrounds coming to college but whereas the belonging intervention emphasizes everyday challenges experienced by all students, difference-education interventions emphasize group-specific challenges, such as those faced uniquely by first-generation college students (Stephens, Hamedani, & Townsend, Chapter 5, this volume). However, both approaches convey that challenges are not specific to the self but normal across a group of people and improve with time, and thus not evidence of a general lack of belonging.

INTERVENTION CONTENT AND IMPLEMENTATION

Belonging Guide

Complete materials from all published studies through 2017 we have coauthored, along with annotations and guidance on customization, are available in the Belonging Guide (Walton, Murphy, Logel, Yeager, & the College Transition Collaborative, 2017; see Appendix 2.1 for annotated materials from Walton and Cohen [2011]).

When and How Is the Intervention Delivered?

There are many opportunities to convey the basic idea in the belonging intervention, that belonging is a normal process that develops over time. In college contexts, this can be done from prior to the first year to during that year, from one-on-one sessions (Walton & Cohen, 2007, 2011) to small-group sessions (Walton et al., 2015) to first-year classes (Binning et al., 2020; Murphy et al., 2020) to online modules (Broda et al., 2018; Yeager et al., 2016; see also Devers et al., 2016). These sessions generally last 30–60 minutes. In middle school, the intervention has been delivered over two 30-minute class sessions early in sixth and seventh grades (Borman et al., 2019; Goyer et al., 2019).

How Is the Intervention Represented?

Generally, the intervention is represented as an effort to learn from students about their experience in the academic transition to benefit future students. Students are told they will review conclusions and stories from older students and share their own experience and expertise with future students to give them a better sense of what the transition will be like. Thus, participants are represented as benefactors and co-creators of an exercise to help others, not as beneficiaries of an intervention or recipients of a persuasive message.

Nuts and Bolts: Of What Does the Intervention Consist?

The intervention includes (1) summary information about the experiences of students in the academic transition, which directly conveys the intervention message; (2) stories from older students that illustrate this message from diverse perspectives; and (3) interactive components that allow students to connect this message to their own experience and articulate it for themselves. These materials convey two broad themes:

1. That it is normal to worry at first about whether you belong in a new school.
2. That these difficulties do not mean that you do not belong; rather, with time and effort, most students typically come to feel at home in the school.

Stories

Most studies of college students have included six to nine stories (~100–150 words per story); those of middle-school students, three stories in each of two sessions (~85 words per story). The stories are represented as typical of diverse students' experience in the transition at hand. They are best understood as parables. Each describes an individual student's trajectory, drawing on past materials and students' experiences gathered in interviews and focus groups with careful editing to address critical themes effectively. As parables, they do not give advice, which could feel prescriptive, presumptuous, or inapplicable (cf. Eskreis-Winkler, Fischbach, & Duckworth, 2018). Instead, they offer multiple models for how a person's experience could develop over time (Lockwood & Kunda, 1997). While they all convey the same theme, they also include some range to increase the likelihood participating students find models who experienced challenges that relate to their own circumstance and see diverse trajectories of growth from these challenges.

DESCRIBING CHALLENGES TO BELONGING

First, the stories articulate specific common worries and everyday negative experiences many students have in an academic transition. Further, they voice the negative thoughts and feelings a student can have in response to these challenges, including feelings of non-belonging (e.g., "I thought professors were scary," Appendix 2.1, B, Story 3). They thus represent experiences, thoughts, and feelings of nonbelonging as normal. These challenges can be attributed explicitly to the difficulty of the transition (e.g., "Still, I think the transition to college is difficult, and it was for me . . . ," Appendix 2.1, B, Story 2). They are not attributed to the school itself. Instead, negative content is placed within a positive overall representation of the school appropriate for the setting (e.g., "I love [school name] and I wouldn't trade my experiences here for anything. . . . Still . . . ," Appendix 2,1, B, Story 2). Thus, the materials validate the pride students often feel in their school, even as they acknowledge normative challenges and doubts.

The challenges described are appropriate to the context. In college, they may include interactions with instructors (e.g., feeling intimidated, receiving critical feedback) and peers in academic contexts (e.g., joining study groups), academic setbacks (a poor grade), challenges making friends, and missing home or older friends. Importantly, the stories do not raise negative experiences or doubts without resolving their implications for belonging; the reader is not left to wonder whether the protagonist in fact does belong. They also do not reify negative norms (e.g., "Everyone is depressed," "Everyone gets drunk all the time") or attribute difficulties to enduring negative qualities of the school (e.g., "There's a lot of pressure here").

The stories are attributed to upper-year students whose seniority affords them a sufficiently long vantage point on the transition, usually through a "tag" at the end of the story that represents his or her identity (see Appendix 2.1). The students are diverse, including both students who are more and less advantaged in the setting. To counter the stereotype that only disadvantaged students question their belonging, the strongest characterization of feelings of nonbelonging (e.g., feeling intimidated in class) are attributed to more advantaged students, such as to Whites in a predominately White college (Walton & Cohen, 2011) or to men in engineering (Walton et al., 2015). These "counterstereotypical" stories render the intervention distinct from approaches that emphasize role models, in which in-group members illustrate a path of growth for the self (cf. Lockwood & Kunda, 1997; Stephens et al., Chapter 5, this volume). Instead, the emphasis is on feelings of nonbelonging that arise from difficulties in the academic transition experienced by all students.

DESCRIBING IMPROVEMENT IN BELONGING WITH TIME

Second, the stories describe trajectories of improvement: How negative experiences and doubts lessen with time, as students find communities and come to feel at home in the school. This improvement is characterized by (1) behaviors that support belonging, such as initiative a student takes to connect with others (e.g., attending office hours) or specific activities or communities he or she joins (e.g., a student organization); (2) the development of relationships that support belonging, such as with instructors or peers; and (3) psychological change that supports belonging. This psychological change includes both new, more adaptive attributions for specific common challenges (e.g., "I had to remind myself that making close friends takes time," Appendix 2.1, B, Story 6; "And I saw that even when professors are critical, or their grading harsh, it didn't mean they looked down on me or that I didn't belong. It was just their way of motivating high-achieving [school name] students," Appendix 2.1, B, Story 3) and the broad belief system targeted by the intervention ("Everybody feels they are different freshman year from everybody else, when really in at least some ways we are all pretty similar. Since I realized that, my experience has been almost one-hundred percent positive," Appendix 2.1, B, Story 1). Thus, the exemplars model new behaviors, new relationships, and new ways of thinking that support belonging.

Improvement is attributed both to the passage of time and to students' efforts, resourcefulness, and resilience. The role of time is significant, as belonging can improve with time as a person gets used to a new place and is receptive to efforts initiated by others. Stories should not emphasize fixed qualities of individuals (e.g., "You have to be outgoing to succeed here") or atypical help, luck, or specific formal resources that may be unavailable to or inappropriate for other students. For example, in a story about feeling intimidated by professors, it would not be helpful to say, "Then I met Professor X and he made all the difference." The stories should not depict saviors but the patience, effective strategies, and persistence all students can use to build belonging (e.g., "I began to take more initiative in going to office hours and meeting with professors. When I made the effort, I found that my professors became quite warm and were invested in me and in my doing well," Appendix 2.1, B, Story 4).

The timeline for improvement should be represented vaguely (e.g., "With time . . . "); otherwise students could worry that they have "missed the boat" if they lack a sense of belonging at a specific future point in time. It could also be problematic to represent improvement in a specific distant future—then challenges may seem insurmountable or not worth waiting out. The stories may also validate challenges or doubts that are ongoing but represent these as not a fundamental threat to belonging (e.g., "Though I still have doubts about myself sometimes they're the kinds of things everybody feels on occasion," Appendix 2.1, B, Story 8).

Although the stories emphasize challenges experienced by all students, they may also acknowledge group-specific challenges (Stephens et al., Chapter 5, this volume). For instance, interviews with upper-year students in engineering revealed that women sometimes felt excluded from male peer groups. A corresponding intervention story validated this experience but curtailed its negative implications for belonging (Walton et al., 2015, Story 7):

> " . . . I remember once in my first term having lunch with some other civil engineers. They spent 90% of the time talking about hockey, about which I know next to nothing. I felt like I didn't belong. It was discouraging. But over time I got to know my classmates better, individually and as a group. Once I remember talking about the TV show *Monster Machines,* which I have to admit I love. We had a great time sharing stories about the different episodes. Even though I don't share their love of hockey, I realized that we do have a lot in common—an interest in how things work—and that's why we're all engineers. . . . "

DETAILS AND COHERENCE

As parables, the stories use specific details in symbolic or illustrative ways to highlight both challenges (e.g., conversation about hockey) and improvement (e.g., *Monster*

Machines; "I realized that. . . . "). These details should be ones that diverse participating students can relate to, not individuating or specific to one person's experience. Details and language style should also be appropriate to the context at hand. And taken together, each story should be internally consistent and coherent, and emphasize a clear theme.

ORDER AND TYPES OF STORIES

The ordering of stories is intentional. For college students, the first story dispels a form of "pluralistic ignorance"—the perception that worries about belonging are specific to oneself (see Prentice & Miller, 1993). Attributed to a member of the group the materials are most designed to reach, such as a Black student at a predominantly White college, the story simply describes a student learning the core idea in the intervention: that early worries and challenges to belonging, which had seemed unique to oneself, are in fact common for all students (Appendix 2.1, B, Story 1). The story does not describe these challenges in any detail. It just implies that whatever difficulties a student experiences are likely to be more common than it might seem.

The next story or two feature counterstereotypical exemplars: students from more advantaged groups, who might seem least likely to worry about belonging, but who describe strong, specific experiences of nonbelonging and how these improved with time (Appendix 2.1, B, Stories 2 and 3). These stories counter the assumption that only members of disadvantaged groups face significant worries about belonging. Later stories address other comon themes in a context, such as teacher–student relationships, friendships, imposter syndrome, and common goals (Appendix 2.1, B, Stories 4–9).

For middle school students, the themes are simplified and interwoven (Goyer et al., 2019). Stories also may not be attributed to a student with a given social identity but presented alongside an array of images of students representing the diversity of the student body, thus implying that the stories reflect the experiences of students in that community as a whole.

Saying Is Believing

After reading the intervention summary and stories, students are asked to describe how their own experience in the transition so far, and/or what they expect in the future, reflects the experiences of the students they read about. These materials, students are told, may be shared with future students to help them better understand what to expect in the transition. In the original study, students wrote an essay describing their experiences of belonging, rewrote this essay into a speech, and then delivered this speech to a video camera to create footage that could be shared in first-year orientation the next year (Walton & Cohen, 2011). In other studies, students have written a personal letter to a future incoming student (Walton et al., 2015; Yeager et al., 2016). As noted earlier, saying-is-believing exercises can promote learning and personalization (see Aronson, 1999; Walton & Wilson, 2018).

Control Conditions

Multiple active control conditions have been tested. These feature the same structure of activities—summary information, student stories, and saying-is-believing task—but lack the critical focus on belonging. They have addressed instead how students (1) get used to the physical environment of a new school (e.g., generic information about the weather, campus, and city; Walton & Cohen, 2011; Yeager et al., 2016), (2) develop study skills (Murphy et al., 2020; Walton et al., 2015), or (3) become used to the school lunchroom and interested in state politics (Goyer et al., 2019). Some studies have also included no-treatment control conditions (Walton et al., 2015). Others supplement randomized control groups with nonrandomized campuswide comparisons (Murphy et al., 2020; Walton & Cohen, 2011; Yeager et al., 2016).

NUANCES AND MISCONCEPTIONS

Not Mostly about Friendships

One misconception is that the intervention focuses on purely social experiences, such as close friendships or feelings of homesickness. To the contrary, the emphasis is on experiences of belonging and nonbelonging *within the core academic context* of school—in classrooms, study groups, lab settings, and in interactions with classmates or instructors. The stories thus address worries about ability, about showing work to others, about being evaluated, and about receiving critical feedback or poor grades. This focus arises from the fact that it is the intellectual abilities and merit of racial-minority students and women in math and science that is most directly impugned by negative stereotypes, not their likability (e.g., Glick & Fiske, 2001). In so doing, the materials seek to convey that worries about belonging and being valued and respected within the core academic contexts of school are normal (experienced by many students) and improve with time.

Not Just Role Models

A second misconception is that the intervention is primarily a role model exercise and, thus, that the most important materials are stories told by ingroup members whose experiences are most relevant to participating students (see Lockwood & Kunda, 1997). To the contrary, an important aspect of the intervention are counterstereotypical stories, which show how majority-group members also worry about belonging.

Acknowledgment of Difference

A third misconception is that the stories ignore group-based differences in students' experience. They do not. They simply emphasize everyday worries about belonging that arise from the difficulty of the transition for all students and how this improves with time. Some variants also highlight group-specific challenges (e.g., the hockey story described above). The saying-is-believing exercise also provides participating students an opportunity to describe challenges they have experienced, including experiences of difference involving one or more of their social identities.

IMPLICATIONS FOR PRACTICE

There are many ways that institutions can convey adaptive ways of thinking about belonging and build a culture that supports this. Here we focus on implementation in school contexts, where most research has been conducted, but similar efforts can and have been undertaken in work contexts. We describe ways schools have found to convey and embody the specific themes of the belonging intervention. These efforts complement broader efforts to promote belonging and inclusion, such as to promote diversity among students, staff, and faculty; to represent and value this diversity; to counter bias, prejudice, and sexual harassment; and to structure communities so people have genuine opportunities to build relationships of value (see Murphy, Kroeper, & Ozier, 2018).

As with any psychological exercise, no implementation of the belonging intervention will be effective if the materials are not delivered in an impactful way, such that recipients pay attention, engage, and connect the material with their lives (see Weiss, Bloom, & Brock, 2014). Psychological interventions are not "a worksheet to be handed out or a lesson to 'get through'" (Yeager & Walton, 2011, p. 289) but a tool to engage people substantively in thinking about themselves or their experience in a new way.

It is also essential to maintain the integrity of the critical message (see Dweck, 2016). Simply handing out school swag or assuring students, "You belong!" does not help students see that everyday challenges are normal and improve with time. Additionally, although it may be helpful to hear adaptive messages about belonging multiple times from multiple sources, the message should always feel authentic, not false or manipulative.

Online Materials: Reflection Modules and Belonging Videos

Online modules can reach thousands of students with high-fidelity materials at low cost (Yeager et al., 2016; see also Devers et al., 2016). As with other psychological interventions, a challenge is to achieve impact at scale (Paunesku et al., 2015). There are two basic risks. First, the content of the materials may be less relevant for larger and more diverse populations. To address this, we discuss the customization of content below. Second, students may engage with materials less seriously when they are delivered online rather than in person. Thus, online sessions should be as attractive and interactive as possible. For instance, all past studies include saying-is-believing components, which engage students and invite them to reflect on how the intervention message is true for them. Some also complement written materials with audio recordings of upper-year students reading the critical intervention stories (Walton et al., 2015; Yeager et al., 2016, Experiment 1).

Another scalable way to convey adaptive ideas about belonging is through online videos. For the past few years, Stanford University has empowered outgoing senior students to create a welcome video for incoming first-year students highlighting key themes about belonging; new students receive this video in the summer before they enter college (see *http://tinyurl.com/pringle2017*). Although this approach has not been formally evaluated, it provides an authentic and impactful means to establish adaptive norms about belonging from the start for an entire cohort of students.

In-Person Experiences

Institutions can also implement in-person experiences to help students contend with challenges to belonging early on. This may involve structured reflections and small-group discussion or specific assignments in first-year classes, each of which has been shown to improve core academic outcomes (e.g., Binning et al., 2020; Murphy et al., 2020). Residential programming offers another opportunity. Stanford created a credit-bearing, discussion-based course, Frosh 101, to extend lessons introduced during new student orientation, including about belonging, into the first year. In a first session, facilitators (more senior students) share challenges to and growth in belonging they experienced in coming to college. First-year students then write anonymously about their own experience, describing why and how it is normal to worry at first about belonging in this transition and how this gets better with time. These writings are then collected and are read aloud without identifying their authors. The group then discusses common themes. The next week, students create mementos that reflect their discussion, such as a poem, a flier, a painting, digital art, or a sculpture, to be displayed in the dorm.

Organizing such in-person experiences may require greater coordination and be more costly per student. There can also be challenges to maintaining the fidelity of the intervention message. Yet they may help shift a school culture.

Customization

Past research testing the social-belonging intervention has incorporated customized content among standard belonging stories in new contexts, under the assumption that distinct challenges to belonging arise in specific contexts.

The aim of the customization process is to understand the challenges to belonging students experience in a particular environment and to identify adaptive and realistic ways students can understand and respond to these challenges in that context. This process generally involves user-centered pilot research, including surveys, interviews, and focus groups with the target population. For women in engineering, it led to the incorporation of new stories addressing feelings of exclusion from male peer groups (the hockey story above) and experiences of sexist disrespect on campus (Walton et al., 2015). For graduates of urban charter schools, pilot research identified a passivity in building belonging in college among students leaving highly structured urban charter school contexts. Story revisions reemphasized the active steps students need to take to build relationships with peers and faculty in college (Yeager et al., 2016). For middle school students, customization led to stories addressing worries about getting lost in a larger school, forgetting a locker combination, how one's stomach hurt the first few months, and a fear of talking to teachers (Goyer et al., 2019).

This customization has typically been carried out within the structure of the intervention outlined above, including the first story emphasizing pluralistic ignorance followed by counterstereotypical exemplar stories. The Belonging Guide mentioned earlier discusses why and how to include customized content (Walton et al., 2017). Doing so may make materials more relevant, authentic, and impactful for a context. However, the customization and writing process requires significant expertise and should not be carried out casually. Effective belonging stories are deceptively complex and difficult to write well. Moreover, basic themes and threats to belonging are often common across diverse contexts—thus, stories addressing core themes may be largely retained across settings. Customizing *some* content does not imply that *all* content should be customized.

PRACTITIONER EXPERIENCES

Appendix 2.2 shares reflections from two practitioners who implemented the social-belonging intervention at their institution through the College Transition Collaborative (*http://collegetransitioncollaborative.org*).

IMPLICATIONS FOR THEORY

First, the belonging intervention illustrates how social-psychological factors can per-petuate inequality (see Steele, 1997, 2010; Sherman et al., Chapter 3, this volume). The intervention does not expand learning opportunities. Nor does it increase students' basic capability (e.g., intelligence, self-control) or motivation to learn, factors commonly cited as causes of inequality (e.g., Herrnstein & Murray, 1994). Instead, it shows that potent social-psychological processes follow from societal disadvantage in the form of pervasive worries about belonging and how these reproduce inequality in school success.

Second, for theories of education, the belonging intervention highlights the untapped capacity for better outcomes present in both many students from socially disadvantaged backgrounds and many school contexts, yet how this potential can go hidden and unreal-ized as a consequence of unaddressed feelings of nonbelonging (Walton & Spencer, 2009).

Third, the intervention highlights the causal role of social-psychological processes for lifespan development. Social psychology is often identified with the "power of the situation," which can seem to imply that people simply bend with the wind of every new context (Ross & Nisbett, 1991). If so, social-psychological processes would not affect life outcomes. Yet worries about belonging can become embedded in the structure of people's lives, forestalling the development of social resources that pay dividends over the life course.

Fourth, for "wise" interventions, the belonging intervention provides a paradigmatic example of how a brief psychological exercise at a key point in time can produce recursive and, thus, lasting change. Here, the intervention, delivered early in college or in middle school improved major life and school outcomes 7–11 and 7 years later, respectively (Brady et al., 2020; Goyer et al., 2019). In each case it did so, it seems, by helping students make sense of and respond to daily experiences more adaptively, improving patterns of social interaction and helping students develop stronger and more trusting relationships, reinforcing feelings of belonging (see Walton & Wilson, 2018).

Fifth, for psychology, the intervention highlights the centrality of belonging for both sustained motivation and achievement (Carr & Walton, 2014; Walton, Cohen, Cwir, & Spencer, 2012) and functioning generally. Although we have focused on academic outcomes, the belonging intervention has also been shown to improve health, happiness, and daily functioning (e.g., higher and more stable self-esteem; Walton & Cohen, 2011; Walton et al., 2015). Such findings suggest that belonging may serve as a psychological "hub" for the self, essential to diverse outcomes (see Baumeister & Leary, 1995). Finally, the intervention illustrates the close relationship between cognitive (attributional) and affective (belonging) processes, and how an attributional approach can help people make sense of their experiences in ways that support better affective outcomes (cf. Marigold, Chapter 17, this volume).

FUTURE DIRECTIONS

An important direction for future research involves better understanding heterogene-ity in the effects of the belonging intervention. In some cases, it has not produced sig-nificant gains where gains might be expected (Broda et al., 2018). With what kinds of students and in what kinds of school contexts is the intervention most likely to improve outcomes? What contexts provoke latent worries about belonging but nonetheless afford opportunities for belonging that students could pursue? We speculate that benefits will be limited in contexts that are too toxic for students to reasonably belong or where genuine opportunity for learning is limited. Such research will inform and potentially integrate psychological and sociological theories of societal inequality.

As we noted, the belonging intervention can also improve health (Walton & Cohen, 2011). Where, for whom, and how do health benefits arise? Future research should include specific health-relevant physiological objective indicators, including measures of both acute stress responses (e.g., cortisol) and functioning over time (e.g., the conserved transcriptional response to adversity). Health and physiological outcomes may or may not track with psychological and academic outcomes (cf. Miller, Cohen, Janicki-Deverts, Brody, & Chen, 2016)—or with each other (see Destin, 2018).

Another important question involves the best way to think about customization and new contexts, both in school contexts and elsewhere. We do not yet understand as well as we need to the contexts in which more or less standard belonging materials will be effective, the contexts in which customization is helpful or necessary, and how to determine this. In many cases, it may be most effective to design high-quality and engaging but standard materials that can be presented to many people in a given kind of context (e.g., the transition to college), and to which recipients can flexibly respond by describing their own experiences (through saying-is-believing prompts or group discussions; à la Walton & Cohen, 2011; Walton et al., 2015; Yeager et al., 2016). In other cases, standard materials may be modified or even replaced by a bottom-up process in which participating students begin by articulating, sharing, and discussing in safe ways their own challenges to and growth in belonging (see Binning et al., 2020).

Finally, even as most research on the belonging intervention to date has focused on school contexts, people also strive to belong in other achievement-related settings, such as work contexts, where doubts about belonging may also undermine outcomes (e.g., Fassiotto et al., 2016). Future research should examine the role of belonging uncertainty and belonging interventions in such settings and how the intervention can improve outcomes and reduce inequalities there.

REFERENCES

Aronson, E. (1999). The power of self-persuasion. *American Psychologist, 54*(11), 875–884.

Aronson, J., & Inzlicht, M. (2004). The ups and downs of attributional ambiguity: Stereotype vulnerability and the academic self-knowledge of African American college students. *Psychological Science, 15*(12), 829–836.

Baumeister, R. F., & Leary, M. (1995). The need to belong: Desire for interpersonal attachments as a fundamental human motivation. *Psychological Bulletin, 117*, 497–529.

Binning, K. R., Kaufmann, N., McGreevy, E. M., Fotuhi, O., Chen, S., Marshman, E., . . . Singh, C. (2020). Changing social contexts to foster equity in college STEM classrooms: An ecological belonging intervention. *Psychological Science.* [Epub ahead of print]

Borman, G. D., Rozek, C. S., Pyne, J., & Hanselman, P. (2019). Reappraising academic and social adversity improves middle school students' academic achievement, behavior, and well-being. *Proceedings of the National Academy of Sciences of the USA, 116*(33), 16286–16291.

Brady, S. T., Cohen, G. L., Jarvis, S. N., & Walton, G. M. (2020). A brief social-belonging intervention in college improves adult outcomes for African Americans. *Science Advances, 6,* eaay3689.

Broda, M., Yun, J., Schneider, B., Yeager, D. S., Walton, G. M., & Diemer, M. (2018). Reducing inequality in academic success for incoming college students: A randomized trial of growth mindset and belonging interventions. *Journal of Research on Educational Effectiveness, 11,* 317–338.

Carr, P. B., & Walton, G. M. (2014). Cues of working together fuel intrinsic motivation. *Journal of Experimental Social Psychology, 53,* 169–184.

Cook, J. E., Purdie-Vaughns, V., Garcia, J., & Cohen, G. L. (2012). Chronic threat and contingent belonging: Protective benefits of values affirmation on identity development. *Journal of Personality and Social Psychology, 102,* 479–496.

Darley, J. M., & Gross, P. H. (1983). A hypothesis-confirming bias in labeling effects. *Journal of Personality and Social Psychology, 44,* 20–33.

Destin, M. (2018). Socioeconomic mobility, identity, and health: Experiences that influence immunology and implications for intervention. *American Psychologist, 74*(2), 207–217.

Devers, C., Daugherty, D., Steenbergh, T., Runyan, J., Oke, L., & Alayan, A. (2016). Enhancing student success: Disseminating a growth-mindset and social-belonging intervention with smartphones. In *Proceedings of EdMedia 2016—World Conference on Educational Media and Technology* (pp. 1674–1677). Vancouver, BC, Canada: Association for the Advancement of Computing in Education (AACE). Retrieved August 28, 2018, from *www.learntechlib. org/primary/p/173171.*

Dweck, C. (2016, January 11). Recognizing and overcoming false growth mindset. Retrieved from *www.edutopia.org/blog/recognizingovercoming-false-growth-mindset-carol-dweck.*

Eskreis-Winkler, L., Fishbach, A., & Duckworth, A. L. (2018). Dear Abby: Should I give advice or receive it? *Psychological Science, 29*(11), 1797–1806.

Fassiotto, M., Hamel, E. O., Ku, M., Correll, S., Grewal, D., Lavori, P., . . . Valantine, H. (2016). Women in academic medicine: Measuring stereotype threat among junior faculty. *Journal of Women's Health, 25,* 292–298.

Garcia, J., & Cohen, G. L. (2013). A social psychological perspective on educational intervention. In E. Shafir (Ed.), *Behavioral foundations of policy* (pp. 329–350). New York: Russell Sage.

Glick, P., & Fiske, S. T. (2001). An ambivalent alliance: Hostile and benevolent sexism as complementary justifications for gender inequality. *American Psychologist, 56,* 109–118.

Goffman, E. (1963). *Stigma: Notes on the management of spoiled identity.* New York: Prentice Hall.

Goyer, J. P., Cohen, G. L., Cook, J. E., Master, A., Apfel, N., Lee, W., . . . Walton, G. M. (2019). Targeted identity-safety interventions cause lasting reductions in discipline citations among negatively stereotyped boys. *Journal of Personality and Social Psychology, 172*(1), 229–259.

Herrnstein, R. J., & Murray, C. (1994). *The bell curve: Intelligence and class structure in American life.* New York: Free Press.

Leitner, J. B., Ayduk, O., Boykin, C. M., & Mendoza-Denton, R. (2018). Reducing negative affect and increasing rapport improve interracial mentorship outcomes. *PLOS ONE, 13,* e0194123.

Lockwood, P., & Kunda, Z. (1997). Superstars and me: Predicting the impact of role models on the self. *Journal of Personality and Social Psychology, 73*(1), 91–103.

Ludden, J., & Weeks, L. (2009, May 26). Sotomayor: "Always looking over my shoulder." Washington, DC: National Public Radio. Retrieved from *www.npr.org/templates/story/story. php?storyId=104538436.*

Mallett, R. K., Mello, Z. R., Wagner, D. E., Worrell, F., Burrow, R. N., & Andretta, J. R. (2011). Do I belong?: It depends on when you ask. *Cultural Diversity and Ethnic Minority Psychology, 17*(4), 432–436.

Marksteiner, T., Janke, S., & Dickhäuser, O. (2019). Effects of a brief psychological intervention on students' sense of belonging and educational outcomes: The role of students' migration and educational background. *Journal of School Psychology, 75,* 41–57.

Mendoza-Denton, R., Downey, G., Purdie, V. J., Davis, A., & Pietrzak, J. (2002). Sensitivity to status-based rejection: Implications for African American students' college experience. *Journal of Personality and Social Psychology, 83*(4), 896–918.

Miller, G. E., Cohen, S., Janicki-Deverts, D., Brody, G. H., & Chen, E. (2016). Viral challenge reveals further evidence of skin-deep resilience in African Americans from disadvantaged backgrounds. *Health Psychology, 35*(11), 1225–1234.

Murphy, M. C., Gopalan, M., Carter, E. R., Emerson, T. U., Bottoms, B. L., & Walton, G. M. (2020). A customized belonging intervention improves retention of socially disadvantaged students at a broad-access university. *Science Advances, 6*, eaba4677.

Murphy, M. C., Kroeper, K. M., & Ozier, E. M. (2018). Prejudiced places: How contexts shape inequality and how policy can change them. *Policy Insights from the Behavioral and Brain Sciences, 5*, 66–74.

Obama, M. (2014). Remarks by the president and first lady at College Opportunity Summit. Retrieved January 5, 2017, from *www.whitehouse.gov/the-pressoffice/2014/01/16/remarks-president-and-first-lady-college-opportunity-summit*.

Paunesku, D., Walton, G. M., Romero, C. L., Smith, E. N., Yeager, D. S., & Dweck, C. S. (2015). Mindset interventions are a scalable treatment for academic underperformance. *Psychological Science, 26*, 784–793.

Perry, R. P., & Hamm, J. M. (2017). An attribution perspective on competence and motivation: Theory and treatment interventions. In A. Elliot, C. Dweck, & D. Yeager (Eds.), *Handbook of competence and motivation: Theory and applications* (2nd ed., pp. 61–84). New York: Guilford Press.

Prentice, D. A., & Miller, D. T. (1993). Pluralistic ignorance and alcohol use on campus: Some consequences of misperceiving the social norm. *Journal of Personality and Social Psychology, 64*(2), 243–256.

Robinson, M. L. (1985). Princeton-educated Blacks and the Black community (Undergraduate thesis), Princeton University, Princeton, NJ. Retrieved from *www.politico.com/pdf/080222_MOPrincetonThesis_1-251.pdf*.

Ross, L., & Nisbett, R. E. (1991). *The person and the situation: Perspectives of social psychology.* New York: McGraw-Hill.

Schmader, T., Johns, M., & Forbes, C. (2008). An integrated process model of stereotype threat effects on performance. *Psychological Review, 115*(2), 336–356.

Sherman, D. K., Hartson, K. A., Binning, K. R., Purdie-Vaughns, V., Garcia, J., Taborsky-Barba, S., . . . Cohen, G. L. (2013). Deflecting the trajectory and changing the narrative: How self-affirmation affects academic performance and motivation under identity threat. *Journal of Personality and Social Psychology, 104*(4), 591–618.

Spencer, S. J., Steele, C. M., & Quinn, D. M. (1999). Stereotype threat and women's math performance. *Journal of Experimental Social Psychology, 35*(1), 4–28.

Steele, C. M. (1997). A threat in the air: How stereotypes shape intellectual identity and performance. *American Psychologist, 52*, 613–629.

Steele, C. M. (2010). *Whistling Vivaldi: How stereotypes affect us and what we can do.* New York: Norton.

Steele, C. M., & Aronson, J. (1995). Stereotype threat and the intellectual test performance of African Americans. *Journal of Personality and Social Psychology, 69*(5), 797–811.

Steele, C. M., Spencer, S. J., & Aronson, J. (2002). Contending with group image: The psychology of stereotype and social identity threat. In M. P. Zanna (Ed.), *Advances in experimental social psychology, Vol. 34* (p. 379–440). San Diego, CA: Academic Press.

Terman, L. M. (1916). *The measurement of intelligence.* Boston: Houghton Mifflin.

Walton, G. M., & Brady, S. T. (2017). The many questions of belonging. In A. Elliot, C. Dweck, & D. Yeager (Eds.), *Handbook of competence and motivation: Theory and application* (2nd ed., pp. 272–293). New York: Guilford Press.

Walton, G. M., & Cohen, G. L. (2007). A question of belonging: Race, social fit, and achievement. *Journal of Personality and Social Psychology, 92,* 82–96.

Walton, G. M., & Cohen, G. L. (2011). A brief social-belonging intervention improves academic and health outcomes of minority students. *Science, 331,* 1447–1451.

Walton, G. M., Cohen, G. L., Cwir, D., & Spencer, S. J. (2012). Mere belonging: The power of social connections. *Journal of Personality and Social Psychology, 102,* 513–532.

Walton, G. M., Logel, C., Peach, J., Spencer, S., & Zanna, M. P. (2015). Two brief interventions to mitigate a "chilly climate" transform women's experience, relationships, and achievement in engineering. *Journal of Educational Psychology, 107,* 468–485.

Walton, G. M., Murphy, M. C., Logel, C., Yeager, D. S., & the College Transition Collaborative. (2017). The social-belonging intervention: A guide for use and customization. Retrieved from *http://collegetransitioncollaborative.org/content/2017/belonging-custom-guide.*

Walton, G. M., & Spencer, S. J. (2009). Latent ability: Grades and test scores systematically underestimate the intellectual ability of negatively stereotyped students. *Psychological Science, 20,* 1132–1139.

Walton, G. M., & Wilson, T. D. (2018). Wise interventions: Psychological remedies for social and personal problems. *Psychological Review, 125,* 617–655.

Walton, G. M., & Yeager, D. S. (2020). Seed and soil: Psychological affordances in contexts help to explain where wise interventions succeed or fail. *Current Directions in Psychological Science, 29,* 219–226.

Weiss, M. J., Bloom, H., & Brock, T. (2014). A conceptual framework for studying the sources of variation in program effects. *Journal of Policy Analysis and Management, 33,* 778–808.

Williams, C. L., Hirschi, Q., Sublett, K. V., Hulleman, C. S., & Wilson, T. D. (2020, March 2). A brief social belonging intervention improves academic outcomes for minoritized high school students. *Motivation Science.* [Epub ahead of print]

Wilson, T. D., Damiani, M., & Shelton, N. (2002). Improving the academic performance of college students with brief attributional interventions. In J. Aronson (Ed.), *Improving academic achievement: Impact of psychological factors on education* (pp. 88–108). San Diego, CA: Academic Press.

Yeager, D. S., Purdie-Vaughns, V., Garcia, J., Apfel, N., Brzustoski, P., Master, A., . . . Cohen, G. L. (2014). Breaking the cycle of mistrust: Wise interventions to provide critical feedback across the racial divide. *Journal of Experimental Psychology: General, 143,* 804–824.

Yeager, D. S., & Walton, G. M. (2011). Social-psychological interventions in education: They're not magic. *Review of Educational Research, 81,* 267–301.

Yeager, D. S., Walton, G. M., Brady, S. T., Akcinar, E. N., Paunesku, D., Keane, L., . . . Dweck, C. S. (2016). Teaching a lay theory before college narrows achievement gaps at scale. *Proceedings of the National Academy of Sciences of the USA, 113,* E3341–E3348.

APPENDIX 2.1. Social-Belonging Intervention Materials from Walton and Cohen (2011)

(A) Prelude and summary. (B) Annotated student stories. (C) Saying-is-believing essay prompt. See Walton, Murphy, Logel, Yeager, and the College Transition Collaborative (2017) for experimenter script and more examples of materials.

A

Junior/Senior Survey: A Summary of Results

Department of Psychology, [school name]

[date]

[page break]

Survey Procedure

504 [school name] Juniors and Seniors completed survey materials in [date]. Participants were randomly sampled from the population of all [school name] Juniors and Seniors. Percentages are accurate within +/- 4 percentage points for the [school name] upperclassmen student body as a whole

Results were consistent across class year and across racial and gender groups.

Quantitative Summary

During their freshman year, many if not most students worry about whether other people at [school name] accept them.
73% - 86% of upperclassmen reported that, during their freshman year, they:
- "sometimes" or "frequently" worried whether other students would accept them in the context of classes and coursework.
- "sometimes" or "frequently" worried that other students at [school name] viewed their abilities negatively.
- were "some" or "a lot" more comfortable working alone rather than working with other students.
- experienced "some" or "a lot" of discomfort forming study groups or finding partners in science and language laboratories.
- experienced "some" or "a lot" of discomfort speaking in class.
- "sometimes" or "frequently" worried that professors at [school name] viewed their abilities negatively
- "sometimes" or "frequently" felt intimidated by [school name] professors.

But after their freshman year, most students come to feel confident that other people at [school name] accept them.
82% - 97% of upperclassmen reported that, since their freshman year
- their comfort in the academic environment at [school name] has improved "some" or "a lot."
- they are "confident" or "certain" that most other students accept them in the context of classes and coursework.
- they are "confident" or "certain" that other students at [school name] view their abilities positively.
- they "rarely" or "never" experience discomfort working with other students.
- they "rarely" or "never" experience discomfort forming study groups or finding partners in science and language laboratories.
- they "rarely" or "never" experience discomfort speaking in class.
- they are "confident" or "certain" that professors at [school name] view their abilities positively.
- they are "confident" or "certain" that professors at [school name] accept them.

B   Illustrative Sample of Free-Response Reports
The quotations below have been selected because they are illustrative of the major finding of the survey. These quotations are representative of the responses of participating students to questions asking them to describe their experience at [school name], and how this experience had changed since their freshman year.

Story	Annotation
(1) "When I first got to [school name], I worried that I was different from other [students at school name]. Everyone else seemed so certain that they were right for [school name], I wasn't sure I fit in. Sometime after my first year, I came to realize that many people come to [school name] uncertain whether they fit in or not. Now it seems ironic – everybody feels they are different freshman year from everybody else, when really in at least some ways we are all pretty similar. Since I realized that, my experience at [school name] has been almost one-hundred percent positive." - Participant #17, [dorm name] senior, African-American female	**Pluralistic ignorance**: Many difficulties in the transition to college are normal, even if they don't seem that way at first. *A story that unfolds over time; vague timeline of improvement;* ← *First-person perspective, development of personal thoughts and feelings, not advice-giving* ← *Does not deny differences in students' experience, even as it emphasizes commonalities* ← *Attribution to the group of greatest concern, implying that challenges people in this group face may be more normative than they may seem*

(continued)

(2) "I love [school name] and I wouldn't trade my experiences here for anything. I've met some close friends, I've had some fantastic experiences, and I've certainly learned a lot. Still, I think the transition to college is difficult, and it was for me. My freshman year I really didn't know what I was doing – I made a lot of casual friends at parties and other social settings and I avoided interacting with professors in class and office hours, I think because I was intimidated by them. It got a lot better once I chose a major I was excited about. I began to make close friends through classes and labs, and I started to get involved in research with one of my professors. Now I am happier than I have ever been at [school name]. It is really rewarding for me to feel like I belong in the intellectual community here."
- Participant #103, [dorm name] senior, White female

Counterstereotypical 1: Counters the stereotype that only members of minority groups question their belonging, featuring strong, specific examples.

← *Places negative experiences in a positive overall context; Attributes difficulties to the challenge of the transition to college*

← *Focus on belonging in the core academic context of college*

← *Vague timeline of improvement; Describes processes of building belonging and student's active role; Illustrative examples*

← *Attribution to a majority group member, who might not otherwise be thought to experience significant worries about belonging*

(3) "I didn't go to a very good high school, and I worried that my high school courses had not prepared me well for college. Honestly, when I got here, I thought professors were scary. I thought they were critical and hard in their grading, and I worried a lot about how they and other students would evaluate me. I was nervous about speaking in class and I didn't like other people to read my papers. Around my sophomore year I felt more comfortable – I began to enjoy my classes more and I found some close friends who I trusted. I also became more comfortable speaking in class, and sometimes I asked my friends to edit my papers for me. And I saw that even when professors are critical, or their grading harsh, it didn't mean they looked down on me or that I didn't belong. It was just their way of motivating high-achieving [school name] students."
- Participant #19, [dorm name] junior, White male

Counterstereotypical 2

← *Focus on belonging in the core academic context of college*

← *Vague timeline of improvement; Role of the passage of time*

← *Describes processes of building belonging and student's active role*

← *Models developing a new, more adaptive interpretation, here of critical feedback*

← *Attribution to a majority group member*

(4) "I had small, close knit classrooms in high school, and so it was hard to adjust to the large, impersonal lectures at [school name]. It's easy to lose the entire teacher-student relationship. It took me a long time to get used to it, and to understand that, just because there were more students, the professors didn't care less about me or think of me as just another number. Once I figured this out I began to take more initiative in going to office hours and meeting with professors. When I made the effort I found that my professors became quite warm and were invested in me and in my doing well. My junior year I became a research assistant with a professor in my major, and I have just loved working with her and her graduate students outside the formal classroom. It is great to actually participate in cutting edge research!"
- Participant #32, [dorm name] junior, African-American male

Teacher-Student Relationships: Addresses worries about belonging in the core academic context for a minority student without confirming stereotypes.

← *Attributes difficulties to the challenge of the transition to college*

← *Focus on belonging in the core academic context of college*

← *Illustrative example*

← *Attribution to a minority-group member, following two stories attributed to majority-group members*

(5) "Initially my transition to [school name] was pretty easy. Going out on [campus location] was easy and fun, and I met a lot of people early on. After Winter Break, things got harder because I realized that all my really good friends were at home and I didn't have friends like that at school. However, I decided that instead of searching for friends, I should pursue my interests and let things fall into place. I got involved in extra-curriculars, and I met people who had common interests and unique perspectives. I also got to know people in class as study partners who became close friends. I found a comfort zone by exploring my interests and taking the leap into an active life at [school name]. But this took time and before I found my niche at [school name] there were times when I felt quite lonely."
- Participant # 77, [dorm name] senior, White female

Close Friendships 1: Addresses challenges developing close friendships in college

← *Conveys that belonging challenges need not arise immediately in college but can come up later; there is no one set process*
← *Validates the common comparison of college to high school friends*

← *Describes processes of building belonging and student's active role*

← *Emphasizes the essential role of time; Validates negative feelings*

← *Attribution to a majority-group member, primarily so the set as a whole is broadly representative of the school student body*

(6) "The most difficult transition from high school to [school name] was coming from a situation in which I knew every student for the past seven years into a new situation in which I did not know one student before I arrived. Freshman year even though I met large numbers of people, I didn't have a small group of close friends. I had to work to find lab partners and people to be in study groups with. I was pretty homesick, and I had to remind myself that making close friends takes time. Since then in classes, clubs, and social activities, I have met people, some of who are now just as close as my friends in high school were."
- Participant #84, [dorm name] junior, Asian-American male

Close Friendships 2

← *Conveys the essential role of time in developing close friends; "Seven years" is intended, an awkward but realistic way a student might refer to both high school and middle school*

← *Focus on belonging concerns in the core academic context of college*

← *Describes growth in belonging in college while validating high school ties, thus not pitting one against the other*

← *Attribution to an Asian American primarily so the set as a whole is broadly representative of the school student body*

(continued)

(7) "Freshman year was a learning experience for me. I was unprepared for the workload and differences in grading at [school name], and I had to learn to budget my time wisely, so I wouldn't have extreme blocks of time studying and of not studying. After getting burned grade-wise several times and feeling stressed out in the process I worried that I wasn't smart enough. Fortunately, a conversation with an upperclassman helped me see that I needed to change my study habits. I learned to study and do my work more effectively than before. Although my start was somewhat rocky, it has felt good to learn from my mistakes, and I am proud of the success I have had."
- Participant #55, [dorm name] junior, White male

Counterstereotypical 3

◄——— *Focus on belonging in the core academic context of college*

◄——— *Models entertaining then rejecting a fixed and pejorative interpretation*

◄——— *Describes processes of building belonging and student's active role*

◄——— *Focus on growth and learning, not mere success*

◄——— *Attribution to a majority group member*

(8) "As excited as I was to come to [school name], I must admit that part of me thought I had been accepted due to a stroke of luck, and would not be able to measure up to the other students. It wasn't until late in my second year that I started to feel comfortable in my own shoes, and to believe that I really was up to par and could totally hold my own. After that, [school name] started to feel a bit like home, and though I still have doubts about myself sometimes they're the kinds of things everybody feels on occasion."
- Participant #60, [dorm name] senior, Hispanic female

Imposter Syndrome: Acknowledges the feeling of being an imposter, normalizes this and represents growth

◄——— *Focus on belonging in the core academic context of college; Vague (and late) timeline of improvement*

◄——— *Acknowledges that doubts can persist but represents these as immaterial to actual belonging*

◄——— *Attribution to a minority group member, following three majority-group members*

(9) "Walking into classes for the first time freshman year was uncomfortable to say the least. Particularly when shopping seminars, the only thing more intimidating than the other students (some of whom were upperclassmen), were the professors, who were all so highly regarded in their fields. Now I feel much more relaxed participating in discussions and asserting my opinions. I think everybody here has a common goal - to share knowledge and to achieve together — and for the most part everyone is respectful and supportive of each others' ideas."
- Participant #8, [dorm name] senior, White female

Counterstereotypical 4/Common Goals

◄——— *Focus on belonging in the core academic context of college; Vague timeline of improvement*

◄——— *Emphasizes common goals around learning; Validates that some individuals may be less than respectful but represents this as not a threat to belonging*

◄——— *Attribution to a majority group member*

C The results of the Junior/Senior Survey suggest that, during freshman year students often worry about whether or not professors and other students at [school name] accept them. However, the survey results also suggest that most students eventually become comfortable at [school name] and find a family of people at [school name] with whom they are close and feel they belong.

In an effort to further understand how the transition to college takes place, we would like to ask you to describe why you think this would be so— that is, why students might feel initially unsure about their acceptance but ultimately overcome these fears. Please be sure to <u>illustrate your essay with examples from your own experiences</u> in classes, seminars, lectures, study groups, and labs. Please take as much time as you like.

Note – your essay may be provided, anonymously, to incoming [school name] freshmen next fall.

[5 lined pages]

Feel free to continue your essay on the opposite sides of these pages

APPENDIX 2.2. Two Practitioners' Experiences Implementing the Social-Belonging Intervention

We asked two practitioners who implemented the social-belonging intervention on their college campus in partnership with the College Transition Collaborative (CTC; *www.collegetransitioncollaborative.org*) to describe their experience.

Kurt A. Boniecki, PhD
Associate Provost for Instructional Support
Associate Professor of Psychology
University of Central Arkansas

As a social psychologist by training, I have been excited to be involved in the application of my discipline to solving the problems that I now face as an academic administrator. At my institution, we've traditionally approached student success by providing academic support services, such as tutoring, corequisite remediation, and supplemental instruction. Although these services are effective, we were still losing nearly 30% of our incoming freshmen within the first year. Understanding why and what we could do about it led us to explore mindset approaches, such as the belonging intervention, that seek to address students' self doubts and their interpretations of the challenges they face in college. In 2014, we joined the College Transition Collaborative and implemented the belonging intervention to two cohorts of incoming freshmen. While it is still too early to determine the long-term effects of the intervention, preliminary results so far are promising and show that disadvantaged students are more likely to complete a full-time load of courses in their first term and first year. Of course, we don't expect the intervention to be a silver bullet that supplants our academic support services, but compared to those services that involve significant training and personnel costs, the belonging intervention is relatively easy to administer and requires very little in terms of resources. That's a selling feature to university administrators on a tight budget. Thus, we will continue to study the long-term effects of the intervention and explore ways to improve it.

One area for improvement is the delivery of the intervention. Though easy to administer online, we struggled with low response rates when using e-mail invitations. As a result, we shifted from students being invited to complete the intervention on their own time to requiring participation as part of students' on-campus summer orientation. That approach has its potential drawbacks though, because students may not have the time or personal space during a summer orientation program to genuinely reflect on and write about their own doubts and how they might overcome them, which is a key component of the intervention. Thus, we are exploring other means of delivery, such as embedding the intervention in online orientation modules and early classroom assignments.

A side benefit of our participation in the CTC has been the awareness it has created among academic support staff of students' mindsets and how these affect their interpretation of academic struggle. We are questioning the idea that "tough love" messages really motivate students to succeed and are recognizing that they are more likely to motivate them to quit. As a result, we are changing how we communicate with students. From advising sessions to probation letters, we are now more cognizant of what we say and how it can help a student overcome a maladaptive mindset. Also, just like the intervention is changing students' mindsets, I believe our participation in the CTC is beginning to change the mindsets that our staff and faculty have of our students. Many staff and faculty are abandoning the belief that some students are not "meant" to go to college for the notion that all students can succeed under the right conditions. A key tenet of the CTC approach is that student success is a process and that academic struggle is a normal part of college life. This idea has influenced the development of other student success initiatives beyond the intervention. For example, our university promotes a campuswide Fail Forward Week in which students, staff, and faculty are encouraged to share their failures publicly. The hope is that students will see their academic struggles as typical and will seek the help they need.

Jerusha Detweiler-Bedell, PhD
Professor of Psychology
Director, Teaching Excellence Program
Lewis & Clark College

Lewis & Clark was the first liberal arts college to implement the CTC's belonging intervention. When the CTC team approached our college with this opportunity, a focus on students' sense of "belonging" was not yet part of the institutional fabric. Yes, we were eager to understand better what kinds of students succeed at Lewis & Clark College, and yes, we were attentive to the importance of growing the diversity of our student body. Yet at that time we hadn't considered the role we needed to play in discussing and normalizing the challenges all undergraduates face in order to help our students not only persist but thrive.

Presenting the CTC's plan to the community required bringing together a large number of stakeholders, ranging from the dean's office to student life staff to faculty to the advising office and more. Initially, there was support for the basic idea, but a great deal of skepticism about using an experimental design for the intervention. "If something like this seems promising, why not provide it to all students right away?" What was harder to understand was the fact that this intervention had never been tested at a primarily undergraduate institution, and even if it had been, our students may be different from those at other schools. We needed to tailor the intervention to our own students and assess its effectiveness before putting the resources into providing it to everyone. These early conversations not only helped members of our institution to understand the wisdom of assessment prior to widespread implementation but also to spread the concept of belongingness throughout our campus community.

Early data demonstrated that our entering first-year students were being affected by the belonging intervention. As one student described, "Through reading about other students' experiences of coming to Lewis & Clark and becoming more comfortable over time, I have recognized that all students are experiencing the same stresses that I am now. There is no easy way to get around the discomfort of starting all over. The best thing to do is embrace the opportunities Lewis & Clark offers and be outgoing. By doing this, I will find myself at home in no time." As data collection progressed and results for the tailored belongingness intervention continued to be promising, Lewis & Clark was able to make an informed choice to implement the intervention for all entering students.

Although there is somewhat of a chicken-and-the-egg problem here, campuswide changes began to be put in place on the heels of the CTC's intervention. For example, a new, required first-year experience called the "Pioneer Success Institute" was initiated the year after the CTC intervention began. At the same time, faculty began to focus more explicitly on inclusive pedagogy and the ways students' struggles in those first few semesters could be normalized in order to make their classrooms more inviting places to be. And perhaps most striking, our institution recently unveiled a new strategic plan, where one of the six key goals echoes the CTC's intervention. As Lewis & Clark's president, Wim Wiewel, said in his inaugural address (October 5, 2018), "The overarching goal is to create an institutional culture of belonging, where all community members can fully participate."

CHAPTER 3

Self-Affirmation Interventions

David K. Sherman, Mohini Lokhande, Tim Müller,
and Geoffrey L. Cohen

A theory-based intervention known as "self-affirmation" provides people with the opportunity to affirm a sense of self-integrity, a global image of moral and adaptive adequacy, at moments of psychological threat. By assuaging threat, affirmations can allay stress and defensive responding. The positive impact of self-affirmations has been shown in many domains where persistent threats to self-integrity can impede adaptive outcomes. Affirmations, by broadening the perceived bases of self-integrity, render these threats less dire. The focus of the present chapter is on affirmations in educational institutions. On the whole, affirmation interventions have been shown to be powerful yet conditional in their effects. They have large and lasting benefits when people are under persistent psychological threat that impedes adaptive outcomes, when the affirmation is well-timed to this threat and activates the self-affirmation process, and where other resources for positive change are available and thus likely to be activated once psychological threat has been assuaged. To illuminate theoretical and practical considerations, a case study is presented from researchers working in a German school system with a large immigrant population; the successful application of affirmation depended on being attentive to the underlying mechanisms and theoretical moderators. In a final section, lingering theoretical and applied questions are discussed.

BACKGROUND

The motive to maintain a positive sense of self pervades social life. Dismissing evidence that one is engaging in risky behavior, reacting defensively to good advice, feeling vigilant and stressed in situations where one feels judged, and avoiding domains where one perceives oneself to be failing seem like discrete phenomena. But they are similar at a psychological level. They all represent the mind's attempt to deal with threats to the self. While the different responses to threats in different arenas protect feelings of personal worth in the short term, they can prove counterproductive in the long run. The attempts people make to protect themselves from threats to self-integrity are understandable and in some cases even adaptive. Given the pervasiveness of threats to self in the various arenas of life, people would lose confidence and grit if their sense of self were constantly under assault. But over time self-protection can have costly effects in many domains, including health, education, relationships, dispute resolution, and career success.

For over three decades, researchers and practitioners have applied self-affirmation theory to understand and change behavior in a wide range of domains. The theory begins with the premise that people are motivated to maintain an image of themselves as "morally and adaptively adequate," as good people who are able to control important outcomes in their lives (Steele, 1988). Claude Steele, the creator of self-affirmation theory, referred to this need as a drive for "self-integrity." Applied to social problems, self-affirmation theory provides a lens for understanding why so many attempts at social and personal change fail. It is because they can inadvertently threaten self-integrity, evoking psychological mechanisms that can shield self-integrity and also impede growth.

Self-affirmation interventions are situational opportunities, sometimes brief, for people to affirm their global self-integrity. Most often they take the form of an opportunity for people to show their fidelity to a cherished value they hold. Because values are central to people's sense of self-integrity, expressing one's fidelity to them is a simple and effective way to affirm self-integrity. Self-affirmation interventions have received the most attention in the domain of education. Indeed, affirmations have been applied in schools around the world. The United States, Germany, and England are three countries where thousands of students and dozens of public schools have participated—or are currently participating—in large field studies evaluating the impact of self-affirmation.

As Kurt Lewin (1951), the father of social psychology, stated, "There is nothing so practical as a good theory." Following his lead, we believe that the most useful intervention of all is the theoretical wisdom that follows from self-affirmation theory. Armed with this theory, educators and other practitioners can craft situations that meet the core needs of the people they serve. For this reason, we first review self-affirmation theory. Then we describe the successes and limitations of one of the most popular interventions derived from this theory—brief writing activities that encourage people to identify and reflect on their cherished values.

PSYCHOLOGICAL PROCESSES

Self-Integrity Maintenance

The theoretical basis of self-affirmation rests on the insight that people are motivated to maintain a global sense of personal adequacy. They strive to be morally and adaptively adequate (Steele, 1988; Cohen & Sherman, 2014). How do people maintain self-integrity in a world where it is continually under threat (Steele, 1988)?[1] When Steele first proposed self-affirmation theory, the prevailing notion in social psychology was that people were motivated to *directly* neutralize threats to the self. A smoker might defensively dismiss the dangers of smoking. An employee might attribute a bad job outcome to an unfair boss. A

---

[1] Although we briefly highlight the key theoretical and conceptual points related to self-affirmation theory, we recommend that any practitioner seeking to implement an affirmation intervention read a trio of review papers to understand the intellectual history and empirical development of self-affirmation theory (Steele, 1988; Sherman & Cohen, 2006; Cohen & Sherman, 2014).

teacher might attribute the underperformance of students to their laziness or lack of ability. Of course, people might also protect their self-integrity not only through cognitive distortions but through behavioral change. The smoker quits. The employee or teacher accepts a measure of personal responsibility and takes a more proactive role in improving the situation. Yet people routinely engage in defensive distortions and biased judgments in response to threats to the self. The "psychological immune system" gets activated and shields people (Gilbert, Pinel, Wilson, Blumberg, & Wheatley, 1998). Motivated reasoning (Kunda, 1987) can lead people to feel good about themselves but to deny important information and feedback that could lead to better outcomes in their lives. Yet, self-affirmation theory suggests that denial and defense are not inevitable outcomes of threat.

People have flexibility in how they respond to threats to the self. They can do so indirectly, and, when they do, this can provide them with the self-protection they need to accept and act on threatening experiences. The cardinal motive of the self-system, according to self-affirmation theory, is global self-integrity. If people feel reassured that, on the whole, they are good, moral people, then they are better able to cope with threatening situations without resorting to defensive justifications and other cognitive distortions that protect self-integrity at the expense of learning. This process likely starts early in life; infants can be consoled by touching and cuddling even when these do little to remedy the source of the distress. Later in life, people are consoled by prayer, religion, and social support—everyday "interventions" that reassure people they are "okay" even while failing to resolve the provoking threat (Steele & Liu, 1983; Steele, 1988).

According to self-affirmation theory, people have a range of creative solutions to the problem of sustaining self-integrity in any situation. A student who feels insecure about her ability might act out in class in an effort to win approval from peers and thus reaffirm self-integrity. The employee who feels alienated at work might decorate his desk with pictures of family and friends. People can create cognitive worlds, tailor-made definitions of success, that put their own qualities in a positive light. As research on the above-average effect shows, most people on average see themselves as "above average" on a range of desirable traits (Dunning, Meyerowitz, & Holzberg, 1989). They are able to do so, in large measure, because they define what it means to be a good "leader," "student," or "scientist" in a way that emphasizes their own idiosyncratic strengths and downplays their weakness (Dunning, 2003; Dunning & Cohen, 1992), a tendency that is amplified when their self-integrity comes under threat (Dunning, Leuenberger, & Sherman, 1995).

The major insight of self-affirmation theory is that people do not simply accept negative identities and stereotypes imposed on them in a situation but instead creatively find ways to convey, in effect, "Even though it may not seem so in this situation, I am a person of integrity." The key practical insight of self-affirmation theory is this: Practitioners should think about the raw materials they can introduce into everyday situations at every level—face-to-face encounters, relationships, and institutions—that help people to maintain a sense of self-integrity in constructive ways. To the extent that people have a range of possibilities for protecting the self in a situation, they will have less need to defensively distort or deny threatening experiences from which they could otherwise learn.

Threat is not intrinsically a bad thing. It is the mind's alert signal that there is a threat in the situation. Indeed, sometimes, as noted earlier, threat can motivate positive behavioral change (see Cohen & Sherman, 2014; Ehret, LaBrie, Santerre, & Sherman, 2015; Walton & Wilson, 2018). For example, when people are made to feel badly for failing to live up to their own professed values, such as practicing healthy behavior, they may subsequently seize an opportunity to redeem themselves—for instance, by making healthful choices (Stone & Focella, 2011). How people respond to threat, and whether their response is adaptive or nonadaptive, depends on many factors but perhaps most of all on the opportunities for course correction and self-affirmation available in the social environment.

Self-affirmation theory offered a challenge to cognitive dissonance theory (Festinger, 1957) and its theoretical elaborations that posited self-consistency as a primary motive (Aronson, 1969). The earliest research in self-affirmation theory showed that people could absorb a psychological inconsistency, even when it implicated a valued self-concept, when their self-integrity was bolstered in unrelated domains. For example, when people affirmed their self-integrity by reflecting on values that were important to them, they no longer rationalized their actions—for instance, by changing their attitudes to bring them in line with regrettable behavior that they had subtly been pressured to engage in (Steele, 1988). This occurred even when the values were unrelated to the threatening action. A person who asserts a love for art, for instance, might no longer need to rationalize smoking behavior.

Research in self-affirmation theory went on to assimilate many of the findings that had previously been ascribed to basic motives for self-consistency (Aronson, Cohen, & Nail, 1999). One of the most heavily researched phenomena in cognitive dissonance was the tendency to resist persuasive information contrary to long-held beliefs. In the health domain, people often dismiss or rationalize away evidence that they are engaging in behavior that puts their health at risk. For example, women who drank coffee were much more critical of an article linking caffeine use with negative health outcomes than women who did not drink coffee (Liberman & Chaiken, 1992). Such defensive processing or "motivated reasoning" has long been a topic of study in psychology (Ditto & Lopez, 1992; Kunda, 1987) but the underlying motivation for it was unclear. Self-affirmation theory suggested it arose from the threat such information poses to global self-integrity. Thus, in one study, people were more open to threatening health information about their unsafe sex practices when they had the opportunity to reflect on important values they held in a different domain (Sherman, Nelson, & Steele, 2000). The opportunity to reflect on the value of kindness or personal relationships, for example, led sexually active students to acknowledge the risks of unsafe sex after viewing an acquired immunodeficiency syndrome (AIDS) educational video, coffee drinkers to be more open to information linking excessive caffeine intake to health risks (Sherman et al., 2000), and female alcohol consumers to be more open to evidence linking alcohol consumption to breast cancer (Harris & Napper, 2005). In the years since these original studies, there have been several meta-analyses (e.g., Epton, Harris, Kane, van Koningsbruggen, & Sheeran, 2015; Ferrer & Cohen, 2019) and narrative reviews of self-affirmation in the health domain (Ehret & Sherman, 2014; Cohen & Sherman, 2014), as well as extensions into other domains, such as intergroup conflict (Sherman, Brookfield, & Ortosky, 2017). Together the research illustrates the impact of self-affirmation on increasing openness to threatening information and promoting positive behavioral change in a wide range of life arenas.

Stress Reduction

The experience of self-threat is like a psychological alarm. It can be triggered by any number of events. This includes exposure to counterattitudinal evidence, negotiations with a political adversary, a mistake, an insult, and so on. There is, in other words, something vital at stake in many seemingly mundane social situations: one's self (Goffman,

1978). Among the most important emotional symptoms of self-threat is stress. The stress response is an adaptive mechanism designed to mobilize the body's resources for an environmental challenge (Sapolsky, 2004). However, when too severe or too chronic, stress can impair performance and well-being. Research on self-affirmation demonstrates that debilitating levels of stress can be forestalled by timely activities that reaffirm self-integrity. For example, when college undergraduates were given self-affirmation activities to complete during winter break of the stressful first year of college, they reported fewer visits to the health center (Keough & Markus, 1999). When people had the chance to reflect on important values before having to give a stressful talk in front of a judgmental audience, they showed less of a spike in the stress hormone cortisol (Creswell et al., 2005), and for those suffering from high levels of chronic stress, performed better under the pressure (Creswell, Dutcher, Klein, Harris, & Levine, 2013). In a field study, college undergraduates who engaged in a self-affirmation exercise the week before their most stress-inducing midterm examination exhibited a less steep rise in urinary catecholamines, another biological marker of the stress response (Sherman, Bunyan, Creswell, & Jaremka, 2009).

Defense of Social Identities

The research described so far shows the ubiquity of self-threat and the self-affirmation process in social life. Another extension of self-affirmation research is to show how the motive to protect the integrity of the self is directly tied to the motive to protect our social or group identities. Affirming or threatening the self affects the way people judge and treat groups, including their own. After completing a self-affirmation activity, people were less likely to recoup lost self-esteem by stereotyping outgroups as inferior (Fein & Spencer, 1997; Badea, Binning, Verlhiac, & Sherman, 2017). They were more charitable when explaining why their sports team won or lost (Sherman & Kim, 2005). They were more willing to acknowledge "hard truths" about the injustices perpetrated by their country against minorities and competing nations (Adams, Tormala, & O'Brien, 2006; Čehajić-Clancy, Effron, Halperin, Liberman, & Ross, 2011; see Badea & Sherman, 2019, for review). They were less likely to denigrate the "other side" in political debates as biased (Binning, Sherman, Cohen, & Heitland, 2010; Cohen, Aronson, & Steele, 2000; see also Binning, Brick, Cohen, & Sherman, 2015; Cohen et al., 2007).

EMPIRICAL EVIDENCE FOR SELF-AFFIRMATION INTERVENTIONS

Self-affirmation works not by giving people something that they lack but by allowing people to manifest what they already have—what they stand for, the psychological commitments that ground their sense of self-integrity. An opportunity to assert one's important values, and to explain why they are important, is an opportunity to express commitments that have been a lifetime in the making. A self-affirmation, in this sense, is a situational channel that facilitates the link between inner assets and their outward expression. (We describe implementation of the intervention in a section below and provide annotated materials in Appendixes 3.1 and 3.2, respectively.) A critical point is that people cannot always go it alone in the self-affirmation process. They are constrained or supported by the situation they are in. Thus, in virtually all of the studies described so far, the self-affirmation takes the form of a question, introduced by the experimenters, that prompts people to reflect on their values and why they are important to them at a moment of threat. Without the question, people may be more constrained in how they can affirm the self, though people can be taught to self-affirm (Brady et al., 2016; Walton, Logel, Peach, Spencer, & Zanna, 2015). Naturally, there are individual differences in how much a person can spontaneously self-affirm (Harris et al., 2019).

Laboratory Outcomes

The range of outcomes along which self-affirmation effects have been documented include (1) acceptance of threatening information in health and politics (Sherman & Cohen, 2002); (2) behavioral compliance with threatening information, such as increases in healthful eating and exercise frequency, and reductions in alcohol consumption among at-risk adults (Harris & Napper, 2005; Ehret & Sherman, 2018; Falk et al., 2015; see Epton et al., 2015; Ferrer & Cohen, 2019, for reviews); (3) reductions in stress, such as stress arising from social evaluation or performance situations (Creswell et al., 2005, 2013); (4) reductions in self-destructive coping behaviors, such as excessive eating (Logel & Cohen, 2012; Logel, Kathmandu, & Cohen, 2019); (5) increases in intergroup understanding, as evidenced by less outgroup denigration (Badea et al., 2017), more compromise in political conflict, and greater willingness to acknowledge wrongdoing on the part of one's group (Čehajić-Clancy et al., 2011); (6) reductions in biased assimilation of new evidence, as evidenced by evenhandedness in political partisans' evaluation of presidential candidates' performance in a debate (Binning et al., 2010); (7) acceptance of threatening changes at the workplace (Jiang, 2018; Wiesenfeld, Brockner, & Martin, 1999); (8) reduction of ingroup favoritism in negotiation contexts (Sivanathan, Molden, Galinsky, & Ku, 2008; Ward, Atkins, Lepper, & Ross, 2011); (9) reduction in self-handicapping in athletic and academic domains (Finez & Sherman, 2012; Siegel, Scillitoe, & Parks-Yancy, 2005); and (10) better performance under stress and social identity threat (Creswell et al., 2013; Martens, Johns, Greenberg, & Schimel, 2006; Shapiro, Williams, & Hambarchyan, 2013). The scope of domains where affirmations have been shown to have ameliorative effects suggests that a similar psychological process, to some extent, underlies them all.

Outcomes from Longitudinal Field Experiments

Although self-affirmation theory has been tested in many contexts, we focus here on the widespread application in schools. Schools are in many ways the ideal field setting to test self-affirmation theory. Many of the outcomes that self-affirmation has been shown to affect in laboratory studies—performance, stress, health, openness to threatening information, prejudice, and social conflict—are priorities for schools throughout the world.

The initial self-affirmation intervention studies in educational contexts were conducted in middle schools, and in particular, with a racially diverse group of children making the transition to seventh grade in a middle class school district. Adolescence is a turbulent period of development (Eccles, Lord, & Midgley, 1991). Children go through dramatic physical and psychological changes, and cope with multiple stressors, including the challenge of forming their identity. The stressors can be especially acute for racial/ethnic-minority students, because they must contend with negative stereotypes about their ability and belonging in school (Steele, 1997). Cohen, Garcia, Apfel, and Master (2006) applied a self-affirmation intervention in this context. They had middle school teachers administer affirmation writing exercises (or control exercises) using a randomized experimental procedure in which teachers were kept unaware of both students' condition assignment and the hypotheses motivating the study. The writing exercises were tailored to be intelligible and engaging for this age group and for the students at this school. Samples of student responses to the values affirmation prompts in various studies are provided in Table 3.1 (Sherman et al., 2013; Ehret & Sherman, 2018). In the original studies, roughly half of the students at the school were of African American descent and the remainder of European American descent. Academic performance was assessed as grade point average (GPA) in core courses (English, math, science, and social studies), obtained through students' transcripts.

TABLE 3.1. Examples of Affirmations That Students Have Written in Experimental Studies

Middle school students (from Sherman et al., 2013, Study 2)

"Creativity is important to me because it allows variety and some fun in my everyday life. This would be important to me when I am trying to think outside the box and when choosing my outfits. Independence is very important to me because I am fairly self-conscious and get very nervous. This would be important when making a speech or doing independent activities. Finally, my relationship with friends and family is important because my friends and family make my day better and better, and when I need some help or confidence they will be there for me."

"Athletic ability is my most important value. I love this value so much because sports are my passion. I love football, baseball, and basketball. For all of these sports you need athletic ability and be able to stay in shape. My second value is I have a sense of humor. Humor is a great thing, it makes people laugh everyone has fun and there is nothing wrong with humor. I love all different kinds of humor and that is why it is one of my values."

"Creativity is important because I have to draw, sing, and, well, be creative! It's fun to be creative because you can see things in other ways as other people wouldn't. I mean, it's so fun to be creative. My relationships with family and friends are EXTREMELY important. Without them, who would I turn to? Who would make me smile and laugh and act how I am today? My last value is a sense of humor because I love to laugh or make people laugh and it just makes everything seem so much more fun."

College students (from Ehret & Sherman, 2018)

"Family and friends I value the most because they are all I got at the end. My family has been there for me every step of the way motivating me to do my best and pushing me to my limits and brining me up when I'm down. Friends will come and go but for the ones that stay are irreplaceable."

"For me it is very important to live in the moment and not take life so serious. Often times when I try to plan something out things do not go the way I wanted and I am just let down and bummed out. By living in the moment and enjoying each day as it coms I have become a much happier person I feel overall. Also I feel that life has a lot of ups and downs and a lot of what happens can not be controlled, by accepting that I have less worries and find myself less stress. I feel that this is a very important value to have in order to make you a more stress free person, which allows you to focus on the more important things in life."

"Athletics are the reason I go to such an amazing school like (school). Without them, I do not know how much life would of turned out. They have kept my head on straight and also caused me to excel in school. They have also helped me grow as a young man because they have taught me life lessons that would of been hard to learn without sports."

Note. See Appendix 3.1 for annotated version of standard prompt for middle school students. Material from Ehret and Sherman (2018). Reprinted with permission from Oxford University Press.

In three sequential studies, the self-affirmation intervention significantly improved the first-term grades of African American students, closing the racial achievement gap by 40% (Cohen et al., 2006; Cohen, Garcia, Purdie-Vaughns, Apfel, & Brzustoski, 2009). The effect was not that evident on performance on the exams immediately after the intervention (see Cohen et al., 2006) but rather emerged on *cumulative* performance as measured by GPA. The affirmation's effects took time to unfold. Small incremental improvements in performance compounded into higher GPAs by the end of the term. Consistent with this mechanism of compounding benefits, follow-up observations found that the effects of affirmation on GPA persisted for the remaining 2 years of middle school. Later research replicated the same positive effects of affirmation among Latino American students over middle school, with effects persisting into high school (Sherman et al., 2013).

Research by independent teams of investigators have documented similar benefits of affirmation among stereotyped groups. Borman, Grigg, Rozek, Hanselman, and Dewey (2018) tested the effects of self-affirmation in a large population of middle school students across an entire school district, finding persistent benefits on minority students' grades that extended years later into high school. Affirmation interventions applied by other research teams have found benefits among economically disadvantaged students—in particular, students who are the first in their family to attend college (Harackiewicz et al., 2014; Tibbetts et al., 2016), "further education" students in the United Kingdom (akin to community college students in the United States) in a preregistered study (Schwalbe et al., 2018, 2019), and female graduate students in business schools (Kinias & Sim, 2016). It is important to recognize that affirmations are not panaceas—they do not work everywhere and all the time. Null replications have been reported (Bratter, Rowley, & Chukhray, 2016; Dee, 2015; de Jong, Jellesma, Koomen, & de Jong, 2016; Hanselman, Rozek, Grigg, & Borman, 2017; Harackiewicz, Canning, Tibbetts, Priniski, & Hyde, 2016; Protzko & Aronson, 2016), a point we return to in a section below on heterogeneity of affirmation effects. Still, there are enough positive results that the ultimate verdict on this intervention, like even the most effective interventions and policies, is that it is powerful but conditional: It has large and lasting benefits under certain conditions.

Also, when affirmation effects occur, they can last for a long time and have ripple effects into other domains of functioning. In a follow-up study to the original cohorts of students in Cohen et al. (2006, 2009), African American students who were originally assigned to the affirmation condition in seventh grade were more likely to attend college years later, and more likely to attend the selective colleges that are key drivers of economic mobility among the disadvantaged (Goyer et al., 2017). Highlighting the breadth of self-affirmation effects in school, a recent study demonstrated that the same intervention lessened disciplinary infractions over students' 3 years of middle school (Binning et al., 2019). Acting out is sometimes, it seems, motivated by a desire to affirm the self. When that motive is fulfilled through alternative routes, students are more likely to trust their teachers and behave (Goyer et al., 2019).

MECHANISMS

Self-affirmation interventions have far-reaching and long-lasting effects through two sets of mechanisms: first, psychological processes that lead to enduring changes in how people perceive social experience and, second, positive feedback loops between the self-system and the social system.[2] Several psychological responses occur as a consequence of a self-affirmation intervention (Cohen & Sherman, 2014; Sherman & Hartson, 2011). First, affirmations evoke a more expansive self-conception (Critcher & Dunning, 2015). Thinking about the value of religion, or the importance of relationships, for example, helps people to realize that they have many sources of self-regard. From this perspective, a threatening event seems more surmountable. People can persist in the face of challenge and resist temptations to which they would otherwise cave because they have a greater confidence in their ability to cope (Burson, Crocker, & Mischkowski, 2012; Logel & Cohen, 2012; Schmeichel & Vohs, 2009).

Beyond increasing the psychological salience of self-resources, self-affirmation interventions also give people a more expansive frame for viewing a specific threat, helping them to "put it in perspective" (Critcher & Dunning, 2015; Sherman et al., 2013; Wakslak & Trope, 2009). When people experience a threatening situation, they tend to fixate on it, a state of vigilance in which the threat commands their attention (Cohen & Garcia, 2008; Kaiser & Major, 2006; Murphy, Steele, & Gross, 2007). In the short term, this kind of vigilance can be adaptive. However, in the long term, it can consume mental resources that could otherwise be expended on learning. It can also undermine psychological and physical health by focusing attention on adversity rather than the "bigger picture." Evidence that self-affirmation facilitates a more expansive view of situational threats is provided by research on the process of "psychological untethering." Under normal circumstances, people who face continual threat due to negative stereotypes, such as African Americans in school, display a tethering between daily adversity on the one hand and their sense of well-being and belonging on the other. They appear, on average, to experience a bad grade or negative feedback not as an isolated incident but as a confirmation of the stereotype, and their well-being and belonging falter as a consequence. However, when affirmed, this tethering is reduced and sometimes eliminated, such that adversity no longer correlates with well-being and belonging (Cook, Purdie-Vaughns, Garcia, & Cohen, 2012; see also Walton & Cohen, 2011). Against the backdrop of a broadened self-view, daily assaults to self-worth loom less large.

This untethering mechanism helps to explain how the self-affirmation process propagates through time, and for that matter how other psychological interventions do so as well (Walton & Cohen, 2011). Although the intervention is objectively brief, its psychological effects are lived and relived in the encoding of social experience (Sherman et al., 2013; Cook et al., 2012).

Longitudinal studies have assessed the untethering process as it plays out over time. Cook and colleagues (2012) found that for African American students in the control condition, feelings of belonging in school were tightly linked with academic performance. They felt less belonging in school when they did poorly rather than well, whereas European Americans' sense of belonging was relatively less conditional on their performance. But for African American students who completed the affirmation, belonging was more stable and relatively less tethered to their performance (Cook et al., 2012).

---

[2]This section on mechanisms is not exhaustive, of course, and mechanistic questions can be addressed at many other levels of analysis beyond what is discussed in this chapter. For example, research has examined a neural reward-related mechanism underlying self-affirmation effects as evidenced by activation of the ventral striatum (Dutcher et al., 2016).

In another longitudinal study, on days when nonaffirmed Latino American students experienced greater daily stress and adversity, they reported feeling more judged in light of their race. And on days when they felt more identity threat—that they were judged as a member of their group—Latino American students in the control condition reported feeling reduced belonging and academic self-efficacy (Sherman et al., 2013).[3] However, among Latino American students who were affirmed, these links between daily adversity and identity threat, and identity threat and academic fit (belonging and efficacy, respectively) were eliminated (Sherman et al., 2013).

On the whole, these studies illustrate the experience of self-threat in institutional settings and how affirmation affects this experience. An individual who contends with a threat based on his or her group identity, in effect, lives in a more symbolically threatening world, where daily adversities can confirm a perception that "people like me" do not belong. This perception can prime people to see their social world as even more threatening, making them more vigilant to threat, in a repeating cycle (Rheinschmidt & Mendoza-Denton, 2014; Yeager et al., 2014). However, an interruption in this cycle, one that expands people's psychological perceptions beyond the threat at a key transition, can have benefits that compound with time.

Effects over Time

The field research shows that the self-affirmation process can perpetuate itself over time. Brief self-affirmations can have effects that persist for days, weeks, months, and years. How? One way is through recursive processes—that is, processes that recur, because they feed off their own consequences (Cohen et al., 2009; Cohen & Sherman, 2014; Wilson & Linville, 1985; Walton & Wilson, 2018). Feeling affirmed, a person performs better. Performing better, the person feels more affirmed, in a repeating cycle (Cohen & Sherman, 2014; Cohen et al., 2009). The opportunity to initiate such a recursive cycle might be especially great at key transitions, such as entry to middle school or college, when early outcomes can have disproportionate effects on trajectories (Elder, 1998).

Another way that self-affirmation processes propagate through time is through its interaction with the social system, which may also be recursive. Self-affirmed, a student may perform better, and performing better, he or she may be recognized and rewarded by teachers. The well-documented effects of teacher expectancies (Rosenthal, 1994) may then carry forward the effects of the affirmation. The student may be given more attention and the benefit of the doubt, held to a higher standard, and deflected into higher-expectation academic tracks, all of which may feed back to further affirm the student.

A formal model of this recursive and interactive change processes is presented in Cohen and Sherman (2014; see also Cohen, Garcia, & Goyer, 2017; Ferrer & Cohen, 2019; Goyer et al., 2017). Figure 3.1 offers a diagrammatic model of a "cycle of adaptive potential." This model was developed to understand the process by which an intervention, such as self-affirmation, or any formative experience, can lead to long-term change.

---

[3] Such studies, of course, are correlational, so there is uncertainty in the direction of the causal arrow. Perhaps adversity causes a decrement in psychological well-being, perhaps the reverse path applies, or perhaps some third variable explains the link. We suspect the relationships are bidirectional and multiply determined. On the whole, however, the tethering effect shows that there is an intercorrelation among variables for those under threat that does not occur for those not under threat and that can be severed through timely affirmation.

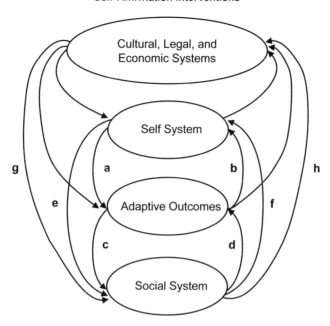

FIGURE 3.1. Cycle of adaptive potential embedded within cultural, legal, and economic contexts. Affirmation effects can propagate themselves over time by leading to changes in the environment that cycle back and augment changes in the self. A student who is affirmed (path A) may perform better initially, and that initial performance may then feed back to the self (path B) such that the student has two sources of affirmation: the original affirming event and the improved performance at school (and the sense of personal accomplishment and efficacy that would create). Doing better at school may lead the teacher to notice, give positive feedback or more challenging material (path C), which then may feed back to the student by leading to further improved performance (path D). The student, performing better and feeling more supported by the teacher or school as a result of this positive social feedback, may then challenge him- or herself further, opting for more difficult courses—for example, leading to a change in his or her social system (path E), which could, in turn, serve as further affirmation that the student belongs within the system (path F). Finally, the entire cycle of adaptive potential between the student, adaptive outcomes, and the social system is embedded in a set of cultural, legal, and economic systems that interact with the other systems (paths G and H, and the four other paths not yet specified).

It is the interaction between psychological processes and social processes, many of which can be recursive in nature, that drives outcomes through time.

From this perspective, an intervention like self-affirmation is a "trigger," the effects of which are "channeled" by the social environment (Goyer et al., 2017; Pawson & Tilly, 1997; Ferrer & Cohen, 2019). Latino American middle school students who completed a self-affirmation earned higher grades, the short-term effects, but then they were also placed into more challenging courses over the long term (Goyer et al., 2017). They were also more likely to be enrolled by their school in an advanced college preparation program. Another study found that some of the lasting effect of affirmation on middle school African Americans' later outcomes was driven by the fact that it deflected them from the remedial track in high school (Cohen et al., 2009; Goyer et al., 2017). Without the institutional channeling process, long-term effects of self-affirmation may not have been found.

Heterogeneity

The evidence of positive affirmation effects seems to suggest the value of "scaling up" the intervention to reach more students. One commentary urged "advancing values affirmation as a scalable strategy for mitigating identity threats and narrowing national achievement gaps" (Borman, 2017). Indeed, this goal is the objective of the affirmation studies in Germany, the United Kingdom, and the United States, as mentioned earlier. However, we think that "scaling up" is not so much a matter of disseminating the same intervention to as many students as possible. Rather it is a matter of targeting the intervention to those contexts where it is most likely to be effective. As noted, several replication efforts have turned up null results. As in medical science, interventions should ideally be targeted to contexts where they are most likely to be effective. Indeed, in medical science, it is increasingly clear that many interventions may have null results overall but still have benefits for a small subgroup of superresponders (Mukherjee, 2015). How do we achieve precise targeting? In short, through the identification of moderators, addressed in the next section. Researchers and practitioners need to identify *when, where,* and *for whom* wise interventions work best—an endeavor where much progress has been made and still more, we suspect, awaits. The following section structures the review of moderators around three factors: psychological threat, the presence of resources, and timeliness.

Psychological Threat

Most obviously, the effect of affirmation hinges on whether the target group in question is under sufficient psychological threat to impede adaptive outcomes (Cohen & Sherman, 2014). The first affirmation studies were conducted with African American students as the focal group. Virtually all their teachers were European American, creating an awareness in these students that the stereotype could be used against them (Inzlicht & Ben-Zeev, 2000; Sekaquaptewa & Thompson, 2003). African Americans in such an environment were expected to be under consistent psychological threat due to the negative stereotypes they contend with (i.e., stereotype threat; Steele, Spencer, & Aronson, 2002). Thus, it was this group that was expected to benefit from the affirmation. Consistent with theorizing, African Americans who were affirmed not only earned higher grades but also exhibited significantly lower racial stereotype activation on a cognitive accessibility task. Similar effects of affirmation on a negatively stereotyped ethnic group, with no effects on European American students, were observed in field interventions conducted with Latino Americans (Sherman et al., 2013). A study by Miyake et al. (2010) found that for female students in an introductory physics course, self-affirmation improved exam scores for those who subscribed relatively more to the stereotype that "men are better at science than women." In short, one key moderator of affirmation effects is whether students are under consistent psychological threat. These consistent psychological threats often arise from the groups to which people belong and the stereotypes that are targeted at them.

Threat may vary not only with students' characteristics but with features of the institution. Researchers conducted an affirmation intervention across 11 middle schools in Madison, Wisconsin (Borman et al., 2018; Borman, Grigg, & Hanselman, 2016). Using the procedures from the original studies, they found that the African American and Latino American students showed an improvement in GPA, with no effect on the European American and Asian participants. Although the overall effect size was smaller than that observed in the previous studies, it varied by school. The researchers found that the improvement in eighth-grade GPA among affirmed minority students was strongest in schools that had more threatening contexts, with threat defined as the degree to which minority students were underrepresented and the degree to which they underperformed relative to their European American peers (see also Hanselman, Bruch, Gamoran, & Borman, 2014).

Of course, there are limits to the level of threat an affirmation can mitigate. If the environment is one of severe threat, where at every turn, racism or sexism is confronted, it seems highly unlikely that affirmation will do much, if anything. Other steps will be necessary. It is mainly where there is a low-level but consistent threat that is impeding adaptive outcomes that affirmation is apt to be most effective. One potential benefit of larger multisite studies is that they enable researchers to identify the ways institutional settings vary in the degree of psychological threat present in them.

One strategy that practitioners and researchers can use to identify which individuals are under consistent psychological threat in a given environment is to assess the degree to which they underperform given their prior levels of achievement and preparation. Is there an underperformance effect? A telltale sign of underperformance is the extent to which a group of people performs worse than others even after prior indicators of success are controlled (Steele, 1997). This suggests that "something else," presumably something in the environment of the school, may be suppressing students' potential. Which group underperforms may vary by context. In the United Kingdom, for example, low-income students display a particularly large underperformance effect. Moreover, a recent study found that low-income students who were in schools where they were mixed with high-income students showed dramatic benefits in academic performance as a result of self-affirmation (Hadden, Easterbrook, Nieuwenhuis, Fox, & Dolan, 2019). Another strategy is to measure psychological threat using validated scales. For example, in Layous et al. (2017), White men were found to have a relatively low level of belonging in school and exhibited the greatest benefit of the affirmation.

Resources

Wise interventions can often be seen as the kick-start to a process that unfolds over time and in a social context (Cohen & Sherman, 2014; Cohen et al., 2017; Goyer et al., 2017). But for that process to unfold, there must be institutional supports to carry it forward. For example, a self-affirmed student might perform better and be more willing to seek out opportunities for learning. She might have the confidence to approach a teacher for help, or to sign up for a more difficult course. What is critical here is the *availability* of the social channels for the psychological currents, triggered by the affirmation, to keep moving forward. One study (Dee, 2015) found null effects of the affirmation intervention overall, but when examining classrooms that were more conducive to cognitive growth (i.e., the ones that displayed large gains in test scores), affirmation led to improved performance among minority students. What kinds of social resources are needed to propagate the effects of self-affirmation and other wise interventions? More research is needed on this question—we would categorize them into two types. First, cognitive resources, in terms of objective opportunities for learning and continued progress; and second, social resources, in the form of social reinforcement and validation (Cohen et al., 2017).

Timeliness

A final key moderator of the benefits of affirmation is its timeliness. For maximal benefit it must be timed to the emergence of threat and the availability of environmental resources for change. In the health domain, Ferrer and Cohen (2019) demonstrate that the timeliness of affirmation along these two dimensions predicts the degree of its benefit. In school, affirmations should be timed to the emergence of threat, which, if unaddressed, might lead to deteriorating outcomes over time. Thus, in the original studies, affirmations were timed to occur at the beginning of the school year and before exams and at a key developmental milestone, the transition to middle school. One study found that even a difference of 2 weeks in the timing of the affirmation—the first week of middle school versus the third week—had a large impact, with earlier timing yielding greater benefit on student grades (Cook et al., 2012). Indeed, the effect of timing in this study equaled the effect of providing the affirmation intervention at all obtained in previous studies. For practitioners and researchers, what matters is not just "what" intervention is used, but also and importantly, "where" and "when."

In summary, the key moderators of any psychological intervention can be distilled into what we refer to as the "three *T*'s" (Cohen et al., 2017; Ferrer & Cohen, 2019). It is *targeted* at the right person (one experiencing threat). It is *tailored* to the need (an affirmation might be effective at addressing threats to self-integrity, but not a lack of skill). And finally, the intervention is *timely* (given at a time and place where threat may hinder access or use of institutional resources). It is the confluence of these three conditions that predicts the positive impact of affirmation, as well, we suspect, of many interventions (Ferrer & Cohen, 2019).

THEORETICAL COUSINS OF SELF-AFFIRMATION INTERVENTIONS

The self-affirmation intervention is related to several other interventions in the social psychological literature. First, it is related to expressive writing interventions, as pioneered in the work of Jamie Pennebaker (Pennebaker & Evans, 2014). These interventions illustrated the power of expressive writing: In particular, people who were encouraged to write about traumatic events, expressing their deepest thoughts and feelings, were found to exhibit better outcomes, including along objective health indices (Pennebaker & Chung, 2011). The affirmation intervention similarly leverages the power of expressive writing but avoids confronting people with negative events. The benefit is that self-affirmation interventions do not cause the short-term decrements in mood sometimes found in the standard expressive writing exercise. Interestingly, one study (Creswell et al., 2007) found that much of the power of conventional expressive writing interventions among breast cancer survivors derived from their ability to focus people on self-affirming thoughts and feelings (e.g., the importance of relationships in their lives). Still, there are presumably contexts where expressive writing about traumatic events is a more effective intervention than self-affirmation. Every intervention has its time and place.

Another cousin (or perhaps aunt or uncle) of the self-affirmation intervention comes out of the seminal research by Rokeach (1973) on values confrontation—research that illustrated the power of *values* in people's psychology. Rokeach found that when people were led to confront a conflict between their values and their actions, it sometimes led to large and lasting self-change. People felt "self-dissatisfied" and as a consequence changed their actions to bring them in line with their values. The intellectual debt that self-affirmation research owes to Rokeach is the notion that values are a powerful source of self-integrity, and perhaps the basic unit of identity. Even in the harshest of circumstances, people can choose what they stand for.

Finally, self-affirmation interventions have an intellectual connection to other interventions that tap into identity and self-perception. "Foot-in-the-door" interventions encourage people to take a small initial step on behalf of a cause, and, under some circumstances, this has been found to increase their willingness to make later larger sacrifices (Freedman & Fraser, 1966; see Burger, 1999, for review). These interventions paved the path for our understanding of how change can persist through time. An initial action causes deep changes in identity and self-perception, with the resulting changes carrying the influence forward through time. A similar intellectual debt is owed to Wilson and Linville's (1985) classic research on attributional training, and their resurrection of the notion of "exacerbation cycles" by Storms and McCaul (1976). The notion was that a small initial change in psychology or behavior could propagate itself by interrupting a negative feedback loop. The self-affirmation field studies complement and go beyond these classic studies by extending the temporal window of observation. Rather than simply stopping the study with the first dependent measure (e.g., the first behavior after an intervention, or grades in the first term after the intervention), several of the field studies featured in self-affirmation research assess a chain of events that unfolds over a significant portion of the life course (Borman et al., 2018; Cohen & Sherman, 2014; Goyer et al., 2017; Tibbetts et al., 2016).

INTERVENTION CONTENT AND IMPLEMENTATION

The implementation of any intervention should occur after careful pilot testing to determine the nature of the psychological threat, constraints in the context in which it is to be administered (such as literacy level), and whether the materials are clear and impactful for the target population. In our experience, this pilot testing period is also a time to build trust with the teachers of the classrooms where the intervention is to be administered and with other key personnel within the school (principal, school psychologist). The self-affirmation intervention that was used in the middle school context in Cohen et al. (2006, 2009) and Sherman et al. (2013) was deployed after such pilot testing. It can be found in Appendix 3.1—the materials are annotated to call out important details and their intent. While there are many inductions of self-affirmation (see McQueen & Klein, 2006, for review; see Napper, Harris, & Epton, 2009, for an alternative method), the values writing exercise is the most commonly used manipulation of self-affirmation. In this activity, participants first read over a list of values and choose the value or values that are personally most important to them (in the affirmation condition) or values that are unimportant to them (in the control condition; several different control conditions have been used). When several affirmations are given over a school year, the content of the activities is varied in order for them to stay fresh for the students. But each one asks participants questions that tap into self-defining values. The writing activities typically take about 10 minutes for students to complete.

There are several aspects to the implementation of the affirmation that, though sometimes subtle, can make a difference. Here, we draw on the long tradition in social psychology that emphasizes the importance of experimental manipulations that are immersive and impactful (Aronson, Ellsworth, Carlsmith, & Gonzales, 1990; Ross, Lepper, & Ward, 2010). One of the distinctive qualities of social psychology is the attention to detail that goes into the creation and implementation of any manipulation, including an intervention. What is critical—and what we are trying to create and duplicate—is not a physical experience of writing about a value but a *psychological* experience of feeling affirmed.

For one, the affirmation activities are described as regular classroom activities and are never presented as an intervention to help students (see Yeager & Walton, 2011). No student is made to feel that he or she is in need of help, a message that may increase psychological threat. Indeed, research suggests that when people are made aware that the affirmation is designed to help them, its impact is attenuated (Sherman, Cohen, et al., 2009). This is not to say that people cannot use affirmation as a personal coping strategy if they are aware of its benefits. As long as they feel they have choice in the decision to use it, they still benefit even when aware of its salutary effects (Silverman, Logel, & Cohen, 2013). Indeed, the lessons of self-affirmation theory can be imparted to students with positive results (Walton et al., 2015).

There are other implementation factors that are important. For example, we suspect that some of the efficacy of the intervention comes from the fact that it appears to be an activity that is from *teachers* or other institutional authorities. Students are thus led to feel that teachers, or other institutional authorities, care about their values and how they are important to them (cf. Bowen, Wegmann, & Webber, 2013). From the students' point of view, their values, and who they are and what they stand for, are welcome (see Walton, Paunesku, & Dweck, 2012). This may help to explain why values affirmations bolster students' sense of belonging in school (Cook et al., 2012). Although speculative, one reason replications may sometimes fail is that they are presented by outsiders rather than by insiders or institutional representatives whose respect students care about (see Protzko & Aronson, 2016). The key condition here is not at the literal or procedural level. It is at the *psychological* level. Sometimes, it may not be possible to present the research activity as a regular classroom activity (we describe one such instance below). What is important is that students *perceive* that their values are respected by people who matter.

Another key detail related to an intervention's implementation is the degree to which it promotes student engagement. In the study in Wisconsin middle schools that featured over 1,000 students, researchers coded the affirmation essays for student engagement, which they operationalized as whether students selected an important value and then discussed its personal importance (Borman et al., 2018). The vast majority (76%) of the potentially threatened students in the affirmation condition were coded as having engaged with the activity, and this group of students showed relatively larger gains. These findings suggest that whether the implementation encourages student engagement, such as by having the teachers convey its importance or by providing a quiet time for students to complete it, is critical.

Implementation details may explain sometimes paradoxical results, as when the affirmation works once but not a second time. When Borman and colleagues (Hanselman et al., 2017) sought to replicate their affirmation effects in the same 11 schools, they found null effects. The authors consider a number of sources for this change, many of them relevant to implementation. The teachers may have been less excited about participating in the study the second time around; the fact that they were on strike may have played a role (see Borman, 2017, for discussion).

NUANCES AND MISCONCEPTIONS

We see self-affirmation interventions as an example of a psychologically wise intervention (Walton, 2014). They target the underlying processes that shape the way people think and feel about their social situation, including themselves, and specifically, their sense of personal adequacy (Cohen & Sherman, 2014; Cohen et al., 2017, Lewin, 1951; Steele, 1997; Walton & Wilson, 2018). Unlike many interventions, wise interventions tend to work not by adding new forces but by activating or unleashing forces that are already present in the situation but dormant. Students' abilities may be inhibited by psychological threat. Lessening that threat, the intervention allows abilities to more fully express themselves.

One common misconception about affirmation interventions is that because they are relatively brief and low cost, the causes of the social problems they ameliorate are small and simple. Health epidemics and illnesses, while caused by the smallest of entities—germs and viruses—are heavily influenced by sanitation, nutrition, biological vulnerability, stress, and so on. Likewise, almost all social problems arise from multiple forces. Achievement gaps based on race, class, or gender are the product of a complex web of systemic, historical, institutional, cultural, and economic factors (see, e.g., Gandara & Contreras, 2009; Mitchell, Ream, Ryan, & Espinoza, 2008; Neal, 2006; Rothstein, 2005). Researchers, practitioners, and policymakers must never lose sight of the important structural factors leading to achievement, such as poverty and unequal distribution of economic and educational resources (Reardon, 2011), immigration policies (Gandara & Contreras, 2009), parenting practices and limitations in English literacy (Lopez, 2009), class size, school demographics, educational policies (Jencks & Phillips, 1998), individual discrimination (Ready & Wright, 2011), and institutional racism (e.g., Voigt et al., 2017). All of these are causes of achievement gaps that must be addressed.

Showing that a psychological intervention lessens the achievement gap does not imply that it has exclusively psychological sources (see Ikizer & Blanton, 2016). It implies that, under some circumstances, psychology can be a key valve through which the influence of cultural, systemic, historical, and institutional forces flow. As we suggested earlier, structural and psychological inequalities can reinforce each other, as when social inequality causes psychological threat in the classroom, which causes underperformance, which in turn propagates social inequality (see also Claro, Paunesku, & Dweck, 2016). Likewise, any psychological intervention, in the absence of structural supports for success, would have little if any effect. Cognitive, social, material, and emotional supports available to students in a social environment will determine whether the spark introduced by a self-affirmation kindles into a lasting change.

IMPLICATIONS FOR PRACTICE: ADAPTING AFFIRMATION INTERVENTIONS FOR AN INTERNATIONAL CONTEXT

We now review a case study that illuminates how many of the considerations laid out above make a practical difference in the field. Whenever researchers and practitioners apply a psychological theory to a novel context, they need to be aware of how the process they seek to intervene on plays out in the specific setting they hope to change. The paragraphs that follow address how two researchers, Mohini Lokhande and Tim Müller, took on this challenge in the German educational system.

Various steps were taken in order to (1) simplify the intervention materials so that they would be understood by students with lower literacy skills; (2) make the affirmation task more engaging so that students would put sufficient effort into thinking about important values in their lives, such as embedding the value activity in an interactive comic strip; (3) make the activity more concrete with specific references not to abstract values but to specific activities (e.g., "spending time with family and friends" instead of "valuing family and friends"); (4) include values that resonate in Germany; (5) break down the essay-writing task into simple steps to make the writing process easier; (6) encourage students to focus on intrinsic values like feelings of belonging rather than extrinsic ones like prestige; and (7) trigger a positive recursive cycle, while accommodating to data protection regulations, by having the researchers provide growth-oriented feedback to students after they completed the initial intervention.

It was necessary to consider who, in this context, was vulnerable to psychological threat. Previous interventions featuring affirmation had been conducted in the United States and were designed to alleviate the stereotype threat that racial minorities feel in school (Cook et al., 2012; Walton & Cohen, 2007). By contrast, in contemporary Europe, the primary stigma centers on immigration. Immigrant students may feel as though they do not even belong in their country, let alone in the classroom, a state of "belonging uncertainty" that has befallen immigrants worldwide (see Walton & Cohen, 2007). Moreover, there exists a fairly pronounced achievement gap between immigrant students and their native peers in Germany (Gebhardt, Rauch, Mang, Sälzer, & Stanat, 2012). The Expert Council of German Foundations on Integration and Migration, a nonpartisan advisory council on whose behalf the study was conducted, sought to address this gap. The purpose of the study was to generate concrete lessons for future educational reforms in Germany.

As the self-affirmation intervention was translated into this new context, there were several implementation details to consider. Attempts were made to retain many of the procedures used in the original interventions, but adjustments had to be made. Knowing the key theoretical considerations, however, made adjustments possible without undermining psychological impact. See Lokhande and Müller (2019) and Müller and Lokhande (2017) for a detailed description of the procedure and results.

The study took place in lower secondary schools (age range 12–13 years) in the state of Berlin. These schools are usually attended by students with lower academic ability and from socially disadvantaged families. Moreover, most schools were ethnically diverse. About two-thirds of the students spoke a language other than German at home. Many had a Turkish, Arabic, or Eastern European background. The research was designed as a large-scale replication study in 11 schools (N = 820). Because ethical guidelines and data protection requirements are strict in Germany, it was not possible to present the study as a regular classroom exercise. Instead, we designed a cover story that integrated the intervention into the classroom as a supportive exercise for all students that, though initiated by outside researchers, was supported by the school. This way, we increased the chances that a key psychological element of the affirmation experience—the sense that "my values" are being recognized and respected by institutional authorities—would be preserved.

The timing and context of the intervention were considered carefully. It was decided to implement the intervention in a mathematics class where psychological threat was expected to be most acute and debilitating (Borman et al., 2016). To interrupt the emergence of recursive cycles, the intervention was administered at the beginning of the new school year and, for seventh graders, right after the transition from primary to secondary school. Also, an exam was administered immediately after the first affirmation, and then 8 weeks later. This way, the effect of the initial affirmation might be immediately channeled into better performance, which might then facilitate better performance on subsequent exams (Cohen et al., 2009). To facilitate this recursive process, students across all conditions received feedback on each of the two exams that emphasized their capacity for growth (see Yeager & Dweck, 2012; all materials can be obtained from the authors upon request).

The intervention was implemented by trained research administrators rather than teachers. On the positive side, this facilitated treatment fidelity, ensuring maximal control over the implementation was obtained. On the negative side, this element of the procedure might undercut certain key psychological elements from the experience. Students might be less engaged by the activity because it was being delivered by outsiders. Accordingly, innovative procedures were introduced to support student engagement. For instance, one novel procedural element was the use of an appealing interactive comic strip to increase students' motivation to write an essay. In the story, an alien wants to learn more about young people on Earth and asks students several questions related to their values. (The annotated and translated materials can be found in Appendix 3.2.) As in the original studies, students were told to write down their thoughts and feelings and told that the assignment was nonevaluative.

Additionally, several *prompts* focused students on the intrinsically rewarding nature of their values (Schimel, Arndt, Banko, & Cook, 2004). Students answered yes/no questions about different statements related to their two chosen values, such as "When I think about [value *x*, value *y*], . . . I'm happy and content." This element was designed to focus students on the intrinsic rationale for their values (Schimel et al., 2004) and on emotional experiences associated with these kinds of rationales (e.g., joy, contentment, lack of anxiety; Rheinberg & Eser, 2018).

Replicating previous results, the affirmation interventions improved the performance of students from an identity-threatened group (Lokhande & Müller, 2019). A significant interaction effect between affirmation condition and ethnic background was obtained. On the first exam, there was a positive effect of the affirmation on the math achievement of immigrant students, though this was confined to Turkish immigrants and did not occur for students of Arabic descent. Eight weeks later, however, both immigrant groups performed significantly better on the second math test. Echoing results of previous studies, no significant effect of the affirmation was found for the nonimmigrant group. Overall, the achievement gap between immigrant and nonimmigrant students was reduced by approximately 40%.

The experience of adapting the value-affirmation procedure to the German context highlights the importance of attention to psychological detail and meaning (see Lee & Luykx, 2005). After the publication of the results (Müller & Lokhande, 2017), many teachers showed an interest in using the intervention materials in their own classrooms. But many thought that it would be a simple matter of handing out the comic strip and, once completed, students would "magically" improve (cf. Yeager & Walton, 2011). As the case study illustrates, implementation fidelity requires the creation of a positive psychological experience, and this requires careful consideration of the meaning that every procedural element will have for students. Implementation fidelity also requires setting the stage so that any initial psychological effects of the intervention can be channeled, sooner rather than later, into performance and the experience of progress.

IMPLICATIONS FOR PSYCHOLOGICAL THEORY

The research reported in this chapter demonstrates the pervasive power of self-integrity in mediating responses to many experiences in social life: confronting threats to one's social identity in social contexts, such as school, coping with regrettable actions, processing medical and political information, and dealing with intergroup divides. When people are able to affirm self-integrity by drawing on alternative self-resources, they are able to tolerate, and even grow, from threatening experiences in their lives. The consistency of affirmation effects across these diverse domains suggests a psychological unity.

Additionally, self-affirmation research has shown how "psyche and structure" interact, propagating outcomes through time (Cohen et al., 2017; Cohen & Sherman, 2014; Goyer et al., 2017). Psychological processes interact with processes in the social environment in recursive feedback loops. Rather than psychologize social problems—or sociologize them—the perspective offered in self-affirmation research suggests that the action is in the interaction between these levels of analysis.

FUTURE DIRECTIONS

There are many questions to be answered. Three form the focus of our concluding section:

1. Under what conditions can self-affirmations have negative effects?
2. How does the self-affirmation process unfold spontaneously, when there is no intervention to trigger it?
3. What are the specific pathways through which the self-affirmation process interacts with the social environment through time?

First, self-affirmations can have negative effects. One type of situation in which this is the case are those where threat has positive effects (Rokeach, 1973; Stone & Focella, 2011), and affirmation could short-circuit that process. In situations where self-protective responses have proved adaptive, affirmation may have negative consequences (e.g., Jessop, Ayers, Burn, & Ryda, 2018). Affirmation is not a panacea. For instance, when people persist on a task because they are motivated to protect their self-integrity, an affirmation could lead to disengagement. After repeated failure on a task where there is little opportunity for improvement, affirmation has been shown to lead people to disengage (Vohs, Park, & Schmeichel, 2013). If a person is persisting on a task because of psychological threat (e.g., "I don't want to look dumb"), affirmation might lift this self-evaluative concern and lead the person to give up.

Another situation where affirmations may backfire is in the absence of psychological threat. For example, in educational contexts, for the most part affirmation intervention studies have had null or negligible mean effects on the academic performance of non-identity-threatened students. In a few studies, however, there appears to be some evidence of negative trends for these groups, at least on the focal outcome (e.g., Brady et al., 2016; Kizilcec, Saltarelli, Reich, & Cohen, 2017). Researchers do not yet know how robust these effects occur or, to the extent that they occur, why (Binning & Browman, 2020). One possibility, however, is that when an individual is not under consistent identity threat, a self-affirmation may introduce alternative processes. For example, perhaps self-affirmation leads people to feel more like an individual than a member of their group; this may lead non-identity-threatened students to benefit less from "stereotype lift," the psychological boost they get from being on the upside of negative stereotypes (Walton & Cohen, 2003). Additionally, insofar as some degree of threat or stress helps performance, perhaps affirmation might lower it to suboptimal levels for some groups (Zajonc, 1965). In research on persuasion, affirmation in nonthreatening contexts has increased self-confidence, causing resistance rather than openness to change (Briñol, Petty, Gallardo, & DeMarree, 2007).

A second question for future research is the spontaneity of the affirmation processes (see Harris et al., 2019). An affirmation intervention—or any wise intervention—is but a spark for a psychological process. That process can occur even without an intervention to trigger it. Some people may engage the self-affirmation process spontaneously (Harris et al., 2019). Indeed, it may be possible to train people to activate the self-affirmation process on their own. Brady and colleagues (2016) examined the self-affirmation process as it occurred spontaneously, by asking people to write down their thoughts after a stress induction. They found that people do indeed differ in the extent to which they spontaneously self-affirm. A strong predictor of this tendency was high self-esteem.

Another study taught female engineering students how to self-affirm spontaneously through a short slide show (Walton et al., 2015). Female students who worked in predominantly male fields of engineering earned higher grades as a result of this training. Harris and colleagues (2019) have also examined individual differences in spontaneous self-affirmation through the use of a self-report measure. Spontaneous self-affirmers exhibit open-mindedness to threatening health information akin to those who complete experimental affirmations (see also Cornil & Chandon, 2013; Ferrer et al., 2015). This research highlights an important new frontier in self-affirmation research: How the process of self-affirmation unfolds spontaneously and how differences in people's ability to spontaneously marshal the self-affirmation process may explain individual differences in resilience, self-esteem, and perhaps clinical outcomes.

A third direction for affirmation research involves further exploring the interactions between the self-affirmation process and the social environment. For example, sometimes a psychological process may have effects on the larger social environment. In one study (Powers et al., 2016), classrooms with a higher proportion of minorities who had been self-affirmed performed better on the whole. The benefits of the self-affirmation intervention did not end with minority students but spilled over to affect the entire classroom. How the environment changed was unclear, but one possibility is that the classroom became more orderly and positive (Binning et al., 2019), enabling teachers to reach a greater number of students, especially low-performing students who might have otherwise been overlooked.

FINAL WORDS

Self-affirmation theory has had a long evolution. It began as a basic theory of how people maintain the integrity of self. It has grown into a theory with applications to a wide range of applied arenas, including education, health, and conflict. On the one hand, the effects of affirmation interventions can be powerful and long lasting. On the other hand, these effects are conditional. They do not occur for all people and in all contexts. "Powerful but conditional" is an apt way to describe them and many other wise interventions. A large dose of humility is thus needed whenever scientists or practitioners apply them. To adapt an intervention to a new context, it is important to understand whether and how psychological threat plays out, for whom, and when. It is important to adapt the intervention so that it is engaging and actually affirming. With these caveats acknowledged, we can also be excited about the range of domains where self-affirmation can be applied—many of which are still yet to be imagined.

REFERENCES

Adams, G., Tormala, T. T., & O'Brien, L. T. (2006). The effect of self-affirmation on perception of racism. *Journal of Experimental Social Psychology, 42,* 616–626.

Aronson, E. (1969). The theory of cognitive dissonance: A current perspective. In L. Berkowitz (Ed.), *Advances in experimental social psychology* (Vol. 4, pp. 1–34). New York: Academic Press.

Aronson, E., Ellsworth, P. C., Carlsmith, J. M., & Gonzales, M. H. (1990). *Methods of research in social psychology.* New York: McGraw-Hill.

Aronson, J., Cohen, G. L., & Nail, P. R. (1999). Self-affirmation theory: An update and appraisal. In E. Harmon-Jones & J. Mills (Eds.), *Cognitive dissonance theory: Revival with revisions and controversies* (pp. 127–147). Washington, DC: American Psychological Association.

Badea, C., Binning, K. R., Verlhiac, J., & Sherman, D. K. (2017). In the aftermath of terrorism: Effects of self- versus group-affirmation on support for discriminatory policies. *Journal of Experimental Social Psychology, 76,* 421–428.

Badea, C., & Sherman, D. K. (2019). Self-affirmation and prejudice reduction: When and why? *Current Directions in Psychological Science, 28,* 40–46.

Binning, K. R., Brick, C., Cohen, G. L., & Sherman, D. K. (2015). Going along versus getting it right: The role of self-integrity in political conformity. *Journal of Experimental Social Psychology, 56,* 73–88.

Binning, K. R., & Browman, A. S. (2020). Theoretical, ethical, and policy implications for conducting social-psychological interventions to close educational achievement gaps. *Social Issues and Policy Review, 14,* 182–216.

Binning, K. R., Cook, J. E., Purdie-Greenaway, V., Garcia, J., Chen, S. Apfel, N., . . . Cohen, G. L. (2019). Bolstering trust and reducing discipline incidents at a diverse middle school: How self-affirmation affects behavioral conduct during the transition to adolescence. *Journal of School Psychology, 75,* 74–88.

Binning, K. R., Sherman, D. K., Cohen, G. L., & Heitland, K. (2010). Seeing the other side: Reducing political partisanship via self-affirmation in the 2008 presidential election. *Analyses of Social Issues and Public Policy, 10,* 276–292.

Borman, G. D. (2017). Advancing values affirmation as a scalable strategy for mitigating identity threats and narrowing national achievement gaps. *Proceedings of the National Academy of Sciences of the USA, 114,* 7486–7488.

Borman, G. D., Grigg, J., & Hanselman, P. (2016). An effort to close achievement gaps at scale through self-affirmation. *Educational Evaluation and Policy Analysis, 38,* 21–42.

Borman, G. D., Grigg, J., Rozek, C. S., Hanselman, P., & Dewey, N. A. (2018). Self-affirmation effects are produced by school context, student engagement with the intervention, and time: Lessons from a district-wide implementation. *Psychological Science, 29,* 1773–1784.

Bowen, N. K., Wegmann, K. M., & Webber, K. C. (2013). Enhancing a brief writing intervention to combat stereotype threat among middle-school students. *Journal of Educational Psychology, 105,* 427–435.

Brady, S. T., Reeves, S. L., Garcia, J., Purdie-Vaughns, V., Cook, J. E., Taborsky-Barba, S., . . . Cohen, G. L. (2016). The psychology of the affirmed learner: Spontaneous self-affirmation in the face of stress. *Journal of Educational Psychology, 108,* 353–373.

Bratter, J. L., Rowley, K. J., & Chukhray, I. (2016). Does a self-affirmation intervention reduce stereotype threat in Black and Hispanic high schools? *Race and Social Problems, 8,* 340–356.

Briñol, P., Petty, R. E., Gallardo, I., & DeMarree, K. G. (2007). The effect of self-affirmation in nonthreatening persuasion domains: Timing affects the process. *Personality and Social Psychology Bulletin, 33,* 1533–1546.

Burger, J. M. (1999). The foot-in-the-door compliance procedure: A multiple-process analysis and review. *Personality and Social Psychology Review, 3,* 303–325.

Burson, A., Crocker, J., & Mischkowski, D. (2012). Two types of value-affirmation: Implications for self-control following social exclusion. *Social Psychological and Personality Science, 3,* 510–516.

Čehajić-Clancy, S., Effron, D. A., Halperin, E., Liberman, V., & Ross, L. D. (2011). Affirmation, acknowledgment of in-group responsibility, group-based guilt, and support for reparative measures. *Journal of Personality and Social Psychology, 101,* 256–270.

Claro, S., Paunesku, D., & Dweck, C. S. (2016). Growth mindset tempers the effects of poverty on academic achievement. *Proceedings of the National Academy of Sciences of the USA, 113,* 8664–8668.

Cohen, G. L., Aronson, J., & Steele, C. M. (2000). When beliefs yield to evidence: Reducing biased evaluation by affirming the self. *Personality and Social Psychology Bulletin, 26,* 1151–1164.

Cohen, G. L., & Garcia, J. (2008). Identity, belonging, and achievement: A model, interventions, implications. *Current Directions in Psychological Science, 17,* 365–369.

Cohen, G. L., Garcia, J., Apfel, N., & Master, A. (2006). Reducing the racial achievement gap: A social-psychological intervention. *Science, 313,* 1307–1310.

Cohen, G. L., Garcia, J., & Goyer, J. P. (2017). Turning point: Targeted, tailored, and timely psychological intervention. In A. J. Elliot, C. S. Dweck, & D. S. Yeager (Eds.), *Handbook of competence and motivation: Theory and application* (pp. 657–686). New York: Guilford Press.

Cohen, G. L., Garcia, J., Purdie-Vaughns, V., Apfel, N., & Brzustoski, P. (2009). Recursive processes in self-affirmation: Intervening to close the minority achievement gap. *Science, 324,* 400–403.

Cohen, G. L., & Sherman, D. K. (2014). The psychology of change: Self-affirmation and social psychological intervention. *Annual Review of Psychology, 65,* 333–371.

Cohen, G. L., Sherman, D. K., Bastardi, A., Hsu, L., McGoey, M., & Ross, L. (2007). Bridging the partisan divide: Self-affirmation reduces ideological closed-mindedness and inflexibility in negotiation. *Journal of Personality and Social Psychology, 93,* 415–430.

Cook, J. E., Purdie-Vaughns, V., Garcia, J., & Cohen, G. L. (2012). Chronic threat and contingent belonging: Protective benefits of values affirmation on identity development. *Journal of Personality and Social Psychology, 102,* 479–496.

Cornil, Y., & Chandon, P. (2013). From fan to fat?: Vicarious losing increases unhealthy eating, but self-affirmation is an effective remedy. *Psychological Science, 24,* 1936–1946.

Creswell, J. D., Dutcher, J. M., Klein, W. M. P., Harris, P. R., & Levine, J. M. (2013). Self-affirmation improves problem-solving under stress. *PLOS ONE, 8*(5), e62593.

Creswell, J. D., Lam, S., Stanton, A. L., Taylor, S. E., Bower, J. E., & Sherman, D. K. (2007). Does self-affirmation, cognitive processing, or discovery of meaning explain cancer-related health benefits of expressive writing? *Personality and Social Psychology Bulletin, 33,* 238–250.

Creswell, J. D., Welch, W. T., Taylor, S. E., Sherman, D. K., Gruenewald, T. L., & Mann, T. (2005). Affirmation of personal values buffers neuroendocrine and psychological stress responses. *Psychological Science, 16,* 846–851.

Critcher, C. R., & Dunning, D. (2015). Self-affirmations provide a broader perspective on self-threat. *Personality and Social Psychology Bulletin, 41,* 3–18.

de Jong, E. M., Jellesma, F. C., Koomen, H. M. Y., & de Jong, P. F. (2016). A values-affirmation intervention does not benefit negatively stereotyped immigrant students in the Netherlands. *Frontiers in Psychology, 7,* 691.

Dee, T. S. (2015). Social identity and achievement gaps: Evidence from an affirmation intervention. *Journal of Research on Educational Effectiveness, 8,* 149–168.

Ditto, P. H., & Lopez, D. F. (1992). Motivated skepticism: Use of differential decision criteria for preferred and nonpreferred conclusions. *Journal of Personality and Social Psychology, 63,* 568–584.

Dunning, D. (2003). The zealous self-affirmer: How and why the self lurks so pervasively behind social judgment. In S. J. Spencer, S. Fein, M. P. Zanna, & J. M. Olson (Eds.), Motivated social perception: The Ontario symposium (Vol. 9, pp. 45–72). Mahwah, NJ: Erlbaum.

Dunning, D., & Cohen, G. L. (1992). Egocentric definitions of traits and abilities in social judgment. *Journal of Personality and Social Psychology, 63,* 341–355.

Dunning, D., Leuenberger, A., & Sherman, D. A. (1995). A new look at motivated inference: Are self-serving theories of success a product of motivational forces? *Journal of Personality and Social Psychology, 69,* 58–68.

Dunning, D., Meyerowitz, J. A., & Holzberg, A. D. (1989). Ambiguity and self-evaluation: The role of idiosyncratic trait definitions in self-serving assessments of ability. *Journal of Personality and Social Psychology, 57,* 1082–1090.

Dutcher, J. M., Creswell, J. D., Pacilio, L. E., Harris, P. R., Klein, W. M., Levine, J. M., . . . Eisenberger, N. I. (2016). Self-affirmation activates the ventral striatum: A possible reward-related mechanism for self-affirmation. *Psychological Science, 27,* 455–466.

Eccles, J. S., Lord, S., & Midgley, C. (1991). What are we doing to early adolescents?: The impact of educational contexts on early adolescents. *American Journal of Education, 99,* 521–542.

Ehret, P. J., LaBrie, J. W., Santerre, C., & Sherman, D. K. (2015). Self-affirmation and motivational interviewing (SAMI): Integrating perspectives to reduce resistance and increase efficacy of alcohol interventions. *Health Psychology Review, 9,* 83–102.

Ehret, P. J., & Sherman, D. K. (2014). Public policy and health: A self-affirmation perspective. *Policy Insights from Behavioral and Brain Sciences, 1,* 222–230.

Ehret, P. J., & Sherman, D. K. (2018). Integrating self-affirmation and implementation intentions: Effects on college student drinking. *Annals of Behavioral Medicine, 52,* 633–644.

Elder, G. H. (1998). The life course as developmental theory. *Child Development, 69,* 1–12.

Epton, T., Harris, P. R., Kane, R., van Koningsbruggen, G. M., & Sheeran, P. (2015). The impact of self-affirmation on health-behavior change: A meta-analysis. *Health Psychology, 34,* 187–196.

Falk, E. B., O'Donnell, M. B., Cascio, C. N., Tinney, F., Kang, Y., Lieberman, M. D., . . . Strecher, V. J. (2015). Self-affirmation alters the brain's response to health messages and subsequent behavior change. *Proceedings of the National Academy of Sciences of the USA, 112,* 1977–1982.

Fein, S., & Spencer, S. J. (1997). Prejudice as self-image maintenance: Affirming the self through derogating others. *Journal of Personality and Social Psychology, 73,* 31–44.

Ferrer, R. A., & Cohen, G. L. (2019). Reconceptualizing self-affirmation with the "trigger-and-channel" framework: Lessons from the health domain. *Personality and Social Psychology Review, 23*(3), 285–304.

Ferrer, R. A., Taber, J. M., Klein, W. M., Harris, P. R., Lewis, K. L., & Biesecker, L. G. (2015). The role of current affect, anticipated affect and spontaneous self-affirmation in decisions to receive self-threatening genetic risk information. *Cognition and Emotion, 29,* 1456–1465.

Festinger, L. (1957). *A theory of cognitive dissonance.* Stanford, CA: Stanford University Press.

Finez, L., & Sherman, D. K. (2012). Train in vain: The role of the self in claimed self-handicapping strategies. *Journal of Sport and Exercise Psychology, 34,* 600–620.

Freedman, J. L., & Fraser, S. C. (1966). Compliance without pressure: The foot-in-the-door technique. *Journal of Personality and Social Psychology, 4*(2), 195–202.

Gandara, P., & Contreras, F. (2009). *The Latino education crisis: The consequences of failed social policies.* Cambridge, MA: Harvard University Press.

Gebhardt, M., Rauch, D., Mang, J., Sälzer, C., & Stanat, P. (2012). Mathematische Kompetenz von Schülerinnen und Schülern mit Zuwanderungshintergrund. In M. Prenzel, C. Sälzer, E. Klieme, & O. Köller (Eds.), *PISA 2012: Fortschritte und herausforderungen in Deutschland* (pp. 275–308). Münster, Germany: Waxmann.

Gilbert, D. T., Pinel, E. C., Wilson, T. D., Blumberg, S. J., & Wheatley, T. P. (1998). Immune neglect: A source of durability bias in affective forecasting. *Journal of Personality and Social Psychology, 75,* 617–638.

Goffman, E. (1978). *The presentation of self in everyday life.* London: Harmondsworth.

Goyer, J. P., Cohen, G. L., Cook, J. E., Master, A., Apfel, N., Lee, W., . . . Walton, G. M. (2019). Targeted identity-safety interventions cause lasting reductions in discipline citations among negatively stereotyped boys. *Journal of Personality and Social Psychology, 117,* 229–259.

Goyer, J. P., Garcia, J., Purdie-Vaughns, V., Binning, K. R., Cook, J. E., Reeves, S. L., . . . Cohen, G. L. (2017). Self-affirmation facilitates minority middle schoolers' progress along college trajectories. *Proceedings of the National Academy of Sciences of the USA, 114,* 7594–7599.

Hadden, I. R., Easterbrook, M. J., Nieuwenhuis, M., Fox, K. J., & Dolan, P. (2019). Self-affirmation reduces the socioeconomic attainment gap in schools in England. *British Journal of Educational Psychology.*

Hanselman, P., Bruch, S. K., Gamoran, A., & Borman, G. D. (2014). Threat in context: School moderation of the impact of social identity threat on racial/ethnic achievement gaps. *Sociology of Education, 87*(2), 106–124.

Hanselman, P., Rozek, C. S., Grigg, J., & Borman, G. D. (2017). New evidence on self-affirmation effects and theorized sources of heterogeneity from large-scale replications. *Journal of Educational Psychology, 109,* 405–424.

Harackiewicz, J. M., Canning, E. A., Tibbetts, Y., Giffen, C. J., Blair, S. S., Rouse, D. I., & Hyde, J. S. (2014). Closing the social class achievement gap for first-generation students in undergraduate biology. *Journal of Educational Psychology, 106,* 375–389.

Harackiewicz, J. M., Canning, E. A., Tibbetts, Y., Priniski, S. J., & Hyde, J. S. (2016). Closing achievement gaps with a utility-value intervention: Disentangling race and social class. *Journal of Personality and Social Psychology, 111,* 745–765.

Harris, P. R., Griffin, D. W., Napper, L. E., Bond, R., Schüz, B., Stride, C., & Brearley, I. (2019). Individual differences in self-affirmation: Distinguishing self-affirmation from positive self-regard. *Self and Identity, 18*(6), 589–630.

Harris, P. R., & Napper, L. (2005). Self-affirmation and the biased processing of threatening health-risk information. *Personality and Social Psychology Bulletin, 31,* 1250–1263.

Ikizer, E. G., & Blanton, H. (2016). Media coverage of "wise" interventions can reduce concern for the disadvantaged. *Journal of Experimental Psychology: Applied, 22,* 135–147.

Inzlicht, M., & Ben-Zeev, T. (2000). A threatening intellectual environment: Why females are susceptible to experiencing problem-solving deficits in the presence of males. *Psychological Science, 11,* 365–371.

Jencks, C., & Phillips, M. (1998). *The Black–White test score gap.* Washington, DC: Brookings Institution Press.

Jessop, D. C., Ayers, S., Burn, F., & Ryda, C. (2018). Can self-affirmation exacerbate adverse reactions to stress under certain conditions? *Psychology and Health, 33,* 827–845.

Jiang, L. (2018). Job insecurity and creativity: The buffering effect of self-affirmation and work-affirmation. *Journal of Applied Social Psychology, 48,* 388–397.

Kaiser, C. R., & Major, B. (2006). A social psychological perspective on perceiving and reporting discrimination. *Law and Social Inquiry, 31,* 801–830.

Keough, K. A., & Markus, H. R. (1999). On being well: The role of the self in building the bridge from philosophy to biology. *Psychological Inquiry, 9,* 49–53.

Kinias, Z., & Sim, J. (2016). Facilitating women's success in business: Interrupting the process of stereotype threat through affirmation of personal values. *Journal of Applied Psychology, 101*(11), 1585–1597.

Kizilcec, R. F., Saltarelli, A. J., Reich, J., & Cohen, G. L. (2017). Closing global achievement gaps in MOOCs. *Science, 355*, 251–252.

Kunda, Z. (1987). Motivated inference: Self-serving generation and evaluation of causal theories. *Journal of Personality and Social Psychology, 53*, 636–647.

Layous, K., Davis, E. M., Garcia, J., Purdie-Vaughns, V., Cook, J. E., & Cohen, G. L. (2017). Feeling left out, but affirmed: Protecting against the negative effects of low belonging in college. *Journal of Experimental Social Psychology, 69*, 227–231.

Lee, O., & Luykx, A. (2005). Dilemmas in scaling up innovations in elementary science instruction with nonmainstream students. *American Educational Research Journal, 42*, 411–438.

Lewin, K. (1951). *Field theory in social science: Selected theoretical papers* (D. Cartwright, Ed.). New York: Harper & Row.

Liberman, A., & Chaiken, S. (1992). Defensive processing of personally relevant health messages. *Personality and Social Psychology Bulletin, 18*, 669–679.

Logel, C., & Cohen, G. L. (2012). The role of the self in physical health: Testing the effect of a values-affirmation intervention on weight loss. *Psychological Science, 23*, 53–55.

Logel, C., Kathmandu, A., & Cohen, G. L. (2019). Affirmation prevents long-term weight gain. *Journal of Experimental Social Psychology, 81*, 70–75.

Lokhande, M., & Müller, T. (2019). Double jeopardy—double remedy?: The effectiveness of self-affirmation for improving doubly disadvantaged students' mathematical performance. *Journal of School Psychology, 75*, 58–73.

Lopez, M. H. (2009). *Latinos and education: Explaining the attainment gap.* Washington, DC: Pew Research Center, Pew Hispanic Center Project. Retrieved from *www.pewhispanic. org/2009/10/07/latinos-and-education-explaining-the-attainment-gap.*

Martens, A., Johns, M., Greenberg, J., & Schimel, J. (2006). Combating stereotype threat: The effect of self-affirmation on women's intellectual performance. *Journal of Experimental Social Psychology, 42*, 236–243.

McQueen, A., & Klein, W. M. (2006). Experimental manipulations of self-affirmation: A systematic review. *Self and Identity, 5*, 289–354.

Mitchell, D. E., Ream, R. K., Ryan, S., & Espinoza, J. (2008). Organizational strategies for addressing California's educational achievement gap (Policy brief prepared by California Department of Education and the University of California). Retrieved from *http://education. ucdavis.edu/sites/main/files/Mitchell_PaperWEBR.pdf.*

Miyake, A., Kost-Smith, L. E., Finkelstein, N. D., Pollock, S. J., Cohen, G. L., & Ito, T. A. (2010). Reducing the gender achievement gap in college science: A classroom study of values affirmation. *Science, 330*, 1234–1237.

Mukherjee, S. (2015). *The laws of medicine: Field notes from an uncertain science.* New York: Simon & Schuster.

Müller, T., & Lokhande, M. (2017). Wider die Stereotypisierung: Bessere Schulleistung durch Selbstbestätigung [Counteracting stereotype threat: Increasing achievement in school by self-affirmation]. In Berlin Institute for Integration and Migration Research (BIM) and Research Unit of the Expert Council of German Foundations on Integration and Migration (SVR—Research Unit; Ed.), Vielfalt im Klassenzimmer. Wie Lehrkräfte gute Leistung fördern können [Diversity in the classroom. How teachers can promote good student achievements]. Berlin. Retrieved from *www.svr-migration.de/publikationen/vielfalt-im-klassenzimmer.*

Murphy, M. C., Steele, C. M., & Gross, J. J. (2007). Signaling threat: How situational cues affect women in math, science, and engineering settings. *Psychological Science, 18*, 879–885.

Napper, L., Harris, P. R., & Epton, T. (2009). Developing and testing a self-affirmation manipulation. *Self and Identity, 8*(1), 45–62.

Neal, D. (2006). Why has Black–White skill convergence stopped? *Handbook of the Economics of Education, 1*, 511–576.

Pawson, R., & Tilley, N. (1997). *Realistic evaluation*. London: SAGE.

Pennebaker, J. W., & Chung, C. K. (2011). Expressive writing: Connections to physical and mental health. In H. S. Friedman (Ed.), *Oxford handbook of health psychology* (pp. 417–437). New York: Oxford University Press.

Pennebaker, J. W., & Evans, J. F. (2014). *Expressive writing: Words that heal: Using expressive writing to overcome traumas and emotional upheavals, resolve issues, improve health, and build resilience*. Enumclaw, WA: Idyll Arbor.

Powers, J., Cook, J. E., Purdie-Vaughns, V., Garcia, J., Apfel, N., & Cohen, G. L. (2016). Changing environments by changing individuals: The emergent effects of psychological intervention. *Psychological Science, 27*, 150–160.

Protzko, J., & Aronson, J. (2016). Context moderates affirmation effects on the ethnic achievement gap. *Social Psychological and Personality Science, 7*, 500–507.

Ready, D. D., & Wright, D. L. (2011). Accuracy and inaccuracy in teachers' perceptions of young children's cognitive abilities: The role of child background and classroom context. *American Educational Research Journal, 48*, 335–360.

Reardon, S. F. (2011). The widening academic achievement gap between the rich and the poor: New evidence and possible explanations. In R. Murnane & G. Duncan (Eds.), *Whither opportunity?: Rising inequality and the uncertain life chances of low-income children* (pp. 91–116). New York: Russell Sage Foundation Press.

Rheinberg, F., & Engeser, S. (2018). Intrinsic motivation and flow. In J. Heckhausen & H. Heckhausen (Eds.), *Motivation and action* (pp. 579–622). Berlin: Springer.

Rheinschmidt, M. L., & Mendoza-Denton, R. (2014). Social class and academic achievement in college: The interplay of rejection sensitivity and entity beliefs. *Journal of Personality and Social Psychology, 107*, 101–121.

Rokeach, M. (1973). *The nature of human values*. New York: Free Press.

Rosenthal, R. (1994). Interpersonal expectancy effects: A 30-year perspective. *Current Directions in Psychological Science, 3*, 176–179.

Ross, L., Lepper, M., & Ward, A. (2010). History of social psychology: Insights, challenges, and contributions to theory and application. In S. T. Fiske, D. T. Gilbert, & G. Lindzey (Eds.), *Handbook of social psychology* (Vol. 2, pp. 3–50). Hoboken, NJ: Wiley.

Rothstein, R. (2005). *Class and schools: Using social, economic, and education reform to close the Black–White achievement gap*. Washington, DC: Economic Policy Institute.

Sapolsky, R. M. (2004). *Why zebras don't get ulcers: The acclaimed guide to stress, stress-related diseases, and coping—now revised and updated*. New York: Holt Paperbacks.

Schimel, J., Arndt, J., Banko, K. M., & Cook, A. (2004). Not all self-affirmations were created equal: The cognitive and social benefits of affirming the intrinsic (vs. extrinsic) self. *Social Cognition, 22*, 75–99.

Schmeichel, B. J., & Vohs, K. D. (2009). Self-affirmation and self-control: Affirming core values counteracts ego depletion. *Journal of Personality and Social Psychology, 96*, 770–782.

Schwalbe, M. C., Barnes, J., O'Reilly, F., Chande, R., Soon, Z. Sanders, M., & Cohen, G. L. (2018). *Improving literacy and numeracy in the UK: Evidence from a registered large-scale values affirmation RCT*. Poster presented at the annual conference of Society of Personality and Social Psychology, Atlanta, GA.

Schwalbe, M., Chande, R., Barnes, J., O'Reilly, F., Sanders, M., Watson, J., & Cohen, G. (2019). *Values affirmation and UK further education college performance*. Charlottesville, VA: Center for Open Science. Retrieved from *osf.io/qh9ep*.

Schwarz, N., Bless, H., Strack, F., Klumpp, G., Rittenauer-Schatka, H., & Simons, A. (1991). Ease of retrieval as information: Another look at the availability heuristic. *Journal of Personality and Social Psychology, 61*, 195–202.

Sekaquaptewa, D., & Thompson, M. (2003). Solo status, stereotype threat, and performance expectancies: Their effects on women's performance. *Journal of Experimental Social Psychology, 39,* 68–74.

Shapiro, J. R., Williams, A. M., & Hambarchyan, M. (2013). Are all interventions created equal?: A multi-threat approach to tailoring stereotype threat interventions. *Journal of Personality and Social Psychology, 104,* 277–288.

Sherman, D. K., Brookfield, J., & Ortosky, L. (2017). Intergroup conflict and barriers to common ground: A self-affirmation perspective. *Social and Personality Psychology Compass, 11*(12).

Sherman, D. K., Bunyan, D. P., Creswell, J. D., & Jaremka, L. M. (2009). Psychological vulnerability and stress: The effects of self-affirmation on sympathetic nervous system responses to naturalistic stressors. *Health Psychology, 28,* 554–562.

Sherman, D. K., & Cohen, G. L. (2002). Accepting threatening information: Self-affirmation and the reduction of defensive biases. *Current Directions in Psychological Science, 11,* 119–123.

Sherman, D. K., & Cohen, G. L. (2006). The psychology of self-defense: Self-affirmation theory. In M. P. Zanna (Ed.), *Advances in experimental social psychology* (Vol. 38, pp. 183–242). San Diego, CA: Academic Press.

Sherman, D. K., Cohen, G. L., Nelson, L. D., Nussbaum, A. D., Bunyan, D. P., & Garcia, J. (2009). Affirmed yet unaware: Exploring the role of awareness in the process of self-affirmation. *Journal of Personality and Social Psychology, 97,* 745–764.

Sherman, D. K., & Hartson, K. A. (2011). Reconciling self-protection with self-improvement: Self-affirmation theory. In M. Alicke & C. Sedikides (Eds.), *The handbook of self-enhancement and self-protection* (pp. 128–151). New York: Guilford Press.

Sherman, D. K., Hartson, K. A., Binning, K. R., Purdie-Vaughns, V., Garcia, J., Taborsky-Barba, S., . . . Cohen, G. L. (2013). Deflecting the trajectory and changing the narrative: How self-affirmation affects academic performance and motivation under identity threat. *Journal of Personality and Social Psychology, 104,* 591–618.

Sherman, D. K., & Kim, H. S. (2005). Is there an "I" in "team"?: The role of the self in group-serving judgments. *Journal of Personality and Social Psychology, 88,* 108–120.

Sherman, D. A. K., Nelson, L. D., & Steele, C. M. (2000). Do messages about health risks threaten the self?: Increasing the acceptance of threatening health messages via self-affirmation. *Personality and Social Psychology Bulletin, 26,* 1046–1058.

Siegel, P. A., Scillitoe, J., & Parks-Yancy, R. (2005). Reducing the tendency to self-handicap: The effect of self-affirmation. *Journal of Experimental Social Psychology, 41,* 589–597.

Silverman, A., Logel, C., & Cohen, G. L. (2013). Self-affirmation as a deliberate coping strategy: The moderating role of choice. *Journal of Experimental Social Psychology, 49,* 93–98.

Sivanathan, N., Molden, D. C., Galinsky, A. D., & Ku, G. (2008). The promise and peril of self-affirmation in de-escalation of commitment. *Organizational Behavior and Human Decision Processes, 107,* 1–14.

Steele, C. M. (1988). The psychology of self-affirmation: Sustaining the integrity of the self. In L. Berkowitz (Ed.), *Advances in experimental social psychology* (Vol. 21, pp. 261–302). San Diego, CA: Academic Press.

Steele, C. M. (1997). A threat in the air: How stereotypes shape intellectual identity and performance. *American Psychologist, 52,* 613–629.

Steele, C. M., & Liu, T. J. (1983). Dissonance processes as self-affirmation. *Journal of Personality and Social Psychology, 45,* 5–19.

Steele, C. M., Spencer, S. J., & Aronson, J. (2002). Contending with group image: The psychology of stereotype and social identity threat. In M. P. Zanna (Ed.), *Advances in experimental social psychology* (Vol. 34, pp. 379–440). San Diego, CA: Academic Press.

Stone, J., & Focella, E. (2011). Hypocrisy, dissonance and the self-regulation processes that improve health. *Self and Identity, 10,* 295–303.

Storms, M. D., & McCaul, K. D. (1976). Attribution processes and emotional exacerbation of dysfunctional behavior. In J. H. Harvey, W. J. Ickes, & R. F. Kidd (Eds.), *New directions in attribution research* (Vol. 1, pp. 143–164). Hillsdale, NJ: Erlbaum.

Tibbetts, Y., Harackiewicz, J. M., Canning, E. A., Boston, J. S., Priniski, S. J., & Hyde, J. S. (2016). Affirming independence: Exploring mechanisms underlying a values affirmation intervention for first-generation students. *Journal of Personality and Social Psychology, 110,* 635–659.

Vohs, K. D., Park, J. K., & Schmeichel, B. J. (2013). Self-affirmation can enable goal disengagement. *Journal of Personality and Social Psychology, 104,* 14–27.

Voigt, R., Camp, N. P., Prabhakaran, V., Hamilton, W. L., Hetey, R. C., Griffiths, C. M., . . . Eberhardt, J. L. (2017). Language from police body camera footage shows racial disparities in officer respect. *Proceedings of the National Academy of Sciences of the USA, 114,* 6521–6526.

Wakslak, C. J., & Trope, Y. (2009). Cognitive consequences of affirming the self: The relationship between self-affirmation and object construal. *Journal of Experimental Social Psychology, 45,* 927–932.

Walton, G. M. (2014). The new science of wise psychological interventions. *Current Directions in Psychological Science, 23,* 73–82.

Walton, G. M., & Cohen, G. L. (2003). Stereotype lift. *Journal of Experimental Social Psychology, 39,* 456–467.

Walton, G. M., & Cohen, G. L. (2007). A question of belonging: Race, social fit, and achievement. *Journal of Personality and Social Psychology, 92,* 82–96.

Walton, G. M., & Cohen, G. L. (2011). A brief social-belonging intervention improves academic and health outcomes of minority students. *Science, 331,* 1447–1451.

Walton, G. M., Logel, C., Peach, J. M., Spencer, S. J., & Zanna, M. P. (2015). Two brief interventions to mitigate a "chilly climate" transform women's experience, relationships, and achievement in engineering. *Journal of Educational Psychology, 107,* 468–485.

Walton, G. M., Paunesku, D., & Dweck, C. S. (2012). Expandable selves. In M. R. Leary & J. P. Tangney (Eds.), *Handbook of self and identity* (pp. 141–154). New York: Guilford Press.

Walton, G. M., & Wilson, T. D. (2018). Wise interventions: Psychological remedies for social and personal problems. *Psychological Review, 125,* 617–655.

Ward, A., Atkins, D. C., Lepper, M. R., & Ross, L. (2011). Affirming the self to promote agreement with another: Lowering a psychological barrier to conflict resolution. *Personality and Social Psychology Bulletin, 37,* 1216–1228.

Wiesenfeld, B. M., Brockner, J., & Martin, C. (1999). A self-affirmation analysis of survivors' reactions to unfair organizational downsizings. *Journal of Experimental Social Psychology, 35,* 441–460.

Wilson, T. D., & Linville, P. W. (1985). Improving the performance of college freshmen with attributional techniques. *Journal of Personality and Social Psychology, 49,* 287–293.

Yeager, D. S., & Dweck, C. S. (2012). Mindsets that promote resilience: When students believe that personal characteristics can be developed. *Educational Psychologist, 47,* 302–314.

Yeager, D. S., Purdie-Vaughns, V., Garcia, J., Apfel, N., Brzustoski, P., Master, A., . . . Cohen, G. L. (2014). Breaking the cycle of mistrust: Wise interventions to provide critical feedback across the racial divide. *Journal of Experimental Psychology: General, 143,* 804–824.

Yeager, D. S., & Walton, G. M. (2011). Social-psychological interventions in education: They're not magic. *Review of Educational Research, 81,* 267–301.

Zajonc, R. B. (1965). Social facilitation. *Science, 149,* 269–274.

APPENDIX 3.1. Annotated Self-Affirmation Materials

Name _____ Date _____ Teacher _____

WHAT ARE YOUR PERSONAL VALUES?

In this assignment you will be answering several questions about your ideas, your beliefs, and your life. **It is important to remember while you are answering these questions that there are no right or wrong answers.**

Please read carefully over this list of personal values and think about each of the values. Then circle the two or three values that are MOST important to you. We understand that all of these values may be important to you. Even if you feel that many of the values are important, please pick **only TWO or THREE** of them to circle.

The **most** important values to me are: (circle two or three)

Athletic Ability

Being Good at Art

Creativity

Independence

Living in the Moment

Membership in a Social Group
   (such as your community, racial group, or school club)

Music

Politics

Relationships with Friends or Family

Religious Values

Sense of Humor

↞ Name signifies self and importance; teacher signifies that the authority is taking students' values seriously.

↞ This prompt conveys that it is not evaluative, and encourages a broad perspective.

↞ For younger or less literate students, prompt was simplified because many did not know what the term value means: "Remember that there are no right or wrong answers to any of these questions. Please read this list carefully. Then circle the TWO or THREE things that are MOST important to you."

↞ Picking two or three things gives students the opportunity to focus on more than one value if they want, so that they don't feel as though they are leaving one out that is important to them.

↞ Although not typically considered a "value," calling music a "value" imbues it with a higher meaning.

↞ This list was originally developed through research with U.S. college students about what matters most to them and then adapted to the middle school context; studies done in different cultures should identify core values/topics that resonate.

↞ The list of values typically excludes the domain most relevant to the threat, school, or academics, at least for the first intervention.

↞ Clip art chosen to appeal to seventh graders, not used for college student affirmations.

(continued)

Used in Cohen, Garcia, Apfel, and Master (2006); Cohen, Garcia, Purdie-Vaughns, Apfel, and Brzustoski (2009); and Sherman et al. (2013).

Directions:

1. Look at the values you picked as most important to you.

2. Think about times when these values were or would be very important to you.

3. In a few sentences, describe why these values are important to you. Focus on your thoughts and feelings, and don't worry about spelling, grammar, or how well written it is.

← Students are encouraged to think about concrete instances when these values served as resources.

← Instructions emphasize nonevaluative nature.

← Ample space provided for expressive writing, but not so much space that students feel intimidated.

(continued)

← Based on theories of ease of retrieval, participants asked for a limited number of reasons why value was important (Schwarz et al., 1991).
← Research suggests that focusing on "why" rather than "how" a value is important is more self-affirming (Schmeichel & Vohs, 2009). This prompt provides another opportunity to focus students on the rationales for their values.

← These statements were constructed to be easy for students to agree with and to reinforce the writing that they did earlier.

(continued)

Again, look at the values you picked as most important. List the top two reasons why these values are important to you:

1.

2.

Make a check mark to show how much you agree with each of the following statements:

1. These values have influenced my life.

Strongly Disagree	Disagree	Somewhat Disagree	Somewhat Agree	Agree	Strongly Agree
___	___	___	___	___	___

2. In general, I try to live up to these values.

Strongly Disagree	Disagree	Somewhat Disagree	Somewhat Agree	Agree	Strongly Agree
___	___	___	___	___	___

3. These values are an important part of who I am.

Strongly Disagree	Disagree	Somewhat Disagree	Somewhat Agree	Agree	Strongly Agree
___	___	___	___	___	___

4. I care about these values.

Strongly Disagree	Disagree	Somewhat Disagree	Somewhat Agree	Agree	Strongly Agree
___	___	___	___	___	___

(continued)

← Control condition designed to appear identical to affirmation condition so that students looking at one another's desks could not detect differences easily.

Name _____ Date _____ Teacher _____

WHAT ARE YOUR PERSONAL VALUES?

In this assignment you will be answering several questions about your ideas, your beliefs, and your life. **It is important to remember while you are answering these questions that there are no right or wrong answers.**

Please read carefully over this list of personal values and think about each of the values. Then circle the two or three values that are LEAST important to you. Even if you feel that several of the values are not very important, please pick only **TWO or THREE** of them to circle.

The **least** important values to me are: (circle two or three)

Athletic Ability

Being Good at Art

Creativity

Independence

Living in the Moment

Membership in a Social Group
    (such as your community, racial group, or school club)

Music

Politics

Relationships with Friends or Family

Religious Values

Sense of Humor

← Several different control conditions have been used. The purpose of this control condition is to have participants engage in values-related writing that is not self-relevant.

Directions:

1. Look at the values you picked as **least** important to you.

2. Think about times when these values would be important to **someone else** (like another student at your school or a person you've heard about).

3. In a few sentences, describe why these values would be important to **someone else** (like another person at your school or a person you've heard about). Focus on your thoughts and feelings, and don't worry about spelling, grammar, or how well written it is.

(continued)

Again, look at your least important values. List the top two reasons why **someone else** (like another student at your school or a person you've heard about) would pick these as their most important value:

1.

2.

Make a check mark to show how much you agree with each of the following statements:

1. These values have influenced some people.

Strongly Disagree	Disagree	Somewhat Disagree	Somewhat Agree	Agree	Strongly Agree
____	____	____	____	____	____

2. In general, some people try to live up to these values.

Strongly Disagree	Disagree	Somewhat Disagree	Somewhat Agree	Agree	Strongly Agree
____	____	____	____	____	____

3. These values are important to some people.

Strongly Disagree	Disagree	Somewhat Disagree	Somewhat Agree	Agree	Strongly Agree
____	____	____	____	____	____

4. Some people care about these values.

Strongly Disagree	Disagree	Somewhat Disagree	Somewhat Agree	Agree	Strongly Agree
____	____	____	____	____	____

APPENDIX 3.2. Annotated Extracts from the Comic Strip in the Intervention Study Conducted in Germany

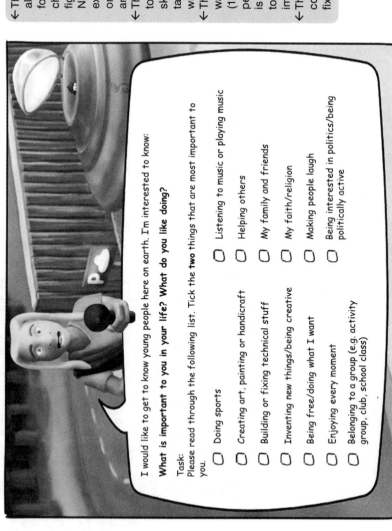

I would like to get to know young people here on earth. I'm interested to know:

What is important to you in your life? What do you like doing?

Task:
Please read through the following list. Tick the **two** things that are most important to you.

- ◻ Doing sports
- ◻ Creating art, painting or handicraft
- ◻ Building or fixing technical stuff
- ◻ Inventing new things/being creative
- ◻ Being free/doing what I want
- ◻ Enjoying every moment
- ◻ Belonging to a group (e.g. activity group, club, school class)
- ◻ Listening to music or playing music
- ◻ Helping others
- ◻ My family and friends
- ◻ My faith/religion
- ◻ Making people laugh
- ◻ Being interested in politics/being politically active

← The character's name is Nari. Nari is introduced as an alien visiting Earth, whose task it is to interview the kids for Nari's (extraterrestrial) school newspaper. An alien character was chosen in order to serve as an identity figure for children from all ethnic or social backgrounds. Nari is not human and therefore does not resemble any existing ethnic/racial group, nationality, or religion. In order for boys and girls to identify equally, Nari also lacks any fixed gender.

← The value affirmation task was strongly simplified in order to match a target group with high variation in literacy skills. Pretests showed that a longer and more complex task led to students being easily bored or unwilling to write a substantial essay.

← The notion of "values" was not adopted here, since it was regarded as a little too abstract for the age group (12–13 years). Furthermore, writing essays about personal values (as opposed to concrete experiences) is a less common task in German schools. We aimed to paraphrase values as concrete actions or things of importance.

← The items were adopted to the German context. In comparison to the U.S. original, we added "building or fixing technical stuff" and "helping others" to the list.

(continued)

Used in Müller and Lokhande (2017). Translated from German. Source: SVR Research Unit/Christian Müller.

The writing task was broken down into several steps to facilitate the writing process, enhance engagement with the task, and support a deeper processing of the chosen items.

The students are first asked to repeat their chosen items and to generate seven words that describe why the two things are important.

In the essay task, the students are then asked to include as many of the previously generated words as they can.

Task:

Write the two things that you picked into the box in the center.

Use the blank spaces to write down at least 7 words that explain:

Why is this important to you?
Why do you like doing this?

1.) _____

2.) _____

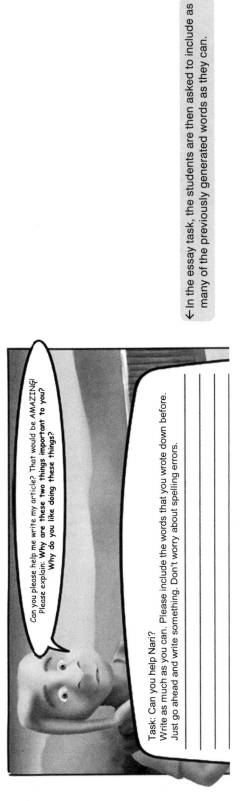

Can you please help me write my article? That would be AMAZING! Please explain: **Why are these two things important to you? Why do you like doing these things?**

Task: Can you help Nari?
Write as much as you can. Please include the words that you wrote down before. Just go ahead and write something. Don't worry about spelling errors.

CHAPTER 4

The Utility-Value Intervention

Chris S. Hulleman and Judith M. Harackiewicz

The utility-value intervention is an interactive, classroom-based assignment designed to help students make connections between the content they are learning and their lives. Across numerous randomized field trials, the intervention has increased learning outcomes, including course-specific performance and interest, and longer-term outcomes, such as course taking and persistence in a major. The intervention has proved to be particularly effective for students at risk for poor performance, including students with a history of low performance, less confidence that they will do well in the course, and students from traditionally marginalized groups. In this chapter, we review the origins of the intervention, which is grounded in the expectancy-value framework of achievement motivation and the real-world experience of educators who are trying to increase student motivation and engagement in their courses. We review the seminal studies demonstrating the effectiveness of the intervention, consider variations of the intervention—including versions created with and implemented by teachers—and discuss implications for theory, research, and practice.

BACKGROUND

In most schools in the United States, educators decide what happens in the classroom. They control the content, the learning activities, which students are in the classroom, and how students interact with one another. Although there are many good reasons for this, including making learning developmentally appropriate and sequenced, instructor-centric environments can rob students of opportunities to engage in learning that is meaningful and interesting to them. For example, nearly every student has wondered at some point, "Why are we learning this?!" Decades of research in educational psychology have revealed that students are more motivated to engage in learning, persist longer, and learn more when they find some type of value in what they are learning (Eccles et al., 1983; Wigfield, Rosenzweig, & Eccles, 2017). One study revealed that 90% of middle school teachers reported that one of the top barriers for student motivation was a lack of value for learning (Hulleman & Barron, 2013). This problem might be particularly pronounced for students already at risk of underperforming, whether due to a lack of confidence, lower levels of prior achievement, or because their cultural backgrounds differ from the educators who have designed the learning context.

Such was the experience of one of us (Hulleman) during his time as an introductory statistics graduate teaching assistant. Most of the students were aspiring psychology majors who could not see why they needed to know statistics to help people. Our intrepid teaching assistant sought to engage students during his weekly discussion sections. He drew on his research focus—motivation—to help his students find value in what they were learning. The expectancy-value framework (Eccles et al., 1983) highlighted three sources of value that helps motivate students: finding an activity enjoyable (i.e., *intrinsic value*); important to one's identity (i.e., *attainment value*); and useful, either now or in the future (i.e., *utility value*). Within the span of a 15-week semester, Hulleman decided to focus on helping students find utility value, connecting what they were learning in the class and their lives. Through the same trial-and-error process that instructors have employed for decades, he developed a series of activities that encouraged students to connect statistics to their lives. He began by encouraging students to look for examples of statistics in popular magazines or online media (e.g., *Redbook, Sports Illustrated,* CNN.com, ESPN.com). He began by setting aside 3–5 minutes each week for students to share their examples. Students struggled at first to make connections, with their lack of confidence in their statistics skills being exacerbated by a lack of value for statistics. But by the end of the semester, students were taking up nearly half the class period talking about the statistics examples they were finding in the popular literature. Students seemed more engaged, confident, and willing to ask questions. The critical insight of this initial work was that students needed to make their own connections between what they were studying and their lives, rather than trying to internalize a message delivered by the instructor. These personally meaningful connections enabled students to find the course content more relevant to their lives, which would energize their learning.

With the help of his colleagues, including his dissertation advisor (one of us: Harackiewicz), these assignments formed the inspiration for what is now known as the utility-value intervention. The utility-value intervention was first formally studied in the lab, where undergraduate students ($N = 107$) learned a new mental math technique (Hulleman, Godes, Hendricks, & Harackiewicz, 2010, Study 1). Students were randomly assigned to generate examples of how the technique applied to their lives (utility-value condition) or summarized the technique they just learned (control condition). Students who wrote about the utility value of the new math technique reported more interest in learning additional mental math techniques, with strongest findings for students who reported low confidence that they could learn the technique.

We then returned to the classroom to test the intervention in introductory psychology ($N = 318$; Hulleman et al., 2010, Study 2). Students either wrote a letter to a significant other (e.g., friend, relative) about how something they were learning in class was relevant to the significant other's life or found an example of how a topic they were studying was used in popular media. Both activities prompted students to create their *own* connections between course material and their lives rather than simply telling them how the course is useful. Initially low-performing students who completed either the letter or the media assignment were more interested in psychology at the end of the semester compared to students in the control condition, who lost interest over the semester (Harackiewicz, Hulleman, & Pastor, 2009).

PSYCHOLOGICAL PROCESSES

Utility Value

As outlined in the original (Eccles et al., 1983) expectancy-value framework, perceiving any type of value in an activity is likely to increase motivation to perform the activity. Reflecting on personal connections between course content and students' lives is expected to increase perceptions of utility value, which subsequently increases the likelihood that students will engage in course-related tasks like studying for an exam. To instigate that utility value, students' responses to the intervention need to have three characteristics.

First, *connections need to be personal.* Intervention activities are most empowering when students are able to create their own connections rather than being told about why they should value material (Canning & Harackiewicz, 2015; Durik & Harackiewicz, 2007; Durik, Schechter, Noh, Rozek, & Harackiewicz, 2015; Hulleman, 2007). Second, *connections need to be specific.* Just as specific goals (e.g., "I want to set a detailed budget by June 1") are more likely to lead to goal attainment than general goals (e.g., "I want to spend less"; Locke & Latham, 2002), specific connections between course content and everyday life is more likely to spur motivation and adaptive outcomes. Prior studies suggest that specific examples in intervention essays partially explain intervention effects (Harackiewicz, Canning, Tibbetts, Prinski, & Hyde, 2016; Rozek, Hyde, Svoboda, Hulleman, & Harackiewicz, 2014). Third, *connections need to be content-relevant.* If the goal of utility-value interventions is to support learning in a specific class, then the connections that students make to their lives need to be relevant to current course content. Figure 4.1 outlines how an exemplar quote is personal, specific, and content-relevant; these are the types of responses researchers or practitioners would ideally scaffold students toward in utility-value interventions.

Intervention Prompt

I would like you to think about how what we have been learning about in this class is important to your life in some way. What connection can you find between one of the topics we have been studying and something that is important in your life? Write a few sentences about that connection below:

Exemplary Quote

It is **personal** and specific and is *content-relevant.*

> "Playing hockey and friction are connected because in hockey while passing or shooting the puck it *slides on the ice which causes friction, slowing down the puck.* Friction could be important to my life because **I can better understand how much force I need** to get the puck to move with the friction moving against it."

Personal: A personal pronoun is used to reference something specific to the student's interest, hobbies, or goals.

Specific: Discusses how friction impacts a specific action in hockey.

Content-relevant: Indicates a linkage to a specific topic in the course in an accurate way.

FIGURE 4.1. Exemplar student quote for utility-value-intervention mechanisms. Data from Hulleman, Hulleman, et al. (2018).

Other Psychological Processes

As listed in Figure 4.2, these *intervention processes* instigate the cascade of psychological processes, beginning with perceived utility value, that lead to the beneficial effects of the utility-value intervention. Although utility value was originally hypothesized to be the key psychological process instigated by utility-value interventions, our recent research has revealed two related aspects of motivation from expectancy-value theory that utility-value interventions also affect. First, when students become engaged in a learning activity in a way that allows them to realize their knowledge of the content, their confidence in their ability to learn in the course is likely to increase (i.e., *success expectancies*). Second, as students perceive value in a course, particularly a content area that is difficult to master, their perceptions of the negative consequences of being in the course are likely to decrease (i.e., *perceived costs*). Decades of research based in the expectancy-value framework of achievement motivation in education (i.e., Eccles et al., 1983) has revealed that students' success expectancies and perceived utility value are positively related to learning, whereas perceived cost is negatively related to learning (e.g., Barron & Hulleman, 2015).

MECHANISMS

Psychological Mechanisms

Motivation researchers have investigated several psychological mechanisms that could explain the effects of utility value on motivation: identification, involvement, and interest. For example, perceiving the relevance of an activity to one's life or future goals may lead an individual to identify with the activity (*identification*), become more actively involved in learning (*involvement*), and develop an enduring *interest* in the topic (e.g., Dewey, 1913; Eccles & Wigfield, 2002; Hidi & Renninger, 2006). First, perceiving utility value in a topic may lead to an increase in the perceived importance of an activity in general, and eventually to the identification of the activity with the individual's self-concept (e.g., attainment value: Eccles et al., 1983; identified regulation: Deci & Ryan, 1985). For example, finding an application for an activity (e.g., quadratic equations and engineering) opens up the possibility of making connections to things that are personally important to the individual (e.g., a career as an engineer). Once these connections have been made, repeated engagement in the activity can lead to the activity becoming incorporated into the individual's self-concept (i.e., identification). Second, perceiving utility value in a topic may promote active task engagement. For example, perceiving a connection between geometry and life may energize an individual to become more actively involved in geometry class by seeking out learning opportunities, putting forth more effort, and becoming more engaged. When students are active contributors to the learning process, then they are more likely to feel in control (deCharms, 1968), self-determined (Deci & Ryan, 1985), and efficacious (Bandura, 1997). Rather than being passive recipients of education, students perceive that they are active participants and become absorbed in the learning process (Harackieiwicz & Sansone, 1991). Third, students are more likely to engage in activities that they find important, and perceiving utility value in a topic can increase their willingness to seek out the activity over time. Repeated engagement facilitates the acquisition of activity-related skills and knowledge, and enhances the experience

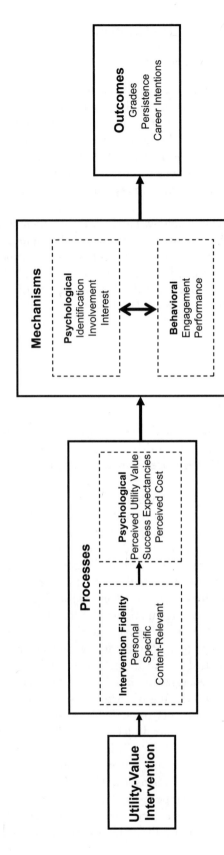

FIGURE 4.2. The utility-value-intervention logic model.

of positive affect. Repeatedly working on an enjoyable, self-relevant task that leads to skill development perfectly defines the necessary antecedent conditions for the development of interest (Hidi & Renninger, 2006). This triad of psychological mechanisms may be particularly empowering when students generate their own examples and connections, because they are personal (instead of regurgitated examples from textbooks and teachers; Dewey, 1913; Hulleman, 2007). Discovering how math applies to life may be especially effective in getting students involved in their learning, and even fostering a sense of identification with the activity, because it supports their autonomy in the classroom. This process may be less likely to occur if the usefulness of the activity is simply explained by a teacher or parent. Furthermore, it's not just that more direct approaches may be less effective; in fact, some research finds that direct approaches may even be counterproductive. In one study, Canning and Harackiewicz (2015) found that experimental utility-value manipulations that emphasized the relevance of a math activity for everyday activities and future careers undermined the interest of students with low ability perceptions.

Behavioral Mechanisms

Co-occurring with the psychological mechanisms outlined above, students who perceive increased utility value are more likely to demonstrate behavioral engagement and increased performance in the activity. In the classroom, behavioral *engagement* includes things like increased attendance, homework completion, and work quality. Increased *performance* includes proximal measures of competence development, such as performance on quizzes, tests, and oral presentations. These behavioral mechanisms work in tandem with the psychological mechanisms. For example, increased attendance can lead to increased learning, which results in increased positive affect toward school. When repeated over time, this can lead to the development of interest. Conversely, experiencing identification with the activity—such as when a student connects learning biology to his or her interest in becoming a paramedic—can lead to an increased interest in classroom activities, which enables the student to complete his or her homework at a higher level. This then leads to better performance on quizzes and tests.

EMPIRICAL EVIDENCE

Outcomes

Since the original intervention studies (Hulleman et al., 2010), the utility-value intervention has been replicated across of a variety of high school and college courses. In a recent meta-analysis of utility-value interventions (Hulleman, Wormington, Tibbetts, & Phillipoom, 2018), we found 33 field studies where 12,478 participants were randomized to a utility-value or control condition. Our meta-analytic results indicated that, on average, the utility-value intervention boosted learning outcomes—such as exam scores, end-of-semester course grades and pass rates, and interest in the topic—by a quarter of a standard deviation ($d = 0.24$). Table 4.1 presents a representative sample of published utility-value intervention studies. For most of these studies, intervention effects were most pronounced for students most likely to experience adverse learning outcomes, such as students with histories of lower achievement (e.g., Hulleman, Kosovich, Barron,

TABLE 4.1. Representative Utility-Value Intervention Randomized Field Experiments

Study	Sample age and context	Sample size	Student moderators	Outcomes
Hulleman & Harackiewicz (2009)	High school general science	262	Success expectations	Grades, interest
Hulleman, Godes, Hendricks, & Harackiewicz (2010)	4-year college psychology	318	Initial exam performance	Utility value interest
Gaspard et al. (2015)	High school math	1,916	Gender	Utility value interest
Harackiewicz, Canning, Tibbetts, Priniski, & Hyde (2016)	4-year college biology	1,040	Prior achievement, success expectations, underrepresented group membership	Grades
Hulleman, Kosovich, Barron, & Daniel (2017)	4-year college psychology	359	Gender, initial exam performance	Final exam scores
Rosenzweig, Wigfield, & Hulleman (2019)	4-year college physics	99	Initial exam performance	Grades
Kosovich, Hulleman, Phelps, & Lee (2019)	2-year college math	180	Gender	Pass rates
Total		4,174		

Note: For a comprehensive review, see a recent meta-analysis of utility-value interventions (Hulleman, Wormington, Tibbetts, & Philipoom, 2018).

& Daniel, 2017), lower success expectancies (e.g., Hulleman & Harackiewicz, 2009), or from traditionally underrepresented groups in higher education (e.g., Harackiewicz et al., 2016).

Two sets of follow-up studies are important to highlight. In our first follow-up study, we implemented the intervention in 30 high school science classrooms taught by 10 different teachers ($N = 262$; Hulleman & Harackiewicz, 2009). The writing activities were shortened to make them developmentally appropriate and to fit into a 45-minute class period. Students randomized to the utility-value condition were simply prompted to write one to two paragraphs about how a topic they were studying in science related to their lives. Students randomized to the control condition were prompted to write a one- to two-paragraph summary of a topic they were studying in class. Students completed the writing activities two to five times per semester depending on the teacher. We found that the intervention enhanced both course grades and subsequent interest in science for low-performing students in the utility-value condition compared to the control condition. For example, less confident students increased their semester grade in the course by over three-quarters of a grade point on a 4-point scale ($d = 0.50$).

In a second set of follow-up studies, Harackiewicz and colleagues (2016; Canning et al., 2018; Priniski et al., 2019; Rosenzweig, Harackiewicz, et al., 2019) implemented a utility-value intervention within a two-semester introductory biology sequence at a research-intensive university. The basic paradigm was the same for all four studies. For each of three units across the semester, students were randomly assigned to receive either a utility-value writing assignment, in which they explained why course material was useful to them personally (or wrote a letter to a friend or family member about how the course material was relevant to them), or a control assignment, in which they summarized course material. These assignments were part of the course curriculum and were graded for credit by biology graduate students blind to condition. In the first published study, Harackiewicz et al. found that the utility-value intervention had an overall, small positive effect on course grades for all students. They also found that the intervention had a more positive effect for students with a history of lower success expectations in the course (replicating the effects of Hulleman & Harackiewicz, 2009), and for underrepresented students, specifically students who were both first-generation and members of underrepresented minority groups.

Effects over Time

Most of the utility-value intervention studies have examined intervention effects in a single semester. This is because the intervention was designed to promote motivation and engagement within a specific learning context; therefore, it seems unlikely that the intervention should have long-lasting direct effects (Harackiewicz & Priniski, 2018). However, it if promotes performance in foundational courses, it may influence broader outcomes indirectly, by helping students succeed in these classes. It is also possible that the intervention might promote identification processes that have implications for subsequent academic choices. Only two published studies have looked at results in subsequent semesters, both in college biology. In the first study (N = 577; Canning et al., 2018), students in the utility-value condition earned higher grades in the course, were more likely to enroll in the second course of the biology sequence, and were less likely to abandon their science, technology, engineering, or math (STEM) major, than students in the control group. In the second study, Hecht, Harackiewicz, et al. (2019) followed students in the original Harackiewicz et al. (2016) study for 2 years after the intervention and examined whether they continued to the next course in the biology sequence and persisted in a bioscience major. They found that the utility-value intervention promoted persistence in the biomedical track for students who entered the introductory biology course with higher levels of confidence in their ability to perform well in the course. In other words, these researchers found a direct effect on long-term persistence, although the pattern of the interaction was different from that observed many times on shorter-term outcomes, such as interest (Hulleman et al., 2010) and course performance (Harackiewicz et al., 2016). Moreover, this effect was mediated through different processes, showing the complexity of understanding long-term effects of a task-specific intervention.

In addition to investigating the extent to which utility-value interventions last over time, and which outcomes are impacted, it is essential to consider how the intervention can have an effect over time. How do the short-term mechanisms translate into broader effects? We can glean some insight from Harackiewicz and colleagues' (2016) college biology intervention. Hecht, Harackiewicz, et al. (2019) found that the process through which the utility-value intervention influenced persistence was distinct from the process through which it promoted course grades. Engagement with the course material was related to course grades, whereas making personal connections to the material was related to persistence in the biology major. These findings suggest that the utility-value intervention may initiate two distinct processes that align with involvement and identification, respectively: (1) helping underperforming students to engage with course material, thereby improving performance, which had a significant indirect effect on persistence in the major; and (2) increasing reflection on the personal relevance of course material, thereby helping confident students see why pursuing that domain may be important.

Heterogeneity

At present, the majority of published utility-value intervention studies have found that the intervention works best for students who are traditionally underrepresented, underserved, or underprepared in the learning context (e.g., students with lower prior achievement, first-generation college students, racial/ethnic minorities; see Table 4.1). Our initial hypothesis was that concerns about academic performance impeded students' capacity to perceive value through a narrowing of attention (Durik & Harackiewicz, 2007; Hulleman, 2007), and that prompting students to make those connections gave them the opportunity they needed to make some initial connections. However, our more recent research demonstrates that for some students, particularly those students who perform poorly early in the course, the utility-value intervention boosts their success expectancies (Hulleman, Kosovich, et al., 2017; Rosenzweig, Wigfield, & Hulleman, 2020). Students who perform poorly initially tend to be more disengaged from the course. As a result, nudging them to see the value in the course by completing utility-value intervention activities may spark them to reengage with course material. Furthermore, students whose values are not aligned with those of the learning context might feel disconnected from the learning context from the beginning (Stephens, Hamedani, & Destin, 2014; Harackiewicz et al., 2016). For example, students from groups traditionally underrepresented in higher education, such as students who belong to a racial/ethnic-minority group, tend to value interdependent and communal goals more than independent and agentic goals (Diekman, Brown, Johnston, & Clark, 2010). The utility-value intervention provides these students an opportunity to identify their own values rather than being told to connect to goals that are not their own (e.g., more independent than interdependent).

An important reason why moderator effects might vary across learning contexts is that utility-value interventions provide an opportunity for students to articulate how their personal goals and values might align with learning in a specific context, rather than being told to connect to goals that are not their own (e.g., more independent than interdependent). This aligns with the core aspects of the Eccles et al. (1983) expectancy-value framework that explicates how student motivation is dependent upon the learning context. Our current corpus of research makes it difficult to test this context-salient hypothesis because interventions have been implemented in contexts with very few traditionally underrepresented students, which makes it difficult to fully examine students' intersectional identities. For example, Harackiewicz and colleagues (2016) needed to collect data across four semesters to have sufficient numbers of first-generation students and racial/ethnic-minority students to conduct their analyses. Testing interventions in new and diverse learning contexts will provide the opportunity to determine whether the intervention logic model and our hypotheses about intervention moderators hold up.

Second, variation in the social context of learning could influence intervention effects. One way of looking at this is by institutional context. Although the interventions have been tested across different types of institutions (e.g., high school, community college, and research-intensive universities) and subject areas (e.g., math, psychology, biology), our meta-analytic review of utility-value interventions did not show significant heterogeneity in intervention effects by context (d's from 0.19 to 0.31). Unfortunately, large studies that include many different learning contexts in a single study have not yet been published with the utility-value intervention. Such studies have the potential to uncover important variations in learning context that could contribute to heterogeneity in intervention impacts (cf. Yeager et al., 2019).

COUSINS

The utility-value intervention is related to several other social-psychological interventions, each of which focuses on how students make meaning of themselves in school.

First, it draws on the *saying-is-believing* aspect of many other social-psychological interventions, including growth mindset (Dweck & Yeager, Chapter 1, this volume), social belonging (Walton & Brady, Chapter 2, this volume), and values affirmation (Sherman, Lokhande, Müller, & Cohen, Chapter 3, this volume). The saying-is-believing aspect of these interventions involves asking students to reflect on the intervention message without having to explicitly endorse it as their own (Aronson, 1999; Walton & Wilson, 2018). This reduces reactance and increases the likelihood that students might be open to internalizing some of the intervention message for themselves.

Second, the utility-value intervention is similar to other interventions designed to help students connect their motives for learning with what they are learning in school. The *communal-value intervention* asks students to reflect on how their communal values, such as helping others, might connect with doing research in biology (Brown, Smith, Thoman, Allen, & Muragishi, 2015). The *prosocial purpose intervention* prompts students to think about how getting an education will enable them to help other people or make a difference in the world (Yeager et al., 2014). Instead of focusing on one type of value, the utility-value intervention allows students to make the choice about how the course connects to their lives. In this way, the utility-value intervention offers students more flexibility in terms of what type of utility value they will perceive in the learning content, whereas the communal and prosocial interventions focus students on those specific aspects of utility value.

Third, the utility-value intervention inspired us to develop a *parent intervention*. We developed materials for parents of high school students that highlighted how STEM courses were related to the students' current and future lives, and provided guidance on how parents could talk to their teens about these connections. This intervention enabled parents to have more nuanced and supportive conversations with their teen about how math and science related to his or her current interests and potential future educational and career pathways, and it increased parents' positive attitudes about the importance of STEM, the number of conversations they had with their teen, and most importantly, the number of STEM courses students took in high school and college (e.g., Harackiewicz, Rozek, Hulleman, & Hyde, 2012; Rozek, Svoboda, Harackiewicz, Hulleman, & Hyde, 2017).

Fourth, the *relevance affirmation intervention* is a combination of the utility-value intervention and the value-affirmation intervention (Kizilcec & Cohen, 2017). In relevance affirmation, students first affirm their core values (by circling their top values from a list), and then they write an essay about how their current educational pathway connects to those core values. The relevance affirmation intervention does not target specific learning content like the utility-value intervention but instead activates more global values that serve to affirm a student's identity, which makes it similar to the prosocial purpose intervention (Yeager et al., 2014).

Fifth, the utility-value intervention is similar to interventions that personalize the learning context. In these *context-personalization interventions* (Cordova & Lepper, 1996), the learning content and tasks are customized for the individual student by using personal details, such as the student's name, or preferences, such as the student's favorite music group. Context-personalization interventions do not provide students the opportunity to actively make connections but instead makes the connection for the student by imbuing the learning context with customized personal details and preferences.

INTERVENTION CONTENT AND IMPLEMENTATION

Versions

Basic Writing Prompt

The original version of the intervention (see Figure 4.3) involved a simple prompt for students to select a topic they are currently studying and write about how it connects to something in their lives (Hulleman et al., 2010, Study 1; Hulleman & Harackiewicz, 2009). This version clearly puts the student perspective as the driver of making connections that are personal and specific to that student. The challenge is that, for many students, making strong connections is difficult without appropriate scaffolds, which is why additional variants of the intervention have been developed. As presented in Figure 4.4, a modified version of the basic prompt was developed for college biology students (Harackiewicz et al., 2016).

Letter

As described previously, the letter version prompts students to write a letter to a significant other—parent, sibling, friend—about how what the student is learning in class could be relevant to his or her significant other's life (i.e., self–other overlap; Aron, Aron, Tudor, & Nelson, 1991). This allows students to endorse a utility value for the material without having to completely endorse it for themselves. It also offers the students an opportunity to become a benefactor of a message intended to help others, instead of being passive recipients of information.

Quotations

Gaspard and colleagues (2015) developed the first version of the utility-value intervention that provided sample quotes from students who had already taken the course. Instead of the instructor explicating the potential value of math, quotations from near-age peers provide a scaffold for students to find their own value. Since their first version

Reflecting on Your Purpose for Learning

Now that we have reviewed the main topics and concepts from this unit, it is time to reflect on one specific topic or concept.

Part A: Pick one of the topics or concepts that we have covered in this unit and briefly summarize the main parts.

Part B: Apply this topic/concept to your life, or to the life of someone you know. How might the information be useful to you, or a friend/relative, in daily life? How does learning about this topic apply to your future plans?

You can either: 1) write about it in at least 5 sentences, 2) draw a concept map with a description, or 3) draw a sketch with a description. If you do a concept map or a sketch, be sure to describe it well enough so that the reader can understand it.

For example, if you were studying nutrition, you could choose a topic such as how food is digested. Briefly summarize the digestive process – how foods are broken down in the mouth, stomach, and intestines to make energy. Then you could write about how this applies to your own life. For example, eating healthy foods helps your body produce energy to play your favorite sport or study for exams.

You could also draw a concept map of how your knowledge of digestion applies to your life. An example is provided below. Remember that you would also need to add a brief written description with a concept map or diagram.

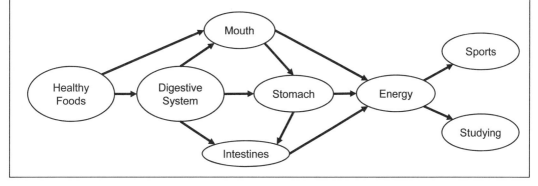

FIGURE 4.3. The basic utility-value-intervention prompt for high school science. From Hulleman and Harackiewicz (2009). Reprinted with permission from the American Association for the Advancement of Science.

of quotations was implemented with ninth-grade math students in Germany, Hulleman, Kosovich, and colleagues (2017) have developed quotation interventions for numerous learning contexts, including high school biology, algebra, and geometry, and community college math. Generally, students read four to six quotations, and then rate the quotations for personal relevance and interest. The major difference between these approaches is that the German version had an additional component where students first participated in an interactive discussion with a researcher about the relevance of math in their lives before engaging with the intervention materials individually. Figure 4.5 presents some sample intervention quotes from a community college math intervention (Kosovich, Hulleman, Phelps, & Lee, 2019).

Writing Assignment #1

Objective: Writing about scientific principles and phenomena is an increasingly important skill in the 21st century. This assignment is designed to help you understand a major concept covered in this unit while also helping you develop your science writing skills. One key to effective science writing is explaining how science can be used in everyday life. You'll do this in a 500–600 word paper. You should:

1) Formulate and answer a question	Sample questions
Select a concept that was covered in lecture and formulate a question. Use this question as the title of your essay.	• What is gene expression and how is it applied in medical research? • What are mutagens and why are they potentially harmful to DNA?
2) Explain how this applies to your life	**Examples of applications**
Write a 500–600 word essay **answering this question**, and discuss **how the information could be useful to you in your own life.** Be sure to include some concrete information that was covered in this unit, explaining *why* the information is relevant to your life and useful for you. Be sure to explain *how* the information applies to you personally and give examples.	• Medical researchers study gene expression patterns to diagnose and treat conditions caused by genetic variants. **In your own life**, you will have access to more effective treatments for any serious illnesses you develop, thanks to these advances. • Farmers use artificial selection to produce plants and animals with the most desirable traits, which can make crops more resilient. Access to cheaper and more abundant crops can save you money on groceries **in your own life**. • UV light is a mutagen that damages DNA by causing thymine mutations, which can lead to cancer. You can reduce the chances of damaging your DNA **in your own life**, by applying sunscreen when in the sun.

3) Structure your essay as suggested below

State your question in the title.

- **1st section:** Give an overview of the answer to your question.
- **2nd section:** Provide the scientific details of the answer to your question. Be sure to select the relevant information from class notes and the textbook.
- **3rd section:** Make it personal. Explain why this information is relevant to your life or useful for you and give examples.

Since you will be writing about science from a personal perspective, you can use personal pronouns (I, we, you, etc.).

FIGURE 4.4. The basic writing prompt for college biology. From Harackiewicz, Canning, Tibbetts, Priniski, and Hyde (2016).

Community College Math

> "As a firefighter/paramedic I use algebra almost every work day. Be it for a patient's weight and drug calculations, or weights when it comes to building materials. For any job that deals with medicine, you need math to save lives! I've had to apologize to all my math teachers for complaining that I would never use this stuff!" —Robin, 22, Firefighter/Paramedic

> "My major is computer arts animation so it requires a considerable amount of mathematics. I use algebra to show the way that an object is rotated and shifted and made larger and smaller—all major actions in animation. For example, let's say you want your Fortnite character to move naturally and realistically. You would have to use a simple set of equations to work out how the character moves in relation to the background and other characters in the game." —Dylan, 19, Computer Arts Animation Major

High School Geometry

> "I used to think Geometry was sort of useless outside of math class, because I want to be a graphic designer and definitely not go into any job where you use a lot of math. But, when I work for a long time on a painting and realize that the whole thing won't fit on the canvas, it really messes up the whole day. Geometry is actually really important for art or graphic design because it can help scale different shapes to avoid making things that are too big." —Omar, 18, high school senior

High School Biology

> "As a high school athlete I knew that lifting weights and eating right would help my performance, but why? I would lift weights without knowing what was actually happening to my muscles. Learning about what my muscles need to get stronger really helped me. I started eating the right food like spinach and broccoli. It made me feel healthier and improved my performance." —Rick, 20

> "During August of last year, I suffered an injury in my right eye. If I didn't go to the doctor, I would have lost my vision. After my surgery, my parents and I went to many doctor visits. Having learned about vision and the anatomy of the eye helped me a lot. I was able to better understand what happened to my eye and how the surgery helped me. I was even able to explain to my parents what exactly happened to me. They seemed really confused, and it felt good to be able to help them understand!" — Sarah, 19

FIGURE 4.5. Sample utility-value-intervention quotations for community college math, high school geometry, and high school biology. Data from Kosovich, Hulleman, Phelps, and Lee (2019); Rosenzweig, Hulleman, Barron, Kosovich, and Wigfield (2019); and Hulleman, Kosovich, Barron, and Daniel (2017).

Instructor Version: Build Connections

We designed the Build Connections activity so that teachers could have an activity that they could lead and be engaged in that would instigate similar psychological processes as the original utility-value intervention. This allows teachers to be the scaffold for learning, and to leverage the social dynamics of the classroom. The Build Connections materials and support guide are freely available online (*https://characterlab.org/activities/build-connections-for-classrooms*) and Figure 4.6 presents an example completed Build Connections worksheet. By putting student interests and goals as the first activity, the Build Connections activity is driven by instructors developing deeper relationships with students. Once they get to know student interests better, and how students are trying to make connections to the material, then instructors can be better equipped to support students in connection making as new material is introduced.

Implementation Factors

There are five important implementation factors for utility-value intervention that have received some level of empirical support in the research literature: participant responsiveness, timing, dosage, length, and choice/variety. However, each of these factors is in need of additional testing across different contexts and student groups.

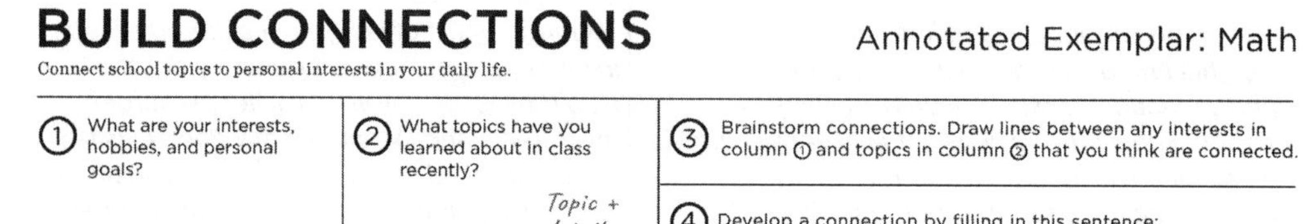
BUILD CONNECTIONS
Annotated Exemplar: Math
Connect school topics to personal interests in your daily life.

① What are your interests, hobbies, and personal goals?
Basketball
Video Games
Texting
Hang out with team
Dogs
Sneakers
Basketball Scholarship
Design my own shoes
Be in a video game
Brainstorms multiple possible connections
Complete/robust range of interests

② What topics have you learned about in class recently?
Topic + details
Functions describe relationships b/w quantities
Defines key terms
Inverse - one decreases as other increases
Example: Higher altitude -> lower temperature
Shows understanding of selected content
Linear - both variables increase at constant rate
Includes content vocabulary

③ Brainstorm connections. Draw lines between any interests in column ① and topics in column ② that you think are connected.

④ Develop a connection by filling in this sentence:
Video games (interest from ①) and linear functions (topic from ②) are connected because I can use a function to decide if I should rent a video game (linear function) or buy it (fixed cost) based on how much I will use it.
Describes connection clearly & precisely

⑤ Think more about your connection by filling in this sentence:
Linear functions (topic from ④) could be important to my life because I can use them to compare different options in the future, like buying or paying a monthly fee for my phone.
Importance is personal & actionable

FIGURE 4.6. The Build Connections intervention exercise for middle school and high school teachers. From Character Lab (2019). Reprinted with permission.

Participant Responsiveness

Several studies show that how responsive students are to the intervention prompts is related to student outcomes. Hulleman and Cordray (2009) found that high school science and college psychology students who made more specific, personal connections in their writing reported more utility value in the course than either students in the utility-value condition who made fewer specific and personal connections, or those in the control group. Nagengast et al. (2018) replicated this finding in their sample of ninth-grade math students in Germany who were randomized to a utility-value or control condition. Harackiewicz et al. (2016) found similar results in their introductory biology sample, such that students who wrote longer essays benefited more from the intervention. Not only did they find that students who made more personal and specific connections were likely to perform better in the course but they also found that students who were more engaged in the activity (as measured by the number of words written) benefited more from the intervention. In addition, two studies (Gaspard et al., 2019; Hulleman & Cordray, 2009) found that teacher engagement in the intervention also influences intervention outcomes.

Timing

The original thinking was that the utility-value intervention is best delivered at the midway point of the course and beyond. Because not all topics are equally relevant or easy to connect to students lives, waiting until midsemester allows students to have learned enough course content so that they can make personally meaningful connections. However, we have subsequently learned that waiting that long has drawbacks, as some students begin to disengage from the learning context early in the semester. In college biology, early assignments are particularly effective for students with a history of poor performance (Canning, Priniski, & Harackiewicz, 2019). As a result, we now implement the intervention as early as the second or third week of the semester.

Dosage

The utility-value intervention is not a one-shot intervention. Rather, it can take repeated experiences for students to appreciate the utility value of course material. Hulleman and Cordray (2009) found that high school science teachers who offered the intervention more times during the semester had better intervention outcomes than teachers who offered it fewer times in the semester. In college science courses, it can be difficult for students to write personal essays because the norms of scientific writing discourage the use of personal pronouns, and multiple assignments provide opportunities for feedback and practice reflecting on connections. For example, Canning et al. (2018) found that three utility-value assignments were more effective than a single assignment. Anecdotally, we have seen teachers try to implement a brief utility-value reflection once a week, with the result that students quickly grew tired of the exercise.

Length

The amount of time one intervention implementation takes students varies based on a host of student factors, including age and reading and writing skills, as well as design constraints of the classroom context. Interventions have ranged from brief homework assignments that take as little as 5 minutes (average of 7 minutes in an online math classroom in Rosenzweig, Hulleman, Barron, Kosovich, & Wigfield, 2019), 15- to 20-minute in-class assignments (e.g., Kosovich et al., 2019), 90-minute sessions that include a 45-minute lesson by an instructor followed by completion of an individual activity (Gaspard et al., 2015), or homework assignments that take several days or weeks to complete (Harackiewicz et al., 2016; Hulleman et al., 2010; Hulleman, Thoman, Dicke, & Harackiewicz, 2017).

Choice/Variety

Choice and variety are known to have powerful effects on motivation and performance (Patall, Cooper, & Wynn, 2010), but these features have only recently been tested in the utility-value intervention paradigm. Utility-value assignments have differed in terms of assignment type (i.e., essay, letter, quotes), but they can also differ in terms of assignment structure (e.g., whether students are exposed to a variety of assignments, whether students are given choices about which assignments to complete). These issues are relevant to consider when there are multiple assignments across a semester. Of course, the utility-value interventions are imbued with choice—students decide what topic to write about and what connections to draw—but the experience of choice can be further enhanced by giving students choices among assignment types. Indeed, many early studies gave students choices (e.g., Hulleman & Harackiewicz, 2009). In the college biology context, we found that higher levels of choice had positive effects on perceived utility value, interest, and performance (Priniski et al., 2019; Rosenzweig, Harackiewicz, et al., 2019), and that having a variety of utility-value assignments enhanced course performance (Priniski et al., 2019).

NUANCES AND MISCONCEPTIONS

Teach It, Don't Preach It

Helping students perceive utility value, and therefore benefit from the intervention, is about allowing students the opportunity to discover the connections between what they are learning and their lives that is *most meaningful to them*. Instead of forcing students to see specific ways in which course material might be useful in some students' lives, they need to be given the opportunity to see it for themselves. This means that instructors should think about the intervention as providing just enough scaffolding for students to make their own personal and specific connections, and no more.

Content Matters

If we want students to be motivated within a specific learning context, then the connections students make need to be specific to the topics they are learning in that context. This means the intervention needs to activate content that is being learned. This usually requires work with instructors to decide on the proper scaffolds, such as sample quotes, and timing the intervention so that there has been enough content learned to make informed connections. College students and students who are more advanced in the content area may need different scaffolds—and even less scaffolding—than students who are younger and less skilled.

It's Not a Stand-Alone Exercise

Unlike some other social-psychological interventions, this intervention needs to be explicitly connected to the learning objectives of the course. Ideally, students will receive some type of course credit to complete it, and the instructor will provide a rationale for why the utility-value activity is being completed. Example rationales include offering students an opportunity to think more deeply about the course, and the assignment being a part of the instructor's ongoing interest in improving the classroom experience for students. Without providing a compelling rationale for engaging in the activity, students are likely to disengage and/or not complete the activity. For college classes in particular, the assignments need to be on the syllabus and part of the curriculum. It's critical that they be perceived as an integral component of their curriculum. As one math instructor commented:

> "You need to come in with the attitude that this is not a superfluous activity. If you don't buy in, then your students won't buy in. You have to value it and make it important. At the beginning, I wasn't as sure what the [utility-value intervention] was. I administered it as extra credit in my classes at first. But with a better understanding of the activities, I made it more of a mandatory part of the course. Now every year, it's just built into my grading."

IMPLICATIONS FOR PRACTICE

The effectiveness of the utility-value intervention suggests that educational contexts can become better contexts for learning by increasing the potential for students to see personal value in what they are learning. In essence, such interventions are a promissory note that if instructors can make substantive, structural, and pedagogical changes to classrooms, then motivation and learning will increase. Here are some key supports instructors will need to make those changes.

Instructor Support

Online Materials

If instructors want to change what they do to help students make more connections, then we need to provide them with ideas and activities that can help. The Build Connections activity is one such activity that is designed for instructors to use with their students, and is freely available online (Character Lab, 2019). There is also supporting documentation, including implementation dos and don'ts (see Figure 4.7). If instructors are interested in providing sample quotations for students, where will they get the quotes? One important resource would be to build a repository of quotations with the help of practitioners, and share them widely.

1	**Acknowledge feelings of frustration or boredom with school.**
	Affirm that students might not find every moment of school relevant, interesting, or exciting.
2	**Create an autonomy-supportive environment.**
	Help students explore and think about how school connects to their life instead of the teacher's life. Avoid telling them why they *"must learn this."* Instead, encourage them to consider how it might connect to different aspects of their life (classroom, family, daily life, careers, helping others).
3	**Provide examples of possible connections.**
	Students may need help initiating examples, so be ready with some ideas of your own connections, or share connections made by other students.
4	**Ask follow-up questions.**
	Students may start with vague connections (*"Learning this will help me in the future."*). Be prepared to ask questions that encourage students to be specific (*"Tell me about the skills needed for your hobby." "What else do you know about this topic?" "Do you know of any examples of anyone else using this in their life?"*).
5	**Provide knowledge of the topic.**
	Students need to have enough exposure to and information about a topic in order to make high quality connections. Allow students to refer to materials they have used or created in class (study guides, notes, etc.) to help them think more deeply about the topic and spark ideas.

FIGURE 4.7. Implementation tips for helping students find utility value in learning.

Training

We can make utility-value intervention materials available to instructors, but how will they know what kinds of scaffolds their students need? Should they use the writing version, the quotes version, or a combination? We need to offer online and in-person training on how to make the design decisions needed to develop effective interventions, and meaningfully integrating activities into the curriculum without overburdening either instructors or students. Ultimately, instructors will need to change some of their practices—beyond simply implementing a utility-value intervention—in order to best help their students find personal value and meaning in learning. Figure 4.8 shares some reflections of middle school teachers after implementing the Build Connections activity with their students.

Other Institutional Opportunities

Although the utility-value intervention was designed to be used by classroom teachers, there are other educators who could make use of the intervention or its variants. For example, academic advisors could use a version of the intervention to learn more about how students are thinking about the connection between the courses they are taking in a semester and their major or career interests. College access counselors could use a version of the intervention to help students make connections between the colleges they are interested in and their future goals. We already have evidence that the Build Connections activity is being used in both of these ways in high schools and community colleges.

Build Connections Helped Teachers Make More Meaningful Connections

"I think I acknowledge more mathematical connections in my everyday life and in turn discuss these connections with my students. Additionally, I do not just discuss connections at the beginning or end of a unit. I try to incorporate connections throughout each unit and then spiral back to these connections throughout the year." – 7th-grade math teacher

"Prior to this, I did try to point out connections to the students' lives, but I wasn't trying to get them to make the connection. Now, I like to ask them about what they are interested in, or what new show they are watching, or new game they are playing, etc., and see if there is a connection. Some topics are way harder than others to find something they can personally relate to, and sometimes I have to do a little research of my own to learn about what the kids are doing to help them find a connection." – 7th-grade science teacher

Build Connections Helped Teachers Understand Their Students' Interests

"I was surprised about some of the interests of my students and things that they are involved in. Seeing the things they are involved in helped me form more conversations and interests with students." – 7th-grade science teacher

"I usually connect skills of reading and writing to what they'll be doing in future EDUCATION classes. This is a good reminder to link it to things they're interested in and will do for the rest of their life." – 9th-grade civics teacher

Build Connections Helped Teachers Make More Meaningful Connections

"My teaching has changed in that I am more intentional in looking for the opportunities to draw connections with content materials and its real-life implication. There are times in which the content materials have pretty clear real-life relevance. There are other times when I feel myself struggling to find real-life connections." – Middle school resource teacher

---

FIGURE 4.8. Teacher feedback on using Build Connections. Data from Hulleman, Hulleman, et al. (2018).

Providing students with a variety of opportunities to find value at different points of their educational journey increases the possibility that they can leverage their education in ways that maximize their motivation and learning outcomes.

IMPLICATIONS FOR PSYCHOLOGICAL THEORY

For the field of psychology, the utility-value intervention serves as an example of the importance of taking a theoretical construct—one found to be predictive of learning outcomes in many longitudinal, correlational studies—and building an intervention based on that construct that is then tested in an applied context. Despite decades of research on the role of motivation in education (Bransford, Brown, & Cocking, 2000), our initial studies (Hulleman et al., 2010; Hulleman & Harackiewicz, 2009) provided the first experimental tests of an educational intervention designed to leverage perceptions of utility value to increase student learning outcomes. Although many educators have based practice on the tenets of expectancy-value theory, the lack of rigorously tested applications of the central constructs is distressing, particularly given the press for researchers to provide explicit recommendations for practitioners based on their findings. In the case of utility-value interventions, one implication of the correlational research was that instructors needed to emphasize the relevance of the learning content to students' lives. However, our early research demonstrated that communicating utility value directly can lead to unintended negative consequences for some students (Durik, Hulleman, & Harackiewicz, 2015), and that allowing students to generate their own connections is likely to be much more effective, particularly for students at risk of academic underperformance. If psychology is to achieve its potential to positively impact society, researchers will need to increasingly conduct applied tests of their theories in the real-world contexts that they desire to improve so that their recommendations are based on causal evidence rather than identifying psychological phenomena that merely co-occur with desired outcomes (Hulleman & Barron, 2016).

Second, the original insight of the utility-value intervention is that students need to discover value in the learning material that matters to them. This led to structuring the intervention so that individual students have a choice about what aspects of the course content to connect to their lives, and which aspects of their lives to connect to the course content. This autonomy-supportive approach to operationalizing the construct of utility value has led to the development of variations of the intervention intended to provide more and different scaffolding so that students can make the most personal and specific connection possible. This work has deepened the definition of what it means to find learning content useful, and how perceiving utility value can lead to increased learning outcomes. The original conceptualization of utility value was considered to be closer to extrinsic motivation, whereas the operationalization of utility value in our intervention is more autonomous. In this way, this operationalization of the utility-value intervention has instigated a theoretical question about whether or not utility value needs to be identified as internal to an individual's self-definition, or if utility value can be related to more external motivations, such as wanting to obtain rewards or avoid punishments.

FUTURE DIRECTIONS

First, although the original intent of the intervention was to boost learning outcomes for students in a specific course, due to the demonstrated efficacy of the intervention it is now imperative to consider how these effects might translate into broader changes in students' educational pathways. However, this leads to the question of how do we get from the perception of value in a very specific context to broader change? It is not clear that we would necessarily expect an intervention that is so context specific to have continued effects beyond that context unless further prompting occurred in the future. Instead, it is more likely that the broader effects of the intervention occur by changing immediate course outcomes—such as performance and interest—which then translate into additional course taking and better performance in those courses. Indeed, many of the intervention studies to date have found significant effects on performance in gateway courses. Improved performance in these foundational courses may initiate recursive processes through which students develop confidence and/or identification with the domain, and then continue to perform better in other courses in the discipline (Cohen & Sherman, 2014; Hecht, Harackiewicz, et al., 2019). In addition, improved course performance may open up new possibilities, such as research experiences and admission to advanced courses that continue to foster engagement, performance, and persistence in the field

(Hecht, Priniski, & Harackiewicz, 2019; Goyer et al., 2017). Although we reviewed some of our initial insight into the pathway of broader effects in the "Empirical Evidence" section, much work remains to follow students in intervention studies as they move through their education pathways. We may gain insights that help us design variants of the utility-value intervention that leverage initial reflections on utility value so that they have the potential to carry over beyond the initial learning context.

Second, as we continue to learn about the role that perceptions of value play in motivating students, emerging findings demonstrate that some types of value are more motivating for some students than others (Diekman et al., 2010; Thoman, Brown, Mason, Harmsen, & Smith, 2015), and that different learning contexts differentially provide the opportunity to find different types of value. For example, Thoman and colleagues have found that research labs in the biomedical sciences tend to highlight individual achievement and accomplishment as the goals of the work, which represent more independent and agentic types of values. In contrast, students from traditionally underrepresented groups in higher education tend to be motivated by careers that highlight more interdependent and prosocial values, like helping others. Thoman et al. have found that this value mismatch partially explains the reasons why students from underrepresented groups choose not to persist in STEM majors, even when controlling for academic performance. These findings encourage us to consider whether utility-value interventions might be more effective for underrepresented students if they were structured in a way so that students were encouraged to make connections between the course content and their interdependent goals (e.g., Yeager et al., 2014; Tibbetts, Harackiewicz, Priniski, & Canning, 2016), or if having the choice would be more effective. In our ongoing community college math work, we have developed interventions prompts that provide sample quotations from students that emphasize both independent and interdependent motives, and we are examining whether students' backgrounds influence the type of connections they make.

Third, there are a variety of implementation factors that we have identified as impacting the effectiveness of the utility-value intervention, including timing, dosage, length, choice, and variety, among others. We have also reviewed different types and structures of utility-value interventions that have evidence of effectiveness, including writing- and quotations-based versions. However, very few studies have been designed as experiments where participants are randomly assigned to different implementation factors or design features of the utility-value intervention (cf. Priniski et al., 2019). Future studies also need to examine whether any of these factors vary as a function of level of education, student demographic characteristics, or other aspects of the learning context. How much customization is necessary in order to implement an effective utility-value intervention in a new context?

Fourth, as we transition the implementation of the utility-value intervention from researchers to instructors and other educational practitioners, how do we adapt and test these utility-value practices while still instigating the targeted psychological processes? For example, although Build Connections was designed based on the efficacy evidence from the utility-value intervention, we still need to test whether this variation works, and whether it works without direct researcher involvement. Clearly, collaborating with practitioners from beginning to end of the translation process will be essential, both to provide supports for implementation and to capture learnings on what does and does not work.

REFERENCES

Aron, A., Aron, E. N., Tudor, M., & Nelson, G. (1991). Close relationships as including other in the self. *Journal of Personality and Social Psychology, 60*(2), 241–253.

Aronson, E. (1999). The power of self-persuasion. *American Psychologist, 54*(11), 875–884.

Bandura, A. (1997). *Self-efficacy: The exercise of control.* New York: Freeman.

Barron, K. E., & Hulleman, C. S. (2015). Expectancy-value-cost model of motivation. In J. D. Wright (Ed.), *International encyclopedia of the social and behavioral sciences* (2nd ed., Vol. 8, pp. 503–509). Oxford, UK: Elsevier.

Bransford, J. D., Brown, A. L., & Cocking, R. R. (2000). *How people learn* (Vol. 11). Washington, DC: National Academy Press.

Brown, E. R., Smith, J. L., Thoman, D. B., Allen, J., & Muragishi, G. (2015). From bench to bedside: A communal utility-value intervention to enhance students' science motivation. *Journal of Educational Psychology, 107*(4), 1116–1135.

Canning, E. A., & Harackiewicz, J. M. (2015). Teach it, don't preach it: The differential effects of directly-communicated and self-generated utility-value information. *Motivation Science, 1*(1), 47–71.

Canning, E. A., Harackiewicz, J. M., Priniski, S. J., Hecht, C. A., Tibbetts, Y., & Hyde, J. S. (2018). Improving performance and retention in introductory biology with a utility-value intervention. *Journal of Educational Psychology, 110*, 834–849.

Canning, E. A., Priniski, S. J., & Harackiewicz, J. M. (2019). Unintended consequences of framing a utility-value intervention in two-year colleges. *Learning and Instruction, 62*, 37–48.

Character Lab. (2019). Build Connections for classrooms. Retrieved from *https://characterlab.org/activities/build-connections-for-classrooms.*

Cohen, G. L., & Sherman, D. K. (2014). The psychology of change: Self-affirmation and social psychological intervention. *Annual Review of Psychology, 65*, 333–371.

Cordova, D. I., & Lepper, M. R. (1996). Intrinsic motivation and the process of learning: Beneficial effects of contextualization, personalization, and choice. *Journal of Educational Psychology, 88*(4), 715–730.

deCharms, R. (1968). *Personal causation.* New York: Academic Press.

Deci, E. L., & Ryan, R. M. (1985). *Self-determination.* New York: Wiley.

Dewey, J. (1913). *Interest and effort in education.* Cambridge, MA: Riverside Press.

Diekman, A. B., Brown, E. R., Johnston, A. M., & Clark, E. K. (2010). Seeking congruity between goals and roles: A new look at why women opt out of science, technology, engineering, and mathematics careers. *Psychological Science, 21*, 1051–1057.

Durik, A. M., & Harackiewicz, J. M. (2007). Different strokes for different folks: How personal interest moderates the effects of situational factors on task interest. *Journal of Educational Psychology, 99*, 597–610.

Durik, A. M., Hulleman, C. S., & Harackiewicz, J. M. (2015). One size fits some: Instructional enhancements to promote interest don't work the same for everyone. In K. A. Renninger, M. Nieswandt, & S. Hidi (Eds.), *Interest in mathematics and science learning* (pp. 49–62). Washington, DC: American Educational Research Association.

Durik, A. M., Shechter, O., Noh, M. S., Rozek, C. S., & Harackiewicz, J. M. (2015). What if I can't?: Perceived competence as a moderator of the effects of utility value information on situational interest and performance. *Motivation and Emotion, 39*, 104–118.

Eccles, J., Adler, T. F., Futterman, R., Goff, S. B., Kaczala, C. M., Meece, J. L., & Midgley, C. (1983). Expectancies, values, and academic behaviors. In J. T. Spence (Ed.), *Achievement and achievement motives: Psychological and sociological approaches* (pp. 75–146). San Francisco: Freeman.

Eccles, J. S., & Wigfield, A. (2002). Motivational beliefs, values, and goals. *Annual Review of Psychology, 53*, 109–132.

Gaspard, H., Dicke, A.-L., Flunger, B., Brisson, B. M., Häfner, I., Nagengast, B., & Trautwein, U. (2015). Fostering adolescents' value beliefs for mathematics with a relevance intervention in the classroom. *Developmental Psychology, 51*(9), 1226–1240.

Gaspard, H., Parrisius, C., Kleinhansl, M., Piesch, H., Wille, E., Nagengast, B., . . . Hulleman, C. S. (2019, June). *Implementing utility-value interventions in mathematics classrooms: The role of implementation fidelity.* Presentation to the Curry School of Education, Charlottesville, VA.

Goyer, J. P., Garcia, J., Purdie-Vaughns, V., Binning, K. R., Cook, J. E., Reeves, S. L., . . ., Cohen, G. L. (2017). Self-affirmation facilitates minority middle schoolers' progress along college trajectories. *Proceedings of the National Academy of Sciences of the USA, 114*(29), 7594–7599.

Harackiewicz, J. M., Canning, E. A., Tibbetts, Y., Priniski, S. J., & Hyde, J. S. (2016). Closing achievement gaps with a utility-value intervention: Disentangling race and social class. *Journal of Personality and Social Psychology, 111*, 745–765.

Harackiewicz, J. M., Hulleman, C. S., & Pastor, D. A. (2009, August). *Developmental trajectories of interest within semester-long courses in high school science and introductory psychology.* Paper presented at the European Association for Research on Learning and Instruction (EARLI) Biennial Conference, Munich, Germany.

Harackiewicz, J. M., & Priniski, S. J. (2018). Improving student outcomes in higher education: The science of targeted intervention. *Annual Review of Psychology, 69*, 409–435.

Harackiewicz, J. M., Rozek, C. S., Hulleman, C. S., & Hyde, J. S. (2012). Helping parents to motivate adolescents in mathematics and science: An experimental test of a utility-value intervention. *Psychological Science, 43*, 899–906.

Harackiewicz, J. M., & Sansone, C. (1991). Goals and intrinsic motivation: You can get there from here. In M. L. Maehr & P. R. Pintrich (Eds.), *Advances in motivation and achievement* (Vol. 7, pp. 21–49). Greenwich, CT: JAI Press.

Hecht, C. A., Harackiewicz, J. M., Priniski, S. J., Canning, E. A., Tibbetts, Y., & Hyde, J. S. (2019). Promoting persistence in the biological and medical sciences: An expectancy-value approach to intervention. *Journal of Educational Psychology, 111*(8), 1462–1477.

Hecht, C. A., Priniski, S. J., & Harackiewicz, J. M. (2019). Understanding long-term effects of motivation interventions in a changing world. In E. Gonida & M. Lemos (Eds.), *Advances in motivation and achievement: Vol. 20. Motivation in education at a time of global change: Theory, research, and implications for practice* (pp. 81–98). Bingley, UK: Emerald Group.

Hidi, S., & Renninger, K. A. (2006). The four-phase model of interest development. *Educational Psychologist, 41*, 111–127.

Hulleman, C. S. (2007). *The role of utility value in the development of interest and achievement.* Unpublished doctoral dissertation, University of Wisconsin–Madison, Madison, WI.

Hulleman, C. S., & Barron, K. E. (2013, April). Teacher perceptions of student motivational challenges and best strategies to enhance motivation. Paper presented in J. Turner (Chair), *Bridging the theory–practice divide: Teacher approaches to motivating students.* Symposium presented at the annual meeting of the American Educational Research Association, San Francisco, CA.

Hulleman, C. S., & Barron, K. E. (2016). Motivation interventions in education: Bridging theory, research, and practice. In L. Corno & E. M. Anderman (Eds.), *Handbook of educational psychology* (3rd ed., pp. 160–171). New York: Routledge, Taylor & Francis.

Hulleman, C. S., & Cordray, D. S. (2009). Moving from the lab to the field: The role of fidelity and achieved relative intervention strength. *Journal of Research on Educational Effectiveness, 2*, 88–110.

Hulleman, C. S., Godes, O., Hendricks, B., & Harackiewicz, J. M. (2010). Enhancing interest and performance with a utility-value intervention. *Journal of Educational Psychology, 102*(4), 880–895.

Hulleman, C. S., & Harackiewicz, J. M. (2009). Promoting interest and performance in high school science classes. *Science, 326,* 1410–1412.

Hulleman, C. S., Hulleman, T. K., Wormington, S. V., Vines, E., Foran, M., & Clayton, K. (2018). *Build Connections: A collaboration to improve a teacher led utility-value intervention.* Charlottesville, VA: Motivate Lab.

Hulleman, C. S., Kosovich, J. J., Barron, K. E., & Daniel, D. (2017). Making connections: Replicating and extending the utility-value intervention in the classroom. *Journal of Educational Psychology, 109*(3), 387–404.

Hulleman, C. S., Thoman, D. B., Dicke, A., & Harackiewicz, J. M. (2017). The promotion and development of interest: The importance of perceived values. In P. O'Keefe & J. M. Harackiewicz (Eds.), *The science of interest* (pp. 189–208). New York: Springer.

Hulleman, C. S., Wormington, S. V., Tibbetts, C. Y., & Philipoom, M. (2018, August). *A meta-analytic synthesis of utility-value interventions in education.* Paper presented at the bi-annual meeting of the International Conference on Motivation, Aarhus, Denmark.

Kizilcec, R. F., & Cohen, G. L. (2017). Eight-minute self-regulation intervention raises educational attainment at scale in individualist but not collectivist cultures. *Proceedings of the National Academy of Sciences of the USA, 114*(17), 4348–4353.

Kosovich, J. J., Hulleman, C. S., Phelps, J., & Lee, M. (2019). Improving algebra success with a utility-value intervention. *Journal of Developmental Education, 42*(2).

Locke, E. A., & Latham, G. P. (2002). Building a practically useful theory of goal setting and task motivation: A 35-year odyssey. *American Psychologist, 57*(9), 705–717.

Nagengast, B., Brisson, B. M., Hulleman, C. S., Gaspard, H., Häfner, I., & Trautwein, U. (2018). Learning more from educational interventions studies: Estimating complier average causal effects in a relevance intervention. *Journal of Experimental Education, 86,* 105–123.

Patall, E. A., Cooper, H., & Wynn, S. R. (2010). The effectiveness and relative importance of choice in the classroom. *Journal of Educational Psychology, 102*(4), 896–915.

Priniski, S. J., Rosenzweig, E. Q., Canning, E. A., Hecht, C. A., Tibbetts, Y., Hyde, J. S., & Harackiewicz, J. M. (2019). The benefits of combining value for the self and others in utility-value interventions. *Journal of Educational Psychology, 111*(8), 1478–1497.

Rosenzweig, E. Q., Harackiewicz, J. M., Priniski, S. J., Hecht, C. A., Canning, E. A., Tibbetts, Y., & Hyde, J. S. (2019). Choose your own intervention: Using choice to enhance the effectiveness of a utility-value intervention. *Motivation Science, 5*(3), 269–276.

Rosenzweig, E. Q., Hulleman, C. S., Barron, K. E., Kosovich, J. J., & Wigfield, A. (2019). Making math matter: Adapting utility-value interventions for online math courses. *Journal of Experimental Education, 87*(2), 332–352.

Rosenzweig, E. Q., Wigfield, A., & Hulleman, C. S. (2020). More useful or not so bad?: Examining the effects of utility value and cost reduction interventions in college physics. *Journal of Educational Psychology, 112*(1), 166–182.

Rozek, C. S., Hyde, J. S., Svoboda, R. C., Hulleman, C. S., & Harackiewicz, J. M. (2014). Gender differences in the effects of a utility-value intervention to help parents motivate adolescents in mathematics and science. *Journal of Educational Psychology, 107*(1), 195–206.

Rozek, C. S., Svoboda, R. C., Harackiewicz, J. M., Hulleman, C. S., & Hyde, J. S. (2017). Utility-value intervention with parents increases students' STEM preparation and career pursuit. *Proceedings of the National Academy of Sciences of the USA, 114,* 909–914.

Stephens, N. M., Hamedani, M. G., & Destin, M. (2014). Closing the social-class achievement gap: A difference-education intervention improves first-generation students' academic performance and all students' college transition. *Psychological Science, 25*(4), 943–953.

Thoman, D. B., Brown, E. R., Mason, A. Z., Harmsen, A. G., & Smith, J. L. (2015). The role of altruistic values in motivating underrepresented minority students for biomedicine. *BioScience, 65,* 183–188.

Tibbetts, Y., Harackiewicz, J. M., Priniski, S. J., & Canning, E. A. (2016). Broadening participation in the life sciences with social–psychological interventions. *CBE-Life Sciences Education, 15*(3), es4.

Walton, G. M., & Wilson, T. D. (2018). Wise interventions: Psychological remedies for social and personal problems. *Psychological Review, 125*(5), 617.

Wigfield, A., Rosenzweig, E. Q., & Eccles, J. S. (2017). Achievement values. In A. Elliot, C. Dweck, & D. Yeager (Eds.), *Handbook of competence and motivation: Theory and application* (pp. 116–134). New York: Guilford Press.

Yeager, D. S., Hanselman, P., Walton, G. M., Murray, J., Crosnoe, R., Muller, C., . . . Dweck, C. S. (2019). A national experiment reveals where a growth mindset improves adolescent achievement. *Nature, 573*(7774), 364–369.

Yeager, D. S., Henderson, M. D., Paunesku, D., Walton, G. M., D'Mello, S., Spitzer, B. J., & Duckworth, A. L. (2014). Boring but important: A self-transcendent purpose for learning fosters academic self-regulation. *Journal of Personality and Social Psychology, 107*(4), 559–580.

CHAPTER 5

Difference-Education

Improving Disadvantaged Students' Academic Outcomes by Changing Their Theory of Difference

Nicole M. Stephens, MarYam G. Hamedani,
and Sarah S. M. Townsend

This chapter provides an overview of *difference-education*: a wise intervention designed to help disadvantaged students overcome the psychological obstacles (i.e., a lack of fit and empowerment) that can negatively impact their opportunity to succeed in college. The defining feature of difference-education is that it teaches students about the contextual nature of social group differences through the stories of successful students from diverse backgrounds. This chapter explains what difference-education is, describes how it can reduce educational disparities, and provides an overview of strategies to implement it effectively. First, we provide an overview of the difference-education intervention approach and describe the literatures that we drew on to develop the methods and theorizing that underlie this approach. Second, we discuss the psychological processes through which difference-education produces its effects and provide an overview of supporting research. Third, we review how difference-education interventions have been implemented in college settings, explain some nuances and misconceptions, and describe potential directions for future research.

Difference-education is a wise intervention designed to help college students who are disadvantaged by mainstream educational settings overcome psychological obstacles that can undermine their opportunity to succeed in college. The defining feature of difference-education is that it teaches students about the contextual nature of social group differences through the contrasting narratives or stories of successful students from diverse backgrounds. We use the term *social group differences* to refer to variation in the experiences, opportunities, and/or outcomes of diverse social groups. The stories that students are exposed to during a difference-education intervention convey a contextual understanding of social group differences by illuminating how students' current experiences in college can vary as a function of their different backgrounds. By being exposed to these stories, intervention participants learn that social group differences are *contextual*—that is, they are a product of students' diverse life experiences and backgrounds. This critical insight can help students understand that their different backgrounds are not a deficiency that holds them back but rather can be a source of strength that they can leverage to fit in with the college community and find their own path to success. As described in this chapter, we designed the first wave of difference-education interventions to examine whether it was possible to use this contextual understanding of social group difference to improve the academic outcomes of first-generation college students (Stephens, Hamedani, & Destin, 2014; Townsend, Stephens, Smallets, & Hamedani, 2018).

BACKGROUND

Even after first-generation college students (i.e., students who do not have parents with 4-year college degrees) defy the odds to gain admission to college, they still confront obstacles to success that continuing-generation students (i.e., students who have at least one parent with a 4-year college degree) face less often. Beyond having fewer economic resources and academic skills (e.g., Horn & Nuñez, 2000; Terenzini, Springer, Yaeger, Pascarella, & Nora, 1996), first-generation students also confront an additional set of psychological or cultural obstacles, such as a lack of fit or empowerment (Astin & Oseguera, 2004; Goudeau & Croizet, 2017; Sirin, 2005). We use the term *fit* to refer to the feeling of being accepted, recognized, welcomed, and included within a setting, such as the college community (e.g., Stephens, Brannon, Markus, & Nelson, 2015).[1] We use the term *empowerment* to refer to (1) the psychological experience of efficacy, ownership, and control; and (2) the resulting willingness to enact the strategies needed to make the most of one's experience. Together these obstacles fuel a persistent *social class achievement gap,* such that first-generation students earn lower grades and more often drop out compared to continuing-generation students (Astin & Oseguera, 2004; Sirin, 2005).

One especially important cultural obstacle is the mismatch between the largely middle-class culture of higher education and the working-class beliefs, norms, and values that many first-generation students bring with them to college (e.g., Stephens, Fryberg, Markus, Johnson, & Covarrubias, 2012). For example, many colleges and universities expect students to pave their own path and express their personal opinions (Fryberg & Markus, 2007), while many working-class students are instead socialized to follow the rules and adhere to socially accepted norms of behavior (e.g., Kohn, 1969). First-generation students are guided by more interdependent norms and may not feel fully comfortable expressing their ideas or opinions in class, or attending office hours to ask a professor for clarification on an assignment or to explain a grade. This cultural mismatch can lead first-generation students to feel excluded from these educational settings and lead them to question whether they fit or belong in college (e.g., Covarrubias & Fryberg, 2015; Ostrove & Long, 2007; Walton & Cohen, 2007). First-generation students can

---

[1] We use the term *social fit,* rather than belonging, to emphasize the relationship between a person's psychological experience and its congruence with a particular context, setting, or environment. This term derives from decades of prior work on cultural fit, as well as person–environment, person–culture, or person–organization fit (e.g., Chatman, 1991; Dawis, 1992; Edwards, Cable, Williamson, Lambert, & Shipp, 2006; Fulmer et al., 2010).

also be unfamiliar with the "rules of the game" that lead to success in higher education, such as how to relate to professors or how to choose a major. This lack of familiarity can undermine their sense of empowerment and efficacy (e.g., Housel & Harvey, 2010; Reay, Crozier, & Clayton, 2009). These obstacles can systematically disadvantage first-generation students and further fuel the social class achievement gap.

Intellectual History

In the first wave of studies, difference-education was designed to reduce the social class achievement gap by helping first-generation students gain a sense of fit and empowerment in college. Difference-education builds on the wise intervention literature in social psychology by using the methodological strategy of changing students' construal or understanding of their experience (Walton & Wilson, 2018)—in this case, their experience of difference. This research area leverages the strategy of changing students' lay theories about ability and achievement to foster success in school (e.g., Wilson, 2011). A *lay theory* is a set of fundamental assumptions about the nature of the self and social world that shapes how people interpret and respond to their experiences (Molden & Dweck, 2006). For example, one popular lay theory intervention provides an understanding that intelligence or ability is malleable and can change over time (e.g., Blackwell, Trzesniewski, & Dweck, 2007). Likewise, we theorize that changing students' lay theories about social group differences—in particular, teaching them a contextual theory of difference—can improve their academic outcomes.

To explain why a contextual theory would improve disadvantaged[2] students' academic outcomes, we drew from diverse literatures in psychology and education that typically do not "talk" to one another. Research in social psychology, on the one hand, has identified two prominent theories of difference—an essentialist theory and a contextual theory—and examined their consequences for intergroup relations. This literature does not examine the effects of a contextual theory on academic outcomes, but instead focuses on its effects on intergroup outcomes. Research in education, on the other hand, theorizes about the academic benefits of teaching students about social group differences, but does not directly isolate or test the causal effects of a contextual theory on these academic outcomes. As such, both literatures provide complementary evidence for our theory, but do not formulate nor test it directly. Below, drawing on the social psychology literature, we first provide an overview of these two lay theories and explain how they can shape the meaning of social group difference and affect intergroup outcomes. Second, we draw on the education literature to provide an overview of research in multicultural and social justice education, which supports the claim that a contextual theory can benefit disadvantaged students academically.

Research in social psychology identifies the meanings and consequences of essentialist versus contextual theories of social group difference for intergroup outcomes. An *essentialist* theory defines social group differences as biologically rooted and therefore relatively fixed or unchanging essences or attributes of individual people or social groups

---

[2]The term *disadvantaged* refers to students who are typically disadvantaged by the mainstream culture of higher education—typically students who are first-generation, low-income, and/or underrepresented racial or ethnic minorities. This term is meant to highlight how institutional environments can negatively impact students' learning experiences and chances for success, not that their backgrounds themselves are deficits.

(Gelman, 2004; Haslam, Rothschild, & Ernst, 2000; Prentice & Miller, 2007). In the United States, the essentialist theory of social group differences is the most common way of understanding difference (e.g., Markus, 2008).

Throughout history, an essentialist theory of social group difference has been used to stigmatize social group differences and to downwardly constitute certain groups as deficient or inferior (Markus, 2008; Markus & Moya, 2010). This essential view of difference means that a social group's differences are likely to be interpreted as an indication of their lower value in society, and this rationale can be used to justify their subjugation and mistreatment. For example, if working-class Americans were to receive lower scores than middle-class Americans on an intelligence test, an essentialist theory would suggest that this difference is an indication of working-class people's inherent inferiority, which could be used to rationalize the act of withholding educational resources from them. Indeed, throughout history, this logic has been used to justify prejudice and discrimination and to exclude, oppress, and withhold opportunities from a wide range of social groups. It has been used to justify the genocide of Native Americans, the enslavement of African Americans, and a wide range of discriminatory policies that excluded immigrants throughout U.S. history (e.g., Markus & Moya, 2010; Omi & Winant, 2015). As a result, an essentialist theory of difference links social group differences with largely negative meanings and stigma, and shapes people's experiences accordingly. When people use this essentialist theory to make sense of social group differences, they often experience differences as a threat, a source of deficiency, or a weakness.

An essentialist perspective contrasts sharply with another way of understanding social group difference: a contextual theory. Well represented in the academy and among the social sciences, this theory asserts that social group differences are not essential but instead socially constructed (e.g., Markus, 2008; Markus & Moya, 2010; Omi & Winant, 2015). According to this theory, social group differences come from the normal process of participating in, adapting, and responding to the diverse sociocultural contexts that people inhabit throughout their lives.[3] Further, considering the contextual origins of difference, this theory implies that differences can change over time with new contextual experiences (see Markus, 2008, for related arguments). The contextual view means that social group differences are normal—that is, they stem from people's different life experiences, rather than some kind of inherent inferiority. As such, these differences can no longer be used to justify the mistreatment of those who are different. For example, if working-class Americans were to receive lower scores than middle-class Americans on an intelligence test, a contextual theory suggests that this difference is an indication of working-class students' disparate levels of preparation or opportunities in schools. This interpretation could then be used to rationalize the act of giving working-class students more resources to develop their skills and abilities. As a result, a contextual theory destigmatizes and normalizes the experience of difference, and shapes people's experiences accordingly. Therefore, when people use a contextual theory to make sense of social group differences, they can experience differences positively, as an asset or strength.

Consistent with this idea, research in psychology suggests that exposure to a contextual theory can improve the quality of intergroup relations. Specifically, research has

---

[3]The term *sociocultural context* refers to a socially and historically constructed environment that contains a set of culture-specific ideas, practices, and institutions (Markus & Hamedani, 2019; Stephens, Markus, & Fryberg, 2012).

shown that a contextual theory compared with an essentialist theory leads to decreased stereotyping and race-based categorization (Bastian & Haslam, 2006; Chao, Hong, & Chiu, 2013; Keller, 2005); more identification and perceived similarity across different groups (No et al., 2008); and higher levels of intergroup trust and desire for intergroup contact (Kung et al., 2018; Williams & Eberhardt, 2008). For example, when confronted with a social problem relevant to race, Williams and Eberhardt found that exposing diverse participants to the idea that race is socially constructed led them to report greater emotional engagement (based on a self-report measure of their mood) than those who were exposed to the idea that race is essential.

Second, research in education—particularly work on multicultural and social justice education—suggests that learning about the contextual nature of social group difference has the potential to foster disadvantaged students' academic engagement and improve their performance in school (e.g., grades). Most of this interdisciplinary research in education is not designed to isolate or test the causal effects of a contextual theory in the way that experimental social psychologists would. Instead, the research tends to examine the effects of multidimensional educational experiences, which typically include a contextual theory as one part of many different ideas and practices. Although this research area does not provide direct causal evidence of the benefits of a contextual theory, it suggests that a contextual theory has the *potential* to benefit disadvantaged students.

Ethnic studies courses are one example of multicultural and social justice education. They encourage students to view social groups, including their own, as socially and historically situated, and highlight how contextual factors, such as institutions, policies, and practices, can shape students' experiences and life outcomes. Research examining the effects of ethnic studies courses demonstrates that these learning experiences are correlated with a variety of academic benefits (see Sleeter, 2011, for a review; see also Bowman, 2010; Cole, Case, Rios, & Curtin, 2011; Denson, 2009; Nelson Laird, 2005). These courses are often associated with improved academic performance and empowerment of disadvantaged students (e.g., Cabrera, Milem, Jaquette, & Marx, 2014; Sleeter, 2011). For example, one study of San Francisco high schools suggested that taking an ethnic studies course in ninth grade led to an increase in ninth-grade attendance, grade-point average (GPA), and credits earned (Dee & Penner, 2016).

Taken together, research from both psychology and education suggests that providing disadvantaged students with a contextual theory of difference could help destigmatize social group differences and therefore help students understand their meanings in a new, more positive way. That new understanding, in turn, could help improve their engagement and performance in school (e.g., grades). In sum, research in psychology helps explain why a contextual theory is likely to yield positive effects relative to an essentialist theory, and education research provides initial evidence to support the idea that more positive responses are likely to translate into improved academic outcomes.

PSYCHOLOGICAL PROCESSES

A contextual theory of difference has the potential to change how students make sense of and respond to their own and others' social group differences. Indeed, upon entering college, students often experience challenges or obstacles associated with social group differences. Research in psychology and education demonstrates the college environment often fails to foster a sense of fit and empowerment for first-generation students (e.g., Ostrove & Long, 2007; Stephens, Brannon, et al., 2015). Illustrating a lack of fit, a first-generation student at Vanderbilt University recounted, "Never before had I truly felt such an extreme sense of estrangement and alienation. . . . I quickly realized that although I may look the part, my cultural and socioeconomic backgrounds were vastly different from those of my predominantly White, affluent peers. I wanted to leave" (Riggs, 2014, para. 2). Describing the experience of feeling disempowered upon entering college, one first-generation student at Cornell University said, "I had no road map for what I was supposed to do once I made it to campus. . . . Aside from a check-in with my financial aid officer . . . I was mostly keeping to myself to hide the fact that I was a very special kind of lost" (Capó Crucet, 2015, para. 15).

A contextual theory of difference can help first-generation students understand their social group differences in a new, more positive light—as a strength, resource, or asset, rather than as a stigma, weakness, or deficiency. Specifically, as shown in Figure 5.1, viewing differences as contextual should change the meaning of difference and help first-generation students gain a sense of fit and empowerment.

Learning that difference is contextual can decrease the stigma attached to difference, and therefore foster disadvantaged students' sense of fit in the college setting. Providing a contextual theory of difference should increase students' sense of fit by conveying that their challenges are informed by their backgrounds and prior experiences, rather than indicating their deficiency as individuals. In other words, the contextual theory should convey the message that "differences are a normal part of the college experience." For example, a first-generation student should understand that having parents without a college education means that it will likely be harder to get advice from one's parents about college (e.g., how to choose a major), and they may need to go to a trusted advisor instead. Accordingly, students should then gain a sense of fit from learning that "my differences will not prevent me from finding my path."

Likewise, learning that difference is contextual can imply that one's experiences of difference are malleable rather than fixed, and therefore foster disadvantaged students' sense of empowerment in college. Providing a contextual theory should help students

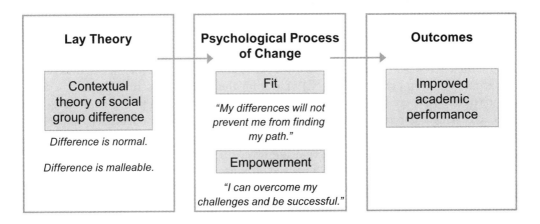

FIGURE 5.1. Psychological processes by which a contextual theory of social group difference improves academic performance.

better understand that their challenges are due to experiences in different contexts (e.g., they attended a less rigorous high school), rather than some individual deficiency. In other words, the contextual theory should convey that "differences are malleable" and can be changed in the future. For example, when confronting background-specific challenges, a first-generation student should understand that struggling in one's classes could be a result of having less preparation in a low-quality high school, rather than less ability to succeed. This should help students feel more efficacious and in control, and also foster their willingness to take full advantage of the resources available to them. Accordingly, students should then gain a sense of empowerment from learning that "I can overcome my challenges and be successful."

EMPIRICAL EVIDENCE

Outcomes

In an initial set of studies conducted at selective colleges, we delivered and tested difference-education in an effort to improve the academic outcomes of incoming first-generation college students. These interventions exposed students to a contextual theory of social group difference during the transition from high school to college by sharing contrasting stories of senior college students from diverse social class backgrounds. The systematic variation in these stories showed intervention participants vivid examples of how their prior social class contexts could inform their experiences in college. As of the publication of this chapter, the intervention has been delivered in two ways: (1) through a student panel that intervention participants attended in person (Stephens et al., 2014), and (2) through a scalable version that intervention participants completed online (Townsend et al., 2018).

Both of these interventions were delivered early on in students' first quarter or semester (see Yeager & Walton, 2011). We examined the outcomes of difference-education by following intervention participants throughout their time in college, obtaining their official grades from the registrar's office, and conducting a series of surveys and an in-person laboratory study (Stephens et al., 2014; Stephens, Townsend, Hamedani, Destin, & Manzo, 2015; Townsend et al., 2018).

Across both the in-person and online interventions, the primary goal was to improve first-generation college students' academic outcomes. First, we examined the impact of the intervention on students' grades. For the in-person intervention, an analysis of students' official first-year grades revealed that first-generation students in the difference-education condition earned higher GPAs during their first years in college than their counterparts in the control condition (Stephens et al., 2014), thereby reducing the social class achievement gap by 63%. In the scalable version in which students read older students' stories online, we examined students' GPAs during the first 2 years of college. This study showed that difference-education improved first-generation students' cumulative GPA throughout their first 2 years of college (Townsend et al., 2018).

We also examined whether students learned the contextual theory of difference that the intervention sought to convey. If the intervention communicated the theory effectively, we reasoned that participants should be able to articulate some of the insights they gained. They should also be able to use the theory to make sense of and respond to social group differences in a more positive way. We explored both of these possibilities.

First, we asked participants to write about what they learned from the student stories that they had listened to in the panel or read about online. Based on our coding of themes that emerged in participants' open-ended responses, we found evidence consistent with the idea that participants learned a contextual theory of difference. Specifically, both first- and continuing-generation participants in the difference-education condition compared to the control were far more likely to report that they had learned about how students' different backgrounds can matter in college (Stephens et al., 2014; Townsend et al., 2018). For example, illustrating her understanding of how someone's background shapes the college experience, one intervention participant said, "People from different backgrounds have different expectations of college." Demonstrating a similar understanding, another intervention participant said, "Everyone comes from such a different background and has different motives for doing well."

Second, we examined whether participants were able to use the theory to make sense of and respond to social group differences in a more positive way. Consistent with the idea that learning a contextual theory of difference conveys a relatively positive meaning of difference, we found that participants in the difference-education condition compared to the control condition reported greater appreciation of difference (e.g., valuing diversity as part of college; Stephens et al., 2014). Furthermore, at the end of the second year in college, we also examined participants' comfort with social group difference in the course of their interactions with other college students (see Stephens, Townsend, et al., 2015, for detailed methods). Specifically, we asked participants from the in-person intervention study to deliver a speech to a college student peer (i.e., a research assistant), focusing on the topic of how their backgrounds could matter in college, and to complete a series of stressful academic tasks. We then coded the content of the speech and also obtained participants' physiological responses. In the course of the speech, difference-education (vs. control) participants showed a greater willingness to talk about the impact of their different background contexts (e.g., family and friends from home), and also were more comfortable while doing so, as indicated by their physiological responses (Stephens, Townsend, et al., 2015). This finding suggests that difference-education encouraged participants to understand and respond to difference in a new, more positive way compared to participants in the control condition.

Mechanism

We theorized that the difference-education intervention improves students' academic performance (e.g., GPA) by helping them to understand that their social group differences are contextual in nature, rather than essential features of people or social groups. Specifically, as explained previously, we theorize that learning a contextual theory of difference should help students to experience not only a greater sense of fit as part of the college community but also a greater sense of empowerment to more fully take advantage of campus resources (see Figure 5.1).

Broadly consistent with our theorizing, we found that difference-education increased both fit and empowerment across the in-person and online interventions. In the in-person study, we found that both first- and continuing-generation students in the difference-education condition reported greater fit than those in the control condition. In the online study, however, we found that greater fit only emerged among first-generation students in the difference-education versus control condition.

As for experiences and behaviors related to empowerment, in the in-person study, we found an increased tendency among first-generation students to take advantage of the campus resources they needed to succeed at their university (e.g., seeking help from professors; Stephens et al., 2014). In the online intervention, we found evidence of a complementary but somewhat different process: first-generation students reported a greater sense of feeling empowered as learners, and also reported higher levels of efficacy, control, and preparation (Townsend et al., 2018). Taken together, and drawing from the literatures reviewed above, we theorize that the intervention increased students' sense of empowerment—the psychological experience of being empowered (e.g., efficacious), coupled with the willingness to take the actions (e.g., seeking resources) necessary to succeed.

When we examined the mechanism through which difference-education produces academic benefits (e.g., improved grades), we found that empowerment—but not fit—helps to explain these effects. In the in-person intervention, seeking campus resources served as one process by which difference-education improved first-generation students' grades. Similarly, in the online intervention study, the psychological experience of empowerment served as one process by which difference-education improved first-generation students' grades.

Effects over Time

As described above, we observed benefits for students' academic outcomes that persisted throughout the first 2 years in college in the online difference-education intervention (Townsend et al., 2018). We are currently examining whether the grades benefits persist throughout the duration of college in both interventions. We theorize that these academic benefits will persist throughout college because of the ways in which a contextual theory initiates a positive, self-reinforcing cycle of experiential and behavioral change (e.g., Miller, Dannals, & Zlatev, 2017; Yeager & Walton, 2011). For example, when a first-generation student confronts a background-specific challenge (e.g., difficulty choosing a major), a contextual theory can help her change how she makes sense of her different experiences in college. Instead of interpreting this challenge as an indication of a fixed deficiency, she can view it as a normal part of coming from her background (e.g., not having college-educated parents to advise her). This interpretation should help foster a sense of fit with the college community. Moreover, using a contextual theory to make sense of her experience should convey that her challenge is not fixed, and that there are steps that she can take to overcome this background-specific challenge and improve her outcomes in college. This interpretation should help foster a sense of empowerment. In turn, these psychological experiences of fit and empowerment should foster positive behavioral changes that have a number of downstream benefits. For example, this student may be more likely to seek help or develop relationships with teachers, which can amplify her psychological experiences of fit and empowerment and also improve her academic performance.

Heterogeneity

Designing an effective psychological intervention requires considering a number of contextual and individual factors. For any psychological intervention to have a positive impact, the people targeted must first have the opportunity (i.e., enough resources or skills) to achieve better outcomes. For example, college students must have enough food and reliable housing to be able to focus on academic pursuits, and they must also have the necessary academic skills so that increased academic effort (e.g., spending more time studying) will translate into better academic outcomes (e.g., Stephens, Markus, et al., 2012). In the case of difference-education, we theorize that providing a contextual theory improves students' academic performance by fostering a greater sense of fit and empowerment. According to this logic, this intervention should be most effective when psychological obstacles play a role in undermining students' performance. In other words, the intervention should be most helpful when people already have a foundation of material resources and academic skills, but are not performing up to their potential because of a lack of fit or empowerment.

Beyond giving students the opportunity to succeed, it is also important to consider the different academic contexts and groups with which the intervention can have the most impact. There is nothing about difference-education that limits it to the context of higher education, nor to the particular focus on first-generation college students. Though future research should explore potential boundary conditions, we expect that difference-education would be effective across different settings and with different social groups (e.g., women or racial or ethnic minorities). The general methodological strategy of difference-education should be the same: the intervention would seek to change people's experiences, behaviors, and outcomes by providing a contextual theory of difference. However, as is the case in any intervention, context matters, and it is critically important to take both the local context and the particular social group into account. In practice, researchers and practitioners must work to understand the existing views and challenges that a particular disadvantaged group faces in a setting, and tailor intervention methods and content to address those particular views, challenges, and identity-based concerns.

In the case of different social groups, an intervention designed to address race or gender (vs. social class) would need to take into account how people's existing views about race and gender may differ from those about social class. Because existing views about race or gender (vs. social class) in the United States are likely more well-defined or more essentialized, and thus more difficult to change (e.g., Destin, Rheinschmidt-Same, & Richeson, 2017), an intervention that seeks to provide a contextual theory about racial or gender differences would need to be tailored to counteract people's existing narratives about race or gender (e.g., as biological features of people). Moreover, since discussions about race and gender (vs. social class) may also be more fraught, these discussions may require additional steps to render them inclusive and empowering, rather than threatening. For example, ethnic studies courses rely on highly trained instructors to talk about these difficult topics, and they typically engage students in these conversations over an extended period of time (e.g., a semester).

Future research should also examine in what kinds of social contexts and with whom the intervention is most likely to be effective. Because we theorize that a difference-education intervention improves students' outcomes by providing a contextual theory of social group difference, we expect that the intervention could be effective in any setting where a contextual theory would represent a significant change in how people would otherwise make sense of their experiences. Specifically, we expect that a difference-education intervention would be far more effective in contexts where essentialist theories are the default understanding of social group difference than in contexts where people are already well versed in a contextual theory. For example, in a given college or university, it is important to consider what diversity efforts are already being implemented. If students have previously engaged in various discussions about the contextual nature of difference (e.g., through an orientation program, a seminar, or an ethnic studies course), they are less likely to benefit from a difference-education intervention.

COUSINS

Difference-education focuses on changing how students construe the meaning and nature of social group differences, which in turn helps improve their academic experience and performance. This focus on changing how people construe their experiences is similar to many other approaches in the wise intervention literature (Dittmann & Stephens, 2017; Walton & Wilson, 2018). Among these interventions, difference-education is perhaps most similar to belongingness interventions in terms of the specific methods used to deliver the message (e.g., Walton & Cohen, 2007). Belongingness interventions seek to change construal by having intervention participants learn from the stories of other successful students at their university. Similar to these methods, difference-education interventions also seek to change construal by exposing intervention participants to student success stories. Belongingness and difference-education diverge, however, in the content of the student stories and thus the nature of the particular lay theory that they provide. Belongingness interventions focus on changing students' lay theory of adversity by signaling that these experiences are *shared in common* with other students and will improve with time (e.g., Walton & Cohen, 2007). In contrast, difference-education focuses on changing students' lay theory of social group difference by helping them to understand it as contextual. Compared to belongingness, difference-education therefore more explicitly shows how students' different backgrounds shape their *different* experiences in college.

Beyond the methodological similarity to other lay theory interventions in social psychology, the key message in difference-education is most similar to Gurin's work on intergroup dialogue learning experiences (Gurin & Nagda, 2006; Gurin, Nagda, & Zúñiga, 2013).

Intergroup dialogues are weekly discussion sessions in which students from diverse backgrounds meet in groups and talk about their commonalities and differences. They are encouraged to critically reflect with other students about the source, nature, and impact of social group differences (Gurin & Nagda, 2006; Gurin et al., 2013). They also discuss topics such as power, inequality, and privilege. These discussions of social group difference make visible how important sociocultural contexts systematically shape people's life experiences and outcomes—that is, the contextual nature of difference (Gurin et al., 2013, p. 155). Indeed, Gurin and colleagues theorize that the dialogues "allow a larger, social truth to emerge between and among individuals in which everyone recognizes themselves as social selves rather than autonomous beings" (p. 78). Participating in these dialogues has been shown to produce psychological tendencies associated with intergroup skills, such as intergroup empathy, perspective taking, and intergroup collaboration (see Gurin et al., 2013). Like intergroup dialogues, difference-education also educates students about the contextual nature of social group differences. However, unlike intergroup dialogues, difference-education provides a more focused message that seeks to isolate the effects of a contextual theory without the more comprehensive learning experience.

INTERVENTION CONTENT AND IMPLEMENTATION: HOW DIFFERENCE-EDUCATION CONVEYS A CONTEXTUAL THEORY

To assess the benefits of difference-education, we randomly assigned half of the participants to attend a difference-education intervention and the other half to attend an active control intervention. In both conditions, incoming students either listened to or read the stories of senior students who discussed how they adjusted to and found success in college. To make this educational experience relevant to everyone, and to also avoid stigmatizing disadvantaged students, the incoming intervention participants and senior students sharing their stories included both first- and continuing-generation students.

In the difference-education intervention, the students' stories linked their social class backgrounds to different experiences they had in college. In particular, their stories revealed how students' different backgrounds can inform their experiences in both positive and negative ways, shaping (1) the challenges or obstacles they were likely to confront, as well as (2) the strengths and strategies they leveraged to be successful. Because part of learning a contextual theory is understanding that social group differences can be positive, it was critical to convey that students' diverse backgrounds could be a source of not only challenges but also strengths.

For instance, to highlight how different social class backgrounds can negatively shape the college experience, one first-generation student said, "Because my parents didn't go to college, they weren't always able to provide me the advice I needed, so it was sometimes hard to figure out which classes to take and what I wanted to do in the future." This story conveys a contextual understanding of difference by linking his previous social class context (i.e., not having college-educated parents) to an obstacle he faced in college (i.e., not knowing which classes to take). Similarly, after previously mentioning her parents' graduate-level degrees, one continuing-generation student said, "I went to a small private school, and it was great college prep. We got lots of one-on-one attention, so it was a big adjustment going into classes with 300 people." Like the first-generation student's story, the continuing-generation student's story links her social class background (i.e., having highly educated parents) to a college obstacle (i.e., having less attention and support in college than in high school).

The intervention also exposed students to examples of how their diverse social class backgrounds can shape the strategies and strengths they use to succeed in college. First- and continuing-generation stories discussed how they worked to address and overcome the particular challenges that they confronted. For instance, after the first-generation student in the example above described the challenge of not being able to get specific advice about college and careers from his parents, he said, "There are other people who can provide that advice, and I learned that I needed to rely on my advisor more than other students." In contrast, after the continuing-generation student described the challenge of being overwhelmed in large classes, she explained, "I felt less overwhelmed when I took the time to get to know other students in the class."

To further convey how one's background can positively shape the college experience, the student stories described how their backgrounds afforded them particular strengths. For instance, one first-generation student said, "I've been through a lot in my life. . . . It gave me perspective that made [university name] a lot easier to tackle. Midterms and papers seem hard, and they are, but at the same time they just seem like another drop in the bucket, and I love that perspective." This first-generation story links the student's social class background (i.e., overcoming adversity due to coming from a family without college education) to a strength (i.e., having a broad perspective), emphasizing the contextual nature of her positive experiences in college. Likewise, after describing her parents as having obtained college degrees, one continuing-generation student said, "My choice to attend [university name] really was supported by everyone in my family. There was no sort of imposition by my parents [saying], 'You need to go to the [school name]' or anything like that. It was like, 'Wherever you want to go we'll fully support you in any way that we really can,' and so they were very open with it."

As in the first-generation story, the continuing-generation story links the student's social class background to a background-specific strength. In this case, having parents who are both college educated and financially secure means that those parents are more likely to be open and supportive about a student's college choices.

Students in the control intervention, in contrast, were exposed to similar stories that also included obstacles, strategies, and strengths. However, these stories did not communicate a contextual theory of difference—that is, the stories did not include background-specific information about how students' social class backgrounds shaped their college experiences. Using the same intervention format, incoming students learned from successful senior students' personal stories about their experiences in college—in particular, the challenges they faced and the strengths and strategies they leveraged to be successful. One story mentioned an obstacle that a student faced in college (e.g., the coursework was difficult) and then suggested a strategy for success, "Go to class, and pay attention. If you don't understand something or have a hard time with the material, meet with your teaching assistant or professor during office hours." As in the difference-education condition, participants in the control condition learned about students' different experiences in college, including the challenges they faced (e.g., a student found coursework to be difficult), and the strengths and strategies that they learned to be successful (e.g., a student found it helpful to meet with a professor). Notably, across both conditions, participants learned the same types of strategies for success, such as seeking help from peers and professors. The key difference between the conditions was that students in the control condition did not learn how their own and others' backgrounds could inform their college experiences (i.e., their obstacles, strengths, or strategies for success).

NUANCES AND MISCONCEPTIONS

By providing a contextual theory of social group difference, difference-education has the potential to improve disadvantaged students' academic achievement throughout college. Yet, given the many challenges that come with addressing social group differences, what are some nuances that practitioners and researchers should consider when delivering a difference-education intervention? In the section that follows, we briefly describe some research-based strategies that can help ensure that difference-education is effective. Although these strategies have not been tested directly in the context of social psychological interventions, a wide range of research findings support their importance.

Avoid Stereotyping

It is critical to avoid stereotyping people based on their social group memberships when discussing social group difference. Intentionally or unintentionally stereotyping students will produce feelings of threat and exclusion, and ultimately undermine their engagement, motivation, and performance (e.g., Major, Spencer, Schmader, Wolfe, & Crocker, 1998; Steele, 2010). Instead, research suggests the importance of recognizing the intersection of multiple identities that is unique to each person, as well as the importance of intragroup variation and diversity (e.g., Cole, 2009; Crenshaw, 1991; Markus & Conner, 2014; Rosenthal, 2016).

In a difference-education intervention, multiple strategies can be used to avoid stereotyping students or communicating limiting characterizations of their social groups. First, it is important to demonstrate variation in students' experiences both across and within social groups; signal that these social differences are tendencies or patterns, rather than one-to-one relationships; and show that social differences can evolve and change with new experiences. We designed the difference-education stories to differ not only across students' social class backgrounds but also within their particular social class background. For example, first-generation students' stories included similar, but not identical, content about their experiences in college. Another strategy is to maintain students' sense of individuality by showing them how the diverse sociocultural contexts of their lives matter in ways that are unique to their particular backgrounds and identities. For example, students' social class, race, gender, and/or other backgrounds can shape their experiences in distinct ways. Although the stories in difference-education focused primarily on social class, they also acknowledged intersectional identities (e.g., being an African American, male, first-generation college student).

Acknowledge Both Negatives and Positives

It is important to acknowledge both negative and positive realities of social group difference. On the one hand, teaching positive content alone (e.g., pride in one's group or identity) would fail to prepare students for the background-specific challenges they are likely to face in college (e.g., Adams, Bell, & Griffin, 2007; Gurin et al., 2013). On the other hand, focusing on negative content alone (e.g., discussing stereotypes about one's group) would likely be highly demotivating for students (e.g., see Ben-Zeev et al., 2017). For example, research on "wise feedback" shows that negative feedback is motivating only when paired with "an invocation of high standards and by an assurance of the student's capacity to reach those standards" (Cohen, Steele, & Ross, 1999, p. 1302).

In a difference-education intervention, it is therefore important to provide students with opportunities to learn about how social group differences can impact their life experiences and outcomes in both positive and negative ways. In the difference-education interventions described above, we balanced students' discussion of the *negative* background-specific challenges they faced with a discussion of the *positive* strengths and strategies (e.g., seeking help from professors) that can provide a path to success. For example, after the stories described students' challenges (e.g., choosing a major), they then discussed ways to overcome them, empowering participants with strategies they can use to be successful.

Make Difference Relevant to Everyone

It is also important to make the experience of learning about social group differences relevant to everyone—both advantaged and disadvantaged students (see Moss-Racusin et al., 2016; Sleeter, 2011). For disadvantaged students, seeing that difference is also relevant to advantaged students can help normalize the experience of difference and reassure them that they are not being singled out (e.g., Hummel & Steele, 1996). At the same time, including advantaged students in discussions of social group difference can help ensure that they will experience the topic of social group difference as self-relevant and important for their own lives and experiences, while also reducing the likelihood that they will perceive difference as a threat (e.g., Dover, Major, & Kaiser, 2016; Plaut, Garnett, Buffardi, & Sanchez-Burks, 2011; Wilkins, Hirsch, Kaiser, & Inkles, 2016).

In a difference-education intervention, one strategy to help all people see difference as self-relevant is to include the contrasting stories of both advantaged and disadvantaged students. In the difference-education interventions described above, the stories of the senior students, as well as the intervention participants, included both first- and continuing-generation students. The contrast between these stories of students from different social class backgrounds can help all students learn how their backgrounds and prior life experiences shape who they are. Including individuals from diverse backgrounds also makes it possible to frame the intervention as a general (rather than group specific) program that can help everyone adjust to a new setting.

Give Voice to Underrepresented Narratives

Giving voice to underrepresented narratives—that is, student stories that are typically excluded from the mainstream—is crucial for fostering a sense of fit and inclusion, as well as the empowerment to find a path to success (e.g., Delgado & Stefancic, 2000; Duncan-Andrade & Morrell, 2008; Mitra, 2004). These narratives should provide diverse perspectives that can help to recognize and validate the life experiences of disadvantaged students.

In a difference-education intervention, it is important to give voice to these underrepresented narratives in two key ways. First, students' stories should enable participants, especially those who are disadvantaged by the setting, to recognize themselves in these stories. In the difference-education interventions described earlier, we presented students' stories in a way that illuminated their diverse experiences and paths to success. Second, it is critical to choose narratives that convey comfort and self-acceptance, rather than discomfort or embarrassment. In the difference-education interventions described above, students discussed difficult topics, but at the same time demonstrated an understanding and acceptance of their own experiences. For example, as one first-generation student confidently shared, "Once I came to [university name], I realized that I didn't have to be strong all of the time and that most people had no expectations of me besides trying my best and putting in effort in classes. After that, I realized that there was no shame in struggling or asking for help."

IMPLICATIONS FOR PRACTICE

We believe that various behind-the-scenes strategies are critical to ensuring that a difference-education intervention will be successful. Key strategies include (1) adapting intervention content to the context of the study, (2) conducting the intervention during a period of transition, and (3) ensuring that participation is voluntary. Although these strategies are relevant to all interventions, they can be applied specifically to difference-education interventions.

First, it is critical to adapt the stories to reflect students' actual experiences in a given college or university setting. To do so, we begin by talking to administrators and interviewing students to better understand the financial, academic, and psychological obstacles they face. We then adapt our intervention materials (i.e., the student stories) so that they reflect the actual experiences of students in that setting. For example, if a vast majority of students are Latinx, then it is critical to ensure that Latinx students' perspectives are well represented in the stories. Beyond representation, the stories should also highlight the common experiences, challenges, activities, and campus resources available there. For example, in a high-ranking university where first-generation college students are frequently a very small minority, these students are likely to confront more questions about belonging than they would if they were attending a lower-ranking university or community college where first-generation students are more highly represented. Student stories should be carefully adapted to include the most common and relevant issues.

Second, it is critical to conduct the intervention during a transitional moment. Whenever possible, we deliver the difference-education intervention at the beginning of the academic year, typically within the first month of the fall semester. We believe that the intervention content is likely to have the greatest impact in changing students' construal when they are still making sense of their experiences in this new setting. For example, when they are still learning about what it means to come from a different background or to have a different experience than other students. This meaning-making process could persist for different lengths of time depending on the context. After students have adjusted to a new setting for many months or years, their understandings of themselves and their experiences may be more difficult to change.

Third, whenever possible, it is critical to ensure that participation in difference-education intervention is voluntary, at least to some extent. As is the case in all interventions, it is important for participants to feel like they have a choice. When students choose to participate, particularly in middle-class U.S. contexts, they are more likely to be fully engaged and motivated to learn (see Patall, Cooper, & Robinson, 2008). Research suggests that forcing students to participate (e.g., in a mandatory program) is more likely to produce reactance and decrease engagement (see Dobbin & Kalev, 2013; Dobbin, Kim, & Kalev, 2011).

IMPLICATIONS FOR PSYCHOLOGICAL THEORY

At first glance, a review of research in mainstream social psychology might suggest that helping disadvantaged students succeed requires avoiding discussions of social group difference altogether. Stemming from the essentialist view of difference, the topic of social group differences is often represented as stigmatizing and a potential threat to avoid. Markus (2008) argues that viewing difference in this negative light permeates much of social psychology. For example, the literatures on intergroup relations, implicit bias, social categorization, and social identity threat reflect this perspective on difference. According to research in these areas, when social group differences become salient, they have the potential to produce negative consequences, such as stereotyping, bias, and discrimination (Brewer & Miller, 1984; Dovidio & Gaertner, 2000; see Gurin & Nagda,

2006; Gurin et al., 2013, for discussion). For example, in the face of negative, essential-izing stereotypes about one's group, disadvantaged students are likely to underperform on achievement tasks (e.g., Steele, 2010).

In contrast to this commonly held negative view of "difference as a threat," research in cultural psychology and the literatures on multicultural and social justice education suggest that acknowledging social group difference need not create the experience of threat. Instead, when viewed from a contextual perspective, social group differences have the potential to serve as an important source of meaning, identity, and motivation (see Markus, 2008; see also Brannon, Taylor, Higginbotham, & Henderson, 2017). Consis-tent with these perspectives, the difference-education intervention presented here sug-gests that consequences of social group difference hinge on how students construe the meanings of difference and how it relates to their experiences as students. Indeed, as we argued throughout this chapter, when difference is represented and understood as contextual—that is, a product of people's ongoing participation in particular sociocul-tural contexts over time—it has the potential to be experienced positively and to help students find a path to success that takes their differences into account.

FUTURE DIRECTIONS

This chapter explains what difference-education is, how to implement it effectively, and why it can be an effective approach to reducing educational disparities. Yet, a number of important questions remain unanswered. As is the case with other successful social psychological interventions, future research on difference-education interventions should further specify the necessary and sufficient components that drive the intervention's ben-efits. One important question is whether role models with similar backgrounds are neces-sary for students to gain a contextual understanding of difference. For example, would intervention participants need to listen to the stories of successful senior students, or could they simply read a research article about the contextual sources of social inequal-ity?

Future research should also investigate the specific ways in which interventions that provide a contextual theory can catalyze psychological and behavioral changes in a recur-sive cycle over time (see Miller et al., 2017; Yeager & Walton, 2011). Based on previous work on multicultural and social justice education, as well as the difference-education studies presented here, we suggest that fit and empowerment are two key processes that explain how a contextual theory changes behavior (e.g., seeking resources) and improves academic performance.

However, further work is needed to unpack precisely how these psychological changes work in both directions to sustain long-term behavioral changes (and vice versa). For example, in one direction, how might the psychological experiences of fit and empowerment work together to initiate key behavioral changes, such as seeking campus resources or developing a relationship with a mentor? And, in the other direction, how do these behavioral changes impact and sustain students' psychological changes over time as they progress through college and encounter new experiences? Research is also needed to better understand when the psychological benefits of fit and empowerment emerge only for the disadvantaged group targeted by the intervention versus when they occur for all students—both disadvantaged and advantaged.

Beyond fit and empowerment, research should consider other possible complementary processes through which learning a contextual theory of difference could catalyze psychological or behavioral change. Although we have shown that difference-education participants are more comfortable discussing their differences with a peer (Stephens, Townsend, et al., 2015), future work might also consider whether students who learn a contextual theory of difference become more culturally intelligent or competent—that is, able to more effectively navigate across different cultural contexts (e.g., Ang & Van Dyne, 2008; Earley & Ang, 2003; Leung, Ang, & Tan, 2014). Likewise, research could ask whether students develop metacognitive skills about how cultures work and how people's thoughts, feelings, and actions can be shaped by their cultures (e.g., Leung, Lee, & Chiu, 2013; Mor, Morris, & Joh, 2013).

In addition, future research should also consider how such a theory might be used to drive cultural change at an institutional level. As in other social psychological interventions (Yeager & Walton, 2011; Wilson, 2011), difference-education focuses on providing a new lay theory (i.e., a contextual theory of social group difference) to change students' psychological experiences (e.g., increase their fit and empowerment) and academic outcomes. We believe that these individual-level changes are not a panacea and may fail to support long-term change if they are not built into and reinforced by the larger college culture. To maintain and support these individual-level changes over time, we must also change institutional-level policies, practices, and resources (e.g., Markus & Conner, 2014; Markus & Hamedani, 2019; Stephens, Markus, & Fryberg, 2012; Walton & Wilson, 2018). For example, universities could communicate a contextual theory of difference in diversity courses; dorm programming or first-year programs or via shared cultural products, such as university websites or student guidebooks. At the same time, because people can shape their cultures (Markus & Hamedani, 2019), providing a contextual theory at an individual level also has the potential to change institutions. Increasing individual-level awareness and understanding of difference has the potential to create a more inclusive and accepting environment in which students are empowered to effect change.

In conclusion, even the most academically prepared first-generation students confront particular psychological obstacles that can fuel the social class achievement gap in higher education. This chapter provided an overview of how difference-education can help disadvantaged students overcome these psychological obstacles and find a path to success that takes their different experiences into account. The research reviewed here suggests that the difference-education approach has the potential to improve the academic outcomes of disadvantaged students by communicating a contextual theory of social group difference. When students learn that their differences are a product of contextual experience, rather than essential features of people or groups, they should experience greater fit and empowerment in college. In turn, their improved experiences in college can help them more fully engage in and take advantage of the resources available to them and ultimately improve their opportunity to succeed.

REFERENCES

Adams, M., Bell, L. A., & Griffin, P. (2007). *Teaching for diversity and social justice* (2nd ed.). New York: Routledge.

Ang, S., & Van Dyne, L. (2008). *Handbook of cultural intelligence: Theory, measurement, and applications.* New York: Routledge.

Astin, A. W., & Oseguera, L. (2004). The declining "equity" of American higher education. *Review of Higher Education, 27,* 321–341.

Bastian, B., & Haslam, N. (2006). Psychological essentialism and stereotype endorsement. *Journal of Experimental Social Psychology, 42,* 228–235.

Ben-Zeev, A., Paluy, Y., Milless, K., Goldstein, E., Wallace, L., Marquez-Magana, L., . . . Estrada, M. (2017). "Speaking truth" protects underrepresented minorities' intellectual performance and safety in STEM. *Education Sciences, 7,* 65.

Blackwell, L. S., Trzesniewski, K. H., & Dweck, C. S. (2007). Implicit theories of intelligence predict achievement across an adolescent transition: A longitudinal study and an intervention. *Child Development, 78,* 246–263.

Bowman, N. A. (2010). Disequilibrium and resolution: The nonlinear effects of diversity courses on wellbeing and orientations toward diversity. *Review of Higher Education, 33,* 543–568.

Brannon, T. N., Taylor, V. J., Higginbotham, G. D., & Henderson, K. (2017). Selves in contact: How integrating perspectives on sociocultural selves and intergroup contact can inform theory and application on reducing inequality. *Social and Personality Psychology Compass, 11*(7), e12326.

Brewer, M. B., & Miller, N. (1984). Beyond the contact hypothesis: Theoretical perspectives on desegregation. In N. Miller & M. Brewer (Eds.), *Groups in contact: The psychology of desegregation* (pp. 281–302). Orlando, FL: Academic Press.

Cabrera, N. L., Milem, J. F., Jaquette, O., & Marx, R. W. (2014). Missing the (student achievement) forest for all the (political) trees: Empiricism and the Mexican American studies controversy in Tucson. *American Educational Research Journal, 51,* 1084–1118.

Capó Crucet, J. (2015, August 22). Taking my parents to college. *New York Times.* Retrieved from *www.nytimes.com.*

Chao, M. M., Hong, Y. Y., & Chiu, C. Y. (2013). Essentializing race: Its implications on racial categorization. *Journal of Personality and Social Psychology, 104,* 619–634.

Chatman, J. (1991). Matching people and organizations: Selection and socialization in public accounting firms. *Administrative Science Quarterly, 36,* 459–484.

Cohen, G. L., Steele, C. M., & Ross, L. D. (1999). The mentor's dilemma: Providing critical feedback across the racial divide. *Personality and Social Psychology Bulletin, 25,* 1302–1318.

Cole, E. R. (2009). Intersectionality and research in psychology. *American Psychologist, 64,* 170–180.

Cole, E. R., Case, K. A., Rios, D., & Curtin, N. (2011). Understanding what students bring to the classroom: Moderators of the effects of diversity courses on student attitudes. *Cultural Diversity and Ethnic Minority Psychology, 17,* 397–405.

Covarrubias, R., & Fryberg, S. (2015). The impact of self-relevant representations on school belonging for disadvantaged Native American students. *Cultural Diversity and Ethnic Minority Psychology, 21,* 10–18.

Crenshaw, K. (1991). Mapping the margins: Intersectionality, identity politics, and violence against women of color. *Stanford Law Review, 43,* 1241–1299.

Dawis, R. V. (1992). Person–environment fit and job satisfaction. In C. Cranny, P. Smith, & E. Stone (Eds.), *Job satisfaction* (pp. 69–88). New York: Lexington Books.

Dee, T., & Penner, E. (2016). The causal effects of cultural relevance: Evidence from an ethnic studies curriculum (Working Paper No. 21865). Retrieved from *www.nber.org/papers/w21865.*

Delgado, R., & Stefancic, J. (2000). *Critical race theory: The cutting edge.* Philadelphia: Temple University Press.

Denson, N. (2009). Do curricular and cocurricular diversity activities influence racial bias?: A meta-analysis. *Review of Educational Research, 79,* 805–838.

Destin, M., Rheinschmidt-Same, M., & Richeson, J. R. (2017). Status-based identity: A conceptual framework integrating the social psychological study of socioeconomic status and identity. *Perspectives on Psychological Science, 12,* 270–289.

Dittmann, A. G., & Stephens, N. M. (2017). Interventions aimed at closing the social class achievement gap: Changing individuals, structures, and construals. *Current Opinion in Psychology, 18,* 111–116.

Dobbin, F., & Kalev, A. (2013). The origins and effects of corporate diversity programs. In Q. M. Roberson (Eds.), *Oxford handbook of diversity and work* (pp. 253–281). New York: Oxford University Press.

Dobbin, F., Kim, S., & Kalev, A. (2011). You can't always get what you need: Organizational determinants of diversity programs. *American Sociological Review, 76,* 386–411.

Dover, T. L., Major, B., & Kaiser, C. R. (2016). Members of high-status groups are threatened by pro-diversity organizational messages. *Journal of Experimental Social Psychology, 62,* 58–67.

Dovidio, J. F., & Gaertner, S. L. (2000). Aversive racism and selection decisions: 1989 and 1999. *Psychological Science, 11,* 315–319.

Duncan-Andrade, J. M. R., & Morrell, E. (2008). *The art of critical pedagogy: Possibilities for moving from theory to practice in urban schools* (Vol. 285). New York: Lang.

Earley, P. C., & Ang, S. (2003). *Cultural intelligence: Individual interactions across cultures.* Stanford, CA: Stanford University Press.

Edwards, J. R., Cable, D. M., Williamson, I. O., Lambert, L. S., & Shipp, A. J. (2006). The phenomenology of fit: Linking the person and environment to the subjective experience of person–environment fit. *Journal of Applied Psychology, 91,* 802–827.

Fryberg, S. A., & Markus, H. R. (2007). Cultural models of education in American Indian, Asian American and European American contexts. *Social Psychology of Education, 10,* 213–246.

Fulmer, C. A., Gelfand, M. J., Kruglanski, A. W., Kim-Prieto, C., Diener, E., Pierro, A., & Higgins, E. T. (2010). On "feeling right" in cultural contexts: How person–culture match affects self-esteem and subjective well-being. *Psychological Science, 21,* 1563–1569.

Gelman, S. A. (2004). Psychological essentialism in children. *Trends in Cognitive Sciences, 8,* 404–409.

Goudeau, S., & Croizet, J. C. (2017). Hidden advantages and disadvantages of social class: How classroom settings reproduce social inequality by staging unfair comparison. *Psychological Science, 28,* 162–170.

Gurin, P., & Nagda, B. (2006). Getting to the what, how, and why of diversity on campus. *Educational Research, 35,* 20–24.

Gurin, P., Nagda, B. A., & Zúñiga, X. (2013). *Dialogue across difference: Practice, theory, and research on intergroup dialogue.* New York: Russell Sage Foundation.

Haslam, N., Rothschild, L., & Ernst, D. (2000). Essentialist beliefs about social categories. *British Journal of Social Psychology, 39,* 113–127.

Horn, L., & Nuñez, A.-M. (2000). *Mapping the road to college: First-generation students' math track, planning strategies, and context of support* (NCES 2000153). Washington, DC: U.S. Government Printing Office.

Housel, T. H., & Harvey, V. L. (2010). *The invisibility factor: Administrators and faculty reach out to first-generation college students.* Boca Raton, FL: Universal.

Hummel, M., & Steele, C. (1996). The learning community: A program to address issues of academic achievement and retention. *Journal of Intergroup Relations, 23,* 28–32.

Keller, J. (2005). In genes we trust: The biological component of psychological essentialism and its relationship to mechanisms of motivated social cognition. *Journal of Personality and Social Psychology, 88,* 686–702.

Kohn, M. (1969). *Class and conformity.* Chicago: University Press.

Kung, F. Y., Chao, M. M., Yao, D. J., Adair, W. L., Fu, J. H., & Tasa, K. (2018). Bridging racial divides: Social constructionist (vs. essentialist) beliefs facilitate trust in intergroup contexts. *Journal of Experimental Social Psychology, 74,* 121–134.

Leung, A. K., Lee, S.-L., & Chiu, C. Y. (2013). Meta-knowledge of culture promotes cultural competence. *Journal of Cross-Cultural Psychology. 44,* 992–1006.

Leung, K., Ang, S., & Tan, M. L. (2014). Intercultural competence. *Annual Review of Organizational Psychology and Organizational Behavior, 1,* 489–519.

Major, B., Spencer, S., Schmader, T., Wolfe, C., & Crocker, J. (1998). Coping with negative stereotypes about intellectual performance: The role of psychological disengagement. *Personality and Social Psychology Bulletin, 24,* 34–50.

Markus, H. R. (2008). Pride, prejudice, and ambivalence: Toward a unified theory of race and ethnicity. *American Psychologist, 63,* 651–667.

Markus, H. R., & Conner, A. (2014). *Clash!: How to thrive in a multicultural world.* New York: Hudson Street Press.

Markus, H. R., & Hamedani, M. G. (2019). People are culturally shaped shapers: The psychological science of culture and culture change. In D. Cohen & S. Kitayama (Eds.), *The handbook of cultural psychology* (2nd ed., pp. 11–52). New York: Guilford Press.

Markus, H. R., & Moya, P. M. (2010). *Doing race: 21 essays for the 21st century.* New York: Norton.

Miller, D. T., Dannals, J. E., & Zlatev, J. J. (2017). Behavioral processes in long-lag intervention studies. *Perspectives on Psychological Science, 12,* 454–467.

Mitra, D. L. (2004). The significance of students: Can increasing "student voice" in schools lead to gains in youth development? *Teachers College Record, 106,* 651–688.

Molden, D. C., & Dweck, C. S. (2006). Finding "meaning" in psychology: A lay theories approach to self-regulation, social perception, and social development. *American Psychologist, 61,* 192–203.

Mor, S., Morris, M., & Joh, J. (2013). Identifying and training adaptive cross-cultural management skills: The crucial role of cultural metacognition. *Academy of Management Learning and Education, 12,* 453–475.

Moss-Racusin, C. A., van der Toorn, J., Dovidio, J. F., Brescoll, V. L., Graham, M. J., & Handelsman, J. (2016). A "scientific diversity" intervention to reduce gender bias in a sample of life scientists. *Life Sciences Education, 15,* 1–11.

Nelson Laird, T. F. (2005). College students' experiences with diversity and their effects on academic self-confidence, social agency, and disposition toward critical thinking. *Research in Higher Education, 46,* 365–388.

No, S., Hong, Y. Y., Liao, H. Y., Lee, K., Wood, D., & Chao, M. M. (2008). Lay theory of race affects and moderates Asian Americans' responses toward American culture. *Journal of Personality and Social Psychology, 95,* 991–1004.

Omi, M., & Winant, H. (2015). *Racial formation in the United States* (3rd ed.). New York: Routledge.

Ostrove, J. M., & Long, S. M. (2007). Social class and belonging: Implications for college adjustment. *Review of Higher Education, 30,* 363–389.

Patall, E. A., Cooper, H., & Robinson, J. C. (2008). The effects of choice on intrinsic motivation and related outcomes: A meta-analysis of research findings. *Psychological Bulletin, 134,* 270–300.

Plaut, V. C., Garnett, F. G., Buffardi, L. E., & Sanchez-Burks, J. (2011). "What about me?": Perceptions of exclusion and Whites' reactions to multiculturalism. *Journal of Personality and Social Psychology, 101,* 337–353.

Prentice, D. A., & Miller, D. T. (2007). Psychological essentialism of human categories. *Current Directions in Psychological Science, 16,* 202–206.

Reay, D., Crozier, G., & Clayton, J. (2009). "Strangers in paradise?": Working-class students in elite universities. *Sociology, 43,* 1103–1121.

Riggs, L. (2014, January 14). What it's like to be the first person in your family to go to college. *The Atlantic*. Retrieved from *www.theatlantic.com*.

Rosenthal, L. (2016). Incorporating intersectionality into psychology: An opportunity to promote social justice and equity. *American Psychologist, 71*, 474–485.

Sirin, S. R. (2005). Socioeconomic status and academic achievement: A meta-analytic review of research. *Review of Educational Research, 75*, 417–453.

Sleeter, C. E. (2011). The academic and social value of ethnic studies: A research review. Retrieved from *www.files.eric.ed.gov/fulltext/ED521869.pdf*.

Steele, C. M. (2010). *Whistling Vivaldi and other clues to how stereotypes affect us*. New York: Norton.

Stephens, N. M., Brannon, T. N., Markus, H. R., & Nelson, J. E. (2015). Feeling at home in college: Fortifying school-relevant selves to reduce social class disparities in higher education. *Social Issues and Policy Review, 9*, 1–24.

Stephens, N. M., Fryberg, S. A., Markus, H. R., Johnson, C. S., & Covarrubias, R. (2012). Unseen disadvantage: How American universities' focus on independence undermines the academic performance of first-generation college students. *Journal of Personality and Social Psychology, 102*(6), 1178–1197.

Stephens, N. M., Hamedani, M. G., & Destin, M. (2014). Closing the social-class achievement gap: A difference-education intervention improves first-generation students' academic performance and all students' college transition. *Psychological Science, 25*, 943–953.

Stephens, N. M., Markus, H. R., & Fryberg, S. A. (2012). Social class disparities in health and education: Reducing inequality by applying a sociocultural self model of behavior. *Psychological Review, 119*, 723–744.

Stephens, N. M., Townsend, S. S. M., Hamedani, M. G., Destin, M., & Manzo, V. (2015). A difference-education intervention equips first-generation college students to thrive in the face of stressful college situations. *Psychological Science, 26*, 1556–1566.

Terenzini, P. T., Springer, L., Yaeger, P., Pascarella, E. T., & Nora, A. (1996). First-generation college students: Characteristics, experiences, and cognitive development. *Research in Higher Education, 37*, 1–22.

Townsend, S. S. M., Stephens, N. M., Smallets, S., & Hamedani, M. G. (2018). Empowerment through difference: An online difference-education intervention closes the social class achievement gap. *Personality and Social Psychology Bulletin, 45*(7), 1068–1083.

Walton, G. M., & Cohen, G. L. (2007). A question of belonging: Race, social fit, and achievement. *Journal of Personality and Social Psychology, 92*, 82–96.

Walton, G. M., & Wilson, T. D. (2018). Wise interventions: Psychological remedies for social and personal problems. *Psychological Review, 125*, 617.

Wilkins, C. L., Hirsch, A. A., Kaiser, C. R., & Inkles, M. P. (2016). The threat of racial progress and the self-protective nature of perceiving anti-White bias. *Group Processes and Intergroup Relations, 20*, 801–812.

Williams, M. J., & Eberhardt, J. L. (2008). Biological conceptions of race and the motivation to cross racial boundaries. *Journal of Personality and Social Psychology, 94*, 1033–1047.

Wilson, T. D. (2011). *Redirect: The surprising new science of psychological change*. New York: Little, Brown and Company.

Yeager, D. S., & Walton, G. M. (2011). Social-psychological interventions in education: They're not magic. *Review of Educational Research, 81*, 267–301.

CHAPTER 6

The Pathways Intervention as a Model to Design Broader Systems of Equitable Student Support

Mesmin Destin and Ivan A. Hernandez

The pathways intervention is built upon the images that young people have of the type of people they might become in the future. Studies related to the pathways intervention demonstrate the importance of guiding students to perceive the path to their desired futures as open or within reach and to develop strategies that will help them progress toward desired future identities. For students from lower-socioeconomic status (SES) backgrounds and racial/ethnic-minority groups, the pathways intervention is particularly well suited to increase the likelihood that they genuinely envision higher education as a part of their future, which helps to support academic motivation through challenges. The pathways intervention and related studies have led students to imagine future identities that are connected to education and have increased students' expected academic performance and planned effort on school tasks. In its full implementation, the intervention has shown significant positive effects on students' academic outcomes and well-being that persisted through a 2-year follow-up period. In this chapter, we describe the theory behind the pathways intervention and related experiments, in addition to empirical evidence for its effects on a variety of outcomes and implications for psychological theory, research, and policy.

BACKGROUND

Students in the United States have very high aspirations for educational and lifetime success, in general. When asked how far they plan to go in school, the vast majority of students express that they want to complete a college degree or beyond, regardless of their socioeconomic background (Mickelson, 1990; Oyserman & Lewis, 2017; Schneider & Stevenson, 1999). In reality, though, students from families with fewer financial resources are less likely to reach college than students from wealthier families (Ma, Pender, & Welch, 2016). This is in large part due to the many ways that having more family financial assets affords students with better-resourced schools, more enriching academic experiences, and increased access to future opportunities (Jackson, Johnson, & Persico, 2016; Lafortune, Rothstein, & Schanzenbach, 2018; Lovenheim, 2011). For example, a student who attends a high school in a wealthy neighborhood is more likely to have regular access to guidance counselors and college preparatory curriculum than a student who attends a school in a segregated, lower-income community (see Corwin, Venegas, Oliverez, & Colyar, 2004; Gamoran & Hannigan, 2000; Kanno & Kangas, 2014). One reason why these resources matter for academic outcomes is that they signal to students what is actually likely for their futures and either reinforce or weaken students' visions of their lives to come. These images of the future, which are sometimes called possible selves or future identities, help to guide students' everyday behaviors and their motivation to engage and persist in school tasks that can lead to reaching high academic goals. The pathways intervention involves a series of activities that are designed to bolster students' developing future identities and their understanding of the path to reach their goals. As a result, pathways helps to support students' school motivation even in contexts that do not otherwise consistently reinforce the images that they have for their futures.

Before offering greater depth regarding the theory, evidence, and application related to the pathways intervention, there are two important caveats or considerations to keep in mind. First, the core issue that pathways aims to address originates at a level that is situated beyond the individual student or psychological processes. The access to resources that students encounter in their schools and neighborhoods provides the foundation for how they imagine their futures and pursue school goals. Ideally, acknowledging and addressing the root manifestations of economic inequality that young people experience should be part of any large-scale effort to improve academic outcomes through future identities. At the very least, though, efforts at psychological intervention should leverage the messages that students receive from their surrounding contexts (e.g., peers, parents, teachers, schools, neighborhoods) in order to amplify the potential effects of individual, student-targeted intervention.

Second, the idea of psychological intervention, itself, can carry certain assumptions that do not always align with the broader goal of increasing educational equity. Psychological intervention can inherently situate the researcher—who is often from a dominant racial/ethnic, socioeconomic, and/or cultural background—as the savior, and the student as the target of the problem without expertise and agency. As described, the pertinent target of intervention rests at a higher level than just the individual student. However, psychological studies can provide strong evidence for how environments and experiences shape people's outlooks, and this evidence can be used to inform the development of systemic interventions that go beyond the individual. Despite these considerations, the term *intervention* is used to describe pathways research for simplicity and consistency with other chapters in the book.

PSYCHOLOGICAL PROCESSES

There are three primary psychological processes theorized to underlie the pathways intervention. The foundation for the pathways intervention and the establishment of these processes were derived from early work detailing the core postulates of identity-based motivation theory, which builds from ideas including the working self-concept, situated cognition, and possible selves (see Markus & Nurius, 1986; Markus & Wurf, 1987; Miller, Brickman, & Bolen, 1975; Smith & Semin, 2007).

Dynamic Construction

Although people often tend to think about their identities as stable over time when describing themselves, there are many important aspects of how individuals view and express themselves that are shaped heavily by the environment in real time. People often automatically bring to mind parts of themselves that are relevant to interacting with the situation at hand (Markus & Wurf, 1987), and the basic ways that our minds process information vary depending on aspects of the environment (Smith & Semin, 2004, 2007). These identities that are constructed and cued in context guide how it feels to engage in particular behaviors, how situations are interpreted, and what behavior seems relevant. The pathways intervention provides students with opportunities to elaborate upon their current and possible future identities that are connected to education in a way that increases their salience across environments and over time (Oyserman, 2015).

Action Readiness

Building upon dynamic construction, when a particular identity is brought to mind, it accompanies a greater likelihood that a person engages in behaviors associated with that identity (Oyserman & Destin, 2010). Specifically, people who articulate images of themselves reaching, or even failing to reach, a desired future (i.e., future identities) are more effective in pursuing their educational and health goals than people who do not bring those possible future identities to mind (Hoyle & Sherrill, 2006; Ruvolo & Markus, 1992). If a student's identity that is connected to education is not cued in context, then engaging in behavior that is relevant to that identity (e.g., schoolwork, studying) does not feel fluent in the moment. The pathways intervention enhances this connection between student identities and specific school behaviors that are relevant to reaching academic goals.

Interpretation of Difficulty

Finally, identities shape how people interpret and respond to experiences of difficulty when pursuing identity-relevant goals (Fisher & Oyserman, 2017; Oyserman, Elmore, Novin, Fisher, & Smith, 2018; Smith & Oyserman, 2015). More specifically, when a task feels connected to a salient and valued identity, people are likely to interpret difficulty during that task as a sign that they are working on something that has meaning and importance. When important identities feel connected to academic achievement, then everyday academic challenges are interpreted as meaning that school tasks are important rather than impossible (Fisher & Oyserman, 2017; Smith & Oyserman, 2015). On the other hand, when a task feels disconnected from any valued identity, encountering difficulty is more likely to signal to a person that the task is impossible for them and that they should relent. For example, lower-SES students who encounter evidence that there are robust opportunities for socioeconomic mobility to reach their desired futures are less likely to interpret academic difficulty as a sign that a school task is impossible (i.e., are more inclined to persist when faced with academic difficulty) than those who encounter evidence that there is not much opportunity to ascend the socioeconomic ladder (Browman, Destin, Carswell, & Svoboda, 2017).

How the Pathways Intervention Fosters Motivation

From a psychological perspective, resources and a supportive environment matter because contexts shape the ways that people view themselves and their possible futures, the corresponding actions that they take, and the ways that they respond to difficulty and setbacks (Oyserman & Destin, 2010). For example, a seventh-grade student who grows up in a neighborhood surrounded by people with many different career pathways and educational backgrounds is likely to vividly imagine pursuing a desirable future career and education, which helps provide meaning to everyday school tasks. For a context to fully support these future identities, it must consistently reinforce self-relevant goals that are connected to school and achievement (Oyserman, Bybee, & Terry, 2006).

The pathways intervention aims to increase the likelihood that people's aspirations translate into the effective pursuit of their future identities by targeting the connections among the contexts, identities, and behaviors described above. Students are more likely to focus sustained effort on educational tasks (e.g., class work, studying) when contexts reinforce their aspirational future identities, including a focus on both the objective and the path to get there. When identity-based motivational processes are activated to support positive student outcomes, the following experiences occur: (1) school-related future goals that are relevant to one's identity come to mind in the academic context (e.g., "I want to graduate from college"); (2) these goals feel within reach and congruent with other important aspects of identity in ways that inspire action (e.g., "Other people from lower-SES backgrounds effectively work toward and succeed in college"); and (3) academic difficulties that are experienced along the way are interpreted as meaning that an education-dependent future is important (e.g., "Studying for this test is difficult, so it must be important for me to do well at it"), not impossible.

The pathways intervention provides students with the opportunity to elaborate upon the images of the types of adults they might like to become in the future (e.g., financially secure adult). The pathways intervention also guides students toward perceiving that the path to their desired futures is open and that there are resources and strategies that will help them reach their desired (and avoid undesired) future identities (Destin, 2017; Destin & Oyserman, 2009). Students who have more elaborate and strategic behavioral plans to reach their goals are more likely to effectively pursue their future identities than those with less concrete strategies (Oyserman, Johnson, & James, 2011). Further, generally emphasizing the idea of education as a journey helps to support school-focused motivation (Landau, Oyserman, Keefer, & Smith, 2014). As described in more detail below, the pathways intervention also shifts students' tendencies toward interpreting obstacles and difficulties in reaching their desired futures as normal and important, while simultaneously strengthening connections between their social identities and images of their possible future identities.

EMPIRICAL EVIDENCE

Outcomes

The pathways intervention and related randomized controlled field experiments have shown positive effects on the academic motivation of students, with most studies focusing on students from lower-SES backgrounds and racial/ethnic-minority groups. The seminal implementation of the pathways intervention was delivered to 264 middle school students from predominantly low-income backgrounds and racial/ethnic-minority groups (Oyserman et al., 2006). Students in this sample were randomly assigned to either a control condition or an intervention condition where they participated in 11 different sessions that were each completed during a single class period. Students in the intervention showed a significantly better trajectory in their academic motivation, standardized test scores, and grades compared with students in the control group. Further, the positive effects of the intervention extended to outcomes including reductions in student absences, misbehavior in school, and depression (Oyserman et al., 2006). These positive effects persisted through a 2-year follow-up period. The pathways intervention effects persist because they aim to shift the way that people view themselves in relation to academic contexts and opportunities, congruent with a wise intervention approach (Walton & Wilson, 2018).

In addition to the main intervention study, smaller-scale field experiments have tested specific aspects of the pathways approach. One series of studies, for example, demonstrated the positive effects of need-based college financial aid information designed to make the pathway to future opportunities feel open rather than closed. Ninety-six seventh-grade students in urban middle schools from predominantly low-income, Black, and Hispanic/Latinx backgrounds were randomly assigned to receive either the experimental materials about financial aid or materials about the costs of college that might act as a barrier or close the path to future goals. The experimental or control materials were delivered during a single class session. The experimental treatment increased students' expected grades and planned effort on homework, studying, and reading (Destin & Oyserman, 2009).

Another randomized controlled field experiment related to the pathways intervention demonstrated the effects of thinking about desired future economic success as connected to education. A sample of 295 seventh-grade students (59% African American or Latinx; 61% of middle school students qualified for free or reduced lunch) were randomly assigned to an experimental treatment condition where they received evidence of the connection between higher education and higher income and a control condition that drew attention to high-earning careers that were not connected to education (e.g., athletes, entertainers, musicians). The experimental or control materials were delivered during a single class session. Students in the experimental treatment condition planned to expend more effort on homework and studying and were more likely to turn in an extra-credit assignment the day after the experiment than students in the control condition (Destin & Oyserman, 2010).

An additional field experiment related to the pathways intervention included a more diverse sample of 156 seventh-grade students from varied socioeconomic backgrounds and racial/ethnic groups. Once again, the materials about need-based financial aid that were designed to make pathways to opportunities feel open had positive effects, this time in comparison to a control group that did not receive any such materials. The materials were delivered during a single class session, and students from lower-SES families who were randomly assigned to the experimental treatment condition showed an increase in their plans to engage in schoolwork compared with those in the control group (Destin, 2017). These studies offer evidence that the pathways intervention has positive effects on students, and that they support academic motivation through the shared mechanism of identity.

Mechanisms

The pathways intervention improves student outcomes by providing students with the opportunity and support to elaborate upon their motivating identities, with a particular emphasis on their developing future identities. In the main intervention study, future identities are measured as possible selves, or written descriptions of who students hope to become or avoid becoming in the future. Participating in pathways led students to articulate future identities that were connected to education and more detailed, plausible, and linked to everyday strategies than control group students, which all activate the processes of identity-based motivation and mediate positive effects on academic achievement. Similarly, the field experiments related to the pathways intervention also activated students' future identities in connection to education in order to support academic motivation. Some experiments directly activated the mechanism by leading students to think about desired successful futures as connected to education (Destin & Oyserman, 2010). Other studies indirectly activated the same mechanism through an emphasis on resources that open the pathway to desired future identities connected to education (Destin & Oyserman, 2009). In a direct test of this theoretical pathway among a sample of lower-SES students, those who were randomly assigned to an experimental condition focused on resources and an open path were more likely to envision future identities that were connected to education than similar students who were randomly assigned to a comparison condition (Destin, 2017). The increased salience of a future identity connected to education mediated positive effects of the experimental treatment on student motivation. Students planned to devote more effort toward their long-term academic goals if they envisioned a salient future identity that included a college education. The experimental manipulation shifted students' perceptions of potential economic barriers and encouraged students to envision a desired future that was likely to include education. In all of these studies, when students from lower-SES backgrounds engage with pathways materials during early adolescence, they are more likely to imagine higher education as a part of their future, which leads to increased academic motivation (see Figure 6.1).

Effects over Time

The majority of the field experiments related to the pathways intervention were not designed to examine long-term effects. In most of the studies, students completed outcome measures immediately after experimental manipulations materials were made salient. However, the most robust evidence of the longitudinal impact of the pathways intervention comes from the seminal implementation among students from predominantly low-income backgrounds and racial/ethnic-minority groups (Oyserman et al., 2006). These students participated in multiple sessions that reinforced key processes (see below for more details). Students in the intervention displayed greater academic motivation,

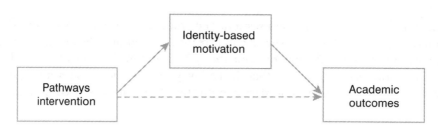

FIGURE 6.1. Identity-based motivation as the primary mechanism of the pathways intervention.

standardized test scores, grades, and also displayed reductions in absences, misbehavior in school, and depression (Oyserman et al., 2006) compared with students in the control group. These positive effects were mediated by shifts in identity and persisted through a 2-year follow-up period.

Heterogeneity

The processes related to identity-based motivation can apply across demographic groups, but the pathways intervention and related experiments tend to be most relevant and effective for students from lower-SES backgrounds and racial/ethnic-minority groups. They are designed to counteract contextual cues that students from these nondominant groups encounter (e.g., financial barriers to higher education) that can weaken identities and motivation. More generally, the pathways intervention matters most for students who perceive barriers to their desired futures or who see a certain social identity as incompatible with that desired future (see Debrosse, Destin, Rossignac-Milon, Taylor, & Rogers, 2018; Debrosse, Rossignac-Milon, Taylor, & Destin, 2018).

RELATED APPROACHES ("COUSINS")

The pathways intervention is related to a number of other social psychological interventions. *Self-affirmation interventions,* for example, also involve reflections on the self. Further, just as pathways allows students to individually bring to mind and articulate a genuinely valued identity, a key aspect of affirmation studies is that content is self-generated and tailored to tap into each student's particular valued identity (Cohen & Sherman, 2014). However, these two interventions are quite different. Self-affirmation interventions aim to improve student outcomes by shifting their perspectives in ways that alleviate potential psychological threats to achievement (e.g., stereotype threat; Steele, 1997; Steele & Aronson, 1995). In the typical paradigm, students select, reflect upon, and write about personally important values (see Sherman, Lokhande, Müller, & Cohen, Chapter 3, this volume; Steele, 1988), which bolsters students' sense of worth, helping to alleviate potential psychological threats to achievement. The pathways intervention, on the other hand, is tailored to activate a more broadly applicable motivational process by linking the individual's present self with future identities. When identity-based motivational processes connect the present self with future identities, individuals engage in important behaviors that facilitate the pursuit or avoidance of that future identity, whereas affirmation interventions can sometimes disengage people from their goal pursuit (e.g., Vohs, Park, & Schmeichel, 2013).

Utility-value interventions may activate similar motivational processes to those activated by the pathways intervention and identity-based motivation. Both perspectives emphasize the ways that goal-related tasks, like schoolwork, are related to students' personal lives. Utility-value experiments ask students to consider how course material or knowledge is useful and relevant for goals or aspects of their life outside of school (Harackiewicz, Canning, Tibbetts, Priniski, & Hyde, 2016). Although related, the pathways intervention is more likely to target students' construal of the social context (e.g., perceived financial barriers to college) that influences the development of their identities, whereas utility-value experiments focus more directly on the construal of the students' schoolwork itself. After making more connections between the course material and their lives, students display greater course achievement expectations, continuing interest in the course, and value the course material more (Hulleman, Kosovich, Barron, & Daniel, 2017). One distinction between utility-value and pathways interventions is that the pathways intervention is more likely to start by invoking students' broad images of their lives in the future and then narrow to specific goal-related content. Utility-value approaches are more likely to first invoke students' specific goals or work on specific tasks that might then broaden to be considered as part of a more complete image of their life in the future. In other words, pathways often starts by asking, "Who do I want to become?," while utility value often asks, "How is this course content relevant to me?"

Growth-mindset-of-intelligence interventions, like the pathways intervention and a number of other notable interventions (e.g., *social-belonging interventions*; see Walton & Brady, Chapter 2, this volume), also target outcomes related to academic motivation and achievement by providing students with new ways to make sense of and respond to their academic experiences. Growth-mindset-of-intelligence interventions might address the question "Am I smart enough to do the work in college?" They often impart in students the belief that they can learn, change, and develop particular skills or traits, such as intelligence. These beliefs alter the way students interpret and respond to academic difficulties, usually leading them to be more resilient and persistent in the face of challenges (e.g., Blackwell, Trzesniewski, & Dweck, 2007; Yeager & Dweck, 2012). Growth-mindset interventions directly convey that struggle is an opportunity for growth and learning (see Paunesku et al., 2015). Similarly, social-belonging interventions help students perceive challenges in their educational experiences as normal and evolving over time. However, social-belonging interventions target the question "Can I come to belong in college?"

The pathways intervention, on the other hand, conveys the meta-message that the schoolwork they are currently engaging in is relevant to both who they are currently and who they can become in the future, indirectly leading school challenges to be seen as important to reaching their desired identity. Other related work directly disrupts students' misperception that experienced difficulties in an academic domain imply that they will never be able to succeed in that domain or that they should pursue a different future goal or identity (Lin-Siegler, Ahn, Chen, Fang, & Luna-Lucero, 2016). Much of this work has been influenced by earlier *attributional-retraining interventions* (e.g., Wilson & Linville, 1982, 1985). The pathways intervention, instead, directly increases the likelihood that students imagine education as a part of their future and guide students to perceive the path toward their desired futures as open, expanding students' perceptions of what is possible for them. When schoolwork feels connected to that salient and valued identity, students interpret difficulty in school as something meaningful and important.

The pathways intervention is concerned with students' successful pursuit of attaining a desired future outcome. As such, pathways is also related to a family of other *goal-setting interventions*. For example, *proximal goal interventions* guide students who are disinterested and displaying significant challenges in math to set proximal goals (vs. distal goals) to accomplish, which leads them to display greater math self-efficacy and actual mastery of mathematical operations (Bandura & Schunk, 1981). Additionally, *implementation-intention interventions* guide students to set "if–then" plans that target the execution of the preset goal intentions, which significantly increase the likelihood that individuals successfully attain their goals (see Gollwitzer & Sheeran, 2006, for meta-analyses and review). Similar to the pathways intervention, these interventions link present behaviors to goal pursuit. However, pathways implements a combination of long-term goals, but with an emphasis on an individual's long-term identity. In the pathways intervention, personal and unique goal setting is also very important. However, goal proximity is a crucial distinction between these two approaches.

Whereas proximal goal interventions are designed to lead students to set short-term small goals that build on one another, the pathways intervention starts by focusing on distal futures (e.g., an adolescent thinking about an aspired adult career) and linking them to more immediate action. Additionally, the pathways intervention shapes students' perceptions about what is possible for them and people like them in the future, whereas proximal goal interventions might more directly target current self-efficacy in a specific domain (e.g., math). Further, whereas implementation intentions are intended to facilitate goal pursuit by setting strategies to overcome obstacles, for example, pathways targets the congruency between the current action and one's future identity (e.g., "*If* I am to be a college graduate, *then* completing this extra-credit assignment is congruent with that identity, and therefore, is meaningful in the moment"). There are a number of other related social-psychological interventions that space here does not allow for comparison (see also Bryan, Walton, Rogers, & Dweck, 2011; Miller et al., 1975; Yeager et al., 2014).

INTERVENTION CONTENT AND IMPLEMENTATION

The pathways intervention may be implemented over several weeks and consists of a series of workshops. The seminal pathways intervention was delivered during 11 different sessions that are each completed during a single class period. Each session had a specific purpose, built on the previous session, and reinforced the primary aims over a 7-week period (see Oyserman, 2015). The goals were to guide students to reflect on and identify their desired adult identities and to describe strategies to attain them. The intervention established a connection between students' future identities and strategies to attain them, shifted the way they interpreted difficulty to focus on the importance of their setbacks in attaining their future identities, and created a link between their social identities and possible futures.

The first two sessions include interactive activities leading students to identify their adult possible selves and to increase their salience and congruence with their social identities. The third session focuses on identifying the role models and people who might be negative forces in their lives. During the fourth session, students draw timelines connecting their current life to their future, including potential obstacles and different opportunities that might arise along the way. The fifth, sixth, and seventh sessions incorporate skill building as students generate strategies that would help them reach their desired futures and avoid their undesired futures. This includes activities and opportunities for students to internalize the idea that difficulty is a normative experience. The final sessions allowed students to reflect on all that they learned, apply that knowledge in small groups, and to discuss each session with a focus on reinforcing the main ideas. The main ideas, or meaning-making meta-messages, include "We all care about school," "We all want a good future," "Everyone faces obstacles and difficulties," and "Failures and setbacks are normal." Throughout the intervention, facilitators establish a structure where students can learn and consistently communicate the meta-messages and underlying themes that permeate every activity that the students complete. The intervention is also designed to convey messages in a manner that will be understood and that is developmentally appropriate. An implementation manual for the pathways intervention can be found in Oyserman (2015).

In addition to the full pathways intervention implementation, several related field experiments have tested specific aspects of the broader intervention during a single middle school class session. These experiments have taken place in homerooms and subject classrooms during the academic term, as well as during summer programs. They differ in content and length but target the same core processes as the main pathways intervention. In the classroom, the teacher introduces the members of the research team as visitors from a local university providing career-related information to young students, and the materials are distributed on paper, including relevant text and figures. These materials include real information, such as current figures of adult earnings without using any form of deception. Students are then asked to complete a brief questionnaire that is ostensibly a separate general survey, which contains the outcome measures and is completed in class.

In one example of a field experiment related to the pathways intervention, students randomly assigned to the treatment condition are introduced to the concept of need-based financial aid and economic resources available to support the pursuit of higher education (see Destin, 2017). The information included statements from sources like the College Board indicating that "there is more financial aid available than ever before—over $154 billion. . . . The financial aid system is based on the goal that anyone should be able to attend college, regardless of financial circumstances. Here is how the system works: Students and their families are expected to contribute to the cost of college to the extent that they are able. If a family is unable to contribute the entire cost, financial aid is available to bridge the gap." In order to increase the likelihood that resources feel within reach, students also learn that more information is available on the Free Application for Federal Student Aid website (*www.fafsa.gov*). Students randomly assigned to a comparison condition, on the other hand, read information about the actual (at the time of the study) costs of attending local universities. The statements include "At 4-year public institutions, tuition costs average $7,605 per year" and "At 4-year private institutions, tuition costs average $27,293 per year." Students then receive examples of what it would cost to attend specific universities in the area. Some versions of the experiment also include a no-information control condition. Students in all conditions complete short writing activities that ask them questions to verify their comprehension of the material before completing subsequent measures of identity and motivation in the moment.

NUANCES AND MISCONCEPTIONS

The pathways intervention generates significant excitement among educators because it resonates with intuitive ideas about how to motivate students. This helps in developing school partnerships, building school buy-in, and in potentially leading school partners to implement lasting changes and programs. However, the intuitive nature of the pathways intervention can also lead researchers and practitioners to overlook the important psychological intricacies and nuance necessary to consistently activate these motivational processes with fidelity. Two key aspects of the pathways intervention that can be easily neglected during implementation are that (1) the students must individually bring to mind and articulate a genuinely valued identity, and (2) the identity and related processes must receive some form of social recognition, reinforcement, or validation.

In studies that ask students to think about their past experiences in certain ways or to imagine particular future possibilities, the most effective prompts provide them with the space and time to draw from their own meaningful experiences and ideas. After they think about a particular challenge that they faced or career that they hope to reach, then more guidance is provided to help them elaborate on that unique core image in a manner that is informed by psychological science. It can be tempting, however, to implement these interventions by telling students what types of past experiences to think about or what types of futures to imagine and pushing the process along. This rushed and depersonalized implementation is far less likely to truly engage individual students or shift the ways that they think about themselves (see Canning & Harackiewicz, 2015).

Once an identity is genuinely brought to mind and then cultivated in a way that supports motivation, it must be strategically reinforced by social interactions or the social context as a whole in order to generate lasting positive effects. As articulated by identity-based motivation theory, identities are constantly reconstructed based on the environment. So, one meaningful shift in how students think about themselves may have an important effect on motivation during key moments, but it might also dissipate if the school, neighborhood, or social environment do not include cues and affordances that reactivate and reinforce that identity. One way to foster social reinforcement is to include small-group activities into the intervention. When students share their ideas with one another, it conveys the message and social norm that they have common experiences with their peers and that their perspectives are valued by others around them. In addition to including peers, a deeper inclusion of parents and teachers into facilitation and implementation provides opportunities for continued reinforcement of motivating identities. It is important to note, though, that identities and motivation are just one step toward positive academic outcomes, and students require opportunities for substantive learning experiences in order to fully express their motivation.

FROM INTERVENTION TO SYSTEMIC CHANGE: IMPLICATIONS FOR PRACTICE

Perhaps the greatest promise of the pathways intervention is in its potential implications for practice across multiple levels of a student's environment, rather than only as an individual intervention. As shown in Figure 6.2, an individual student's identity, psychological processes, and motivation are embedded within multiple systems of contextual influence (see Bronfenbrenner, 1977, 1979). From the peer to teacher to parent to broader institutional climate, these various levels of contextual influence provide different opportunities to translate pathways into a variety of other practical programs to support academic equity. Several experiments have begun to systematically show how specific types of actions and programs at each of these levels can support positive student outcomes.

At the peer level, a recent experiment built from the pathways intervention to train high school student near peers as mentors for eighth-grade student participants (Destin, Castillo, & Meissner, 2018). In a cascading mentorship model, a random group of high school student near-peer mentors completed five sessions of training by college student research assistants. The randomly selected high school student mentors prepared to facilitate a series of discussions and activities with eighth-grade participants that were modified from the pathways intervention (Oyserman, 2015; Oyserman et al., 2006). After the 5 days of training, the high school student mentors were each matched with a small group of eighth-grade student mentees. For the next 5 days, they facilitated the programming focused on topics including images for the future, timelines and obstacles, and encountering and responding to difficulty, similar to the approach detailed in the pathways "Intervention Content and Implementation" section. Before and after the 5-day program, eighth-grade student mentees completed key measures of motivation. Eighth-grade students who were randomly assigned to participate in the near-peer identity-based mentoring showed increased academic persistence at the end of the sessions compared with a control group that were instead randomly assigned to receive basic homework help from high school tutors (Destin et al., 2018). The experiment demonstrated that peers can influence identity-based processes that shape motivation and provided insight for the development of programming that expands on the original pathways intervention. Although not evaluated in this study, other studies have also demonstrated positive effects for high school or college student mentors themselves (e.g., Schreier, Schonert-Reichl, & Chen, 2013).

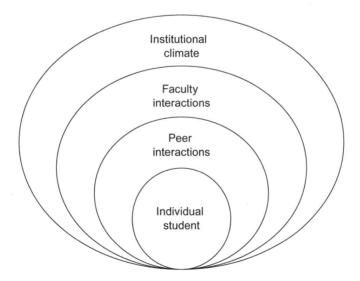

FIGURE 6.2. Examples of levels of context with potential for programs that expand the pathways intervention and influence identity-based motivational processes.

The key insight from the near-peer experiment is that taking the effort to connect adolescents with those who are slightly older than them can be beneficial. The high school students and eighth-grade students attended different schools in the same community. This allowed the high school students to facilitate vivid and authentic conversations about their lives and possible futures. It is important to note, however, that simply connecting students with one another without mentorship guidance was not as beneficial, as shown by the homework-help tutoring condition. Instead, relevant, identity-based guidance is necessary. Further, the experimental demonstration had immediate effects on student motivation and indirect effects on their grades, but there were no direct effects on their academic performance. It is likely that sustained interactions with near-peer mentors can lead to sustained positive effects on academic outcomes.

One level of contextual influence that does include more sustained interaction is the teacher level. In another recent study that expanded on the pathways intervention, researchers provided all participating teachers with a 2-day training in identity-based motivation (Horowitz, Sorensen, Yoder, & Oyserman, 2018). This study included several rigorous checks to evaluate the extent to which trained teachers delivered the content of the intervention with fidelity. The content was well received by teachers and students, and fidelity reached high levels. Importantly, surpassing fidelity thresholds in facilitation of the content predicted important student outcomes, including higher grades and reduced course failure. The study was not a randomized controlled trial designed to test causal effects but rather demonstrated the potential of the pathways intervention to inform the training and development of teachers as a way to shape this extremely influential aspect of student context.

In addition to teachers, parents can also be a consistent level of contextual influence for students. In a parent-focused experiment expanding on the pathways intervention, researchers recruited parents of current eighth-grade students to participate in a study where they would observe a panel of parents whose students had already progressed beyond eighth grade in the same community (Destin & Svoboda, 2017). The parents who served as panelists provided predetermined answers to a series of questions about their own children's journeys, how they helped their children think about different aspects of their possible futures, and how they responded to their children's experiences of academic difficulty. The intervention was implemented toward the beginning of the school year. Participants observed the rich discussion and completed an evaluation at the end of the panel that included some key measures of attitudes and behavioral intentions. After the panel, parents of current eighth graders planned to talk with their children sooner about certain aspects of the future and they interpreted academic difficulty as a greater sign of a task's importance compared to parents in a control group. Further, the grades of students whose parents were randomly assigned to observe the panel increased significantly over the course of the school year compared with students whose parents were in the control group. Similar to the teacher study, this parent study demonstrated the enormous potential in expanding the pathways intervention to strategically reaching adults who regularly interact with students. The study also demonstrated the power of including the stories and insights of actual community members into the pathways intervention to influence student outcomes.

Finally, a higher and somewhat more abstract level of contextual influence where the effects of the pathways intervention can be expanded comes from the school or institutional climate that students encounter. Institutional climate can be especially influential for students from groups that are nondominant in society or who are the minority within a particular setting (Cheryan, Plaut, Davies, & Steele, 2009; Murphy, Steele, & Gross, 2007). One series of lab experiments demonstrated the effect of the institutional climate in higher education on the identities and motivation of students from lower-SES family backgrounds (Browman & Destin, 2016). College students from diverse backgrounds were randomly assigned to encounter information that led them to perceive the institutional climate as "warm" or "chilly" toward socioeconomic diversity. In the warm condition, information focused on how the institution is proud and supportive of its socioeconomic diversity as exemplified through its commitment of various financial resources. In the chilly condition, information focused on how the institution is generally content to be a wealthy community as exemplified through its network of large donors and students who are able to pay full financial aid. Lower-SES students felt more motivated and more likely to succeed after encountering the warm climate compared with the chilly climate (Browman & Destin, 2016). These types of cues within educational settings and institutions (e.g., in their programming, resources, and everyday messaging) can complement the pathways intervention to influence the success of students from lower-SES backgrounds and other nondominant groups in society.

The pathways intervention and processes related to identity-based motivation theory are well situated to inform the development of many different types of programs focused on student outcomes because of the inherent link between various levels of context and individual identities. As described, existing evidence provides specific guidance at the peer, teacher, parent, and institutional climate levels. These studies, however, provide just a few examples of how the pathways intervention can inform the development of efforts to influence various levels of an individual student's context.

IMPLICATIONS FOR THEORY

The pathways intervention and related work demonstrate the importance of young people's views of themselves and their possible futures in shaping their current school engagement and outcomes. The studies also show the inherent malleability of these influential identities and the many different types of experiences and social forces that play a role in how young people come to see themselves from moment to moment. Importantly, the identities that students articulate in the studies remain self-generated because the explicit imposition of a particular life path by researchers would likely weaken genuine student motivation. The pathways intervention illustrates a need to provide the resources, opportunities, and supports for students to explore, express, and elaborate upon ideas about themselves and their futures.

As mentioned at the outset, another implication is that studies related to the pathways intervention should not be considered interventions simply because they aim to influence outcomes for participants from diverse and often underserved backgrounds or because they are conducted in field settings. The idea of intervention can sometimes inherently imply that researchers unlock the definitive answer to solving some persistent social issue or fixing misguided behaviors of individuals or groups. Instead, the pathways intervention and related studies contribute to theory building in a similar manner to studies including members of more dominant and privileged groups in society. They often, however, also have a more externally valid conceptualization of context and the results can have more directly applicable implications. The results of these studies, though, have the greatest implications in how they can inform broader efforts to reduce inequality rather than as independent interventions that are not included in systematic initiatives to influence multiple levels of context.

FUTURE DIRECTIONS

The study of other possible levels of context, such as the neighborhood level, in addition to the potential effects of multiple coordinated efforts spanning different levels of context, can continue to advance insight in this area of research. In other words, there may be ways that approaches at certain levels can supplement approaches at other levels. For example, parent or teacher programming might be coordinated with a direct-to-student approach. Similarly, an attempt to shift institutional climates might be meaningfully paired with a neighborhood-focused initiative. By increasing the likelihood that students receive congruent messages that reinforce one another, their identities that support motivation may develop in a more stable, cohesive, and integrated manner. Future work may study how the effects of a traditional pathways intervention may expand when linked to systemic changes and supports.

Another way to advance this area of work is to systematically test the specific types of financial and learning resources that are necessary to maximize the potential positive effects of interventions that target various levels of context. Further, a movement toward intervention characterized by more systemic and coordinated efforts opens the possibilities to more holistically evaluate the ways that contexts and identities influence a wider range of outcomes for individuals, including health and well-being, across the lifespan (Destin, 2019).

Finally, perhaps the most important area for continued advancement is greater interface with social and public policy (Destin, 2018). Policies have the potential to shape aspects of the broader overarching context in addition to specific aspects of the lives of students and their families. On the positive end, researchers can provide tools and frameworks to help policymakers think about the various ways that policies can influence broader contexts with implications for the identities and lives of individuals. On the negative end, if researchers fail to interface with policy, individual programming and intervention will remain inherently limited in its ability to reduce systemic and persistent inequities. Insight from the pathways intervention can guide the development of a wide range of policies, practices, and individual interactions that support students in drawing deeper connections between their aspirations and real-life circumstances.

REFERENCES

Bandura, A., & Schunk, D. H. (1981). Cultivating competence, self-efficacy, and intrinsic interest through proximal self-motivation. *Journal of Personality and Social Psychology, 41*(3), 586–598.

Blackwell, L. S., Trzesniewski, K. H., & Dweck, C. S. (2007). Implicit theories of intelligence predict achievement across an adolescent transition: A longitudinal study and an intervention. *Child Development, 78*(1), 246–263.

Bronfenbrenner, U. (1977). Toward an experimental ecology of human development. *American Psychologist, 32*(7), 513–531.

Bronfenbrenner, U. (1979). *The ecology of human development.* Cambridge, MA: Harvard University Press.

Browman, A. S., & Destin, M. (2016). The effects of a warm or chilly climate towards socioeconomic diversity on academic motivation and self-concept. *Personality and Social Psychology Bulletin, 42*(2), 172–187.

Browman, A. S., Destin, M., Carswell, K. L., & Svoboda, R. C. (2017). Perceptions of socioeconomic mobility influence academic persistence among low socioeconomic status students. *Journal of Experimental Social Psychology, 72,* 45–52.

Bryan, C. J., Walton, G. M., Rogers, T., & Dweck, C. S. (2011). Motivating voter turnout by invoking the self. *Proceedings of the National Academy of Sciences of the USA, 108*(31), 12653–12656.

Canning, E. A., & Harackiewicz, J. M. (2015). Teach it, don't preach it: The differential effects of directly-communicated and self-generated utility-value information. *Motivation Science, 1*(1), 47–71.

Cheryan, S., Plaut, V. C., Davies, P. G., & Steele, C. M. (2009). Ambient belonging: How stereotypical cues impact gender participation in computer science. *Journal of Personality and Social Psychology, 97*(6), 1045–1060.

Cohen, G. L., & Sherman, D. K. (2014). The psychology of change: Self-affirmation and social psychological intervention. *Annual Review of Psychology, 65*(1), 333–371.

Corwin, Z. B., Venegas, K. M., Oliverez, P. M., & Colyar, J. E. (2004). School counsel: How appropriate guidance affects educational equity. *Urban Education, 39*(4), 442–457.

Debrosse, R., Destin, M., Rossignac-Milon, M., Taylor, D., & Rogers, L. O. (2018). Immigrant adolescents' roots and dreams: Perceived mismatches between ethnic identities and aspirational selves predict engagement. *Self and Identity, 1,* 1–15.

Debrosse, R., Rossignac-Milon, M., Taylor, D. M., & Destin, M. (2018). Can identity conflicts impede the success of ethnic minority students?: Consequences of discrepancies between ethnic and ideal selves. *Personality and Social Psychology Bulletin, 44*(12), 1725–1738.

Destin, M. (2017). An open path to the future: Perceived financial resources and school motivation. *Journal of Early Adolescence, 37*(7), 1004–1031.

Destin, M. (2018). *Leveraging psychological factors: A necessary component to improving student outcomes.* Washington, DC: American Enterprise Institute & Third Way.

Destin, M. (2019). Socioeconomic mobility, identity, and health: Experiences that influence immunology and implications for intervention. *American Psychologist, 74*(2), 207–217.

Destin, M., Castillo, C., & Meissner, L. (2018). A field experiment demonstrates near peer mentorship as an effective support for student persistence. *Basic and Applied Social Psychology, 40*(5), 269–278.

Destin, M., & Oyserman, D. (2009). From assets to school outcomes: How finances shape children's perceived possibilities and intentions. *Psychological Science, 20*(4), 414–418.

Destin, M., & Oyserman, D. (2010). Incentivizing education: Seeing schoolwork as an investment, not a chore. *Journal of Experimental Social Psychology, 46*(5), 846–849.

Destin, M., & Svoboda, R. (2017). A brief randomized controlled intervention targeting parents improves grades during middle school. *Journal of Adolescence, 56,* 157–161.

Fisher, O., & Oyserman, D. (2017). Assessing interpretations of experienced ease and difficulty as motivational constructs. *Motivation Science, 3*(2), 133–163.

Gamoran, A., & Hannigan, E. C. (2000). Algebra for everyone?: Benefits of college-preparatory mathematics for students with diverse abilities in early secondary school. *Educational Evaluation and Policy Analysis, 22*(3), 241–254.

Gollwitzer, P. M., & Sheeran, P. (2006). Implementation intentions and goal achievement: A meta-analysis of effects and processes. In M. P. Zanna (Ed.), *Advances in experimental social psychology* (Vol. 38, pp. 69–119). San Diego, CA: Academic Press.

Harackiewicz, J. M., Canning, E. A., Tibbetts, Y., Priniski, S. J., & Hyde, J. S. (2016). Closing achievement gaps with a utility-value intervention: Disentangling race and social class. *Journal of Personality and Social Psychology, 111*(5), 745–765.

Horowitz, E., Sorensen, N., Yoder, N., & Oyserman, D. (2018). Teachers can do it: Scalable identity-based motivation intervention in the classroom. *Contemporary Educational Psychology, 54,* 12–28.

Hoyle, R. H., & Sherrill, M. R. (2006). Future orientation in the self-system: Possible selves, self-regulation, and behavior. *Journal of Personality, 74*(6), 1673–1696.

Hulleman, C. S., Kosovich, J. J., Barron, K. E., & Daniel, D. B. (2017). Making connections: Replicating and extending the utility value intervention in the classroom. *Journal of Educational Psychology, 109*(3), 387–404.

Jackson, C. K., Johnson, R. C., & Persico, C. (2016). The effects of school spending on educational and economic outcomes: Evidence from school finance reforms. *Quarterly Journal of Economics, 131*(1), 157–218.

Kanno, Y., & Kangas, S. E. N. (2014). "I'm not going to be, like, for the AP": English language learners' limited access to advanced college-preparatory courses in high school. *American Educational Research Journal, 51*(5), 848–878.

Lafortune, J., Rothstein, J., & Schanzenbach, D. W. (2018). School finance reform and the distribution of student achievement. *American Economic Journal: Applied Economics, 10*(2), 1–26.

Landau, M. J., Oyserman, D., Keefer, L. A., & Smith, G. C. (2014). The college journey and academic engagement: How metaphor use enhances identity-based motivation. *Journal of Personality and Social Psychology, 106*(5), 679–698.

Lin-Siegler, X., Ahn, J. N., Chen, J., Fang, F. F. A., & Luna-Lucero, M. (2016). Even Einstein struggled: Effects of learning about great scientists' struggles on high school students' motivation to learn science. *Journal of Educational Psychology, 108*(3), 314–328.

Lovenheim, M. F. (2011). The effect of liquid housing wealth on college enrollment. *Journal of Labor Economics, 29*(4), 741–771.

Ma, J., Pender, M., & Welch, M. (2016). *Education pays 2016.* New York: College Board.

Markus, H. R., & Nurius, P. (1986). Possible selves. *American Psychologist, 41*(9), 954–969.

Markus, H. R., & Wurf, E. (1987). The dynamic self-concept: A social psychological perspective. *Annual Review of Psychology, 38*(1), 299–337.

Mickelson, R. A. (1990). The attitude-achievement paradox among Black adolescents. *Sociology of Education, 63*(1), 44–61.

Miller, R. L., Brickman, P., & Bolen, D. (1975). Attribution versus persuasion as a means for modifying behavior. *Journal of Personality and Social Psychology, 31*(3), 430–441.

Murphy, M. C., Steele, C. M., & Gross, J. J. (2007). Signaling threat: How situational cues affect women in math, science, and engineering settings. *Psychological Science, 18*(10), 879–885.

Oyserman, D. (2015). *Pathways to success through identity-based motivation.* New York: Oxford University Press.

Oyserman, D., Bybee, D., & Terry, K. (2006). Possible selves and academic outcomes: How and when possible selves impel action. *Journal of Personality and Social Psychology, 91*(1), 188–204.

Oyserman, D., & Destin, M. (2010). Identity-based motivation: Implications for intervention. *The Counseling Psychologist, 38*(7), 1001–1043.

Oyserman, D., Elmore, K., Novin, S., Fisher, O., & Smith, G. C. (2018). Guiding people to interpret their experienced difficulty as importance highlights their academic possibilities and improves their academic performance. *Frontiers in Psychology, 9.*

Oyserman, D., Johnson, E., & James, L. (2011). Seeing the destination but not the path: Effects of socioeconomic disadvantage on school-focused possible self content and linked behavioral strategies. *Self and Identity, 10*(4), 474–492.

Oyserman, D., & Lewis, N. A. (2017). Seeing the destination and the path: Using identity-based motivation to understand and reduce racial disparities in academic achievement. *Social Issues and Policy Review, 11*(1), 159–194.

Paunesku, D., Walton, G. M., Romero, C., Smith, E. N., Yeager, D. S., & Dweck, C. S. (2015). Mind-set interventions are a scalable treatment for academic underachievement. *Psychological Science, 26*(6), 784–793.

Ruvolo, A. P., & Markus, H. R. (1992). Possible selves and performance: The power of self-relevant imagery. *Social Cognition, 10*(1), 95–124.

Schneider, B., & Stevenson, D. (1999). The ambitious generation. *Educational Leadership, 57*(4), 22–25.

Schreier, H. M. C., Schonert-Reichl, K. A., & Chen, E. (2013). Effect of volunteering on risk factors for cardiovascular disease in adolescents: A randomized controlled trial. *JAMA Pediatrics, 167*(4), 327–332.

Smith, E. R., & Semin, G. R. (2004). Socially situated cognition: Cognition in its social context. *Advances in Experimental Social Psychology, 36*, 53–117.

Smith, E. R., & Semin, G. R. (2007). Situated social cognition. *Current Directions in Psychological Science, 16*(3), 132–135.

Smith, G. C., & Oyserman, D. (2015). Just not worth my time?: Experienced difficulty and time investment. *Social Cognition, 33*(2), 1–18.

Steele, C. M. (1988). The psychology of self-affirmation: Sustaining the integrity of the self. *Advances in Experimental Social Psychology, 21*, 261–302.

Steele, C. M. (1997). A threat in the air: How stereotypes shape intellectual identity and performance. *American Psychologist, 52*(6), 613–629.

Steele, C. M., & Aronson, J. (1995). Stereotype threat and the intellectual test performance of African Americans. *Journal of Personality and Social Psychology, 69*(5), 797–811.

Vohs, K. D., Park, J. K., & Schmeichel, B. J. (2013). Self-affirmation can enable goal disengagement. *Journal of Personality and Social Psychology, 104*(1), 14–27.

Walton, G. M., & Wilson, T. D. (2018). Wise interventions: Psychological remedies for social and personal problems. *Psychological Review, 125*(5), 617–655.

Wilson, T. D., & Linville, P. W. (1982). Improving the academic performance of college freshmen: Attribution therapy revisited. *Journal of Personality and Social Psychology, 42*(2), 367–376.

Wilson, T. D., & Linville, P. W. (1985). Improving the performance of college freshmen with attributional techniques. *Journal of Personality and Social Psychology, 49*(1), 287–293.

Yeager, D. S., & Dweck, C. S. (2012). Mindsets that promote resilience: When students believe that personal characteristics can be developed. *Educational Psychologist, 47*(4), 302–314.

Yeager, D. S., Henderson, M. D., Paunesku, D., Walton, G. M., D'Mello, S., Spitzer, B. J., & Duckworth, A. L. (2014). Boring but important: A self-transcendent purpose for learning fosters academic self-regulation. *Journal of Personality and Social Psychology, 107*(4), 559–580.

CHAPTER 7

The Strategic Resource Use Intervention

Patricia Chen

Improving learning is not just about working harder, but also about how *effectively* learners direct their efforts. Many learners fall short of achieving their potential, not necessarily because they are unable or unwilling to put in the effort but because they are not strategic in the way they use their learning resources to build mastery. We showed that an online, self-administered "strategic resource use" intervention, which guided learners to self-reflect on how they would effectively use their resources to study for their exams, significantly improved academic performance. The intervention guided them through the psychological process of strategizing *what* to use and *why* (for what purpose), and planning *when, where,* and *how* to learn effectively. Carrying out such reflection was related to more effective resource use reported during learning, and in turn, to better academic performance. Our research brings together principles from self-regulated learning theory, effective goal pursuit, and wise intervention methods to demonstrate the important causal relationship between strategic resource use and academic achievement. More consequentially, we show that this psychology can be changed in a scalable way to empower many learners.

> I keep six honest serving-men
> (They taught me all I knew);
> Their names are What and Why and When
> And How and Where and Who.
> —RUDYARD KIPLING (1902)

BACKGROUND

Every year, millions of dollars are spent by governments worldwide on improving education through the provision of new or better-quality resources for learners (Organisation for Economic Co-operation and Development, 2018; World Bank Group, 2018). These might include, but are not limited to, textbooks, course pack readings, workbooks with practice problems, online encyclopedias, discussion forums, practice exam questions, supplementary or remedial classes, workshops on study skills, and more. In schools, teachers and school administrators never stop finding ways to create, evaluate, and choose educational resources to support student learning. Because of all these efforts, many learners in our developed world today have excellent learning resources at their fingertips (or at least attainable with some initiative on their parts). However, providing students with resources does not directly improve mastery. Instead, students have to select and use the resources wisely when learning to reap the pedagogical benefits that they bring.

The problem is that many students do not exercise such self-regulation in their learning (Pintrich, Smith, Garcia, & McKeachie, 1991; Zimmerman, 2011; Zimmerman & Martinez-Pons, 1988). For example, when I asked two undergraduate students of mine to describe the way that they generally studied for exams, one answered, "How do I prepare for my exams? I just take out my textbook and start reading." Another described the process of studying as "You just take out your notes and the textbook and . . . start looking through them." The process of studying for exams, it seems, is often construed by these students as a passive, unplanned activity that one begins without much forethought or strategizing. This is in stark contrast to the way teachers and researchers conceive of effective, self-regulated learning as an active process of trial and self-reflection (Bembenutty, 2011; Chen, Ong, & Coppola, 2019).

When students do not approach their learning strategically—or in a self-reflective and goal-directed manner—they may not learn or perform to their potential. As psychologists, educators, school administrators, members of government, and parents, it behooves us to do something to help maximize, rather than waste, our society's human potential.

PSYCHOLOGICAL PROCESS

Metacognition

How can we help our learners use the resources available to them to learn effectively? A key is the psychological process of "metacognitive self-regulation," or "metacognition" for short—defined as thinking about one's approaches to learning (Pintrich, 2002; Pintrich et al., 1991). Exercising metacognition goes beyond being aware of and knowing how to execute specific study skills (such as elaboration and organization)—it also involves changing the way learners think about and approach their learning (Pintrich, 2002; Zimmerman, 1989). This involves strategizing what approaches might be appropriate to the task, monitoring how effective these approaches are, fine-tuning and changing approaches when unproductive, and reflecting on feedback (Chen, Chavez, Ong, & Gunderson, 2017; Chen, Powers, Katragadda, Cohen, & Dweck, 2020; Pintrich, 2002; Pintrich et al., 1991). Importantly, practicing metacognition during learning relates to many important learning processes and outcomes, including greater self-efficacy, higher levels of motivation, more effective learning strategies, higher exam performance, and even better academic trajectories over time (Chen et al., 2017; Chen, Ong, et al., 2019; Pintrich, Smith, Garcia, & McKeachie, 1993; Pintrich & De Groot, 1990).

To date, metacognition has been widely applied to many learning processes—including how learners assess the extent of their learning, estimate the ease or difficulty of a new learning task, and switch cognitive strategies when in error (Dunlosky & Bjork, 2008; Dunlosky & Metcalfe, 2009; Fleming & Frith, 2014). However, a comparatively understudied, albeit immensely important, part of the metacognitive process is how learners manage their resource use in a self-reflective and purposeful manner. This has been called "resource regulation" or "resource management"—and it is the psychological process that I refer to when I describe people as being strategic in their resource use (Chen et al., 2017; Chen, Ong, et al., 2019; Pintrich et al., 1991).

Resource Regulation

Resource regulation involves knowing what resources are available, but also the conditional knowledge about when and how to use them effectively (Pintrich, 2002; Pintrich & Garcia, 1994). Students who are not strategic in their resource use may be aware of the various resources available to them, but they might not think about which specific resources could be more or less conducive to learning for particular subjects and exam formats; they might not deliberately think about the purpose for which they would use each resource; or they might not be planful about how they could use each resource effectively. Learners who practice strategic resource use, on the other hand, tend to consider what they are expected to know when taking the exam, they strategize which resources they should use to make their learning effective, they know the purpose for which they intend to use each resource, and they are intentional and planful about how to use each resource effectively. Although resources broadly encompass both internal (e.g., motivation levels, emotions, attention) and external resources (e.g., books, online websites, classmates, discussion forum members, teachers, academic advisors), in this chapter and in our strategic resource use intervention, I focus on students' use of their external resources during learning.

Prior work on students' self-regulation of external resources has generally measured resource regulation through retrospective self-reports of how they use their study time, how strategically they select their study environments, how well they stick to their study schedule, and whether they seek help appropriately (Bergin, Reilly, & Traynor, 2005; Karabenick, 2003; Pintrich et al., 1991). For example, students respond to items such as "I make good use of my study time for this course" and "I usually study in a place where I can concentrate on my coursework" on scales from 1 (*Not at all true of me*) to 7 (*Very true of me*). Such research on resource regulation has mostly been correlational in nature (e.g., Bergin et al., 2005; Chen, Ong, et al., 2019; Pintrich et al., 1991, 1993; Valle et al., 2008). Importantly, the findings show that students who report being more strategic in their resource use tend to be more intrinsically motivated, and they perform better in their classes (Karabenick, 2003; Pintrich et al., 1991). However, they leave open questions about causality—whether promoting more strategic resource use can causally enhance learning and academic performance.

Promoting Resource Regulation with the Strategic Resource Use Intervention

Our research aimed to test whether an intervention that targets this process of resource regulation can causally improve students' academic performance. To this end, we designed the strategic resource use intervention to guide people to be more metacognitive about how to make effective use of their resources when studying for an exam (Chen et al., 2017). The intervention has been represented as a survey on student learning in the class, and presented as a series of short messages and questions that students answer on their own before they start studying for an exam. It prompts students to ask themselves—and to answer for themselves: "What am I expected to master by the upcoming exam?"; "What kinds of resources are available to me?"; "Which resources should I use to study effectively, and which resources may not be as helpful?"; "Why will each resource I have chosen to use be useful for my learning?"; and "How should I plan to use the resources to study?"

In other words, the intervention does not teach students study strategies, tell them how they should be studying, or prescribe what resources they should use—instead, it guides students through the process of self-reflection by providing questions that encourage metacognition and model answers to scaffold their responses. This way, students are empowered to take ownership of their strategies and plans (Janis & King, 1954; Walton & Cohen, 2011; Wilson, 1990).

The strategic resource use intervention approach resonates with the "wise intervention" approach in social psychology, because it targets how students make sense of their learning process to improve how effectively they leverage their resources when learning (Walton, 2014; Walton & Wilson, 2018). Our approach is also consistent with the spirit of self-regulated learning, which involves a self-directed, agentic process of shaping one's own learning (Zimmerman, 2002).

EMPIRICAL EVIDENCE

Outcomes

So far, two classroom experiments have tested the strategic resource use intervention and yielded promising results (Chen et al., 2017). Two double-blind, randomized, controlled experiments were conducted in an introductory college statistics course of a large, public Midwestern university. Each experiment recruited separate cohorts of students, 1 year apart. Students took the intervention (or a control) online as part of a survey on student learning in the class, which took about 15 minutes to complete. They were invited to do this about a week before each of their two class exams. Upon accessing the online survey, students were randomly assigned to receive either the strategic resource use intervention (treatment condition) or a control message (control condition). Those in the control condition read a "business-as-usual" exam reminder, which informed them about their upcoming exam in the way that their class instructor usually announced exam reminders (and also consistent with the way that other instructors at that university generally reminded their students about upcoming exams). Students randomly assigned to the treatment condition also received that exam reminder and then completed a short exercise that prompted them to strategize and plan out their resource use for their upcoming exam (see the "Intervention Content and Implementation" section for more details). Students in both conditions were comparable on their prior achievement levels (i.e., high school grade-point average [GPA] and college GPA), their desired grades on each exam, their levels of motivation to achieve their desired grades, how important these grades were to them, and their confidence in attaining their desired grades.

In both experiments, students who were randomly assigned to the treatment condition outperformed their peers in the control condition on both class exams, and by an average of one-third of a letter grade in the class. In Experiments 1 and 2, respectively, there was an average difference of 3.64 and 4.21% in students' final course grades between those randomly assigned to the treatment and control conditions (Chen et al., 2017). To illustrate this in practical terms, students who would have otherwise achieved a B in the class instead performed at the level of a B+ if they were randomly assigned to the intervention condition, and students who would otherwise have gotten a B+ instead attained an A– in the intervention condition.

These intervention effects were not significantly moderated by students' academic achievement levels prior to starting the class, gender, race, or class standing. Although a lack of moderation might seem surprising in light of other social-psychological interventions that tend to target and benefit one group of students more than another, there was no reason for us to believe a priori that different groups of students in that class were already carrying out self-reflective resource use to different extents. Our findings (corroborating observations of students in the class before the study) seem to suggest that the self-reflective process our intervention targeted is one that many students were generally unaware of or not practicing optimally on their own, at least with this student population in this class context. Thus, the strategic resource use intervention had the potential to benefit many learners in this class.

Mechanisms

What mechanisms might explain the intervention effects? The strategic resource use intervention was designed to prompt students to self-reflect on how to approach their learning effectively, so that they would direct their resource use in a more effective manner when studying. We assessed these hypothesized mechanisms of self-reflection and effective resource use. We measured self-reflection at the end of the class (to prevent priming these ideas among the control group midway through the class) with items such as "As I studied for the class, I kept monitoring whether or not the way I was studying was effective" and "I actively evaluated how well certain study techniques were working for me in this class." Through postexam surveys administered after each exam, we measured students' reports of how effective their resource use was when studying, and averaged this across both exams to compute a proxy for how effectively they were using their resources over the course of the class, on average.

Consistent with the psychological process described earlier, we found that students in the treatment group reported being more self-reflective about their learning during the class, compared to those in the control group. In other words, they reported actively tailoring how they studied to the class context, monitoring how effectively they were studying, changing the way they were studying when unproductive, and reflecting on their performance during the class at a greater frequency, compared to controls. The more students exercised such self-reflective learning, the higher the reported effectiveness of their resource use, which in turn, related to better overall class performance (see Figure 7.1; Chen et al., 2017).

In addition to making students more self-reflective, we found that the strategic resource use intervention also reduced negative feelings that students had about their upcoming exams and increased their perceived control over their exam performance

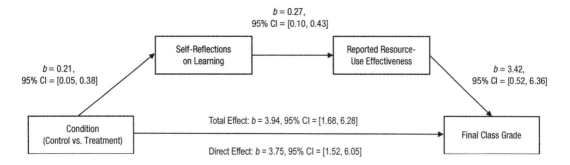

FIGURE 7.1. Modeling the process by which the intervention affects students' final course performance, mediated by their self-reflections on learning and the reported effectiveness of their resource use when studying. Condition is coded as follows: control = 0, treatment = 1. CI represents the confidence interval. Residual error terms are not included in this figure. Reprinted with permission from Chen, Chavez, Ong, and Gunderson (2017).

(Chen et al., 2017). Although not the main hypothesized mechanisms of the intervention, these additional motivational effects of the intervention are worth noting, given that exam-oriented negative affect (such as math anxiety) and perceptions of controllability contribute to student achievement (Ashcraft, 2002; Ashcraft & Kirk, 2001; Skinner, Wellborn, & Connell, 1990).

Importantly, the intervention did not just make students use more resources—in fact, students in the treatment condition reported using fewer resources, on average, than those in the control condition (Chen et al., 2017). This suggests that students in the treatment condition were using their resources *more effectively* by reflecting on how to approach their learning, rather than just using a greater number of resources. These results are consistent with our goal of making learners more *strategic* (i.e., self-reflective and goal directed)—not just getting them to study harder in a thoughtless, ineffective manner.

The Role of Strategizing and Follow-Through

To further understand the effects of the intervention, we addressed two additional questions: Out of all the resources that students reported using, how much did it matter if they had purposefully selected these resources in the intervention ahead of time? To what extent was it important that students followed through with their plans, beyond just making plans?

Among those in the treatment condition (these data were not available for those in the control condition), we found that it was indeed important for students to strategically select the resources that they were to use ahead of time: The number of resources that students had selected in advance and used ("planned-and-used" resources) positively related to their exam performance, whereas the number of resources that students had used but not strategized a priori ("unplanned-and-used" resources) was unrelated to their performance in the same model. At least among those in the treatment condition, these findings underscore the importance of exercising strategic forethought in carefully selecting one's learning resources. When it came to planning, our results also highlighted that follow-through mattered. Only the number of resources that students had planned to use and reported using ("planned-and-used" resources) positively related to their exam performance, but not the number of resources that students had planned to use but did not follow through with ("planned-but-did-not-use" resources). The takeaway is that students should make practical plans about their resource use in advance, and also make it a point to follow through with their plans.

Taken together, our two field experiments demonstrated that promoting strategic resource use can causally enhance learning and performance, and our findings provide evidence for the psychological process by which it does so.

Effects over Time

Currently, the intervention design has focused on preparing students for their upcoming exams within a particular class. At least within the same class context, the intervention seems to work well. But can we create a version of the intervention that might enable students to generalize the psychological process of resource regulation beyond the class in which it was administered? This could involve asking students how they would apply this psychological process to their other classes, or asking them how they might use this in other domains of learning outside school (e.g., learning how to play a musical instrument or a new sports skill). Our ongoing research is looking into how we might be able to adapt the current intervention design to encourage transfer.

Heterogeneity, Moderation, and Durability

The strategic resource use intervention is meant to complement—but not replace—existing measures that many educational institutions and government policies have in place to provide resources to learners. In fact, our intervention is predicated on the assumption that the necessary resources for learning are available to learners. After all, many student-centered interventions, like this one, depend on the availability of learning resources (e.g., mentors, peer study groups, and academic support services) in the environment for students to leverage (Cohen, Garcia, Apfel, & Master, 2006; Paunesku et al., 2015; Walton & Wilson, 2018; Yeager et al., 2016, 2019). Certainly, if a basic repertoire of resources is not even available, then providing that should be the priority. Once learners do have access to the learning resources, however, the next important step is to ensure that they use these resources effectively. For example, this second step can be a challenge for many college freshmen, who often feel overwhelmed and unsure about how best to prioritize and utilize the many, varied resources available on their university campuses. The goal of the strategic resource use intervention is to inculcate the psychological process of strategic resource use, so that people can be more thoughtful about how they might leverage the various resources available to them effectively.

To reap the full benefits of the intervention, students need to engage in the self-reflective process of strategizing and planning their resource use. Our findings suggest that they should especially craft strategic plans that are (1) focused on *maximizing mastery,* (2) *tailored* to the upcoming exam format, and (3) concrete about *when* and *how* they will use the resources to study (Chen et al., 2017). These were the key ingredients of students' open-ended responses to the intervention that were positively (and reliably) related to their class performance across our experiments. Our results suggest that students who do not pay attention to or engage with the intervention in these meaningful ways may not receive as much benefit as those who do. Future iterations of the intervention could emphasize even more than we have previously done on how students might include these psychological elements as they self-reflect on their resource use.

Because the intervention targets students' self-reflection about their resource use, it is plausible that the intervention confers more benefits to those who do not already carry out this metacognitive process on their own. Although we did not measure this in our previous studies, this could be an important moderator of the intervention effects that future studies should assess.

Learning to proactively self-reflect on one's resource use could be especially relevant during developmental transitions that involve moving from learning in a more structured environment to an environment that requires greater independence and autonomy, or changing from a familiar context to a new context that requires different strategies to be effective. One such example is the transition from high school, where learning is generally more structured and guided by the teacher, to college—a new learning environment where students are expected to navigate multiple, varied resources, to manage their time on their own, and to figure out how to master the content independently. Another example is the transition from school to the workforce, where many supervisors expect employees to be resourceful and autonomous in picking up the necessary skills to get the job done well. During these transitions, old ways of doing things may no longer work as well in the new contexts. Hence, many people often feel overwhelmed by the experience that their familiar methods are no longer as effective, by the number and variety of new options to try, by the lack of structured guidance, and by the fact that there may not always be a clear best way to learn. It is in these very moments that the strategic resource use intervention might be especially useful.

Although we did not explicitly test this, I believe that students should want to invest the effort to learn for the intervention to be effective. Without at least a basic amount of motivation to try, neither strategizing nor planning how to use one's resources for learning might be fruitful. This is related to the idea of follow-through described earlier, where the number of resources that students planned and followed through mattered for performance, but not the number of resources that they planned but did not see through. Specifically, this intervention is not targeted at motivating unmotivated students to study—instead, it helps students who already have some motivation to learn to channel their efforts productively. It is conceivable that pairing this intervention with one that boosts motivation, such as a growth mindset intervention, a purpose intervention, or a utility-value intervention (e.g., Blackwell, Trzesniewski, & Dweck, 2007; Hulleman & Harackiewicz, 2009; Yeager et al., 2014), might better help students who lack self-reflection and who also need some motivating.

COUSINS

The strategic resource use intervention differs in a number of ways from most traditional study skills interventions that focus on telling students what learning strategies (e.g., highlighting, rehearsal, elaboration, organization, self-testing) are more or less effective for the average learner (Hattie, 2009; Wingate, 2006). First, training cognitive learning strategies, which increases learners' awareness of various study strategies and how to execute them, is generally considered skill building, whereas the strategic resource use intervention is a self-reflection exercise that walks learners through the metacognitive process of strategizing and planning out how to maximize their resource use to learn (Chen et al., 2017; Pintrich, 2002). The self-regulated learning literature clearly contrasts this meta-cognitive process of "planning, monitoring, and regulating" learning (Pintrich, 2002, p. 220) against just having the knowledge about various learning strategies. Second, while many study skills interventions are often prescriptive in nature, the strategic resource use intervention avoids telling students how they should study, but rather, guides them through a process of effective strategizing and planning. Third, study skills interventions in many schools are often taught in a general manner that is divorced from specific subject knowledge (Wingate, 2006), but the strategic resource use intervention is designed to teach metacognitive principles through application within a specific class context.

The strategic resource use intervention belongs to a family of social-psychological interventions that change the way people think about their goals and how they pursue them (Walton & Wilson, 2018). Specifically, the intervention helps learners reflect on how they might use the resources available to them in a purposeful, effective manner to achieve their academic goals. Other interventions of this kind engage people in active reflection about the goal pursuit process by asking them to commit to when, where, and how they would take a desired action, or by having them anticipate obstacles that they might encounter and describing what they would do to overcome these obstacles when working toward their goals (Gollwitzer, 1999; Gollwitzer & Brandstätter, 1997; Oettingen & Gollwitzer, 2010). Such interventions have been effective at increasing the likelihood that people actually carry out the desirable behaviors, and also effective at producing significant gains in goal achievement (Duckworth, Grant, Loew, Oettingen, & Gollwitzer, 2011; Duckworth, Kirby, Gollwitzer, & Oettingen, 2013; Gollwitzer, 1999). The strategic resource use intervention leverages this wisdom by getting people to commit to when, where, and how they will take action on their goals. However, it is also unique in asking people to reflect on which specific resources would be effective for their goal pursuit and why.

The strategic resource use intervention is similar to growth mindset of intelligence interventions in that both focus on orienting people toward generating and employing effective strategies that are associated with internal and controllable attributions. Growth mindset interventions focus on changing students' beliefs about their intelligence by teaching them that intelligence is controllable and malleable through hard work, effective strategies, and help from others (Aronson, Fried, & Good, 2002; Blackwell et al., 2007; Paunesku et al., 2015; Yeager et al., 2019). These growth mindset interventions have been very effective at changing learners' beliefs about intelligence and improving their academic achievement trajectories. The strategic resource use intervention and the growth mindset interventions, however, differ in their main goals and mechanisms. By changing people's beliefs about the malleability of intelligence, growth mindset interventions incline people toward a mastery orientation in their learning. This focus on mastery orients people toward searching for effective strategies and greater persistence in times of challenge or difficulty. The strategic resource use intervention, however, does not aim to change people's beliefs about their intelligence, but it targets their metacognition about their resource use. Specifically, this intervention prompts people to reflect and plan what strategies to employ, monitor their strategies as they learn, and switch strategies if they are ineffective.

INTERVENTION CONTENT AND IMPLEMENTATION

Context and Timing

To date, we have published two randomized, controlled experiments on the strategic resource use intervention that was conducted in an introductory statistics course at a large, public Midwestern university (Chen et al., 2017). The statistics course was an important prerequisite course to many majors in the natural sciences, social sciences, business school, and premedicine track, and it additionally satisfied a quantitative skill requirement at the undergraduate level. Therefore, students enrolled in the class generally took their learning and performance seriously. All students in the class were taught by the same instructor during the spring semesters when we conducted our studies, ensuring that the instructional content and style were consistent across all our participants. Students who consented to participate were randomized via the survey software to either a treatment condition (where they would receive a business-as-usual exam reminder, the strategic resource use intervention exercise, and survey questions) or a control condition (where they would receive the same business-as-usual exam reminder and survey questions, but not the intervention).

The intervention was distributed online via "preexam surveys" to students in the class about 10 days before each of their two class exams, with a participation deadline of about 7 days prior to each exam. We chose this timing for this specific class context with the instructor because students in the class during the spring semester typically started studying about a week before their exams. Distributing the intervention at this time gave students the opportunity to think about how they would approach their studying before most of them actually started studying. It was also not too far in advance of their exams so as to render the self-reflection exercise irrelevant to them.

Representation

We represented our intervention as a survey to understand student learning in the class. The online intervention interface was modeled to look like a generic survey about students' goals, motivations, and feelings about the exam, along with an exam reminder and open-ended questions about students' study plans. It took about 15 minutes to complete online.

Intervention Content

Overview

The survey began with an exam reminder that all students in the class typically received from the instructor: "Your exam is coming up on [day and date]. You might want to start preparing for it." Students then completed our brief strategic resource use intervention exercise where they were prompted to actively think about their upcoming exam format; select which resources out of the many available to them they would use to study effectively; explain why each resource would be useful to their learning; and plan out when, where, and how they would use the resources. Next, I describe more details about each of these components of the intervention exercise.

Details

The strategic resource use exercise started with a message emphasizing scientific findings that high-achieving students use their resources strategically when preparing for exams. Students were then prompted to consider the kinds of questions that they expected on their upcoming exam, and to think through what resources (including study materials and people who can help them) would help them prepare for the exam most effectively. These brief messages were meant to motivate them to engage in the intervention and to initiate their self-reflection in an open-ended way, before the scaffolding that followed.

Following these general messages, students received more specific questions about strategizing and planning out their resource use within their given class context. Students were presented with a comprehensive checklist of all the class resources available to them, and they were asked to select the resources out of this checklist that would help them prepare for their upcoming exam effectively. For example, some resources that students in the statistics course had were lecture notes, practice exam questions, past homework problems, textbook readings, yellow formula card, online problem-solving applet, discussions with other students in the class (e.g., peer study groups), office hours held by the lecture instructor, and office hours held by the graduate student instructor (i.e., teaching assistant). This means that students had to reflect on which resources would be effective for developing mastery and which resources might not be so effective for their own learning, thereby prioritizing their resource use. We generated this comprehensive list of resources through discussions with the class instructor and teaching assistants, focus groups with students who had previously taken the class, and student surveys.

After making their selections, students were asked to describe *why they thought each resource they selected would be useful* for their exam preparation. Prompting students to consider and make explicit the purpose for which they will use each of the resources they had chosen is an important step in the self-reflective process, because it helps them better channel their resource use more effectively toward those specific goals when they are studying. This reflection may also make students aware of when they may not be using a resource for its intended purpose. However, not all students may know how to give a thoughtful answer to the question "Why do you think these resources would be useful for your exam preparation?" without some guidance, even when they might be motivated to self-reflect. Thus, immediately after students read the question, they were given a model example to scaffold their responses:

> "Doing practice exam questions will allow me to practice on problems similar to what I will encounter on my exam. While doing the problems, I will look out for how I am expected to apply my knowledge. This will give me an idea of what material I should review in the lecture notes and how to apply the formulas I learn."

The model example guided their responses by showing them how they might think through the purposes for which they would use the various resources chosen (Collins, Brown, & Holum, 1991; Schunk, 1981).

We observed from students' responses that they indeed seemed to be using the model examples provided to scaffold their own thought processes and responses to the prompt. Here is an example of one student's answer:

"Lecture notes, past HW problems, practice exam questions: these will be helpful for me because I can see the steps necessary for completing a problem and I can practice doing the problems with a guide (my lecture notes) and follow the steps on those until I can do them without using my lecture notes.

"Discussions, private tutoring: These will help me to verbally talk through my problems so that I can make sure I know what I am talking about when I do the problems on my own."

The final step was *planning when, where,* and *how* they would use their resources. The purpose of this planning component was to increase the likelihood that students would actually follow through with their proposed strategies, rather than just building castles in the air that they never implement (Leventhal, Singer, & Jones, 1965; Gollwitzer, 1999). As Ross and Nisbett (2011, p. 227) aptly put it, concrete planning helps to "(facilitate) the link between positive intentions and constructive actions." Students were asked to plan out how they would use their resources to study, and again, they were given a model example to guide their planning that showed specific, concrete plans of when, where, and how a student might use their resources:

"Wednesday, 3/18, 3:00 P.M.–5:00 P.M., Library: Practice exam questions from 1 past exam."

"Friday, 3/20, 1:00 P.M.–3:00 P.M., Home: Read lecture notes for 2 topics."

Here is an example of a student's plan, which clearly shows in its structure and content that they used the model example to guide their own response:

"Sunday 5/25—home: relistening to lectures I had trouble with and looking over lecture notes."

"Monday 5/26—home: look over old homework and listen to more lectures, start HW 3."

"Tuesday 5/27—library: finish HW 3 and do problem roulette."

Importantly, this plan includes concrete descriptions of when, where, and how the student intends to use the resources to study.

Control Condition

In each of the two published experiments (Chen et al., 2017), we compared the students who were randomly assigned to the treatment condition to their peers who were randomly assigned to the control condition. The control presented students with a business-as-usual exam reminder that students typically received. After this, students filled out survey questions. They were not exposed to any of the active ingredients of the strategic resource use intervention in their surveys. We designed the control to be as close to business as usual in the class, making sure that we did not take away anything from the class that the instructor or students would normally do if the study had not been conducted. As mentioned earlier, students randomly assigned to the control condition were comparable to those assigned to the treatment before the intervention.

NUANCES AND MISCONCEPTIONS

Not Just Awareness of Resources

Although the intervention provides students with a list of the learning resources available to them, it is unlikely that the effects in our experiments were primarily due to increasing the accessibility of the resources available to students. In the statistics class where our intervention was tested, students were given frequent reminders by the instructor about the various resources available to them. In fact, they received a weekly "Get Things Done" list via e-mail, which reminded them about their deadlines for that week and included a list of the class resources they had. Therefore, within this class context, it is more likely that students in the treatment condition benefited from the intervention because they were prompted to self-reflect, rather than because they were exposed to one or two more reminders about the resources available.

Not Just about Studying More

Importantly, our intervention does not just tell students to study more or to use a larger number of resources to study. Our strategic resource use intervention focused on guiding students to be more self-reflective and goal-directed—and therefore effective—in their resource use, rather than just encouraging them to use more resources. While some students can benefit from studying harder, the active psychological ingredient in our intervention is to study more *strategically*. As described earlier, students in our intervention treatment group reported using fewer resources to study, on average, than students in the control group (Chen et al., 2017). This resonates with findings from research on study time, which suggest that it is usually not the duration of time spent studying that matters most for performance, but what really matters is how *effectively* students spend their study time (Plant, Ericsson, Hill, & Asberg, 2005; Schuman, Walsh, Olson, & Etheridge, 1985).

Not Just Planning

Although the strategic resource use intervention does involve a planning component, it is not just another planning intervention. First, the mechanisms of the strategic resource use intervention involve increasing students' self-reflection on their learning and, in turn, more effective resource use. Traditional planning interventions do not target these mechanisms (e.g., Gollwitzer, 1999; Oettingen & Gollwitzer, 2010). Second, we found that the active psychological ingredients in students' responses to the intervention, which were positively related to their final course grades, went beyond planning: The more strategically students chose their resources (1) by taking the format of the upcoming exam into consideration, and (2) by focusing on the goal of maximizing mastery, the better they performed in the class. Our findings underscore that the psychology of our intervention goes beyond committing to a plan of action.

IMPLICATIONS FOR PRACTICE

The efficacy of the strategic resource use intervention is testimony to the wisdom that learning is more effective when it is carried out in a strategic (rather than a passive or an unregulated) manner. This is wisdom that many educators and psychologists already have; yet it is also an idea that is sometimes challenging to convey to students in a way that they can execute on their own. The strategic resource use intervention is one bite-sized, online, and self-administered approach that educators and students can use to empower learners.

Administration Format

Because of its brief, online, and self-administered nature, the strategic resource use intervention can be conveniently disseminated to many students. Students access the intervention via a survey link, or through an online learning platform (e.g., Electronic Coach [ECoach] learning platform; Huberth, Chen, Tritz, & McKay, 2015). This online administration makes the intervention easily scalable and it also caters to the preferences of many learners among today's Internet-savvy generation. Although we have not tried implementing the intervention through pen-and-paper format, it is possible that administration through this means could also be effective if the core components of the intervention are retained.

Customization

When applying the intervention to a new class context, it is important to retain the key psychological ingredients of strategic resource use, while also tailoring the intervention content to be relevant to the class. Table 7.1 summarizes the key parts of the intervention and provides examples of answers that exemplify the metacognitive process each part targets. These are important parts of the psychological process that should be conceptually replicated in the new class context. At the same time, the details of the resource checklist and model examples in the intervention should be tailored to make sure that they are relevant to students' learning within the specific class. This class-specific tailoring also applies to the exam reminder that precedes the strategic resource use exercise. For instance, the following is part of the planning model example that we tailored for a different college chemistry class in ongoing, unpublished research (Cheng et al., 2019):

> "Saturday, 10/7, 1:00 P.M.–3:30 P.M., Home: Redo tough problems in lab section and write-ups, do extra practice problems on Canvas."

> "Sunday, 10/8, 3:00 P.M.–5:30 P.M., Library: Do timed practice exam, try to find other examples of questions that I got stuck on."

> "Monday, 10/9, 10:00 A.M.–11:30 A.M., Chemistry Gazebo: Attend office hours with the problems I had difficulty with."

As this example illustrates, the dates, times, study locations, resources, and their use are specific to the chemistry course and relevant to the timing of the students' upcoming exam. In short, designing the intervention involves integrating general principles of

TABLE 7.1. Summary of Key Components of the Strategic Resource Use Intervention

Components	Key self-reflective questions	Examples of answers that exemplify the psychological process
1. Clarify goals.	"What grade am I aiming for?"	"I am aiming for an A on this exam, which means a score of 90 or higher."
	"For the exam, what am I expected to know and do well?"	"I am expected to master the topics from Chapters 1 to 6."
	"How is the exam formatted and what kinds of questions will I expect on the exam?"	"I need to explain the processes of geological formations in open-ended essay questions."
2. Consider all available resources.	"*What* are all the resources that are available to me?"	• Textbook • Lecture notes • Teacher's office hours • Dictionary • Online search engine • Discussion forum • Peer study group • Homework problems • Practice exam questions
3. Identify and commit to resources that would make learning effective.	"*Which* resources should I use to master the content effectively?"	• Textbook • Homework problems • Practice exam questions • Discussion forum • Teacher's office hours • Peer study group
4. Explain the purpose for which each resource is used.	"*Why* would each resource be useful to my learning?"	"Trying the practice exam under timed conditions will give me practice on problems similar to the kind that I will encounter on my actual exam and also practice answering them within the 75-minute time limit. As I do the exam, I will look out for how I am expected to apply my knowledge, so that I know what content I should review later."
	"For what purpose do I intend to use each resource?"	"I will do the extra practice assignments, as well as the online practice problems, especially for topics that I find difficult. This will help me solidify my confidence to handle the kinds of problems that I find most challenging."
5. Plan concretely how to use the resources.	"*When, where,* and *how* will I use each resource?"	"This Wednesday between 4 P.M. and 6 P.M. in the library, I plan to finish reading Chapters 5 and 6 of my textbook. That same day after dinner between 8 P.M. and 10 P.M., I will then meet with my study group in the dorm study room to try practice exam questions for Chapters 5 and 6. We will try the questions independently and then discuss those that each of us got wrong."

strategic resource use with the concrete, class-specific application of these principles to make sure that the intervention is relevant.

Previous Mistakes in Implementation

Previously, we have shared the intervention materials with educators and researchers who were interested in trying it out in their own classes. From observing the way that some administer the intervention, I have noticed a few issues in the implementation of the intervention that can be avoided. These generally occurred in cases where people modified parts of the intervention without sufficiently anticipating how students might respond to the questions or without fully understanding the psychology behind the intervention. For example, one implementation required students to fill out the "why useful" open-ended question for each resource separately, rather than giving them the flexibility to group resources by function. This caused a few problems that the designer had not foreseen: first, it penalized students for choosing more rather than fewer resources, and second, by separating students' answers to each resource, it did not encourage students to consider how the resources would work together synergistically.

In another (suboptimal) implementation, the designer asked students to plan out when, where, and how they would study with each resource, but only offered them an interface where they were expected to respond to each resource separately (e.g., "For resource X that you selected, please indicate when, where, and how you will use this" and "For resource Y that you selected, please indicate when, where, and how you will use this."). This approach makes it difficult for students to plan how they might use various resources within the same study session. For example, as students study in a study group, they may read their textbook, refer to their notes, and discuss among themselves questions about the content that arise. When students plan their study time, they rarely ask themselves "When, where, and how should I use my textbook?," followed by "When, where, and how should I use my homework assignments?," and so on, which is how the ineffective implementation of the planning question forces students to plan. Instead, effective students often consider what they want to accomplish in a particular study session, then decide when and where that session might be and what resources they should use during that session. A third issue with this approach is that it penalizes students who select more resources to use. Some students who were faced with a long list of open-ended response boxes actually stopped responding after a few boxes.

By contrast, the strategic resource use intervention asks students to plan out how they would prepare for their upcoming exam, provides them with a model example, and offers them an open-ended box to freely describe their plans. This directs students to structure their plans like the model example, which includes when, where, and how to use various resources, and it also allows students the freedom to write as lengthy or as concise plans as they wish, without overwhelming them with a multitude of open-ended response boxes. If necessary, future iterations of the intervention could be even more explicit about asking students to include the when, where, and how components of planning.

These aforementioned problems—and many others—can be avoided by considering the psychology of the intervention and how it is meant to improve learning. Table 7.1 provides a schematic that summarizes the psychological process and the kinds of exemplary responses that we are trying to move students toward as they learn on their own. Having said this, some mistakes are inevitable during the trial-and-error process of designing and testing any new intervention. As we further develop the strategic resource use intervention and test it in new class contexts, we can expect to make some mistakes that we might not have foreseen; but importantly, we can all sensibly learn from such trial and error along the way.

Testing Scaling and Distribution

At the end of the day, interventions are designed and tested to be made available to educators and learners to benefit learning. Our goal is aligned with supporting learners' effective self-regulation of their own learning. Naturally, we are interested in understanding how and how effectively learners would make use of the intervention on their own if it is freely available to them and presented as an effective tool that they could use (rather than couched as a survey from researchers about their class experiences). We also want to know how students would make use of this intervention if it were sourced and authored centrally in the university, rather than represented as coming from their instructors—as this would be a practical way to scale this to many students at a school in the future. To this end, we have started actively testing how students make use of the intervention when it is freely available as an exam preparatory tool through an online platform that is widely distributed at a large, public university.

My research team has worked with designers and programmers to incorporate the strategic resource use intervention as an "Exam Playbook" in an ECoach platform at the University of Michigan (Huberth et al., 2015). Students who access the online platform have access to a range of educational tools, including the strategic resource use intervention, that they can freely choose to use (or not). ECoach is now available to students in multiple science, technology, engineering, and mathematics classes across the university, and it has over 10,000 student users to date. It includes personalized reminders to students that resources are available to them. For example, it might remind a student in a physics course that her midterm exam for the class is coming up in 2 weeks' time, and that she might want to check out the Exam Playbook to help her prepare for her exam. These timely messages function as reminders and encouragements to facilitate students' own decision making about their learning—they do not force students to use the online tools but present the tools as beneficial resources that students could tap into if they choose to. This research collaboration offers an excellent opportunity to monitor and evaluate how students are using the strategic resource use intervention out of their own initiative, when the intervention is released "in the wild" (so to speak).

Although we have yet to finish analyzing or to publish the data from these ongoing research efforts, I am keen to share some anecdotes from student users that we have collected so far. User experience design testers conducted focus groups at the end of the semester with students from various classes in which ECoach was made available. Feedback from the user experience testing team indicated that students seemed to find the Exam Playbook helpful to their learning: "The Exam Playbook was mentioned in nearly every interview as the students' most useful and memorable feature in ECoach"—for example, "[David[1]] really appreciated the reflection component of the Exam Playbook.

---

[1]The real identities of students have been replaced by fictitious identities in brackets, to protect their anonymity.

He said this was the first time he ever really took a step back and thought seriously about his study habits and why he's using particular resources." These preliminary feedback seem to suggest to us that students do make use of the Exam Playbook, and that they find it helpful. Such feedback has been encouraging to us, as we continue to seek teacher and school partners to further test, refine, and distribute the intervention.

IMPLICATIONS FOR PSYCHOLOGICAL THEORY

Goal Pursuit Occurs in the Context of Resources

The effectiveness of our strategic resource use intervention provides causal evidence that strategic resource regulation—an important yet understudied part of the metacognitive learning process—promotes achievement (Chen et al., 2017). Importantly, our findings underscore that goal pursuit does not take place in a vacuum. As people pursue their goals, they are often surrounded by resources that are either already available or that can be sought out with some initiative (e.g., forming study groups, looking for a coach). The more people are able to recognize the resources that are relevant to their goals, strategize which resources are useful to them, and commit to using these resources effectively, the more empowered people will be to achieve their goals. I hope that this research will springboard more work on the psychological process of resource regulation, which is evidently important in helping people pursue their goals effectively.

Strategy: The Neglected Attribution

Our research places the spotlight back on an attribution that has been well studied among learners in cognitive and educational psychology, but relatively neglected in social psychology: strategy. The takeaway here is not about the importance of raw intellect or sheer effort (e.g., how many hours a student studies or how many resources a student uses)—although these are certainly important. Instead, our findings focus on the importance of self-reflective and goal-directed resource use during learning. Regardless of how capable and effortful they may be, students may still not perform to their full potential if they do not approach their learning strategically. The good news is that guiding the average learner to become more strategic empowers them to learn more effectively and to perform at a level higher than what they otherwise might be able to achieve (Chen et al., 2017).

Complementing Growth Mindset Messages

Relatedly, nurturing students to be more strategic on their own could complement growth mindset messages. Growth mindset of intelligence interventions often teach learners that they can grow their intelligence through effort and effective strategies (Paunesku et al., 2015; Yeager et al., 2019). These interventions convey that students can continually develop themselves as learners over time, and offer suggestions about how they might do so. Similarly, the strategic resource use intervention represents learning as an evolving, controllable process: It prompts students to generate their own strategies for learning, to monitor their strategy use, and to change strategies when unproductive, empowering them to take control of and manage their learning. Given these complementary self-regulatory processes, one might imagine that students might benefit all the more from marrying a growth mindset message with guided prompts that encourage them to generate their own ways of investing effort strategically.

The Student's Perspective

To date, education research has made giant strides in enhancing curriculum and pedagogy, especially from the perspective of the teacher or administrator (e.g., "How can we teach better?"; Hattie, 2009). However, quite a significant portion of work on the psychology of the student focuses on individual differences (e.g., personality, intelligence, conscientiousness, working memory capacity), prior educational background, and demographic differences (Hattie, 2009). While these are valuable research directions, have we been neglecting what learning means and how learning occurs from the perspective of the student?

As students learn, develop, and encounter challenges as they grow, many of them inevitably ask themselves questions such as, "Does this matter?" (e.g., Hulleman & Harackiewicz, 2009; Yeager et al., 2014), "Am I dumb?" (e.g., Molden & Dweck, 2006; Paunesku et al., 2015), and "Do I belong here?" (e.g., Walton & Cohen, 2011). Social-psychological interventions address how frequently students are asking these questions, and just as important, how they are answering them (Walton, 2014; Walton & Wilson, 2018). However, when it comes to managing their own learning, many students are not asking themselves self-reflective questions about their learning enough—for example, "How will I learn this subject?" (e.g., Zimmerman, 2002), "How should I plan my study time?" (Gollwitzer, 1999), and "How will I study effectively for this upcoming exam?" (Chen et al., 2017). The strategic resource use intervention aims to encourage more of such self-reflection in students, and to scaffold their answers to important questions like these.

FUTURE DIRECTIONS

Although we know that the strategic resource use intervention was effective for many learners in one class context, there is still much to do to better understand the generalizability of its effects to different kinds of students and other learning contexts. For now, we cannot yet conclude how well the effects of the intervention generalize to other types of students (e.g., students of different ages, education levels, or cognitive abilities), subjects (e.g., an English literature class vs. a statistics class), class structures (e.g., multiple smaller tests rather than a few big exams, curved grading systems vs. noncurved grading systems), exam formats (e.g., multiple-choice tests vs. open-ended essay questions), or teaching styles (e.g., teaching students to study in a tightly structured manner vs. giving students more autonomy over their own learning). Research in these areas will be valuable for building a better understanding of the possible heterogeneity of the intervention effects and its boundary conditions. Importantly, we will also learn how to tailor the current intervention design to better cater to different students and learning contexts.

Another exciting question for this area of research is: How can we adapt the intervention to facilitate transfer of these self-regulatory principles? With the current class-specific design, we might not expect students to naturally generalize this metacognitive process on their own to other learning contexts. The challenge is to teach resource regulation in a way that concretely relates to students' learning in their classes, but that at that same time comes across as applicable to their learning more broadly. The good news is that we have started thinking about ways to adapt the current intervention design to promote transfer. As aforementioned, we are trying out methods such as asking students to apply the same strategic planning process to another challenging class of theirs, asking students to teach strategic resource use in a way that is applicable to another student who is learning a different skill (e.g., music or sports), and instilling a mindset that orients people toward being metacognitive more generally (Chen et al., 2020). This question about transfer is important to pin down if we want to make scientifically informed judgments about the dosage and design of the intervention to foster extensive, long-lasting benefits for learners.

Another future direction is to lower the barriers for teachers to customize the intervention for their students. At present, customization involves a close partnership between the researchers and instructors to produce a comprehensive resource checklist, to identify how students are typically reminded to study for their exams in the class, and to edit the model examples if they are not as relevant. The time and effort involved in this collaboration might be a barrier to some teachers offering the intervention to their students. If we can find ways to lower these barriers—such as by making the model examples more generalizable, offering teachers a tool that allows them to easily self-customize the intervention and distribute it to their classes, or creating a general version of the intervention that is not specific to a subject or class—we might be able to make this more accessible to teachers and students.

In our studies, we found that the intervention did not only boost self-reflection but it also decreased students' negative affect toward their upcoming exams, and increased their perceived control over their exam grades. Might there be other effects of the intervention that we have not measured or considered? It would be fruitful for future studies to examine how the intervention might affect students' classroom behaviors (Are they engaging with their homework assignments, laboratory exercises, and class discussion forums differently?), their motivation to learn (Are they more inclined toward a mastery orientation in their learning?), their growth mindset (Does the intervention change their fundamental beliefs about intelligence?), and their interactions with their peers and teachers (Are they seeking help from others in a more effective manner?). These and other factors are theoretically plausible, but unexplored, mechanisms of the intervention that could contribute to students' learning and academic performance across class contexts and in an enduring manner.

CONCLUDING THOUGHTS

The fact that so much is being done by so many—including teachers, parents, schools, governments—across the world is testimony to how much we all value learning. We cannot afford to waste all these efforts to improve students' learning on mindless, ineffective resource use. My hope is that, with more research and interventions like the strategic resource use intervention, our psychological science will keep finding new and better ways to help our learners use their resources wisely and effectively to learn.

REFERENCES

Aronson, J., Fried, C. B., & Good, C. (2002). Reducing the effects of stereotype threat on African American college students by shaping theories of intelligence. *Journal of Experimental Social Psychology, 38,* 113–125.

Ashcraft, M. H. (2002). Math anxiety: Personal, educational, and cognitive consequences. *Current Directions in Psychological Science, 11,* 181–185.

Ashcraft, M. H., & Kirk, E. P. (2001). The relationships among working memory, math anxiety, and performance. *Journal of Experimental Psychology: General, 130,* 224–237.

Bembenutty, H. (2011). *Self-regulated learning.* Danvers, MA: Wiley Periodicals.

Bergin, S., Reilly, R., & Traynor, D. (2005). Examining the role of self-regulated learning on introductory programming performance. In *Proceedings of the first international workshop on computing education research* (pp. 81–86). New York: Association of Computing Machinery.

Blackwell, L. A., Trzesniewski, K. H., & Dweck, C. S. (2007). Theories of intelligence and achievement across the junior high school transition: A longitudinal study and an intervention. *Child Development, 78,* 246–263.

Chen, P., Chavez, O., Ong, D. C., & Gunderson, B. (2017). Strategic resource use for learning: A self-administered intervention that guides self-reflection on effective resource use enhances academic performance. *Psychological Science, 28,* 774–785.

Chen, P., Ong, D. C., & Coppola, B. C. (2019). *Explore, exploit, and prune in the classroom: Modeling the decision processes behind learners' resource regulation.* Manuscript under review.

Chen, P., Powers, J. T., Katragadda, K. R., Cohen, G. L., & Dweck, C. S. (2020). A strategic mindset: An orientation toward strategic behavior during goal pursuit. *Proceedings of the National Academy of Sciences of the USA, 117,* 14066–14072.

Cheng, K. M., Chen, P., Schwartz-Poehlmann, J., Pfalzgraff, W., Ren, F., Katragadda, K. R., . . . Schwartz, D. L. (2019). *Getting a GRIP on resource regulation: Tailoring and testing the strategic resource-use intervention in college chemistry classes.* Manuscript in preparation.

Cohen, G. L., Garcia, J., Apfel, N., & Master, A. (2006). Reducing the racial achievement gap: A social-psychological intervention. *Science, 313,* 1307–1310.

Collins, A., Brown, J. S., & Holum, A. (1991). Cognitive apprenticeship: Making thinking visible. *American Educator, 15,* 6–11.

Duckworth, A. L., Grant, H., Loew, B., Oettingen, G., & Gollwitzer, P. M. (2011). Self-regulation strategies improve self-discipline in adolescents: Benefits of mental contrasting and implementation intentions. *Educational Psychology, 31,* 17–26.

Duckworth, A. L., Kirby, T., Gollwitzer, A., & Oettingen, G. (2013). From fantasy to action: Mental contrasting with implementation intentions (MCII) improves academic performance in children. *Social Psychological and Personality Science, 4,* 745–753.

Dunlosky, J., & Bjork, R. A. (2008). *Handbook of metamemory and memory.* New York: Psychology Press Taylor & Francis Group.

Dunlosky, J., & Metcalfe, J. (2009). *Metacognition.* Thousand Oaks, CA: SAGE.

Fleming, S. M., & Frith, C. D. (2014). *The cognitive neuroscience of metacognition.* Berlin: Springer.

Gollwitzer, P. M. (1999). Implementation intentions: Strong effects of simple plans. *American Psychologist, 54,* 493–503.

Gollwitzer, P. M., & Brandstätter, V. (1997). Implementation intentions and effective goal pursuit. *Journal of Personality and Social Psychology, 73,* 186–199.

Hattie, J. (2009). *Visible learning: A synthesis of over 800 meta-analyses relating to achievement.* New York: Routledge.

Huberth, M., Chen, P., Tritz, J., & McKay, T. A. (2015). E2Coach: Computer-tailored student support in introductory physics. *PLOS ONE, 10,* e0137001.

Hulleman, C. S., & Harackiewicz, J. M. (2009). Promoting interest and performance in high school science classes. *Science, 326,* 1410–1412.

Janis, I. L., & King, B. T. (1954). The influence of role playing on opinion change. *Journal of Abnormal and Social Psychology, 49*(2), 211–218.

Karabenick, S. A. (2003). Seeking help in large college classes: A person-centered approach. *Contemporary Educational Psychology, 28,* 37–58.

Kipling, R. (1902). *The elephant's child.* London: Macmillan.

Leventhal, H., Singer, R., & Jones, S. (1965). Effects of fear and specificity of recommendation upon attitudes and behavior. *Journal of Personality and Social Psychology, 2,* 20–29.

Molden, D. C., & Dweck, C. S. (2006). Finding "meaning" in psychology: A lay theories approach to self-regulation, social perception, and social development. *American Psychologist, 61*(3), 192–203.

Oettingen, G., & Gollwitzer, P. (2010). Strategies of setting and implementing goals: Mental contrasting and implementation intentions. In J. E. Maddux & J. P. Tangney (Eds.), *Social psychological foundations of clinical psychology* (pp. 114–135). New York: Guilford Press.

Organisation for Economic Co-operation and Development. (2018). Education spending. Retrieved March 16, 2018, from *https://data.oecd.org/eduresource/education-spending.htm#indicator-chart.*

Paunesku, D., Walton, G. M., Romero, C., Smith, E. N., Yeager, D. S., & Dweck, C. S. (2015). Mind-set interventions are a scalable treatment for academic underachievement. *Psychological Science, 26,* 784–793.

Pintrich, P. R. (2002). The role of metacognitive knowledge in learning, teaching, and assessing. *Theory into Practice, 41,* 219–225.

Pintrich, P. R., & De Groot, E. V. (1990). Motivational and self-regulated learning components of classroom academic performance. *Journal of Educational Psychology, 82,* 33–40.

Pintrich, P. R., & Garcia, T. (1994). Self-regulated learning in college stdents: Knowledge, strategies, and motivation. In P. Pintrich, D. Brown, & C. Weinstein (Eds.), *Student motivation, cognition, and learning* (pp. 113–133). Hillsdale, NJ: Erlbaum.

Pintrich, P. R., Smith, D. A. F., Garcia, T., & McKeachie, W. J. (1991). A manual for the use of the Motivated Strategies for Learning Questionnaire (MSLQ). Retrieved from *http://eric.ed.gov/?id=ED338122.*

Pintrich, P. R., Smith, D. A. F., Garcia, T., & McKeachie, W. J. (1993). Reliability and predictive validity of the Motivated Strategies for Learning Questionnaire (MSLQ). *Educational and Psychological Measurement, 53,* 801–813.

Plant, E. A., Ericsson, K. A., Hill, L., & Asberg, K. (2005). Why study time does not predict grade point average across college students: Implications of deliberate practice for academic performance. *Contemporary Educational Psychology, 30,* 96–116.

Ross, L., & Nisbett, R. E. (2011). *The person and the situation: Perspectives of social psychology.* London: Pinter & Martin.

Schuman, H., Walsh, E., Olson, C., & Etheridge, B. (1985). Effort and reward: The assumption that college grades are affected by quantity of study. *Social Forces, 63,* 945–966.

Schunk, D. H. (1981). Modeling and attribution effects on children's development: A self-efficacy analysis. *Journal of Educational Psychology, 75,* 93–105.

Skinner, E. A., Wellborn, J. G., & Connell, J. P. (1990). What it takes to do well in school and whether I've got it: A process model of perceived control and children's engagement and achievement in school. *Journal of Educational Psychology, 82,* 22–32.

Valle, A., Núñez, J. C., Cabanach, R. G., González-Pienda, J. A., Rodríguez, S., Rosário, P., . . . Múnoz-Cadavid, M. A. (2008). Self-regulated profiles and academic achievement. *Psicothema, 20*(4), 724–731.

Walton, G. M. (2014). The new science of wise psychological interventions. *Current Directions in Psychological Science, 23,* 73–82.

Walton, G. M., & Cohen, G. L. (2011). A brief social-belonging intervention improves academic and health outcomes of minority students. *Science, 331,* 1447–1451.

Walton, G. M., & Wilson, T. D. (2018). Wise interventions: Psychological remedies for social and personal problems. *Psychological Review, 125,* 617–655.

Wilson, T. D. (1990). Self-persuasion via self-reflection. In J. M. Olson & M. P. Zanna (Eds.), *Self-inference processes: The Ontario symposium* (Vol. 6, pp. 43–68). Hillsdale, NJ: Erlbaum.

Wingate, U. (2006). Doing away with "study skills." *Teaching in Higher Education, 11,* 457–469.

World Bank Group. (2018). Government expenditure on education, total (% of GDP). Retrieved March 16, 2018, from *https://data.worldbank.org/indicator/SE.XPD.TOTL.GD.ZS.*

Yeager, D. S., Hanselman, P., Walton, G. M., Crosnoe, R., Muller, C., Tipton, E., . . . Dweck, C. S. (2019). A national experiment reveals where a growth mindset improves achievement. *Nature: Human Behavior, 573,* 364–369.

Yeager, D. S., Henderson, M. D., Paunesku, D., Walton, G. M., D'Mello, S., Spitzer, B. J., & Duckworth, A. L. (2014). Boring but important: A self-transcendent purpose for learning fosters academic self-regulation. *Journal of Personality and Social Psychology, 107,* 559–580.

Zimmerman, B. J. (1989). A social cognitive view of self-regulated academic learning *Journal of Educational Psychology, 81*(3), 329–339.

Zimmerman, B. J. (2002). Becoming a self-regulated learner: An overview. *Theory into Practice, 41,* 64–70.

Zimmerman, B. J. (2011). Motivational sources and outcomes of self-regulated learning and performance. In B. J. Zimmerman & D. H. Schunk (Eds.), *Handbook of self-regulation of learning and performance* (pp. 49–64). New York: Routledge.

Zimmerman, B. J., & Martinez-Pons, M. (1988). Construct validation of a strategy model of student self-regulated learning. *Journal of Educational Psychology, 80,* 284–290.

PART II

HEALTH AND WELL-BEING

CHAPTER 8

Happiness Interventions

Kristin Layous

The content of happiness interventions ranges widely (e.g., expressing gratitude, performing kind acts, focusing on one's strengths), but all variations seek to address the same underlying potential—that people can increase their own happiness. Across dozens of experiments, happiness interventions have successfully boosted well-being, often via changes in how people perceive themselves, their situations, and their relationships. Here I review empirical evidence demonstrating the efficacy of happiness interventions, the conditions that make happiness interventions more or less effective (e.g., person-activity fit), the instructions for particular happiness interventions, and some of the nuances and misconceptions surrounding their implementation. In addition, I discuss the process by which happiness interventions may affect long-term changes in happiness and other outcomes, as well as the potential for happiness interventions to contribute to broader psychological theory.

Happiness interventions are brief, often self-guided, reflective or behavioral activities designed to boost people's happiness (i.e., their overriding sense of emotional and cognitive well-being) by prompting them to mimic the thoughts and behaviors of naturally happy people. Researchers often use the terms *positive psychology interventions* (PPIs) or *positive activity interventions* (PAIs), with the former being an umbrella term that includes happiness interventions performed in the context of group- and individual-level therapy, as well as self-guided formats, and the latter being a term specific to the self-guided format. By self-guided, I mean that a person receives activity instructions (maybe from a researcher, website, app, or book) and then engages in the activity without therapeutic supervision. Lyubomirsky and Layous (2013) also use the term *positive activities* instead of *positive activity interventions* to refer to the naturalistic practice of happiness-promoting activities outside the context of an experiment.

BACKGROUND

Across the globe, people report happiness as an important goal for themselves (Diener, 2000) and their children (Diener & Lucas, 2004). Extensive research demonstrates that happiness is not only a pleasant emotional and cognitive experience, but is also predictive of and causally related to positive outcomes in relationships, career, and physical health (Lyubomirsky, King, & Diener, 2005). Thus, happiness aids success in important life domains, which likely feeds back into one's happiness in a virtuous recursive cycle.

Therapists have been attempting to relieve patients' psychological suffering by modifying maladaptive thoughts and behaviors since the late 1800s (see Smith & Glass, 1977, for the efficacy of therapy), but a direct focus on increasing happiness, rather than simply alleviating distress, is relatively new (Seligman & Csiksentmihalyi, 2000; but see Fordyce, 1977, 1983). Critics of happiness pursuit warned that "trying to be happier is as futile as trying to be taller" (Lykken & Tellegen, 1996, p. 189), but, in their seminal work, Lyubomirsky, Sheldon, and Schkade (2005) refuted this and other sources of pessimism regarding happiness pursuit. They argued that, despite relatively stable influences on happiness like genetics and life circumstances (estimated to explain about 50 and 10% of individual differences in happiness, respectively), a large proportion of happiness is left unexplained by these factors and is likely subject to change by altering how one behaves and how one perceives him- or herself and his or her social world. Indeed, during the last two decades, research on happiness interventions has burgeoned, demonstrating that increasing happiness is possible, even with brief and cost-effective strategies (Bolier et al., 2013; Sin & Lyubomirsky, 2009).

To explore ways to promote happiness, Lyubomirsky, Sheldon, et al. (2005) analyzed the thought patterns and behaviors of naturally happy people (see also Fordyce, 1977, 1983). For example, past research has demonstrated that happy people think gratefully, perform kind acts, and strive for personally meaningful goals, so Lyubomirsky, Sheldon, et al. (2005) reasoned that prompting people to engage in these types of thoughts or behaviors might boost their well-being. They demonstrated that instructing people to think gratefully or perform kind acts increased happiness relative to a control group (see also Emmons & McCullough, 2003; Seligman, Steen, Park, & Peterson, 2005, for concurrent happiness intervention studies). These findings provided proof of their concept that engaging in certain types of thoughts and behaviors—which can be under one's control—boosts happiness.

Thus, initial happiness interventions were empirically, not theoretically, driven—researchers explored whether the correlates of happiness could be packaged and administered to cause increases in happiness. That said, Walton and Wilson (2018) offer a helpful theoretical framework to understand why these happiness interventions work. They propose that "wise interventions" are psychologically wise to the way people see themselves, other people, or a particular situation, and use precise theory- and research-informed strategies to alter these meanings. They reason that almost every situation is open to some type of interpretation and it is the inferences that people draw that most proximally drives behavior. Thus, if meanings can be changed, so can behaviors and, ultimately, changes in objective life circumstances may follow.

Happiness interventions can readily be interpreted through this wise intervention framework. First, happiness interventions are wise to the particular thoughts and behaviors that promote happiness. Second, via structured reflection exercises or the enactment of new behaviors, happiness interventions help people make meaning of themselves and their social world in ways that promote happiness. Third, although the initial change within a person is subjective (i.e., they view themselves, their relationships, or their circumstances more positively), this altered state may lead to changes in behavior that builds on itself in a self-enhancing recursive cycle.

In contrast with other wise interventions in this volume, happiness interventions are quite varied in content, focusing on different behaviors or thought processes entirely (e.g., gratitude, kindness, optimism). Nevertheless, all happiness interventions seek to address the same underlying potential—that people can increase their own happiness. In this chapter, I highlight some unifying threads among happiness interventions, as well as specific information about two types of interventions with strong empirical support: those that focus on gratitude and kindness.

PSYCHOLOGICAL PROCESSES

Walton and Wilson (2018) argue that, in order to alter potentially problematic ways of viewing the self and the social world, researchers need to consider three basic motives that underlie people's meaning-making processes: the need to understand oneself and one's surroundings (including their social relationships), the need for self-integrity, and the need to belong. Promoting psychological need satisfaction may be particularly important in the context of happiness interventions because psychological need fulfillment relates directly to happiness, which is the primary desired outcome of happiness interventions (Ryan & Deci, 2000).

The Need to Understand

People have a fundamental need to make sense of themselves and others and they do their best to make inferences that match their own experiences and the information available to them (Walton & Wilson, 2018). For example, if parents, mentors, or friends tell a child that happiness is determined at birth, the child may hold the perception that happiness is fixed—there is no use trying to live a happier life. In this instance, trusted sources have informed the child how to understand happiness and this belief may hold long after the child remembers how the belief was initially instilled. Thus, a happiness intervention that conveys the knowledge that happiness is malleable, rather than fixed, could drastically change a person's meaning-making process around happiness. Indeed, those who hold a growth mindset toward happiness (a belief that happiness can grow through effort) are happier than those who hold a more fixed perspective (Van Tongeren & Burnette, 2018). In a causal test of the effect of growth mindset on happiness, participants randomly assigned to receive information about the malleability (vs. the stability) of happiness reported higher growth mindsets toward happiness, which in turn related to greater happiness (Van Tongeren & Burnette, 2018). Thus, altering the understanding of happiness as malleable rather than fixed promotes greater happiness.

In addition, due at least partially to individual differences in inborn personality traits (Larsen & Ketelaar, 1991) or learned tendencies from parents who model emotion regulation (Eisenberg, Cumberland, & Spinrad, 1998), people are predisposed to view the world and respond to it in ways that either promote or detract from their happiness (Lyubomirsky, 2001). As noted by Walton and Wilson (2018), almost every situation is open for interpretation and some people interpret the situation in a way that promotes their happiness, whereas others do not. Happiness interventions redirect people's attention to the positive in their lives and help them view themselves and their social world in happiness-promoting ways. Thus, even if people are predisposed to view situations in a way that undermines their happiness, happiness interventions can alter these thought processes and behaviors.

For example, happiness interventions focused on gratitude, such as listing what one is grateful for (in a journal-type framework; Emmons & McCullough, 2003) or writing a letter of gratitude to someone who has done something for you (e.g., Lyubomirsky, Dickerhoof, Boehm, & Sheldon, 2011), amplify people's recognition and appreciation of the good things they already have, helping them construe their lives as more positive than they did before.

Emmons and McCullough (2003) provided the following examples from people's gratitude lists: "waking up this morning," "the generosity of friends," "for wonderful parents," "to the Lord for just another day," and "to the Rolling Stones." None of these blessings were new positive events happening to participants, but the gratitude activity helped them actively appreciate aspects of their lives they likely take for granted on most days. Although this initial change in perception is subjective, over time, this shift in perspective may help people take action that leads to more enduring changes in their objective circumstances (more on this in the "Effects over Time" section).

Similarly, when writing a gratitude letter, people actively appreciate the influential relationships they already have (or have had in the past). Common themes include close others giving letter writers unconditional love or social support in times of adversity, as well as believing wholeheartedly in their ability to succeed. These letters also often reveal a drive to work hard to prove that their benefactor's efforts were not wasted, which may point to ways in which gratitude can affect future behavior. Below are two excerpts from letters that were representative of many written by college students (unpublished excerpts from the Layous, Lee, Choi, and Lyubomirsky [2013] study).

Dear [High School Teacher],

If it wasn't for your [English] class in high school, I probably wouldn't be the person I am today. I feel that after I took your class I grew up so much more. I became a better person in regards to forming my own opinions about life. You were a strict teacher, you pushed us to our limits, but never did you ever tell us we couldn't handle it. I know that you pushed us to our limits because you had so much confidence in us. You had so much belief in us as individuals and that you pushed us because you wanted us to know that we are capable of becoming the best that [our school] had to offer. . . . Thank you for believing in my capabilities. Thank you for pushing me to my limits. Thank you for making me believe in myself. Thank you for teaching me to like myself for who I am. Thank you for changing my life for the better.

Sincerely,
Student

Brother,

I wanted to write to you to let you know how grateful I am for everything you have done for me. You are an amazing brother and mentor, someone who I look up to. I hope one day I can come close to achieving the goals you have hoped I accomplish. You did not have to be there for me like you were when we were younger. With mom and dad always being gone, you raised me and [our other brother], something that would not be easy for anyone to do, you only being 9 years old when I was born. I will never forget the nights you stayed home to help me with my homework instead of being a typical teenager who enjoyed the life with friends, parties, and living carefree. . . . Every day I go to school knowing I have to work hard, and then work harder, not to let you down. You have never placed worry or pressure on me to succeed in life, but I know deep down, that that is all you want. I look at you not only as a brother, but as a role model, a father figure, and one of my best friends. I refuse to mess up my life, and make unforgettable mistakes, knowing you sacrificed so much just for me to be able to do so. I am forever in debt to you, in the most loving way possible. I want to do well in school, personal relationships, work and in life, so I can make myself proud, and you proud. I don't think I have ever written out on paper just what exactly you have done for me, or how thankful deep down I really am. So thank you [brother], thank you so much. If it weren't for you, I honestly don't know what I would be doing. I promise I won't let you down, [we're] so close to accomplishing our life dreams.

I love you . . . [you're] an amazing brother and you will be an amazing father one day.

Your sister

One study clearly illustrated the ability of happiness interventions to change people's construal of their life events. Participants were randomly assigned to one of two happiness interventions or a control condition (Dickerhoof, 2007). In all three conditions, people were asked to write down personally satisfying experiences from the week (e.g., "I went on a job interview, and I got the job on the spot!") and then participants and independent coders rated how satisfying the experiences were. Participants in the happiness intervention conditions reported that their experiences were becoming marginally more satisfying over time compared to participants in the control group. Alternatively, independent coders actually rated participant experiences as becoming less satisfying over time, indicating that participant perceptions of increased satisfaction were not objective—they were due to improved construal of these situations. This perception of satisfaction mediated the relationship between condition and well-being, indicating that an important way in which happiness interventions boost well-being is by improving people's perception of the events in their lives. Importantly, this altered view of one's experiences is likely to lead to altered behavior—perhaps trying new activities or taking on new challenges—that feeds back into one's happiness is a recursive cycle. The altered understanding of one's life is just the first step to changing cycles of unhappiness.

Need for Self-Integrity

People also have the need to view themselves as capable, competent agents in the world—morally and adaptively adequate (Bandura, 1997; Cohen & Sherman, 2014). The gratitude letter examples demonstrate that people often write to close others who have believed in them. Although the gratitude letter prompt does not explicitly ask participants to write about others who have made them feel worthy, implicit in the activity is writing to someone who has invested in the letter writer, thus demonstrating the target's view of the letter writer as worthy.

Whereas gratitude interventions prompt reflection as a first step, kindness interventions first prompt a behavior and then leave it up to the participants to reflect upon the meaning of that behavior. One way in which performing acts of kindness boosts happiness is likely by fostering a sense of accomplishment in the performer (e.g., he or she feels like a good person). For example, across three experiments, participants prompted to help others increased in positive self-evaluations relative to those who did not help (Williamson & Clark, 1989). The self-evaluations included a variety of personal characteristics that may make up one's sense of self as morally and adaptively adequate (e.g., successful, helpful, trustworthy, considerate, useful, and kind). In one specific type of kindness intervention, participants were randomly assigned to "make someone else happy" throughout the week for 4 weeks (excerpts from Layous, Kurtz, Margolis, Chancellor, and Lyubomirsky [2018] included below). A consistent theme across these entries was the person performing kind acts feeling proud of him- or herself for investing in others.

> "I chose to make my boyfriend happier last week. I made him dinner and tried to be nicer to him and not be so critical of him. I chose this person because he's the person I spend most of my free time with. I knew treating him nicely would make him happy because a lot of times when I'm stressed I take it out on him. He was much more appreciative toward me. I was very proud of myself that I could make him as happy as I did."

> "This week I chose one of my friends and housemates. During the week we don't have much time to hang out, so this weekend I made sure we did. We went out together Friday night and had a movie night the next night. I chose [friend] because we've been friends for a long time, and I knew she was someone I really cared about. I knew just spending time with her would make her happy. She was excited when she realized I wanted to spend so much time with her. I felt proud of myself that I took time away from doing things only for myself. I think I was successful in making her happy."

Need to Belong

People also have the fundamental need to belong—to feel close and connected with others (Baumeister & Leary, 1995; Ryan & Deci, 2000). Importantly, people's relationships with others are also open for interpretation with people pondering questions such as "Does my significant other truly love me?" or "Does this social group really care if I'm here?" (Walton & Wilson, 2018).

Both gratitude and kindness interventions highlight positive relationships in one's life. Gratitude journaling is a private activity, but people often bring to mind their valued social relationships. Similarly, although gratitude letters often go undelivered in experiments to isolate the effect of simply writing the letter, the activity brings to mind important others in one's life and highlights the investment of others in the letter writer's life. Whereas gratitude activities typically simply bring to mind positive social relationships (but see Walsh & Lyubomirsky, 2018, for the additional benefit of delivering the gratitude letter), kindness interventions prompt people to behave in positive ways toward others: strangers, acquaintances, or close others. Not surprisingly, both gratitude interventions and kindness interventions boost people's sense of connectedness to others (e.g., Kerr, O'Donovan, & Pepping, 2015). Research suggests that even interactions with strangers, like your coffee shop barista, promote belonging and happiness (Sandstrom & Dunn, 2014), and investing in close relationships provides even more of a boost in happiness than investing in acquaintances (Aknin, Sandstrom, Dunn, & Norton, 2011), perhaps because of the potential to trigger a positive feedback loop in your close relationships.

Importantly, performing kind acts and expressing gratitude may work in tandem to promote positivity in one's relationships. In the above excerpt, the person who invested time into making her boyfriend happier noted how appreciative he was of her efforts. Past theory and research has demonstrated that those who feel grateful toward their partner are more likely to engage in behaviors that strengthen the relationship (e.g., spending quality time with one's partner; Algoe, 2012). Thus, the initial kind act from Partner *A* may trigger gratitude in Partner *B*, which stimulates Partner *B* to invest further in the relationship, triggering an upward spiral of gratitude, positive relationship behaviors, and relationship satisfaction in Partner *A* and Partner *B* (Algoe, 2012). Although a great deal of gratitude research has taken place in the context of romantic relationships, research has also demonstrated the positive effects of gratitude in close friendships (e.g., Lambert & Fincham, 2011), indicating that gratitude has a role across relationship type, promoting fulfilling relationships (Algoe, 2012). Given people's inherent need to feel close to others, it is no surprise that activities that promote positive relationships also contribute to happiness.

EMPIRICAL EVIDENCE

Outcomes

The primary outcomes of happiness interventions are subjective well-being and depression. In the tradition of Diener (1984), subjective well-being includes three primary components: positive affect, negative affect, and life satisfaction—sometimes reported separately and sometimes reported as part of a composite with negative affect reverse-scored (Busseri & Sadava, 2011). In the literature, subjective well-being and "happiness" are used interchangeably, and *subjective well-being* is often used as an umbrella term that subsumes measures that ask participants directly about their happiness (e.g., Lyubomirsky & Lepper, 1999). Sometimes researchers also measure participants' eudaimonic well-being—their sense of purpose and meaning in life—but research suggests that subjective and eudaimonic well-being have so much overlap that differences between the two are more conceptual than empirical (e.g., Disabato, Goodman, Kashdan, Short, & Jarden, 2016). Thus, for simplicity, I focus mainly on the subjective well-being and depression results.

Two meta-analyses have investigated the efficacy of happiness interventions. The first included 51 studies and found that the effect of PPIs is moderate on subjective well-being and depression (Sin & Lyubomirsky, 2009). With stricter inclusion criteria (e.g., only peer-reviewed publications, only studies with randomization to condition), the second meta-analysis included 39 studies and found that the effect of PPIs is small but significant on subjective well-being and depression at postintervention, with the small effects on subjective well-being persisting 3–6 months later (Bolier et al., 2013).

Recent papers also explored the effects of gratitude and kindness interventions specifically. A meta-analysis of gratitude interventions included 38 studies with 282 effect sizes from various outcome variables and comparison conditions (Dickens, 2017; see also Davis et al., 2016). Compared to a neutral control condition, people who engaged in a gratitude intervention reported higher quality of relationships, grateful mood and disposition, life satisfaction, positive affect, happiness, well-being, and optimism, and lower depression at postintervention, with all effect sizes being small to moderate. The differences between the gratitude and control conditions remained at follow-up for well-being, happiness, positive affect, and depression, with the follow-up period varying from 2 weeks to 6 months. A meta-analysis of kindness interventions included 27 studies with 52 effect sizes comparing the effect of performing kind acts versus various controls. Collapsing across comparison condition types and various indicators of subjective well-being, the effect of kindness interventions on the well-being of the actor was small to medium (Curry et al., 2018).

In addition to boosting subjective well-being, happiness interventions also have positive effects on relationships, work, and physical health either directly or via increases in happiness. As mentioned before, happiness interventions promote feelings of connection with others (Dickens, 2017; Kerr et al., 2015) and may trigger positive feedback loops within one's relationships (Algoe, 2012). People induced into a positive mood are also better workers in a variety of ways—they set higher goals, persevere at challenging tasks longer, complete a greater amount of work with no decline in quality, and come up with more mutually beneficial solutions in negotiations (Walsh, Boehm, & Lyubomirsky, 2018). In addition, happiness is related to physical health (Pressman, Jenkins, & Moskowitz, 2019), and people who engage in happiness interventions have reported fewer symptoms of physical illness (Burton & King, 2008; Emmons & McCullough, 2003, Study 1), and even fewer visits to the doctor (Burton & King, 2004; King, 2001) than comparison groups.

Research on happiness interventions suggests potential pathways by which happiness may affect physical health. Specifically, participants who engage in happiness interventions (vs. various comparison conditions) have reported greater sleep duration (Emmons & McCullough, 2003, Study 3) and sleep quality (Jackowska, Brown, Ronaldson, & Steptoe, 2016), decreased diastolic blood pressure (Jackowska et al., 2016) and inflammation (Redwine et al., 2016), and healthier eating (Fritz, Armenta, Walsh, & Lyubomirsky, 2019). Thus, happiness interventions may improve physical health by increasing the healthy cardiovascular profile associated with positive emotions (Boehm & Kubzansky, 2012) and by promoting healthier behaviors (e.g., better eating and sleep habits).

Mechanisms

To understand how happiness interventions can affect long-term changes in well-being, we must first explore the feelings, thoughts, and behaviors of people directly following their engagement in a happiness intervention. In the "Psychological Processes" section of this chapter, I focus on the potential for happiness interventions to change the way people construe themselves, their relationships, and their circumstances in general, which likely feed back into greater happiness over time in a recursive process. Here I focus on some evidence of these proximal changes in the way people understand their current circumstances and relationships (need to understand), feel about themselves (need for self-efficacy), and feel connected to others (need for belonging).

Immediately following a gratitude expression activity, participants felt more grateful (Lambert, Fincham, & Stillman, 2012; Layous et al., 2017), more positive overall (Layous et al., 2017; Watkins, Woodward, Stone, & Kolts, 2003), more connected to others (Layous et al., 2017), and more emotionally and cognitively engaged at school (King & Datu, 2018) than comparison groups. Directly after performing an act of kindness, participants felt more positive overall and evaluated themselves more positively on a variety of personal characteristics (e.g., successful, trustworthy) than participants who did not perform an act of kindness (Williamson & Clark, 1989). Importantly, participants reported these feelings directly after the activity—there had been no time for objective life circumstances to change. This means that participants' construal of themselves, their relationships, and their circumstances had changed to view their life in a more positive light. These immediate shifts in construal, positivity, and psychological need satisfaction likely drive longer-term changes in well-being (Fredrickson, 2013; Layous & Lyubomirsky, 2014; Lyubomirsky & Layous, 2013).

Another possibility ripe for future exploration is that happiness interventions drive immediate changes in behavior (i.e., not just construal), which then feed back into happiness. For example, people induced into a grateful state are more likely to perform acts of kindness (Bartlett & DeSteno, 2006), a behavior that also leads to higher happiness (see Miller, Dannals, & Zlatev, 2017). More research needs to explore the proximal changes in feelings, thoughts, and behaviors that promote happiness change well after the initial intervention.

Effects over Time

Theoretically, happiness interventions may affect long-term well-being and related outcomes (e.g., relationship closeness, workplace success, and physical health) via two non-mutually exclusive pathways: recursive processes and continued practice. Regarding recursive processes, the broaden-and-build theory of positive emotions states that positive emotions broaden people's attention and prompt engagement in approach-oriented behaviors (e.g., playing, exploring, learning, engaging with new activities or people; Fredrickson, 2013). Although the boost in positive emotions is temporary, this broadened, exploratory state allows people to take actions that may lead to durable changes in well-being. For example, if a woman engages in a happiness intervention and feels more positive as a result, she may feel energized to attend a gym class. While at this gym class, she may meet someone with common interests who becomes a friend and an enduring source of social support. Thus, the initial positive state promoted actions that created an objective and stable happiness-promoting change—a new friend (see Fredrickson, Cohn, Coffey, Pek, & Finkel, 2008, for empirical evidence).

Fredrickson (2013) focuses on positive emotions as the fuel that drives these happiness-promoting actions, but based on the psychological processes and mechanisms discussed earlier, I posit that other mediators are also at play (e.g., construal, psychological need satisfaction, or positive behaviors). Regardless of the precise mechanism, a happiness intervention may trigger a series of events that promotes sustained happiness (see also Cohen & Sherman, 2014; Yeager & Walton, 2011; Walton & Wilson, 2018, for a discussion of recursive processes). Although possible, the above scenario relies on a chain of fortuitous events that may not happen—perhaps no one is particularly friendly at the gym that day and therefore the upward spiral of positivity (i.e., the recursive process) is not triggered. Indeed, Walton and Wilson (2018) note the importance of a receptive environment for recursive processes to unfold.

This is where the second pathway, continued practice, comes into play. If, instead of engaging in a happiness intervention only once—or only during a prescribed intervention period (e.g., over 6 weeks)—a person decides to continue his gratitude practice indefinitely, he increases the chance that this gratitude practice will set off a chain of positive events in his life, thus sustaining his happiness. Whereas at first, the gratitude intervention may only have changed his subjective construal of his life, eventually, this subjective construal leads to positive actions that will improve objective circumstances (e.g., more high-quality social relationships) when met with a receptive environment. An objective circumstance like more high-quality social relationships would itself promote greater happiness.

Another possibility is that the continued practice itself reinforces happiness by helping people actively appreciate their lives as they are. Indeed, happiness researchers have posited that continued practice is necessary to sustainably boost happiness and therefore if the gratitude practice stopped, so would the associated gains in well-being (Lyubomirsky, Sheldon, et al., 2005, but see Cohn & Fredrickson, 2010). Researchers also theorize that if continued practice is sustained long enough, the practice may become habitual, thus sustaining boosts in well-being without effortful practice (Lyubomirsky, Shedon, et al., 2005). Thus, for example, someone who practices gratitude over time may eventually have his or her immediate response to a situation be one of gratitude rather than dismay. This person may then resemble people who are naturally grateful due to personality or early learned tendencies. No research has been conducted yet to determine whether happiness interventions can become habitual after a certain amount of time and therefore sustain boosts in well-being.

More research also needs to explore evidence for whether recursive processes, continued practice, or both drive long-term changes in well-being. If continued practice is necessary, you may expect longer intervention periods (e.g., 10 weeks vs. 4 weeks) to have similar (or even perhaps greater) gains in well-being than shorter interventions. Indeed, a meta-analysis found that interventions that were longer had larger effect sizes than those that were shorter, but this finding was confounded by the fact that many of the longer interventions also took place in group or individual therapy, another factor that boosted efficacy (Sin & Lyubomirsky, 2009). In my own work, I have seen evidence of a quadratic effect whereby the intervention boosts well-being out to a certain point (e.g., 3 weeks in), but does not sustain the boosts for everyone out to the end of the intervention (e.g., 6 weeks in; Layous, Kurtz, Wildschut, & Sedikides, 2020). Thus, continued practice alone does not seem to maintain boosts in well-being.

Some studies have measured the degree to which people continue to practice the intervention of their own free will after the prescribed intervention period and found that continued practice was related to sustained increases in well-being (Dickerhoof, 2007; Proyer, Wellenzohn, Gander, & Ruch, 2015; Seligman et al., 2005; Sheldon & Lyubomirsky, 2006). Unfortunately, most of these studies do not provide enough information to know whether the continued practice was necessary to maintain sustained well-being increases, or were merely additionally beneficial.

Complicating matters, most of the evidence on continued practice is correlational, so the relationship between continued practice and sustained well-being could be due to other factors. For example, Sheldon and Lyubomirsky (2006) found that continued practice was related to participant self-reports of self-concordance with their activity (e.g., the degree to which they enjoyed the activity and identified with its importance vs. felt forced to engage in the activity by external forces or guilt). Similarly, Cohn and Fredrickson (2010) noted that those who continued their happiness-promoting practice were also the ones who reacted more strongly in the initial weeks of the intervention. This early reactivity could be an indication of fit between the person and the happiness intervention. Thus, quite rationally, those who felt the intervention working for them were more likely to continue practicing it beyond the prescribed intervention period and those who were slower to react (not reaping benefits until near the end of the intervention and reaping fewer benefits overall) stopped the practice when the study stopped. Nevertheless, Cohn and Fredrickson noted that what little gains the noncontinuers reaped in the initial intervention were sustained at the follow-up, indicating continued practice may not be necessary because it is possible the intervention helps the person build other sources of positivity in their lives that sustain well-being regardless of continued practice.

All of this is to say that more research needs to be conducted to explore the degree to which continued practice is necessary and under which conditions (e.g., under optimal person-activity fit) continued practice is most beneficial. Following recommendations by Miller and colleagues (2017), more research also needs to measure behavioral changes following happiness interventions and how those behavioral changes may sustain boosts in well-being in a recursive process.

Adding to the difficulty of exploring the "how" of well-being change over time, many happiness interventions include either no follow-up after the intervention or a relatively short follow-up (e.g., 1 month). Given how difficult behavior change is, longer follow-up periods are needed to know whether and how the changes instigated by happiness interventions stick beyond the prescribed intervention period. Nevertheless, some articles point to the potential longevity of these effects. Bolier and colleagues (2013) found nine happiness interventions that examined follow-up effects from 3 to 6 months after the intervention and found a small but significant effect of the interventions (vs. control) on well-being at the follow-up.

Heterogeneity

Theory and research proposes various aspects of the happiness intervention (e.g., its dosage) and the people practicing it (e.g., their personality) that moderate the degree to which the activity works to increase well-being (Layous & Lyubomirsky, 2014; Lyubomirsky & Layous, 2013). For example, one study found that a gratitude exercise was more effective if performed once per week rather than three times a week and another study found that a kindness intervention was more effective if all kind acts were done in 1 day during the week rather than spread out across the week (Lyubomirsky, Sheldon, et al., 2005). The authors later reasoned that both studies suggest that happiness interventions performed once per week are most effective, perhaps because many cultural routines are performed weekly (e.g., church, television programs; Lyubomirsky & Layous, 2013). Although the authors cannot be sure why these patterns of implementation were the most effective, at the very least, these studies point to the dosage of the intervention affecting its efficacy. Lyubomirsky and Layous discuss various other aspects of happiness intervention implementation that may affect its efficacy (e.g., variety, built-in social support).

In addition, research points to aspects of the person that might make him or her more likely to improve in well-being following a happiness intervention. For example, in one study, people who were relatively more extraverted gained more in well-being from happiness interventions indicating the role of personality (Senf & Liau, 2013). Past research has demonstrated that extraverted people consistently experience more positive emotions than their more introverted counterparts (Costa & McCrae, 1980), perhaps because they react more positively to similar daily events (Larsen & Ketelaar, 1991). Thus, it seems that extraverted people are predisposed to construe events as positive and, when given overtly positive material like a happiness intervention, they benefit more than their peers. Lyubomirsky and Layous (2013) discuss other characteristics of people that may affect their likelihood of gaining in well-being following a happiness intervention (e.g., how motivated they are to boost their happiness, how much they believe that happiness interventions can increase well-being).

Importantly, the optimal dosage of a happiness intervention (i.e., how often it is practiced) may vary by person, and whether particular personality profiles (i.e., extraversion) gain more in well-being from a happiness intervention may depend on the happiness intervention itself. Thus, perhaps more important than the main effects of activity or person characteristics is the fit between a particular person and a particular activity (i.e., person–activity fit; Lyubomirsky & Layous, 2013). For example, giving random acts of kindness to complete strangers may not be the best intervention for introverted people (Pressman, Kraft, & Cross, 2015). Indeed, participants who indicate that an activity feels relatively more natural and enjoyable to them are more likely to increase well-being over time (Dickerhoof, 2007) and to continue practicing the intervention beyond the prescribed period (Sheldon & Lyubomirsky, 2006). Similarly, people who indicate a good fit with the happiness intervention are more likely to sustain benefits to well-being (Proyer et al., 2015; see also Cohn & Fredrickson, 2010). More research needs to address the issue of person–activity fit to best maximize well-being benefits for happiness seekers.

COUSINS

Happiness interventions incorporate a broad range of activities, both inside (e.g., Fava & Ruini, 2003; Seligman, Rashid, & Parks, 2006) and outside (e.g., Seligman et al., 2005) of therapy, so I am not able to discuss all of them here. The activities mentioned below (and the gratitude and kindness activities already mentioned) are similar in that they all help people view themselves, their relationships, or their environments in ways that promote happiness, but they are different in the exact way they focus attention.

Various interventions—broadly classified as savoring interventions—direct people's attention to the positive in their past, present, or future experiences. Some researchers characterize *savoring* as an umbrella term that encompasses gratitude, with gratitude being a specific type of savoring in which one recognizes and appreciates a direct benefit received from the goodwill of another person (Adler & Fagley, 2005). Many savoring interventions have successfully boosted positive emotions by prompting people to remember positive experiences from their past (e.g., Burton & King, 2004; Sedikides et al., 2015). Perhaps unsurprisingly given the fundamental need for humans to feel connected to others (e.g., Baumeister & Leary, 1995), the two most frequent subjects of these positive memories is close others and momentous events (e.g., weddings, graduations) during which close others are an important part (Wildschut, Sedikdies, Arndt, & Routledge, 2006). Following this theme, the boost in positivity following the recollection of positive memories was predicted by an increased sense of connectedness to others, as well as an increased sense of meaning in life, self-esteem, and self-continuity (one's sense that they are connected with their past and that their personality has remained the same across time; Sedikides et al., 2015).

Other savoring interventions attempt to direct people's attention to the positivity in their present experience by engaging in activities like taking pictures of their surroundings in a thoughtful way (i.e., looking for and appreciating beauty; Kurtz, 2015) or sharing positive news with a significant other (Gable, Reis, Impett, & Asher, 2004). Counterintuitively, many savoring interventions induce a sense of scarcity to promote present savoring—either by having people mentally subtract someone important from their lives (Koo, Algoe, Wilson, & Gilbert, 2008) or by framing time as scarce in a given location (i.e., at their college campus; Kurtz, 2008; Layous, Kurtz, Chancellor, & Lyubomimrsky, 2018; see also Carstensen, Isaacowitz, & Charles, 1999). In one study, inducing a sense of time scarcity boosted feelings of psychological need satisfaction in the moment (feelings of autonomy, competence, and connectedness) that predicted boosts in well-being over time (Layous, Kurtz, Chancellor, et al., 2018). Thus, imagining time as scarce made people construe their current environments as more fulfilling than they previously had.

Anticipating positive future events also boosts happiness (Quoidbach, Hansenne, & Mottet, 2008). In a specific type of positive future anticipation, people "visualize their best possible future self," imagining that everything in their lives has gone as well as it possibly can, and then write about what they envision (King, 2001). Common themes that arise in these essays are job success, self-improvement, marriage and family, and home ownership—success in career and social relationships. Researchers also adapted the "best possible self" activity into a multiweek intervention, with each week focusing on a specific domain of life (e.g., family, friends, career, or health; Boehm, Lyubomirsky, & Sheldon, 2011; Layous, Nelson, & Lyubomirsky, 2013). Although the "best possible self" intervention is often viewed as a self-oriented activity compared to more socially oriented activities like expressing gratitude (e.g., Boehm et al., 2011), when discussing their ideal future life, people spontaneously bring up close others, indicating their central importance to visions of future success (King, 2001). Indeed, participants randomly assigned to a "best possible self" condition not only reported greater positive affect than a control condition but also marginally greater connectedness (Layous, Nelson, et al., 2013).

Another happiness intervention often viewed as self-oriented assesses participants' strengths with the Values in Action Inventory (Peterson & Seligman, 2004) and then prompts participants to use one of their top strengths in a new way (Seligman et al., 2005; Senf & Liau, 2013). Importantly, on this particular strengths assessment, many of the strengths that participants may have are inherently socially oriented, like gratitude, kindness, love, social intelligence, or teamwork, so this activity may not actually be as self-focused as it may seem on the surface. Past research has shown that this activity is effective in boosting happiness and decreasing depressive symptoms (Seligman et al., 2005; Senf & Liau, 2013), but more research needs to be conducted to explore the exact mechanisms of the effect. For example, do the socially relevant strengths drive the effect on well-being or can focusing solely on individualistic strengths also benefit well-being?

Meditation has also been found to boost happiness. Many meditation programs are meant to boost mindfulness—a nonjudgmental present awareness of one's experience (Kabat-Zinn, 2003). Mindfulness-based meditation practices do not focus on boosting positivity—they are meant to adjust people's inherent tendency to evaluate each experience as good or bad. Nevertheless, evidence suggests that mindfulness-based meditation practices not only reduce negativity, but also boost positivity (Davidson et al., 2003). Other meditation practices directly focus on boosting positivity. For example, loving-kindness meditation prompts participants to direct love and compassion toward themselves, loved ones, acquaintances, strangers, and all living beings, and increases positive emotions, mindfulness, meaning in life, perceptions of social support, and perceptions of physical health (Fredrickson et al., 2008).

A theme in all of the above interventions is the importance of social relationships for happiness. Many other wise interventions also focus on helping people view their relationships in a positive light, although not typically with the primary goal of increasing personal happiness. For example, across multiple studies, the social-belonging intervention has helped students construe their challenges as normal and temporary, not as a sign they do not belong in their educational setting (e.g., Walton & Cohen, 2011). The primary goal of the social-belonging intervention is to improve academic achievement among marginalized groups, but it also boosts happiness and physical health (Walton & Cohen, 2011). Thus, a common theme across wise interventions, including happiness interventions, is the focus on positive social relationships.

INTERVENTION CONTENT AND IMPLEMENTATION

Happiness interventions within therapy can be quite intensive (Fava & Ruini, 2003; Seligman et al., 2006), but the self-guided variety are often brief and typically performed once per week for about 6 weeks (although 6 weeks is an arbitrary time frame to permit completion of a study during a school term). Writing activities (e.g., gratitude) are often scheduled for as few as 2 minutes (Burton & King, 2008) to as many as 15 minutes (Lyubomirsky et al., 2011), whereas kindness activities can take much longer with participants often reporting spending quality time with loved ones.

Gratitude interventions typically focus on either keeping a gratitude journal (e.g., "counting blessings" or "three good things"; Emmons & McCullough, 2003; Seligman et al., 2005) or writing gratitude letters (e.g., Layous, Lee, et al., 2013; Lyubomirsky et al., 2011).

Typical instructions for keeping a gratitude journal are as follows: "There are many things in our lives, both large and small, that we might be grateful about. Think back over the past week and write down on the lines below up to five things in your life that you are grateful or thankful for" (Emmons & McCullough, 2003). This activity prompts participants to reflect upon and appreciate aspects of their lives that they may take for granted, giving them an opportunity to extract positivity from mundane experiences that they otherwise would have taken for granted.

Typical instructions for a gratitude letter writing activity are as follows:

> "Please take a moment to think back over the past several years of your life and remember an instance when someone did something for you for which you are extremely grateful. For example, think of the people—parents, relatives, friends, teachers, coaches, teammates, employers, and so on—who have been especially kind to you but have never heard you express your gratitude. Although you should try to write your letter of gratitude to a new person each week; if you prefer, you can write another letter to the same person you wrote to previously."

Then, participants are given a list of more specific instructions (abbreviated): (1) Write in a letter format, (2) Do not worry about perfect grammar or spelling, (3) Describe in specific terms why you are grateful to this individual and how the individual's behavior affected your life, and (4) Describe what you are doing now and how you often remember their efforts. Participants are also reminded that their letter will be completely confidential. Although the typical instructions ask the participant to write in a letter format, research suggests that simply writing about the person in a nonletter format is equally effective (Layous et al., 2017). In many gratitude letter writing interventions, the letter is not shared with the target to isolate the causal effect of the gratitude expression itself, but recent research suggests that delivering the gratitude letter boosts well-being more than simply writing it and, as an added bonus, also boosts the well-being of the recipient (Walsh & Lyubomirsky, 2018).

Kindness interventions prompt participants to perform three (e.g., Layous, Lee, et al., 2013; Nelson, Layous, Cole, & Lyubomirsky, 2016) or five (Lyubomirsky, Sheldon, et al., 2005; Nelson et al., 2015) acts of kindness during the week, all in 1 day (Lyubomirsky, Sheldon, et al., 2005). Typical instructions are as follows (with the last sentence undoubtedly coming from the Institutional Review Board):

"In our daily lives, we all perform acts of kindness for others. These acts may be large or small and the person for whom the act is performed may or may not be aware of the act. Examples include helping your parents cook dinner, doing a chore for your sister or brother, helping a friend with homework, visiting an elderly relative, or writing a thank you letter. During one day this week (any day you choose), please perform five acts of kindness—all five in one day. The acts do not need to be for the same person, the person may or may not be aware of the act, and the act may or may not be similar to the acts listed above. Next week you will report what acts of kindness you chose to perform. Please do not perform any acts that may place yourself or others in danger."

Asking people to report the kind acts they performed (i.e., the kindness check-in) has two purposes. The first purpose is to hold people accountable. Researchers do not want participants to blow off the activity, so they remind them that they will report their kind acts the following week. If participants do not perform kind acts, they can leave the kindness check-in blank and the researcher can decide whether to include them in the analyses. That said, even if participants did not purposely perform kind acts during the week, they likely still did nice things for others that they might report. Research suggests that recounting the kindnesses one has performed throughout the day boosts well-being (Kerr et al., 2015; Otake, Shimai, Tanaka-Matsumi, Otsui, & Fredrickson, 2006). Thus, the second purpose of the kindness check-in is to give participants one more chance to benefit. Kindness interventions that ask people to go out and intentionally do kind acts cannot be sure that participants actually did anything additional to what they usually do, but, by asking participants to report their kind acts, they can be sure that participants who report their kind acts are becoming more aware of the kindnesses they perform.

For a comprehensive list of happiness-promoting activities, visit the Greater Good in Action website (*https://ggia.berkeley.edu*), part of the Greater Good Science Center at the University of California, Berkeley, which houses 58 research-tested practices for boosting well-being.

NUANCES AND MISCONCEPTIONS

Research has found that valuing happiness to an extreme degree actually undermines it, so there seems to be a risk in people endorsing statements like "If I don't feel happy, maybe there is something wrong with me," and "I am concerned about my happiness even when I feel happy" (Mauss, Tamir, Anderson, & Savino, 2011). Alternatively, research also suggests that simply prioritizing positivity as an important part of daily life (e.g., "A priority for me is experiencing happiness in everyday life") is predictive of well-being (Catalino, Algoe, & Fredrickson, 2014). Thus, Catalino et al. demonstrate that the explicit intention to pursue happiness is likely positive, but Mauss et al. demonstrates that overvaluing happiness is distinct from a simple intention and can be detrimental. These two different approaches to thinking about happiness and their distinct relationships with well-being inform the administration of happiness interventions.

Indeed, most happiness interventions do not focus participants directly on their own happiness (e.g., "Go make yourself happy") but instead prompt participants to engage in activities that take the focus off of their personal happiness (e.g., write a gratitude letter, perform kind acts). A person engaging in these research-tested practices is obviously showing signs of prioritizing positivity by seeking out happiness-promoting strategies, but, when engaged in the activity itself, will not be thinking about their own happiness in an "Are we there yet?" unhealthy way. Indeed, in general, self-focus is related to negative affect, particularly when that self-focus involves ruminative thoughts like "Why do I feel the way I do?" (Mor & Winquist, 2002). Thus, happiness interventions like gratitude and kindness often take the focus off the self and direct it to others. This is a nuance of happiness interventions that has not been discussed much, but I think may be an important part of their success—happiness interventions do not typically focus directly on happiness.

Simply telling people to make themselves happy without giving them efficacious happiness-promoting activities may not work because people often do not know what will make them happy. For example, many people engage in retail therapy to boost their mood, but research has shown that experiential purchases promote greater happiness than materialistic ones, likely because experiential purchases are more open to positive reinterpretation and contribute to social relationships (Van Boven & Gilovich, 2003; see also Kasser & Ryan, 1993). In another experiment, participants randomly assigned to perform kind acts for others reported greater flourishing than those assigned to perform kind acts for themselves (Nelson et al., 2016). Presumably, the self-kindness group engaged in activities meant to boost their well-being, but they were unsuccessful in doing so. Thus, people may want to pursue happiness, but they may not know what will actually make them happy.

Although people may not know exactly what to do to pursue their happiness, theory suggests that their intention to pursue happiness is important to their success, as happiness pursuit takes at least some effort (Lyubomirsky, Sheldon, et al., 2005). In one test of this theory, researchers advertised their study as either a "happiness intervention" or a "cognitive exercises" study (Lyubomirsky et al., 2011). Researchers thought that participants who signed up for the happiness intervention study were likely motivated to pursue their own happiness and had the intention of doing so, whereas participants who signed up for the cognitive exercises were less motivated and had no explicit intention to pursue their happiness. Regardless of how participants initially entered the study (via happiness intervention or cognitive exercises title), all were randomly assigned to complete one of two happiness interventions or a control activity weekly for 6 weeks. Participants who were motivated to improve their happiness and were assigned to one of the happiness interventions reported greater increases in well-being than those who practiced happiness interventions but were not motivated, or the control groups. Researchers concluded that participants needed both a will (i.e., motivation/intention to pursue happiness) and a proper way (i.e., an efficacious happiness-promoting activity) to increase well-being (Lyubomirsky et al., 2011; see also Ferguson & Sheldon, 2013, for a replication with a completely experimental design).

The positive effects of intention during happiness pursuit is interesting compared to other wise interventions in which the purpose is rarely made explicit to participants. For example, some research suggests that making the purpose of self-affirmation interventions known undermines their effect (Sherman et al., 2009), but upon further examination, the awareness may only be detrimental if the activity is viewed to be externally imposed rather than internally chosen (Silverman, Logel, & Cohen, 2013). I further discuss the importance of intrinsic motivation later in this section.

One reason intention to pursue happiness may predict higher happiness following a happiness intervention is because intentional happiness seekers may put more effort into happiness-increasing activities. Lyubomirsky and colleagues (2011) had independent coders rate the degree to which participants put effort into completing their assigned activities (either the happiness interventions or the control activity). Regardless of whether participants self-selected into the happiness activity or not, those who put more effort into the happiness interventions (but not the control activity) saw greater increases in well-being. This again supports the "will and proper way" logic—participants needed to put effort into an efficacious activity. Unfortunately, Lyubomirsky and colleagues did not report whether those who self-selected into the happiness intervention study also put forth more effort. Possibly, anyone who puts effort into happiness-promoting activities will reap the benefits, with or without the explicit intention to become happier.

The Ferguson and Sheldon (2013) and Lyubomirsky and colleagues' (2011) studies suggest that intentionality is an important component of benefiting from a happiness intervention, but many questions remain. For example, can the effect of intention and effort be disentangled and, if so, which is more important? What exactly needs to be intentional—the pursuit of happiness more generally or just intentionality toward the practice of a specific happiness-promoting activity (e.g., intentionally practicing gratitude or kindness)? I suspect that the latter would be just as effective as the former, but no research to my knowledge has disentangled these effects. At what stage in happiness pursuit is intentionality necessary? In light of the potential for recursive processes to unfold, maybe intentionality is only necessary at the beginning of a happiness pursuit, but ceases to become necessary when activities either become habitual or trigger other positive processes that contribute to happiness. Finally, even at the beginning of a happiness intervention, is intention truly necessary, or is it merely helpful? I suspect if a group of nonhappiness seekers (i.e., people who do not have the goal of improving their happiness) started writing in a gratitude journal weekly, at least some of them would experience improvements in well-being, indicating that the initial intention to pursue happiness was not necessary for some. Similarly, in an experiment described earlier, participants randomly assigned to read information about happiness being malleable (vs. fixed) reported higher happiness despite never expressing any intention to pursue happiness (Van Tongeren &

Burnette, 2018). Thus, although initial theory suggested that intentionality is necessary for happiness pursuit (Lyubomirsky, Sheldon, et al., 2005), many questions surround the exact nature of this intentionality.

Another nuance is that, as much as possible, happiness interventions need to be autonomy supportive (see also Silverman et al., 2013; Vansteenkiste, Simons, Lens, Sheldon, & Deci, 2004). People need to engage in happiness interventions because they want to and because the activities feel natural and enjoyable to them (intrinsically motivating). Even if people hold personal happiness as an intrinsically motivated goal because it feels good in and of itself, the way one pursues happiness (e.g., via gratitude expression or prosocial behavior) could start to feel unnatural or forced. Similarly, if people hold happiness as a goal only because others seem happier than they do or because society expects them to be happy, happiness pursuit may also feel mandated by extrinsic forces or by one's own guilt or shame (cf. Crocker & Park, 2004). Thus, as much as possible, people need to come to happiness pursuit on their own terms and the happiness interventions themselves need to underscore this autonomy. One experiment randomly assigned both U.S. and South Korean students to perform kind acts or focus on their academics (the control group) and then either provided autonomy-supportive messages from a peer who purportedly completed this study previously (e.g., "Just wanted to let ya know that where u do these acts and who u do them for is totally up to u. Feel free to do this however u want! :) "), or just provided the other instructions with no peer support messages (i.e., no autonomy support; Nelson et al., 2015). Regardless of culture, the autonomy-supportive/ kindness group showed greater linear improvements in well-being over the 6-week intervention than the other three groups, indicating that autonomy support boosted the efficacy of the kindness activity, but not the control group.

IMPLICATIONS FOR PRACTICE

Happiness interventions are quite scalable, as online versions of interventions have showed comparable results to in-person versions (Layous, Nelson et al., 2013) and preliminary results from a multicomponent happiness intervention program show that the online version was even more successful than the in-person version (Heintzelman, 2018). Similarly, an iPhone application called Live Happy features various happiness-promoting strategies and has shown increases in mood and global happiness in users, particularly those who engaged more frequently with the application and tried more of the activities (Parks, Della Porta, Pierce, Zilca, & Lyubomirsky, 2012). Given the self-guided, nonclinical nature of many happiness interventions, they are easy to implement in a variety of settings.

That said, one potential cause for concern about the implementation of happiness interventions in the public is whether particular activities could backfire among particular people (Fritz & Lyubomirsky, 2018). For example, one study found that a subset of participants actually decreased in happiness following a kindness intervention (Pressman et al., 2015). This kindness intervention was highly public—participants spent 90 minutes performing kind acts for strangers (e.g., giving a compliment, holding the door open, offering to carry something). Qualitative evidence revealed that participants who decreased in happiness reported being shy and uncomfortable engaging with strangers or reported being sad when they did not receive a positive response to their kind acts.

The majority of kindness interventions give participants a choice in how they perform their kind acts, thus the likelihood of person-activity fit and autonomous motivation is higher. Researchers and practitioners need to consider the participants in their happiness interventions and what type of complications they may experience, as well as leave enough flexibility in their administration as to give participants control and choice in their implementation.

In another example of a backfiring effect, one study found that writing gratitude letters actually decreased well-being among mildly depressed participants (Sin, Della Porta, & Lyubomirsky, 2011; see also Layous, Lee, et al., 2013, for the null effect of gratitude letters among South Koreans). The authors reasoned that writing a letter of gratitude might have been too taxing for depressed participants. Indeed, in casual conversations with clinical psychologists, they caution that some of their patients with depression find it difficult to think of people in their lives who care about them, or, alternatively, if they can think of someone, patients quickly feel guilty about their family and friends wasting time on them (see also Layous et al., 2017). In a clinical setting, therapists can guide patients into a different way of thinking, but if people with depression are completing the gratitude letter activity by themselves, they may not have the proper support or wherewithal to benefit from the activity. Over half of happiness seekers on the Internet qualify as clinically depressed (Parks et al., 2012), so researchers need to be careful about which activities they recommend and which caveats they may place. In one successful customization, researchers adapted the "visualize your best possible self" instructions for chronic pain patients by acknowledging their pain in the instructions (Peters et al., 2017). Thus, participants were asked to imagine their good life in the future "despite their pain." This small customization may have made participants feel understood and may have made the activity feel less unreasonable given their current difficult circumstances.

IMPLICATIONS FOR PSYCHOLOGICAL THEORY

First, happiness interventions inform the degree to which a relatively stable and genetically influenced aspect of one's personality—happiness—can be meaningfully and sustainably changed through intentional practice. Although the heritability of happiness is well established at about 40–50%, empirical evidence indicates that even identical twins can have substantially different well-being trajectories due to nonshared environmental influences (which could include intentional practice; see Layous, 2018, for a review). Many view heritability estimates to be concrete and deterministic, but they are highly influenced by nongenetic factors, like variability in the environment and variability in the trait across people in the sample. Even if happiness was 100% heritable, improving environmental factors could still raise happiness in an entire population, boosting people's well-being relative to their own levels. For example, in one multiweek happiness intervention among identical and fraternal twins, the average well-being across the whole sample improved even though the estimates of the genetic effects on happiness remained consistent across the study (Haworth et al., 2016). Genetically sensitive designs with an experimental intervention component can continue to help researchers understand the interplay between genes and environment on happiness and other personality processes.

Second, intervening to improve happiness among people in different cultures helps psychologists learn about processes of well-being that are culturally specific and those that might be more universally important. For example, although gratitude interventions consistently boost well-being among Western samples, one study found that gratitude letters were not effective in boosting well-being in a South Korean sample (e.g., Layous, Lee, et al., 2013). On the other hand, kindness interventions have been equally effective among Eastern (South Korean) and Western (U.S.) samples (Layous, Lee, et al., 2013; Nelson et al., 2015), suggesting a universality not characteristic of gratitude letters. Exploring what activities do or do not boost happiness among different cultures, and the psychological processes by which they do so, can promote theory development surrounding what leads to thriving in different cultures.

Lastly, intervening to improve happiness could develop theory in clinical psychology by pointing to the role of positive affect in the manifestation and treatment of mental illness. Currently, treatment for depression largely relies on drug therapy or cognitive-behavioral therapy, approaches that have been successful, but perhaps incomplete and not a fit for all patients. Researchers have speculated that drug therapy, cognitive-behavioral therapy, and happiness interventions act on different neural circuitry (Layous, Chancellor, Lyubomirsky, Wang, & Doraiswamy, 2011). A three-arm randomized trial comparing changes in brain functioning among depressed patients undergoing happiness interventions, cognitive-behavioral therapy, or drug therapy could reveal whether the theorized neural circuitry is supported. Future studies could also test the combination of one or more of these therapies to explore whether addressing multiple neural circuits at once has an additive effect on depression outcomes.

In addition, adding happiness interventions to existing therapeutic approaches could address limitations of current treatment. For example, it takes several weeks for patients to respond to drug therapy, but, on average, people respond to happiness interventions quickly, showing immediate boosts to mood (e.g., Seligman et al., 2005). Thus, happiness interventions may complement slower-acting drug therapies. Similarly, happiness interventions help focus people's attention on the positive in their lives, so may be a good complement to cognitive-behavioral therapy's focus on reducing maladaptive thoughts (e.g., Beck, 2011). More research will further our understanding of the neural circuitry surrounding depression and the way that happiness interventions could be incorporated into existing treatment plans or even act as an effective stand-alone treatment (e.g., Seligman et al., 2006).

FUTURE DIRECTIONS

The late Chris Peterson, a prominent thought leader in positive psychology, summarized positive psychology with three words: "other people matter" (Peterson, 2006). Although the happiness interventions reported in this chapter have leveraged the perception of positive relationships with others to increase personal happiness, very few have explored the effect of happiness interventions on relationships and functioning in closed networks like workplaces and schools (but see Chancellor, Margolis, Jacobs Bao, & Lyubomirsky, 2018; Layous, Nelson, Oberle, Schonert-Reichl, & Lyubomirsky, 2012). Theoretically, improving perceptions of relationships within a closed network could trigger positive recursive processes that build upon each other quickly, reaping immediate relational and well-being benefits. Thus, a ripe area for future research is intervening to improve happiness among closed networks and exploring the cumulative effects on individual or group-level happiness, as well as other important outcomes, like academic achievement or workplace productivity.

Another important future direction in happiness intervention research is for more studies to include longer follow-ups. So far, the literature as a whole has demonstrated promising short-term gains in well-being, even out to 6 months (Bolier et al., 2013), but longer periods are needed to truly claim stable changes. Similarly, more research needs to explore the process of long-term change to consider the role of recursive processes and continued practice in promoting durable changes in happiness, as well as the downstream consequences of these changes.

Happiness intervention researchers should also measure objective outcomes that may result either directly or indirectly from happiness interventions. Researchers of other wise interventions (e.g., belonging and self-affirmation) have done an excellent job demonstrating their intervention's effect on important objective outcomes like grade-point average, whereas happiness interventions thus far have been more likely to focus on subjective changes (e.g., self-reports of happiness, but see Burton & King, 2004; King, 2001).

Lastly, given the importance of fit between the happiness seeker and the happiness-promoting activity (i.e., person-activity fit), I think the most promising direction of future happiness intervention research lies in the exploration of the types of activities that work for different types of people, as well as ways to predict best-fitting practices to individualize interventions for maximum efficacy. A truly wise intervention would be one that hits the right lever for the right person at the right time, setting off a promising upward trajectory toward greater well-being.

REFERENCES

Adler, M. G., & Fagley, N. S. (2005). Appreciation: Individual differences in finding value and meaning as a unique predictor of subjective well-being. *Journal of Personality, 73*(1), 79–114.

Aknin, L. B., Sandstrom, G. M., Dunn, E. W., & Norton, M. I. (2011). It's the recipient that counts: Spending money on strong social ties leads to greater happiness than spending on weak social ties. *PLOS ONE, 6*(2), e17018.

Algoe, S. B. (2012). Find, remind, and bind: The functions of gratitude in everyday relationships. *Social and Personality Psychology Compass, 6*(6), 455–469.

Bandura, A. (1997). *Self-efficacy: The exercise of control.* New York: Freeman.

Bartlett, M. Y., & DeSteno, D. (2006). Gratitude and prosocial behavior: Helping when it costs you. *Psychological Science, 17*(4), 319–325.

Baumeister, R. F., & Leary, M. R. (1995). The need to belong: Desire for interpersonal attachments as a fundamental human motivation. *Psychological Bulletin, 117,* 497–529.

Beck, J. S. (2011). *Cognitive behavior therapy: Basics and beyond* (2nd ed.). New York: Guilford Press.

Boehm, J. K., & Kubzansky, L. D. (2012). The heart's content: The association between positive psychological well-being and cardiovascular health. *Psychological Bulletin, 138*(4), 655–691.

Boehm, J. K., Lyubomirsky, S., & Sheldon, K. M. (2011). A longitudinal experimental study comparing the effectiveness of happiness-enhancing strategies in Anglo Americans and Asian Americans. *Cognition and Emotion, 25,* 1263–1272.

Bolier, L., Haverman, M., Westerhof, G. J., Riper, H., Smit, F., & Bohlmeijer, E. (2013). Positive psychology interventions: A meta-analysis of randomized controlled studies. *BMC Public Health, 13*(1), 119–139.

Burton, C. M., & King, L. A. (2004). The health benefits of writing about intensely positive experiences. *Journal of Research in Personality, 38*(2), 150–163.

Burton, C. M., & King, L. A. (2008). Effects of (very) brief writing on health: The two-minute miracle. *British Journal of Health Psychology, 13*(1), 9–14.

Busseri, M. A., & Sadava, S. W. (2011). A review of the tripartite structure of subjective well-being: Implications for conceptualization, operationalization, analysis, and synthesis. *Personality and Social Psychology Review, 15*(3), 290–314.

Carstensen, L. L., Isaacowitz, D. M., & Charles, S. T. (1999). Taking time seriously: A theory of socioemotional selectivity. *American Psychologist, 54*(3), 165–181.

Catalino, L. I., Algoe, S. B., & Fredrickson, B. L. (2014). Prioritizing positivity: An effective approach to pursuing happiness? *Emotion, 14*(6), 1155–1161.

Chancellor, J., Margolis, S., Jacobs Bao, K., & Lyubomirsky, S. (2018). Everyday prosociality in the workplace: The reinforcing benefits of giving, getting, and glimpsing. *Emotion, 18*(4), 507–517.

Cohen, G. L., & Sherman, D. K. (2014). The psychology of change: Self-affirmation and social psychological intervention. *Annual Review of Psychology, 65,* 333–371.

Cohn, M. A., & Fredrickson, B. L. (2010). In search of durable positive psychology interventions: Predictors and consequences of long-term positive behavior change. *Journal of Positive Psychology, 5*(5), 355–366.

Costa, P. T., & McCrae, R. R. (1980). Influence of extraversion and neuroticism on subjective well-being: Happy and unhappy people. *Journal of Personality and Social Psychology, 38*(4), 668–678.

Crocker, J., & Park, L. E. (2004). The costly pursuit of self-esteem. *Psychological Bulletin, 130*(3), 392–414.

Curry, O. S., Rowland, L. A., Van Lissa, C. J., Zlotowitz, S., McAlaney, J., & Whitehouse, H. (2018). Happy to help?: A systematic review and meta-analysis of the effects of performing acts of kindness on the well-being of the actor. *Journal of Experimental Social Psychology, 76,* 320–329.

Davidson, R. J., Kabat-Zinn, J., Schumacher, J., Rosenkranz, M., Muller, D., Santorelli, S. F., . . . Sheridan, J. F. (2003). Alterations in brain and immune function produced by mindfulness meditation. *Psychosomatic Medicine, 65*(4), 564–570.

Davis, D. E., Choe, E., Meyers, J., Wade, N., Varjas, K., Gifford, A., . . . Worthington, E. L., Jr. (2016). Thankful for the little things: A meta-analysis of gratitude interventions. *Journal of Counseling Psychology, 63*(1), 20–31.

Dickens, L. R. (2017). Using gratitude to promote positive change: A series of meta-analyses investigating the effectiveness of gratitude interventions. *Basic and Applied Social Psychology, 39*(4), 193–208.

Dickerhoof, R. M. (2007). Expressing optimism and gratitude: A longitudinal investigation of cognitive strategies to increase well-being. *Dissertation Abstracts International, 68,* 4174 (UMI No. 3270426).

Diener, E. (1984). Subjective well-being. *Psychological Bulletin, 95*(3), 542–575.

Diener, E. (2000). Subjective well-being: The science of happiness and a proposal for a national index. *American Psychologist, 55,* 34–43.

Diener, M. L., & Lucas, R. E. (2004). Adults' desires for children's emotions across 48 countries. *Journal of Cross-Cultural Psychology, 35,* 525–547.

Disabato, D. J., Goodman, F. R., Kashdan, T. B., Short, J. L., & Jarden, A. (2016). Different types of well-being?: A cross-cultural examination of hedonic and eudaimonic well-being. *Psychological Assessment, 28*(5), 471–482.

Eisenberg, N., Cumberland, A., & Spinrad, T. L. (1998). Parental socialization of emotion. *Psychological Inquiry, 9*(4), 241–273.

Emmons, R. A., & McCullough, M. E. (2003). Counting blessings versus burdens: An experimental investigation of gratitude and subjective well-being in daily life. *Journal of Personality and Social Psychology, 84*(2), 377–389.

Fava, G. A., & Ruini, C. (2003). Development and characteristics of a well-being enhancing psychotherapeutic strategy: Well-being therapy. *Journal of Behavior Therapy and Experimental Psychiatry, 34*(1), 45–63.

Ferguson, Y. L., & Sheldon, K. M. (2013). Trying to be happier really can work: Two experimental studies. *Journal of Positive Psychology, 8*(1), 23–33.

Fordyce, M. W. (1977). Development of a program to increase personal happiness. *Journal of Counseling Psychology, 24*(6), 511–521.

Fordyce, M. W. (1983). A program to increase happiness: Further studies. *Journal of Counseling Psychology, 30*(4), 483–498.

Fredrickson, B. L. (2013). Positive emotions broaden and build. *Advances in Experimental Social Psychology, 47*(1), 1–53.

Fredrickson, B. L., Cohn, M. A., Coffey, K. A., Pek, J., & Finkel, S. M. (2008). Open hearts build lives: Positive emotions, induced through loving-kindness meditation, build consequential personal resources. *Journal of Personality and Social Psychology, 95*(5), 1045–1062.

Fritz, M. M., Armenta, C. N., Walsh, L. C., & Lyubomirsky, S. (2019). Gratitude facilitates healthy eating behavior in adolescents and young adults. *Journal of Experimental Social Psychology, 81*, 4–14.

Fritz, M. M., & Lyubomirsky, S. (2018). Whither happiness?: When, how, and why might positive activities undermine well-being. In J. P. Forgas & R. F. Baumeister (Eds.), *The social psychology of living well* (pp. 101–115). New York: Psychology Press.

Gable, S. L., Reis, H. T., Impett, E. A., & Asher, E. R. (2004). What do you do when things go right?: The intrapersonal and interpersonal benefits of sharing positive events. *Journal of Personality and Social Psychology, 87*(2), 228–245.

Haworth, C. M., Nelson, S. K., Layous, K., Carter, K., Bao, K. J., Lyubomirsky, S., & Plomin, R. (2016). Stability and change in genetic and environmental influences on well-being in response to an intervention. *PLOS ONE, 11*(5), e0155538.

Heintzelman, S. J. (2018). *ENHANCE: Evidence for the efficacy of a comprehensive intervention program to promote durable changes in subjective well-being.* Presented at the Happiness and Well-Being Preconference at the annual meeting of the Society of Personality and Social Psychologists, Atlanta, GA.

Jackowska, M., Brown, J., Ronaldson, A., & Steptoe, A. (2016). The impact of a brief gratitude intervention on subjective well-being, biology and sleep. *Journal of Health Psychology, 21*(10), 2207–2217.

Kabat-Zinn, J. (2003). Mindfulness-based interventions in context: Past, present, and future. *Clinical Psychology: Science and Practice, 10*(2), 144–156.

Kasser, T., & Ryan, R. M. (1993). A dark side of the American dream: Correlates of financial success as a central life aspiration. *Journal of Personality and Social Psychology, 65*(2), 410–422.

Kerr, S. L., O'Donovan, A., & Pepping, C. A. (2015). Can gratitude and kindness interventions enhance well-being in a clinical sample? *Journal of Happiness Studies, 16*(1), 17–36.

King, L. A. (2001). The health benefits of writing about life goals. *Personality and Social Psychology Bulletin, 27*(7), 798–807.

King, R. B., & Datu, J. A. D. (2018). Grateful students are motivated, engaged, and successful in school: Cross-sectional, longitudinal, and experimental evidence. *Journal of School Psychology, 70*, 105–122.

Koo, M., Algoe, S. B., Wilson, T. D., & Gilbert, D. T. (2008). It's a wonderful life: Mentally subtracting positive events improves people's affective states, contrary to their affective forecasts. *Journal of Personality and Social Psychology, 95*(5), 1217–1224.

Kurtz, J. L. (2008). Looking to the future to appreciate the present: The benefits of perceived temporal scarcity. *Psychological Science, 19*(12), 1238–1241.

Kurtz, J. L. (2015). Seeing through new eyes: An experimental investigation of the benefits of photography. *Journal of Basic and Applied Sciences, 11*, 354–358.

Lambert, N. M., & Fincham, F. D. (2011). Expressing gratitude to a partner leads to more relationship maintenance behavior. *Emotion, 11*(1), 52–60.

Lambert, N. M., Fincham, F. D., & Stillman, T. F. (2012). Gratitude and depressive symptoms: The role of positive reframing and positive emotion. *Cognition and Emotion, 26*(4), 615–633.

Larsen, R. J., & Ketelaar, T. (1991). Personality and susceptibility to positive and negative emotional states. *Journal of Personality and Social Psychology, 61*(1), 132–140.

Layous, K. (2018). Malleability and intentional activities. In E. Diener, S. Oishi, & L. Tay (Eds.), *E-handbook of well-being.* Salt Lake City, UT: DEF.

Layous, K., Chancellor, J., Lyubomirsky, S., Wang, L., & Doraiswamy, P. M. (2011). Delivering happiness: Translating positive psychology intervention research for treating major and minor depressive disorders. *Journal of Alternative and Complementary Medicine, 17*(8), 675–683.

Layous, K., Kurtz, J., Chancellor, J., & Lyubomirsky, S. (2018). Reframing the ordinary: Imagining time as scarce increases well-being. *Journal of Positive Psychology, 13*(3), 301–308.

Layous, K., Kurtz, J., Margolis, S., Chancellor, J., & Lyubomirsky, S. (2018). *Make someone happy and you will be happy too: An other-oriented path to well-being.* Unpublished manuscript.

Layous, K., Kurtz, J., Wildschut, T., & Sedikides, C. (2020). *The effect of a multi-week nostalgia intervention on well-being: Mechanisms and moderation.* Manuscript under revision.

Layous, K., Lee, H., Choi, I., & Lyubomirsky, S. (2013). Culture matters when designing a successful happiness-increasing activity: A comparison of the United States and South Korea. *Journal of Cross-Cultural Psychology, 44*, 1294–1303.

Layous, K., & Lyubomirsky, S. (2014). The how, what, when, and why of happiness: Mechanisms underlying the success of positive interventions. In J. Gruber & J. Moskowitz (Eds.), *Positive emotion: Integrating the light sides and dark sides* (pp. 473–495). New York: Oxford University Press.

Layous, K., Nelson, S. K., & Lyubomirsky, S. (2013). What is the optimal way to deliver a positive activity intervention?: The case of writing about one's best possible selves. *Journal of Happiness Studies, 16*, 635–654.

Layous, K., Nelson, S. K., Oberle, E., Schonert-Reichl, K. A., & Lyubomirsky, S. (2012). Kindness counts: Prompting prosocial behavior in preadolescents boosts peer acceptance and well-being. *PLOS ONE, 7*(12), e51380.

Layous, K., Sweeny, K., Armenta, C., Na, S., Choi, I., & Lyubomirsky, S. (2017). The proximal experience of gratitude. *PLOS ONE, 12*(7), e0179123.

Lykken, D., & Tellegen, A. (1996). Happiness is a stochastic phenomenon. *Psychological Science, 7*(3), 186–189.

Lyubomirsky, S. (2001). Why are some people happier than others?: The role of cognitive and motivational processes in well-being. *American Psychologist, 56*(3), 239–249.

Lyubomirsky, S., Dickerhoof, R., Boehm, J. K., & Sheldon, K. M. (2011). Becoming happier takes both a will and a proper way: An experimental longitudinal intervention to boost well-being. *Emotion, 11*, 391–402.

Lyubomirsky, S., King, L., & Diener, E. (2005). The benefits of frequent positive affect: Does happiness lead to success? *Psychological Bulletin, 131*(6), 803–855.

Lyubomirsky, S., & Layous, K. (2013). How do simple positive activities increase well-being? *Current Directions in Psychological Science, 22*(1), 57–62.

Lyubomirsky, S., & Lepper, H. S. (1999). A measure of subjective happiness: Preliminary reliability and construct validation. *Social Indicators Research, 46*(2), 137–155.

Lyubomirsky, S., Sheldon, K. M., & Schkade, D. (2005). Pursuing happiness: The architecture of sustainable change. *Review of General Psychology, 9*(2), 111–131.

Mauss, I. B., Tamir, M., Anderson, C. L., & Savino, N. S. (2011). Can seeking happiness make people unhappy?: Paradoxical effects of valuing happiness. *Emotion, 11*(4), 807–815.

Miller, D. T., Dannals, J. E., & Zlatev, J. J. (2017). Behavioral processes in long-lag intervention studies. *Perspectives on Psychological Science, 12*(3), 454–467.

Mor, N., & Winquist, J. (2002). Self-focused attention and negative affect: A meta-analysis. *Psychological Bulletin, 128*(4), 638–662.

Nelson, S. K., Della Porta, M. D., Jacobs Bao, K., Lee, H. C., Choi, I., & Lyubomirsky, S. (2015). "It's up to you": Experimentally manipulated autonomy support for prosocial behavior improves well-being in two cultures over six weeks. *Journal of Positive Psychology, 10*, 463–476.

Nelson, S. K., Layous, K., Cole, S. W., & Lyubomirsky, S. (2016). Do unto others or treat yourself?: The effects of prosocial and self-focused behavior on psychological flourishing. *Emotion, 16*(6), 850–861.

Otake, K., Shimai, S., Tanaka-Matsumi, J., Otsui, K., & Fredrickson, B. L. (2006). Happy people become happier through kindness: A counting kindnesses intervention. *Journal of Happiness Studies, 7*(3), 361–375.

Parks, A. C., Della Porta, M. D., Pierce, R. S., Zilca, R., & Lyubomirsky, S. (2012). Pursuing happiness in everyday life: The characteristics and behaviors of online happiness seekers. *Emotion, 12*(6), 1222–1234.

Peters, M. L., Smeets, E., Feijge, M., van Breukelen, G., Andersson, G., Buhrman, M., & Linton, S. J. (2017). Happy despite pain: A randomized controlled trial of an 8-week Internet-delivered positive psychology intervention for enhancing well-being in patients with chronic pain. *Clinical Journal of Pain, 33*(11), 962–975.

Peterson, C. (2006). *A primer in positive psychology.* Oxford, UK: Oxford University Press.

Peterson, C., & Seligman, M. (2004). *Character strengths and virtues: A handbook and classification.* Washington, DC: American Psychological Association Press.

Pressman, S. D., Jenkins, B. N., & Moskowitz, J. T. (2019). Positive affect and health: What do we know and where next should we go? *Annual Review of Psychology, 70*, 627–650.

Pressman, S. D., Kraft, T. L., & Cross, M. P. (2015). It's good to do good and receive good: The impact of a "pay it forward" style kindness intervention on giver and receiver well-being. *Journal of Positive Psychology, 10*(4), 293–302.

Proyer, R. T., Wellenzohn, S., Gander, F., & Ruch, W. (2015). Toward a better understanding of what makes positive psychology interventions work: Predicting happiness and depression from the person × intervention fit in a follow-up after 3.5 years. *Applied Psychology: Health and Well-Being, 7*(1), 108–128.

Quoidbach, J., Hansenne, M., & Mottet, C. (2008). Personality and mental time travel: A differential approach to autonoetic consciousness. *Consciousness and Cognition, 17*(4), 1082–1092.

Redwine, L., Henry, B. L., Pung, M. A., Wilson, K., Chinh, K., Knight, B., . . . Mills, P. J. (2016). A pilot randomized study of a gratitude journaling intervention on HRV and inflammatory biomarkers in stage B heart failure patients. *Psychosomatic Medicine, 78*(6), 667–676.

Ryan, R. M., & Deci, E. L. (2000). Self-determination theory and the facilitation of intrinsic motivation, social development, and well-being. *American Psychologist, 55*(1), 68–78.

Sandstrom, G. M., & Dunn, E. W. (2014). Social interactions and well-being: The surprising power of weak ties. *Personality and Social Psychology Bulletin, 40*(7), 910–922.

Sedikides, C., Wildschut, T., Routledge, C., Arndt, J., Hepper, E. G., & Zhou, X. (2015). To nostalgize: Mixing memory with affect and desire. *Advances in Experimental Social Psychology, 51*(10), 189–273.

Seligman, M. E. P., & Csikszentmihalyi, M. (2000). Positive psychology: An introduction. *American Psychologist, 55*, 5–14.

Seligman, M. E. P., Rashid, T., & Parks, A. C. (2006). Positive psychotherapy. *American Psychologist, 61*(8), 774–788.

Seligman, M. E. P., Steen, T. A., Park, N., & Peterson, C. (2005). Positive psychology progress: Empirical validation of interventions. *American Psychologist, 60,* 410–421.

Senf, K., & Liau, A. K. (2013). The effects of positive interventions on happiness and depressive symptoms, with an examination of personality as a moderator. *Journal of Happiness Studies, 14*(2), 591–612.

Sheldon, K. M., & Lyubomirsky, S. (2006). How to increase and sustain positive emotion: The effects of expressing gratitude and visualizing best possible selves. *Journal of Positive Psychology, 1*(2), 73–82.

Sherman, D. K., Cohen, G. L., Nelson, L. D., Nussbaum, A. D., Bunyan, D. P., & Garcia, J. (2009). Affirmed yet unaware: Exploring the role of awareness in the process of self-affirmation. *Journal of Personality and Social Psychology, 97*(5), 745–764.

Silverman, A., Logel, C., & Cohen, G. L. (2013). Self-affirmation as a deliberate coping strategy: The moderating role of choice. *Journal of Experimental Social Psychology, 49*(1), 93–98.

Sin, N. L., Della Porta, M. D., & Lyubomirsky, S. (2011). Tailoring positive psychology interventions to treat depressed individuals. In S. I. Donaldson, M. Csikszentmihalyi, & J. Nakamura (Eds.), *Applied positive psychology: Improving everyday life, health, schools, work, and society* (pp. 79–96). New York: Routledge.

Sin, N. L., & Lyubomirsky, S. (2009). Enhancing well-being and alleviating depressive symptoms with positive psychology interventions: A practice-friendly meta-analysis. *Journal of Clinical Psychology, 65*(5), 467–487.

Smith, M. L., & Glass, G. V. (1977). Meta-analysis of psychotherapy outcome studies. *American Psychologist, 32*(9), 752–760.

Van Boven, L., & Gilovich, T. (2003). To do or to have?: That is the question. *Journal of Personality and Social Psychology, 85*(6), 1193–1202.

Van Tongeren, D. R., & Burnette, J. L. (2018). Do you believe happiness can change?: An investigation of the relationship between happiness mindsets, well-being, and satisfaction. *Journal of Positive Psychology, 13*(2), 101–109.

Vansteenkiste, M., Simons, J., Lens, W., Sheldon, K. M., & Deci, E. L. (2004). Motivating learning, performance, and persistence: The synergistic effects of intrinsic goal contents and autonomy-supportive contexts. *Journal of Personality and Social Psychology, 87*(2), 246–260.

Walsh, L. C., Boehm, J. K., & Lyubomirsky, S. (2018). Does happiness promote career success?: Revisiting the evidence. *Journal of Career Assessment, 26*(2), 199–219.

Walsh, L. C., & Lyubomirsky, S. (2018). *To share or not to share?: The effects of sharing gratitude on actors and targets.* Poster presented at the annual meeting of the Society for Personality and Social Psychologists, Atlanta, GA.

Walton, G. M., & Cohen, G. L. (2011). A brief social-belonging intervention improves academic and health outcomes of minority students. *Science, 331*(6023), 1447–1451.

Walton, G. M., & Wilson, T. D. (2018). Wise interventions: Psychological remedies for social and personal problems. *Psychological Review, 125*(5), 617–655.

Watkins, P. C., Woodward, K., Stone, T., & Kolts, R. L. (2003). Gratitude and happiness: Development of a measure of gratitude, and relationships with subjective well-being. *Social Behavior and Personality: An International Journal, 31*(5), 431–451.

Wildschut, T., Sedikides, C., Arndt, J., & Routledge, C. (2006). Nostalgia: Content, triggers, functions. *Journal of Personality and Social Psychology, 91*(5), 975–993.

Williamson, G. M., & Clark, M. S. (1989). Providing help and desired relationship type as determinants of changes in moods and self-evaluations. *Journal of Personality and Social Psychology, 56*(5), 722–734.

Yeager, D. S., & Walton, G. M. (2011). Social-psychological interventions in education: They're not magic. *Review of Educational Research, 81*(2), 267–301.

CHAPTER 9

The Stress-Mindset Intervention

Alia J. Crum, Isaac J. Handley-Miner, and Eric N. Smith

The substantial body of research depicting the damaging effects of stress has spurred a decidedly negative cultural narrative around stress. There is also considerable evidence, however, that stress can improve people's health, well-being, and performance. In this chapter, we detail an intervention designed to shift people's mindset about stress from the prevailing mindset that stress is debilitating to the mindset that stress can be enhancing. We describe several lab- and field-based studies that demonstrate improvements in health, well-being, and performance from this mindset intervention via attentional, affective, motivational, and physiological mechanisms. Situating this intervention in the wise intervention framework, we detail the structure and content of the intervention, outline important considerations for implementing the intervention, and discuss the intervention's contribution to existing psychological theory.

BACKGROUND

Hans Selye, often referred to as the "father of stress," began his career as a medical student in Prague in the 1920s. During his medical training, he noted a specific sickly appearance of his patients; regardless of their diagnosis or circumstance, they all displayed the same haggard quality. These observations inspired his experimental work with rats at McGill University in the 1930s and 1940s, leading to his exploration of the stress response, or "Selye's syndrome," as he sometimes referred to it (Jackson, 2014; Selye, 1974). Selye notes in his seminal 1936 letter to the editor in *Nature*—considered by many historians as the inception of modern research on the biological and psychological effects of stress—that the experience of stress triggered by "non-specific nocuous agents" (e.g., physical injury, extreme amounts of exercise, exposure to cold) causes rats to undergo a consistent and predictable physiological response (p. 32). He describes this "general adaptation syndrome" as consisting of three stages: an alarm reaction as the body prepares to defend itself, a period of resistance as the body begins adapting to the heightened alarm state, and, ultimately, exhaustion as the body can no longer sustain the taxing effects of the alarm state (Selye, 1936, p. 32). Selye's work, documented in the roughly 1,500 articles and 32 books he authored over his lifetime, came to dominate the field of stress research (Jackson, 2014; Szabo, Tache, & Somogyi, 2012).

Although stress can be defined neutrally as the experience or anticipation of challenge or threat in one's goal-related efforts, much of the research following in the wake of Selye's depiction of stress documented damaging physiological and psychological effects of stress. For example, research has demonstrated that chronic stress can lead to memory loss (Sapolsky, 1996), posttraumatic stress disorder (Lupien, McEwen, Gunnar, & Heim, 2009), and depression (Hammen, 2005). Stress has also been linked to greater susceptibility to upper respiratory viruses, faster progression of HIV to acquired immunodeficiency syndrome (AIDS), and higher incidence of cardiovascular disease (Schneiderman, Ironson, & Siegel, 2005). Spurred by this research, popular media outlets have enthusiastically saddled up for the war on stress with headlines declaring, "Even the Youngest of Us Need to Learn to Battle Stress" (*Newsweek,* 2018) and "Work-Related Stress Can Kill, Study Finds" (Kahn, 2008).

The notoriety of these research findings and the media attention they inspired have spawned the rigid cultural perspective that stress is bad. Accompanying this attitude, scores of stress management programs have cropped up, promising to help people mitigate stress and its negative effects. The idea of stress management can be attributed in part to the critical insight that the outcomes of stress are not driven only by the sheer amount of stress one experiences but also by how one copes with that stress—in other words, the manner in which people appraise stress and mobilize cognitive and behavioral resources to combat stress (Billings & Moos, 1981; Carver, Scheier, & Weintraub, 1989; Folkman & Lazarus, 1980; Lazarus & Folkman, 1984; Penley, Tomaka, & Wiebe, 2002). Yet, stress management programs all too often focus solely on reducing stress, and while a few stress management programs have shown promising results (e.g., the mindfulness-based stress-reduction program; Creswell, 2017), many of them have failed to produce reliable benefits (Somerfield & McCrae, 2000).

A stress-reduction approach has several practical shortcomings. First, some stress may be too significant or variable to be effectively reduced though coping mechanisms. Poverty, for example, is notoriously difficult to escape and can sprout a host of additional stressors and cognitive demands (Mullainathan & Shafir, 2013), rendering the stress associated with it a poor candidate for "reduction" techniques. Second, a life of avoiding stress would likely leave one without much of what people treasure most—getting an education, pursuing a career, maintaining strong friendships, and raising children, among other meaningful goals; all generally involve experiencing some degree of stress. Last, the irony of the stress-reduction movement is that it may be inadvertently adding to the stress many people experience. Experiencing stress, while being bombarded with the message that stress is bad, can cause people to worry about the negative effects of that stress (Brady, Hard, & Gross, 2018), and similar types of recurring and intrusive thoughts, and the cognitive resources they take up, have been shown to have negative outcomes (e.g., Logel, Iserman, Davies, Quinn, & Spencer, 2009; Schmader, Johns, & Forbes, 2008). McGonigal (2015) captures this stressed-about-stress phenomenon in the book *The Upside of Stress*: "When a friend of mine was pregnant with her first child, she saw a study online that put her in a panic. The headline warned that a mother's stress during pregnancy is passed on to the baby. My friend was under a lot of pressure at work, and she began to worry. Was she permanently harming her baby by not going on early maternity leave?" (p. 43). This "meta-stress" is an ironic and unfortunate by-product of well-intentioned attempts to help people reduce their stress.

What has come of this negative portrayal of stress in our culture? We spend vast amounts of money on stress management programs, but people's stress levels do not seem to be improving (Gallup Daily: U.S. Mood, 2018; Saad, 2017). Of course, there are a multitude of ecological, societal, and cultural factors influencing stress levels, but we have little encouraging evidence that our current stress-reduction culture is living up to its promise. Furthermore, by focusing on the negative outcomes of stress, we have inadvertently created a culture that is now stressed about stress.

A "NEW" PERSPECTIVE ON STRESS

It stands to reason that Selye's early work would have focused on the negative consequences of stress. As a medical student, Selye observed sick people day after day, and the people he saw regularly were those who remained patients. What perspective might he have adopted had he continued to observe the people who made swift recoveries from the same conditions that plagued those still bedridden in his hospital? Or what about those who never entered his hospital?

Later in his career, Selye (1976) recognized another form stress could take: eustress, or "good" stress. Selye noted the importance of distinguishing between *eu*stress and *dis*tress—"the former being agreeable or healthy, and the latter, disagreeable or pathogenic" (p. 54)—and even attributed his own health and well-being to eustress: "What is important is to live so that one's distress is converted into eustress. In any event, that is what has kept me healthy and happy" (p. 55). Despite Selye's endorsement, public attention around eustress was far outpaced by that around distress. As the concept of eustress faded to academic obscurity, stress and distress soon became synonymous for most practitioners and consumers of stress research.

There is a strong body of research demonstrating the beneficial effects of stress as Selye's distinction suggests. Stress has been linked with enhanced cognitive performance, personal initiative, and emotional stability (Dienstbier, 1989; Epel, McEwen, & Ickovics, 1998; Fay & Sonnentag, 2002). Stress can promote physiological thriving, facilitating the healing response and enhancing immunity (Dienstbier, 1989; Epel et al., 1998). Research on "posttraumatic growth" has even shown that severe bouts of stress triggered by traumas, such as life-threatening illness or military combat, can, in some instances, have positive outcomes, such as improved relationships, greater appreciation for life, and enhanced perceptions of personal strength (Tedeschi & Calhoun, 2004).

This research on the benefits of stress does not render the research illustrating the harmful effects of stress any less important or real. Rather, it suggests that the effects of stress are paradoxical: stress has the capability to either help or harm our health, well-being, and performance. The question then is: What is the distinguishing factor that determines whether the stress we experience will manifest in positive or negative outcomes?

This chapter reviews the manner in which mindset serves as a moderating factor in determining the stress response. In the tradition of wise interventions (Walton & Wilson,

2018), the stress-mindset intervention was designed to change the subjective meaning people ascribe to stress in order to influence how stress affects their health, well-being, and performance. Specifically, this intervention educates people about the ways in which stress can have enhancing effects in their daily lives in order to shift people's mindsets from the prevailing view that stress is harmful (a "stress-is-debilitating mindset") to the view that stress can be beneficial to health, well-being, and performance (a "stress-can-be-enhancing mindset").

PSYCHOLOGICAL PROCESSES

The core psychological process theorized to underlie this intervention is shifting mindsets—beliefs or theories about the nature and workings of things and processes in the world (Dweck, 2006). The world is complex and inherently subjective; mindsets serve organizing, orienting, and activating purposes, guiding people's attention, motivation, affect, and physiology, sometimes in ways that lead to self-fulfilling effects (Crum, Salovey, & Achor, 2013).

A plethora of research demonstrates that the mindsets people hold influence health and behavior in numerous domains. Our work on stress mindset was inspired by research on mindsets about intelligence. In this work, students who are encouraged through intervention to adopt the mindset that intelligence is malleable—something that can be grown and developed—are more likely to take steps toward building their intelligence, such as choosing more challenging tasks (Yeager et al., 2016) and seeking out and attending to feedback (Mangels, Butterfield, Lamb, Good, & Dweck, 2006). Furthermore, it appears that certain mindsets can directly affect physiology without measurable changes in behavior. For example, a group of hotel room attendants who adopted the mindset that their work was good exercise lost weight and had lower blood pressure 4 weeks later (Crum & Langer, 2007). In another study, participants who were told a milkshake they drank was "decadent" (e.g., containing lots of fat, sugar, and calories) experienced a greater drop in the hunger hormone ghrelin compared to those who believed the same milkshake was "sensible" (e.g., containing minimal fat, sugar, and calories; Crum, Corbin, Brownell, & Salovey, 2011).

A core feature of mindset research, as is core to wise interventions more broadly (Walton & Wilson, 2018), is that mindset interventions do not need to alter the objective qualities of people or situations in order to promote benefit. This suggests that improving people's response to stress does not require changing or reducing the amount of stress they are experiencing or equipping them with an improved skill set—rather, changing people's interpretation of what experiencing stress means can improve their response to stress. Thus, the stress-mindset intervention is designed to alter peoples' mindset about stress by providing them with information on how stress can be enhancing. This is in direct contrast to other interventions that offer strategies to reduce and/or cope with stress. The theory is that establishing this stress-can-be-enhancing mindset will lead to improved health, well-being, and performance by altering the emotional states people experience during times of stress, what people attend to and are motivated to do when in a state of stress, and how the body responds hormonally to stress, as discussed in the "Mechanisms" section below.

The core psychological construct of stress mindset can be measured by the Stress Mindset Measure (SMM; Crum et al., 2013), an eight-item measure that asks participants the extent to which they agree or disagree with a series of statements about the consequences of stress for health and vitality, learning and growth, and performance and productivity. This measure has been validated and explored in a number of samples, including college students (Crum, Akinola, Martin, & Fath, 2017; Goyer, Akinola, Grunberg, & Crum, 2019), employees at a large financial firm (Crum et al., 2013) and a large technology firm (Crum et al., 2019), Navy SEALs (Smith, Young, & Crum, 2019), and a sample of middle school students (tested using a youth version of the SMM; Park et al., 2017). Most research suggests that, prior to intervention, people typically fall on the "stress-is-debilitating" side of the scale, reflecting our cultural milieu. The SMM can be accessed at *https://mbl.stanford.edu/materials-measures/stress-mindset-measure*.

EMPIRICAL EVIDENCE

Outcomes

Evidence from existing stress-mindset research indicates that preexisting stress mindsets are associated with health, well-being, and performance outcomes. Having a stress-can-be-enhancing mindset has been tied to improved self-reported health and energy levels, reduced symptoms of anxiety and depression, and greater life satisfaction and performance at work (Crum et al., 2013). While these initial results were correlational, subsequent randomized controlled trials established causal links between stress-can-be-enhancing mindsets and these domains (Crum et al., 2019; Crum et al., 2013, 2017; Goyer et al., 2019).

In the initial experimental study manipulating stress mindsets, a randomly assigned group of employees at a large Fortune 500 company watched a series of short videos about the positive effects of stress. Meanwhile, another group watched videos on the negative effects of stress that presented similar information to what they might encounter reading a news article or participating in a traditional stress management workshop and a third control group watched no videos. Participants in the treatment group adopted more of a stress-can-be-enhancing mindset (as assessed by the SMM) and, 1 week later, reported fewer negative health symptoms associated with depression and anxiety than both of the other groups (Crum et al., 2013). As this intervention took place in a work setting, we also investigated the effects of adopting a stress-can-be-enhancing mindset on people's self-reported work performance. One week after the video intervention, those in the treatment group reported stronger performance on composite measures of both "hard" skills—those related to productivity, including the quality, quantity, accuracy, and efficiency of their work; and "soft" skills—those related to the abilities to sustain focus, communicate effectively, generate new ideas, and contribute to the overall work environment (Crum et al., 2013).

In a pair of follow-up studies to the seminal intervention, we tested many of the same primary outcomes, but implemented more involved versions of the intervention. In the first study, employees were recruited from a large financial institution shortly after the 2008 financial collapse to participate in a 2-hour live training on stress mindset. In the second study, employees from a large technology company took a 90-minute online training about stress mindset. (See the "Intervention Content and Implementation" section for more information on the features of this intervention approach compared to the approach used in earlier studies.) Both randomized interventions found positive effects on symptoms of anxiety and depression, and participants from the financial institution also reported higher satisfaction with their physical health 4 weeks after the intervention (Crum et al., 2019). Furthermore, results from these interventions again suggested that shifting stress mindsets has the potential to influence hard and soft skills in the workplace (Crum et al., 2019).

We also adapted our intervention messages for an education setting by conducting a study with low-income, ethnic-minority students entering an elite university. This population of students is especially likely to experience stress and pressure in a collegiate setting. One objective of this study was to compare the stress-mindset intervention to a traditional stress management program. As such, there were four conditions: (1) the treatment condition in which students received an in-person stress-mindset intervention similar to that used with the employees from the large financial institution described above; (2) a stress management intervention condition in which students received an in-person stress management training of comparable length and format to the treatment condition; (3) a low-socioeconomic status (SES), no-treatment control group; and (4) a high-SES, no-treatment control group. Results showed that participants in the mindset condition experienced higher levels of positive affect during periods of high stress—in this case, finals weeks—than college students who received either no intervention or a traditional stress management intervention (Goyer et al., 2019). Furthermore, in the low-SES, no-treatment control condition, there was a significant negative relationship between levels of perceived stress immediately before the freshman final exam week and self-reported exam scores, such that higher perceived stress prior to the final exam week was associated with lower exam performance; the same relationship was nonsignificant for those in the stress-mindset, stress management, and high-SES conditions. This suggests that the stress-mindset intervention may have helped mitigate the negative association between perceived stress and exam performance for low-SES students.

This series of experimental studies offer substantial evidence that we can make significant differences in people's lived experiences by encouraging them to revise the subjective meaning they assign to stress. The next section explores how a shift in mindset can produce these changes in health, well-being, and performance.

Mechanisms

We theorize that individuals' mindsets about the nature of stress can impact health, well-being, and performance outcomes through four mechanisms: attention, affect, motivation, and physiology. We review each of these mechanisms below. Although these mechanisms represent simplified theoretical pathways, we suspect that a set of recursive processes occur in which each of these mechanisms mutually reinforce one another. Furthermore, we recognize that many of the proposed mechanisms are important outcomes in and of themselves depending on the research question, but provide them here with a focus on how these mechanisms might affect global levels of psychological and physical flourishing. An illustration of the mechanisms of stress mindset can be found in Figure 9.1.

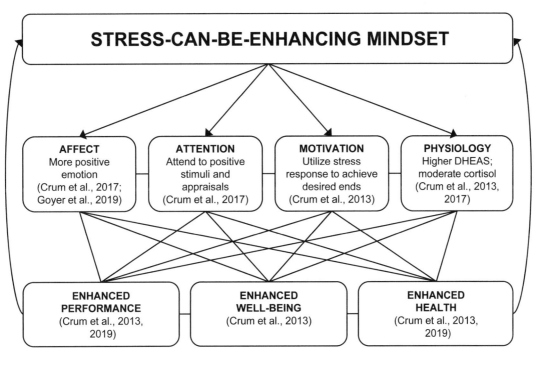

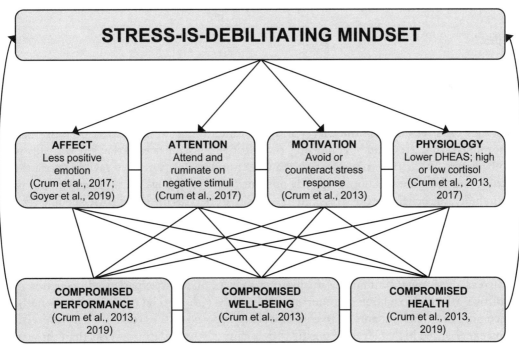

FIGURE 9.1. Theorized mechanisms of the stress-mindset intervention.

Attention

When experiencing stress, the mindset people have about whether it is debilitating or enhancing is likely to influence attention in logical ways. In theory, having a stress-is-debilitating mindset will lead people to focus on all the ways stress might be a negative force in their life, whereas having a stress-can-be-enhancing mindset will lead them to look for and be more mindful of the ways stress has positive effects. Indeed, research suggests that people who are led to adopt a stress-can-be-enhancing mindset are more likely to display an attentional bias toward positive stimuli (Crum et al., 2017).

More generally, we posit attention as an important mechanism of stress-mindset interventions because what people attend to (and how they think about what they attend to) has been shown to impact performance (e.g., attending to information critical to succeeding at a particular task; Chajut & Algom, 2003), mental health and well-being (e.g., not ruminating on negative events or self-perceptions; Nilly & Winquist, 2002), and even physical health (e.g., attending to stimuli that reinforce or bring to mind positive expectations about healing; Zion & Crum, 2018). Given these straightforward pathways and the encouraging experimental results reported above, more research should be conducted on the specific attentional outcomes of stress-mindset interventions. We would expect changes in both what one focuses on as well as how—and how long—he or she thinks about it. Such attributional and rumination patterns are likely to differ depending on one's mindset about stress (see Amirkhan, 1990), but these mechanisms have not yet been tested in experimental settings.

Affect

The second mechanism through which stress mindsets are expected to impact health, well-being, and performance outcomes is changing how people feel when stressed. Again, the logic is fairly straightforward. If people hold the mindset that stress is debilitating, then they are likely to experience stress even more negatively because not only are they stressed but they are stressed about the effects of stress. If that same stress is experienced through the mindset that stress can be enhancing, the affective consequences of that stress are likely to be better. While the stress-can-be-enhancing mindset does not necessarily remove the stress, and therefore will not completely mitigate negative feelings, such as nervousness or irritability, the belief that the stress can have positive effects is likely to provide people with more positive affect, such as feelings of excitement, determination, and inspiration.

Indeed, research supports these mindset-based alterations in affect. Participants completing a mock job interview who were taught about the enhancing aspects of stress experienced increases in positive affect when confronted with the stressful experience, whereas those taught about the debilitating aspects of stress experienced decreases in positive affect throughout the course of the study (Crum et al., 2017). Additionally, incoming first-year students at an elite university exposed to the stress-mindset intervention experienced higher levels of positive affect during stressful exam weeks than those in the stress management and no-treatment control groups (Goyer et al., 2019). These two studies found no evidence of changes in negative affect. Employees at the large technology company who participated in the stress-mindset intervention experienced a small trending decrease in negative effect, which could reflect a reduction in stress about stress since they also reported lower levels of perceived distress, but future research should investigate this link further (Crum et al., 2019). Across studies, observed changes in positive affect have been much stronger and more robust than changes in negative affect, indicating that viewing stress as enhancing boosts positive emotions, but does not necessarily eliminate the stress and the negative affect stress produces.

Such mindset-generated improvements in positive affect during stress can be a critical determinant in shaping whether or not stress will have lasting effects on physiological health and well-being. A wealth of research supports the benefits of positive affect for mental and physical health, including psychological resilience, physiological immunity, and healthier behavior (see Fredrickson & Joiner, 2018; Salovey, Rothman, Detweiler, & Steward, 2000, for an overview). Positive affect has also been shown to promote a host of skills and behaviors associated with performance in a broad range of contexts, including creativity and problem solving (see Lyubomirsky, King, & Diener, 2005, for an overview).

Motivation

Another mechanism that we propose underlies the outcomes of stress-mindset interventions is what people are motivated to do when in a state of stress. People demonstrate a range of behavioral responses to stress, but a simple, yet highly meaningful dimension of these responses is the degree to which individuals approach or avoid stressful information and events (Roth & Cohen, 1986). If people view stress as enhancing, it stands to reason that they would be motivated to approach and actively address a stressful situation, whereas those who view stress as debilitating would be motivated to reduce, avoid, or distance themselves from the stressful situation.

To test these proposed mechanisms, Crum and colleagues (2013) measured the stress mindsets of a group of college students taking an introductory psychology class. Several weeks later, these students were told that a number of them would be selected to give presentations during that class session. Students were then asked whether they would like to receive feedback on their presentation from their peers and/or experts at the business school. Individuals who had a stress-can-be-enhancing mindset were significantly more likely than those with a stress-is-debilitating mindset to request feedback, which represented a more approach-motivated response to the stressful act of public speaking (Crum et al., 2013). While this finding is only correlational, it provides initial evidence that approach motivation may contribute to the positive outcomes we see from stress-mindset interventions. Indeed, research suggests that for stressors that are recurring and can be addressed, actively approaching the stressor (in this case, seeking feedback so as to improve one's public speaking skills) generally results in less long-term distress than avoiding the stressor (in this case, opting out of feedback so as to avoid thinking further about the stressful event), primarily because the latter approach does nothing to resolve the cause of the stress (Carver & Connor-Smith, 2010).

Physiology

The final mechanism we propose as core to the success of stress-mindset interventions is direct physiological effects. Research on placebo and nocebo effects has demonstrated the power of our associations and expectations to elicit physiological change, even without behavioral change (see Zion & Crum, 2018, for a review). Because our mindset about stress will, almost by definition, influence the associations and expectations we hold for stress, we expected shifts in stress mindsets to have measurable physiological consequences.

When in a state of stress, our bodies release catabolic and anabolic hormones. Catabolic hormones, such as cortisol, stimulate the breakdown of proteins to generate energy for the body, but prolonged exposure can be damaging, leading to conditions such as osteoporosis, hypertension, and cardiovascular disease. Anabolic hormones such as dehydroepiandrosterone sulfate (DHEA-S) act in opposition to catabolic hormones, stimulating cell repair to facilitate healing processes (Charney, 2004; Epel et al., 1998). In one study, we measured the salivary cortisol levels of students who were told they might be selected to give an impromptu presentation to their class. Results revealed that among students with a stress-can-be-enhancing mindset during this task, those with a high baseline cortisol response experienced reduced cortisol levels and those with a low baseline cortisol response experienced increased cortisol levels (Crum et al., 2013). As suggested by Crum et al., this moderating effect may represent a more adaptive response than a simple across-the-board decrease in cortisol levels because deficient cortisol levels have been associated with negative outcomes, such as increased susceptibility to inflammatory and autoimmune diseases (Sternberg, 2001), and moderate levels of arousal tend to promote peak performance (Yerkes & Dodson, 1908). While correlational, these findings hint at a connection between stress mindsets and physiological responses to stress.

Moreover, in the study in which participants engaged in a mock job interview, salivary DHEA-S and cortisol levels were also measured. While those in the stress-can-be-enhancing condition did not experience a significant change in cortisol levels in response to the challenge,[1] they did experience a boost in the anabolic hormone DHEA-S (Crum et al., 2017), again suggesting a more adaptive response to stress. In addition to facilitating healing responses, DHEA-S is thought to protect neurons in the hippocampus from some of the harmful effects of cortisol and evidence suggests that it may promote psychological resilience (Charney, 2004). More research is needed to understand the physiological mechanisms of stress mindsets.

Effects over Time

Although little data exist on the long-term effects of stress-mindset interventions, the limited data we do have hints that effects of the intervention hold up over time. Crum et al. (2019) report positive outcomes 4 weeks postintervention—however, these findings do not indicate how the effects might diminish or extend past this point. The strongest test of longitudinal efficacy over multiple time points comes from the intervention conducted with low-income students beginning college at an elite university. These students received the stress-mindset intervention during the summer before their freshman year and then received a "booster" version of the intervention during the fall semester of their freshman year. Compared to both a group that received a traditional stress management training and a no-treatment control group, those who received the stress-mindset intervention

---

[1] The effects of cortisol in this study were in response to an acute stressor on a single day. Because we did not have cortisol response on a baseline day, we were unable to test the more complex reactivity pattern found in Crum et al. (2013) in which a stress-can-be-enhancing mindset was associated with elevated cortisol for hyporesponders and decreased cortisol for hyperresponders.

experienced higher levels of positive affect during the finals weeks of both their freshman spring and sophomore spring. In fact, the difference between the stress-mindset group and the other two groups was directionally larger the second year—a difference of 0.43 standard deviation between the no-treatment control and the stress-mindset intervention the first year and a difference of 0.48 standard deviation the second year (Goyer et al., 2019).

These results align with the theory behind mindset interventions, which predicts that mindset interventions can have lasting—and perhaps even compounding—effects. If after partaking in a stress-mindset intervention an individual construes a new bout of stress as enhancing, he or she should be more likely to think and behave in ways that make him or her more likely to experience positive outcomes from that stress. Experiencing positive outcomes, in turn, should bolster his or her stress mindset. This recursive process, characteristic of wise interventions (Walton & Wilson, 2018), may explain why the gap in positive affect between students who took part in the stress-mindset intervention and students in the other two conditions increased between freshman and sophomore year, even though these students did not receive a stress-mindset booster in that time frame. Nevertheless, more research is needed before we can say with confidence how this intervention impacts long-term outcomes.

Heterogeneity

While there has been very little exploration to date of potential moderators of the stress-mindset intervention (Jamieson, Crum, Goyer, Marisa, & Akinola, 2018), our theory suggests that stress itself could be a moderator. If people are not experiencing stress, their newfound stress-can-be-enhancing mindset would have no fuel to produce meaningful outcomes. Similarly, we would expect that the more stress a person is experiencing, the bigger the effects of this intervention would be, which exploratory analyses have supported (Smith et al., 2019). However, if people are particularly obstinate in their view that stress is debilitating—perhaps due to a lifetime spent attributing stress as the cause of negative events—they may not benefit from this intervention. Additionally, a rather obvious point that nonetheless bears stating is that this intervention would also be unlikely to have an effect if participants already hold a strong stress-can-be-enhancing mindset. As such, this intervention may be less effective in the aggregate among cultures or subpopulations that already have a more positive view of stress. On the other hand, in line with wise intervention theory (Walton & Wilson, 2018), people in these populations who do not yet have a stress-can-be-enhancing mindset might see longer-lasting benefits from stress-mindset interventions because the cultural messaging they are exposed to on a daily basis will help maintain and bolster a stress-can-be-enhancing perspective. Future research should directly test these hypotheses.

COUSINS

This work draws on decades of research on the impact of mindsets (sometimes referred to as "implicit theories") that people hold about the nature and workings of things and processes in the world, such as the nature of intelligence (Dweck & Leggett, 1988), personality (Chiu, Hong, & Dweck, 1997), and emotions (Romero, Master, Paunesku, Dweck, &

Gross, 2014). Stress-mindset work is similar in that it further demonstrates that mindsets can affect behavior (Dweck & Leggett, 1988), well-being (Smith et al., 2018), and performance (Blackwell, Trzesniewski, & Dweck, 2007), and that these mindsets are malleable through intervention (e.g., Paunesku et al., 2015; Yeager et al., 2016). It also extends this research by showing that mindsets need not reflect only beliefs about the extent to which something is fixed versus malleable, but can also reflect beliefs about other characteristics, such as whether something will have enhancing or debilitating effects.

Research on stress mindsets, akin to research on mindset more generally, is related to but distinct from research and theory on attributions and appraisals (see Wilson & Linville, 1982). Mindsets are similar to appraisals in that they are subjective judgments regarding a complex and ambiguous reality. Mindsets are distinct, however, in that they can exist in the mind (consciously or subconsciously) in an ever-ready fashion, whereas appraisals and attributions occur in response to a specific situation. More precisely, stress mindset encompasses the beliefs one ascribes to stress, whether they are currently in a stressful situation or not. Appraisals refer to situation-specific evaluations, such as how much stress one perceives and the degree to which one evaluates it as a threat (appraised demands exceed appraised resources) versus a challenge (appraised resources meet appraised demands; see Blascovich et al., 2003; Blascovich, Mendes, Hunter, & Lickel, 2000).

The stress reappraisal intervention is especially similar to the stress-mindset intervention. Described in more detail by Jamieson and Hangen (Chapter 10, this volume), this intervention teaches people that the physiological arousal they may experience while stressed can be useful (as opposed to detrimental). For example, students who were informed about the potential benefits that physiological arousal can have on performance prior to taking a practice Graduate Record Examination (GRE) not only performed better on the math portion in that lab setting but went on to report higher scores on the actual GRE (Jamieson, Mendes, Blackstock, & Schmader, 2010; see also Brady et al., 2018; Jamieson, Peters, Greenwood, & Altose, 2016; Jamieson & Hangen, Chapter 10, this volume). This can be seen as a targeted substantiation of stress-can-be-enhancing mindset, in which one particular indicator of stress (physiological arousal) in one particular instance (during tests) improves one particular outcome (performance). This approach could also be applied more broadly, and indeed, our recent theory and research is focusing on synergizing these two interventions into what we call "stress optimization" (Crum, Jamieson, & Akinola, 2020; Jamieson et al., 2018).

INTERVENTION CONTENT AND IMPLEMENTATION

The stress-mindset intervention aims to expose participants to the many ways that stress can, in fact, be enhancing—a perspective that counters the prevailing cultural narrative on stress. Using examples from a variety of domains, the intervention seeks to broaden people's understanding of how stress can enhance everyday experiences, such as focus and productivity, recovery from illness, and appreciation for life. To date, the intervention has been delivered using two different structures: (1) a series of short videos that review selective facts about the effects of stress (Crum et al., 2013, 2017), and (2) a 1- to 2-hour training employing a metacognitive approach that provides a balanced view of the positive and negative effects of stress and incorporates personal reflection exercises (Crum et al., 2019).

Stress-Mindset Intervention 1.0

The shorter, selective-information approach first employed by Crum et al. (2013) included three 3-minute videos on the topics of health, performance, and learning and growth. The videos contained a combination of music, images, and text, and delivered messages such as "The secretion of stress hormones does more than just protect the body from harm. These hormones help rebuild cells, synthesize proteins, and enhance immunity." In Crum et al. (2017), only one 3-minute video on the topic of cognitive performance was used to shift mindsets, and included messages such as "This stress response is designed to enhance your focus, decision making, memory, [and] performance." Table 9.1 provides

TABLE 9.1. **Messages Delivered in Stress-Mindset Manipulation Videos and Example Evidence Provided to Participants**

	Stress is debilitating	Stress can be enhancing
Health and vitality (Crum, Salovey, & Achor, 2013)	*Message:* Stress harms your physical health.	*Message:* Stress can make you stronger and healthier.
	Example evidence: Stress has been linked with frequent colds, hypertension, and cardiovascular disease.	*Example evidence:* Stress leads to the secretion of growth hormones that rebuild cells, synthesize proteins, and enhance immunity.
	Herbert & Cohen (1993); Sapolsky (1996); Schneiderman, Ironson, & Siegel (2005)	Dienstbier (1989); Epel, McEwen, & Ickovics (1998)
Learning and growth (Crum et al., 2013)	*Message:* Stress threatens your well-being.	*Message:* Stress can help you grow.
	Example evidence: Stress can lead to irritability, emotional exhaustion, low morale/self-esteem, loss of enjoyment, and memory loss.	*Example evidence:* The experience of stress and adversity can promote deeper relationships, new perspectives, and greater appreciation for life.
	Schneiderman et al. (2005); Shapiro, Brown, & Biegel (2007); Shapiro, Shapiro, & Schwartz (2000)	Park, Cohen, & Murch (1996); Park & Helgeson (2006); Tedeschi & Calhoun (2004)
Performance and productivity (Crum et al., 2013)	*Message:* Stress makes you perform worse.	*Message:* Stress can help you perform better.
	Example evidence: Stress deteriorates your focus and decision making.	*Example evidence:* Stress enhances your focus and drive.
	Keinan (1987); McEwen & Sapolsky (1995); Schwabe & Wolf (2010)	Cahill, Gorski, & Le (2003); Fay & Sonnentag (2002); Hancock & Weaver (2005)
Cognitive performance (Crum, Akinola, Martin, & Fath, 2017)	*Message:* Stress deteriorates your cognitive performance.	*Message:* Stress can improve your cognitive performance.
	Example evidence: Feeling anxious while completing cognitive tasks can hurt performance.	*Example evidence:* Feeling anxious while engaging in cognitive performance tasks can help performance.
	Keinan (1987); McEwen & Sapolsky (1995); Schwabe & Wolf (2010)	Cahill et al. (2003); Hancock & Weaver (2005); Jamieson, Mendes, Blackstock, & Schmader (2010)

an overview of the messages delivered in each video, including the stress-is-debilitating videos employed as controls. All videos used in Crum et al. (2013, 2017) can be viewed at *https://mbl.stanford.edu/instruments/stress-mindset-manipulation-videos*.

Stress-Mindset Intervention 2.0

Although the interventions described above were short, easy to administer, and effectively shifted participants' mindsets, there were a handful of potential shortcomings. First, the original stress-mindset interventions delivered selective information—in this case, touting the positive effects of stress but not volunteering the negative effects. In reality, stress can be both enhancing and debilitating, and we may lose credence as scientists if we do not acknowledge these conflicting messages. Authenticity and noncoercive messages have been found to be important in past intervention work (e.g., Bryan et al., 2016; Yeager, Dahl, & Dweck, 2018), and thus we may discover interventions are more effective when they acknowledge the paradoxical nature of stress (see Crum et al., 2019).

Moreover, as psychological interventions are only a small portion of people's full psychological experience, participants will likely come across inconsistent evidence against a single-sided mindset intervention. For example, a participant of a stress-can-be-enhancing intervention who reads a news article on the negative health effects of stress or experiences a dip in his or her work performance due to stress may start to question the mindset the intervention intended to communicate. Thus, another limitation is that once people leave the context of the intervention and are inevitably assailed with information about the ill effects of stress, their mindset might drift back to its preintervention state.

And finally, employing informational videos that confer a single viewpoint is an inherently passive approach that does not offer people much agency over their mindsets. On the other hand, conveying the message that mindsets are changeable and offering people the opportunity to choose their own mindset might help interventions produce long-term shifts in participants' mindsets.

To patch these shortcomings, Study 1 of Crum et al. (2019) tested a new version of the stress-mindset intervention: a 2-hour live training consisting of three modules. Module 1 targeted the limitations of providing a one-sided view of stress by introducing the paradox of stress—the fact that stress can simultaneously have enhancing and debilitating effects on health, well-being, and performance. In addition to providing a more complete account of stress, this module was designed to help inoculate participants against future stress-is-debilitating messages. Addressing both sides of stress allows participants to reconcile this contrasting information in their mindsets. Additionally, in line with research on self-persuasion (Aronson, 1999), the module prompted participants to actively reflect on personal experiences in which stress was beneficial to make these messages more personally meaningful and more likely to be internalized.

Modules 2 and 3 addressed the lack-of-agency shortcoming by demonstrating the self-fulfilling nature of mindsets and empowering participants with a concrete technique for incorporating the information and shifting their stress mindset. Module 2 taught participants that mindsets can become self-fulfilling such that believing that stress can be enhancing can increase its beneficial effects. Likening the consequences of mindsets to the placebo effect, the training explored the power of mindsets with several examples of self-fulfilling physiological effects in contexts such as healing, aging, and exercising.

Finally, Module 3 coached participants to actively and deliberately adopt an adaptive stress mindset by (1) acknowledging any stress they were experiencing; (2) embracing the ways in which that stress may be important to their goals and values; and (3) utilizing the stress to improve their health, well-being, and performance. This intervention has since been transformed into a toolkit that includes videos and reflection questions and is available at *www.sparqtools.org/rethinkingstress*.

NUANCES AND MISCONCEPTIONS

Stress versus Stressors

When delivering a stress-mindset intervention, it is important to distinguish between stress and stressors. Stress is the experience or anticipation of challenge or threat in one's goal-related efforts and stressors are any events or conditions that lead to this anticipation. The stress-mindset intervention makes no claim that individual stressors are good things—rather, the intervention emphasizes that the stress that emanates from a stressor can, in some cases, have enhancing outcomes. At first blush, this may seem an inconsequential distinction. One might argue that if a stressor causes stress, and if that stress can be enhancing, then surely the stressor should be considered a good thing. But this view neglects the other outcomes that stressors can spawn. Take the loss of a loved one, for example. The occurrence itself is, of course, not a good thing. However, the resultant stress could be harnessed to motivate someone to seek out a support group where they then might develop strong new friendships. Or perhaps the stress could give them the impetus to make a change in their life that they had been meaning to make for a while (e.g., change jobs, rekindle a lost friendship, move to a new area). But accompanying that stress are likely many other outcomes—perhaps loneliness, fear, or loss of meaning. Although the *stress* from losing a loved one might have led to positive outcomes, such as new friends and a better job, it does not mean that this *stressor* was a positive thing. Many stressors—poverty, divorce, illness—are not in and of themselves good things, yet the process of undergoing these experiences can have enhancing outcomes (Tedeschi & Calhoun, 2004).

Managing versus Utilizing Stress

Given the popularity of stress management and reduction programs, participants may assume that an unspoken objective of the stress-mindset intervention is to diminish the amount of stress people are experiencing or to help people cope with the negative effects of stress. On the contrary, the goal is to help people adopt a mindset that will allow them to harness the stress that they will inevitably encounter in their daily lives. The focus, then, is on utilizing—not managing or reducing—the stress response to achieve improvements in health, well-being, and performance. One could channel the stress associated with a moral dilemma into connecting more deeply with their values. One could embrace the stress of rehabilitating an injury as an opportunity to grow more resilient. One could convert the stress of a difficult project at work into motivation and focus to complete the project faster. None of these examples involve reducing stress—rather, the goal is to refocus the energy inherent to stress so that your stress response can better serve you.

Seeking Out Stress

Although the intervention centers on utilizing stress, it is not meant to encourage taking on additional stress. While it is likely the case that additional stress could be useful in some circumstances, like attempting a challenging task or taking on a new role, the intervention clarifies that stress can have simultaneous positive and negative effects so it is not necessarily a good idea to seek out more stress for its enhancing properties. From an organizational perspective, just as this intervention is not an endorsement of taking on extra stress, it also should not come across as a rationale for the perpetuation of a stressful work, school, or caregiving environment. For example, in workplace settings, these interventions would backfire if employees felt that the implicit goal of the intervention was to get employees to work harder. It is important that this intervention comes from a place of care and a genuine desire to help people utilize inevitable and/or necessary stress in their lives, not a desire to help them pile on more. This may require a targeted and purposeful introduction to the intervention to make it clear to participants why this intervention is valuable and how the organization hopes its members will benefit from it.

IMPLICATIONS FOR PRACTICE

Together, this research suggests that stress management approaches may be substantially improved to the degree that they foster more useful mindsets about the nature of stress. To better disseminate a stress-can-be-enhancing mindset, we need to (1) collaborate with global organizations and technological platforms to deliver scaled-up interventions, (2) create trainings for practitioners (train the trainer) on methods of delivering these messages to reach broader audiences, and (3) influence health organizations (e.g., National Institutes of Health, World Health Organization) to be more mindful of what mindsets their messages convey.

In doing so, it is important to acknowledge that many people have spent their entire lives considering stress as harmful and something to be avoided whenever possible. Some participants may therefore experience knee-jerk skepticism to the notion that stress can be enhancing. To combat this response, the intervention incorporates a discussion of the paradox of stress, emphasizing that stress is by no means always good, and in fact can have simultaneous negative and positive consequences. However, organizations and practitioners hoping to capitalize on these ideas should ensure they do not suggest that people *should* hold a stress-can-be-enhancing mindset, but rather present scientific evidence for its benefits and allow participants to come to their own conclusion without coercion or condescension. As Walton and Wilson (2018) note, interventions are likely to be less effective when they are prescriptive—rather, participants should be given the space to generate their own narrative and incorporate these ideas in ways they find personally meaningful.

Of course, it is also important to note that this intervention is not a cure-all across any context in which we might deploy it. Research has suggested that stress-can-be-enhancing mindsets are impactful during times of stress (e.g., layoffs, military training; Crum et al., 2013; Smith et al., 2019), but little work has examined the impact of these mindsets in settings where stress may be less salient. As mentioned earlier, exploratory analyses have suggested that stress-can-be-enhancing mindsets may be more beneficial to those reporting greater amounts of stress (Smith et al., 2019), indicating that these messages may be less impactful for those not experiencing stress when participating in the intervention. Some participants may even feel concerned that their health, well-being, or performance could be hampered by their lack of stress, which could be similarly counterproductive. For example, a student given a stress-can-be-enhancing intervention may be worried that *not* being stressed about an exam could result in worse performance. Thus, paying attention to context is necessary, as with the deployment of any intervention.

IMPLICATIONS FOR PSYCHOLOGICAL THEORY

Mindsets Are Powerful and Pervasive

Stress-is-debilitating mindsets are just one example of pervasive mindsets that may be holding people back from their full potential. Our culture perpetuates a number of maladaptive or unhelpful mindsets when it comes to our health—that healthy foods are less indulgent (Turnwald, Jurafsky, Conner, & Crum, 2017), that adequate exercise cannot be attained through everyday activities (Crum & Langer, 2007), and that health is primarily the absence of illness (Conner, Boles, Markus, Eberhardt, & Crum, 2018). Even though these mindsets may dominate our culture, research on stress mindsets suggests that promoting counternormative narratives of competing mindsets may be beneficial. In this vein, we must understand which mindsets are possible to hold in order to better understand mindsets that are currently invisible but of great importance to our lives. Culturally echoed mindsets will remain hidden until more systematic evaluations of mindsets are conducted.

"Negative" Experiences Can, and Should, Be Embraced

The interventions discussed in this chapter suggest the importance of reevaluating negative assumptions of daily occurrences. For example, demonizing stress and focusing only on ways to reduce the amount of stress in our lives may further exacerbate the negative effects it can have, causing people distress about being stressed and leading to negative recursive processes (see Brady et al., 2018). Stress does not need to be a solely negative force in people's lives. We encourage researchers to reevaluate cultural assumptions on "negative" experiences, as there may be optimistic narratives that capitalize on these experiences. With the right mindset, these experiences may be harnessed to promote health, well-being, performance, and other meaningful outcomes.

FUTURE DIRECTIONS

Several questions should be explored in future research, including how stress mindsets are developed and how stress mindsets function in different types of stress, including acute versus chronic, as well as more severe conditions, such as anxiety disorders and depression. Of particular interest from an intervention standpoint is to reconsider the use of biased information to convey mindset messages. Although an unbiased narrative of conflicting mindsets may be less powerful in some contexts and populations given the difficulty of incorporating paradoxical beliefs (e.g., Yeager et al., 2016), other interventions may be limited in both their application and long-term impact when they do not address the paradoxical and ambiguous nature of life. In these cases, "meta-mindsets" or mindsets about the nature of mindsets may themselves be impactful. Targeting these beliefs may be an effective path to improve future interventions, as it suggests a more agentic pathway to mindset activation. For example, people who believe that mindsets are self-fulfilling (i.e., those who hold a "self-fulfilling meta-mindset") might be more likely to actively recognize and deliberately switch on adaptive mindsets. Further research is needed to determine what happens when someone thinks stress is generally debilitating but believes that activating a stress-can-be-enhancing mindset can benefit their performance. Will this person be motivated to activate this mindset and will it prove self-fulfilling? Or are there psychological barriers to utilizing mindsets when not fully believed? In addition, rather than explicitly stating how stress-can-be-enhancing mindsets can help participants (as this message has the potential to undermine effects; see Sherman et al., 2009; Yeager et al., 2016), future interventions could convey information about meta-mindsets and the nature of stress, then allow participants to act on that information without explicit influence.

CONCLUSION

Throughout this chapter, we suggested that the predominant view in our society is that stress is something that should be avoided or mitigated, and we have proposed that a shift in mindsets, in which stress can be a motivating and energizing force, will promote optimal functioning. By shifting the mindset we hold about stress, we can begin noticing and attending to the ways stress benefits our daily lives, experiencing better emotional responses to stress, motivating ourselves to actively make use of the stressors in our lives, and benefiting from the physiological reactions stress induces—ultimately achieving improved health, well-being, and performance.

While seeking to reduce our stress levels is not inherently bad—unless it leads to further stress about stress or reinforces a stronger stress-is-debilitating mindset—it is counterproductive to believe that we could simply eradicate stress from our lives. Hans Selye (1974), whose early work arguably precipitated our cultural adoption of a stress-is-debilitating mindset, noted toward the end of his career: "Above all, stress is not something to be necessarily avoided. It is associated with the expression of all our innate drives. . . . Indeed, complete freedom from stress is death!" (p. 137). We humbly propose one tweak to this sentiment: above all, stress is not something to be necessarily avoided *but rather something to be harnessed.*

REFERENCES

Amirkhan, J. H. (1990). Applying attribution theory to the study of stress and coping. In S. Graham & V. S. Folkes (Eds.), *Attribution theory: Applications to achievement, mental health, and interpersonal conflict* (pp. 79–102). New York: Psychology Press.

Aronson, E. (1999). The power of self-persuasion. *American Psychologist, 54*(11), 875–884.

Billings, A. G., & Moos, R. H. (1981). The role of coping responses and social resources in attenuating the stress of life events. *Journal of Behavioral Medicine, 4*(2), 139–157.

Blackwell, K. L., Trzesniewski, K. H., & Dweck, C. S. (2007). Implicit theories of intelligence predict achievement across an adolescent transition: A longitudinal study and an intervention. *Child Development, 78*(1), 246–263.

Blascovich, J., Mendes, W. B., Hunter, S. B., & Lickel, B. (2000). Stigma, threat, and social interactions. In T. F. Heatherton, R. E. Kleck, M. R. Hebl, & J. G. Hull (Eds.), *The social psychology of stigma* (pp. 307–333). New York: Guilford Press.

Blascovich, J., Mendes, W. B., Tomaka, J., Salomon, K., Seery, M., Kemeny, M., . . . Haley, D. (2003). The robust nature of the biopsychosocial model challenge and threat: A reply to Wright and Kirby. *Personality and Social Psychology Review, 3*(3), 234–243.

Brady, S. T., Hard, B. M., & Gross, J. J. (2018). Reappraising test anxiety increases academic performance of first-year college students. *Journal of Educational Psychology, 110*(3), 395–406.

Bryan, C. J., Yeager, D. S., Hinojosa, C. P., Chabot, A., Bergen, H., Kawamura, M., & Steubing, F. (2016). Harnessing adolescent values to motivate healthier eating. *Proceedings of the National Academy of Sciences of the USA, 113*(39), 10830–10835.

Cahill, L., Gorski, L., & Le, K. (2003). Enhanced human memory consolidation with post-learning stress: Interaction with the degree of arousal at encoding. *Learning and Memory, 10*(4), 270–274.

Carver, C. S., & Connor-Smith, J. (2010). Personality and coping. *Annual Review of Psychology, 61*, 679–704.

Carver, C. S., Scheier, M. F., & Weintraub, J. K. (1989). Assessing coping strategies: A theoretically based approach. *Journal of Personality and Social Psychology, 56*(2), 267–283.

Chajut, E., & Algom, D. (2003). Selective attention improves under stress: Implications for theories of social cognition. *Journal of Personality and Social Psychology, 85*(2), 231–248.

Charney, D. S. (2004). Psychobiological mechanisms of resilience and vulnerability: Implications for successful adaptations to extreme stress. *American Journal of Psychiatry, 161*(2), 195–216.

Chiu, C., Hong, Y., & Dweck, C. S. (1997). Lay dispositionism and implicit theories of personality. *Journal of Personality and Social Psychology, 73*(1), 19–30.

Conner, A. L., Boles, D. Z., Markus, H. R., Eberhardt, J. L., & Crum, A. J. (2018). Americans' health mindsets: Content, cultural patterning, and associations with physical and mental health. *Annals of Behavioral Medicine, 53*(4), 321–332.

Creswell, J. D. (2017). Mindfulness interventions. *Annual Review of Psychology, 68*, 491–516.

Crum, A. J., Akinola, M., Martin, A., & Fath, S. (2017). The role of stress mindset in shaping cognitive, emotional, and physiological responses to challenging and threatening stress. *Anxiety, Stress, and Coping, 30*(4), 379–395.

Crum, A. J., Corbin, W. R., Brownell, K. D., & Salovey, P. (2011). Mind over milkshakes: Mindsets, not just nutrients, determine ghrelin response. *Health Psychology, 30*(4), 424–429.

Crum, A. J., Jamieson, J. P., & Akinola, M. (2020). Optimizing stress: An integrated intervention for regulating stress responses. *Emotion, 20*(1), 120–125.

Crum, A. J., & Langer, E. J. (2007). Mind-set matters: Exercise and the placebo effect. *Psychological Science, 18*(2), 165–171.

Crum, A. J., Salovey, P., & Achor, S. (2013). Rethinking stress: The role of mindsets in determining the stress response. *Journal of Personality and Social Psychology, 104*(4), 716–733.

Crum, A. J., Santoro, E. W., Smith, E. N., Achor, S., Moraveji, N., & Salovey, P. (2019). *Evaluation of a metacognitive stress mindset intervention.* Manuscript submitted for publication.

Dienstbier, R. A. (1989). Arousal and physiological toughness: Implications for mental and physical health. *Psychological Review, 96*(1), 84–100.

Dweck, C. S. (2006). *Mindset: The new psychology of success.* New York: Random House.

Dweck, C. S., & Leggett, E. L. (1988). A social-cognitive approach to motivation and personality. *Psychological Review, 95*(2), 256–273.

Epel, E. S., McEwen, B. S., & Ickovics, J. R. (1998). Embodying psychological thriving: Physical thriving in response to stress. *Journal of Social Issues, 54*(2), 301–322.

Even the youngest of us need to learn to battle stress. (2018). *Newsweek.* Retrieved from *www.newsweek.com/even-youngest-us-need-learn-battle-stress-932282.*

Fay, D., & Sonnentag, S. (2002). Rethinking the effects of stressors: A longitudinal study on personal initiative. *Journal of Occupational Health Psychology, 7*(3), 221–234.

Folkman, S., & Lazarus, R. S. (1980). An analysis of coping in a middle-aged community sample. *Journal of Health and Social Behaviour, 21*(3), 219–239.

Fredrickson, B. L., & Joiner, T. (2018). Reflections on positive emotions and upward spirals. *Perspectives on Psychological Science, 13*(2), 194–199.

Gallup Daily: U.S. Mood. (2018). Retrieved October 31, 2018, from *https://news.gallup.com/poll/106915/gallup-daily-us-mood.aspx.*

Goyer, J. P., Akinola, M., Grunberg, R., & Crum, A. J. (2019). *A stress mindset intervention improves affect for minority students during exam periods in freshman and sophomore years.* Manuscript in preparation.

Hammen, C. (2005). Stress and depression. *Annual Review of Clinical Psychology, 1,* 293–319.

Hancock, P. A., & Weaver, J. L. (2005). On time distortion under stress. *Theoretical Issues in Ergonomics Science, 6*(2), 193–211.

Herbert, T. B., & Cohen, S. (1993). Stress and immunity in humans: A meta-analytic review. *Psychosomatic Medicine, 55,* 364–379.

Jackson, M. (2014). Evaluating the role of Hans Selye in the modern history of stress. In D. Cantor & E. Ramsden (Eds.), *Stress, shock, and adaptation in the twentieth century* (pp. 21–48). Rochester, NY: University of Rochester Press.

Jamieson, J. P., Crum, A. J., Goyer, J. P., Marisa, E. M., & Akinola, M. (2018). Optimizing stress responses with reappraisal and mindset interventions: An integrated model. *Anxiety, Stress, and Coping, 31*(3), 245–261.

Jamieson, J. P., Mendes, W. B., Blackstock, E., & Schmader, T. (2010). Turning the knots in your stomach into bows: Reappraising arousal improves performance on the GRE. *Journal of Experimental Social Psychology, 46,* 208–212.

Jamieson, J. P., Peters, B. J., Greenwood, E. J., & Altose, A. J. (2016). Reappraising stress arousal improves performance and reduces evaluation anxiety in classroom exam situations. *Social Psychological and Personality Science, 7*(6), 579–587.

Kahn, M. (2008). Work-related stress can kill, study finds. *Reuters.* Retrieved from *www.reuters.com/article/us-heart-stress/work-related-stress-can-kill-study-finds-idUSL2284632220080123.*

Keinan, G. (1987). Decision making under stress: Scanning of alternatives under physical threat. *Journal of Personality and Social Psychology, 52*(3), 639–644.

Lazarus, R. S., & Folkman, S. (1984). *Stress, appraisal, and coping.* New York: Springer.

Logel, C., Iserman, E. C., Davies, P. G., Quinn, D. M., & Spencer, S. J. (2009). The perils of double consciousness: The role of thought suppression in stereotype threat. *Journal of Experimental Social Psychology, 45*(2), 299–312.

Lupien, S. J., McEwen, B. S., Gunnar, M. R., & Heim, C. (2009). Effects of stress throughout the lifespan on the brain, behaviour and cognition. *Nature Reviews Neuroscience, 10*(6), 434–445.

Lyubomirsky, S., King, L., & Diener, E. (2005). The benefits of frequent positive affect: Does happiness lead to success? *Psychological Bulletin, 131*(6), 803–855.

Mangels, J. A., Butterfield, B., Lamb, J., Good, C., & Dweck, C. S. (2006). Why do beliefs about intelligence influence learning success?: A social cognitive neuroscience model. *Social Cognitive and Affective Neuroscience, 1,* 75–86.

McEwen, B. S., & Sapolsky, R. M. (1995). Stress and cognitive function. *Current Opinion in Neurobiology, 5*(2), 205–216.

McGonigal, K. (2015). *The upside of stress: Why stress is good for you, and how to get good at it.* New York: Penguin Random House.

Mullainathan, S., & Shafir, E. (2013). *Scarcity: Why having too little means so much.* New York: Holt.

Nilly, M., & Winquist, J. (2002). Self-focused attention and negative affect: A meta-analysis. *Psychological Bulletin, 128*(4), 638–662.

Park, C. L., Cohen, L. H., & Murch, R. L. (1996). Assessment and prediction of stress-related growth. *Journal of Personality, 64*(1), 71–105.

Park, C. L., & Helgeson, V. S. (2006). Introduction to the special section: Growth following highly stressful life events—current status and future directions. *Journal of Consulting and Clinical Psychology, 74*(5), 791–796.

Park, D., Yu, A., Metz, S. E., Tsukayama, E., Crum, A. J., & Duckworth, A. L. (2017). Beliefs about stress attenuate the relation among adverse life events, perceived distress, and self-control. *Child Development, 89*(6), 2059–2069.

Paunesku, D., Walton, G. M., Romero, C., Smith, E. N., Yeager, D. S., & Dweck, C. S. (2015). Mind-set interventions are a scalable treatment for academic underachievement. *Psychological Science, 26*(6), 784–793.

Penley, J. A., Tomaka, J., & Wiebe, J. S. (2002). The association of coping to physical and psychological health outcomes: A meta-analytic review. *Journal of Behavioral Medicine, 25*(6), 551–603.

Romero, C., Master, A., Paunesku, D., Dweck, C. S., & Gross, J. J. (2014). Academic and emotional functioning in middle school: The role of implicit theories. *Emotion, 14*(2), 227–234.

Roth, S., & Cohen, L. J. (1986). Approach, avoidance, and coping with stress. *American Psychologist, 41*(7), 813–819.

Saad, L. (2017, December 20). Eight in 10 Americans afflicted by stress. Retrieved from *https://news.gallup.com/poll/224336/eight-americans-afflicted-stress.aspx.*

Salovey, P., Rothman, A., Detweiler, J., & Steward, W. (2000). Emotional states and physical health. *American Psychologist, 55*(1), 110–121.

Sapolsky, R. M. (1996). Stress, glucocorticoids, and damage to the nervous system: The current state of confusion. *Stress, 1,* 1–19.

Schmader, T., Johns, M., & Forbes, C. (2008). An integrated process model of stereotype threat effects on performance. *Psychological Review, 115*(2), 336–356.

Schneiderman, N., Ironson, G., & Siegel, S. D. (2005). Stress and health: Psychological, behavioral, and biological determinants. *Annual Review of Clinical Psychology, 1,* 607–628.

Schwabe, L., & Wolf, O. T. (2010). Learning under stress impairs memory formation. *Neurobiology of Learning and Memory, 93*(2), 183–188.

Selye, H. (1936). A syndrome produced by diverse nocuous agents. *Nature, 138,* 32.

Selye, H. (1974). Stress without distress. In G. Serban (Ed.), *Psychopathology of human adaptation* (pp. 137–146). Boston: Springer.

Selye, H. (1976). Forty years of stress research: Principal remaining problems and misconceptions. *Canadian Medical Association Journal, 115,* 53–56.

Shapiro, S. L., Brown, K. W., & Biegel, G. M. (2007). Teaching self-care to caregivers: Effects of mindfulness-based stress reduction on the mental health of therapists in training. *Training and Education in Professional Psychology, 1*(2), 105–115.

Shapiro, S. L., Shapiro, D. E., & Schwartz, G. E. R. (2000). Stress management in medical education: A review of the literature. *Academic Medicine, 75*(7), 748–759.

Sherman, D. K., Cohen, G. L., Nelson, L. D., Nussbaum, A. D., Bunyan, D. P., & Garcia, J. (2009). Affirmed yet unaware: Exploring the role of awareness in the process of self-affirmation. *Journal of Personality and Social Psychology, 97*(5), 745–764.

Smith, E. N., Romero, C., Donovan, B., Herter, R., Paunesku, D., Cohen, G. L., . . . Gross, J. J.

(2018). Emotion theories and adolescent well-being: Results of an online intervention. *Emotion, 18*(6), 781–788.

Smith, E. N., Young, M. D., & Crum, A. J. (2019). Stress, mindsets, and success in Navy SEALs special warfare training. *Frontiers in Psychology, 10,* 2962.

Somerfield, M. R., & McCrae, R. R. (2000). Stress and coping research: Methodological challenges, theoretical advances, and clinical applications. *American Psychologist, 55*(6), 620–625.

Sternberg, E. M. (2001). Neuroendocrine regulation of autoimmune/inflammatory disease. *Journal of Endocrinology, 169,* 429–435.

Szabo, S., Tache, Y., & Somogyi, A. (2012). The legacy of Hans Selye and the origins of stress research: A retrospective 75 years after his landmark brief "letter" to the editor of *Nature Stress, 15*(5), 472–478.

Tedeschi, R. G., & Calhoun, L. C. (2004). Posttraumatic growth: Conceptual foundations and empirical evidence. *Psychological Inquiry, 15*(1), 1–18.

Turnwald, B. P., Jurafsky, D., Conner, A., & Crum, A. J. (2017). Reading between the menu lines: Are restaurants' descriptions of "healthy" foods unappealing? *Health Psychology, 36*(11), 1034–1037.

Walton, G. M., & Wilson, T. D. (2018). Wise interventions: Psychological remedies for social and personal problems. *Psychological Review, 125*(5), 617–655.

Wilson, T. D., & Linville, P. W. (1982). Improving the academic performance of college freshmen: Attribution therapy revisited. *Journal of Personality and Social Psychology, 42*(2), 367–376.

Yeager, D. S., Dahl, R. E., & Dweck, C. S. (2018). Why interventions to influence adolescent behavior often fail but could succeed. *Perspectives on Psychological Science, 13*(1), 101–122.

Yeager, D. S., Romero, C., Paunesku, D., Hulleman, C. S., Schneider, B., Hinojosa, C., . . . Dweck, C. S. (2016). Using design thinking to improve psychological interventions: The case of the growth mindset during the transition to high school. *Journal of Educational Psychology, 108*(3), 374–391.

Yerkes, R. M., & Dodson, J. D. (1908). The relation of strength of stimulus to rapidity of habit-formation. *Journal of Comparative Neurology and Psychology, 18*(5), 459–482.

Zion, S. R., & Crum, A. J. (2018). Mindsets matter: A new framework for harnessing the placebo effect in modern medicine. In *International review of neurobiology* (Vol. 138, pp. 137–160). London: Elsevier.

CHAPTER 10

Stress Reappraisal Interventions
Improving Acute Stress Responses in Motivated Performance Contexts

Jeremy P. Jamieson and Emily J. Hangen

Stress is typically perceived as having negative effects on health and performance, and people exert substantial efforts to reduce or avoid experiencing stress. Contrary to lay beliefs, however, stress is not only a negative state to be unilaterally avoided. Adaptive stress responses can also facilitate performance, help people achieve goals, and even confer protective health benefits. This chapter presents stress reappraisal, a psychological intervention developed to help optimize stress responses, and reap performance, cognitive, and health benefits. Rather than reducing or down-regulating stress arousal, stress reappraisal educates individuals about the adaptive benefits of stress such that bodily signs of stress (e.g., racing heart) are conceptualized as coping resources. Reappraising stress arousal as functional and adaptive increases appraisals of coping resources, which in turn, improve downstream outcomes. This chapter reviews the extant literature on the background, mechanisms, and outcomes of the intervention, and discusses heterogeneity, implementation, and implications of the intervention.

Acute social stressors rooted in achievement pressures or social interactions are ubiquitous in modern society. For instance, in educational settings, nearly all students experience testing situations as negative stressors (Bradley et al., 2010). Beyond the economic and performance costs of stress, the accumulation of acute, maladaptive stress has substantial health consequences. Notably, repeated maladaptive acute stress responses are associated with increased rates of cardiovascular disease, reduced immune function, and cognitive impairment, to name a few outcomes (e.g., Jefferson et al., 2010; Lundberg, 2005; Matthews, Gump, Block, & Allen, 1997).

Although stress is typically perceived and experienced as negative and maladaptive, stress can also facilitate cognitive performance, promote active coping, and protect the body against the damaging effects of catabolic hormones (e.g., Dienstbier, 1989; Jamieson, Crum, Goyer, Marotta, & Akinola, 2018; Mendes, Gray, Mendoza-Denton, Major, & Epel, 2007). Thus, without experiencing the benefits of (the right kind of) stress, people can underachieve, miss opportunities for growth, and even suffer negative health outcomes. The notion that stress can have facilitative *and* debilitative effects (Crum, Akinola, Martin, & Fath, 2017), however, is not represented in lay theories. People typically only consider the negative facets of stress and equate stress with distress. This perspective is even echoed by social scientists. Scales developed to measure stress are overwhelmingly constructed of negative-valence items that present stress as a negative state (e.g., Cohen, Kamarck, & Mermelstein, 1983). The result is that people believe that efforts to cope with stressors should focus on eliminating or avoiding stress altogether rather than seeking to promote adaptive stress responses (Brooks, 2014).

Given the societal costs of negative stress responses, what can be done to discourage maladaptive responses and promote thriving during acute stress contexts? Toward this end, the stress reappraisal intervention reviewed here posits that the way people think about stress responses can unlock adaptive benefits and attenuate costs. Stress reappraisal focuses on promoting more adaptive stress response profiles by altering cognitive appraisal processes (Jamieson, Hangen, Lee, & Yeager, 2018). Specifically, this intervention presents the arousal experienced during stressful situations as a functional coping resource that aids performance—that is, signs of stress arousal (e.g., racing heart) are interpreted as coping tools that facilitate adaptive patterns of cognitive appraisals to affect subsequent physiological, affective, and motivational processes. For example, consider a job applicant sitting down for an important interview with a prospective employer. The applicant's heart is racing and his or her palms are sweaty. These bodily responses could be interpreted as signs the applicant is nervous and that stress levels need to be reduced through, for instance, deep breathing. Alternatively, the bodily stress responses could be interpreted as signs the applicant is "amped up" and ready to perform. Whereas the former interprets stress as maladaptive and to be avoided, the later interprets stress as functional and to be optimized. Contrary to traditional relaxation techniques that seek to reduce stress, stress reappraisal seeks to help individuals make meaning of their stress responses as helpful. The extant literature suggests that this intervention can improve physiological responses, facilitate performance, and reduce attention for negative cues in acute stress contexts.

BACKGROUND

Stress reappraisal grew directly out of the biopsychosocial (BPS) model of challenge and threat (Blascovich, 1992). Challenge and threat theory, in turn, built on the framework provided by the appraisal theory of emotion (Lazarus, 1991) and mapped the biological underpinnings of acute stress responses (upstream appraisal processes) onto downstream health, behavior, and decision outcomes in "motivated performance situations," which are goal-relevant performance situations requiring instrumental (i.e., active) responses (Blascovich, Mendes, Hunter, & Salomon, 1999; Blascovich & Mendes, 2010; Mendes, 2009). For instance, job interviews, academic exams, performance reviews, public speeches, and negotiations are all examples of motivated performance situations.

A core contribution of the BPS model of challenge and threat is specifying the psychological processes underpinning stress responses. Specifically, in challenge and threat theory, cognitive appraisals of demands (e.g., perceptions of uncertainty, danger, and required effort) and resources (e.g., perceptions of familiarity, knowledge, skills/ability, dispositional factors, and social support) interact to elicit challenge- and threat-type psychological states when individuals are actively engaged (Mendes & Park, 2014). Challenge states are experienced when appraisals of coping resources exceed perceived situational demands. Alternatively, threat manifests when perceived demands exceed resources (see Figure 10.1).

Importantly for understanding appraisals in the context of the BPS model, "demands" and "resources" are multidimensional. Demands consist of perceptions of uncertainty, danger, and/or effort, and these facets can be independent or intertwined. For example, consider an unfamiliar social-evaluative situation, such as a student taking an important placement exam. The test taker may not know the layout of the exam and would certainly not know the exact questions (i.e., uncertainty), which would require the test taker to devote effort to parsing the format/instructions. Thus, uncertainty and effort dimensions of demand appraisals are intertwined—however, placement test situations also include the potential for negative evaluation and social harm (i.e., "danger" dimension of demand appraisals), which are not necessarily tied to appraisals of effort or uncertainty.

A large corpus of research from the BPS literature demonstrates that challenge and threat patterns of appraisals have direct consequences for outcomes. For example, challenge and threat states demonstrate differential motivational response patterns. Whereas challenge is generally associated with appetitive approach motivation, threat elicits

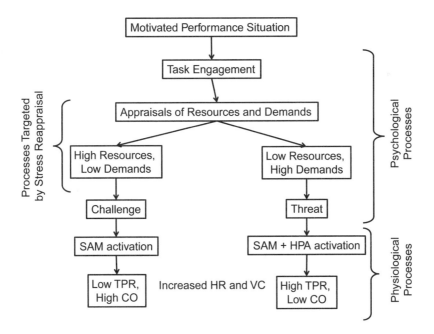

FIGURE 10.1. Overview of the psychological and physiological processes of the biopsychosocial model of challenge and threat. Stress reappraisal seeks to promote challenge responses via highlighting the adaptive benefits of stress. SAM, sympathetic–adrenal–medullary axis; HPA, hypothalamic–pituitary–adrenal axis; HR, heart rate; VC, ventricular contractility; TPR, total peripheral resistance; CO, cardiac output.

aversive, avoidance motivation (e.g., Jamieson, Valdesolo, & Peters, 2014). Downstream, challenge predicts positive behavioral and performance outcomes (e.g., Blascovich et al., 1999), but threat impairs decision making, and is associated with cognitive decline and cardiovascular disease (Jefferson et al., 2010; Matthews et al., 1997). Moreover, in a study that directly informed the development of stress reappraisal, individuals who were assigned to appraise a speech preparation task as a challenge experienced more positive emotions (Tugade & Fredrickson, 2004).

Together this research suggests that manipulating or modifying resource and demand appraisal processes has the potential to improve physiological stress responses and cognitive and behavioral outcomes. Indeed, a growing literature on stress reappraisal provides support for the idea that acute stress responses can, indeed, be improved via modifying appraisal processes (e.g., Beltzer, Nock, Peters, & Jamieson, 2014; Brady, Hard, & Gross, 2018; Hangen, Elliot, & Jamieson, 2019; Jacquart, Papini, Freeman, Bartholomew, & Smits, 2020; Jamieson et al., 2020; Jamieson, Mendes, Blackstock, & Schmader, 2010; Jamieson, Mendes, & Nock, 2013; Jamieson, Nock, & Mendes, 2012, 2013; Jamieson, Peters, Greenwood, & Altose, 2016; John-Henderson, Rheinschmidt, & Mendoza-Denton, 2015; Moore, Vine, Wilson, & Freeman, 2015; Rozek, Ramirez, Fine, & Beilock, 2019; Sammy et al., 2017; Oveis, Gu, Ocampo, Hangen, & Jamieson, 2020).

PSYCHOLOGICAL PROCESSES

The focal goal of the stress reappraisal intervention is to increase resource appraisals by defining the stress response itself as a coping resource (e.g., Jamieson, 2017). In the stress reappraisal intervention literature, individuals are provided with instructions that present the arousal experienced during stressful situations as a functional coping resource that can facilitate performance. The theory is that this information will alter the ratio of resources and demands such that the individual is more likely to view the stress as a challenge as opposed to a threat.

Contrary to other stress management approaches, the stress reappraisal intervention is not aimed at convincing individuals that stressful situations are not demanding—that is, reappraising stress does not decrease perceptions of effort required to address stressors. The focus of stress reappraisal manipulations on resource appraisals is an important mechanistic distinction when individuals encounter acutely stressful situations that cannot be avoided or mitigated. For example, in the U.S. (and many others) educational system, students frequently must take evaluative exams (i.e., a stressful situation); these exams have important consequences for grades, placements, and applications, and are generally unavoidable. However, students who reframe stress responses as functional can help optimize performance in stressful academic testing contexts (e.g., Brady et al., 2018; Jamieson et al., 2010, 2016, 2020).

PHYSIOLOGICAL PROCESSES

Importantly for the effectiveness of the stress reappraisal intervention, challenge and threat psychological states are associated with patterns of physiological responding (see Mendes & Park, 2014, for a biologically oriented review). Dienstbier's (1989) work on physiological toughness helped to provide the organization for the physiological response patterns delineated by challenge and threat. Specifically, challenge and threat physiological responses derive from activation of the sympathetic–adrenal–medullary (SAM) and hypothalamic–pituitary–adrenal (HPA) axes. Both challenge- and threat-type responses are accompanied by SAM activation, which leads to the synthesis and secretion of catecholamines, particularly epinephrine (or adrenaline) and norepinephrine. More downstream, catecholamines increase ventricular contractility (decreasing preejection period and increasing heart rate), constrict veins (facilitating venous return of blood to the heart), and dilate atrial blood vessels (via binding of epinephrine to beta-2 receptors; Brownley, Hurwitz, & Schneiderman, 2000). Challenge-type responses, which are dominated by SAM activation, are thus characterized by increased cardiac output (CO)—the volume of blood pumped by the heart across a period of time (usually 1 minute)—and decreased resistance in the total peripheral vasculature resistance (TPR). Challenge-type responses also allow for a rapid onset and offset of responses: Resources are mobilized rapidly and individuals return to homeostasis quickly after stress offset.

In addition to activating the SAM axis, threat also strongly activates the HPA axis, which is frequently assessed by measuring cortisol (its end product). Given the shorter half-lives of catecholamines relative to cortisol (e.g., a few minutes vs. 1+ hours, respectively), HPA activation elicits more prolonged stress responses after stress offset relative to SAM-dominated challenge responses. HPA activation also tempers effects of the SAM axis and results in reduced (or little change in) CO and increased TPR downstream in the cardiovascular system (see Figure 10.1). Thus, the end consequences of the cardiovascular changes accompanying challenge and threat states is that challenge results in more oxygenated blood being delivered to peripheral sites, such as the brain, whereas blood is concentrated in the core of the body when individuals experience threat.

As patterns of appraisals shift from more threat oriented to more challenge oriented (i.e., as resource appraisals increase relative to demand appraisals, respectively), stress axes are differentially recruited to direct downstream stress responses—thus, by increasing appraisals of resources, the stress reappraisal intervention seeks to elicit SAM-dominated patterns of stress that facilitate thriving under stress.

EMPIRICAL EVIDENCE

Outcomes

Initial findings from the stress reappraisal literature suggest that the intervention improves outcomes in acute stress contexts. The first empirical test of the intervention was a combined laboratory/field experiment (Jamieson et al., 2010). In this study, students preparing to take the Graduate Record Examination (GRE) were first recruited for a laboratory practice GRE session. They were randomly assigned to receive stress reappraisal instructions or no instructions prior to taking practice exams. Reappraisal participants outperformed controls on the quantitative section of the practice GRE. Then, 1–3 months after the practice exam, participants provided score reports from their actual, real GRE tests. Again, reappraisal participants outperformed controls on the quantitative section. Reappraisal participants also reported that stress arousal was more beneficial for performance.

In a follow-up laboratory experiment designed to elucidate basic effects, participants were randomly assigned to receive stress reappraisal, placebo control ("ignore stress"), or no instruction materials prior to giving a speech about their personal strengths and weaknesses, and performing mental arithmetic in front of an evaluative audience followed (the Trier Social Stress Test; Kirschbaum, Pirke, & Hellhammer, 1993; Jamieson et al., 2012). *During* the stressful social-evaluative tasks (e.g., public speaking and math problem-solving tasks), participants assigned to the reappraisal condition exhibited more adaptive (i.e., challenge-like) cardiovascular responses relative to participants assigned to the control conditions. Following the public speaking task, an emotional Stroop task (Williams, Mathews, & MacLeod, 1996) was used to assess attentional bias for negative cues. Reappraisal participants were less vigilant for negative cues compared to control participants. These first experimental tests of the stress reappraisal intervention demonstrated the potential for the intervention to improve outcomes.

Mechanisms

Although initial stress reappraisal studies focused on assessing the effects of the intervention on downstream outcomes, subsequent work has more clearly elucidated the mechanisms underlying these effects. As touched on previously, appraisals of resources (rather than demands) are the focal psychological mechanisms of stress reappraisal. To demonstrate, in a double-blind field experiment, community college students completed either stress reappraisal or placebo control materials prior to taking an in-class mathematics exam (Jamieson et al., 2016). Reappraisal instructions educated students about the adaptive benefits of stress arousal, whereas placebo materials instructed students to ignore stress. After the instruction materials, math anxiety and stress appraisals were assessed. Consistent with performance effects observed previously, reappraisal participants scored higher on their exams, and also reported less math evaluation anxiety and higher resource appraisals. Bootstrap mediation analyses suggested the effect of the intervention on exam performance manifested through appraisals of resources.

The emphasis on changing cognitive appraisals of coping resources can also be seen in a laboratory study (Beltzer et al., 2014). Prior to performing a stressful public speaking task, participants were randomly assigned stress reappraisal or were given no instructions, and then reported on their stress appraisals in anticipation of speaking. Relative to controls, reappraisal participants displayed less anxiety. The effect of reappraisal on behavioral displays of anxiety was mediated by the ratio of resources to demands, such that the higher resources were relative to demands, the less anxiety participants displayed while speaking.

Taken together, the extant literature suggests that stress appraisals, and resource appraisals in particular, are core mechanisms of the stress reappraisal intervention (see Jamieson, 2017, for a review of stress appraisals). To date, however, all direct tests of mechanisms have relied on self-reports of appraisals, which have inherent shortcomings. Notably, stress appraisals are processed both consciously and unconsciously/automatically (Blascovich, 2008). Thus, individuals may or may not have access to all components of multifaceted psychological appraisal processes when completing explicit self-reports. Moreover, self-reports cannot be obtained *in vivo* during stressful situations. For these reasons (and others; see Blascovich, 2008, for a review), research grounded in challenge and threat theory—and by extension, the stress reappraisal intervention—has emphasized mapping psychological processes (e.g., challenge and threat, appraisal patterns) by measuring physiological responses (e.g., Blascovich et al., 1999)—that is, if appraisals of resources exceed demands, this pattern of psychological responding will necessitate challenge-type physiological responses (see Figure 10.1), even if the individual cannot (retro- or proactively) report on the full array of his or her appraisals with a high degree of accuracy. Future lines of research on stress reappraisal, and other BPS-oriented research, could seek to develop implicit measures of appraisals to more tightly yoke psychological mechanisms to downstream outcomes.

Effects over Time

Beyond the basic questions of an intervention's effectiveness it is important to consider how long effects persist, and how effects unfold over time. An effective intervention that produces brief effects requiring repeated delivery to maintain the effects has limited efficacy for producing lasting change. Addressing questions of the duration and dynamics of intervention effects necessitates elucidating mechanisms. Although the majority of stress reappraisal research focuses on *in vivo* stress processes, research has observed subsequent effects of the intervention following stressful contexts. As noted previously, reappraising stress arousal reduced attention for emotionally negative cues in a laboratory setting (Jamieson et al., 2012)—that is, reappraisal participants exhibited less vigilance for negative cues than control participants even though there was no evaluative pressure (i.e., no social stress) during the attention task. Thus, the effects of the intervention on attentional processes persisted after stress offset.

Research has also examined longer-term performance effects of stress reappraisal in educational contexts. In initial examinations of duration of effects in an educational context, students were randomly presented with reappraisal or control instructions embedded in an e-mail message delivered prior to exams, and performance was measured across an academic semester. Reappraisal instructions led to higher end-of-semester course grades relative to controls via reducing exam worries (Brady et al., 2018). Moreover, as touched on previously, a study with students taking the GRE observed performance benefits as a function of the intervention up to 3 months after initial delivery without boosters (Jamieson et al., 2010). Taken together, these lagged effects of the stress reappraisal intervention suggest students are capable of applying instructions beyond the specific context in which the intervention is delivered. However, these studies do not elucidate the mechanisms underlying precisely *how* stress reappraisal might feed forward to impact future outcomes.

Exploring processes in longitudinal designs to answer mechanistic questions of temporal dynamics is potentially important because challenge/threat appraisals are not encapsulated to specific situations or within individuals—rather, prior appraisals influence future appraisals in subsequent similar (or even unfamiliar) situations (e.g., Gross, 2015). Toward this end, a recently completed study examined temporal dynamics of stress reappraisal in an educational setting. More specifically, a double-blind field experiment examined how stress reappraisal impacts students across several exam situations (Jamieson et al., 2020). To do so, students were randomly assigned to receive stress reappraisal or expectancy control instructions immediately prior to their second in-class exams (to allow for comparisons to Exam 1). Then, psychological processes—stress appraisals, achievement goals (Elliot, 1999), and procrastination (Steel, 2010)—were assessed between Exams 2 and 3 with the aim of examining how stress reappraisal might impact psychological processes outside of classroom exam situations, and how these processes might feed forward to affect future academic performance and neuroendocrine responses. Preliminary results suggest that teaching students that stress is functional and adaptive improved academic performance and neuroendocrine functioning during Exam 2. Importantly for understanding temporal dynamics, students using reappraisal reported they procrastinated less and had more performance-approach goals in at-home diary measures, which then directly predicted subsequent Exam 3 scores (e.g., more procrastination led to lower scores). Thus, reappraisal may not only improve proximal stress responses and performance but also improve psychological processes that are predictive of longer-term academic success as has been seen in other interventions reported throughout this volume.

Heterogeneity of Effects

Like all psychological interventions, stress reappraisal is not a "silver bullet" for improving stress outcomes. The effectiveness of reappraising stress arousal on outcomes depends on myriad factors, including demographics, individual differences, and contextual factors, to name a few. This section focuses on reviewing and proposing moderating factors of the intervention, including both situational and individual difference factors. The proposed moderating factors were developed from an understanding of how stress reappraisal counters traditional lay beliefs—namely, presenting stress arousal (and even subsequent negative affective experiences of anxiety) as a coping resource stands in stark contrast to how people typically attempt to manage stress. In other words, stress reappraisal is not aimed at eliminating or dampening stress arousal. It does not encourage relaxation or reduction of sympathetic arousal as most stress management approaches do, but instead focuses on changing the type of stress response experienced (threat → challenge). In fact, negative lay conceptualizations of stress play an important role in why stress reappraisal is effective. If people already believed stress was beneficial for coping, teaching them to reappraise stress as functional and adaptive would do little to impact challenge and threat responses.

Context and Situational Factors

Given typical "stress-is-bad" perspectives, the classic stress regulation literature has often (but not always) instructed individuals to reappraise external cues to decrease stress arousal in passive situations (e.g., Gross, 2002). However, situational factors are important to consider when implementing classic reappraisal methods or arousal-maintaining stress reappraisal methods. For instance, in clinically relevant samples/situations, the arousal experienced is often not appropriate/functional. To demonstrate, an individual with posttraumatic stress disorder may experience a stress response in situations that are not acutely demanding but include trauma-inducing cues, such as a veteran responding to hearing a car backfire because it resembles the noise of a gunshot. Thus, reappraising stress arousal as beneficial in these situations is not appropriate because arousal is not needed to actively address acute task demands. Acutely stressful motivated performance situations, however, necessitate instrumental responding where increased sympathetic arousal can be functional. Notably, stress reappraisal provides a method for regulating affective responses in demanding situations because it focuses on changing the type of stress response experienced in order to effectively address the demands of the situation. In sum, if there are no situational demands that need to be addressed, stress reappraisal will likely be ineffective at improving outcomes.

Not only must situations present acute task demands but individuals must also engage with the situation for stress reappraisal to be maximally effective. In the BPS model of challenge and threat, a prerequisite to experiencing challenge and threat states is engagement, which requires active attention and reflects goal relevance (Seery, Weisbuch, & Blascovich, 2009). Typically assessed with measures of sympathetic arousal (e.g., preejection period), engagement is important for understanding stress reappraisal effects because without sympathetic arousal, there would be no physiological experience of stress to reappraise. Consider students about to take an important, difficult exam at the frontier of their knowledge and ability. Students experiencing threat can reappraise the stress they experience and, in turn, improve their performance (Brady et al., 2018; Jamieson et al., 2010, 2016). However, a disengaged student who chooses to opt out or not seriously work on the exam will not experience a stress response and therefore, cannot reappraise any stress arousal. This lack of engagement in acute stress contexts could result from a learned helplessness effect (e.g., Jesus & Lens, 2005), whereby an individual believes that it is not worth trying in a given context because failure will result regardless. Stress reappraisal techniques would likely be ineffective at increasing engagement in such contexts.

Demographic Factors and Individual Differences

Not all individuals should be expected to benefit similarly from stress reappraisal interventions. The "first wave" of stress reappraisal research focused on demonstrating group-level effects, usually in comparison to control conditions (e.g., Jamieson et al., 2012). More recent work, however, has begun to elucidate person-level moderators. For instance, a study examining the effects of stress reappraisal during an interpersonal competition observed group-level intervention effects on physiological responses, but also observed notable moderation by participant gender (Hangen et al., 2019). More specifically, during an interpersonal mathematics competition, reappraisal instructions were effective for improving physiological functioning and facilitating performance for men, but women were unaffected. This study was the first to observe gender differences as a function of stress reappraisal. In fact, stress reappraisal has specifically been shown to alleviate stereotype threat effects in women (John-Henderson et al., 2015; cf. Schmader, Forbes, Zhang, & Mendes, 2009). Thus, concluding that stress reappraisal interventions work better for males may be misguided. Rather, gender differences in effectiveness could be rooted in contextual factors. In competition contexts, for example, a stereotype exists that males are more competitive than females (e.g., Kray, Thompson, & Galinsky, 2001), and compared to men, women are more reluctant to engage in interpersonal competitions (Croson & Gneezy, 2009) and are less confident about their abilities to compete (Niederle & Vesterlund, 2007). If females avoid stressful, competitive contexts or seek to disengage when placed in such situations, there would be no active, acute stress to reappraise and thus limited benefits of the intervention.

Other research on moderators of stress reappraisal suggests anxiety processes derived from uncertainty processes may play an important role (Brady et al., 2018).

To illustrate, students in an introductory psychology class were randomly assigned to receive stress reappraisal or control materials. Reappraisal instructions led to higher exam scores and less worry, but only for first-year students. Unlike upperclassmen, first-year students are navigating a novel academic environment and are inexperienced in university-level testing situations, and thus experience more uncertainty and test anxiety compared to upperclassmen. These data suggest that stress reappraisal may be particularly effective at facilitating coping and improving performance for individuals experiencing particularly potent negative affective responses in acute stress contexts (cf. Jamieson et al., 2016).

Although research on psychological moderators of stress reappraisal effects is limited, there are interesting avenues for exploration. For instance, patterns of stress responding following aversive events can be governed by causal attributions (Abramson, Seligman, & Teasdale, 1978; Mendes, Major, McCoy, & Blascovich, 2008). Internal stable attributions—believing that aversive events originate from properties of the self—lead to avoidance-motivated responses, such as threat. On the other hand, external attributions—placing the cause for aversive events on factors outside the self—are associated with approach-motivated responses, such as anger (Jamieson, Koslov, Nock, & Mendes, 2013). Thus, stress reappraisal manipulations may be more effective for individuals who tend to make external attributions because presenting stress as facilitative aligns with the motivational orientation (approach) typically experienced by those making external relative to internal attributions.

Another likely individual-level moderator of stress reappraisal is stress mindsets: whether stress is believed to have enhancing or debilitating consequences (Crum, Salovey, & Achor, 2013). As covered in more depth in the following "Cousins" section, situation-specific stress appraisals can be shaped by more general belief systems about stress. Individuals with a more stress-is-enhancing mindset could be expected to benefit more from stress reappraisal manipulations. Conversely, individuals who hold strong stress-is-debilitating mindsets might be resistant to stress reappraisal interventions because the materials align poorly with their worldview.

COUSINS

The stress reappraisal intervention seeks to harness the power of cognitive appraisal processes to promote active coping with acute stressors. Resource and demand appraisal processes, however, target *specific* stressful situations, and can (and often do) fluctuate substantially from situation to situation. For instance, one may consider oneself an adept skier. Presented with a demanding trail (e.g., steep, icy, and narrow), the expert skier perceives his or her coping resources (ability, skills, familiarity, etc.) to exceed task demands. However, when the same expert skier is placed in a mathematics achievement context, such as taking an important standardized test, he or she may perceive the demands (high difficulty of problems, uncertainty processes, etc.) as exceeding the ability to cope (poor math knowledge, little experience, etc.). Thus, the effectiveness of any intervention for which appraisal processes are focal mechanisms will likely vary from situation to situation because of differences in basal appraisal patterns and affective response tendencies. To improve the likelihood of observing effects across many different contexts, other cognitive processes (in addition to appraisals) can be harnessed.

Notably, research from the mindsets literature suggests another avenue for intervention. In addition to targeting domain-specific appraisal processes, improving stress responses can also be achieved by targeting domain-general, more meta-level beliefs. For example, research on *stress mindsets,* which are beliefs about the nature of stress in general not tied to specific situations—demonstrates how manipulating mindsets can produce downstream benefits (e.g., Crum et al., 2013). Individuals holding a "stress-is-enhancing mindset" believe that stress can have enhancing effects, whereas those holding a "stress-is-debilitating mindset" believe that stress has debilitating effects. Although the stress can have either or both enhancing and/or debilitating effects, these stress mindsets orient individuals to a set of expectations and motivations.

Similar to effects observed in the stress reappraisal literature, experimental mindset research demonstrates that intervention materials that teach a stress-is-enhancing mindset can improve stress responses, performance, and health outcomes. To demonstrate, employees taught about the enhancing nature of stress self-reported greater improvements in work performance and general health compared to employees taught about the debilitating effects of stress and no instruction controls (Crum et al., 2013). Subsequent research has observed longer-term effects of stress-mindset training across weeks or possibly even years. For instance, employees taught a stress-is-enhancing mindset reported better health and well-being up to 4 weeks after intervention delivery (Crum et al., 2019), and in a college student sample, a stress-is-enhancing mindset intervention delivered prior to the start of college predicted positive outcomes across students' freshman and sophomore years (Goyer, Akinola, Grunberg, & Crum, 2018).

Importantly for research on stress reappraisal, altering general beliefs about stress may benefit outcomes by shaping situation-specific appraisal processes (cf. Yeager, Lee, & Jamieson, 2017). Individuals with a more stress-is-enhancing mindset could be expected to benefit more from stress reappraisal manipulations because they are already "preconditioned" to appraise stress responses as functional and adaptive. Conversely, individuals who hold strong stress-is-debilitating mindsets might be resistant to stress reappraisal interventions because the materials align poorly with their worldview that stress is harmful for them.

To date, only one study has explored stress mindsets and appraisal processes in the same design (Crum et al., 2019). Compared to a stress-is-debilitating mindset, a stress-is-enhancing mindset improved affective responses in a negative social-evaluative situation that elicited threat appraisals. As might be expected, however, optimal outcomes were observed when mindsets and appraisals aligned: participants who both held a stress-is-enhancing mindset *and* received positive feedback that elicited challenge appraisals experienced the most benefits. However, appraisals and mindsets were not integrated. Taken together, the growing literature on stress mindsets suggests that stress responses can be improved by altering meta-level belief systems. This approach provides a nice complement to the situationally grounded stress reappraisal approach, and suggests avenues for potential integrations of the two interventions to optimize effects (see Jamieson et al., 2018, for a review).

In addition to focal grounding in challenge and threat theory, the development of stress reappraisal methods have relied on the *theory of constructed emotion* (Barrett, 2017) and the *extended process model of emotion regulation* (Gross, 2015). Constructionist models of emotion posit that emotions (e.g., anxiety or excitement) are experienced when categorized using knowledge from cognitive concepts. Thus, emotions are "situated conceptualizations" (Barrett, Wilson-Mendenhall, & Barsalou, 2014; Wilson-Mendenhall, Barrett, Simmons, & Barsalou, 2011). Appraisals (among other processes) help transform internal states into emotions (or stress responses) by integrating bodily changes with external sensory information and knowledge of the situation to encourage behavioral response patterns (Barrett, 2006). Moreover, constructionist theorizing is consistent with the strong monist—the idea that the brain and body operate in concert—emphasized in stress reappraisal approaches.

Challenge and threat appraisals also fit well with the conceptualization of "valuation" processes in the extended process model of emotion regulation. A valuation system includes aspects of the social and external environment, perceptions of internal and external states, valuations of perceptions, and goal-directed actions (Gross, 2015). Stress appraisals may be considered perceptual processes that inform valuations with the goal of modifying actions (stress responses), and stress reappraisal processes can operate within second-level valuation systems that have as their targets first-level valuation systems focused on constructing emotional experiences and stress responses. In addition, the importance of agency captured in emotion regulation process models also manifests in stress reappraisal methods (Gross & Barrett, 2011)—that is, it would be difficult to actively regulate stress responses without agency.

The integration of concepts from constructionist models of emotion and dynamical models of emotion regulation has informed ongoing research on the social dynamics of stress reappraisal. Specifically, melding processes from challenge and threat theory and the extended process model of emotion regulation with research on *coregulation*—the reciprocal maintenance of physiological response patterns (Sbarra & Hazan, 2008)—has the potential to better specify how appraisals and subsequent physiological responses help create and maintain healthy relationships, and promote adaptive social behaviors (e.g., responsiveness; Reis, Clark, & Holmes, 2004). To examine interpersonal dynamics of stress reappraisal, recent research examined how instructing one member of a team to reappraise stress impacted their teammate (Oveis et al., 2020). To do so, teammates engaged in a collaborative product design task followed by an individual product pitch delivered to evaluators. Prior to collaborative performance, one person received stress reappraisal instructions. Consistent with predictions, stress reappraisal elicited more challenge-like physiological responses relative to controls. Critically, this improvement manifested in *both* teammates. The nonmanipulated teammate exhibited improved stress responses simply by interacting with a person who reappraised the stress arousal as functional. Notably, reappraisal improved nonmanipulated teammates' stress responses during both collaborative work—a period in which the manipulated and nonmanipulated teammates constantly communicated face-to-face—*and* later during an individual performance period. Mediation analysis suggests that the effect of reappraisal on nonmanipulated teammates' stress responses during individual performance stemmed from the improved stress responses experienced during collaborative work.

Future research on the underlying processes of how contagion of stress reappraisal transmits across teammates could be informed by research on emotion coregulation (Butler & Randall, 2013) and physiological linkage (Waters, West, Karnilowicz, & Mendes, 2017). For instance, research from the coregulation literature indicates that the experience of threat-type stress responses impairs individuals' capacity to be responsive to their partners, and this lack of responsiveness can result in threat responses in the partner (Peters, Reis, & Jamieson, 2018).

NUANCES AND MISCONCEPTIONS

One misconception about stress reappraisal is that it is a stress reduction or stress management technique—that is, traditional efforts to regulate stress responses have focused on reducing or "managing" stress responses because lay conceptualizations of stress are overwhelmingly negative (e.g., Brooks, 2014). However, as noted previously, stress reappraisal interventions do not seek to attenuate arousal or reduce perceptions of situational demands. Informing individuals about the functional benefits of stress responses (e.g., increased heart rate helps to deliver oxygenated blood to the brain and periphery) does not imply that stressful situations are devoid of demands, nor does this approach suggest the best method for coping with stressful experiences is to down-regulate arousal and "keep calm." Consider an athlete about to compete in an important match. Stress experienced in anticipation of performing can be appraised as challenging, such as "I possess the necessary training and ability to beat my competitor" (i.e., resources outweigh demands), or threatening, such as "I worry that I cannot beat this difficult opponent" (i.e., demands exceed resources). Stress reappraisal seeks to encourage the athlete to appraise as the stress experienced in anticipation of and during performance as a resource that will help him or her achieve victory (i.e., boosting resource appraisals). The aim of this intervention is not to encourage the athlete to view his or her competitors as worse, or the match as less important or meaningful (i.e., reducing demand appraisals).

Another misconception of stress reappraisal is that it is easily applied across all individuals and all stressful domains. As touched on previously in the "Heterogeneity" section, though, a prerequisite to exhibiting acute stress responses in challenge and threat theory is engagement. People must care about performing, coping, and so on in a particular stressful context for challenge and threat responses to manifest. If an individual does not care, invest effort, or disengages, he or she is not actively responding to the stressor. Only when individuals actively engage is stress reappraisal hypothesized to help improve responses—that is, stress reappraisal is unlikely to benefit individuals when there is no stress to appraise/reappraise. For example, consider a stressful standardized exam situation. A student could not care about the standardized test, disengage with the situation, and walk out of the room without answering any questions. Such a response pattern would not be associated with any stress response because there are no situational demands, and thus no resources are needed to cope with demands. The stressful task (the standardized test) is simply avoided before appraisal processes are engaged. Reappraising stress arousal is unlikely to promote initial engagement with a stressful situation unless levels of anxiety (or a similar affective state) are so high in anticipation of the stressor that the negative affect leads to complete avoidance of the stress context (cf. Peters, Overall, & Jamieson, 2014). The prior example, however, is not a particularly realistic depiction of how the vast majority of students engage with and respond to testing situations. To advance through educational systems, students must take exams and cannot simply remove themselves from situations. Thus, students must engage, which explains why nearly all students experience exams as stressful (Bradley et al., 2010). Once engaged, appraisal processes come online to evaluate personal coping resources relative to situational demands (Blascovich & Mendes, 2010). Stress reappraisal can then help improve responses by increasing the ratio of resources to demands.

Another nuance of the stress reappraisal intervention is the kind of stress targeted. The research reviewed here provides empirical evidence for the benefits of stress reappraisal in *acute* stress contexts. However, prolonged exposure to stress, or repeated activation of stress systems (i.e., *chronic* stress), has the potential to cause allostatic load and elicit negative health outcomes (Juster, McEwen, & Lupien, 2010). To date, however, potential effects of stress reappraisal on chronic stress processes are unknown because this intervention has not been studied in long-term longitudinal paradigms. As research progresses in this area, it is our hope that stress reappraisal and other interventions for optimizing acute stress responses can help modulate experiences of chronic stress through recursive and reciprocal processes. First, given the longer half-life of catabolic hormones that mark threat responses relative to anabolic hormones that mark challenge responses, promoting challenge should allow participants to return to homeostasis more quickly after stress offset, thus potentially reducing allostatic load. Second, learning how to cope with acute stress in one context has the potential to transmit to other contexts via altering second-level valuation systems (Gross, 2015). This can lead to repeated adaptive stress responses. Finally, extant stress reappraisal research indicates that improving acute stress responses can impact attentional systems as well (Jamieson et al., 2012). If this approach reduces attention for negative cues, it is possible that future ambiguous situations will not be perceived as stressful or threatening.

IMPLICATIONS FOR PRACTICE

To date, laboratory and field research has utilized two general forms of stress reappraisal: (1) a ~10-minute reading exercise comprising summaries of scientific articles on the adaptive benefits of stress responses and responding to questions aimed at encouraging endorsement of the material via "saying-is-believing" processes (e.g., Jamieson et al., 2012; see Walton & Wilson, 2018, for a discussion; materials available for download at *http://socialstresslab.wixsite.com/urochester/research*); and (2) a "short-form," single-paragraph instruction presented below (see also John-Henderson et al., 2015). For instance, Jamieson and colleagues (2010) used the following short-form instructions to manipulate stress appraisals prior to GRE tests:

> "People think that feeling anxious while taking a standardized test will make them do poorly on the test. However, recent research suggests that arousal doesn't hurt performance on these tests and can even help performance . . . people who feel 'anxious' during a test might actually do better. This means that you shouldn't feel concerned if you do feel anxious while taking today's GRE test. If you find yourself feeling anxious, simply remind yourself that your arousal could be helping you do well."

It is important to highlight that stress reappraisal materials have, to date, relied on time-sensitive deliveries. A common thread throughout the extant research on stress reappraisal is that intervention materials have been delivered either during or immediately before acutely stressful motivated performance contexts. Materials were not administrated days or weeks before effects are typically tested; rather, participants are immersed in stressful experiences—both in the lab (e.g., Jamieson et al., 2012) and in naturalistic settings (e.g., Jamieson et al., 2016)—and are administered stress reappraisal intervention materials while stress arousal levels are high. Thus, participants can immediately apply the instructions that are provided to them. To demonstrate, a field experiment found that teaching community college students to appraise their stress arousal as a coping tool immediately before an exam reduced their test anxiety and improved performance (Jamieson et al., 2016). In this experiment, the research team visited participating classrooms on the days of exams and administered the intervention materials immediately prior to students taking their exams, which required substantial coordination between the research team and instructors, as well as steps to ensure that instructors administering and scoring exams remained blind to condition assignment and hypotheses.

This targeted approach requires that practitioners seeking to implement this intervention should be cognizant of when the materials are delivered. If a disconnection exists between when/where materials are completed and when/where stress is experienced, there is a possibility that some effectiveness of the intervention will be lost. However, it should be noted that one prior study used a more distal and passive delivery method—students were e-mailed the "short-form" intervention materials the night before an exam—and still observed psychological and performance effects of the intervention (Brady et al., 2018). Thus, it may be possible to use a less immersive delivery method, though care should be taken to ensure that intervention materials are recalled or applied in the same context where effects are measured.

IMPLICATIONS FOR PSYCHOLOGICAL THEORY

In addition to emerging from research on the BPS model of challenge and threat, stress reappraisal also has roots in concepts derived from emotion regulation and achievement goal theories. Because of these shared underlying processes, research on stress reappraisal has the potential to inform the development of these broader models. For example, the classic process model of emotion regulation highlights "cognitive change" processes such as reappraisal as effective (and heavily studied) methods for regulating emotional experiences (Gross, 2002). Along these lines, stress reappraisal changes cognitive factors (appraisals) to regulate emotional experiences (stress responses). Recent advances in emotion regulation theory have emphasized the importance of *valuations*: when an event/experience/situation is "good for me" versus "bad for me" (Gross, 2015). Importantly for regulating stress responses, reappraising stress as functional and adaptive has the potential to promote the valuation that stress can be "good for me." In this way, stress reappraisal can be conceptualized as an emotion regulation tool operating within the framework provided by the extended process model.

The emphasis of stress reappraisal on improving physiological, cognitive, and performance outcomes in performance contexts makes it ripe for integration with research on achievement goals: cognitive representations of future competence-based outcomes that one approaches or avoids (Elliot & Fryer, 2008). Crossing dimensions of evaluative standard and valence yields four basic goals: mastery-approach goals (focused on doing well relative to task requirements or one's own performance trajectory), performance-approach goals (focused on doing well relative to others), mastery-avoidance goals (focused on not doing poorly relative to task requirements or one's own performance trajectory), and performance-avoidance goals (focused on not doing poorly relative to others; Elliot, 1999). Importantly for integration with stress reappraisal, achievement goals are situation-specific, self-regulatory processes.

Once instantiated, achievement goals can then create a framework through which people interpret and experience future achievement situations (e.g., Dweck, 1986). For instance, reappraising stress arousal can increase subsequent performance-approach goals (Jamieson et al., 2019). The commitment to pursuing these approach goals may then influence a multitude of affective, cognitive, and behavioral processes and outcomes. Along these lines, in one set of studies, the positive focus stemming from performance-approach goals of attaining academic competence was linked to appraising a specific course or exam as a challenge (McGregor & Elliot, 2002). Moreover, as with cyclical emotion regulation processes (Gross, 2015), achievement scenarios are usually not one-off experiences but instead operate in sequences. Thus, with regard to integrating goals with stress reappraisal, achievement goals may operate as both antecedents of appraisal processes and consequences of challenge–threat responses resulting from stress reappraisal manipulations. Moreover, it is possible that goals could serve both these roles sequentially and reciprocally.

CONCLUSIONS AND FUTURE DIRECTIONS

Lay conceptualizations of stress are generally negative. In fact, when asked to choose the best advice for optimally performing in an upcoming stressful task, 91% of people indicated that remaining calm and relaxed (i.e., trying not to be "stressed") was the best option (Brooks, 2014). This negative conceptualization of stress can play an important role in maintaining and promoting negative health and well-being outcomes associated with stressful experiences because appraisals and perceptions of stress directly impact biological responses (e.g., Crum et al., 2013; Blascovich & Mendes, 2010; Jamieson et al., 2018). Thus, intervening to change how people appraise and engage with stressful situations can help improve acute stress responses. This review highlights the physiological, cognitive, and performance benefits of reappraising stress arousal. In this line of research, stress responses are presented as a functional coping resource that aids performance—that is, signs of stress arousal are interpreted as coping tools that facilitate challenge appraisals to affect outcomes.

Although this chapter focuses on stress reappraisal interventions, we advocate for an integrative approach—advancing research by synthesizing and consolidating existing models—to develop interventions to facilitate active coping. Rather than "discovering islands" by creating new models, a potentially more efficacious approach suggested herein may be building bridges by integrating processes, constructs, and themes across multiple models (i.e., "connecting islands"). As highlighted in the "Cousins" section, stress reappraisal and stress mindsets are ideal candidates for integration into a unified stress optimization intervention. Such an intervention would have the potential to combine domain-general benefits of mindset interventions with tools for optimizing coping in specific stressful situations emphasized by stress reappraisal. These potentially additive effects could be disseminated with little to no cost to recipients as well. Future research, however, is needed to explicate basic effects of an integrated stress optimization intervention, and subsequently, to maximize efficiency to scale the intervention for widespread dissemination.

In sum, the research on stress reappraisal reviewed here contributes to a growing corpus of evidence demonstrating the efficacy of brief, social-psychological interventions for improving health and well-being outcomes (see Walton & Wilson, 2018, for a review). As emphasized by Yeager and Walton (2011), however, these interventions are not "magic" panaceas—rather, social-psychological interventions, such as stress reappraisal, target specific processes to enact positive change. Ultimately, it is our hope that this and other intervention approaches can be integrated, scaled, and disseminated to potentially improve people's lives at near zero cost.

REFERENCES

Abramson, L. Y., Seligman, M. E., & Teasdale, J. D. (1978). Learned helplessness in humans: Critique and reformulation. *Journal of Abnormal Psychology, 87,* 49–74.

Barrett, L. F. (2006). Are emotions natural kinds? *Perspectives on Psychological Science, 1*(1), 28–58.

Barrett, L. F. (2017). The theory of constructed emotion: An active inference account of interoception and categorization. *Social Cognitive and Affective Neuroscience, 12*(1), 1–23.

Barrett, L. F., Wilson-Mendenhall, C. D., & Barsalou, L. W. (2014). A psychological construction account of emotion regulation and dysregulation: The role of situated conceptualizations. In J. J. Gross (Ed.), *Handbook of emotion regulation* (2nd ed., pp. 447–465). New York: Guilford Press.

Beltzer, M. L., Nock, M. K., Peters, B. J., & Jamieson, J. P. (2014). Rethinking butterflies: The affective, physiological, and performance effects of reappraising arousal during social evaluation. *Emotion, 14,* 761–768.

Blascovich, J. (1992). A biopsychosocial approach to arousal regulation. *Journal of Social and Clinical Psychology, 11*(3), 213–237.

Blascovich, J. (2008). Challenge, threat, and health. In J. Y. Shah & W. L. Gardner (Eds.), *Handbook of motivation science* (pp. 481–493). New York: Guilford Press.

Blascovich, J., & Mendes, W. B. (2010). Social psychophysiology and embodiment. In S. T. Fiske, D. T. Gilbert, & L. Gardner (Eds.), *Handbook of social psychology* (pp. 194–227). Hoboken, NJ: Wiley.

Blascovich, J., Mendes, W. B., Hunter, S. B., & Salomon, K. (1999). Social "facilitation" as challenge and threat. *Journal of Personality and Social Psychology, 77,* 68–77.

Bradley, R. T., McCraty, R., Atkinson, M., Tomasino, D., Daugherty, A., & Arguelles, L. (2010). Emotion self-regulation, psychophysiological coherence, and test anxiety: Results from an experiment using electrophysiological measures. *Applied Psychophysiology and Biofeedback, 35*(4), 261–283.

Brady, S. T., Hard, B. M., & Gross, J. J. (2018). Reappraising test anxiety increases academic performance of first-year college students. *Journal of Educational Psychology, 110*(3), 395–406.

Brooks, A. W. (2014). Get excited: Reappraising pre-performance anxiety as excitement. *Journal of Experimental Psychology: General, 143*(3), 1144–1158.

Brownley, K. A., Hurwitz, B. E., & Schneiderman, N. (2000). Cardiovascular psychophysiology. In J. T. Cacioppo, L. G., Tassinary, & G. G. Berntson (Eds.), *Handbook of psychophysiology* (2nd ed., pp. 224–264). New York: Cambridge University Press.

Butler, E. A., & Randall, A. K. (2013). Emotional coregulation in close relationships. *Emotion Review, 5*(2), 202–210.

Cohen, S., Kamarck, T., & Mermelstein, R. (1983). A global measure of perceived stress. *Journal of Health and Social Behavior, 24,* 385–396.

Croson, R., & Gneezy, U. (2009). Gender differences in preferences. *Journal of Economic Literature, 47*(2), 448–474.

Crum, A. J., Akinola, M., Martin, A., & Fath, S. (2017). The role of stress mindset in shaping cognitive, emotional, and physiological responses to challenging and threatening stress. *Anxiety, Stress, and Coping, 30*(4), 379–395.

Crum, A. J., Salovey, P., & Achor, S. (2013). Rethinking stress: The role of mindsets in determining the stress response. *Journal of Personality and Social Psychology, 104*(4), 716–733.

Crum, A. J., Santoro, E., Smith, E. N., Salovey, P., Achor, S., & Mooraveji, N. (2020). *Rethinking stress: Changing mindsets to harness the enhancing effects of stress.* Manuscript under review.

Dienstbier, R. A. (1989). Arousal and physiological toughness: Implications for mental and physical health. *Psychological Review, 96*(1), 84–100.

Dweck, C. S. (1986). Motivational processes affecting learning. *American Psychologist, 41*(10), 1040–1048.

Elliot, A. J. (1999). Approach and avoidance motivation and achievement goals. *Educational Psychologist, 34*(3), 169–189.

Elliot, A. J., & Fryer, J. W. (2008). The goal concept in psychology. In J. Shah & W. Gardner (Eds.), *Handbook of motivational science* (pp. 235–250). New York: Guilford Press.

Goyer, J. P., Akinola, M., Grunberg, R., & Crum, A. J. (2018). *Evaluation of a stress mindset intervention to improve performance and wellbeing in underrepresented minority college students at a selective institution.* Manuscript in preparation.

Gross, J. J. (2002). Emotion regulation: Affective, cognitive, and social consequences. *Psychophysiology, 39*(3), 281–291.

Gross, J. J. (2015). The extended process model of emotion regulation: Elaborations, applications, and future directions. *Psychological Inquiry, 26*(1), 130–137.

Gross, J. J., & Barrett, L. F. (2011). Emotion generation and emotion regulation: One or two depends on your point of view. *Emotion Review, 3*(1), 8–16.

Hangen, E. J., Elliot, A. J., & Jamieson, J. P. (2019). Stress reappraisal during a mathematics competition: Testing effects on cardiovascular approach-oriented states and exploring the moderating role of gender. *Anxiety, Stress, and Coping, 32*(1), 95–108.

Jacquart, J., Papini, S., Freeman, Z., Bartholomew, J. B., & Smits, J. A. (2020). Using exercise to facilitate arousal reappraisal and reduce stress reactivity: A randomized controlled trial. *Mental Health and Physical Activity, 18,* 100324.

Jamieson, J. P. (2017). Challenge and threat appraisals. In A. J. Elliot, C. Dweck, & D. Yeager (Eds.), *Handbook of motivation and cognition* (2nd ed., pp. 175–191). New York: Guilford Press.

Jamieson, J. P., Black, A. E., Pelaia, L. E., Gravelding, H., Gordils, J., Altose, A. J., & Reis, H. R. (2020). *The effects of reappraising stress arousal in a naturalistic academic context.* Manuscript under review.

Jamieson, J. P., Crum, A. J., Goyer, J. P., Marotta, M. E., & Akinola, M. (2018). Optimizing stress responses with reappraisal and mindset interventions: An integrated model. *Anxiety, Stress, and Coping, 31*(3), 245–261.

Jamieson, J. P., Hangen, E. J., Lee, H. Y., & Yeager, D. S. (2018). Capitalizing on appraisal processes to improve social stress responses. *Emotion Review, 10,* 30–39.

Jamieson, J. P., Koslov, K., Nock, M. K., & Mendes, W. B. (2013). Experiencing discrimination increases risk taking. *Psychological Science, 24*(2), 131–139.

Jamieson, J. P., Mendes, W. B., Blackstock, E., & Schmader, T. (2010). Turning the knots in your stomach into bows: Reappraising arousal improves performance on the GRE. *Journal of Experimental Social Psychology, 46*(1), 208–212.

Jamieson, J. P., Mendes, W. B., & Nock, M. K. (2013). Improving acute stress responses the power of reappraisal. *Current Directions in Psychological Science, 22,* 51–56.

Jamieson, J. P., Nock, M. K., & Mendes, W. B. (2012). Mind over matter: Reappraising arousal improves cardiovascular and cognitive responses to stress. *Journal of Experimental Psychology: General, 141*(3), 417.

Jamieson, J. P., Nock, M. K., & Mendes, W. B. (2013). Changing the conceptualization of stress in social anxiety disorder affective and physiological consequences. *Clinical Psychological Science, 1*(4), 363–374.

Jamieson, J. P., Peters, B. J., Greenwood, E. J., & Altose, A. J. (2016). Reappraising stress arousal improves performance and reduces evaluation anxiety in classroom exam situations. *Social Psychological and Personality Science, 7*(6), 579–587.

Jamieson, J. P., Valdesolo, P., & Peters, B. J. (2014). Sympathy for the devil?: The physiological and psychological effects of being an agent (and target) of dissent during intragroup conflict. *Journal of Experimental Social Psychology, 55*, 221–227.

Jefferson, A. L., Himali, J. J., Beiser, A. S., Au, R., Massaro, J. M., Seshadri, S., . . . Manning, W. J. (2010). Cardiac index is associated with brain aging: The Framingham Heart Study. *Circulation, 122*, 690–697.

Jesus, S. N., & Lens, W. (2005). An integrated model for the study of teacher motivation. *Applied Psychology: An International Review, 54*(1), 119–134.

John-Henderson, N. A., Rheinschmidt, M. L., & Mendoza-Denton, R. (2015). Cytokine responses and math performance: The role of stereotype threat and anxiety reappraisals. *Journal of Experimental Social Psychology, 56*, 203–206.

Juster, R. P., McEwen, B. S., & Lupien, S. J. (2010). Allostatic load biomarkers of chronic stress and impact on health and cognition. *Neuroscience and Biobehavioral Reviews, 35*(1), 2–16.

Kirschbaum, C., Pirke, K. M., & Hellhammer, D. H. (1993). The "Trier Social Stress Test"—a tool for investigating psychobiological stress responses in a laboratory setting. *Neuropsychobiology, 28*(1–2), 76–81.

Kray, L. J., Thompson, L., & Galinsky, A. (2001). Battle of the sexes: Gender stereotype confirmation and reactance in negotiations. *Journal of Personality and Social Psychology, 80*(6), 942–958.

Lazarus, R. S. (1991). Progress on a cognitive–motivational–relational theory of emotion. *American Psychologist, 46*(8), 819–834.

Lundberg, U. (2005). Stress hormones in health and illness: The roles of work and gender. *Psychoneuroendocrinology, 30*(10), 1017–1021.

Matthews, K. A., Gump, B. B., Block, D. R., & Allen, M. T. (1997). Does background stress heighten or dampen children's cardiovascular responses to acute stress? *Psychosomatic Medicine, 59*(5), 488–496.

McGregor, H. A., & Elliot, A. J. (2002). Achievement goals as predictors of achievement-relevant processes prior to task engagement. *Journal of Educational Psychology, 94*(2), 381–395.

Mendes, W. B. (2009). Assessing autonomic nervous system activity. In E. Harmon-Jones & J. S. Beer (Eds.), *Methods in social neuroscience* (pp. 118–147). New York: Guilford Press.

Mendes, W. B., Gray, H. M., Mendoza-Denton, R., Major, B., & Epel, E. S. (2007). Why egalitarianism might be good for your health: Physiological thriving during stressful intergroup encounters. *Psychological Science, 18*(11), 991–998.

Mendes, W. B., Major, B., McCoy, S., & Blascovich, J. (2008). How attributional ambiguity shapes physiological and emotional responses to social rejection and acceptance. *Journal of Personality and Social Psychology, 94*(2), 278–291.

Mendes, W. B., & Park, J. (2014). Neurobiological concomitants of motivational states. In A. J. Elliot (Ed.), *Advances in motivation science* (pp. 233–270). New York: Academic Press.

Moore, L. J., Vine, S. J., Wilson, M. R., & Freeman, P. (2015). Reappraising threat: How to optimize performance under pressure. *Journal of Sport and Exercise Psychology, 37*(3), 339–343.

Niederle, M., & Vesterlund, L. (2007). Do women shy away from competition?: Do men compete too much? *Quarterly Journal of Economics, 122*(3), 1067–1101.

Oveis, C., Gu, Y., Ocampo, J. M., Hangen, E. J., & Jamieson, J. P. (2020). Emotion regulation contagion: Stress reappraisal promotes challenge responses in teammates. *Journal of Experimental Psychology: General*. [Epub ahead of print]

Peters, B. J., Overall, N. C., & Jamieson, J. P. (2014). Physiological and cognitive consequences of suppressing and expressing emotion in dyadic interactions. *International Journal of Psychophysiology, 94*(1), 100–107.

Peters, B. J., Reis, H. T., & Jamieson, J. P. (2018). Cardiovascular indexes of threat impair responsiveness in situations of conflicting interests. *International Journal of Psychophysiology, 123*, 1–7.

Reis, H. T., Clark, M. S., & Holmes, J. G. (2004). Perceived partner responsiveness as an organizing construct in the study of closeness and intimacy. In D. J. Mashek & A. Aron (Eds.), *Handbook of closeness and intimacy* (pp. 201–225). Mahwah, NJ: Erlbaum.

Rozek, C. S., Ramirez, G., Fine, R. D., & Beilock, S. (2019). Reducing sociodemographic disparities in the STEM pipeline through student emotion regulation. *Proceedings of the National Academy of Sciences of the USA, 116*(5), 1553–1558.

Sammy, N., Anstiss, P. A., Moore, L. J., Freeman, P., Wilson, M. R., & Vine, S. J. (2017). The effects of arousal reappraisal on stress responses, performance and attention. *Anxiety, Stress, and Coping, 30*(6), 619–629.

Sbarra, D. A., & Hazan, C. (2008). Coregulation, dysregulation, self-regulation: An integrative analysis and empirical agenda for understanding adult attachment, separation, loss, and recovery. *Personality and Social Psychology Review, 12*, 141–167.

Schmader, T., Forbes, C. E., Zhang, S., & Mendes, W. B. (2009). A metacognitive perspective on the cognitive deficits experienced in intellectually threatening environments. *Personality and Social Psychology Bulletin, 35*(5), 584–596.

Seery, M. D., Weisbuch, M., & Blascovich, J. (2009). Something to gain, something to lose: The cardiovascular consequences of outcome framing. *International Journal of Psychophysiology, 73*(3), 308–312.

Steel, P. (2010). *The procrastination equation: How to stop putting things off and start getting stuff done.* Toronto: Random House Canada.

Tugade, M. M., & Fredrickson, B. L. (2004). Resilient individuals use positive emotions to bounce back from negative emotional experiences. *Journal of Personality and Social Psychology, 86*(2), 320–333.

Walton, G. M., & Wilson, T. D. (2018). Wise interventions: Psychological remedies for social and personal problems. *Psychological Review, 125*(5), 617–655.

Waters, S. F., West, T. V., Karnilowicz, H. R., & Mendes, W. B. (2017). Affect contagion between mothers and infants: Examining valence and touch. *Journal of Experimental Psychology: General, 146*(7), 1043–1051.

Williams, J. M. G., Mathews, A., & MacLeod, C. (1996). The emotional Stroop task and psychopathology. *Psychological Bulletin, 120*(1), 3–24.

Wilson-Mendenhall, C. D., Barrett, L. F., Simmons, W. K., & Barsalou, L. W. (2011). Grounding emotion in situated conceptualization. *Neuropsychologia, 49*, 1105–1127.

Yeager, D. S., Lee, H. Y., & Jamieson, J. P. (2016). How to improve adolescent stress responses: Insights from integrating implicit theories of personality and biopsychosocial models. *Psychological Science, 27*(8), 1078–1091.

Yeager, D. S., & Walton, G. M. (2011). Social-psychological interventions in education: They're not magic. *Review of Educational Research, 81*(2), 267–301.

CHAPTER 11

Values-Alignment Interventions
An Alternative to Pragmatic Appeals for Behavior Change

Christopher J. Bryan

The science of behavior change has become an increasingly important frontier in the quest to improve human health and well-being. Recognition of this is now widespread in the scientific community, but the science of behavior change—the development of effective, empirically validated techniques for producing lasting, internalized motivation for the behavior choices people know they should be making but usually do not—is still badly underdeveloped. Most public appeals to engage in such "should" behaviors (e.g., exercise, eat healthily, save for the future, conserve energy) focus on the pragmatic reasons why those behaviors are important. The problem with this approach is that such pragmatic appeals lack the motivational immediacy to drive the needed changes in behavior for reasons psychologists have understood for decades. Here, I suggest an alternative approach: reframing should behaviors in terms that emphasize how those behaviors serve the values that are *already* immediate and important to the people whose behavior one seeks to change. I demonstrate the potential of this approach using the example of an intervention to get adolescents to adopt healthier dietary habits by framing manipulative food marketing as a subversion of important adolescent values, including autonomy from adult control and social justice.

BACKGROUND

Perhaps now more than ever before, human thriving depends on individual behavior choices. To effectively address problems ranging from climate change to obesity, we must find ways to foster sustained changes in behavior on a population scale. In particular, we need good ways to create sustained motivation for "should" behaviors—the things people know they should be doing but struggle to muster the motivation for. We see public appeals for should behaviors every day; we are encouraged to get a flu shot, eat more vegetables, exercise, conserve energy, and put our phones away while driving. And those

259

appeals almost always focus on the pragmatic reasons for should behaviors; they emphasize how those behaviors will make us healthier, safer, and more financially secure in the future. This is not an effective approach. The big problem with it is that psychologists (and many economists) have known for decades that people tend to overvalue immediate outcomes relative to those in the future (Ainslie & Haslam, 1992; Berns, Laibson, & Loewenstein, 2007). So, if people see should behavior as the sacrifice of a reward in the immediate term (e.g., enjoying dessert, having money to spend right now) for a reward in the future (e.g., health, financial security), they are unlikely to be motivated to choose them—even if they know they should. This is a problem because, in fact, should behaviors usually *do* require forgoing an immediate reward in favor of one in the future. So what's the alternative?

In this chapter, I describe a new approach to creating sustained, internalized motivation for should behaviors, called values alignment. Values alignment involves identifying values that have *motivational immediacy* for people and that could plausibly be served by the behavior one seeks to motivate, then framing appeals for the behavior in terms of those values. In particular, values that are central to people's (culturally defined) conception of what makes someone deserving of acceptance, approval, or admiration from the members of their important social reference groups tend to be powerful motivators because seeing oneself as living up to those values is critical to self-integrity—the sense that one is a worthwhile person (Leary & Baumeister, 2000; Sherman & Cohen, 2006; Steele, 1988).

Although values alignment is a general approach to motivating should behaviors in a wide range of domains, the theory largely grew out of work on a specific intervention aimed at motivating adolescents to adopt healthier eating habits by framing them as consistent with the important adolescent values of autonomy from adult control and the pursuit of social justice (Bryan, Yeager, & Hinojosa, 2019; Bryan et al., 2016). That intervention is the central focus of this chapter. My collaborators and I framed healthy eating as rebellious and autonomy assertive by teaching adolescents about deceptive food marketing designed to manipulate them and others into eating junk food. We framed healthy eating as social justice-oriented behavior by emphasizing the ways in which food marketers deliberately target vulnerable groups, like very young children and the poor. Our goal was to portray healthy eating not as a way to be healthier in the future—a pragmatic motive that lacks motivational immediacy—but rather as a way to be a "good teenager" who stands up against unjust adult authority. We hypothesized that the reward of knowing they were living up to the important values they share with their peers would have the motivational immediacy to compete with the reward of eating junk food.

PSYCHOLOGICAL PROCESS

The psychological process behind values alignment relies on two basic psychological phenomena: myopia and construal.

Myopia: A Persistent Barrier to Delay of Gratification

Few phenomena in psychology are as thoroughly documented: people consistently overvalue immediate costs and rewards and undervalue those in the future (Ainslie, 1992;

Berns et al., 2007; Frederick, Loewenstein, & O'Donoghue, 2002; Loewenstein, 1996; Mischel & Staub, 1965; Thaler, 1981). Often referred to as myopia, this "pervasive devaluation of the future" (Ainslie & Haslam, 1992, p. 59), helps to explain why the long-term benefits of should behaviors seem to provide such a weak incentive for people to make the immediate sacrifices those behaviors typically require.

Compounding this challenge, motivation to delay gratification depends on people's confidence that the distant reward will eventually be achieved (Kidd, Palmeri, & Aslin, 2013; Mischel, Cantor, & Feldman, 1996; Mischel & Staub, 1965). And people generally have enough experience with temptation to realize that even if they manage to delay gratification in a given instance, the likelihood that they will be able to do so in a sustained and consistent enough way to reap long-term benefits is quite low. These psychological realities impose a persistent barrier to the effective motivation of should behaviors. The values-alignment approach draws on one of social psychology's earliest and most powerful insights to circumvent this barrier: the central role of construal in shaping people's experiences and decisions.

Construal: A Hidden Step between Stimulus and Response

Although people tend to think of themselves as responding directly to objective reality (Ross & Ward, 1996), in fact what they respond to is their internal representation, or *construal,* of that reality (Asch, 1940; Koffka, 2013; Lewin, 1935). The far-reaching implications of this insight become clearer when considering how susceptible one's construal of the world often is to influence from subtle contextual cues. For example, in one classic study (Liberman, Samuels, & Ross, 2004), college undergraduates were invited to play an economic game that required them to adopt either a cooperative or a competitive strategy. The researchers manipulated how participants construed the game simply by giving it different names. Some were introduced to it as the "Community Game," while others were told it was called the "Wall Street Game." The name was irrelevant to the rules of the game or the monetary values associated with different strategies, but it transformed what participants saw as the *point* of the game—whether it was about cooperating with a partner or competing with an opponent. This simple construal manipulation had a big effect on how participants played. More than two-thirds of participants in the "Community Game" condition adopted a cooperative strategy, while fully two-thirds of participants in the "Wall Street Game" condition played competitively.

Upon reflection, it is easy to see why people's construal processes would be so susceptible to influence from contextual cues. Most situations we encounter are relatively ambiguous and we must fill in missing information to make sense of them before we know how to respond. Our construal of a situation influences what information we fill in. All of this happens outside of our awareness, so once we have filled in information based on our construal, it just becomes part of what we perceive to be objective reality (Ross & Ward, 1996).

Values Alignment Circumvents Myopia by Shifting Construal

The key insight behind values alignment is that the obstacle to should behaviors posed by myopia is largely a product of people's construal of those behaviors as being in service of long-term pragmatic benefits. That is, in the mind of a person who construes the purpose of should behaviors as the pursuit of a pragmatic benefit in the distant future, myopia necessarily undermines motivation for those behaviors: Most decisions about should behavior pit an immediate hedonic reward (e.g., enjoying junk food) that people are predisposed to overvalue against a distant pragmatic benefit (e.g., being healthy) that people are predisposed to undervalue.

The aim of values alignment is to circumvent the myopia problem by shifting people away from the pragmatic construal. When you see a should behavior as an expression of your existing deeply held values, this introduces a new reason to perform it: the powerful eudaimonic reward that comes from feeling that you are living up to your important values. And, critically, because this reward is mostly abstract and symbolic, it is experienced immediately so its motivational power is not blunted by myopia (see Figure 11.1). In addition to the immediate reward for choosing should behavior, the values-aligned construal introduces a eudaimonic *cost* for succumbing to temptation and not choosing should behavior. Because the should behavior is now construed as an expression of one's important values, not engaging in that behavior is now construed as *inconsistent* with those values. So when a person fails to choose should behavior, she not only forgoes the reward of living up to her values but must incur the cost of knowing that she is making a choice that is inconsistent with those values.

Applying the Theory: Framing Healthy Eating as an Expression of Adolescent Values

With David Yeager, a developmental psychologist at the University of Texas, Austin, Cintia Hinojosa, a behavioral scientist at the University of Chicago, and others, I implemented these theoretical ideas in the design of a classroom-based intervention to motivate adolescents to make healthier dietary choices (Bryan et al., 2016; Bryan, Yeager, & Hinojosa, 2019). Trying to motivate teenagers to reject junk food in favor of healthier options is an especially tough behavior change challenge. Adolescents tend to overvalue the present and undervalue the future even more extremely than adults do (Braams, van Duijvenvoorde, Peper, & Crone, 2015; Casey & Caudle, 2013; Crone & Dahl, 2012; Steinberg, 2007), and junk food is deliberately formulated by food companies to provide an extraordinarily strong (immediate) hedonic reward (Kessler, 2009; Moss, 2013). So under the conventional long-term health-benefit construal, in order to choose healthier diets, adolescents must pass up a powerful, immediate hedonic reward in service of a long-term goal that is not important to them. Considering this, it is perhaps not surprising that, despite more than 30 years of concerted effort by the scientific community to develop an intervention that improves people's dietary habits, personal dietary choices

FIGURE 11.1. Theoretical psychological process by which values alignment motivates should behavior.

are currently the single leading cause of premature death and disease in the developed world (Forouzanfar et al., 2015; Gakidou et al., 2017).

The two values the intervention was designed to harness—autonomy from adult control and the pursuit of social justice—have been shown in past research to be especially important to adolescents. The first will come as no surprise; adolescents are famously (or infamously, depending on your perspective) rebellious against adult authority (Lee, Siegle, Dahl, Hooley, & Silk, 2014; Vansteenkiste, Simons, Lens, Sheldon, & Deci, 2004). This psychology likely hampers the success of many traditional health interventions, which typically involve adults advising adolescents about what they should be eating for their own good—just the sort of message that tends to provoke teens' rebellious impulses. The second is less widely appreciated but adolescence is a time when people tend to become especially concerned about fairness, social justice, and beyond-the-self aims (Damon, Menon, & Bronk, 2003; Robinson, 2010; Yeager et al., 2014). For the first time in their lives, adolescents are beginning to feel like independent agents in the world and they want to make a difference (Robinson, 2010; Yeager et al., 2014).

To connect to the autonomy value, we framed the intervention as an exposé of manipulative food-industry marketing practices designed to inveigle people into consuming more junk food than they would otherwise be inclined to consume. This includes practices like using deceptive labeling to conceal the sugar content in foods or devoting huge research budgets to discovering new ways to make junk foods maximally addictive (Kessler, 2009; Moss, 2013). To connect to the social justice value, we emphasized the ways in which food marketing contributes to injustice. This refers to practices like disproportionately targeting vulnerable populations (e.g., very young children, the poor, and minority groups) with marketing of the unhealthiest products (Kessler, 2009). Through this framing, we sought to replace what we imagined was adolescents' default construal of healthy eating—something like "Healthy eaters are lame nerds who do what adults tell them to do"—with an alternative construal: "Healthy eaters are independent-minded people who are fighting to make the world a fairer place." This construal, we theorized, would provide adolescents with the immediate symbolic reward of feeling like they were living up to the important values they share with their peers every time they made a healthy dietary choice. Perhaps equally important, every time adolescents made an unhealthy dietary choice, it would impose the immediate symbolic cost of knowing they were not living up to their important values.

EMPIRICAL EVIDENCE

Outcomes

Using randomized, controlled field experimental methods, the values-alignment healthy-eating intervention has been shown to improve adolescents' dietary choices in naturalistic school settings that they believed were unconnected to the research. The first test of its effectiveness (Bryan et al., 2016) was conducted in a rural/suburban middle school in Texas with the entire eighth-grade class in 2 consecutive years ($N = 536$). Participants were randomly assigned, at the individual level, to read one of three short informational articles: an exposé article that linked healthy dietary choices to adolescent values, an active control article based on current best practices that used material from middle school health curricula and the U.S. government's health education website and emphasized the long-term health consequences of healthy and unhealthy diets, or a "no-treatment" control article that was similar to the other two in length but did not deal with food or diet. After reading their respective articles, all students completed a series of survey questions measuring the extent to which they construed healthy eating as relevant to the two target adolescent values and some brief writing exercises to help them internalize the key messages of the article they read (Aronson, 1999).

The day after the intervention session we measured participants' dietary choices in a situation they believed to be unconnected with the research. This was possible thanks to the school principal, who adapted his yearly practice of giving students a "snack pack" each spring as a reward for their hard work in preparing for the statewide standardized tests. To ensure students would not see the snack pack as part of the research, we asked the principal to announce it to students in his normal fashion, long before the research took place (and long before any student at the school knew about the study). Then, the morning after the study, during homeroom period (which was a different class from the one the intervention was administered in), the principal announced over the school public address (PA) system that students would be receiving their snack packs that day. Homeroom teachers distributed order forms and the principal explained that snack packs containing the items they selected would be waiting for them at the main office at the end of the school day. Students were invited to select two snacks and one drink. The snack options included three healthy choices (baby carrots, fresh-cut fruit, and nuts with dried fruit) and three unhealthy choices (cookies, potato chips, and cheese puffs). Drink options included two healthy choices (bottled water and sparkling mineral water) and three unhealthy choices (two sodas and a sweetened fruit drink).

Our primary measure of dietary choices was simply the number of unhealthy options participants chose to include in their snack packs. We found that participants who received the values-aligned exposé intervention ordered slightly but significantly fewer unhealthy options ($M = 1.38$ unhealthy selections) than those who received either of the control articles ($M = 1.49$ unhealthy selections).

There was no significant difference in the number of unhealthy choices participants made after reading the traditional health education intervention (active control) versus the article that was unrelated to diet or nutrition (no-treatment control). The lack of difference between these two control conditions is itself notable: even just 1 day later, we found no evidence that traditional health and nutrition education had any effect on participants' dietary choices. Although this is not surprising in light of the psychological barriers preventing people from choosing should behaviors under the traditional pragmatic construal of that behavior, it is still a striking indictment of the approach that schools and governments currently invest enormous resources in.

There are various ways to quantify the exposé intervention's effect on participants' snack pack choices and each provides a different and complementary perspective on the intervention's effects. For example, examining the percentage of participants in each group who ordered snack packs that were entirely composed of unhealthy options sheds light on how effectively the exposé intervention motivated participants to make at least some sacrifice of their hedonic experience and take a step in the direction of healthier diets. In the two control conditions, 57% of participants chose the maximum possible number of unhealthy options (three). Adolescents who read the values-aligned exposé article were substantially more willing to forgo a tempting, unhealthy treat in favor of something healthier but much less hedonically rewarding: only 46% of them chose snack packs that contained the maximum of three unhealthy options.

The reduction in the number of unhealthy choices among adolescents who received the exposé intervention also translated into differences in the overall nutritional content of the snack packs they ordered. While participants in the two control conditions ordered snack packs with an average of 40.4 total grams of sugar and 60.2 total grams of carbohydrates, those who received the exposé treatment ordered items containing 3.6 fewer grams of sugar and 4.3 fewer grams of carbohydrates, on average.

Although I have argued strongly that emphasizing the practical benefits of should behaviors is an ineffective way to motivate those behaviors, practical outcomes are of course still the most relevant criterion when evaluating an intervention from a policy perspective. Although improving the nutritional content of a single meal or snack cannot possibly have any meaningful impact on long-term health, it is possible to estimate what the health significance would be of differences of the size observed in this experiment if they were sustained over months and years. For example, a relative reduction in carbohydrate consumption of the size observed in this study, if sustained, would translate into roughly 1 pound of body fat lost (or not gained) every 6–8 weeks in adolescents of this age.[1] So can a values-alignment intervention produce *lasting* changes in adolescents' daily dietary choices? We examined this in a second experiment.

Effects over Time

Our first iteration of the values-aligned healthy-eating intervention provided "proof of concept" for the values-alignment approach: It got adolescents to care enough about healthy eating that they were willing to forgo rewarding junk food in favor of healthier but less rewarding options 1 day later in a situation they believed was unrelated. To go beyond that and produce lasting changes in adolescents' daily dietary choices, we must overcome some additional obstacles. Perhaps most daunting among those is that adolescents' lives are pervaded by junk food marketing. This marketing fosters strong positive emotional associations with unhealthy food and drives overconsumption (Harris, Pomeranz, Lobstein, & Brownell, 2009; Hastings & Cairns, 2010; Kessler, 2009; Moss, 2013; Nestle, 2006; Swinburn et al., 2011). So, are the changes prompted by our relatively brief intervention doomed to be wiped away by the barrage of pro-junk food messaging participants are exposed to in their daily lives? Not necessarily. After all, the exposé intervention is designed to change participants' construal of junk food and of junk food marketing. If it is effective at changing the meaning adolescents attach to the junk food marketing messages they are exposed to, maybe it can neutralize their effect—or possibly even harness their ubiquity to support the intervention's message. Imagine if every time adolescents saw an ad for junk food, it served as a reminder of unjust, controlling manipulation by the food industry instead of acting as a tempting inducement to consume the product.

---

[1]Because participants' snack pack choices were limited to a small set of options, the size of the reduction in carbohydrate content must be considered an imprecise estimate of the reduction we might see if participants were choosing from the universe of food and drink options available to them in their daily lives.

In a second randomized, controlled field experiment, David Yeager, Cintia Hinojosa, and I tested a modified version of the exposé intervention that was designed to achieve this (Bryan, Yeager, & Hinojosa, 2019). We again recruited the entire eighth-grade class (*N* = 362) at a middle school in Texas. As in the first experiment, participants were given an informational article to read—either an exposé of manipulative food marketing or a traditional health education message. (We dropped the no-treatment control in this second study because in the first study its effect was indistinguishable from the traditional health education control condition.) This time, however, we added a second intervention session the day after the first session in which participants completed an activity designed to reinforce their negative construal of junk food marketing in particular. Participants in the exposé condition were presented with images of junk food advertisements on tablet computers using software that let them draw or write on the images. Participants were instructed to cross things out, write or draw things on the image—whatever they needed to do to take the dishonest ad and make it more honest. The activity, called "Make It True," was intentionally evocative of the subversive adolescent thrill of using graffiti to rebel against authority (see Figure 11.2). Participants in the traditional health education condition completed a similarly interactive tablet-based activity, created by expert professionals who specialize in media and health communication, in which they spun a virtual *Wheel of Fortune*-style wheel and learned how much physical activity it takes to burn the calories in their favorite foods (New Mexico State University Learning Games Lab, 2015). We called this control activity "Make It Fun."

We assessed the intervention's effect on dietary choices by looking at what participants bought at the school cafeteria. Students pay for their cafeteria purchases by swiping their school identification (ID) cards; the school provided us with records of every participant's daily purchases for the whole school year. The intervention took place in mid-February so we had data on participants' purchases for approximately 6 months before the intervention and 3 months after, allowing us to assess any changes in their dietary choices as a result of their intervention condition, as well as how long any such changes persisted (up to 3 months).

FIGURE 11.2. Examples of changes participants made to food advertisements in the Make It True activity. In the right-most image, the speech bubble reads, "I do not actually like it."

As we predicted, participants in the exposé condition showed a significant reduction in their daily purchases of unhealthy snacks and drinks (e.g., chips, cookies, sugary juices) and a significant increase in their purchases of healthy items (e.g., fruit, milk, water) from the preintervention period to the postintervention period, relative to those who received the control intervention. An exploratory follow-up analysis revealed an unexpected effect as well: the overall improvements in participants' daily dietary choices caused by the exposé intervention were only apparent in boys—that is, what initially appeared to be a small but significant improvement in the health profile of daily dietary choices for all participants in the exposé condition was, in fact, a quite large improvement in boys' purchases (e.g., a 31% relative reduction in junk food purchases) and no improvement at all in girls' purchases, relative to the traditional health education control. If anything, there were hints that girls' dietary choices in the cafeteria might have improved slightly more following the *control* intervention. It is important to be clear that only the effect on cafeteria purchases was moderated by gender in this way. Boys' and girls' psychological responses to the exposé intervention were indistinguishable, but those psychological changes translated into documented improvements in dietary habits only for boys.

Why might this have been the case? Two nonmutually exclusive explanations seem plausible: First, it is important to recall that the lack of any improvement in girls' dietary choices relative to the control condition does not mean it was ineffective—only that it was not *more* effective than the control condition. This is important because the control condition in this experiment was not inert; it was a traditional health education intervention. And one feature of this second iteration of the traditional health-education control intervention might plausibly have influenced girls' dietary choices but not those of boys: the reference to calories (and how much physical activity is required to burn off those calories) in the Make It Fun activity. Because girls are subjected to much more pressure to be thin than boys (Thompson, Heinberg, Altabe, & Tantleff-Dunn, 1999), it seems plausible that this reminder of the link between diet and thinness might have induced girls but not boys in the active control condition to make healthier choices. To have confidence in this explanation, a new experiment will be needed with a no-treatment control condition that does not risk triggering girls' body image concerns. Note that this explanation of the gender difference is entirely consistent with the theory of values alignment: girls value thinness much more than boys (because our culture essentially forces them to) and the proposed explanation is that the active control intervention (inadvertently) aligned healthy eating with that value. Although this does qualify as an instance of values alignment, it relies on, and possibly reinforces, a culturally imposed value that can cause real psychological harm to girls (e.g., Strahan et al., 2008). Note also that this explanation would suggest that the values-aligned exposé intervention is more effective than traditional health education in boys and roughly as effective as traditional health education in girls but without triggering body image-related pressure or shame.

The second possible explanation is that the rebellious "stick-it-to-the-man" spirit of the exposé intervention is simply less compelling to girls than it is to boys. We know girls were as persuaded by the exposé intervention as boys were at least insofar as they showed all the same psychological changes following the intervention that boys did. But it is possible that these psychological changes energized behavior to a lesser degree in girls. Again, a new study that includes a no-treatment control condition will be needed to gain more clarity about these and other possible explanations.

Mechanism

Shifting Construal of Healthy Eating

In the "Psychological Process" section of this chapter, above, I argued that values alignment motivates sustained increases in should behavior by changing people's construal of that behavior in ways that circumvent the barriers imposed by myopia. Was the exposé intervention successful in doing this? In both field experiments I described, we measured the extent to which participants in the treatment and control conditions construed healthy eating as consistent with the values of autonomy and social justice. Participants were asked, for example, how much they agreed with statements like "Eating healthy is a way to stand up to people who are trying to control us" (autonomy) and "When I eat healthy, I'm doing my part to protect kids who are being controlled by food companies" (social justice). As expected, we found that participants in the exposé (values-aligned) condition agreed more strongly with both the autonomy and social justice construals of healthy eating than those in either the no-treatment or the traditional health education control group.

Introduction of Symbolic Reward

I also argued that the construal of should behavior that is produced by values alignment creates a reward for choosing should behavior that comes from knowing one is living up to his or her core values. Because this reward is largely symbolic, it can be experienced immediately—likely before the relevant behavior (e.g., healthy or unhealthy eating) even happens in some cases, since the symbolic implications of a behavior can presumably be experienced in an anticipatory form as soon as one decides to perform it. And because this reward for choosing should behavior is experienced immediately, its power is not undermined by myopia and it can compete with the hedonic rewards that would come from eating rich, unhealthy foods. Essentially, this theoretical argument boils down to a claim that values alignment makes should behavior feel more (immediately) rewarding.

It is difficult to measure a symbolic reward directly but we were able to obtain data that provide indirect support for this hypothesis. We obtained saliva samples from approximately half of the participants in the second intervention experiment a few weeks before the intervention was administered and assayed them for testosterone (T) levels (Medrano et al., 2019). Levels of T increase dramatically in adolescence (for boys and girls) as a result of pubertal development and T is known to increase the brain's sensitivity to reward (Braams et al., 2015). T has also been shown to motivate reward-seeking behavior. Both correlational and experimental studies in animals and in humans have shown that increased levels of T drive increases in behaviors that are expected to be rewarding (Casey, 2015; van Duijvenvoorde, Peters, Braams, & Crone, 2016). So if values alignment motivates should behavior by making that behavior feel more immediately rewarding, it should be most effective in people who experience reward most intensely.

It is worth noting that this is quite a bold prediction. Unhealthy food is also powerfully rewarding, so people with higher levels of T should also be the people who are most powerfully attracted to junk food under the traditional pragmatic construal of healthy eating. Nevertheless, we found, as predicted, that the values-aligned exposé intervention was most effective at motivating healthy eating among those with higher levels of T.

Because the effect of the intervention on daily cafeteria choices was limited to boys, we focus on boys in this analysis as well. First, consistent with our assumption that, under the traditional pragmatic construal, T should attract boys more strongly to the hedonic reward of eating junk food, we found that T levels were positively associated with junk food purchases among boys in the control condition. But the key test of the theoretical process model is whether the exposé intervention was more effective at reducing junk food purchases among boys who were higher in T than among boys who were lower in T. This prediction was also supported by the data; the exposé intervention was significantly more effective among boys with higher levels of T (Medrano et al., 2019). The difference was striking: while higher levels of T were associated with higher rates of unhealthy, hedonically rewarding purchases among boys in the control condition, boys in the exposé condition made relatively few daily junk food purchases irrespective of their T levels (see Figure 11.3). Among boys in the exposé condition, although the hedonic reward of junk food undoubtedly remained a powerful motivator, it was countered by a powerful eudaimonic reward for making healthier choices.

Altering Construal of Junk Food Marketing

Recall that the major modification of the exposé intervention for the second experiment was that we added the Make It True exercise (in which participants modified images of real food ads to make them more honest). The primary purpose of this exercise was to help students to internalize a negative construal of junk food marketing. Our hope was that we could link that marketing so strongly, in participants' minds, with the food industry's attempts to deceive and manipulate that it no longer had the power to create positive emotional associations with junk food and drive overconsumption. How successful were we in neutralizing food marketing?

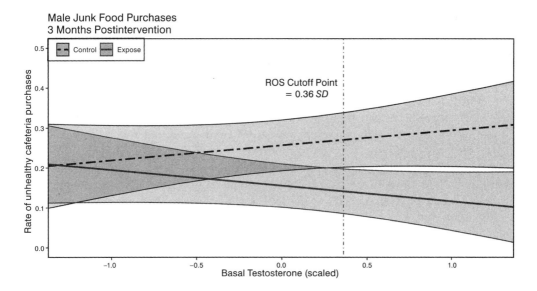

FIGURE 11.3. Interaction of T × condition on boys' junk food purchases. Values along the *y*-axis represent fitted values with our covariates (age, date, and body mass index [BMI]). The dashed vertical line indicates the region of significance (ROS) cutoff point: To the right of the line, the control and expose conditions are significantly different.

We assessed the intervention's effect on participants' implicit affective associations: their immediate, gut-level emotional reactions to junk food marketing, junk food, and healthy food with a widely used and thoroughly validated measure called the affect misattribution procedure (AMP; Payne, Cheng, Govorun, & Stewart, 2005; Payne & Lundberg, 2014). Administered on tablet computers, the AMP measures these implicit associations by asking participants to judge how pleasant an unfamiliar, emotionally neutral image (e.g., a Chinese character) is compared with other similar images after they have just been exposed to a very brief (75 milliseconds)[2] presentation of the target object (e.g., an image of a junk food ad; see Figure 11.4). The logic of the measure is simple: participants' affective response to the target object automatically influences their judgment of the neutral character that follows. Across many trials, the procedure captures participants' affective associations with the target category. Participants completed this task once 2 weeks postintervention and again at the end of the school year (3 months postintervention).

Results strongly validated our theoretical predictions. Compared with the traditional health education intervention, the exposé intervention caused participants' affective associations with both junk food marketing and junk food to become significantly more negative and their affective associations with healthy food to become significantly more positive. These changes were evident both 2 weeks and 3 months postintervention. Moreover, these changes were just as strong for girls as they were for boys, further supporting the interpretation that the exposé intervention successfully aligned healthy eating with girls' values, too. This finding is also consistent with my suggestion that the exposé intervention may have failed to produce healthier cafeteria choices in girls relative to the traditional health education control intervention because the latter was inadvertently aligned with the toxic but high-priority value of thinness that our culture imposes on girls.

Heterogeneity

We have already seen two cases of heterogeneity in the effect of the exposé intervention: its effectiveness at improving daily dietary choices (relative to traditional health education) in boys but not in girls and among boys with high, but not low, levels of T. Each of these instances of heterogeneity helped us learn something important, providing empirical support for the underlying theory in one case (T) and suggesting updates to our theory in the other case (gender). This is an important lesson: We frequently think of treatment effect heterogeneity in primarily practical terms—as "boundary conditions" that set limits on how broadly the usefulness of an intervention generalizes. Although true, this misses the point that identifying sources of heterogeneity in an intervention's effect is often a good way to develop and test the underlying theory about how the intervention works and what adjustments might allow it to work more effectively, or in different segments of the target population. The two sources of heterogeneity I have discussed so far are individual differences, but another sort of heterogeneity—in context—can also have important effects that are often equally useful in testing theory (Spencer, Zanna, &

---

[2]This presentation duration is just barely above the threshold for conscious processing. Participants are instructed not to let the initial image influence their evaluation of the neutral image but they can only control influence of the initial image that they are consciously aware of.

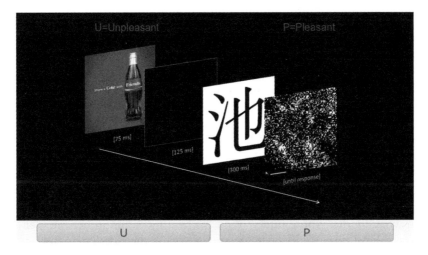

FIGURE 11.4. Representation of a single AMP trial. The target object here is the Coke ad. Participants are presented with it for 75 milliseconds, followed by a dark screen for 125 milliseconds, then the neutral character they are asked to judge for 300 milliseconds before it is replaced with a visual mask, which remains on screen until the participant responds by tapping either the U or the P (to indicate whether they judge the neutral character to be unpleasant or pleasant, respectively, relative to other such characters).

Fong, 2005). So far, we have not had the opportunity to study systematically how this intervention might be affected by context but I describe some anecdotal evidence below in the "Nuances and Misconceptions" section that suggests contextual variation is also likely important for this intervention.

COUSINS

One close intervention cousin to the values-aligned healthy-eating intervention is the taste-focused-labeling intervention (see Turnwald & Crum, Chapter 12, this volume; Turnwald et al., 2019). Taste-focused labeling entails describing healthy dishes in ways that emphasize their tastiness rather than their healthiness. This change in emphasis is important because it helps overcome the strong cultural preconception that healthy foods are less enjoyable to eat than unhealthy foods.[3] The taste-focused-labeling intervention is similar to values alignment in that it too motivates healthy eating by changing the way people construe the purpose of eating healthy foods—emphasizing the (immediate) enjoyment of eating them instead of long-term health benefits. The two interventions differ primarily in the source of the immediate reward they rely on to motivate healthy eating. Whereas values alignment relies on the more abstract, eudaimonic reward of living in accordance with one's important values, taste-focused labeling relies on the

---

[3]This belief may be caused at least in part by the misguided emphasis on pragmatic appeals for should behaviors that I described at the start of this chapter. Emphasizing health as the primary reason to eat foods like fruits and vegetables might inadvertently suggest to people that this is the *only* reason one would want to eat those foods.

concrete, hedonic reward of a pleasurable taste experience. One interesting question for future research is whether these two approaches could be combined in a way that would allow them to reinforce each other. For example, by emphasizing the appealing hedonic properties of healthy foods, taste-focused labeling might make it easier for adolescents to make dietary choices that are consistent with their values. Moreover, once the exposé intervention successfully prompts adolescents to decide that they will make healthier choices by harnessing their important values, adolescents might become more amenable to beliefs (e.g., "Healthy foods are delicious too") that support the wisdom of that decision (Kunda, 1990).

The exposé intervention to influence dietary choices is one instantiation of the broader values-alignment approach to motivating should behaviors. Although the theoretical framework for values alignment that I have articulated here was developed in the context of work on the exposé intervention for healthy eating, other interventions that came before it have employed values alignment even if their designers did not conceive of them explicitly in those terms. One example is an intervention to increase high school students' motivation for tedious schoolwork by linking education to a self-transcendent prosocial purpose (Yeager et al., 2014). In this intervention, adolescents are encouraged to think of a way in which they believe the world could be a better place (e.g., less hunger, disease, or prejudice). Once they have identified a self-transcendent purpose they personally care about, the intervention reframes the sometimes-boring work they are required to do in high school as teaching them skills that they can use to make a positive contribution to the world. Compared with control treatments that either provide useful advice about navigating high school life or that emphasized self-interested motives for learning, the self-transcendent-purpose intervention increased participants' willingness to invest effort in learning difficult material—even in the face of tempting alternatives like watching viral videos—and, in one study, produced a substantial improvement in students' science and math grades. Like the values-aligned healthy-eating intervention, the self-transcendent-purpose intervention works by shifting participants' construal of a should behavior—devoting energy to schoolwork students find boring—such that it is seen as serving a deeply held value. The most obvious difference between the two interventions is that the healthy-eating intervention identified specific values that we knew, from previous research, tend to be important in adolescence. In contrast, the self-transcendent-purpose intervention invites participants to identify their *own* specific value and then encourages them to think about how their schoolwork might serve that value. According to our theory, one advantage of the former approach is that harnessing a shared group value enhances an intervention's power by drawing on the desire people generally feel to fit within their social groups (e.g., Asch, 1956). On the other hand, focusing on a value that is tailored to each individual's personal priorities might allow the intervention to tap into values that participants are especially passionate about. More research is needed to test these hypotheses and assess which contexts, behaviors, or types of people each approach is best suited to.

Another example is a classic intervention by psychologist Milton Rokeach (1971) that used values alignment to increase White undergraduates' support for African Americans' civil rights in the late 1960s by confronting them with inconsistencies in their own constellation of values and attitudes. Rokeach had participants rank a list of 18 human values (e.g., freedom, happiness, a world at peace, equality). He then showed them fabricated data indicating (1) that students at their school, on average, ranked freedom much more highly than equality; and (2) that students who were supportive of civil rights, on average, ranked those two values almost identically, while students who were less supportive of civil rights ranked freedom much more highly than equality. Rokeach then highlighted the hypocrisy of the latter ranking, saying, "This raises the question as to whether those who are *against* civil rights are really saying that they care a great deal about *their own* freedom but are indifferent to other people's freedom" (p. 454). Highlighting this hypocrisy had a profound and lasting effect on students. Three to 5 months later, when they received a letter inviting them to join the National Association for the Advancement of Colored People (NAACP), they were substantially more likely to send in the $1 membership dues. In the 17 months following this intervention, participants also updated their ranking of the two focal values, prioritizing freedom less and equality more. What deeply held and widely shared value did this intervention harness to motivate these increases in support for civil rights? Although the values of freedom and equality were central features of the intervention, I would argue that neither was the critical driver of motivation—rather, I believe it was the strong desire not to feel like or be seen as a hypocrite (see also Stone, Aronson, Crain, Winslow, & Fried, 1994). Rokeach's intervention caused a shift in how participants construed the significance of prioritizing freedom so far above equality. Highlighting the hypocrisy of this disparity caused participants to feel substantial discomfort, which Rokeach then channeled to motivate support for civil rights.

Another class of related interventions uses a subtle linguistic cue to frame behavior as having implications for identity. In a series of experiments, my collaborators and I have shown how referring to should behaviors with a predicate noun instead of a verb (e.g., "be a voter" vs. "vote"; "don't be a cheater" vs. "don't cheat"; "be a helper" vs. "help") can cause people to behave more in accordance with their values—to exert the effort to vote and to help others, and to resist the temptation to cheat (Bryan, Adams, & Monin, 2013; Bryan, Master, & Walton, 2014; Bryan, Walton, Rogers, & Dweck, 2011; Bryan, Yeager, & O'Brien, 2019). Using nouns in this way frames should behavior as a reflection of the *kind of person* one would reveal oneself to be by performing it—it signals that the behavior is reflective of a person's essential, underlying identity (Gelman & Heyman, 1999; Gelman, Hollander, Star, & Heyman, 2000). By signaling that elements of one's identity hinge on a behavior choice, noun wording causes people to behave more in accordance with the core values that constitute their (culturally informed) standards for what constitutes a "good" or worthy person.

INTERVENTION CONTENT AND IMPLEMENTATION

Context and Logistics

The values-aligned food marketing exposé intervention is delivered in a classroom setting and introduced as material being considered for inclusion in future middle school health curricula. Because it is critical not to threaten participants' sense of autonomy, the purpose of the classroom session is described in autonomy-supportive terms, as a request for feedback from participants about whether the material will be seen as engaging to other students of their age. The intervention consists of an informational article that describes the core content (read on a tablet computer with narration through earphones), a pair of brief writing exercises to reinforce the lessons of the article, and the Make It True activity, described above, in which participants modify images of real junk food ads to make them more accurate.

Core Content

The content comes mostly from journalistic accounts of the ways in which food marketers intentionally mislead and manipulate consumers into buying and eating more unhealthy, processed foods than they otherwise would; the harm this does to people's health and well-being; and the ways in which that harmful influence is disproportionately targeted at vulnerable populations, including very young children and the poor (e.g., Kessler, 2009; Moss, 2013). The content is described in terms that make clear and obvious the link to adolescents' drive for autonomy from adult control. For example, see the following excerpt from the informational article:

> The companies that make the unhealthy food spend billions of dollars trying to get people to overeat. The reason is simple: the more people eat, the more money they make. If people only ate when they were actually hungry—if corporations just let you choose what you and your body wanted to eat—they would make a lot less money. So, instead they spend lots of money to come up with new ways to trick our brains into eating more than our bodies want, and more than our bodies can handle.

The direct reference to the counterfactual in this passage ("if corporations just let you choose what you and your body wanted to eat . . .") helps cast food marketing in clear opposition to adolescent autonomy. Tone and language are important here, too. The use of simple, direct language ("just let you choose"; "trick our brains") prevents readers from feeling they are being talked down to, which could provoke autonomy threat or defensiveness. The importance of making the reader feel respected is evident in the following passage as well:

> Why do the companies go after kids? Previous company executives have admitted that it's because they are easy targets. Children that young usually believe what adults tell them. Corporations put ads on Saturday morning cartoons for the most sugar-packed, addictive junk foods. They teach kids as young as 3 and 4—who don't know any better—that eating lots of junk food is cool, fun and normal.

The above excerpt is obviously intended to provoke a prosocial concern for social justice but it accomplishes another goal, too. Focusing on the intended effects of food marketing on very young children makes it possible to portray a belief likely held by many of the readers "that eating lots of junk food is cool, fun and normal" as childish and naïve without insulting the reader or provoking defensiveness.

We also sought to link the desire for the hedonic reward of junk food directly with food marketers' subversion of the reader's autonomy. That was the purpose of the following passage, for example:

> Our brains are naturally designed to tell us to stop eating when we've had enough. But they have laboratories and hire scientists to figure out the brain's blind spots. Then they create foods that cause the brain to crave more and more sugar and fat, even when we're not hungry.

This passage helps to externalize even the internal experience of craving junk food. We worried that if participants construed their desire for junk food as coming from within, they would feel compelled to justify the validity of those cravings (Aronson, 1969; Festinger, 1957; Festinger & Carlsmith, 1959). Externalizing those cravings makes clear that they are threats to autonomy rather than genuine internal desires.

The article also contains examples of real food industry executives, all middle-age White men, to serve as objects of the reader's rebellion. These executives were featured because, in addition to representing a controlling adult authority, they have all been identified as avoiding their own companies' products for health reasons. One such example is John Ruff who, the article explains, "is an executive at Kraft (maker of Kool-Aid, Tang, Oreos, and lots of other high-sugar, high-fat snacks). He dropped high fat and high calorie snacks to stay healthy. His diet calls for avoiding his company's snacks. He continues to sell them to others." Mentioning this hypocrisy helped underscore the ways in which junk food marketing directly undermines the values of autonomy and social justice. This was expected to provoke righteous outrage and fuel participants' motivation for behavior change to defend those core adolescent values.

Supporting Psychology

As is common in many wise interventions, the core content of the exposé intervention is complemented with components designed to evoke supportive psychological processes (Walton, 2014; Walton & Wilson, 2018). To communicate a descriptive norm (Cialdini, 2003; Goldstein, Cialdini, & Griskevicius, 2008) supportive of the intervention's core message, participants read about a survey of the previous year's ninth graders in which "almost all" respondents were "shocked and angry" about food marketers' manipulation and planned to "fight back against the companies by eating less of their processed foods." Those survey results were followed by quotes from previous participants reiterating key points from the article and explaining how they planned to fight back by avoiding junk food.

Next, participants completed a pair of short writing activities in which they were asked why they thought so many people were "outraged and upset" about food marketers' manipulation, invited to share their own feelings on the topic, and finally to describe what kinds of food choices "students like [them]" could make, starting right away, to fight back against this injustice. These activities were designed to serve a self-persuasion function—to help students internalize and feel ownership over the persuasive arguments in the article (Aronson, 1999).

Make It True Exercise

The primary goal of the Make It True exercise was to highlight the role of food ads in supporting the deception and manipulation of the food industry. The activity was framed in terms that recalled the key messages we had communicated the day before:

> "What is advertising? It's a way for companies to sell their products (and make money). A big problem is that junk food ads often target young kids and don't tell the whole truth. How? Companies use bright colors and cartoons to paint a fake picture about their food. And they put these ads everywhere—in children's TV shows,

schools, websites, and even phone apps. Surrounding little kids with these ads is a big way that companies try to take over their power to think for themselves. But we don't have to let a big company do the thinking for them."

Note again the emphasis on protecting young children from marketing, which simultaneously reinforces the alignment of our message with prosocial justice and allows us to call out the food industry's deception with less risk that we might provoke defensiveness by making participants themselves feel like dupes. Next, we provided examples of marked-up ads that the previous year's eighth graders had produced during piloting to help inspire participants. To scaffold participants' creative process, we also provided thought questions (e.g., "When you pick an ad, ask yourself . . . does it seem false or like it's hiding part of the truth?"; "Does it seem like it's trying to make junk food seem way more fun than it really is?") and suggested ways they might modify the ads (e.g., "Add speech or thought bubbles"; "Cross out words to make a point"; "Do a play on words"; and "Add a whole new slogan that shows the reality of the product").

NUANCES AND MISCONCEPTIONS

Wise interventions can be extraordinarily powerful. Examples of psychologically sophisticated interventions that "move the needle" on important outcomes that have been stubbornly resistant to change from other approaches are increasingly common (Walton & Wilson, 2018). In light of these striking successes, it can be tempting to think of wise interventions as "magic bullets"—to distill them to simple, one-dimensional versions of their core idea and expect them to work across a wide range of contexts (Yeager & Walton, 2011). The truth is that such interventions can indeed improve outcomes in a wide range of contexts but, in order to be effective, they are often intricately tailored to the specific context in which they are meant to be implemented. To extend them effectively to novel contexts, one must think carefully about how well the intervention, as it was originally conceived, fits those other contexts. In the case of values alignment, one important question is whether the specific values the intervention was designed to harness are as important and widely shared in the new context. Here, I describe a learning experience my collaborators and I had in the early stages of piloting the food marketing exposé intervention that drove this lesson home for me.

Initially, we piloted the exposé intervention in two middle schools in the New York City area: one in a wealthy North Bronx neighborhood that serves an upper-middle class, primarily White and Asian student body; and one in a poor South Bronx neighborhood that serves a mostly Black and Latinx student body. Students at both schools read an early draft of the exposé article about food industry manipulation and disproportionate targeting of very young children and the poor. Both groups of students read the article with focused interest but their reactions to it were quite different. Students at the upscale North Bronx school reacted with outrage, many spontaneously beginning to plan the ways they would fight back against this unfair behavior by the food companies (e.g., "When I get home, I'm going to make kale chips with my mom!"). Students at the poorer South Bronx school had much more muted reactions. They agreed the behavior of the food companies was unfair but this did not energize them to combat the injustice in the same way. Further discussion with those students, and subsequent reflection, made clear that the exposé intervention as we had drafted it (and as we have tested it so far) was well aligned with *White, middle class* adolescent values in particular. In relying on the published research literature to characterize adolescent values, we likely fell prey to a common and persistent misconception implicit in most psychological literature: the characterization of "human" psychology from research that is based overwhelmingly on samples of White, Western, relatively educated, middle class people (Henrich, Heine, & Norenzayan, 2010; Sears, 1986). The social-psychological literature on social class makes clear why an intervention designed to motivate action by triggering the desire for personal autonomy might be less well aligned with the values of adolescents from working-class backgrounds—namely, working-class culture tends to value individual choice less than middle-class culture does, privileging interdependence among ingroup members and attentiveness to the needs of others in one's group (Stephens, Fryberg, & Markus, 2011; Stephens, Hamedani, Markus, Bergsieker, & Eloul, 2009; Stephens, Markus, & Townsend, 2007).

In addition to this major misalignment of the exposé intervention with the values of lower-socioeconomic status (SES) students, the social justice component of the intervention, which discusses the ways in which the food industry disproportionately targets low-income communities, has a very different meaning to low-SES adolescents than it does to middle-class adolescents. This material is designed to create a sense of prosocial purpose for rejecting junk food in participants by emphasizing the ways in which groups more vulnerable than participants themselves are being targeted. It is well suited to that purpose when the audience is middle class; not so when the audience is the low-income group being targeted by companies.

This analysis makes clear why the current version of the exposé intervention seemed to resonate less strongly with the pilot participants from the low-SES school in the South Bronx. It also suggests ways in which relatively minor modifications might help align that intervention better with the values of lower-SES adolescents. If the emphasis were on the ways in which the food industry targets very young members of low-income communities and communities of color, the call to action in the intervention could be framed less in terms of "sticking it to the man" or "taking back control" and more in terms of the importance of being role models and "protecting the younger members of our community" from harmful outside influence. Pilot work and rigorous testing are needed to be confident that such a modified framing would be effective in lower-SES communities of color but, as a starting place, this framing certainly seems better aligned with values in those communities.

Another nuance that is relevant to values-alignment interventions generally is worth noting. I have emphasized that values alignment involves framing should behavior in terms of values other than long-term pragmatic benefit. But this does not mean that the pragmatic benefits of should behavior are made to seem irrelevant; the difference between pragmatic and values-aligned appeals is about emphasis. The health implications of junk food consumption, for example, are still important to the logic of the exposé intervention but they are not emphasized as the sole or central reason to make healthier choices. Instead, they help motivate why deceptive marketing undermines the values of autonomy and social justice, which are the central focus of the intervention—that is, the food industry's manipulation of people's choices and its targeting of vulnerable populations feel like such violations of these values in part because greedy executives are profiting by undermining people's well-being. Pragmatic concerns play a similar role in other values-aligned interventions: In the purpose-for-learning intervention (Yeager et al., 2014), the emphasis is on making a positive contribution to the world but learning useful skills and getting a job is understood to be how people can do that; in the noun-wording intervention, the identities "voter" and "helper" are so appealing because of the pragmatic value those behaviors are understood to have. The point is not that people are uninterested in pragmatic outcomes; rather, it is that those pragmatic outcomes—especially if they are uncertain or in the distant future—lack the motivational immediacy, on their own, to overcome the barriers to action.

IMPLICATIONS FOR PRACTICE

Research on values alignment more generally and on the food marketing exposé in particular, is still at a relatively early stage and more research is needed before it is possible to offer a comprehensive set of guidelines to practitioners. In the case of the food marketing exposé intervention, one key principle is the importance of supporting the autonomy of participants (Yeager, Dahl, & Dweck, 2018). The conceit we used to achieve this in the studies—framing the content as draft material for future middle school health courses—would not likely wear well as subsequent classes of students received the same material year after year. But an alternative framing of the material, simply as facts that food companies try to conceal but that participants have a right to know about, would likely accomplish the same purpose and be more sustainable.

More broadly, as illustrated by the example of how the exposé intervention seemed much less resonant for students of color in a low-SES school, the question of how to identify the right values to focus on in a values-alignment intervention is an important and difficult one. Especially in Western, educated populations, psychological literature can sometimes inform answers to this question. But for many populations and in many contexts, existing literature does not provide a sufficient basis for designing an intervention. I believe a big part of the answer is that we must begin to incorporate qualitative approaches, borrowed from ethnography, into the intervention-design process. As more research is conducted on values alignment, a systematic, scalable process for this can be developed and serve as a guide to researchers and practitioners. For now, I suggest the guiding principle (which I have alluded to throughout this chapter) that values that are central to a culture's conception of what makes a "good" member of the social group, worthy of respect and admiration from other group members (Leary & Baumeister, 2000), tend to be powerful motivators.

IMPLICATIONS FOR PSYCHOLOGICAL THEORY

In using construal processes to tackle challenges related to myopia, this work brings together two important lines of theory that, historically, have mostly existed separately from each other. The pervasiveness and stubborn consistency with which people discount the value of the future and the negative consequences this tendency has for people's health and well-being has made it a major topic of research in psychology, economics, and related fields. Research on ways to encourage more future-oriented behavior has been intense and has resulted in numerous discoveries of methods for reducing the influence of myopic discounting on behavioral decisions. These include interventions that allow people to precommit to a more farsighted decision long enough before that decision is implemented that they do not yet feel the hedonic pull of the more shortsighted choice (e.g., Thaler & Benartzi, 2004) and ones that use computer simulation or other techniques to increase the vividness with which people are able to imagine the effects of shortsighted decisions on their "future self" (Hershfield, John, & Reiff, 2018; see also Weber et al., 2007). Although interventions in these veins have been effective at changing decisions in a given moment, none has shown potential to reorient people toward farsighted decision making in an ongoing manner.

The extraordinary power of the subjectivist approach to psychology, and of construal processes in particular, is that they afford the possibility of changing what situation people understand themselves to be responding to (Asch, 1940). So rather than trying to find ways to overcome discounting by "bridging the gap" between the present and distant future, values alignment simply alters people's perceptions of what the rewards and costs are for choosing should behaviors versus not choosing them. By realigning this decision to be compatible with people's existing psychological predispositions, values alignment makes it possible to simply circumvent the obstacle of myopia and achieve a more enduring reorientation toward preferring should behavior.

And, of course, the potential to change people's understanding of the situation they are responding to has implications that go far beyond overcoming temporal discounting. So, a more general theoretical lesson of this work is that interventions that take advantage of flexibility in how people construe their worlds are a powerful tool for changing behavior and for addressing vexing social problems (Walton & Wilson, 2018). Finally, the success of the values-alignment approach in fostering lasting change in adolescents' dietary preferences suggests that the overwhelmingly dominant theoretical focus, in conventional scholarship, on material self-interest as the central motivator of behavior might not be appropriate. Self-interest is unquestionably an important motivator but there are also many situations in which people happily privilege other important values over their own self-interest (e.g., Olivola & Shafir, 2013). In behavior change situations where self-interest proves not to be an effective motivator, those working to foment change should consider alternative approaches.

FUTURE DIRECTIONS

The work I have described in this chapter constitutes an initial demonstration that values alignment can generate enduring motivation for should behavior. Much more research is needed to take this from a promising idea to a viable, scalable program. I have already mentioned two high-priority directions for future research in earlier sections. First, to better understand the reason for the gender difference in the effect of the exposé intervention on cafeteria purchases in the second intervention study, a follow-up experiment that includes both a traditional nutrition education control *and* a no-treatment control is a high priority. Second, my theorizing about why the exposé intervention material seemed to resonate less strongly with low-SES adolescents of color and how the intervention could be amended to be effective in that population cries out for testing. Improving dietary habits and health outcomes in the communities most affected by food marketing should be a high priority.

Another high-priority question is whether the effects of the food marketing exposé intervention could be made even stronger by incorporating social components. For reasons of methodological rigor, the intervention studies we have conducted to date have used individual-level random assignment to experimental conditions, within classrooms. Because roughly half of the participants in each classroom were in the exposé condition and the other half in the control condition, we had to take steps to prevent participants from discussing the intervention material with one another (to prevent cross-contamination). But an intervention like this one, which is predicated on linking dietary choices to the important values adolescents share with one another, might have even stronger and longer-lasting effects if participants felt like they were part of a social movement to take a stand against the manipulation and injustice perpetrated by a heinous group of adult authority figures (see Paluck, Shepherd, & Aronow, 2016). Testing this would require a much larger scale than has been possible in experiments to date, with enough schools to allow classroom, or preferably, school-level random assignment.

In addition, one constraint on improvement in the health profile of students' cafeteria purchases in the last study was a lack of appealing healthy options. Combining the food marketing exposé intervention with a program that made more appealing healthy options available in the school cafeteria might result in an even greater improvement in nutritional outcomes. Indeed, this suggestion could even be combined with the previous one. The intervention could be amended to encourage students to lobby their school to make healthier options available. This combination might have the dual benefits of introducing a sense of group cohesion around a constructive purpose (thus fostering stronger commitment to the cause) and increasing students' commitment to healthier diets because they had to work hard to gain access to them (Aronson, 1969; Aronson & Mills, 1959).

And, of course, the values-alignment approach is not specific to autonomy and social justice or to influencing dietary preferences and choices. It is a general theoretical framework for fostering lasting, internalized motivation for a wide range of should behaviors. For example, in a newer line of research with Ashley Whillans, a psychologist at Harvard and Liz Dunn, a psychologist at the University of British Columbia, I am exploring whether values related to parenting can be harnessed to motivate charitable giving. This work is predicated on the observation that most people can only afford to donate amounts of money that feel trivial relative to the massive scope of the need and that this may prevent many people from giving at all. So we are examining whether emphasizing to parents of young children that giving can serve a purpose other than charitable impact might motivate them to give more often. In particular, we frame giving as a way to create a teachable moment for their children. We encourage parents to include their young children in the giving process and to use this as an opportunity to teach their children about the importance of caring about the needs of others. In a series of laboratory studies, we have found that inviting parents to consider giving to a charitable cause along with their children (vs. on their own while a researcher entertained their children) made them more willing to give to the cause and to share their e-mail address with the charitable organization for solicitation of future donations. We are currently conducting a field experiment, in partnership with a large online charitable giving organization, to test whether a version of this teachable-moment framing could motivate parents to make ongoing, monthly donations. Parents who visit the site are encouraged to begin giving their young children a "charitable allowance" and sit down with their children each month to discuss the different causes they could donate the money to.

CONCLUSION

In the coming decades, human thriving is likely to depend on finding ways to produce consistent changes in the everyday behavior choices that are behind many of our most daunting problems. Values alignment offers a way to produce lasting, internalized motivation for such changes. It does this by circumventing the persistent psychological barriers that often prevent people from making the daily choices they know they should be making. Much more research will be needed before this approach can begin to offer scalable solutions to the many challenges humanity is faced with, but results so far are cause for optimism that this goal can be achieved.

REFERENCES

Ainslie, G. (1992). *Picoeconomics: The strategic interaction of successive motivational states within the person.* Cambridge, UK: Cambridge University Press.

Ainslie, G., & Haslam, N. (1992). Hyperbolic discounting. In G. Loewenstein & J. Elster (Eds.), *Choice over time* (pp. 57–92). New York: Russell Sage Foundation.

Aronson, E. (1969). The theory of cognitive dissonance: A current perspective. In L. Berkowitz (Ed.), *Advances in experimental social psychology* (Vol. 4, pp. 1–34). London: Academic Press.

Aronson, E. (1999). The power of self-persuasion. *American Psychologist, 54*(11), 875–884.

Aronson, E., & Mills, J. (1959). The effect of severity of initiation on liking for a group. *Journal of Abnormal and Social Psychology, 59*(2), 177–181.

Asch, S. E. (1940). Studies in the principles of judgments and attitudes: II. Determination of judgments by group and by ego standards. *Journal of Social Psychology, 12*(2), 433–465.

Asch, S. E. (1956). Studies of independence and conformity: I. A minority of one against a unanimous majority. *Psychological Monographs: General and Applied, 70*(9), 1–70.

Berns, G. S., Laibson, D., & Loewenstein, G. (2007). Intertemporal choice—toward an integrative framework. *Trends in Cognitive Sciences, 11*(11), 482–488.

Braams, B. R., van Duijvenvoorde, A. C. K., Peper, J. S., & Crone, E. A. (2015). Longitudinal changes in adolescent risk-taking: A comprehensive study of neural responses to rewards, pubertal development, and risk-taking behavior. *Journal of Neuroscience, 35*(18), 7226–7238.

Bryan, C. J., Adams, G. S., & Monin, B. (2013). When cheating would make you a cheater: Implicating the self prevents unethical behavior. *Journal of Experimental Psychology: General, 142*(4), 1001–1005.

Bryan, C. J., Master, A., & Walton, G. M. (2014). "Helping" versus "being a helper": Invoking the self to increase helping in young children. *Child Development, 85*(5), 1836–1842.

Bryan, C. J., Walton, G. M., Rogers, T., & Dweck, C. S. (2011). Motivating voter turnout by invoking the self. *Proceedings of the National Academy of Sciences of the USA, 108*(31), 12653–12656.

Bryan, C. J., Yeager, D. S., & Hinojosa, C. P. (2019). A values-alignment intervention protects adolescents from the effects of food marketing. *Nature Human Behaviour, 3*(6), 596–603.

Bryan, C. J., Yeager, D. S., Hinojosa, C. P., Chabot, A., Bergen, H., Kawamura, M., & Steubing, F. (2016). Harnessing adolescent values to motivate healthier eating. *Proceedings of the National Academy of Sciences of the USA, 113*(39), 10830–10835.

Bryan, C. J., Yeager, D. S., & O'Brien, J. (2019). Replicator degrees of freedom allow publication of misleading failures to replicate. *Proceedings of the National Academy of Sciences of the USA, 116*, 25535–25545.

Casey, B. J. (2015). Beyond simple models of self-control to circuit-based accounts of adolescent behavior. *Annual Review of Psychology, 66*(1), 295–319.

Casey, B. J., & Caudle, K. (2013). The teenage brain: Self control. *Current Directions in Psychological Science, 22*(2), 82–87.

Cialdini, R. B. (2003). Crafting normative messages to protect the environment. *Current Directions in Psychological Science, 12*(4), 105–109.

Crone, E. A., & Dahl, R. E. (2012). Understanding adolescence as a period of social-affective engagement and goal flexibility. *Nature Reviews Neuroscience, 13*, 636–650.

Damon, W., Menon, J., & Bronk, K. C. (2003). The development of purpose during adolescence. *Applied Developmental Science, 7*(3), 119–128.

Festinger, L. (1957). *A theory of cognitive dissonance.* Redwood City, CA: Stanford University Press.

Festinger, L., & Carlsmith, J. M. (1959). Cognitive consequences of forced compliance. *Journal of Abnormal and Social Psychology, 58*(2), 203–210.

Forouzanfar, M. H., Alexander, L., Anderson, H. R., Bachman, V. F., Biryukov, S., Brauer, M., . . . Murray, C. J. (2015). Global, regional, and national comparative risk assessment of 79 behavioural, environmental and occupational, and metabolic risks or clusters of risks in 188 countries, 1990–2013: A systematic analysis for the Global Burden of Disease Study 2013. *Lancet, 386*(10010), 2287–2323.

Frederick, S., Loewenstein, G., & O'Donoghue, T. (2002). Time discounting and time preference: A critical review. *Journal of Economic Literature, 40*(2), 351–401.

Gakidou, E., Afshin, A., Abajobir, A. A., Abate, K. H., Abbafati, C., Abbas, K. M., . . . Murray, C. J. L. (2017). Global, regional, and national comparative risk assessment of 84 behavioural, environmental and occupational, and metabolic risks or clusters of risks, 1990–2016: A systematic analysis for the Global Burden of Disease Study 2016. *Lancet, 390*(10100), 1345–1422.

Gelman, S. A., & Heyman, G. D. (1999). Carrot-eaters and creature-believers: The effects of lexicalization on children's inferences about social categories. *Psychological Science, 10*(6), 489–493.

Gelman, S. A., Hollander, M., Star, J., & Heyman, G. D. (2000). The role of language in the construction of kinds. In D. L. Medin (Ed.), *Psychology of learning and motivation* (Vol. 39, pp. 201–263). New York: Elsevier.

Goldstein, N. J., Cialdini, R. B., & Griskevicius, V. (2008). A room with a viewpoint: Using social norms to motivate environmental conservation in hotels. *Journal of Consumer Research, 35*(3), 472–482.

Harris, J. L., Pomeranz, J. L., Lobstein, T., & Brownell, K. D. (2009). A crisis in the marketplace: How food marketing contributes to childhood obesity and what can be done. *Annual Review of Public Health, 30*(1), 211–225.

Hastings, G., & Cairns, G. (2010). Food and beverage marketing to children. In E. Waters, B. A. Swinburn, J. C. Seidell, & R. Uauy (Eds.), *Preventing childhood obesity: Evidence policy and practice* (pp. 120–128). Oxford, UK: Blackwell.

Henrich, J., Heine, S. J., & Norenzayan, A. (2010). The weirdest people in the world? *Behavioral and Brain Sciences, 33*(2–3), 61–83.

Hershfield, H. E., John, E. M., & Reiff, J. S. (2018). Using vividness interventions to improve financial decision making. *Policy Insights from the Behavioral and Brain Sciences, 5*(2), 209–215.

Kessler, D. A. (2009). *The end of overeating: Taking control of the insatiable American appetite* New York: Rodale Books.

Kidd, C., Palmeri, H., & Aslin, R. N. (2013). Rational snacking: Young children's decision-making on the marshmallow task is moderated by beliefs about environmental reliability. *Cognition, 126*(1), 109–114.

Koffka, K. (2013). *Principles of gestalt psychology*. London: Routledge.

Kunda, Z. (1990). The case for motivated reasoning. *Psychological Bulletin, 108*(3), 480–498.

Leary, M. R., & Baumeister, R. F. (2000). The nature and function of self-esteem: Sociometer theory. In M. P. Zanna (Ed.), *Advances in experimental social psychology* (Vol. 32, pp. 1–62). New York: Elsevier.

Lee, K. H., Siegle, G. J., Dahl, R. E., Hooley, J. M., & Silk, J. S. (2014). Neural responses to maternal criticism in healthy youth. *Social Cognitive and Affective Neuroscience, 10*(7), 902–912.

Lewin, K. (1935). *A dynamic theory of personality*. New York: McGraw-Hill.

Liberman, V., Samuels, S. M., & Ross, L. (2004). The name of the game: Predictive power of reputations versus situational labels in determining prisoner's dilemma game moves. *Personality and Social Psychology Bulletin, 30*(9), 1175–1185.

Loewenstein, G. (1996). Out of control: Visceral influences on behavior. *Organizational Behavior and Human Decision Processes, 65*(3), 272–292.

Medrano, F. N., Bryan, C. J., Josephs, R., Hinojosa, C. P., Dahl, R. E., & Yeager, D. S. (2019). *Endogenous testosterone helps uncover the mechanism of a successful adolescent behavior change intervention*. Austin: University of Texas, Austin.

Mischel, W., Cantor, N., & Feldman, S. (1996). Principles of self-regulation: The nature of willpower and self-control. In E. T. Higgins & A. W. Kruglanski (Eds.), *Social psychology: Handbook of basic principles* (pp. 329–360). New York: Guilford Press.

Mischel, W., & Staub, E. (1965). Effects of expectancy on working and waiting for larger reward. *Journal of Personality and Social Psychology, 2*(5), 625.

Moss, M. (2013). *Salt, sugar, fat: How the food giants hooked us*. New York: Random House.

Nestle, M. (2006). Food marketing and childhood obesity—a matter of policy. *New England Journal of Medicine, 354*(24), 2527–2529.

New Mexico State University Learning Games Lab. (2015). *Eat and move o-matic*. New Mexico: Author.

Olivola, C. Y., & Shafir, E. (2013). The martyrdom effect: When pain and effort increase prosocial contributions. *Journal of Behavioral Decision Making, 26*(1), 91–105.

Paluck, E. L., Shepherd, H., & Aronow, P. M. (2016). Changing climates of conflict: A social network experiment in 56 schools. *Proceedings of the National Academy of Sciences of the USA, 113*(3), 566–571.

Payne, K., Cheng, C. M., Govorun, O., & Stewart, B. D. (2005). An inkblot for attitudes: Affect misattribution as implicit measurement. *Journal of Personality and Social Psychology, 89*(3), 277–293.

Payne, K., & Lundberg, K. (2014). The affect misattribution procedure: Ten years of evidence on reliability, validity, and mechanisms. *Social and Personality Psychology Compass, 8*(12), 672–686.

Robinson, T. N. (2010). Save the world, prevent obesity: Piggybacking on existing social and ideological movements. *Obesity, 18*(S1), 17–22.

Rokeach, M. (1971). Long-range experimental modification of values, attitudes, and behavior. *American Psychologist, 26*(5), 453–459.

Ross, L., & Ward, A. (1996). Naive realism in everyday life: Implications for social conflict and misunderstanding. In E. S. Reed, E. Turiel, & T. Brown (Eds.), *Values and knowledge* (pp. 103–135). Hillsdale, NJ: Erlbaum.

Sears, D. O. (1986). College sophomores in the laboratory: Influences of a narrow data base on social psychology's view of human nature. *Journal of Personality and Social Psychology, 51*(3), 515–530.

Sherman, D. K., & Cohen, G. L. (2006). The psychology of self-defense: Self-affirmation theory. In M. P. Zanna (Ed.), *Advances in experimental social psychology* (Vol. 38, pp. 183–242). New York: Elsevier.

Spencer, S. J., Zanna, M. P., & Fong, G. T. (2005). Establishing a causal chain: Why experiments are often more effective than mediational analyses in examining psychological processes. *Journal of Personality and Social Psychology, 89*(6), 845–851.

Steele, C. M. (1988). The psychology of self-affirmation: Sustaining the integrity of the self. In L. Berkowitz (Ed.), *Advances in experimental social psychology* (Vol. 21, pp. 261–302). New York: Elsevier.

Steinberg, L. (2007). Risk taking in adolescence: New perspectives from brain and behavioral science. *Current Directions in Psychological Science, 16*(2), 55–59.

Stephens, N. M., Fryberg, S. A., & Markus, H. R. (2011). When choice does not equal freedom: A sociocultural analysis of agency in working-class American contexts. *Social Psychological and Personality Science, 2*(1), 33–41.

Stephens, N. M., Hamedani, M. G., Markus, H. R., Bergsieker, H. B., & Eloul, L. (2009). Why did they "choose" to stay?: Perspectives of Hurricane Katrina observers and survivors. *Psychological Science, 20*(7), 878–886.

Stephens, N. M., Markus, H. R., & Townsend, S. S. M. (2007). Choice as an act of meaning: The case of social class. *Journal of Personality and Social Psychology, 93*(5), 814–830.

Stone, J., Aronson, E., Crain, A. L., Winslow, M. P., & Fried, C. B. (1994). Inducing hypocrisy as a means of encouraging young adults to use condoms. *Personality and Social Psychology Bulletin, 20*(1), 116–128.

Strahan, E. J., Lafrance, A., Wilson, A. E., Ethier, N., Spencer, S. J., & Zanna, M. P. (2008). Victoria's dirty secret: How sociocultural norms influence adolescent girls and women. *Personality and Social Psychology Bulletin, 34*(2), 288–301.

Swinburn, B. A., Sacks, G., Hall, K. D., McPherson, K., Finegood, D. T., Moodie, M. L., & Gortmaker, S. L. (2011). The global obesity pandemic: Shaped by global drivers and local environments. *Lancet, 378*(9793), 804–814.

Thaler, R. H. (1981). Some empirical evidence on dynamic inconsistency. *Economics Letters, 8*(3), 201–207.

Thaler, R. H., & Benartzi, S. (2004). Save more tomorrow: Using behavioral economics to increase employee saving. *Journal of Political Economy, 112*(S1), S164–S187.

Thompson, J. K., Heinberg, L. J., Altabe, M., & Tantleff-Dunn, S. (1999). *Exacting beauty: Theory, assessment, and treatment of body image disturbance.* Washington, DC: American Psychological Association.

Turnwald, B. P., Bertoldo, J. D., Perry, M. A., Policastro, P., Timmons, M., Bosso, C., . . . Crum, A. J. (2019). Increasing vegetable intake by emphasizing tasty and enjoyable attributes: A randomized controlled multi-site intervention for taste-focused labeling. *Psychological Science, 30*(11), 1603–1615.

van Duijvenvoorde, A. C. K., Peters, S., Braams, B. R., & Crone, E. A. (2016). What motivates adolescents?: Neural responses to rewards and their influence on adolescents' risk taking, learning, and cognitive control. *Neuroscience and Biobehavioral Reviews, 70*, 135–147.

Vansteenkiste, M., Simons, J., Lens, W., Sheldon, K. M., & Deci, E. L. (2004). Motivating learning, performance, and persistence: The synergistic effects of intrinsic goal contents and autonomy-supportive contexts. *Journal of Personality and Social Psychology, 87*(2), 246–260.

Walton, G. M. (2014). The new science of wise psychological interventions. *Current Directions in Psychological Science, 23*(1), 73–82.

Walton, G. M., & Wilson, T. D. (2018). Wise interventions: Psychological remedies for social and personal problems. *Psychological Review, 125*(5), 617–655.

Weber, E. U., Johnson, E. J., Milch, K. F., Chang, H., Brodscholl, J. C., & Goldstein, D. G. (2007). Asymmetric discounting in intertemporal choice: A query–theory account. *Psychological Science, 18*(6), 516–523.

Yeager, D. S., Dahl, R. E., & Dweck, C. S. (2018). Why interventions to influence adolescent behavior often fail but could succeed. *Perspectives on Psychological Science, 13*(1), 101–122.

Yeager, D. S., Henderson, M. D., Paunesku, D., Walton, G. M., D'Mello, S., Spitzer, B. J., & Duckworth, A. L. (2014). Boring but important: A self-transcendent purpose for learning fosters academic self-regulation. *Journal of Personality and Social Psychology, 107*(4), 559–580.

Yeager, D. S., & Walton, G. M. (2011). Social-psychological interventions in education: They're not magic. *Review of Educational Research, 81*(2), 267–301.

CHAPTER 12

The Taste-Focused-Labeling Intervention

Emphasizing the Tasty and Enjoyable Attributes of Healthy Foods

Bradley P. Turnwald and Alia J. Crum

Rising rates of obesity, diabetes, and cardiovascular disease call for interventions that promote healthier dietary intake. While most interventions emphasize the long-term importance of eating healthily and highlight the nutritional benefits of healthy options, these health-focused approaches have had limited success. Here we discuss a novel intervention that focuses instead on promoting healthy foods based on their tasty and enjoyable characteristics—qualities that most people prioritize over healthiness in the moment of food choice. Highlighting tasty and enjoyable properties changes people's reason for choosing healthy foods from a choice that is perceived as effortful, instrumental, and misaligned with taste priorities to a choice that is aligned with the short-term goal of choosing tasty and enjoyable food. Compared to the classic approach of emphasizing health qualities and benefits, taste-focused labeling increases the proportion of people who choose healthy foods across a range of field settings and for a variety of vegetables and plant-based foods. In this chapter, we describe (1) theoretical foundations that led to the formulation of the taste-focused-labeling intervention, (2) experimental evidence that it increases healthy food choices, (3) mechanisms and moderators of the effects, (4) how to implement the taste-focused-labeling intervention, and (5) directions for future research.

BACKGROUND

Poor dietary intake (diet low in fruits and vegetables and high in sugar, sodium, and saturated fat) is a major driver of chronic disease (Lim et al., 2013). An estimated 45% of deaths associated with heart disease, stroke, and type 2 diabetes can be attributed to unhealthy eating (Micha et al., 2017), and nearly half of Americans' dietary intake qualifies as "poor" (Rehm, Penalvo, Afshin, & Mozaffarian, 2016). Improving the health qualities of the foods that Americans choose to eat is a public health priority.

To promote healthier eating, three major approaches have been emphasized: (1) educating individuals so that they understand what constitutes a healthy diet and the importance of consuming a healthy diet (e.g., nutrition education programs), (2) using nutritional labeling (e.g., calorie labeling, traffic light labeling, warning labels) so that people can more easily identify healthy choices, and (3) changing aspects of the food choice environment to make healthy choices more accessible or likely (e.g., access to healthy foods in disadvantaged communities, monetary incentives, nudging, and choice architecture). Despite each of these approaches improving attitudes, intentions, or behaviors in some studies or for some populations, substantial progress on improving dietary intake or slowing obesity rates has not been made (Gortmaker et al., 2011; Hawkes et al., 2015; Mann, Tomiyama, & Ward, 2015; Roberto et al., 2015).

One potential explanation for the limited success of many health-focused approaches is a shared underlying feature: reliance on a fundamental assumption that most people will prioritize healthiness above other motives in the moment of food choice if they can simply identify what the healthy choice is. This seemingly logical assumption is, more often than not, flawed. People certainly must have access to healthy foods, but large national surveys across decades show that most Americans prioritize tastiness more than healthiness when making food choices (Aggarwal, Rehm, Monsivais, & Drewnowski, 2016; Glanz, Basil, Maibach, Goldberg, & Snyder, 1998). Making matters worse, many Americans perceive healthy foods as less tasty (Raghunathan, Naylor, & Hoyer, 2006) and less filling (Suher, Raghunathan, & Hoyer, 2016) compared with unhealthy foods. Given such preferences and expectations, it is not surprising that in spite of improved education, access, and nutritional labeling, people forgo healthy options and opt instead for unhealthier foods that they expect will be tastier and more satisfying.

Are healthy foods objectively less tasty, filling, and appealing than unhealthier foods? The notion that healthy foods are not tasty is not an objective fact but rather a mindset—a core assumption about the nature and processes about something (in this case, healthy foods) that is culturally developed and psychologically informed, and orients people toward a particular set of expectations, associations, and attributions (Crum, Salovey, & Achor, 2013; Dweck, 2008). Research shows that experiences with food are shaped by prior experiences, information, and culture. First, food preferences are learned, change over time, and improve with repeated exposure (Aldridge, Dovey, & Halford, 2009; Birch, 1998; Wardle & Cooke, 2008). Second, foods can be experienced as more or less tasty, filling, physiologically satiating, and neurologically rewarding depending upon how they are labeled or framed. Specifically, when the same food is labeled as healthy (vs. not), people experience it as less tasty (Fenko, Kersten, & Bialkova, 2016; Lähteenmäki et al., 2010; Raghunathan et al., 2006), less filling (Finkelstein & Fishbach, 2010; Suher et al., 2016), less appealing (Fenko et al., 2016; Lähteenmäki et al., 2010), less physiologically satiating, (Crum, Corbin, Brownell, & Salovey, 2011), and less neurologically rewarding (Veldhuizen, Nachtigal, Flammer, de Araujo, & Small 2013). Third, culture, rather than objective nutrients alone, influences the foods that people experience as most pleasing. While Americans believe that the healthier the food, the less tasty (Raghunathan et al., 2006), Indian populations endorse this mindset to a lesser degree (Dube, Fatemi, Lu, & Hertzer, 2016), and the French endorse the opposite mindset—that the healthier the food, the tastier it is (Werle, Trendel, & Ardito, 2013). Together, this body of research shows that, like other mindsets, while the mindset that healthy foods are not tasty or enjoyable is not necessarily true or false, it has an impact. By orienting people to a particular set of associations, expectations, and motivational responses, the mindset that healthy food is not tasty or satisfying can create the reality that is implied.

If not from objective qualities of the food itself, how are these mindsets formed? Negative mindsets about healthy foods are, in part, rooted in and reinforced by American cultural messages. For example, national fruit and vegetable promotion campaigns (e.g., "5 A Day," "Fruits and Veggies: More Matters") place more emphasis on the importance of eating healthy foods for fighting disease than on tasty and enjoyable attributes (Marty, Chambaron, Nicklaus, & Monnery-Patris, 2018; Pettigrew, 2016). In contrast, unhealthy foods are promoted in more appealing ways than healthier foods on restaurant menus (Turnwald, Jurafsky, Conner, & Crum, 2017; Turnwald, Anderson, Jurafsky, & Crum, in press), through celebrity endorsements (Bragg, Miller, Elizee, Dighe, & Elbel, 2016), popular character endorsements (Kelly et al., 2010), television advertisements (Harris, Bargh, & Brownell, 2009; Kelly et al., 2010), and major sports sponsorships (Bragg et al., 2018). Emerging work demonstrates a systematic bias in how healthy versus unhealthy foods are portrayed even in nonadvertisement contexts. Unhealthy foods are systematically portrayed with less exciting, indulgent, social, and overall appealing language than healthy foods across America's top-selling movies, television shows, social media outlets, and food reviews (Turnwald et al., 2020). These social, marketing, and informational influences in American culture shape and reinforce the mindset that healthy foods are not tasty or enjoyable.

In this chapter, we present the taste-focused-labeling intervention. In contrast to traditional health-focused approaches, taste-focused-labeling challenges negative mindsets about healthy foods by highlighting the tasty and enjoyable characteristics of healthy dishes. This intervention is designed to not only align healthier foods with diners' taste motives in the moment of food choice but to also improve people's mindsets about healthy foods as a general category by changing the traditional health-focused lens through which they think about them. In the following sections, we describe the psychological processes involved, experimental evidence, mechanisms and moderators, implementation instructions, and questions for future research.

PSYCHOLOGICAL PROCESSES

Taste-focused labeling is a wise intervention (Walton & Wilson, 2018) that works to improve both people's momentary expectation of how tasty and enjoyable a specific healthy dish will be and to broadly improve people's mindsets about all healthy foods. Figure 12.1 summarizes the hypothesized psychological processes through which the taste-focused-labeling intervention operates.

Describing the solid line paths from left to right, promoting the tasty and enjoyable attributes of healthy foods enhances people's expectations of how delicious the food will taste (Liem, Aydin, & Zandstra, 2012; Turnwald et al., 2019). Since most people

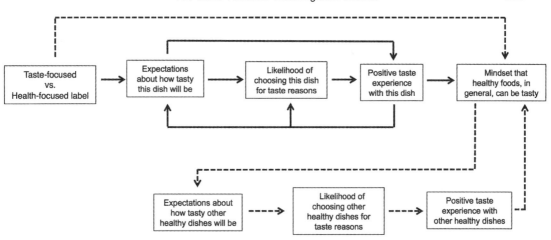

FIGURE 12.1. Conceptual model of how taste-focused labeling works. Solid arrows represent paths that are empirically tested. Dashed arrows represent hypothesized paths.

prioritize tastiness when making food decisions, increased expected tastiness of the dish leads more people to choose it.[1] It also shifts people's reason for choosing a healthy food toward choosing for a tasty experience rather than for long-term health benefits, thereby aligning a healthy choice more closely with taste priorities. Since the subjective experience of taste is a combination of a food's qualities and one's expectations, expecting that a food will taste better can enhance the actual experienced taste of foods (Maimaran & Fishbach, 2014; Raghunathan et al., 2006; Turnwald & Crum, 2019). For this specific healthy food with a taste-focused label, a positive taste experience makes consumption of that same healthy food with a taste-focused label on repeated occasions more likely because people have learned that it tastes good. Moreover, a positive taste experience with this healthy food (labeled as taste focused) has the potential to influence mindsets that healthy foods, as a general category, can be tasty and enjoyable. This is because a positive taste experience with a healthy food can challenge the mindset that healthy foods are not tasty or satisfying by providing a personally experienced counterexample.

Within this process, there are two important questions for future research, as we later describe and as depicted in the model with dashed lines. First, does a positive mindset shift transfer to a person's subsequent experiences with the same healthy foods and other healthy foods (with and without taste-focused labels)? An improvement in the mindset that healthy foods can be tasty could increase a person's expectations about how tasty healthy foods in new environments are and increase the likelihood of choosing healthy foods for taste reasons in new environments, particularly if those foods also have taste-focused labels. Second, does a positive mindset shift occur only after a positive taste experience or can exposure to the label alone shift mindsets about how tasty healthy foods can be?

---

[1]In the "Heterogeneity" section, we address moderators in this model, including one's prior experiences with a particular dish or setting, the extent to which one prioritizes tastiness more than healthiness, and how flavorfully dishes are prepared.

EMPIRICAL EVIDENCE

Three experiments and one multisite replication experiment tested whether labeling could change food choices in real-world contexts. Table 12.1 presents a summary of these experiments and key results.

The first experiment tested whether more students in a university dining hall sampled a small bowl of raw vegetables with dipping sauce when labeled and promoted as taste focused versus health focused. On each of two test days, two cafeteria staff members prompted each diner (total $N = 1,116$) upon entry to try a serving of mixed vegetables (carrots, jicama, and green beans) with miso dipping sauce. On one day, the vegetable dish was labeled as "Fiber-Packed Vegetables with Nutritional Miso Sauce" and verbally advertised as "healthy," "nutritious," and "good for you" by staff. On the other day, the same dish was labeled with a taste-focused description ("Crispy Veggie Straws with Decadent Miso Dip") and verbally promoted as "delicious" and "tasty" by staff. We found that 49% more diners chose the vegetables when labeled as taste focused compared to health focused (Turnwald & Crum, 2019).

The second experiment expanded to a lunch-buffet setting in which healthy foods (salad, vegetable wrap) competed among other food choices to test the hypothesis. Participants ($N = 202$) walked through one of two lunch-buffet lines and had their choice of salad, quinoa, vegetable wrap, turkey or steak sandwich, and dessert. On one serving line, the salad and vegetable wrap were labeled as health focused ("Light n' Healthy Salad," "Healthy Choice Vegetable Wrap"), and on the other as taste focused ("Indulgent Creations Deluxe Salad," "Mouthwatering Grilled Vegetable Wrap"). Other items were given the same, nondescriptive labels on both lines, and labels were not visible to diners

TABLE 12.1. Effect Sizes by Study

Study	N	Setting	Outcome	Food	Duration	Increase
1	1,116 diners	Field: Taste-test table in university dining hall	Proportion of diners choosing	Raw vegetables and dip	1 day	49%
2	202 diners	Field: Self-serve buffet at a conference	Proportion of diners choosing	Salad	1 day	18%
				Vegetarian wrap		84%
3	27,833 diners	Field: Self-serve buffet in university dining hall	Proportion of diners choosing	Hot vegetables	Over 10 weeks	41%
			Mass of food chosen			33%
4	137,842 diners	Field: Self-serve buffet in five university dining halls	Proportion of diners choosing	Hot vegetables	Over 12 weeks	29%
			Mass of food chosen			35%
			Mass of food consumed			39%

Note. All studies were conducted at lunchtime. *N* represents the total number of diner choices observed in each study. Duration represents the number of days for which data were collected in the study, and % increase represents the percent increase in the outcome (proportion of diners choosing healthy foods, mass of food chosen, or mass of food consumed) when labeled taste focused versus health focused.

prior to selecting a buffet line. We observed that 18% more participants chose salad and 84% more participants chose the vegetable wrap when labeled as taste focused compared to health focused (Turnwald & Crum, 2019).

These two experiments showed that, on a single occasion in a naturalistic field setting, a greater proportion of diners chose various healthy foods when labeled as taste focused than as health focused. However, these results do not inform whether this intervention has lasting effects, whether food choices revert to baseline on repeated exposure due to novelty effects, or whether they might reverse due to potential backfire effects. To drive improvements in dietary intake and health, this intervention must sustain healthy food choices over the long term. Therefore, we scaled the intervention to test the effect of repeated exposure to taste-focused and health-focused labeling over the course of several months.

The third experiment assessed whether taste-focused labeling impacted healthy food choices in a naturalistic field setting on repeated exposures over a 10-week period with a large sample (Turnwald, Boles, & Crum, 2017). We also tested whether the type of healthy language impacted choice (restriction-focused healthy language vs. positive-focused healthy language). Across 46 days of data collection in a university dining hall in which 27,933 diner food choices were observed, taste-focused labeling (e.g., "Dynamite Chili and Lime-Seasoned Beets") increased the proportion of diners choosing vegetables by 25% compared to basic labeling (e.g., "Beets"), 35% compared to healthy-positive labeling (e.g., "Vitamin-Packed Beets"), and 41% compared to healthy-restrictive labeling (e.g., "Low-Carb Beets"). The healthy-positive and healthy-restrictive labeling did not differ from each other, demonstrating that a focus on healthiness decreased choice even when the health-focused language was positive. Additionally, we measured the weight of vegetables that diners chose each day, and found that, similarly, a 16–33% greater mass of vegetables was chosen on days that vegetables were labeled as taste focused compared to basic, healthy-positive, and healthy-restrictive labels. Importantly, the benefits of taste-focused labeling were stable over time. There was no label condition × time interaction on the proportion of diners selecting vegetables or the mass of vegetables selected for taste-focused labeling compared to any of the other three labeling types.

In a fourth experiment, we replicated the taste-focused-labeling intervention in five universities across the United States to test whether taste-focused labeling was scalable, whether the effects would replicate, and to test for heterogeneity (Turnwald et al., 2019). Each day, the five university dining halls labeled their main-course vegetable as taste focused, basic, or health focused, and measured the number of diners who chose the vegetable. Results showed that across 137,842 diners, 185 days, and 71 different preparations involving 24 different types of vegetables, taste-focused labeling increased the proportion of diners choosing vegetables by 29%. Once again, the beneficial effect of taste-focused labeling compared to health-focused labeling on vegetable selection did not change over time at any of the five research sites.

At one of the sites in this experiment, we also measured how much of the vegetables people were actually eating, as it is possible that people were taking more vegetables when labeled as taste focused but then throwing them away. To measure the total mass of vegetables that diners served themselves, we weighed the serving dishes each time they were filled throughout the lunch period. We then collected each diner's plate waste at the entrance to the dining hall waste rooms and scraped off any of the remaining daily vegetable on their plate into a separate trash pail. Since we removed all other trash pails from the dining hall, the total mass of vegetables selected minus the total mass of vegetables wasted represented the mass of vegetables that diners actually consumed. Using these methods on each of 16 days revealed that taste-focused labeling significantly increased actual consumption of vegetables by 39% per day, on average. This effect on actual vegetable consumption was also stable over time. Together, these studies provide strong evidence that taste-focused labeling increases people's choice of a large variety of healthy foods (e.g., raw vegetables, hot vegetable dishes, vegetarian wraps, salads) across a variety of institutional field settings (tasting tables, buffet lines, and dining halls).

MECHANISM AND EFFECTS OVER TIME

How does taste-focused labeling work? The first part of our theory (solid black paths in Figure 12.1) is that taste-focused labeling increases diners' expectations of having a positive taste experience with a particular healthy food, which increases the likelihood that they will choose that food for taste reasons and have a positive taste experience. Although many of the field studies measured behavior and not psychological processes, several follow-up studies provide evidence in support of this hypothesis. In two independent preregistered experiments with online participant samples, taste-focused labels significantly increased participants' expectations of a positive taste experience compared to basic and health-focused labels (Turnwald et al., 2019). Furthermore, in all samples, the effect of taste-focused labeling on increased likelihood of choosing was fully mediated by increased expectations of a positive taste experience. Evidence from our longitudinal behavior experiments (see the "Empirical Evidence" section Study 3 and multisite replication) also supports this first part of the mechanism. The effects of taste-focused labeling compared to health-focused labeling on vegetable selection did not diminish over time when the same group of diners were exposed to different healthy dishes with different taste-focused labels over the course of 10–12 weeks, suggesting that this process may occur with each new exposure to a healthy food with a taste-focused label.

We also found that taste-focused labels change the reason why people say they would choose a vegetable dish. When participants in an online study were asked why they would choose a variety of vegetable dishes (on a scale of 1 = *For health benefits* to 5 = *For a tasty experience*), they indicated that it would be primarily for health benefits when these vegetable dishes had basic labels (e.g., "Broccoli," "Carrots"). When these same dishes were presented with health-focused labels, participants were even more likely to indicate that they would choose these dishes primarily for health benefits. However, when we presented these same dishes with taste-focused labels, participants shifted their reason to be primarily for a tasty experience (above the midpoint of the scale; Turnwald et al., 2019). This provides evidence that participants view healthy foods with taste-focused labels as being less in conflict with their taste goals.

To confirm that taste-focused labeling can enhance the actual taste experience of consuming healthy foods, we asked participants ($N = 203$) in a large university dining hall to taste green beans labeled as health focused ("Light n' Low-Carb Green Beans and Shallots") or taste focused ("Sweet Sizzlin' Green Beans and Crispy Shallots"). Compared to individuals who tasted green beans with the health-focused label, those who tasted green beans with the taste-focused label rated them as more delicious. They also endorsed the mindset that "in general, healthy foods taste delicious" postconsumption to a greater extent than individuals who ate the same green beans labeled as health focused (Turnwald & Crum, 2019).

These data preliminarily speak to the effect that choosing a healthy food with a taste-focused label can lead to a more positive taste experience and improve mindsets about the tastiness of healthy foods as a category. Yet more work is needed to understand this process. Does the improved mindset result from merely seeing healthy foods with taste-focused labels, or can this change be cemented only after having a positive taste experience with a tastily labeled healthy food? Does this mindset improvement increase how tasty a person expects other healthy foods to be (with and without taste-focused labels) and, if so, for how long do the effects last? Future work is needed to understand these questions.

HETEROGENEITY

Our research to date suggests at least three important moderating factors of the taste-focused-labeling intervention: (1) how deliciously the foods are prepared, (2) a person's priorities when making food decisions, and (3) a person's cultural background.

First, taste-focused labeling is more effective in settings that serve tastier vegetable dishes. Taste is an interaction between its qualities and expectations and thus both matter. Prior lab research (Woolley & Fishbach, 2016) showed that priming taste goals increased participants' consumption of a raw vegetable compared to priming health goals, but this effect was moderated by how tasty the food was (e.g., apple vs. raw spinach). Our multisite intervention extended these findings to field settings by showing that taste-focused labeling was more effective at schools that served tastier vegetable recipes on average than schools that served more bland preparations (Turnwald et al., 2019). Moderation at the level of setting occurs because one's belief regarding whether this particular distributor or setting generally serves tasty food influences how credible the taste-focused label is in this setting. Further downstream in the model depicted in Figure 12.1, once a diner has chosen the dish, how flavorfully this dish is prepared may moderate the extent to which a positive taste experience occurs because the actual experienced taste must meet expectations set by the label. Backfire effects could occur in cases where blandly prepared vegetables do not meet expectations, disappointing diners and confirming existing negative mindsets that healthy foods are not tasty.

A second factor that influences the efficacy of taste-focused labeling is the extent to which a person prioritizes tastiness and healthiness when making food decisions. Many Americans prioritize tastiness over healthiness (Glanz et al., 1998; Aggarwal et al., 2016). Yet a relatively small proportion of people, such as dieters and restrictive eaters, do prioritize healthiness in the moment of food choice and may be more attracted to health-focused labels because they affirm intentions to choose something that is, above all else, healthy (Irmak, Vallen, & Robinson, 2011; Papies & Veling, 2013). In an online sample of participants ($N = 277$), we found that those who prioritized healthiness to a greater extent were more likely to say that they would order foods with health-focused language than those who prioritized healthiness to a lesser extent, consistent with this moderation hypothesis and with prior studies on health-focused-labeling effects on dieters (Irmak et al., 2011; Papies & Veling, 2013).

Third, other studies suggest that culture and geography likely influence the effects of health-focused and taste-focused labeling. The model depicted in Figure 12.1 assumes an American context. While the mindset that healthy is not tasty or filling was observed in American contexts (Raghunathan et al., 2006; Suher et al., 2016), other cultures do not endorse this mindset to the same degree (Dube et al., 2016; Werle et al., 2013). For any group that already holds positive mindsets about the tastiness of healthy foods, the theory would predict that taste-focused labeling would have a smaller effect because there is little room for improvement in the mindset. However, even for people who have the general mindset that healthy foods are tasty, taste-focused labeling may still help in cases of individual foods that they do not like (e.g., for someone who has the mindset that healthy foods, in general, are tasty except for asparagus). While this list is not exhaustive, these moderators are important to consider when implementing taste-focused labeling for various populations and settings.

COUSINS

The closest intervention "cousins" to taste-focused labeling include interventions that associate foods with other desirable qualities. One such example in young children (ages 4–6) is to make healthy eating more desirable by placing cartoon characters on the label, packaging, or promotional materials of healthier foods (e.g., Hanks, Just, & Brumberg, 2016; Roberto, Baik, Harris, & Brownell, 2010). This strategy increased the likelihood of children choosing healthier foods (Hanks et al., 2016; Roberto et al., 2010) and improved the taste of carrots (Letona, Chacon, Roberto, & Barnoya, 2014; Roberto et al., 2010). Similar to taste-focused labeling, using branded characters associates healthy foods with a desirable quality that is salient to a target population. It differs from taste-focused labeling in that instead of using words related to a positive taste experience, children are attracted to familiar characters that they like and associate tastiness with the presence of these characters on food products.

Another related approach to taste-focused-labeling harnesses the values of rebellion and autonomy in teens to avoid junk food (Bryan et al., 2016). In this values-alignment intervention (see Bryan, Chapter 11, this volume), avoiding unhealthy foods was framed as a status-enhancing behavior that allows one to "stick it to the man," be an informed autonomous being who resists controlling authority figures, and stand up against the social injustices of targeting vulnerable populations. This intervention cousin is similar to taste-focused labeling in that it changes the meaning-making process of choosing a healthier versus unhealthier food. However, it differs in that it harnesses social values of adolescents and presents unhealthy foods as misaligned with these important values. In contrast, taste-focused labeling aligns healthier eating with the more general value of prioritizing tastiness and encourages individuals to approach healthy foods rather than avoid unhealthy foods.

Outside of the food context, the taste-focused labeling intervention harnesses a similar psychological approach as utility value (e.g., Hulleman & Harackiewicz, 2009), prosocial purpose (e.g., Yeager et al., 2014), and social meaning at work (e.g., Grant & Hofmann, 2011) interventions. Although the domains are different, all of these interventions help endow things that are instrumental, long-term pursuits that may otherwise lack much positive meaning to the person (e.g., school lessons, homework, work, safety) with meaning or relevance to motivate greater engagement in the process. For example, high school students improved their math and science grades when asked how course material might be useful to them or a close other three to five times throughout the term

(Hulleman & Harackiewicz, 2009). Yeager and colleagues showed that identifying an important social problem, reading motivational stories from other students who were driven by a desire to contribute positively to the world, and writing their own motivational story for future students also improved high school students' grades. In a health care context, Grant and Hofmann demonstrated that health care providers increased their soap use when primed with messages about protecting patients' health compared to messages about protecting their own health. Because goal pursuit in education and health contexts typically involves sustained effort over the course of years, imbuing the daily processes with pleasure or meaning beyond the long-term instrumental benefits is a useful psychological approach that can inform future work in these domains.

INTERVENTION CONTENT AND IMPLEMENTATION

We created a toolkit called "Edgy Veggies" (*http://sparqtools.org/edgyveggies*) in partnership with Stanford Psychological Answers to Real World Questions (SPARQ) for implementing taste-focused labeling in dining settings. This toolkit contains step-by-step instructions for how to implement taste-focused labeling, many example taste-focused labels, and recipe suggestions that may further enhance the benefits of taste-focused labels. The first step to implementing taste-focused labeling is to identify which foods to promote. This intervention is designed to promote healthy foods. Unhealthier foods typically already have taste-focused descriptions and do not need any added boosts. These healthier foods could be vegetable side dishes, healthier entrees, plant-based or vegetarian/vegan dishes, or healthier preparations of classic favorites. Raw, whole fruits and vegetables can still be promoted by emphasizing tasty and enjoyable properties (Woolley & Fishbach, 2016), although options for taste-focused words are slimmer without the possibility of drawing on preparation methods, ingredients, or unique spins on a composed dish.

The second step is to consider how the foods are prepared. It is important that the dishes are prepared flavorfully for two reasons: (1) it provides more options to choose from when constructing the taste-focused label because there are more ingredients, exciting preparation methods, or flavors to highlight, and (2) the flavor of the dish must at least meet the expectations set by the taste-focused label, otherwise diners may feel disappointed or misled. The flavor of dishes is often enhanced by the addition of herbs, spices, salt, pepper, olive oil, or sauces, and these additions do not have to make the dish less healthy.

The third step is to choose an enticing, taste-focused description for the dish. As described in Turnwald and colleagues (2019), taste-focused labels (e.g., "Herb n' Honey Balsamic-Glazed Turnips," "Sizzlin' Szechuan Green Beans with Toasted Garlic") are designed to elevate diners' expectations of a positive taste experience with healthy dishes. To do so, each taste-focused label is tailored to each dish to provide expectations of specific flavors (i.e., words that describe the taste, preparation methods, or specific ingredients) and at least one other theme designed to elevate expectations of a positive experience (e.g., exciting, indulgent, traditional, location words). This second component of elevating expectations of a positive experience is intentionally flexible to allow labels to draw on a variety of themes that may better fit some specific dishes or contexts than others. For example, dishes may elevate expectations of a positive experience by using (1) exciting words (e.g., *twisted, sizzlin', splashed, boldly, inspired*) if a unique ingredient or preparation method is used; (2) indulgent words (e.g., *glazed, creamy, mouthwatering, caramelized, juicy*) if a sauce is used or the dish is particularly satisfying; (3) traditional words (e.g., *old-fashioned, classic, countryside, Abuelita's, homestyle, Mama's*) if the dish is hearty, comforting, nostalgic, or rooted in tradition; or (4) location-based words (e.g., *New Orleans, Shanghai, tavern style, Thai, Provence*) if the dish draws from ingredients or preparation methods that are positively associated with a particular culture, location, or setting.

NUANCES AND MISCONCEPTIONS

There are three common misconceptions about taste-focused labeling. A first common misconception is that any fancy or positive word would work just as well as taste-focused labels. However, taste-focused labeling increased diners' expectations of how delicious healthy foods will taste and their hypothetical choices of vegetable dishes compared to fancy labels (e.g., "Viridescent," "Ebullient") and vague-positive labels (e.g., "Awesome," "Incredible"; Turnwald et al., 2019). While vague-positive labels and fancy labels may sound novel because people are not used to seeing vegetables described with vague-positive or fancy words, these words do not provide specific flavor expectations and so are less effective than taste-focused labels.

A second common misconception is that this approach is merely a behavioral nudge. Nudges are aspects of the choice architecture that alter people's behavior in a predictable way without forbidding any options or significantly changing their economic incentives (Thaler & Sunstein, 2008). However, nudges are limited in that they try to influence behavior without considering how people make sense of the choices before them. In contrast, taste-focused labeling was informed both by people's taste goals in the moment of food choice and the psychological obstacles (e.g., culturally entrenched mindsets that healthy foods are not tasty) that may prevent them from construing healthy foods as consistent with those goals.

A third common misconception regards the moderator of preparing vegetable dishes more flavorfully. Taste-focused labels work better when applied to vegetable dishes that are prepared flavorfully, but some may feel that preparing vegetable dishes with flavorful ingredients may reduce their nutritional benefits. Ingredients that are perceived as unhealthy (e.g., cheese, butter, salt) can be mindfully incorporated into vegetable dishes in small amounts that enhance flavor but do not override health benefits. Vegetables in our studies were often prepared with ingredients that enhance both flavor and health benefits, such as plant oils, herbs, and spices. Since dieting and restriction are ineffective long-term strategies (Mann et al., 2007), preparing healthier foods more flavorfully using chefs' culinary strategies (Cohen et al., 2015; Spencer, Kurzer, Cienfuegos, & Guinard, 2018) and labeling them in enticing ways to highlight those flavors are both important steps for enhancing vegetable consumption in ways that last.

IMPLICATIONS FOR PRACTICE

Taste-focused labeling improves people's food choices in real-world settings. Jaclyn Bertoldo, nutritionist at Stanford University Residential and Dining Enterprises and partner on this research, provides an operator's perspective on implementing this intervention in major dining operations:

"This research reinforces what I have experienced in the field—the more that I emphasize the health aspects of a food, the less enthused people are to eat it. Taste-focused labeling is an exciting strategy because it is relatively easy and inexpensive to implement, and it has the potential to boost customer satisfaction and positively enhance the dining experience. Plant-based options are also less expensive than meat-based options. Using this strategy to increase the extent to which customers choose plant-based foods and actually enjoy eating them is a win–win–win for food service operators and food companies concerned about their bottom line."

Taste-focused labels are flexible and can be tailored to dining environments in an array of settings. However, there are important differences to consider across dining environments. For example, taste-focused labels on restaurant menus and in other settings in which foods are not visible to customers before choosing what to eat may be particularly effective because diners only have the descriptions to base decisions on. In settings such as cafeterias, dining halls, or school lunchrooms in which diners can see the food prior to making a decision, we expect labeling effects to be weaker because people likely attend less to labels when they can see the food. These settings also typically feature repeat diners who have built habits that may be more difficult to change compared to diners in new settings.

It is also important to consider the audience. Special care should be taken to ensure that foods and ingredients are not being misrepresented and that descriptive language is culturally sensitive in all contexts—some themes are better suited for certain contexts than others. There may be more liberty to play with words like *finger licking* or *Grandma's special recipe* if the dining setting is a Southern barbecue restaurant compared to an upscale steakhouse or an elementary school cafeteria. The important thing is to match the enticing descriptions that are already being used to describe a setting's most popular dishes and to apply those same themes to the healthiest dishes. It is helpful to ask oneself which words would make a dish sound appealing to patrons in the dining setting of interest and use that as a jumping-off point for the label-brainstorming activities presented earlier in the chapter in the Edgy Veggies toolkit.

Incorporating chefs into the idea-generation stage when designing the labels can also provide a greater wealth of ingredients and words to choose from, as the chefs have the most intimate relationship with the food. According to Bertoldo:

"One of the most important lessons we've learned in our operations is the importance of engaging chefs in the process. Not only do they have a lot of creative insight for generating delicious names, but they also play a critical role in developing healthy dishes that taste and look as delicious as they sound."

IMPLICATIONS FOR PSYCHOLOGICAL THEORY

This intervention has implications for psychological theory regarding health promotional approaches. Most interventions to improve healthy behaviors have focused on educating people to identify healthy choices or about the importance of making healthy choices. They have also assumed that a long-term desire to be healthy will be enough to prioritize healthiness among many competing desires in the moment of food choice (e.g., tastiness). However, taste-focused labeling capitalizes on emphasizing the attributes of healthy foods that align with most people's top priority in the moment of food choice: tastiness. Instead of leading with healthiness, which people associate with poorer taste, this intervention changes how foods that are healthy are construed to the individual, shifting his or her mindset by providing a new lens through which to experience and perceive these foods—as delicious and enjoyable. As mentioned in the "Cousins" section of this chapter, taste-focused labels are also similar to a class of interventions that help endow instrumental, long-term pursuits (e.g., school lessons, homework, work, safety) with meaning or relevance to motivate greater engagement in the process.

Broadly, this intervention suggests that health interventions may be more effective when they match how target health behaviors are portrayed with people's intrinsic, short-term motives and priorities (Woolley & Fishbach, 2016, 2017). Research and policy approaches have called for limiting appealing advertising of *unhealthy* foods (Kelly et al., 2010), using labeling strategies like calorie labels or warning labels that make it easy to recognize *unhealthy* foods (e.g., Block & Roberto, 2014; Donnelly, Zatz, Svirsky, & John, 2018; Thorndike, Gelsomin, McCurley, & Levy, 2019), or teaching cognitive training strategies that emphasize health consequences of choosing *unhealthy* foods (Boswell, Sun, Suzuki, & Kober, 2018; Van Dessel, Hughes, & De Houwer, 2018). However, few approaches leverage tasty and enticing components of healthier foods. The present research shows that it is possible to increase the lure of healthy foods by changing the experience that people expect to have when eating them and making available the interpretation that healthy foods *can* satisfy taste motives. Because we need people to not only avoid healthy foods but to choose healthy foods, these efforts are just as critical as the large body of research on strategies for decreasing the appeal of unhealthy foods.

FUTURE DIRECTIONS

Expanding to Other Settings

Are there certain locations, dining settings, or food types that taste-focused labeling is especially effective or not effective for? We hypothesize that labels may be most effective when they are the only piece of information upon which to make decisions (e.g., menus) and when a diner is in a new situation compared to when the label is only one of multiple sources of information (e.g., dining halls in which one can see the dish, smell the dish, see others choosing or avoiding the dish), or when the diner has prior experience with a dish. Much of the work to date is limited in that it was conducted in dining settings within a college campus and all within a North American cultural context with participants who are likely younger and more educated than the general population. More research is needed across different populations and commercial settings.

Understanding Differences by Race, Culture, Socioeconomic Status, and Other Demographic Differences

It is especially important to understand whether taste-focused labeling may be an effective intervention among groups of lower-socioeconomic status (SES) and non-White groups that traditionally have poorer dietary intake. Studies on identity-based motivation (Oyserman, Fryberg, & Yoder, 2007) suggest that health-focused labeling may be ineffective for groups of low-SES or minority groups because healthy behaviors, such as healthy eating, are not seen as congruent with group identity (see also Berger & Rand,

2008; Nosek, Banaji, & Greenwald, 2002, for work on the importance of identity relevance in other domains). This potentially could mean that taste-focused labeling may better align with groups that have the least healthy diets and for whom emphasis on health is counter to their cultural values, but research is needed to test these ideas thoroughly. It remains to be tested whether these differences also depend upon which themes are used in a taste-focused label to elevate expectations of a positive experience (e.g., exciting, indulgent, traditional) because some themes may be more identity relevant for some groups.

Exploring the Broader Impact of Taste-Focused Labels on Mindsets about Healthy Foods as a General Category

Future work is needed to continue to understand the extent to which taste-focused labels may cause mindset shifts in how healthy foods, as a general category, are perceived. Does the improved mindset result from merely seeing healthy foods with taste-focused labels, or can this change be cemented only after having a positive taste experience with a tastily labeled healthy food? Does this mindset improvement increase how tasty a person expects other healthy foods to be (with and without taste-focused labels)? How long do the effects last? Do diners perceive healthy foods with taste-focused labels as healthy foods that are tasty, or do they no longer perceive them as healthy foods?

Testing Longitudinal Effects of Exposure to Taste-Focused Labeling on Health Consequences

While our research shows that taste-focused labels can increase healthy food choices after a single exposure and repeated exposures, no work has tested whether the improved healthy food choices impact health. Future work is needed to test whether health improves as a result of extended exposure to taste-focused labels, such as physiological (blood pressure, heart rate, body mass index [BMI]), subjective (e.g., well-being), and other indices of health (e.g., doctor visits, number of work days missed due to illness).

CONCLUSION

In summary, taste-focused labeling is a psychologically wise intervention that increases the proportion of people who choose healthy foods across a range of settings and for a variety of vegetables, plant-based foods, and healthier restaurant offerings compared to the classic approach of emphasizing health qualities and benefits of healthy foods. It does so by promoting healthy foods based on their delicious and enjoyable characteristics—qualities that most people prioritize over food healthiness in the moment of food choice. This scalable intervention shifts what it means to choose healthy foods from a long-term goal of health to a short-term taste goal. This shift has the potential to evoke lasting benefits in healthy food choices and mindsets about healthy foods.

REFERENCES

Aggarwal, A., Rehm, C. D., Monsivais, P., & Drewnowski, A. (2016). Importance of taste, nutrition, cost and conveniece in relation to diet quality: Evidence of nutrition resilience among

US adults using National Health and Nutrition Examination Survey (NHANES) 2007–2010. *Preventive Medicine, 90,* 184–192.

Aldridge, V., Dovey, T. M., & Halford, J. C. G. (2009). The role of familiarity in dietary development. *Developmental Review, 29*(1), 32–44.

Berger, J., & Rand, L. (2008). Shifting signals to help health: Using identity signaling to reduce risky health behaviors. *Journal of Consumer Research, 35*(3), 509–518.

Birch, L. L. (1998). Development of food acceptance patterns in the first years of life. *Proceedings of the Nutritional Society, 57,* 617–624.

Block, J. P., & Roberto, C. A. (2014). Potential benefits of calorie labeling in restaurants. *Journal of the American Medical Association, 312,* 887–888.

Boswell, R. G., Sun, W., Suzuki, S., & Kober, H. (2018). Training in cognitive strategies reduces eating and improves food choice. *Proceedings of the National Academy of Sciences of the USA, 115*(48), E11238–E11247.

Bragg, M. A., Miller, A. N., Elizee, J., Dighe, S., & Elbel, B. D. (2016). Popular music celebrity endorsements in food and nonalcoholic beverage marketing. *Pediatrics, 138*(1), e20153977.

Bragg, M. A., Miller, A. N., Roberto, C. A., Sam, R., Sarda, V., Harris, J. L., & Brownell, K. D. (2018). Sports sponsorships of food and nonalcoholic beverages. *Pediatrics, 141*(4), e20172822.

Bryan, C. J., Yeager, D. S., Hinojosa, C. P., Chabot, A., Bergen, H., Kawamura, M., & Steubing, F. (2016). Harnessing adolescent values to motivate healthier eating. *Proceedings of the National Academy of Sciences of the USA, 113*(39), 10830–10835.

Cohen, J. F. W., Richardon, S. A., Cluggish, S. A., Parker, E., Catalano, P. J., & Rimm, E. B. (2015). Effects of choice architecture and chef-enhanced meals on the selection and consumption of healthier schools foods: A randomized clinical trial. *JAMA Pediatrics, 169*(5), 431–437.

Crum, A. J., Corbin, W. R., Brownell, K. D., & Salovey, P. (2011). Mind over milkshakes: Mindsets, not just nutrients, determine ghrelin response. *Health Psychology, 30*(4), 424–429.

Crum, A. J., Salovey, P., & Achor, S. (2013). Rethinking stress: The role of mindsets in determining the stress response. *Journal of Personality and Social Psychology, 104*(4), 716–733.

Donnelly, G. E., Zatz, L. Y., Svirsky, D., & John, L. K. (2018). The effect of graphic warnings on sugary-drink purchasing. *Psychological Science, 29*(8), 1321–1333.

Dube, L., Fatemi, H., Lu, J., & Hertzer, C. (2016). The healthier the tastier?: USA–Inda comparison studies on consumer perception of a nutritious agricultural product at different food processing levels. *Frontiers in Public Health, 4,* 6.

Dweck, C. S. (2008). *Mindset: The new psychology of success.* New York: Random House Digital.

Fenko, A., Kersten, L., & Bialkova, S. (2016). Overcoming consumer scepticism toward food labels: The role of multisensory experience. *Food Quality and Preference, 48,* 81–92.

Finkelstein, S. R., & Fishbach, A. (2010). When healthy food makes you hungry. *Journal of Consumer Research, 37,* 357–367.

Glanz, K., Basil, M., Maibach, E., Goldberg, J., & Snyder, D. (1998). Why Americans eat what they do: Taste, nutrition, cost, convenience, and weight control concerns as influences on food consumption. *Journal of the American Dietetic Association, 98*(10), 1118–1126.

Gortmaker, S. L., Swinburn, B. A., Levy, D., Carter, R., Mabry, P. L., Finegood, D., . . . Moodie, M. (2011). Changing the future of obesity: Science, policy, and action. *Lancet, 378*(9793), 838–847.

Grant, A. M., & Hofmann, D. A. (2011). It's not all about me: Motivating hand hygiene among health care professionals by focusing on patients. *Psychological Science, 22*(12), 1494–1499.

Hanks, A. S., Just, D. R., & Brumberg, A. (2016). Marketing vegetables in elementary school cafeterias to increase uptake. *Pediatrics, 138*(2), e20151720.

Harris, J. L., Bargh, J. A., & Brownell, K. D. (2009). Priming effects of television food advertising on eating behavior. *Health Psychology, 28*(4), 404–413.

Hawkes, C., Smith, T. G., Jewell, J., Wardle, J., Hammond, R. A., Friel, S., . . . Kain, J. K. (2015). Smart food policies for obesity prevention. *Lancet, 385*(9985), 2410–2421.

Hulleman, C. S., & Harackiewicz, J. M. (2009). Promoting interest and performance in high school science classes. *Science, 326*(5958), 1410–1412.

Irmak, C., Vallen, B., & Robinson, S. R. (2011). The impact of product name on dieters' and non-dieters' food evaluations and consumption. *Journal of Consumer Research, 38*(2), 390–405.

Kelly, B., Halford, J. C., Boyland, E. J., Chapman, K., Bautista-Castano, I., Berg, C., . . . Summerbell, C. (2010). Television food advertising to children: A global perspective. *American Journal of Public Health, 100*(9), 1730–1736.

Lähteenmäki, L., Lampila, P., Grunert, K., Boztug, Y., Ueland, Ø., Åström, A., & Martinsdóttir, E. (2010). Impact of health-related claims on the perception of other product attributes. *Food Policy, 35*(3), 230–239.

Letona, P., Chacon, V., Roberto, C., & Barnoya, J. (2014). Effects of licensed characters on children's taste and snack preferences in Guatemala, a low/middle income country. *International Journal of Obesity, 38*(11), 1466–1469.

Liem, D., Aydin, N. T., & Zandstra, E. (2012). Effects of health labels on expected and actual taste perception of soup. *Food Quality and Preference, 25*(2), 192–197.

Lim, S. S., Vos, T., Flaxman, A. D., Danaei, G., Shibuya, K., Adair-Rohani, H., . . . Memish, Z. A. (2013). A comparative risk assessment of burden of disease and injury attributable to 67 risk factors and risk factor clusters in 21 regions, 1990–2010: A systematic analysis for the Global Burden of Disease Study 2010. *Lancet, 380*(9859), 2224–2260.

Maimaran, M., & Fishbach, A. (2014). If it's useful and you know it, do you eat?: Preschoolers refrain from instrumental food. *Journal of Consumer Research, 41*(3), 642–655.

Mann, T., Tomiyama, A. J., & Ward, A. (2015). Promoting public health in the context of the "obesity epidemic": False starts and promising new directions. *Perspectives on Psychological Science, 10,* 706–710.

Mann, T., Tomiyama, A. J., Westling, E., Lew, A. M., Samuels, B., & Chatman, J. (2007). Medicare's search for effective obesity treatments: Diets are not the answer. *American Psychologist, 62*(3), 220–233.

Marty, L., Chambaron, S., Nicklaus, S., & Monnery-Patris, S. (2018). Learned pleasure from eating: An opportunity to promote healthy eating in children? *Appetite, 120,* 265–274.

Micha, R., Penalvo, J. L., Cudhea, F., Imamura, F., Rehm, C. D., & Mozaffarian, D. (2017). Association between dietary factors and mortality from heart disease, stroke, and type 2 diabetes in the United States. *Journal of the American Medical Association, 317*(9), 912–924.

Nosek, B. A., Banaji, M. R., & Greenwald, A. G. (2002). Math = male, me = female, therefore math ≠ me. *Journal of Personality and Social Psychology, 83*(1), 44–59.

Oyserman, D., Fryberg, S. A., & Yoder, N. (2007). Identity-based motivation and health. *Journal of Personality and Social Psychology, 93*(6), 1011–1027.

Papies, E. K., & Veling, H. (2013). Healthy dining: Subtle diet reminders at the point of purchase increase low-calorie food choices among both chronic and current dieters. *Appetite, 61,* 1–7.

Pettigrew, S. (2016). Pleasure: An under-utilised "P" in social marketing for healthy eating. *Appetite, 104,* 60–69.

Raghunathan, R., Naylor, R. W., & Hoyer, W. D. (2006). The unhealthy = tasty intuition and its effects on taste inferences, enjoyment, and choice of food products. *Journal of Marketing, 70*(4), 170–184.

Rehm, C. D., Penalvo, J. L., Afshin, A., & Mozaffarian, D. (2016). Dietary intake among US adults, 1999–2012. *Journal of the American Medical Association, 315*(23), 2542–2553.

Roberto, C. A., Baik, J., Harris, J. L., & Brownell, K. D. (2010). Influence of licensed characters on children's taste and snack preferences. *Pediatrics, 126*(1), 88–93.

Roberto, C. A., Swinburn, B., Hawkes, C., Huang, T. T., Costa, S. A., Ashe, M., . . . Brownell, K. D. (2015). Patchy progress on obesity prevention: Emerging examples, entrenched barriers, and new thinking. *Lancet, 385*(9985), 2400–2409.

Spencer, M., Kurzer, A., Cienfuegos, C., & Guinard, J.-X. (2018). Student–consumer acceptance of plant-forward burrito bowls in which two-thirds of the meat has been replaced with legumes and vegetables: The Flexitarian Flip in university dining venues. *Appetite, 131,* 14–27.

Suher, J., Raghunathan, R., & Hoyer, W. D. (2016). Eating healthy or feeling empty?: How the "healthy = less filling" intuition influences satiety. *Journal of the Association for Consumer Research, 1*(1), 26–40.

Thaler, R. H., & Sunstein, C. R. (2008). *Nudge: Improving decisions about health, wealth, and happiness.* New Haven, CT: Yale University Press.

Thorndike, A. N., Gelsomin, E. D., McCurley, J. L., & Levy, D. E. (2019). Calories purchased by hospital employees after implementation of a cafeteria traffic light-labeling and choice architecture program. *JAMA Network Open, 2*(7), e196789.

Turnwald, B. P., Anderson, K. G., Jurafsky, D., & Crum, A. J. (in press). Five-star prices, appealing healthy item descriptions?: Expensive restaurants' descriptive menu language. *Health Psychology.*

Turnwald, B. P., Bertoldo, J. D., Perry, M. A., Policastro, P., Timmons, M., Bosso, C., . . . Crum, A. J. (2019). Increasing vegetable intake by emphasizing tasty and enjoyable attributes: A randomized controlled multisite intervention for taste-focused labeling. *Psychological Science, 30*(11), 1603–1615.

Turnwald, B. P., Boles, D. Z., & Crum, A. J. (2017). Association between indulgent descriptions and vegetable consumption: Twisted carrots and dynamite beets. *JAMA Internal Medicine, 177*(8), 1216–1218.

Turnwald, B. P., & Crum, A. J. (2019). Smart food policy for healthy food labeling: Leading with taste, not healthiness, to shift consumption and enjoyment of healthy foods. *Preventive Medicine, 119,* 7–13.

Turnwald, B. P., Jurafsky, D., Conner, A., & Crum, A. J. (2017). Reading between the menu lines: Are restaurants' descriptions of "healthy" foods unappealing? *Health Psychology, 36*(11), 1034–1037.

Turnwald, B. P., Perry, M. A., Jurgens, D., Prabhakaran, V., Jurafsky, D., Markus, H. R., & Crum, A. J. (2020). *Healthy food cast as unappealing in language of American movies, television, restaurants, government websites, and users on social media.* Manuscript in preparation.

Van Dessel, P., Hughes, S., & De Houwer, J. (2018). Consequence-based approach–avoidance training: A new and improved method for changing behavior. *Psychological Science, 29*(12), 1899–1910.

Veldhuizen, M. G., Nachtigal, D. J., Flammer, L. J., de Araujo, I. E., & Small, D. M. (2013). Verbal descriptors influence hypothalamic response to low-calorie drinks. *Molecular Metabolism, 2*(3), 270–280.

Walton, G. M., & Wilson, T. D. (2018). Wise interventions: Psychological remedies for social and personal problems. *Psychological Review, 125*(5), 617–655.

Wardle, J., & Cooke, I. (2008). Genetic and environmental determinants of children's food preferences. *British Journal of Nutrition, 99,* S15–S21.

Werle, C. O. C., Trendel, O., & Ardito, G. (2013). Unhealthy food is not tastier for everybody: The "healthy = tasty" French intuition. *Food Quality and Preference, 28*(1), 116–121.

Woolley, K., & Fishbach, A. (2016). For the fun of it: Harnessing immediate rewards to increase persistence in long-term goals. *Journal of Consumer Research, 42,* 952–966.

Woolley, K., & Fishbach, A. (2017). Immediate rewards predict adherence to long-term goals. *Personality and Social Pscyhology Bulletin, 43*(2), 151–162.

Yeager, D. S., Henderson, M. D., Paunesku, D., Walton, G. M., D'Mello, S., Spitzer, B. J., & Duckworth, A. L. (2014). Boring but important: A self-transcendent purpose for learning fosters academic self-regulation. *Journal of Personality and Social Psychology, 107*(4), 559–580.

PART III

CONFLICT AND RELATIONSHIPS

CHAPTER 13

The Incremental Theory of Personality Intervention

David S. Yeager and Hae Yeon Lee

This chapter explains how an incremental theory of personality—the belief that people can change their socially relevant characteristics—can cause people to cope with their social difficulties more effectively. We review evidence from randomized trials showing that even short exposures to an intervention teaching an incremental theory of personality can shift people's construals, so that adolescents see social difficulties as experiences that could be changed with time and therefore as less threatening. Our interventions have improved adolescents' maladaptive stress responses, mental health, and academic achievement. We explain how the incremental theory of personality intervention works through attributional and biopsychosocial mechanisms. We conclude with a discussion of future directions for research and practice, such as the implications of implicit theories of personality for school or home environments and for theories of stress and coping.

Making the transition to high school typically comes with social challenges. In some of our studies, we asked ninth-grade students every day for several days in the first month of high school to tell us about negative events that happened to them that day (e.g., Yeager, Lee, & Jamieson, 2016). It was common for students to write about events such as these:

"Well sometimes people call me fat or stupid . . . I didn't want to tell them, but it killed me inside."

"This morning I was walking by and all the person could do was act as if I weren't there. Seeing them and they just look you in the face without a 'hi' or a smile made me feel invisible."

"All my friends were acting weird and wouldn't tell me why. I feel out of place since they're all keeping something from me."

"I had an old friend look at me with disgust, even though I'm not the one who did anything wrong."

"In lunch I only see people in groups of 3–10, never alone. I feel extremely lonely again."

What can be done to help adolescents deal with these challenges and others like them? We developed the incremental theory of personality intervention to answer this question.

The core assumption underlying our intervention is that the meaning of stressful experiences can be ambiguous. Are they happening to me because of something wrong with me or my context, or are they normal events that I can learn from? The incremental theory of personality intervention offers people a new lens for seeing the world—one that focuses on humanity's potential for dynamism and change. In doing so, the intervention gives people reason to expect that even socially painful experiences, such as peer victimization or exclusion, are not causes for despair, because they might get better with time.

The effect of inviting people into this more dynamic worldview has been to improve adolescents' emotional and academic lives, as they confront the inevitable social adversities that accompany a difficult life transition. As we will see, randomized trials have evaluated the intervention and have documented improvements in adolescents' behavior, well-being, and grades. Now that the intervention has shown effects in the context of high school bullying and social exclusion, the stage is set for research to generalize the intervention to other socially challenging periods of life and to test it in more—and more diverse—settings.

BACKGROUND

Quite often, adolescents jockey for social status in a way that harms their peers (Coleman, 1961; Crosnoe, 2011; Hawley, 1999). Aggressive behaviors can range from bullying, defined as a repeated use of aggression against someone with lower social power (Hong & Espelage, 2012), to more subtle forms of relational aggression, such as targeting others' reputations or weakening their social networks through indirect insults, rumors, or exclusion (Prinstein, Boergers, & Vernberg, 2001). Adolescents are not only victims of these behaviors but are also initiators of them. Some young people perceive a need to protect their status and signal their social power before others do the same to them. Many seek revenge after victimization.

Managing social challenges such as these can feel like more than one can handle. As such, the normative difficulties of adolescence can evoke maladaptive stress responses that feed into symptoms of anxiety and depression (Hammen, 2005). Epidemiological data suggest that recent birth cohorts of adolescents may be even more affected by this than previous cohorts (Twenge, Joiner, Rogers, & Martin, 2017) perhaps because connected technologies (e.g., social media) have made it easier than ever for students to engage in relational aggression, such as targeting others' reputations (George & Odgers, 2015; Underwood & Ehrenreich, 2017).

To make matters worse, social difficulties co-occur with academic difficulties. Adolescents have been said to have two jobs in secondary school: the job of doing well socially and the job of doing well academically (Coleman, 1961; Crosnoe, 2011). When the first job is going poorly, it can compromise adolescents' cognitive ability to do the second.

Worries about social status can interfere with the basic cognitive processing required to perform well in classes (Yang, Lee, Crosnoe, & Yeager, 2020), and threats to social belonging in a setting can undermine motivation to learn (Deci & Ryan, 1985; Walton, Cohen, Cwir, & Spencer, 2012). In sum, adolescents' reactions to social status threats can act as a "psychological hub" that connects diverse outcomes, from aggressive behavior to mental health to academic achievement.

The incremental theory of personality intervention targets a belief system, the entity theory of personality, that lies underneath this "psychological hub," and in doing so it simultaneously affects a number of related outcomes (see Yeager et al., 2014, for a discussion). The entity theory of personality is the belief that people cannot change. High school students with an entity theory have been prone to despair, as we explain below. The incremental theory of personality intervention seeks to neutralize the entity theory and improve adolescents' coping with social stressors by teaching a simple belief: *People can change and improve their personal characteristics, under the right conditions, with the right experiences, and with social support.*

The effectiveness of this message grows out of the insight that adolescents who think that current social challenges are permanent will cope more poorly with them. That poorer coping in turn can spill over into their social behavior, well-being, and academic achievement. But if adolescents can put their ongoing social difficulties into perspective—if they can see that social difficulties are temporary and not indicative of people's core character traits—then adolescents may cope more effectively. By coping better, adolescents may show more prosocial behavior and better mental health and academic performance.

PSYCHOLOGICAL PROCESSES

The Entity Theory of Personality "Meaning System"

As stated, an incremental theory of personality is the belief that people's basic social (or moral) characteristics are malleable and can be developed (Dweck, Chiu, & Hong, 1995; Plaks, 2017; Yeager & Dweck, 2012). It is contrasted with the *entity theory of personality,* which is the belief that people's basic characteristics cannot be changed (Dweck et al., 1995; Plaks, 2017; Yeager & Dweck, 2012). These beliefs—called *implicit theories* (or *mindsets) of personality*—have been the subject of a great deal of basic research in social, developmental, and personality psychology. The implicit theories model first focused on the context of academic achievement (Dweck & Leggett, 1988), and later was extended to moral and social judgments (Dweck et al., 1995; Molden, Plaks, & Dweck, 2006), social stereotyping (Levy & Dweck, 1999; Levy, Stroessner, & Dweck, 1998), intergroup conflict (Halperin, Russell, Trzesniewski, Gross, & Dweck, 2011), and more (see Dweck & Yeager, 2019, for a review).

The two implicit theories—entity and incremental—imply different "meaning systems" that shape construals of social situations and goal pursuit within them (Dweck & Yeager, 2019; see also Dweck & Yeager, Chapter 1, this volume). In an entity theory, individuals tend to endorse the goal of "proving" or demonstrating their social competence, rather than improving it (i.e., social "approach" and "avoidance" goals; Erdley, Loomis, Cain, & Dumas-Hines, 1997; see also Ryan & Shim, 2008, for a discussion of social goals). When judging others, an entity theory furthermore creates a heightened focus on underlying traits as causes of behavior, as well as the expectation that traits will remain consistent far into the future. This leads to surprise when traits are not shown to be the most important determinants of individuals' behavior or when they change (see Plaks, 2017, for a review). Then, when confronted with others' social failures, those with more of an entity theory respond in ways that condemn or exclude the targets, as opposed to working productively to educate or change the targets (Rattan & Dweck, 2010).

An incremental theory of personality intervention seeks to target and change the entity theory meaning system. To understand how and why this is effective, below we preview two mediators of an entity theory's effects on behavior and stress responses: attributions and stress appraisals. (These will show up again when we review the mediators of the intervention's effects.)

Attributions

One psychological process affected by implicit theories of personality is a person's *attributions* concerning the causes of ongoing difficulties (Dweck, 1975; Weiner, 1985). This is an important psychological process because the start of high school is a moment with excessive attributional ambiguity.

The attributional ambiguity of high school is illustrated well by a 16-year-old author, Florida Frenz (2013), in her inspiring book *How to Be Human*. Frenz is on the autism spectrum and is a sophisticated observer of the high school transition:

> Some [friends] have abruptly decided they don't want to hang out with me. . . . But more often "friends" indicate their disinterest more subtly. They may not nod or wave at me anymore. Their eyes may wander or glaze over when I try to talk to them. Their replies may go from being stories or jokes to terse answers such as "uh-huh" or "oh." *The gray areas are most frustrating. Is this about me . . . or her? Will my friendships with the other members of the group start fraying as well? Is this a phase or a permanent thing?* (emphasis added)

The sentences in italics highlight the attributional questions. Prior research has shown that how adolescents answer those questions can have important effects on how they cope. When individuals attribute an event such as being socially excluded or being targeted by bullying to factors that are stable and outside of one's control (e.g., the flawed moral character of one's peers or one's own inherent social inadequacy), then they may be expected to cope more poorly, for instance, by showing signs of helplessness or despair (Chiu, Hong, & Dweck, 1997; Gervey, Chiu, Hong, & Dweck, 1999; see also Janoff-Bulman, 1979). But when a person attributes an event such as social rejection or bullying to factors that could be changed (e.g., others' more temporary motivations or erroneous beliefs, or one's misunderstanding of the current social milieu), then the person may be expected to cope better, and may be willing to proactively solve the problem (Yeager & Miu, 2011). Thus, whether one construes social difficulties as stemming from fixed versus malleable causes can be an important determinant of how one responds to the event (Beck, 2008; Janoff-Bulman, 1979; Weiner, 1985), and in particular whether one copes well or poorly.

In past correlational studies, individuals who endorsed more of an entity theory of personality—for instance, agreeing with items such as "Your personality is something about you that you can't change very much"—were more likely to report fixed, stable attributions for their own social difficulties or others' negative social behavior. In one study, children with an entity theory who were led to believe that they had not yet been chosen by a peer for a social interaction were more likely to report wondering whether they were not "a likable person" (Erdley et al., 1997). In another study, adolescents with more of an entity theory who read a story about peers who bullied others were more likely to say that the peers were "bad people" (Yeager, Trzesniewski, Tirri, Nokelainen, & Dweck, 2011).

Recent research (Seo et al., 2019) supported these earlier findings in two ways: first, with a raw-data meta-analysis of all past studies we conducted and, second, with a replication study conducted in a national sample of 25 public high schools (total $N \sim 6,000$). As expected, in both cases, an entity theory of personality predicted a tendency to make fixed-trait attributions about the self ("Maybe I'm not a likable person") and about others ("They are bad people") following socially challenging situations, such as bullying or exclusion. As shown in clinical psychology research (Beck, 2008; Dweck, 1975; Slavich, O'Donovan, Epel, & Kemeny, 2010) the tendency to make fixed-trait attributions predicted higher internalizing symptoms (global stress and depression) and externalizing symptoms (desire for revenge and willingness to proactively use social aggression to protect one's social status). Thus, an entity theory of personality can predict problematic behavior and poorer well-being via attributional processes. Schleider, Abel, and Weisz (2015) also report meta-analytic evidence concerning the link between implicit theories and internalizing/externalizing symptoms.

Physiological Stress Responses

The fixed-trait attributional styles that follow from an entity theory of personality can give rise to maladaptive physiological stress responses that may explain how individuals who differ in their implicit theories of personality go on to show differences in symptoms over time (Schleider & Weisz, 2016; Yeager et al., 2016). The key to understanding why is to recognize that adolescents are not simply disinterested observers of the causes of their social world. The attributions for social difficulties that they make flow directly into their assessments of whether they are likely to be able to deal with or change stressors such as peer victimization or exclusion. Illustrating this fact is a quotation from a high school student participating in a focus group we conducted for one of the original incremental theory studies:

> "I'm in my first month of high school and I have already had one or two melt downs. . . . It is already getting to be a bit much to handle all at once. *I can already see I am in a heck of a ride for high school. . . .* "

What stands out to us in this quotation is how students' predictions about the future—whether their stressors are likely to continue throughout high school—seem closely linked to their appraisals of whether they have what it takes to handle the stressors. Quotations like this one led us to test the hypothesis that individuals with more of an entity theory of personality may tend to construe their social stressors as demands that they do not have sufficient resources to handle what is called a *threat* state in the *biopsychosocial* (BPS) *model of challenge and threat* (Blascovich & Tomaka, 1996; Jamieson, Hangen, Lee, & Yeager, 2018).

Threat-type responses to stressors, which we now know are more likely to grow out of the entity theory meaning system in which negative social stressors are construed as demands that cannot be changed, have been known for some time to contribute to long-term physical and mental health problems (Jamieson et al., 2018; Juster, McEwen, & Lupien, 2010). Threat states elicit greater cortisol responses, greater constriction of the blood vessels, and less efficient cardiac output, all of which could help the body to survive acute physical trauma but are poorly suited for physical and mental health in the absence of acute physical threats (Jamieson et al., 2018; Mendes & Park, 2014).

Daily diary data have shown that an entity theory of personality elicits threat-type stress responses and this can explain why an entity theory might be related to down-stream health outcomes (Seo et al., 2019). Threat-type stress responses, such as elevated cortisol levels, tend to linger and become self-reinforcing (Lee, Jamieson, Miu, Josephs, & Yeager, 2019), and predict the onset of more global outcomes like depression (Dickerson & Kemeny, 2004) or poorer cognitive performance (Lupien, McEwen, Gunnar, & Heim, 2009). Hence, if an incremental theory of personality intervention could reduce threat-type responses—by leading adolescents to perceive their stressors as things that they can handle—then the intervention could result in better long-term outcomes via its effects on physiological stress responses.

How the Incremental Theory Intervention Counteracts the Entity Theory of Personality

The incremental theory of personality intervention seeks to convey this message: *People behave in mean ways not because of the kind of person they are but because of thoughts and feelings that they have—thoughts and feelings that live in the brain. Because we know that the brain can change and mature over time, and thoughts and feelings can change too, then people's behaviors and habits can change as well.* We note that the intervention does not try to make the strong argument that your own personal bullies can change—instead, it makes the argument that people, in general, can change for the better, and then participants complete guided exercises that allow them to apply the message to their own social relationships (see Halperin et al., 2011, for an intervention that took a related approach in the context of intractable conflict).

The intervention follows the basic "grammar" of "wise interventions" that seek to change mindsets (Walton & Wilson, 2018; Yeager & Walton, 2011). The intervention draws on scientific evidence, "sticky" (or memorable) examples, stories from upper-year students, and an opportunity to internalize the new mindset by writing a persuasive letter to future students in the school. We review this content in greater detail as we present the evidence.

The tone and tenor of the intervention is autonomy supportive (Vansteenkiste, Simons, Lens, Sheldon, & Deci, 2004; Yeager, Dahl, & Dweck, 2018)—that is, the intervention does not seek to "tell" adolescents what beliefs they should hold. It invites young people to try on the lens of the incremental theory of personality, and asks them to explain how it could work for them. This may be an important element. The autonomy-supportive approach avoids the disrespectful implication that the intervening parties view the adolescents' beliefs or adjustment to be deficient (Yeager et al., 2018). It can also make the intervention more credible; adolescents who are told to believe that bullies can change may begin to think of specific bullies who may never change. Adolescents may have a more optimistic response when they are asked to generate an argument about why peers who are sometimes mean could potentially change.

EMPIRICAL EVIDENCE

Outcomes

The incremental theory of personality intervention has reduced both externalizing behavior (e.g., aggression) and internalizing symptoms (e.g., maladaptive stress responses and depression). In a few studies, it improved adolescents' academic performance.

Externalizing Behavior

The first incremental theory of personality intervention sought to reduce adolescents' aggressive retaliation in response to a peer provocation (Yeager, Trzesniewski, & Dweck, 2013). The intervention took the form of a multisession classroom workshop delivered to ninth- and tenth-grade students (total $N = 230$) at a relatively lower-achieving school with rather high levels of peer conflict. It occurred over 3 weeks, in six classroom sessions each lasting under 50 minutes. Adolescents were presented with scientific information about changes in the brain and in personality—that changes were always *possible,* even if they were not automatic or easy. They read stories from older students who had learned about the incremental theory of personality (during a pilot study) and completed activities (skits, games, small-group discussions) that allowed them to use the incremental theory for specific, hypothetical instances of victimization or exclusion. Like growth-mindset-of-intelligence interventions (Aronson, Fried, & Good, 2002), participants were guided to internalize the message by completing a writing exercise—a "saying-is-believing" exercise—in which they wrote a letter to a future student encouraging him or her to remember that people can change (Aronson, 1999).

In the first trial, the primary behavioral measure of aggression was assessed 1 month after the end of the intervention. Behavior was measured via a standardized task adapted from social psychology: the number of grams of hot sauce participants allocated to a peer to consume when they believed that the peer had excluded them in an online game, and that the peer strongly disliked spicy food (Lieberman, Solomon, Greenberg, & McGregor, 1999; i.e., Cyberball; Williams & Jarvis, 2006). In truth, there was no peer (the provocation was controlled by a computer) and no one actually ate the hot sauce. Yeager, Trzesniewski, et al. (2013) showed that adolescents who received the incremental theory of personality intervention, compared to two separate control groups allocated about 40% less hot sauce. Improvement was also visible in students' daily behaviors in schools. Three months after the intervention, those who received the incremental theory of personality intervention were more likely to be nominated by their teachers (who were unaware of students' conditions) for having improved their social behavior in school.

Subsequent studies have shortened the intervention and made it easier to replicate in larger samples, taking it from six sessions led by trained facilitators to one session self-administered either on paper or via an online module (Yeager et al., 2014; Yeager, Miu, Powers, & Dweck, 2013). The shortened intervention kept the same basic elements—scientific evidence about the brain's and personality's potential for change, stories from upper-year students who received and endorsed the incremental theory of personality, and the "saying-is-believing" letter to a peer—but the content was communicated more efficiently. Two experiments found that this shortened, self-administered incremental theory of personality intervention effectively reduced adolescents' willingness to respond aggressively to a hypothetical scenario relative to a control group, via changes in attributional tendencies (Yeager, Miu, et al., 2013).

It may seem surprising that a briefer version of the intervention could show measurable effects. But an inspection of the letters students wrote to a peer shows that they often processed the message and found it to be powerful. Here are two examples from one of our recent studies:

> "All the people that are mean and hurtful to you are just missing out on a good friend they could've had. But with all that said people can change and learn what they did and said are wrong. Just because someone is one way right now doesn't mean they can't change at all in time. Because in reality they can change."

> "When we were starting the school year I went [to] where my friends hang out. Then they just looked at me and kept on talking. . . . I felt really left out especially because we were all really good friends in middle school . . . [Although] it may seem like your life is crashing down, and that nothing will ever get better, it is not the end of the world. Your life will not be like this forever. . . . People can change. It's only your first day of school."

Internalizing Symptoms

The first evaluation of the incremental theory of personality intervention found an effect on symptoms of depression (Yeager, Trzesniewski, et al., 2013), even though, at the time, it was designed primarily to reduce aggression. That study showed that although in the control condition adolescents who were more victimized were also more depressed, this was not the case in the intervention condition. With an incremental theory of personality, depression was lower for victimized adolescents compared to control participants who were victimized.

Why did the effect on internalizing symptoms appear? We began to dig into this result more deeply, which led us to the theoretical synthesis with the BPS model of challenge and threat described above. We conducted new studies focusing on internalizing symptoms in general and maladaptive stress responses in particular (e.g., Yeager et al., 2014), and we found that the one-session incremental theory of personality intervention could reduce negative stress responses to an experimenter-controlled social challenge (again, exclusion via Cyberball; Williams & Jarvis, 2006). Then in a field experiment that tracked students' levels of cortisol over 1 week after the intervention—which, as noted, represents one hormonal indicator of threat-type responses to social stressors—Yeager and colleagues (2016, Study 2) found that the incremental theory intervention reduced cortisol among adolescents who reported more intensely negative social stressors.

Can the short-term reductions in threat-type stress responses from the incremental theory of personality last? Evidence is beginning to show that they can. Yeager et al. (2014, Studies 2 and 3) reported two experiments showing that at a 9-month follow-up there were lower levels of global negative stress responses (measured via the Perceived Stress Scale; Cohen, Kamarck, & Mermelstein, 1983) among those who had received the incremental theory of personality at the beginning of the school year.

Could the incremental theory go on to reduce clinically significant depressive symptoms? Individuals who appraise a social stressor as something that they can handle should, in principle, be less likely to show increases in their depressive symptoms (Hammen, 2005)—therefore, an intervention to improve social stress coping might prevent those increases in depression. Consistent with this logic, Miu and Yeager (2015) reported 9-month effects of the incremental theory intervention on self-reported depressive symptoms (measured via a short form of the Children's Depression Inventory [CDI]; Kovacs, 2003).

Two teams have recently found significant effects of the incremental theory intervention on clinical symptoms of depression. Schleider and colleagues (2015) found that an incremental theory of personality intervention led to lower levels of depressive symptoms, compared to controls, in a longitudinal study conducted with clinical populations of adolescents who reported elevated symptoms prior to random assignment to condition. Calvete and colleagues (2019), conducting a replication study with adolescents in Spain (between ages 13 and 18), reported lower levels of depressive symptoms at 6- and 12-month follow-up among those receiving the incremental theory intervention, compared to controls—but this result was moderated by age in unpredicted ways that would ideally lead to additional replication studies.

Academic Performance

The incremental theory of personality intervention was designed to improve responses to social stressors, and did not have an academic component—that is, the short intervention made no mention of trying harder in school. Therefore, initially we did not expect to find that the incremental theory of personality intervention would improve grades, but because social success is so closely tied to academic success in high school, we thought it would be worth testing. In the three studies we conducted so far that tested for it, we found evidence for effects on grades (Yeager et al., 2014, Studies 2 and 3; Yeager et al., 2016, Study 2). This result was conceptually replicated in a laboratory study focusing on performance on a speech and math task (Yeager et al., 2016, Study 1). Thus, an intriguing result is that an intervention that focuses primarily on helping adolescents to deal with their social lives has also produced cross-domain benefits for academic outcomes as well. This supports the "psychological hub" idea that we described above.

Mechanisms

Several experiments have generated preliminary evidence in support of psychological mechanisms growing out of the two theoretical models reviewed earlier: attribution theory and the BPS model of challenge and threat.

Changes in Construals: Attributions and Appraisals

Implicit theories of personality can cause individuals to construe the meaning of the demanding situation differently, make a different appraisal of their resources to deal with the situation, and therefore show different coping responses.

In a randomized field experiment (Lee et al., 2020), ninth-grade adolescents (N = 138) completed a task that involved ostracism on social media (Wolf et al., 2015), which is an experimentally controlled social-evaluative demand. Individuals received fewer *likes* than peers in response to their social media posts, or more *likes* (randomly assigned). Lee and colleagues (2020) found that adolescents who had been exposed to the single session, online incremental theory of personality and who had previously held an entity theory of personality ended up reporting fewer maladaptive appraisals (e.g., "I felt rejected by others") and fewer fixed self-attributions (e.g., "Maybe I'm not a likable person"; "I felt bad about who I am") when they got fewer *likes* than their peers.

Yeager et al. (2016, Study 1) induced an experimentally controlled social-evaluative stressor after randomized assignment of the incremental theory of personality intervention. The stressor was the Trier Social Stress Test (TSST; Kirschbaum, Pirke, & Hellhammer, 1993), which involves giving a public speech and doing mental math in front of unsupportive peers (in actuality, confederates). Teens who had been assigned to an incremental theory of personality intervention reported reduced threat-type appraisals of the social stressor (e.g., saying they can confidently handle the demands of the public speech task) relative to controls—that is, the incremental theory of personality intervention has reduced two of the purported mediators of the negative effects of the entity theory of personality: fixed trait attributions and threat-type appraisals of stressors.

Stress Physiology

The effects of the incremental theory intervention have also appeared on physiological responses to social stress—responses that are thought to lead to long-run differences in well-being (Goodyer, Park, Netherton, & Herbert, 2001; Gunnar & Quevedo, 2007; Sapolsky, 2000; Staufenbiel, Penninx, Spijker, Elzinga, & van Rossum, 2013). In the first experiment described in the previous section, adolescents receiving the incremental theory of personality intervention and undergoing the TSST showed more adaptive cardiovascular responses relative to controls, in the form of greater vascular dilation and cardiac efficiency, and also more adaptive adrenal responses (i.e., lower cortisol response; Yeager et al., 2016). A similar pattern of results emerged in an experiment conducted by Schleider and Weisz (2016), which also showed improvements in acute physiological responses to an experimentally induced stressor within a population of adolescents already showing higher depression at baseline.

Could stress physiology improvements explain the effects of the incremental theory of personality on academic performance? A correlational mediation analysis reported by Yeager and colleagues (2016, supplemental online material), reproduced in Figure 13.1, found that the intervention's effect on lower threat-type appraisals of the stressor predicted changes in vascular dilation from baseline to during the stressor (i.e., reactivity in "total peripheral resistance" [TPR]), and this difference in stress reactivity in turn predicted performance on the public speech and mental math tasks. This is consistent with

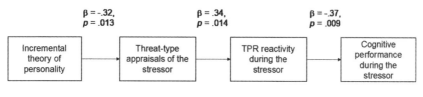

Indirect effect of condition on performance via
TPR: β = -.13, CI: .02, .32, p = .02

FIGURE 13.1. Mediation model showing the path from the incremental theory of personality intervention to improved cognitive performance during a social stressor (the Trier Social Stress Test [TSST]). Coefficients represent standardized estimates. TPR, total peripheral resistance, an indication of vascular constriction, which is a physiological indication of threat-type stress responses. N = 52. Data from Yeager, Lee, and Jamieson (2016, Study 1).

the conclusion that adolescents who received the incremental theory intervention circulated more oxygenated blood to their brains, resulting in better cognitive performance.

Effects over Time

So far, the incremental theory of personality intervention has been evaluated for the length of one school year—usually 9 months (e.g., Miu & Yeager, 2015). This was intentional; students are far less likely to transfer or drop out of high school within ninth grade relative to between ninth and tenth grade. However, a critical question is how and whether the effects persist beyond the 1-year period.

Heterogeneity: Mindset × Context Theory

The incremental theory of personality intervention has usually been evaluated as a universal, preventative intervention, not a targeted intervention (though see Schleider et al., 2015, for a clinical application). This means the intervention is typically given to people regardless of their levels of risk prior to the experiment, and therefore there are likely to be unmeasured moderators of the treatment effects (Greenberg & Abenavoli, 2017). We are now carrying out new intervention experiments to examine heterogeneity. The model we are working from was developed in the context of growth-mindset-of-*intelligence* interventions (see Dweck & Yeager, Chapter 1, this volume).

Our model, which we call mindset × context theory, makes the prediction that wise interventions will show meaningful treatment effects when they are *suitable* (well tailored to the population at hand), when they target *susceptible* individuals (those whose mental health would be compromised if not for the intervention), and when they are delivered in *sustaining* environments (those in which the context could plausibly support a recursive process). Concretely, this leads to the prediction that there should be larger effects of the incremental theory of personality intervention for individuals with prior vulnerabilities (prior entity theories, prior victimization, or prior chronic stress) in contexts where the message that "people can change" feels "true" (perhaps schools where victimization tends to "get better" over time).

COUSINS

The incremental theory of personality intervention owes much to the incremental theory of *intelligence* intervention (also known as the growth-mindset-of-intelligence intervention; see Aronson et al., 2002; Dweck & Yeager, 2019; Yeager & Dweck, 2012). And the "grammar" of wise interventions that it implements comes directly from interventions to address belonging uncertainty (Walton & Cohen, 2011).

Like the social-belonging intervention (see Walton & Brady, Chapter 2, this volume), the incremental theory of personality intervention targets the "psychological hub" of social relationships during a challenging life transition. Both interventions rely on the possibility of attributional ambiguity in the meaning of everyday adversities, and seek to tilt patterns of attributions in favor of changeable causes rather than fixed causes of difficulty. And both interventions have shown evidence of affecting both academic and health outcomes (see Walton & Cohen, 2011). One way to distinguish the two interventions is in the arguments they make about how adversities can change. The incremental theory of personality intervention conveys evidence that people's internal traits change (e.g., via changes in the brain that come with development and experience), whereas the social-belonging intervention argues that people's social circumstances change (e.g., by joining study groups or meeting with professors during office hours). A second way that the interventions differ is in who is targeted by the message and who tends to benefit. The incremental theory of personality intervention targets students who are undergoing social difficulties in general (e.g., bullying or exclusion), but the social-belonging intervention focuses on alleviating identity threat (e.g., students facing stereotype threat). Therefore, we do not expect the incremental theory of personality intervention to be moderated by race, ethnicity, or socioeconomic status unless in a given sample these are correlated with the vulnerability targeted by the intervention (i.e., prior susceptibility to social adversity). But the social-belonging intervention should be moderated by groups that tend to experience identity threat, because it is designed to clear up attributional ambiguity for identity-threatened individuals.

The incremental theory of personality was also informed by interventions seeking to reduce the "hostile attributional bias," which is the tendency for aggressive individuals to attribute causally ambiguous social difficulties to hostile intent (Dodge & Frame, 1982; Dodge, Godwin, & Conduct Problems Prevention Research Group, 2013). The incremental theory of personality intervention targeted a belief system that was thought to give rise to a pattern of attributions, but did not attempt to directly change hostile intent attributions.

The incremental theory has some alignment with the stress-is-enhancing mindset (Crum, Salovey, & Achor, 2013). The latter involves the mindset that one's stress responses can be positive and energizing and can help one address and overcome the stressor. This should also reduce "threat-type" responses to stressors, and yield patterns of cortisol reactivity that are analogous to the incremental theory of personality. The difference between the two is that the incremental theory of personality focuses on people's appraisals of the external stimulus (the stressful event) and the stress-is-enhancing mindset focuses on people's appraisals of the internal stimulus (your ongoing stress response). An interesting future direction could be to combine these two approaches into a single intervention; such an intervention would presumably convey that negative, stressful events *and* negative stress responses can be changed and improved over time.

NUANCES AND MISCONCEPTIONS

Although the incremental theory of personality intervention can have replicable effects, it relies on a number of nuances that we think are important for its effectiveness. The first is that the intervention does not seek to teach an extreme incremental theory of personality so much as it seeks to reduce the extreme entity theory. Said differently, for the intervention to work adolescents do not need to believe that *all* people can *greatly* change at any time or in any social circumstances—instead, they probably only need to have a reasonable doubt about the assumption that people's characteristics cannot *ever* change. The former might be tough for many students to believe; the latter might provide a basis for optimistic outlooks. The intervention simply conveys that it is *possible* for people to change, under the right conditions, with the right support, and with sufficient motivation on behalf of the person seeking to change.

Another nuance is that the intervention does not argue that you deserve to be bullied or excluded (which could imply you have weak social skills that need to be improved) or that you are responsible for changing every peer who is unkind or aggressive. Such a message could have two negative side effects: It could cause adolescents to blame themselves if their peers do not change, or it could cause adolescents to put themselves into dangerous situations where change is unlikely but harm at the hands of the peer is likely. The incremental theory of personality intervention makes the argument that change happens in many ways—sometimes, just through chronological maturation, or natural life transitions—and it is not any one person's responsibility to change another person. But, regardless of how change happens, it is always possible.

Finally, as the intervention begins to be tested in clinical settings (Schleider & Weisz, 2016), one open question concerns how the intervention is presented to participants. In the universal, preventative settings where the intervention was initially tested, it has been framed as a survey about the transition to high school, but participants have not been told that they are getting an "intervention" designed to help them. The goal, as noted, is to be autonomy supportive and prevent reactance (see also Yeager et al., 2018). However, adolescents who are seeking treatment for clinically elevated mental health problems, such as depression and anxiety, may be aware that they are being treated and actively seek out treatment. An intriguing question is whether the intervention needs to be "stealthy" or not (see Walton & Wilson, 2018; Yeager & Walton, 2011, for discussions). (We are grateful to Jessica Schleider, a psychological scientist at Stony Brook University, for suggesting this important future direction for research.)

IMPLICATIONS FOR PRACTICE

This research has implications for how schools and parents talk about and address bullying. Research on *essentialism* (Gelman, 2004), which refers to social judgments that focus on a person's or group's fixed "essence," raises the concern that describing socially aggressive students with generic noun phrases (e.g., "bullies" or "victims" or "troublemakers") could contribute to an entity theory culture and climate. Using generic phrases, defined as statements that take the form "bullies do X" (or, in past studies, "bears eat ants") to describe the characteristics or behaviors of groups of individuals, has led listeners to infer that the group's characteristics or behaviors are rooted in a deep-seated, inherent "essence" that cannot be changed (Cimpian & Markman, 2011; Gelman, Star, & Flukes, 2002). Such judgments are at the root of the entity theory of personality.

An implication of our research, then, is that school policies seeking to reduce bullying and improve coping with social conflict, but that describes the behavior of "bullies," could contribute to the consequences of an entity theory—consequences such as a desire for revenge or poorer coping. Indeed, a related argument has been made in the context of youth violence in the 1990s, including the use of fixed labels (e.g., "superpredator") to describe deviant youth (Dodge, 2008; see also Yeager & Miu, 2011). It may be more effective for schools and parents to focus on *behaviors,* not *people* (i.e., "bullying" not "bullies") and also to focus on the underlying, malleable reasons why some of their peers might engage in that behavior—such as their misguided desire to make themselves feel better, or their insecurity with their own social status.

IMPLICATIONS FOR PSYCHOLOGICAL THEORY

The research on the incremental theory of intervention has contributed to psychological theory by offering a means for bridging prominent theoretical models in different areas of psychology. The first bridge has been between implicit theories models of coping (Dweck & Leggett, 1988) and attribution theory (Kelley, 1973; Weiner, 1985). Fixed-trait attributions (vs. modifiable-cause attributions) for a specific situation have long held a prominent place in cognitive models of depression (Beck, 2008). But a challenge for the application of attribution theory to the treatment of internalizing or externalizing has been to devise methods that are not case based but instead lead individuals to chronically make modifiable-cause attributions across situations. A theoretical contribution of implicit theories models has been to describe the "meaning system" in which attributions reside (Molden & Dweck, 2006), and that can shape attributions in specific situations that are distinct from the situations discussed during a reattribution manipulation.

A second bridge has been between the implicit theories models of coping and the BPS model of challenge and threat (Blascovich & Tomaka, 1996; Jamieson et al., 2018; Yeager et al., 2016). This has been one of our most exciting and generative advances in recent years, because it has led to new theoretical insights in both models—in addition to the new, integrative perspective on stress and coping. As noted, key to the BPS model is an individual's appraisal of the demand (the stressor) and the resources (the ability to cope with the stressor); the ratio of these two appraisals determines physiological responses that are characteristic of "threat" versus "challenge." But the BPS model has not focused on why some individuals might chronically make the appraisal that they do not have the resources to meet the demands they are facing. The integration with implicit theories models (e.g., Jamieson et al., 2018) provides one means to explain this. Second, research on implicit theories of personality had previously found that this very socially focused intervention had surprising effects on academic outcomes (Yeager et al., 2014). This was a bit of a puzzle, since the intervention did not mention academic motivation or performance. The BPS model, however, provided theoretical grounding for it; as mentioned, mediation analysis conducted with data collected by Jamieson (Yeager et al., 2016, Study 1) identified psychobiological mechanisms, such as reductions in the experience of lingering threat-type stress responses to social stressors that could interfere with cognition and performance.

FUTURE DIRECTIONS

Apart from research on the implications for practice and theory noted above, we see at least three exciting avenues for future research. The first is to continue to replicate the effects of the intervention and identify the subgroups and school contexts where effects are weaker and stronger. This will be critical for understanding the public health impact of the intervention, but it is also for advancing mindset × context theory, which may apply to many kinds of wise interventions.

The second future direction is to continue to understand the recursive (or self-reinforcing) processes (Cohen, Garcia, Purdie-Vaughns, Apfel, & Brzustoski, 2009; Walton & Wilson, 2018) that sustain the treatment effects long after the treatment administration has ended. One way to do so is by carrying out finer-grained research on moment-to-moment stress processes. This could co-occur with ambulatory measurement of cardiovascular responses to provide a more precise picture about when implicit theories improve coping outcomes over time.

Another way to examine recursive processes is to measure the emergent social interactions and access to resources that might result from an incremental theory. Presumably, an intervention that promotes more adaptive stress responses might also embolden adolescents to seek out new and more variable social relationships. Those relationships might then provide a buffer from real-world adversities, or even reduce the prevalence of bullying or exclusion. In general, an important possible mechanism for enduring effects of the intervention is changes in the social world brought about by personal agency (see Walton & Wilson, 2018, Figure 1C).

A primary future direction for our research groups is to think more about developmental timing (Dahl, Allen, Wilbrecht, & Suleiman, 2018; Yeager et al., 2018). What is the optimal time—in terms of chronological age, in terms of pubertal maturation, and in terms of educational or professional transitions—to change mindsets? We have presumed that the change in mindset is best done at the beginning of a school transition (Miu & Yeager, 2015; Yeager et al., 2014), but this has not been directly tested in a sample that controls for differences across school systems. Should implicit theories be changed preventatively, well before the socially challenging start of high school? Could this depend on pubertal timing—and therefore, vary across gender, racial, and ethnic groups since groups differ in the onset of pubertal maturation? Advances in hormone assays that indicate pubertal maturation (i.e., testosterone and estradiol) and validation of self-reported pubertal indices will make tests of these questions more feasible than before. Now that the intervention can be made precise, lasting one session, then research can be carried out on when and how it can best be administered and how it interacts with development.

Finally, now that the intervention and its mechanisms have been studied in the context of one socially trying circumstance—peer victimization and exclusion during the transition to high school—we think an important future direction is to examine its application to other social difficulties. How could the intervention help individuals transitioning to college or the workplace and struggling to feel included? We are excited to see how the intervention could be adapted and evaluated in these or other contexts.

ACKNOWLEDGMENTS

Support for writing this chapter came in part from the Eunice Kennedy Shriver National Institute of Child Health and Human Development (R01 HD084772-01), the Raikes Foundation, the William T. Grant Foundation, and Hope Lab. This research was supported by grant, P2CHD042849, Population Research Center, awarded to the Population Research Center at The University of Texas at Austin by the Eunice Kennedy Shriver National Institute of Child Health and Human Development. The content is solely the responsibility of the authors and does not necessarily represent the official views of the National Institutes of Health.

REFERENCES

Aronson, E. (1999). The power of self-persuasion. *American Psychologist, 54*(11), 875–884.

Aronson, J. M., Fried, C. B., & Good, C. (2002). Reducing the effects of stereotype threat on African American college students by shaping theories of intelligence. *Journal of Experimental Social Psychology, 38*(2), 113–125.

Beck, A. T. (2008). The evolution of the cognitive model of depression and its neurobiological correlates. *American Journal of Psychiatry, 165*(8), 969–977.

Blascovich, J., & Tomaka, J. (1996). The biopsychosocial model of arousal regulation. In M. P. Zanna (Ed.), *Advances in experimental social psychology* (Vol. 28, pp. 1–51). Cambridge, MA: Academic Press.

Calvete, E., Fernández-Gonzalez, L., Orue, I., Echezarraga, A., Royuela-Colomer, E., Cortazar, N., . . . Yeager, D. S. (2019). The effect of an intervention teaching adolescents that people can change on depressive symptoms, cognitive schemas, and hypothalamic-pituitary–adrenal axis hormones. *Journal of Abnormal Child Psychology, 47,* 1533–1546.

Chiu, C., Hong, Y., & Dweck, C. S. (1997). Lay dispositionism and implicit theories of personality. *Journal of Personality and Social Psychology, 73*(1), 19–30.

Cimpian, A., & Markman, E. M. (2011). The generic/nongeneric distinction influences how children interpret new information about social others. *Child Development, 82*(2), 471–492.

Cohen, G. L., Garcia, J., Purdie-Vaughns, V., Apfel, N., & Brzustoski, P. (2009). Recursive processes in self-affirmation: Intervening to close the minority achievement gap. *Science, 324*(5925), 400–403.

Cohen, S., Kamarck, T., & Mermelstein, R. (1983). A global measure of perceived stress. *Journal of Health and Social Behavior, 24*(4), 385–396.

Coleman, J. S. (1961). *The adolescent society.* New York: Free Press of Glencoe.

Crosnoe, R. (2011). *Fitting in, standing out: Navigating the social challenges of high school to get an education.* New York: Cambridge University Press.

Crum, A. J., Salovey, P., & Achor, S. (2013). Rethinking stress: The role of mindsets in determining the stress response. *Journal of Personality and Social Psychology, 104*(4), 716–733.

Dahl, R. E., Allen, N. B., Wilbrecht, L., & Suleiman, A. B. (2018). Importance of investing in adolescence from a developmental science perspective. *Nature, 554*(7693), 441–450.

Deci, E. L., & Ryan, R. M. (1985). *Intrinsic motivation and self-determination in human behavior.* New York: Plenum Press.

Dickerson, S. S., & Kemeny, M. E. (2004). Acute stressors and cortisol responses: A theoretical integration and synthesis of laboratory research. *Psychological Bulletin, 130*(3), 355–391.

Dodge, K. A. (2008). Framing public policy and prevention of chronic violence in American youths. *American Psychologist, 63*(7), 573–590.

Dodge, K. A., & Frame, C. L. (1982). Social cognitive biases and deficits in aggressive boys. *Child Development, 53*(3), 620–635.

Dodge, K. A., Godwin, J., & Conduct Problems Prevention Research Group. (2013).

Social-information-processing patterns mediate the impact of preventive intervention on adolescent antisocial behavior. *Psychological Science, 24*(4), 456–465.

Dweck, C. S. (1975). The role of expectations and attributions in the alleviation of learned helplessness. *Journal of Personality and Social Psychology, 31*(4), 674–685.

Dweck, C. S., Chiu, C., & Hong, Y. (1995). Implicit theories and their role in judgments and reactions: A world from two perspectives. *Psychological Inquiry, 6*(4), 267–285.

Dweck, C. S., & Leggett, E. L. (1988). A social-cognitive approach to motivation and personality. *Psychological Review, 95*(2), 256–273.

Dweck, C. S., & Yeager, D. S. (2019). Mindsets: A view from two eras. *Perspectives on Psychological Science, 14*(3), 481–496.

Erdley, C. A., Loomis, C. C., Cain, K. M., & Dumas-Hines, F. (1997). Relations among children's social goals, implicit personality theories, and responses to social failure. *Developmental Psychology, 33*(2), 263–272.

Frenz, F. (2013). *How to be human: Diary of an autistic girl.* Berkeley, CA: Creston Books.

Gelman, S. A. (2004). Psychological essentialism in children. *Trends in Cognitive Sciences, 8*(9), 404–409.

Gelman, S. A., Star, J. R., & Flukes, J. (2002). Children's use of generics in inductive inferences. *Journal of Cognition and Development, 3*(2), 179–199.

George, M. J., & Odgers, C. L. (2015). Seven fears and the science of how mobile technologies may be influencing adolescents in the digital age. *Perspectives on Psychological Science, 10*(6), 832–851.

Gervey, B. M., Chiu, C.-Y., Hong, Y.-Y., & Dweck, C. S. (1999). Differential use of person information in decisions about guilt versus innocence: The role of implicit theories. *Personality and Social Psychology Bulletin, 25*(1), 17–27.

Goodyer, I. M., Park, R. J., Netherton, C. M., & Herbert, J. (2001). Possible role of cortisol and dehydroepiandrosterone in human development and psychopathology. *British Journal of Psychiatry, 179*(3), 243–249.

Greenberg, M. T., & Abenavoli, R. (2017). Universal interventions: Fully exploring their impacts and potential to produce population-level impacts. *Journal of Research on Educational Effectiveness, 10*(1), 40–67.

Gunnar, M. R., & Quevedo, K. (2007). The neurobiology of stress and development. *Annual Review of Psychology, 58*(1), 145–173.

Halperin, E., Russell, A. G., Trzesniewski, K. H., Gross, J. J., & Dweck, C. S. (2011). Promoting the Middle East peace process by changing beliefs about group malleability. *Science, 333*(6050), 1767–1769.

Hammen, C. (2005). Stress and depression. *Annual Review of Clinical Psychology, 1*(1), 293–319.

Hawley, P. H. (1999). The ontogenesis of social dominance: A strategy-based evolutionary perspective. *Developmental Review, 19*(1), 97–132.

Hong, J. S., & Espelage, D. L. (2012). A review of research on bullying and peer victimization in school: An ecological system analysis. *Aggression and Violent Behavior, 17*(4), 311–322.

Jamieson, J. P., Hangen, E. J., Lee, H. Y., & Yeager, D. S. (2018). Capitalizing on appraisal processes to improve affective responses to social stress. *Emotion Review, 10*(1), 30–39.

Janoff-Bulman, R. (1979). Characterological versus behavioral self-blame: Inquiries into depression and rape. *Journal of Personality and Social Psychology, 37*(10), 1798–1809.

Juster, R.-P., McEwen, B. S., & Lupien, S. J. (2010). Allostatic load biomarkers of chronic stress and impact on health and cognition. *Neuroscience and Biobehavioral Reviews, 35*(1), 2–16.

Kelley, H. H. (1973). The processes of causal attribution. *American Psychologist, 28*(2), 107–128.

Kirschbaum, C., Pirke, K.-M., & Hellhammer, D. H. (1993). The "Trier Social Stress Test"—a tool for investigating psychobiological stress responses in a laboratory setting. *Neuropsychobiology, 28*(1–2), 76–81.

Kovacs, M. (2003). *Children's Depression Inventory (CDI): Technical manual update.* North Tonawanda, NY: Multi-Health Systems.

Lee, H. Y., Jamieson, J. P., Josephs, R. A., Reis, H. T., Beevers, C. G., & Yeager, D. S. (2020). *Adolescents' implicit theories of personality shape their responses to social media stressors.* Unpublished manuscript, University of Texas at Austin, Austin, TX.

Lee, H. Y., Jamieson, J. P., Miu, A. S., Josephs, R. A., & Yeager, D. S. (2019). An entity theory of intelligence predicts higher cortisol levels when high school grades are declining. *Child Development, 90,* e849–e867.

Levy, S. R., & Dweck, C. S. (1999). The impact of children's static versus dynamic conceptions of people on stereotype formation. *Child Development, 70*(5), 1163–1180.

Levy, S. R., Stroessner, S. J., & Dweck, C. S. (1998). Stereotype formation and endorsement: The role of implicit theories. *Journal of Personality and Social Psychology, 74*(6), 1421–1436.

Lieberman, J. D., Solomon, S., Greenberg, J., & McGregor, H. A. (1999). A hot new way to measure aggression: Hot sauce allocation. *Aggressive Behavior, 25*(5), 331–348.

Lupien, S. J., McEwen, B. S., Gunnar, M. R., & Heim, C. (2009). Effects of stress throughout the lifespan on the brain, behaviour and cognition. *Nature Reviews Neuroscience, 10*(6), 434–445.

Mendes, W. B., & Park, J. (2014). Neurobiological concomitants of motivational states. In A. J. Elliot (Ed.), *Advances in motivation science* (pp. 233–270). Waltham, MA: Elsevier.

Miu, A. S., & Yeager, D. S. (2015). Preventing symptoms of depression by teaching adolescents that people can change: Effects of a brief incremental theory of personality intervention at 9-month follow-up. *Clinical Psychological Science, 3*(5), 726–743.

Molden, D. C., & Dweck, C. S. (2006). Finding "meaning" in psychology: A lay theories approach to self-regulation, social perception, and social development. *American Psychologist, 61*(3), 192–203.

Molden, D. C., Plaks, J. E., & Dweck, C. S. (2006). "Meaningful" social inferences: Effects of implicit theories on inferential processes. *Journal of Experimental Social Psychology, 42*(6), 738–752.

Plaks, J. E. (2017). Implicit theories: Assumptions that shape social and moral cognition. In J. M. Olson (Ed.), *Advances in experimental social psychology* (Vol. 56, pp. 259–310). Cambridge, MA: Academic Press.

Prinstein, M. J., Boergers, J., & Vernberg, E. M. (2001). Overt and relational aggression in adolescents: Social-psychological adjustment of aggressors and victims. *Journal of Clinical Child Psychology, 30*(4), 479–491.

Rattan, A., & Dweck, C. S. (2010). Who confronts prejudice?: The role of implicit theories in the motivation to confront prejudice. *Psychological Science, 21*(7), 952–959.

Ryan, A. M., & Shim, S. S. (2008). An exploration of young adolescents' social achievement goals and social adjustment in middle school. *Journal of Educational Psychology, 100*(3), 672–687.

Sapolsky, R. M. (2000). Stress hormones: Good and bad. *Neurobiology of Disease, 7*(5), 540–542.

Schleider, J. L., Abel, M. R., & Weisz, J. R. (2015). Implicit theories and youth mental health problems: A random-effects meta-analysis. *Clinical Psychology Review, 35,* 1–9.

Schleider, J. L., & Weisz, J. R. (2016). Reducing risk for anxiety and depression in adolescents: Effects of a single-session intervention teaching that personality can change. *Behaviour Research and Therapy, 87,* 170–181.

Seo, E. J., Lee, H. Y., Jamieson, J., Beevers, C., Reis, H., Josephs, R., & Yeager, D. S. (2019). *Trait attributions and threat appraisals explain why an entity theory of personality predicts greater internalizing symptoms during adolescence.* Unpublished manuscript, University of Texas at Austin.

Slavich, G. M., O'Donovan, A., Epel, E. S., & Kemeny, M. E. (2010). Black sheep get the blues: A psychobiological model of social rejection and depression. *Neuroscience and Biobehavioral Reviews, 35*(1), 39–45.

Staufenbiel, S. M., Penninx, B. W., Spijker, A. T., Elzinga, B. M., & van Rossum, E. F. (2013). Hair cortisol, stress exposure, and mental health in humans: A systematic review. *Psychoneuroendocrinology, 38*(8), 1220–1235.

Twenge, J. M., Joiner, T. E., Rogers, M. L., & Martin, G. N. (2017). Increases in depressive symptoms, suicide-related outcomes, and suicide rates among US adolescents after 2010 and links to increased new media screen time. *Clinical Psychological Science, 6*(1), 3–17.

Underwood, M. K., & Ehrenreich, S. E. (2017). The power and the pain of adolescents' digital communication: Cyber victimization and the perils of lurking. *American Psychologist, 72*(2), 144–158.

Vansteenkiste, M., Simons, J., Lens, W., Sheldon, K. M., & Deci, E. L. (2004). Motivating learning, performance, and persistence: The synergistic effects of intrinsic goal contents and autonomy-supportive contexts. *Journal of Personality and Social Psychology, 87*(2), 246–260.

Walton, G. M., & Cohen, G. L. (2011). A brief social-belonging intervention improves academic and health outcomes of minority students. *Science, 331*(6023), 1447–1451.

Walton, G. M., Cohen, G. L., Cwir, D., & Spencer, S. J. (2012). Mere belonging: The power of social connections. *Journal of Personality and Social Psychology, 102*(3), 513–532.

Walton, G. M., & Wilson, T. D. (2018). Wise interventions: Psychological remedies for social and personal problems. *Psychological Review, 125*(5), 617–655.

Weiner, B. (1985). An attributional theory of emotion and motivation. *Psychological Review, 92*(4), 548–573.

Williams, K. D., & Jarvis, B. (2006). Cyberball: A program for use in research on interpersonal ostracism and acceptance. *Behavior Research Methods, Instruments, and Computers, 38*(1), 174–180.

Wolf, W., Levordashka, A., Ruff, J. R., Kraaijeveld, S., Lueckmann, J.-M., & Williams, K. D. (2015). Ostracism online: A social media ostracism paradigm. *Behavior Research Methods, 47*(2), 361–373.

Yang, M., Lee, H. Y., Crosnoe, R., & Yeager, D. S. (2020). *The cognitive cost of thinking you're popular in high school.* Unpublished manuscript, University of Texas at Austin, Austin, TX.

Yeager, D. S., Dahl, R. E., & Dweck, C. S. (2018). Why interventions to influence adolescent behavior often fail but could succeed. *Perspectives on Psychological Science, 13*(1), 101–122.

Yeager, D. S., & Dweck, C. S. (2012). Mindsets that promote resilience: When students believe that personal characteristics can be developed. *Educational Psychologist, 47*(4), 302–314.

Yeager, D. S., Johnson, R., Spitzer, B. J., Trzesniewski, K. H., Powers, J., & Dweck, C. S. (2014). The far-reaching effects of believing people can change: Implicit theories of personality shape stress, health, and achievement during adolescence. *Journal of Personality and Social Psychology, 106*(6), 867–884.

Yeager, D. S., Lee, H. Y., & Jamieson, J. P. (2016). How to improve adolescent stress responses: Insights from integrating implicit theories of personality and biopsychosocial models. *Psychological Science, 27*(8), 1078–1091.

Yeager, D. S., & Miu, A. S. (2011). Implicit theories of personality predict motivation to use prosocial coping strategies after bullying in high school. In E. Frydenberg & G. Reevy (Eds.), *Personality, stress and coping: Implications for education* (pp. 47–62). Charlotte, NC: Information Age.

Yeager, D. S., Miu, A. S., Powers, J., & Dweck, C. S. (2013). Implicit theories of personality and attributions of hostile intent: A meta-analysis, an experiment, and a longitudinal intervention. *Child Development, 84*(5), 1651–1667.

Yeager, D. S., Trzesniewski, K. H., & Dweck, C. S. (2013). An implicit theories of personality intervention reduces adolescent aggression in response to victimization and exclusion. *Child Development, 84*(3), 970–988.

Yeager, D. S., Trzesniewski, K. H., Tirri, K., Nokelainen, P., & Dweck, C. S. (2011). Adolescents' implicit theories predict desire for vengeance after peer conflicts: Correlational and experimental evidence. *Developmental Psychology, 47*(4), 1090–1107.

Yeager, D. S., & Walton, G. M. (2011). Social-psychological interventions in education: They're not magic. *Review of Educational Research, 81*(2), 267–301.

CHAPTER 14

The Empathic-Discipline Intervention

Jason Anthony Okonofua and Michael Ruiz

Suspensions are the most common form of exclusionary discipline, discipline that removes students from the learning environment. They are associated with a negative consequence for education and life outcomes. Research suggests that suspensions result from a default punitive approach to curb student misbehavior. In this chapter, we detail an intervention designed to shift teachers' mindsets about misbehavior to show more empathy. An empathic mindset is one in which teachers value students' perspectives, nurture students' growth, and prioritize the maintenance of positive relationships with students. We describe lab studies and a large-scale field experiment that demonstrate how the shift from a punitive to empathic mindset can produce more productive outcomes for both teachers and students. The intervention ultimately halved suspension rates in middle school across three school districts (*N* = 1,682 students) and helped students with a history of suspension to maintain a perception of respect from adults at their school. This chapter situates the intervention in the wise intervention framework with information about the content and delivery of the intervention and the mechanisms by which it operates. We end with details about implications of the intervention for theory and integration with policy and practice.

BACKGROUND

Students across the United States are removed from learning environments by way of suspensions at an alarming rate. In 2011, more than 5 million students were suspended from schools throughout the United States, which marked a substantial increase since a few decades ago when less than 2 million students were suspended in 1974 (Losen & Wald, 2003; U.S. Department of Education, Office for Civil Rights, 2016). These rates are of particular concern, because suspensions are an exclusionary discipline that removes students from environments where learning is the priority. And some students, especially those with multiple suspensions, are placed in an environment where they are more likely to enter a life trajectory of school dropout, unemployment, mental and physical illness, and incarceration—a process called the "school-to-prison pipeline" (Jordan, Lara, & McPartland, 1996; Gottfried, 2010; Couch & Fairlie, 2010; Pager, Western, & Sugie, 2009; Boynton, O'Hara, Covault, Scott, & Tennen, 2014; Rocque & Paternoster, 2011). Further, one student's discipline problems can affect other students' outcomes in the classroom (Bill and Melinda Gates Foundation, 2013; Ferguson, 2012). The effects of discipline problems can also extend beyond the school. Recent research showed that taxpayers must contribute millions of dollars to offset the lifetime consequences of school suspensions for society at large—by way of incarceration costs and lower future earnings and tax revenue (Rumberger & Losen, 2017).

These effects have exploded concurrently with zero-tolerance policies put in place to deter threats to school safety with punitive repercussions. An unexpected drawback lies in how suspensions have become a more common response to relatively minor and ambiguous misbehaviors compared to weapon or drug possession (Skiba, 2014). In recent years, the most common reasons for office referrals that result in suspensions are for misbehaviors classified as insubordination or classroom disruption. However, according to Skiba, "no data exist to show that out-of-school suspensions and expulsions reduce disruption or improve school climate" (p. 27).

Stigmatized groups are impacted by these school policies at a disproportionate rate (Pager et al., 2009). Research has shown that lesbian, bisexual, gay, transgender, Black, Latinx, Native American, and students in special education are at a heightened risk for suspension from school (U.S. Department of Education, 2014; Himmelstein & Bruckner, 2011; Poteat, Scheer, & Chong, 2015). For example, Black students are two to three times more likely to be suspended than their White peers (Fabelo et al., 2011). These disparities exist from preschool through high school (Skiba et al., 2011) with Black preschoolers being 3.6 times more likely to receive a suspension than White preschoolers (U.S. Department of Education, Office for Civil Rights, 2016).

Teacher–student relationships suffer under these punitive—nonempathic—conditions. For teachers, they become disheartened when they feel that dealing with misbehavior gets in the way of their teaching goals (Johnson, Yarrow, Rochkind, & Ott, 2009). For students, they can feel threatened and question their teachers' intentions when teachers are more likely to critically respond to them without communicating that they care (e.g., Yeager et al., 2014). This process can be of particular risk for students from stigmatized groups who may already be vigilant to cues that they do not belong at school (Goyer et al., 2019) or will not receive fair treatment (Mendoza-Denton, Downey, Purdie, Davis, & Pietrzak, 2002; Steele, 1997). Students tend to behave with more defiance and less cooperation when they perceive a teacher to be an untrustworthy authority figure (Fenning & Rose, 2007; Gregory & Weinstein, 2008)—a process that is exacerbated for stigmatized students who may already expect unfair treatment. In this way, the default punitive context can deteriorate the quality of teacher–student relationships and cause both teachers and students to feel their goals cannot be reached in school (Okonofua, Walton, & Eberhardt, 2016). Discipline problems can then arise, a process also especially likely for students from stigmatized groups.

Public and private institutions have attempted a variety of strategies to curb the exorbitant rates of exclusionary discipline. From a policy standpoint, many states have enacted laws that prohibit schools from suspending students for reasons such as insubordination or "defiance" (Pupil Discipline . . . , 2015). From a skill-building standpoint, companies and organizations have partnered with school districts to invest in sweeping professional development and structural changes through programs like positive behavioral interventions and supports (Reinke, Herman, & Stormont, 2013). Pointedly, these efforts do not precisely address a major source and effect of discipline problems: fraught teacher–student relationships. Approaches from these standpoints rightfully curb a punitive component of the context, yet lack a promotion of enhanced interpersonal communication (e.g., empathy) to take its place.

The empathic-discipline intervention aims to address that lack of an interpersonal approach head-on with an aim to help teachers sustain high-quality, trusting teacher–student relationships over time to prevent discipline problems. The theory underlying the intervention is based on two core findings about the role of teachers: (1) over time, processes of labeling students can contribute to discipline problems, and (2) valuing students' perspectives and reappraising responses to students' misbehavior can disrupt label-making processes in relationships. Across these aspects of the intervention, teachers are viewed as pivotal "gatekeepers" who are in a position to construct the context for better relationships for entire classrooms of students. The goal of the intervention is to reduce the likelihood that a punitive mindset will lead teachers to label misbehaving students as troublemakers and respond to them with severe discipline (see Figure 14.1).

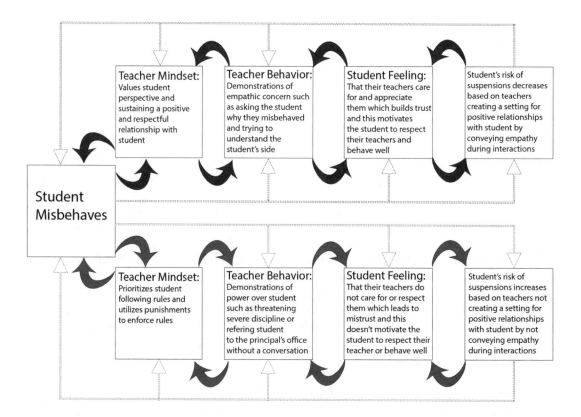

FIGURE 14.1. Empathic discipline (top path) activates empathic mindset, as opposed to default punitive mindset (bottom path). In turn, a more productive recursive cycle ensues.

What is the default punitive mindset? Teacher responses to misbehavior can be shaped by the extent to which a teacher thinks the misbehavior will be an ongoing or consistent hindrance. Teachers can come to think misbehavior will be ongoing when they attribute the misbehavior to an inherent characteristic of the student. We refer to this belief as a "punitive mindset." In turn, teachers may seek more punitive discipline, often discipline that removes the student from the learning environment (e.g., referral to the principal's office). Researchers evidenced such a belief and process in a series of experiments about race disparities in disciplinary action (Okonofua & Eberhardt, 2015). Teachers were presented with a series of misbehaviors by a student and were asked questions about how they would respond. Teachers were more likely to respond to a student they labeled as a troublemaker with a desire for more severe discipline and were more likely to see the student being suspended in the future. The troublemaker labeling was thus pivotal in the discipline process and it was a process that played out over the course of multiple misbehaviors. Further, teachers became more distressed and wanted more severe discipline from one misbehavior to the next, and this escalation was steeper for students viewed as troublemakers. All of these effects were most pronounced if the student was assumed to be Black, because the student was more likely to be a troublemaker if assumed to be Black as compared to White. However, for either a Black or White student, being labeled a troublemaker predicted the process of harsh responses to misbehavior. The empathic-discipline intervention seeks to replace this punitive mindset with an empathic mindset, one that appreciates the potential for students to behave better and for relationships with students to improve over time.

PSYCHOLOGICAL PROCESSES

The adoption of the empathic mindset creates opportunity to build respect, rather than mistrust, in a teacher's relationship with a student who has misbehaved. Over time, each mindset (punitive or empathic) can contribute to recursive cycles such that either the relationship deteriorates and thus discipline problems grow, or a positive relationship remains intact and thus future conflict is prevented (see Figure 14.1). In this section, we describe the process by which a psychological component (a teacher's mindset and a student's feeling of respect) and a behavioral component (how a teacher and a student then respond to each other) can contribute to recursive cycles that ultimately lead to severe exclusionary discipline, or not.

A teacher can have distinct mindsets or models for dealing with student misbehavior. As mentioned, a teacher's punitive mindset can lead him or her to view misbehavior as a stable pattern and thus respond with severe or exclusionary punishment. Also, due to many teachers entering the profession with a desire to support and help children grow (Johnson et al., 2009), that same teacher might also harbor an empathic mindset, one that prioritizes the maintenance of high-quality and productive relationships with students who struggle, including students who misbehave. Each mindset can be activated and affects the way a teacher will respond to misbehavior. When the empathic mindset is activated teachers are less likely to label a misbehaving student as a troublemaker and are more likely to want to find out more about why the student misbehaved.

The researchers conducted an initial experiment to determine whether a targeted exercise could activate distinct mindsets in teachers and in turn shift their responses to a student's misbehavior. K–12 teachers (N = 39) were randomly assigned to engage with reminders of how punishment (punitive mindset) or good teacher–student relationships (empathic mindset) is the solution to misbehavior (Okonofua, Paunesku, & Walton, 2016). It is important to note that, on average, these teachers had 14 years of experience as teachers. The brief article did not include information that was likely new to the teachers—rather, the article served as a structured reminder, a primer of a preexisting representation of quality relationships with students. Teachers in the empathic mindset condition were less likely to label the hypothetical student a troublemaker following the misbehavior. Further, when asked how they would respond to the misbehavior, teachers were more considerate of the student's perspective (e.g., "Ask the student why he or she was misbehaving") in the empathic-mindset condition. In the control condition, teachers were more punitive (e.g., threaten the student, assign detention, or involve the principal).

Students make sense of and respond to different kinds of treatment from teachers. For example, the extent to which students question their sense of belonging at school is associated with how they feel teachers treat them (Goyer et al., 2019). Students' responses can be directly connected to the mindsets that teachers act on in response to misbehavior. When a teacher's punitive mindset is activated, his or her response can lead a student to feel less respect for the teacher and less motivation to behave well. When teachers act on an empathic mindset in response to a student's misbehavior, might that process be curbed?

In a second experiment, the researchers sought to determine the impact on students of teachers' punitive or empathic mindsets. Might students feel more respect for a teacher and more motivation to behave well when a teacher responded to their misbehavior with an activated empathic mindset?

College students (N = 302) were prompted to reflect on their experiences as middle school students and answered questions about how they would feel in a hypothetical scenario about their misbehavior in class. Each participant was randomly assigned to either read that the teacher threatened him or her, assigned detention, and involved the principal (punitive control) or read that the teacher asked why the misbehavior occurred and rearranged the classroom to make it more conducive to better behavior (empathic mindset). Compared to the control condition, participants who read about a teacher with the empathic mindset were more likely to think the teacher deserved respect and were more motivated to behave well and follow instructions. While there were some limitations to this experiment,[1] these findings were noteworthy. The findings suggest that a student response to the default punitive mindset is less respect and motivation to behave well. Further, this response can be reversed when teachers' empathic mindset is activated.

These preliminary experiments provide theoretical insight into how distinct teacher mindsets can be activated through a strategic reminder of their values and the benefits of valuing students' perspectives. It also shows how an empathic mindset can set forth a cycle of more productive behaviors from both the teacher and student thereafter. When teachers' empathic mindset was activated, they were more likely to want to get perspective (e.g., have a conversation with the student) and to respond to the student's situation (e.g., rearrange the physical structure of the classroom). In turn, the student felt more respect in the relationship and became more interested in behaving well. Taken together,

---

[1] Ideally, middle school students would have been the participants in this study. However, we decided that college students would be better able to express how they would have felt in the situation.

while the findings are short term—based in scenarios—they suggest that a productive recursive process would ensue between the teacher and student.

The productive recursive process is coined "empathic discipline" and as a whole makes way for a mindset shift and a behavioral shift in the effects of discipline. The mindset shift pertains to the change in teachers' beliefs about students and their behavior. When teachers engage with materials that remind them of the powerful positive impact of quality teacher–student relationships—as opposed to a default punitive mindset—they become less likely to attribute a student's behavior to a rigid component of the student's character (i.e., labeling the student as a troublemaker). In turn, the student respects the teacher more and is more motivated to behave well in class in the future.

The behavioral component is evident in how the teacher and student interact in their behaviors toward each other. The teacher seeks to find out more about the student's perspective and how to use discipline as a vehicle to gain or maintain the student's respect and trust in the relationship. The student wants to follow the teacher's instructions and to behave well in the future. Over time, the quality of the teacher–student relationship is protected and there is a reduced likelihood of conflict in the future due to these intertwined mindset and behavioral shifts.

The empathic-discipline intervention is geared to offset the punitive path to discipline problems. It aims to shift teachers' mindsets away from default troublemaker labeling and punitive responses to misbehavior. Instead, it strategically highlights (1) listening to and seeking to understand students' perspective in periods of misbehavior, even when this perspective is not productive; (2) prioritizing and sustaining positive relationships with students, especially in times of misbehavior; and (3) helping students grow and improve within the context of a trusting relationship. The intervention seeks to remind teachers that they are in a unique position to do each of these three things, which will allow them to make meaningful contributions to their students' lives. In turn, teachers will create a context for students to feel more respect in the teacher–student relationship and be more motivated to behave well.

EMPIRICAL EVIDENCE

The researchers conducted a randomized controlled field experiment to test whether the effects described in the previous section can extend to actual teacher–student relationships and discipline rates. Can an opportunity for teachers to reflect on, articulate, and commit to an empathic mindset cause reductions in discipline problems?

Outcomes

The experiment was evaluated at five middle schools in three California districts with math teachers ($N = 31$) and students ($N = 1,682$; 52% female; 17% Asian, 2% Black, 54% Latino, 7% White, 20% other/unknown). The schools varied in the percentage of their student population that received free or reduced-price lunch, an indicator of socio-economic status (37%, 68%, 70%, 61%, and 62%, in order of largest to smallest total student enrollment at each of the five schools that participated).

In the experiment, math teachers were randomly assigned to engage either with modules about how technology use is important in involving students (control) or with modules about the importance of sustaining positive relationships with students by way of valuing and seeking to understand their perspectives, especially when students misbehave. In each module, teachers read brief articles and narratives about the topic, and answered questions about their understanding and experiences related to the topic.

Math teachers completed two online modules, a 45-minute session in the fall (October–November) and a 25-minute session in the winter (January–February).[2] All materials were delivered online such that teachers completed the sessions from their own computers and did so at their convenience during a 2-week window. The fall and spring time line was chosen to ensure that teachers had experiences with their current students before engaging in the first module—that is, teachers would be able to engage with the materials in a meaningful way that would directly apply to their students. The second module was designed to serve as a booster, or reminder, when the school year reconvened after holiday breaks.

As described earlier, suspensions are especially impactful because they remove students from the learning environment and they are significantly more common than other exclusionary disciplines, like expulsions or referrals to law enforcement. Further, this was the only discipline outcome schools tracked across each school district. This intervention halved year-long student suspension rates from 9.6 to 4.8% (see Figure 14.2). Similar to national suspension rates, control-condition suspension rates were highest among boys, Black and Latinx students, and students with a history of suspensions. The reduction in suspension rates was comparably large for the following groups: boys, from 14.6 to 8.4%; African Americans and Latinx, from 12.3 to 6.3%; and previously suspended students, from 51.2 to 29.4%.

There was also a notable shift in students' experiences of respect. Students were asked the extent to which they agreed with the statement "Teachers and other adults at my school treat me with respect." The intervention bolstered the respect of the most at-risk students and previously suspended students, perceived from all teachers and adults at their school. It is important to note that the felt respect was not solely from their math teacher but rather all teachers at the school. This point is further explained in the next section.

Mechanism

Did suspensions drop solely due to a change in math teachers' interactions or discipline standards with students, or did they drop, as well, because students experienced fewer suspensions from interactions with adults across school contexts (e.g., nonmath teachers)? Evidence suggests the latter.

Not only did students report experiencing greater respect from all their teachers at school (not just their math teacher) but records also indicated that the fewer suspensions were not likely due solely to fewer referrals for discipline from math teachers. One school district in the sample kept records of the faculty member who referred a student for ultimate suspension. Students from this school accounted for 33% of the full student sample.

---

[2]Math teachers were recruited because all students at the schools had one math teacher only. This allowed for a design that determines efficacy of the treatment with only one of the students' teachers. Otherwise, it would be difficult to determine effects on students if they had some teachers randomly assigned to the treatment condition and others to the control condition.

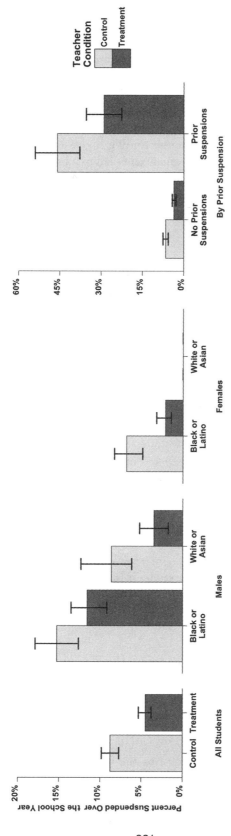

FIGURE 14.2. Middle school students (N = 1,682) whose math teacher (N = 31) completed the empathic-mindset intervention as compared to randomized control materials were half as likely to be suspended over the school year. From Okonofua, Paunesu, and Walton (2016). Error bars represent 95% confidence intervals after 10,000 bootstraps. Reprinted with permission from the authors.

In this school, students of math teachers who received the intervention were 55% less likely to be suspended from school (treatment = 5.4%, control = 12.1%). Yet, the effect was not due to a change only in math class. Only 7.4% of suspensions were referred by math teachers. Furthermore, all students referred for suspension by a math teacher were also referred for suspension by other faculty (e.g., a science teacher). Thus, even excluding suspensions referred by math teachers from the analysis yields an identical reduction in suspension rates. This supplemental finding suggests that, at least in this school, improving the experience with at least one teacher led to a broad improvement in student behavior across diverse classroom contexts. It notably also suggests that the effect was not merely due to math teachers being more lenient in their discipline practices nor to an improvement in students' behavior solely in math classes—rather, students' perceptions of and experiences in the entire school context became more productive and less conducive to discipline problems.

These findings suggest that part of the effect results from a shift in students' perceptions and experiences throughout the school and the school day. Students' entire school experiences can be improved when a single teacher presumably treats them as more deserving of respect and as having a valuable perspective. This is consistent with the aforementioned recursive process of respect in teacher–student relationships (see Figure 14.1). This is also consistent with the finding that the most at-risk students, those with a history of suspensions, were less likely to lose respect for adults at their school when they had a teacher who received the empathic-discipline intervention. It also suggests the importance of students' perspectives in this process (see Goyer et al., 2019).

Effects over Time

The intervention's effects lasted for several months. Teachers began participation in October and suspension records were evaluated for that entire school year. The sustained effects seem to also be associated with protecting teacher–student relationships from deterioration. This is evident in how, several months after the intervention, students with a history of suspension perceived more respect from adults at their school when they have a teacher with the empathic mindset, as opposed to not having it. Future research might explore outcomes beyond the year of the intervention, such as how teachers interact with new students in following years or how students interact with new teachers in the following years.

Heterogeneity

In the initial test of the intervention, the proportional reduction in suspension rates was comparable for all students. Also, due to certain groups being more at risk of receiving suspensions, the absolute impact was relatively larger for them (males: from 14.6 to 8.4%; African American and Latinos: from 12.3 to 6.3%; and previously suspended students: from 51.2 to 29.4%). The intervention was tested at only five schools and with only the math faculty at those schools ($N = 31$; 77% female; 39% sixth grade, 29% seventh grade, 32% eighth grade). While this can attest to the intervention's strength to bring about large and lasting effects with a small sample of high-impact players, it does not allow for definitive heterogeneity information.

Future research is needed to confirm more specific conditions for the intervention's efficacy. For example, randomized controlled trials are currently in place to evaluate the effects of teacher characteristics (e.g., race, gender, and stress) and school characteristics (e.g., school size, student demographics, and grade levels) on the extent to which the intervention reduces suspension rates (see "Future Directions" section).

COUSINS

The empathic-discipline intervention is a psychologically wise intervention (see Walton & Wilson, 2018) that focuses on relationships between teachers and students. How can the quality of these relationships be maintained over time? The value of pursuing answers to this question is not unique to school settings. For example, other interventions have focused on how to maintain relationship quality in marriages.

There are notable differences between the empathic-discipline intervention and interventions for romantic relationships. Romantic relationships involve equal status between partners and partners who have chosen to be connected. Further, the interventions often administer the treatment to both partners. However, teacher–student relationships are hierarchal in nature with teachers in a superior position to students. Teachers and students typically do not choose their relationships—rather, they are assigned. Yet, the similarities in the relationships (e.g., sustained contact over time, stress from interpersonal contact, and interconnected goals) can make interventions similar in theory.

Targeted psychological interventions can mitigate the deleterious effects of conflict in relationships. In one randomized controlled trial, researchers aimed to curb the decline in marital quality (Finkel, Slotter, Luchies, Walton, & Gross, 2013). Couples ($N = 120$) were assigned to either engage with control materials or engage with a treatment that encouraged them to consider a perspective other than their own as a way to reappraise their emotional responses to conflict in their relationship. Every 4 months for 24 months, all couples completed checkup activities about marital quality (e.g., satisfaction, trust). After the first 8 months, couples also completed activities to describe a "significant disagreement" or conflict during the preceding 4 months and reported how distressed they felt by answering questions such as "I am angry at my partner for his/her behavior during this conflict." At months 12, 16, and 20, couples in the treatment condition reappraised the conflict they reported for the preceding 4 months by responding to prompts that guided them to view the conflict as a "third party . . . who sees things from a neutral point of view." It also guided them to reflect on obstacles to getting that perspective and to make plans to make the best of disagreements by taking this kind of perspective during the next 4 months. Compared to couples in the control condition, couples that reappraised conflict by considering a perspective other than their own showed a significantly mitigated decline in relationship quality.

Why might getting a perspective other than one's own protect relationships from reductions in quality? In the reappraisal intervention, the researchers found that the benefits of the intervention were due to a reduction in conflict-related distress over time. The researchers also suggest that the effect was due to the couples in the reappraisal condition adopting an "adaptive framework" of wanting the best for all involved in the relationship (see Libby & Eibach, 2011, p. 234).

The empathic-discipline intervention and the reappraisal intervention are similar in key ways. They both focus on relationship-based processes that unfold over time, target shifts in how people make sense of conflict and distress, and use perspective-getting and empathic intentions to protect relationship quality. First, like the reappraisal intervention, the empathic-discipline intervention aims to combat a decline in relationship quality over time. Similar to marital quality, research shows that the quality of teacher–student relationships declines over time and ultimately contributes to discipline problems (e.g., Hamre & Pianta, 2001). Second, in both marital and teacher–student relationships, the decline in quality is connected to stress in times of conflict (e.g., when one or both persons feel disrespected; e.g., Johnson et al., 2009). Third, both interventions leverage a consideration of another person's perspective and an adaptive framework as a means to protect the quality of the relationship. Albeit, the reappraisal intervention involves considering the perspective of a neutral third-party's perspective of the relationship; both interventions aim for a person to think beyond his or her own perspective or the imagined perspective of the other person in the relationship. As in the reappraisal intervention, teachers exposed to the empathic-discipline intervention engaged in activities to remind them and guide them through the importance and benefits of getting students' perspectives—and not solely imagining them. Teachers were reminded to think about doing so especially when conflicts arise. Further, in both interventions, this was presented as something that can be difficult to do but worthwhile—and the worthwhile component is framed as such for all parties involved. Teachers who engaged with the empathic mindset were reminded that high-quality teacher–student relationships enhance both teachers' capacity to reach their teaching and career goals and students' capacity to reach their learning and life goals (see Okonofua, Walton, et al., 2016).

An underlying component of the similarities between these interventions lies in their focus on processes that unfold over time. Relationships are not one-time encounters—rather, they play out over time. Conflict early in a relationship can contribute to later conflict such that the magnitude of its detriment grows. The cycle of reverberating attitudes and behaviors exists in martial relationships and also in how teachers and students view and treat each other. It is critical for interventions to consider this dynamic (see Cohen, Garcia, Purdie-Vaughns, Apfel, & Brzustoski, 2009; Rosenthal & Jacobson, 1968; Walton & Cohen, 2011).

INTERVENTION CONTENT AND IMPLEMENTATION

Framing

Following past social-psychological interventions (e.g., Walton & Cohen, 2011), teachers were not told that they were receiving an intervention, that the exercise was intended to reduce discipline problems, or that teachers are biased in their discipline practices. Teachers could have interpreted that framing as controlling or as stigmatizing. Instead, teachers were treated as experts asked to offer their feedback on best practices and how to not show bias in discipline. They were told that the researchers were interested in learning more from them about effective discipline practice so they could pass on their insights to new teachers.

The intervention was delivered through a 45-minute online session in the fall and a 25-minute online session in the winter. Each session was introduced as an opportunity for future teachers to learn from participants' past experiences as teachers and that the researchers would present them with brief articles and stories to guide their feedback. These different forms of reflection were geared to cohesively remind teachers of the three primary themes for empathic discipline: (1) seek to understand students' perspective when misbehavior occurs, (2) prioritize the maintenance of positive relationships with students, and (3) help students develop and control their behaviors.

Articles

The articles detailed how it is important for teachers to bring out the best in their students through communication of care and respect relationships. They highlighted how situational factors such as stigma and puberty can cause students to worry about unfair treatment and can affect their behavior. A student can also come to feel less threatened in school and more motivated to behave well when teachers consider situational factors and value the student's perspective. The following is an example of language used in the articles:

> Of course, it takes more time to reach some students than others because their previous experiences and expectations differ. Some students have had good experiences with teachers. Others have had negative experiences. . . . But teachers who consistently reach out and engage students do make a difference. They help students see that they do have a fair shot and that people in authority are there to help them grow and develop, not stand in their way.

Last, the articles explain how this consideration is especially important in the heat of the moment, when conflicts or misbehavior arise. One article states:

> Teachers told us that some of the greatest challenges they faced—and some of their best opportunities for helping students—occurred after students misbehaved or struggled academically. These situations offer teachers an opportunity to talk with students and help them understand their experiences in class and in middle school more positively.

Turmoil is an opportunity to show students care and respect in a way that can be especially meaningful for students and impactful for long-term gains in quality teacher–student relationships.

Stories

The content also included brief stories to drive home major points in the articles. The stories were told from the perspectives of various students and a teacher, and they each included multiple psychological methods to persuasively remind teachers of how key themes emphasized in the articles play out in real-life situations (see Table 14.1). For example, norms were established in most of the stories. These norms ranged from how many students misbehave when they feel anxious to how students become less anxious when they feel they receive care and respect, especially from teachers. The objective was to remind teachers that misbehavior is to be expected from growing children and a normal response is to show care to students. Research shows that establishing norms in this way can lead a person to change his or her behavior to avoid deviating from it (Goldstein, Cialdini, & Griskevicius, 2008).

TABLE 14.1.   Psychological Approaches through Stories in the Intervention Content from the Study by Okonofua, Paunesku, and Walton (2016)

Story	Reminder strategy
Messages: Teachers seek and value students' perspectives; it helps when discipline prioritizes respect.	
Student quotation "In middle school, I didn't feel like I belonged. . . . So I didn't pay attention in class and sometimes I got in trouble. One day I got detention and, instead of just sitting there, my teacher talked with me about what happened. He really listened to me. . . . It felt good to know I had someone I could trust in school."	1. Reminder that any given student can be in a situation to misbehave and that misbehavior can be due to context (e.g., worries about belonging at school). 2. Encourage teacher to listen to student to gain perspective and show respect. 3. Show how a student's perception of a caring teacher is pivotal to development.
Student quotation "One time, after I got in trouble in 7th grade, I still remember how my teacher took me aside later and listened to my side of the story. . . . Even though I still got a detention, I was glad that she didn't just dismiss what I had to say, like other teachers sometimes did. . . ."	1. Show how efforts to seriously understand a student's perspective can communicate respect. 2. Show that discipline can be administered in a mutually respectful manner that protects the integrity and trust in the teacher–student relationship.
Teacher quotation "When I was a child, I remember worrying about how I would be treated by teachers at my school. But I will always remember Ms. McBride, who treated me with respect and trust. She showed me that teachers could make all the difference in how students feel about school."	1. Show it is normal for a student to crave respect, trust, and care, especially from adults in their lives. 2. Show how teachers' own past experiences can allow for common ground with students and their perspectives.
Messages: Students worry about respect; stigma can affect students' perspectives.	
Racially stigmatized student quotation "Whenever I get a new teacher, I think 'Is she gonna treat me fairly? Does she call on the White students more? Does she expect them to know the right answers and us to get them wrong?'"	1. Show that it is normal for students to worry about unfair treatment and how that feeling can be heightened by risk of discrimination due to a student's background. 2. Provide an example of how a teacher's intentions may not always be clear to a student.
Racially stigmatized student quotation "I always thought school wasn't for me, or for people like me. It seemed that people like me just get in trouble in school. But my 6th-grade math teacher really changed my mind. She told us that she knew that every one of us could learn and that she would work hard to help us get there. . . ."	1. Show that students from stigmatized groups may expect unfair treatment. 2. Place teachers in the perspective of a student to help him or her remember the situational reasons why a student might misbehave. 3. Provide an example of how a teacher can help a stigmatized student to feel more certain that he or she can belong at school.

Saying Is Believing

After reading and reflecting on the materials, teachers wrote essays describing how they use the kinds of practices described to build positive relationships with students during difficult disciplinary contexts. For instance, one participating teacher wrote, "I NEVER hold grudges. I try to remember that they are all the son or daughter of someone who loves them more than anything in the world. They are the light of someone's life" (see Table 14.2 for more teacher quotations). Teachers were told that these essays would be shared with new teachers to help them in their practice. This procedure, in which people freely advocate for an idea to a receptive audience ("saying is believing"), is a powerful persuasive technique. It makes the experience active, not passive, promoting deep processing. It also encourages people to commit themselves to an idea and to connect this idea to their own lives and practice (Walton & Wilson, 2018; Yeager & Walton, 2011).

TABLE 14.2. Sample Teacher Responses about Building Positive Relationships with Students from the Study by Okonofua, Paunesku, and Walton (2016)

Teacher responses to *"What are some of the ways that you try to build positive relationships with your students, or things that you would like to try in the future to improve your relationships with your students?"*

1. "At the start of the year I introduce myself to each student individually. We do several journal and other assignments that allow me to learn more about my students. I write comments on the pages so the students know that I actually do read their work. I take note of anything my students share that I may want to reference in conversation."

2. "I make myself available to students after school to provide them with more personalized support. When students are struggling I try to get on their level and find out what is going on not focusing on what they are doing wrong but trying to focus more on what I can do to ameliorate the situation and look for solutions moving forward. I also try to attend events like sports or theatre that they are interested in and talk to them about the things they like."

3. "I feel that one way to build positive relationships is to talk to the students. Often times students feel that they are judged even before they walk into the classroom. So if you listen to them and talk with them they are willing to work for you."

4. "We share good news each week—building a strong classroom community. Each student who wants to share can share. No one is left out. I am fair. I say hello to each student as they walk through the classroom door. I also try and say good-bye to students as they leave. I smile at each student as they enter the classroom. I also try to listen to what a student is telling me and try to be fair and consistent in my discipline in the classroom."

5. "Pull students aside to talk with them about behavior or grades; help students set goals and create steps for meeting them; incorporating student interests into activities and lessons; giving students choice in projects (i.e., students can select, research, focus, determine format for presenting information, etc.); allowing students to create own groups for work; chatting with students about their interests and their daily lives."

6. "I try to find out interests and hobbies outside of school. I attend these activities and talk with parents to build relationships. I talk to the students back at school about the activity that I attended."

7. "I do ice-breaker activities & ask students their hobbies and interests. I also make a point of letting the class know that I am human & make mistakes as well. Our motto is It's OK to make a mistake as [long] as you have grown from it. That could mean apologizing, fixing or having the Ah-Ha moment. We also have 'Bad Day' plans and students can let me know if it is a Bad Day and I will work with their comfort level for participation."

Control Condition

In the randomized controlled trial, half of the math teachers were assigned to a "technology-engagement" control condition. The content of this condition was about how to leverage technology to engage students in lessons and assignments. Thus, like the treatment condition, it was about means to improve student outcomes. The key difference is that this condition did not talk about seeking students' perspectives or ways to think about student misbehavior.

The control condition was similar in structure and in time to complete. Like the treatment condition, the control condition consisted of two online sessions: a 45-minute session in the fall and a 25-minute session in the winter. Also, the content was delivered in the form of articles, stories, and exercises similar in length.

NUANCES AND MISCONCEPTIONS

The empathic-discipline intervention is still not fully understood. Current and future research is needed to determine the specifics for implementation and expectations for effects in various contexts. So far, there is one major nuance or misconception about the intervention. The psychological message is about seeking to understand a student's perspective when the student misbehaves, not merely imagining or assuming his or her perspective.

The Empathic Mindset Leads Teachers to *Get* Perspective, Not *Take* Perspective

Second, the intervention is about getting perspective. It is not about a teacher's ability to guess what a student thinks or feels. It is more about the act of learning a student's perspective (e.g., by listening to him or her) and what that act can communicate to the student (e.g., respect).

The intervention is about the process of finding out more about a student or why a student misbehaved. It is about understanding the student—even if the student's perspective is unproductive. For example, if a student is distressed, a teacher mirroring this emotion could escalate the conflict. Also, it is not necessarily about sharing a student's opinions or agreeing with a student's interpretations of his or her surroundings. If a student thinks that school is a waste of time, it could be problematic and ethically questionable for a teacher to agree with the student—rather, it is about showing that one cares to know about and values the perspective and works from that perspective to productively respond to misbehavior. This can lead a student to feel less threat and more respect. For example, when a teacher asks a student why he or she behaved a certain way (i.e., his or her thoughts and feelings predicating the behavior), it communicates that the teacher thinks the student is more than a collection of behaviors (e.g., troublemaker) but rather a person with thoughts and feelings behind those actions. It communicates that the teacher cares about and respects the student as a person. The question and understanding are the key points, not necessarily that a teacher agrees that a student's thoughts or feelings should continue to manifest in a certain behavior. In fact, many times, discipline requires teachers to guide students to better manage their thoughts and feelings, a key lesson in child development.

IMPLICATIONS FOR PRACTICE

It is important to be cautious when introducing to real-world context interventions that are based on effects studied in lab settings. Lab experiments are particularly informative because they control conditions (e.g., a set and specific student misbehavior) in a way that makes it possible to detect specific effects (e.g., different understandings of misbehavior) of a given treatment (e.g., reminder to value students' perspectives). The empathic-discipline research reports from both lab experiments and experimentation in actual classrooms. It thus provides noteworthy insights about how context matters for practical implication (Ross & Nisbett, 1991).

Scalability

The empathic-discipline intervention was administered with teachers in five schools across three school districts. This required a focus on scalability that maintained fidelity to the treatment—in other words, it was important to make sure the cohesion of the psychological experience was sufficient while also done in a way that can be administered across many contexts. This form of consideration is key for future steps to increase the scalability of the intervention.

Critical components for scalability was that the intervention could be administered online and at teachers' convenience. By constructing the intervention materials in an online forum, it could be implemented remotely from the research base—the location of the research team. The intervention was thus able to be administered at schools in different cities while still being able to be monitored in a single location.

The online platform also made it possible for teachers to participate in the intervention at their convenience within a 3-week window. As mentioned, context matters. Schools have varying schedules and planning in place that determine teachers' day-to-day schedules. For example, in some schools, teachers have planning periods when participation would work best. In other schools, teachers have dedicated times for professional development meetings when participation would work best. While a strict participation schedule (e.g., all participation at a single time and in a single place) would allow for more control over the delivery of the materials and fidelity to the participation procedure, it could disrupt schools', teachers', and students' regular working and learning schedules. In turn, it could lead teachers to not appropriately engage with the materials or opt to not participate at all. The implementation schedule of providing a set number of weeks for teachers to participate at their leisure allowed for relative control over timing of implementation while also being flexible to schools' various schedules.

Context Matters

As with all psychological interventions, the context matters. Schools have different policies in place and different theories for how to approach improvements to student outcomes. The empathic-discipline intervention will likely work best when tactfully integrated with policy and skill-building approaches. While future empirical research is needed to confirm the efficacy of integration, theory suggests that it will be beneficial in contexts with certain policy and skill-building interventions in place.

In modern times, research suggests that schools can have a default punitive climate in which teachers become more likely to respond to misbehavior with punishment instead of care. In this social climate, teachers can come to view a misbehaving student in terms of a label (e.g., a "troublemaker" or a "bad kid"; Okonofua & Eberhardt, 2015; Okonofua, Walton, et al., 2016). Their discipline might then focus on getting rid of the student as opposed to adjust the context to make it more conducive to better behavior. The intervention takes a psychological approach (i.e., how teachers interpret student misbehavior) to shift classrooms from the default punitive social climate to one that is more conducive to teachers and students feeling less disgruntled or threatened. Therefore, the intervention may be particularly beneficial in school contexts that can provide time and space for teachers and students to nurture their relationships. Put differently, teacher–student relationships can be strengthened and discipline problems reduced when policies are in place to enable local or district leaders to effectively create nonpunitive social climates in schools.

Integration with Policy and Skill Building

There have been promising developments in discipline policy and skill building, and the researchers predict that this psychological intervention will work best when integrated with those approaches. For example, many states have adopted policies to restrict office referrals or suspensions for defiance or disrespect (see Pre-K Student Discipline Amendment Act of 2015; Pupil Discipline . . . , 2015). This can lead teachers to experience a loss of a tool in their toolkit to respond to misbehavior. The empathic-discipline intervention can remind teachers of the importance of seeking new tools that can help them get students' perspectives and to respond to misbehavior in a manner that is mindful of students' worries about respect and fair treatment. Together, these approaches can reduce the likelihood of punitive mindsets guiding discipline decisions.

Unlike skill-building approaches, the empathic-discipline intervention does not teach teachers new information about pedagogy or curriculum. However, the intervention might work best when coupled with such information and training. The content of the intervention is intended to encourage teachers to actively seek an understanding of students' perspectives (Eyal, Steffel, & Epley, 2018). The intervention aims to increase teachers' motivation to seek out new or more effective tools—strategies that show students they care for and respect them—to put in their discipline toolkit. This encouragement and motivation can increase the likelihood that teachers seek and meaningfully engage with relevant skill-building professional development. For example, *cultural competency* is a skill-based approach that has received a great deal of attention in how it might bridge the cultural gap between teachers and students from different backgrounds (Prater, Wilder, & Dyches, 2008; see also Dee & Penner, 2016). A teacher who remembers the importance of connecting with students—especially those who might fear they will not receive fair treatment—might engage with this kind of professional development in a more meaningful way that is likely to stick with them and apply it when interacting with students from stigmatized cultural groups.

As individual approaches—psychological, policy, or skill building—they might do some work to reduce discipline problems and inequity in their rates of occurrence. The largest and most lasting effects will likely result when these approaches are strategically integrated with a common aim. The empathic-discipline intervention should be understood and employed with attention placed on how it fits in a broader range of approaches that combat the default punitive climate in many school contexts.

IMPLICATIONS FOR PSYCHOLOGICAL THEORY

Many psychological interventions have shown large positive effects from a direct focus on students' own mindsets about their experiences. Empathic discipline advances that work with evidence for how a focus on students' environments (i.e., teachers' responses to their students' behavior) can also improve student outcomes. This intervention attests to the power of the situation to affect outcomes, for better or for worse (Ross & Nisbett, 1991). This is most apparent in how the intervention highlights the default punitive context in schools. Lab studies show that when teachers are reminded that punishment is critical for students to learn self-control, the teachers are more likely to view a student as a troublemaker when he or she misbehaves. They are also more likely to start students on a path to suspension and less likely to try to find out more about the cause of the misbehavior. The default context is so normalized that a brief intervention that reminds teachers to value students' perspectives and to help students perceive respect from them can significantly change the likelihood of a student getting in trouble throughout the school day.

Second, psychologically wise interventions can contribute to lasting change in real-world outcomes. These interventions are low cost and brief, which can cause them to be interpreted as magic (Yeager & Walton, 2011). However, they are carefully crafted to shift how people interpret their experiences in a way that can build on itself with new experiences over time (see Walton & Wilson, 2018). This is the case with empathic discipline. It shifts the way teachers interpret misbehavior and the students who misbehave. Over time, this can change the way teachers interact with students, and students can come to feel more respected at school. In this way, the intervention provides an example of how a strategic nudge can be embedded in patterns of interaction such that it can build on itself and ultimately influence an entire context (see Harackiewicz, Rozek, Hulleman, & Hyde, 2012; Outes, Sanchez, & Vakis, 2017; Paluck, Shepherd, & Aronow, 2016; Powers et al., 2016, for other examples).

FUTURE DIRECTIONS

The high-priority next steps for the empathic-discipline intervention include investigations of mechanisms by which the intervention's effects benefit teachers, benefit students, and persist over time, and also include explorations of conditions in which the intervention is most effective, or not.

How might the intervention affect teachers? The preliminary findings indicate that teachers who engage with the empathic mindset or participate in the empathic-discipline intervention are less likely to view students as troublemakers and more likely to respond to misbehavior in ways that communicate respect to students. Previous research suggests higher levels of empathy are associated with decreased teacher stress (Platsidou & Agaliotis, 2017). Other research indicates that decreases in teachers' stress (e.g., by way of less perceived threat in teacher–student relationships) are associated with fewer discipline problems for their students (O'Brennan, Pas, & Bradshaw, 2017; Pas, Bradshaw, Hershfeldt, & Leaf, 2010). Might the empathic-discipline intervention's effect on relationships be in part associated with reductions in less anxiety or stress? Further, research shows that people's perception, judgment, and decision making are more likely to be shaped by stereotypes when they lack cognitive resources (e.g., when stressed or exhausted; see Spencer, Charbonneau, & Glaser, 2016). If the intervention's effects are associated with reductions in stress, might it also reduce the likelihood of stereotyping, as is suggested by the reduction of troublemaker labeling?

How might the intervention affect students? When college students imagined themselves as receiving treatment from a teacher with the empathic mindset, they felt more respect in the relationship and more motivation to behave well. Also, previously suspended students of teachers who received the empathic-discipline intervention were more likely to feel respect in their relationships with all adults at their school. These findings suggest that students might experience a shift in their construal of respect throughout the school day. Might the intervention lead students to feel less stress or anxiety in their relationships with teachers or in school at large? Recent research suggests that such a shift in construal can lead to long-term reductions in discipline problems (Goyer et al., 2019).

How might the intervention's effects extend beyond single teacher–student relationships? Preliminary results mark a 50% reduction in year-long suspension rates. Also, previously suspended students reported a heightened perception of respect several months after teachers participated in the intervention. Might future students (e.g., the next year) of a teacher who receives the intervention also be less likely to be suspended and more likely to feel respect with adults at their school? Also, might students of teachers who receive the intervention continue to be less likely to be suspended and more likely to feel respect in future years with new teachers?

Under what conditions might the intervention not work? So far, the empathic-discipline intervention has been tested in middle schools in adjacent districts that serve racially diverse student populations (17% Asian, 2% Black, 54% Latino, 7% White, 20% other/unknown). Future research is needed to determine the intervention's efficacy in other middle school contexts and at other grade levels. For example, it will be useful to discover how well the intervention works in schools with (1) more or less racial and socioeconomic status diversity in the student population (e.g., more Black students); (2) various default cultural contexts, such as policies for responses to student misbehavior (see Pre-K Student Discipline Amendment Act of 2015) and school structure and support (see Gregory, Cornell, & Fan, 2011); and (3) various teacher characteristics, such as their race (see Egalite, Kisida, & Winters, 2015), stress levels, job satisfaction, and burnout—each of which has been associated with the quality of teacher–student relationships (Johnson et al., 2009). Research suggests that factors like punitive policies and stressed teachers are associated with more suspensions for students. The empathic-discipline intervention may then be especially effective for teachers affected by these factors.

Answers to these questions will provide a better understanding of the mechanisms that lead to the overall shift in how teachers and students view each other following the intervention. It is important to better understand these mechanisms to ensure it can predictably improve teacher and student outcomes in various contexts throughout the country that suffer from high and disproportionate rates of discipline problems.

REFERENCES

Bill and Melinda Gates Foundation. (2013). Learning about teaching: Initial findings from the Measures of Effective Teaching project. Retrieved from *www.metproject.org/downloads/Preliminary_Findings-Research_Paper.pdf*.

Boynton, M. H., O'Hara, R. E., Covault, J., Scott, D., & Tennen, H. (2014). A mediation model of racial discrimination and alcohol-related problems among African American students. *Journal of Studies on Alcohol and Drugs, 76*(2), 229–236.

Cohen, G., Garcia, J., Purdie-Vaughns, V., Apfel, N., & Brzustoski, P. (2009). Recursive processes in self-affirmation: Intervening to close the minority achievement gap. *Science, 324,* 400–403.

Couch, K. A., & Fairlie, R. (2010). Last hired, first fired? Black–white unemployment and the business cycle. *Demography, 47*(1), 227–247.

Dee, T., & Penner, E. (2016). *The causal effects of cultural relevance: Evidence from an ethnic studies curriculum* (CEPA Working Paper No. 16-01). Stanford, CA: Stanford Center for Education Policy Analysis.

Egalite, A. J., Kisida, B., & Winters, M. A. (2015). Representation in the classroom: The effect of own-race teachers on student achievement. *Economics of Education Review, 45,* 44–52.

Eyal, T., Steffel, M., & Epley, N. (2018). Perspective mistaking: Accurately understanding the mind of another requires getting perspective, not taking perspective. *Journal of Personality and Social Psychology, 114*(4), 547–571.

Fabelo, T., Thompson, M. D., Plotkin, M., Carmichael, D., Marchbanks, M. P., III, & Booth, E. A. (2011). Breaking schools' rules: A statewide study of how school discipline relates to students' success and juvenile justice involvement. Retrieved from *http://justicecenter.csg.org/resources/juveniles*.

Fenning, P., & Rose, J. (2007). Overrepresentation of African American students in exclusionary discipline: The role of school policy. *Urban Education, 42*(6), 536–559.

Ferguson, R. F. (2012). Can student surveys measure teaching quality? *Phi Delta Kappan, 94*(3), 24–28.

Finkel, E. J., Slotter, E. B., Luchies, L. B., Walton, G. M., & Gross, J. J. (2013). A brief intervention to promote conflict reappraisal preserves marital quality over time. *Psychological Science, 24*(8), 1595–1601.

Goldstein, N. J., Cialdini, R. B., & Griskevicius, V. (2008). A room with a viewpoint: Using social norms to motivate environmental conservation in hotels. *Journal of Consumer Research, 35*(3), 472–482.

Gottfried, M. A. (2010). Evaluating the relationship between student attendance and achievement in urban elementary and middle schools: An instrumental variables approach. *American Educational Research Journal, 47*(2), 434–465.

Gregory, A., Cornell, D., & Fan, X. (2011). The relationship of school structure and support to suspension rates for Black and White high school students. *American Educational Research Journal, 48,* 904.

Gregory, A., & Weinstein, R. S. (2008). The discipline gap and African Americans: Defiance or cooperation in the high school classroom. *Journal of School Psychology, 46,* 455–475.

Goyer, J. P., Cohen, G. L., Cook, J. E., Master, A., Apfel, N., Lee, W., . . . Walton, G. M. (2019). Targeted identity-safety interventions cause lasting reductions in discipline citations among negatively stereotyped boys. *Journal of Personality and Social Psychology, 117*(2), 229–259.

Hamre, B. K., & Pianta, R. C. (2001). Early teacher–child relationships and the trajectory of children's school outcomes through eighth grade. *Child Development, 72*(2), 625–638.

Harackiewicz, J. M., Rozek, C. S., Hulleman, C. S., & Hyde, J. S. (2012). Helping parents to motivate adolescents in mathematics and science: An experimental test of a utility-value intervention. *Psychological Science, 23*(8), 899–906.

Himmelstein, K. E. W., & Bruckner, H. (2011). Criminal-justice and school sanctions against non-heterosexual youth: A national longitudinal study. *Pediatrics, 127,* 49–57.

Johnson, J., Yarrow, A., Rochkind, J., & Ott, A. N. (2009). Teaching for a living: How teachers see the profession today. Public Agenda. Retrieved from *www.publicagenda.org/pages/teaching-for-a-living.*

Jordan, W. J., Lara, J., & McPartland, J. M. (1996). Exploring the causes of early dropout among race-ethnic and gender groups. *Youth and Society, 28*(1), 62–94.

Libby, L. K., & Eibach, R. P. (2011). Visual perspective in mental imagery: A representational tool that functions in judgment, emotion, and self-insight. In M. Zanna & J. Olson (Series Eds.), *Advances in experimental social psychology* (Vol. 44, pp. 185–245). San Diego, CA: Academic Press.

Losen, D. J., & Wald, J. M. (2003). *Deconstructing the school-to-prison pipeline.* San Francisco: Jossey-Bass.

Mendoza-Denton, R., Downey, G., Purdie, V. J., Davis, A., & Pietrzak, J. (2002). Sensitivity to status-based rejection: Implications for African American students' college experience. *Journal of Personality and Social Psychology, 83,* 896–918.

O'Brennan, L., Pas, E., & Bradshaw, C. (2017). Multilevel examination of burnout among high school staff: Importance of staff and school factors. *School Psychology Review, 46*(2), 165–176.

Okonofua, J. A., & Eberhardt, J. L. (2015). Two strikes: Race and the disciplining of young students. *Psychological Science, 26*(5), 617–624.

Okonofua, J. A., Paunesku, D., & Walton, G. M. (2016). Brief intervention to encourage empathic discipline cuts suspension rates in half among adolescents. *Proceedings of the National Academy of Sciences of the USA, 113*(19), 5221–5226.

Okonofua, J. A., Walton, G. M., & Eberhardt, J. L. (2016). A vicious cycle: A social-psychological account of extreme racial disparities in school discipline. *Perspectives on Psychological Science, 11*(3), 381–398.

Outes, I., Sanchez, A., & Vakis, R. (2017). Project: Growth mindset at scale-increasing school attainment by affecting the mindset of pupils and teachers. Retrieved from *www.riseprogramme.org/sites/www.riseprogramme.org/files/65%20Outes-Leon,%20Ingo,%20Sanchez,%20 Alan,%20Vakis,%20Renos.%20%20Project-%20Growth%20Mindset%20at%20Scale.pdf.*

Pager, D., Western, B., & Sugie, N. (2009). Sequencing disadvantage: Barriers to employment facing young Black and White men with criminal records. *Annals of the American Academy of Social and Political Science, 623,* 195–213.

Paluck, E. L., Shepherd, H., & Aronow, P. M. (2016). Changing climates of conflict: A social network experiment in 56 schools. *Proceedings of the National Academy of Sciences of the USA, 113,* 566–571.

Pas, E. T., Bradshaw, C. P., Hershfeldt, P. A., & Leaf, P. J. (2010). A multilevel exploration of the influence of teacher efficacy and burnout on response to student problem behavior and school-based service use. *School Psychology Quarterly, 25*(1), 13.

Platsidou, M., & Agaliotis, I. (2017). Does empathy predict instructional assignment-related stress?: A study in special and general education teachers. *International Journal of Disability, Development and Education, 64*(1), 57–75.

Poteat, V. P., Scheer, J. R., & Chong, E. S. K. (2015). Sexual orientation-based disparities in school and juvenile justice discipline: A multiple group comparison of contributing factors. *Journal of Educational Psychology, 108,* 229–241.

Powers, J. T., Cook, J. E., Purdie-Vaughns, V., Garcia, J., Apfel, N., & Cohen, G. L. (2016). Changing environments by changing individuals: The emergent effects of psychological intervention. *Psychological Science, 27,* 150–160.

Prater, M. A., Wilder, L. K., & Dyches, T. T. (2008). Shaping one traditional special educator preparation program toward more cultural competence. *Teaching Education, 19*(2), 137–151.

Pre-K Student Discipline Amendment Act of 2015. D.C. Assemb B, 21-0001 (2014-2015).

Pupil Discipline: Suspensions and Expulsions: Willful Defiance. Cal. Education Code §8900(k) (2015).

Reinke, W. M., Herman, K. C., & Stormont, M. (2013). Classroom-level positive behavior supports in schools implementing SW-PBIS: Identifying areas for enhancement. *Journal of Positive Behavior Interventions, 15*(1), 39–50.

Rocque, M., & Paternoster, R. (2011). Understanding the antecedents of the "school-to-jail" link: The relationship between race and school discipline. *Journal of Criminal Law Criminology, 101*(2), 633–666.

Rosenthal, R., & Jacobson, L. (1968). *Pygmalion in the classroom.* New York: Holt, Rinehart & Winston.

Ross, L., & Nisbett, R. E. (1991). *Person and the situation: Perspectives of social psychology.* New York: McGraw-Hill.

Rumberger, R. W., & Losen, D. J. (2017). The hidden costs of California's harsh school discipline: And the localized economic benefits from suspending fewer high school students (Civil Rights Project/Proyecto Derechos Civiles). Los Angeles: Civil Rights Project/Proyecto Derechos Civiles.

Skiba, R. J. (2014). The failure of zero tolerance. *Reclaiming Children and Youth, 22*(4), 27.

Skiba, R. J., Horner, R. H., Chung, C., Rausch, M. K., May, S. L., & Tobin, T. (2011). Race is not neutral: A national investigation of African American and Latino disproportionality in school discipline. *School Psychological Review, 40*(1), 85–107.

Spencer, K. B., Charbonneau, A. K., & Glaser, J. (2016). Implicit bias and policing. *Social and Personality Psychology Compass, 10*(1), 50–63.

Steele, C. M. (1997). A threat in the air: How stereotypes shape intellectual identity and performance. *American Psychologist, 52*(6), 613–629.

U.S. Department of Education, Office of Civil Rights. (2016, June). 2013–2014 Civil rights data collection: Key data highlights on equity and opportunity gaps in our nation's public schools. Retrieved from *www2.ed.gov/about/offices/list/ocr/docs/crdc-2013-14.html.*

U.S. Government Department of Education. (2014). *Guided principles: A resource guide for improving school climate and discipline.* Washington, DC: Author.

Walton, G. M., & Cohen, G. L. (2011). A brief social-belonging intervention improves academic and health outcomes among minority students. *Science, 331,* 1447–1451.

Walton, G. M., & Wilson, T. D. (2018). Wise interventions: Psychological remedies for social and personal problems. *Psychological Review, 125*(5), 617.

Yeager, D. S., Purdie-Vaughns, V., Garcia, J., Apfel, N., Brzustoski, P., Master, A., . . . Williams, M. E. (2014). Breaking the cycle of mistrust: Wise interventions to provide critical feedback across the racial divide. *Journal of Experimental Psychology: General, 143*(2), 804–824.

Yeager, D. S., & Walton, G. M. (2011). Social-psychological interventions in education: They're not magic. *Review of Educational Research, 81,* 267–301.

CHAPTER 15

The Group-Malleability Intervention
Addressing Intergroup Conflicts by Changing Perceptions of Outgroup Malleability

Amit Goldenberg, James J. Gross, and Eran Halperin

In the past few decades, social scientists have sought new tools to address and change psychological barriers to conflict resolution. One such barrier is group members' resistance to changes that promote peace, due to the fear that such changes may lead to disappointment or be perceived as weakness by the outgroup. A suggested solution to this barrier involves manipulating individuals' beliefs regarding the possibility for group change. In the present study, a field intervention involving Israelis ($N = 508$) from three locations in Israel extended previous lab findings by testing the durability of a group-malleability intervention over a 6-month period of frequent violence. Three different 5-hour interventions were administered as leadership workshops: The group-malleability intervention was compared to a neutral coping-with-stress intervention and, importantly, to a state-of-the-art perspective-taking intervention. The group-malleability intervention proved superior to the coping intervention in improving attitudes, hope, and willingness to make concessions, and maintained this advantage over a 6-month period of intense intergroup conflict. Moreover, it was as good as, and in some respects superior to, the perspective-taking intervention. These findings provide the first naturalistic examination of the potential of a group-malleability intervention to increase openness to conflict resolution.

BACKGROUND

Work on psychological interventions to reduce intergroup tensions is assuming new importance in light of recent developments in conflict regions around the world. Millions of refugees are fleeing their homes, and the resulting humanitarian crisis is being felt worldwide, transforming local or regional conflicts into an urgent global challenge.

Recent analyses suggest that the number of state-based armed conflicts has reached a new peak since the collapse of the Soviet Union (Melander, Pettersson, & Themner, 2016), supporting the notion that we are in the midst of a global escalation of intergroup conflicts. These recent developments emphasize the importance of finding ways to attenuate the destructive effects of intergroup conflicts.

In the past few decades, social scientists have sought new tools to address and change psychological barriers to conflict resolution (Hameiri, Porat, Bar-Tal, Bieler, & Halperin, 2014; Paluck, 2009). The assumption that undergirds this approach is that conflicts are fueled and perpetuated by certain psychological barriers that may arise as an attempt to cope with the challenging reality of living in a conflict (Bar-Tal, 2007; Ross & Stittinger, 1991). One such barrier is the resistance to change toward peace, due to the fear that any change would lead to disappointment or be perceived as weakness and be taken advantage of by the outgroup (Bar-Tal, 2013; Bar-Tal, Oren, & Nets-Zehngut, 2014). The goal of the current intervention is to attempt to influence a belief that seems to be central to groups' resistance to change, which is the belief that the other side will never change.

PSYCHOLOGICAL PROCESSES

One central mindset commonly held by members of groups involved in intractable conflicts is the notion that the other side is inherently malevolent and will never change (Halperin, 2008; Peterson, 2002). Believing that the other side will never change serves a variety of adaptive functions. First, it shields the individual from disappointment. If one expects nothing from the other side, one cannot be disappointed by any violent or harmful actions taken by the other side (Norem & Cantor, 1986). Second, it helps the individual to justify aggression and violence that are perpetrated by one's own group toward the other side (Bar-Tal, 2013; Bar-Tal et al., 2014). If those on the other side are inherently evil and will never change, they must be resisted by force if necessary, and no other means (e.g., negotiations, gestures) can be beneficial.

The mindset that the other side cannot change is central to the narratives of groups involved in intractable conflicts. Indeed, this mindset is often echoed by the leaders of these groups—for example, take the famous quote by former Israeli Prime Minister Yitzhak Shamir, who, on the brink of the Madrid Peace Conference in 1991, said, "The sea is the same sea, and the Arabs are the same Arabs," implying that just as the sea never changes, so too will the Palestinians never change (Goldenberg, 2012). In 2012, Israeli Prime Minister Binyamin Netanyahu reiterated Shamir's quote, suggesting he was right in his evaluations of the Palestinians (Podolsky, 2012). These quotes by Israeli leaders represent a narrative held by many people in Israel and in other countries involved in conflicts, which is that the other side will never change.

Believing that the other side will always stay the same is a psychological moat that helps to keep victims of conflicts away from the stress and distress of the conflict, but also one that hinders progress toward peace. If there is no chance that the Palestinians will change, why even try (Bar-Tal & Halperin, 2011; Bar-Tal, Halperin, & Pliskin, 2015)? If one believes that the other side can never change, investing efforts in actions that may lead to a reduction in violence or even to reconciliation is perceived as useless. Instead, it makes more sense to invest resources in order to eliminate potential threats using force and aggression. The belief that the other side will not change may serve short-term goals of self-justification, well-being, and avoidance of disappointment, but may hinder the possibility of a long-term solution to the conflict (Halperin, 2008; Halperin, Russell, Trzesniewski, Gross, & Dweck, 2011). Influencing beliefs about the possibility of change may therefore be a precondition for any type of action that brings conflict resolution.

The potential impact of group-malleability mindsets in an intergroup conflict context has led researchers to become interested in empirically examining the causal role of perceived group malleability in motivating support for conflict resolution (Halperin et al., 2011; Rydell, Hugenberg, Ray, & Mackie, 2007). The idea behind this approach was that convincing people that groups can change and develop may increase the motivation of those involved in intractable conflicts to change their attitudes, emotions, and behavior toward the other side (Halperin, Cohen-Chen, & Goldenberg, 2014).

In an attempt to understand the psychological processes related to perceived group malleability, Halperin and colleagues (2011) manipulated perceptions of group malleability among both Israeli and Palestinian samples by asking them to read a mock scientific report that discussed the possibility of group change. In the malleability condition, participants read that groups do not have a fixed, inherent nature, but rather are capable of positive change (with no mention of Israelis or Palestinians). In the fixed condition, participants read a similar article that made the exact opposite arguments (i.e., that groups are fixed and do not tend to change). Halperin and colleagues predicted that the psychological mechanism that would be most affected by the manipulation would be negative attitudes toward the other side, and particularly the belief that the other side is inherently malevolent. This prediction was based on the assumption that if participants believe that groups can change, there is less chance that they would think that groups would have a malevolent nature. Therefore, following this brief manipulation, participants completed a survey that examined both these attitudes toward the outgroup and their willingness to make the appropriate concessions for peace. Results suggested that those in the group-malleability condition expressed less negative attitudes toward the outgroup—particularly attitudes related to the inherent evil nature of the other side—and these negative attitudes mediated support for willingness to make the appropriate concessions for peace. Results were similar among both Jewish Israeli and Palestinian participants.

This encouraging set of lab studies was followed by additional studies that were designed to further understand the mechanisms and potential outcomes related to group-malleability manipulations. Focusing their attention on an emotional mechanism, Cohen-Chen, Crisp, and Halperin (2016) suggested that hope—often activated by the appraisal that situations are dynamic—may be the main affective outcome of changing perceptions of group malleability. Indeed, studies by Cohen-Chen and colleagues (Cohen-Chen, Crisp, & Halperin, 2015; Cohen-Chen et al., 2016) showed that changes in perceived malleability mainly influenced participants' hope for the possibility of conflict resolution, which in turn increased their willingness to support concessions.

Other studies were designed to examine whether perceived malleability may lead to constructive outcomes relevant to intergroup conflicts other than support for concessions. In one such study, Halperin and colleagues (2012) showed that perceived group malleability led to an increased desire to interact with the other side. Further research examining this question showed that increasing perceptions of group malleability not only improved the motivation for intergroup interactions but also the quality of such interactions (Goldenberg et al., 2017). Finally, a set of studies by Wohl and colleagues (2015) showed not only that group malleability affects the motivation to meet with the other side but also that perceived malleability can increase the chance that collective apology by the outgroup would lead to intergroup forgiveness. This research laid the psychological foundation from which the group-malleability intervention was designed.

EMPIRICAL EVIDENCE

Although there has been ample lab-based evidence for the effectiveness of a group-malleability intervention, to date there has not been any intervention in a field setting that examined the long-term effects of a group-malleability manipulation. This intervention was therefore initiated in order to learn more about the potential of using group malleability as a tool to change conflict-related attitudes, emotions, and perhaps even willingness to make concessions in the field. The group-malleability intervention was compared to two other interventions. The first one was a perspective-taking intervention, which focused on the importance of taking the other side's perspective when leading a group, even in challenging situations. It was chosen because of its suggested potential for conflict resolution and prejudice reduction (Bilali & Vollhardt, 2013; Galinsky & Moskowitz, 2000). However, after a series of three pilot studies, it was altered to enhance its effectiveness by de-emphasizing perspective taking in the local Israeli–Palestinian context (which evoked resistance from some participants; Sassenrath, Hodges, & Pfattheicher, 2016; Vorauer & Sasaki, 2009; Zaki & Cikara, 2015) and instead discussed the importance of perspective taking in general. The second intervention was a coping-with-stress intervention that was chosen as a control comparison to both the group-malleability and perspective-taking interventions. The coping-with-stress intervention was designed to teach participants useful coping skills to overcome stressors that leaders often encounter. Coping was chosen and prepiloted as a control condition because it provided useful leadership-related skills, but also because it was unrelated to group-malleability or conflict resolution. Furthermore, a similar workshop has been used as a neutral control condition for a malleability intervention (Yeager, Trzesniewski, & Dweck, 2013). In order to examine the longer-term effects of these interventions, participants' attitudes and behavior were measured in five time points, up to 6 months after the intervention.

Outcomes

We recruited a sample of Jewish–Israeli participants ($N = 508$) from around the country with diverse backgrounds, ages, and political affiliations (191 males and 317 females, $M = 28.81$ years, $SD = 8.69$). Participants' attitudes, hope, and support for conciliatory behavior were measured one time before the intervention and four times following the intervention: postworkshop, 2 weeks, 2 months, and 6 months after the intervention. Some participants dropped out of the study during each follow-up period, leaving us with 59% of the sample in the 6-month follow-up ($N = 300$). However, no differences were found in attrition rate between the groups. The period in which the data were collected was relatively a tumultuous period in Israel, often referred to as the "silent intifada" (Caspit, 2014), in which there were multiple terrorist attacks in Israel, conducted primarily by desperate individual Palestinians who were not directly sent by a known terrorist organization.

We first examined differences in participants' negative attitudes toward the Palestinians. The scale that was used to estimate these negative attitudes was similar to the one used in Halperin and colleagues' (2011) lab study. The scale focused primarily on the perception that Palestinians are inherently malevolent and included items such as "To what extent would you say that the Palestinians are evil?" Looking first at the differences between our three conditions after the intervention, results suggested that participants in the malleability intervention held significantly fewer negative attitudes compared to the control coping intervention (see Figure 15.1, Panel A). Analysis suggested no difference between the group-malleability intervention and the perspective-taking intervention (which was also significantly better compared to the control condition).

Following this comparison of participants' negative attitudes, we examined differences in participants' hope regarding a shared future with the Palestinians. We focused our attention on hope, as previous work suggested that it was an important outcome of group-malleability manipulations (Cohen-Chen, Halperin, Saguy, & van Zomeren, 2014; Wohl et al., 2015). Comparing the group-malleability and coping conditions following the intervention suggested that participants in the group-malleability intervention reported significantly higher hope compared to the control coping intervention (see Figure 15.1, Panel B). Unlike in the case of negative attitudes, we did find a significant difference between the two interventions. These findings point to at least one outcome that seems to differentiate between our group-malleability and perspective-taking interventions.

Influencing psychological constructs, such as negative attitudes and hope for the future, do not necessarily translate into change in support for conciliatory behavior. We therefore examined three such measures. The first was a scale that examined support for a two-state solution. A two-state solution represented the most popular solution for the Israeli–Palestinian conflict when the original study was conducted in 2011. The general principles of the two-state solution include an establishment of a Palestinian state, a division of Jerusalem, territory exchanges between Israel and Palestine, and a symbolic payment of reparations by Israel to Palestinian refugees. Between 2010 and the end of 2014 (which is when our intervention was conducted), dramatic changes in public opinion led

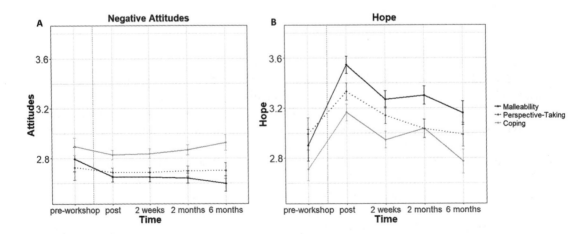

FIGURE 15.1. Average ratings of participants' negative attitudes (A) and hope (B) at each point for all three conditions, obtained from the longitudinal model. Error bars are standard errors. For the sake of simplicity, the distance between points has been constrained to be equal despite the differences in time.

to shifts in terms of public support for that idea, which rendered the items on our old scale obsolete (Hilal, 2007). This is because some major parties in the Israeli government had completely abandoned the two-state solution as a viable resolution to the conflict. Looking at differences among all of our intervention participants' support for a two-state solution revealed no difference between any of our conditions. To overcome this limitation, we created a more timely measure of concessions that included symbolic gestures, such as acknowledgment of Palestine as an independent and sovereign country, and allowing the Palestinian soccer team to play in international games. Indeed, our modified concession scales revealed a significant difference between the group-malleability and the coping interventions, but not between the perspective-taking and group-malleability interventions, providing initial evidence that our intervention was able to shift at least more symbolic concessions compared to the traditional two-state solution measure.

In addition to our concession measures, we wanted to examine whether our intervention actually affected participants' decisions involving dividing resources between Israelis and Palestinians. We therefore added two conciliatory behavior measures that were influenced by economics games. The first such measure was a dictator game (Bolton, Katok, & Zwick, 1998), in which participants were asked to divide resources worth hundreds of millions of Israeli shekels (NIS) between Israelis and Palestinians. Similar to our revised concessions measure, we found significant differences between the group-malleability and the coping interventions, but no differences between the group-malleability and the perspective-taking interventions (see Figure 15.2). Our second measure was modeled on a trust game (Berg, Dickhaut, & McCabe, 1995), in which participants were actually given 10 NIS (approximately $3.00), and were asked to transfer some or all of the amount to a Palestinian player, in the hope that the Palestinian player would reciprocate. Participants were told that any amount that would be given back to them by their Palestinian confederate would be tripled before being given to them. Therefore, if they trusted that their partner would reciprocate, it made sense to share all of their money with their confederate with the hope that they would make more than the initial 10 NIS that were given to them. Results suggested that participants in the group-malleability intervention gave significantly more money to their Palestinian confederate than participants in either the coping intervention or the perspective-taking intervention (see Figure 15.2).

Overall, these results point to the difference between the malleability and coping conditions on all measures except for support for a two-state solution. We found significant differences between the group-malleability and perspective-taking interventions only in participants' hope and in the trust game. Further research should be done to examine whether these effects are replicated in other field interventions—however, both of these results point to a difference in participants' ability to be optimistic in estimating outcomes from interacting with the other side. These findings are congruent with recent work that shows that a group-malleability intervention mainly influenced Israeli and Palestinian participants' ability to cooperate with each other (Goldenberg et al., 2017).

Mechanisms

The group-malleability intervention influenced participants' perceptions regarding the possibility of group change (assessed in a manipulation check). We believe that this general perception is relatively easy to influence, as it is an implicit belief that is not constantly reevaluated and reaffirmed as are other beliefs, such as ideology or religiosity

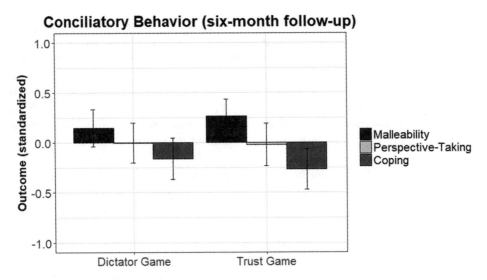

FIGURE 15.2. Performance in two decision-making tasks (standardized) at the 6-month follow-up. Error bars are 95% confidence intervals.

(Rydell et al., 2007). Participants' acknowledgment in the possibility of group change is then applied to specific cases that are relevant to participants, such as the Israeli–Palestinian conflict. Mentioning the specific details of the conflict in our pilot studies did not lead to optimal outcomes (reported below), suggesting that it is better to let participants make the connection between general perceptions of malleability and the specific context in which they are in.

The theoretical connection between group malleability and the outcomes measured in our interventions is easy to explain. Belief in the possibility of group change leads to more hope, as hope is an emotion driven by the appraisal that the world is dynamic and could change for the better (Cohen-Chen et al., 2016). The connection of perceived group malleability to negative attitudes, and particularly attitudes related to groups' inherently malevolent nature is also straightforward. If one believes that groups can change, it is much harder to believe that some people have an inherently evil nature. Following that rationale, believing in the possibility of change should increase the motivation to try and influence an outgroup's change by offering concessions that will help them strive and succeed. Indeed, these findings have been suggested in previous works (Cohen-Chen, Halperin, Crisp, & Gross, 2014; Halperin et al., 2011).

In light of these previous findings, we examined two potential mediation models. In the first model, perceived group malleability following the workshop led to changes in hope and negative attitudes right after the workshop, which in turn led to changes in support for conciliatory behavior 6 months after the workshop. In the second model, perceived group malleability following the workshops mediated all outcomes during the 6-month follow-up. Although both models led to significant results, it was the simple model that was better at predicting the existing data (see Figure 15.3). Below, we provide coefficients of the direct, indirect, and total effects, including confidence intervals for each mediator. As some outcomes differ in their scales, we standardized all of the presented outcomes. Furthermore, due to the simplicity of the model, model fit estimates

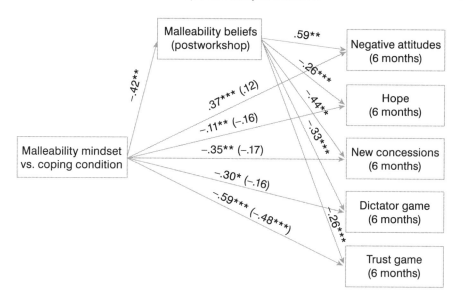

FIGURE 15.3. Mediation model for all outcomes measured at the 6-month follow-up. We used the postworkshop measure of malleability beliefs as a mediator of outcomes at the 6-month follow-up. Results suggested a significant indirect effect for all measured outcomes. $p \le .10$, $p \le .05^*$, $p \le .01^{**}$, $p \le .001^{***}$.

were irrelevant and therefore are not presented. Overall, results suggest significant indirect effects for all of our outcomes, indicating that differences in malleability beliefs between the malleability and coping conditions in the postworkshop measure mediated all of the outcomes in the 6-month follow-up.

Effects over Time

So far, we have compared the three interventions by aggregating all postworkshop measures that were taken following the intervention. However, since we have four measures that were taken after the workshops (postworkshop, 2 weeks, 2 months, and 6 months), we can also examine changes in our outcomes over time. We focused our analyses on participants' hope and negative attitudes toward Palestinians, which were measured during these four follow-ups. Importantly, in our analysis, we examined models that allowed varied changes across time points (growth curve analysis). However, in most of these cases, model comparisons suggested that a simple linear model was strongest compared to all other models. Finally, similar to all other analyses, we controlled for premeasures of each outcome in the analysis.

Results revealed no change over time in negative attitudes in the group-malleability condition, suggesting that the changes that occurred following the intervention were sustained over time. Indeed, comparing negative attitudes in the 6-month follow-ups between the group-malleability and coping interventions suggested that differences were still significant. There were still no differences between the group-malleability and perspective-taking conditions (which were also significantly lower than the control condition; see Figure 15.1, Panel A). Unlike negative attitudes, participants' hope did seem to significantly decline in the postworkshop measures. One potential reason for this decrease is the increase in terrorist attacks that occurred during these 6 months that may have specifically affected participants' hope regarding the future. However, even after this decline, participants' ratings were still significantly higher compared to the preworkshop measures and compared to both the perspective-taking and coping interventions.

Heterogeneity

One important question regarding the heterogeneity of the group-malleability intervention is whether its impact differs among participants with different political affiliations. Two opposite hypotheses are offered. First, it is possible that liberals are more influenced by a group-malleability intervention, as a plethora of work suggests that liberals are more susceptible to the notion of change (Graham, Haidt, & Nosek, 2009; Jost, Federico, & Napier, 2009; Schein & Gray, 2015). However, liberals' susceptibility to the notion of change may mean that the impact of the intervention is weaker, since perceptions of malleability are already an integral part of their thinking (Kahn et al., 2018). The current sample is big enough to examine this important question, which bears on the target audience of such an intervention.

To address this question, we divided our participants into three political groups: liberals, centrists, and conservatives. We decided to use a centrist group because unlike the United States, the Israeli political system includes many different parties and a large portion of the population considers itself as centrist. For each of these three groups, we compared the levels of hope and negative attitudes across the group-malleability and control coping interventions. Results suggest that the difference between the incremental and coping intervention groups was mainly driven by differences within rightists and centrists. In both cases, we found no significant difference between the incremental and coping conditions for liberals. These results suggest that the malleability intervention may be especially useful for conservatives, which suggests the possibility that targeting conservatives might lead to maximal changes.

COUSINS

The idea that changing perceptions of group malleability can influence people's emotions, attitudes, and behaviors toward other group members can be associated with two types of cousins. The first and most obvious cousin is an intervention that is focused on changing perceptions of malleability of the self and others as a tool to motivate individuals to confront challenging situations. The second cousin is an intervention that is focused on changing one's perception of the outgroup, either through interaction or through perspective taking. Here we review both of these approaches.

The idea that perceptions of malleability can serve as a tool for intervention was developed by Carol Dweck, who suggested that beliefs regarding one's own malleability were a factor influencing people's motivation, especially in light of challenging tasks (see Dweck, 2006, 2012, for reviews). Focusing initially on the domain of education, Dweck argued and showed that children who perceived their intelligence as malleable (compared to those who perceived their intelligence as fixed) were more motivated to overcome educational challenges that threatened their sense of self (Hong, Chiu, Dweck, Lin, & Wan,

1999; Nussbaum & Dweck, 2008). These children therefore showed improved performance in school compared to children who perceived their intelligence as fixed. Dweck not only showed that believing in malleability is associated with group performance but also that this belief can be manipulated, and that changing students' malleability beliefs can thus improve their performance in school (Blackwell, Trzesniewski, & Dweck, 2007; Kamins & Dweck, 1999).

Dweck's insights in the domain of education were then examined in the context of interpersonal relations. For example, in a series of studies, Chiu, Dweck, Tong, and Fu (1997) showed that people who perceived others' personalities as fixed tended to make more strict trait judgments regarding other people, whereas those with incremental beliefs were more lenient in their judgment of others (Chiu, Hong, & Dweck, 1997). Further interventions were conducted by Yeager and colleagues, exploring the contribution of perceived malleability to interpersonal relations. In a series of projects, Yeager and colleagues showed that convincing participants that other people can change was associated with reduced aggression (Yeager, Trzesniewski, et al., 2013), hostility (Yeager, Miu, Powers, & Dweck, 2013), and vengeance after peer conflict (Yeager, Trzesniewski, Tirri, Nokelainen, & Dweck, 2011). Overall, this large body of work provides ample evidence of the potential of perceived malleability in improving interpersonal relations, especially in cases of challenging interactions. We assume some overlap between the individual and the group-malleability interventions. Naturally, to believe that groups can change one has to believe in change among individuals as well. At the same time, we believe that changes in intergroup emotions and beliefs are driven mainly by people's views regarding groups as separate entities and that explains part of the potential embedded in the group-malleability interventions, as supported by the data presented above.

Beyond interventions that focus on the notion of malleability of individuals and groups, there are many intergroup interventions that attempt to change people's inherent perception of their outgroup, often with an emphasis on the similarities between one's ingroup and the outgroup. These interventions can be divided into a few subtypes. The first type involves attempting to convince group members that they are actually similar to the outgroup. For example, priming common ingroup identity among racial groups leads to a reduction in intergroup bias (see Gaertner, Dovidio, Anastasio, Bachman, & Rust, 1993, for a review). Even convincing rival groups that they have genetic similarities can also reduce explicit bias and in turn lead to an increase in support for peacemaking (Kimel, Huesmann, Kunst, & Halperin, 2016). Eliciting a sense of similarity seems to be efficient in blurring intergroup boundaries and thus changing group members' perceptions of their ingroup.

A second and related type of intervention does not explicitly try to convince group members of similarity to the outgroup but rather asks group members to take the perspective of the outgroup, either with or without the presence of the outgroup. This is done with the hope that taking the other side's perspective would either lead to emphasizing the similarities between the experiences of both groups or at least to a greater understanding of their position. For example, in a study by Broockman and Kalla (2016), canvassers asked voters to think about a time when they themselves were judged negatively for being different, in order to emphasize their similarity with transgender people, showing that this had an effect on attitudes toward transgendered individuals. In general, perspective-taking interventions seem to lead to a variety of positive outcomes, including decreases in prejudice (Galinsky & Moskowitz, 2000), increases in ingroup help (Batson, Chang,

Orr, & Rowland, 2002; Bilewicz, 2009), and increased willingness to engage in contact (Wang, Kenneth, Ku, & Galinsky, 2014). Importantly, however, some research suggests that perspective-taking interventions may backfire. One reason for this is that when participants are asked to take the perspective of the outgroup, they either realize how big the gap in views between them and their outgroup actually is, or focus on how much effort would be required to bridge the gap between the two groups (see Maoz, 2011; Sassenrath et al., 2016; Vorauer & Sasaki, 2009; Zaki & Cikara, 2015, for similar arguments).

The perspective-taking workshop used in the current project took advantage of insights from these studies. Participants were told that taking others' perspective is an important way to understand their motivations and needs and therefore an extremely important tool for decision making. Indeed, we found that our perspective-taking intervention led to reduced negative attitudes compared to our control coping intervention and to increased willingness to make concessions. We did find in our pilot studies, however, that mentioning the local context of the conflict led to a reversed order and to an increase in negative attitudes. These findings reveal a potential moderator to perspective-taking outcomes.

INTERVENTION CONTENT AND IMPLEMENTATION

Each group-malleability workshop was 5 hours long and included a preworkshop questionnaire (30 minutes), general leadership content (similar to all conditions, 1.5 hours), and the relevant content of each condition (3 hours; see Table 15.1). The general leadership content section was identical in all three groups and was inspired by a leadership development model created by the Harvard Kennedy School's Center for Public Leadership. Participants learned about transformational leaders (Bass, 1985) and how different leadership styles influence group performance. After the general leadership content, the

TABLE 15.1. Summary of the Workshop Schedule

9:00–9:30	Preworkshop questionnaire	Measurement of personality traits and potential moderators. All relevant outcomes were measured in another premeasure 2–4 days before the intervention.
9:30–10:30	General leadership content	Identical in all three groups and inspired by a leadership development model created by the Harvard Kennedy School's Center for Public Leadership.
10:30–11:00	Break	
11:00–12:15	Intervention content, part 1	Introduction of the central idea of the intervention using a story line, a video, and an active discussion.
12:15–12:30	Break	
12:30–1:30	Intervention content, part 2	Examining historical examples and practicing implementing the ideas of the intervention using a simulation between management and employees of a factory.
1:30–2:00	Postworkshop questionnaire	

workshop shifted to fit with each of the conditions. The structure of the interventions was similar for all conditions in terms of schedule and type of activities—however, the main message of each intervention was tailored to each condition. In addition to making sure that the structure of the interventions would be similar, a second goal was that these three interventions would be similar in how much they were engaging and entertaining for participants. Indeed, our tests of participants' engagements suggested that participants enjoyed our interventions in a similar way.

The malleability workshop focused on the benefits of remaining a relevant leader in an ever-changing context, highlighting the importance of identifying and encouraging change in groups. In the first part of this section of the workshop, participants were told that they would focus on a specific aspect of leadership—namely, the ability to identify and facilitate group change. To open this segment, the instructors presented the story of Amir, head of a research and development group in a large company who failed to recognize positive changes in his employees. Ignoring his employees' changes decreased Amir's relevance and eventually led to a deterioration in his relationship with them. After going over the story, instructors led a discussion on the importance of believing in change, identifying it, and facilitating it. Next, participants were introduced to the concept of change in human development and then learned about brain plasticity (by watching a short video). Moving from the individual to the group level, participants learned about the possibility of change in groups, focusing on different aspects that groups could change, such as their stereotypes of others or of themselves, their ideologies, and their lifestyle. Participants were asked to provide examples in each domain following a discussion with the group. Instructors then provided participants with their own examples for each of these domains.

The second part of the workshop (after the second break) focused on group change and leadership. Workshop instructors emphasized the fact that change is never easy, and that leaders must be willing to embrace and facilitate transformations in order to remain relevant. Participants were given three examples of leaders who were able to identify and amplify group change: Steve Jobs, Martin Luther King Jr., and Ellen Johnson Sirleaf. Steve Jobs, Apple's legendary chief executive officer (CEO), recognized changes in consumer preference in the domain of personal computing and developed products that fit these emerging needs. Martin Luther King Jr., a leader and activist for race equality in the United States, was able to recognize that affordances created societal changes within the United States that allowed him to lead a successful collective action movement calling for equality. Ellen Johnson Sirleaf, the first female head of state in Africa, was able to recognize and capitalize on important changes in her home country of Liberia and lead the country to a better future. We chose these three figures as they could serve as excellent examples not only for the group-malleability interventions but also to the perspective-taking and coping interventions. Indeed, in each workshop we used the same three people, focusing the participants' attention on different aspects in these three figures' biography, behaviors, and statements.

Following this section, participants took part in a simulated negotiation between the management group of a paper facility and the facility's union representatives. The context of the negotiation was the need to cut costs in order to improve the facility's profits. Participants were divided into three groups: management, employees, and observers. Each group was given different materials prior to the negotiation. After conducting the negotiation, participants analyzed the position of each group, emphasizing the notion of group change. For example, one of the key points during the negotiation was management's belief in the employees' ability to change a few crucial work-related norms in order to improve production.

Finally, to conclude the workshop, we focused on the change in groups that can lead to improved intergroup relations. A few historical examples were used, including changes in European countries such as England and France that led to tremendous improvements in their relationship, changes in Arab society that led to the Arab Spring, and the conflict in Ireland. For example, when examining the story of the Irish conflict, participants learned about the bloody history between the unionists (mostly Protestants) and the Irish nationalists (mostly Catholics). They then learned about changes occurring in Ireland, and especially change in the approach of the Sinn Féin political party that led to a greater willingness for peace. Participants observed the processes that occurred within each group, leading to these intergroup changes.

NUANCES AND MISCONCEPTIONS

Two nuances played an important role in the success of our group-malleability intervention. The first nuance is that the workshops were framed as a leadership workshop rather than a conflict-resolution intervention. Both during the recruiting and during the workshops, participants were explicitly told that they were taking part in a pilot study designed to examine the utility of different leadership workshops. Leadership was chosen as a focus to provide an appealing framework that would be broad enough to encompass all three interventions. We believe that using the leadership framework was a good strategy, as it reduced potential reactance to the notion of conflict resolution (Bar-Tal & Halperin, 2011; Brehm, 1966).

The second and perhaps more important nuance of our workshop is that we did not mention the specific context of the Israeli–Palestinian conflict throughout the intervention but rather talked about group malleability in general and used examples that were far from the local context. This decision was made after we conducted two pilot studies to test whether mentioning the Israeli–Palestinian conflict would be helpful or harmful. Results of our pilot studies indicated that not mentioning the Israeli context yielded the best outcomes in changing participants' negative attitudes toward Palestinians, increasing participants' hope regarding a mutual future, and increasing willingness to make concessions. In fact, in pilot studies in which the Israeli–Palestinian conflict was highly emphasized during the intervention, we even saw an increase in negative attitudes for some of the participants. We therefore believe that not mentioning the specific context of the conflict was crucial to the success of our intervention.

IMPLICATIONS FOR PRACTICE

Our findings provide encouraging evidence for the possibility of using the group-malleability intervention to reduce negative attitudes, increase hope, and increase the willingness to make concessions necessary to promote the resolution of protracted intergroup conflict. Our longitudinal analysis suggests that changing people's perceptions of group malleability may have long-lasting effects. With this knowledge at hand, it is important to consider how our intervention can be adapted by practitioners and used in tandem with other known interventions. Next we examine some of these opportunities.

Adoption at Scale

As part of the process of adopting our interventions with a larger audience, we are enthusiastic about the possibility of examining the effects of our group-malleability intervention in other challenging intergroup contexts. For example, our workshop could potentially be used to train professionals who are vulnerable to developing intergroup bias in their daily lives. Police officers, teachers, nurses and doctors, judges, and many other professionals whose work is highly affected by their relations to negatively stereotyped groups could potentially benefit from our workshops. The general message of the workshop has the advantage, as discussed above, that it does not raise the resistance that these professionals may have to (or the offense they might take from) a direct message about changing their attitudes or reducing their prejudice (Paluck, 2009). We have already started using such workshops in Israel, as part of the work of aChord: Social Psychology for Social Change, a research-based organization aimed at promoting tolerant equal and respectful relations among different groups within the Israeli society. Under the umbrella of that organization, training and workshops are provided to school principals, teachers, and business managers in an attempt to reduce stereotypes and promote less biased and more harmonious relations among different identity groups within the Israeli society.

In addition to using our workshops in a classroom setting, another area of growth for our intervention is in finding ways to convey the message of our intervention using other modes of communication. The most readily available option is to conduct the group-malleability intervention online. Indeed, there has been recent growth in the use of psychological interventions—and specifically mindset interventions—online (Paunesku et al., 2015; Yeager et al., 2016). We believe that as in those studies, the general message of group malleability can be effective even if disseminated online. However, future work should examine the aspects of the intervention that are lost in the transition to an online intervention. For example, based on our initial analysis, it seems that participants who came to our workshop with someone they knew were more affected by its content. Such effects are probably less strong in online interventions, which might diminish the overall impact of a group-malleability intervention delivered online.

In addition to conducting our intervention online, the general message of group malleability might be disseminated in other ways that could reach a larger audience. For example, one of the big supporters of the idea of group malleability as a motivating tool for conflict resolution is the Israeli president Reuven Rivlin, who initiated a large social initiative focusing on change beliefs under the name "Israeli Hope." In a recent speech, Rivlin (2015) said, "I stand as one who really believes. Not because there is no choice, but because right before my eyes I see a process of change taking place." In addition to being used by public figures, our interventions might also be used as an advertising campaign for organizations interested in using efficient messaging in order to change population-level attitudes in the contexts of conflicts (see, e.g., Hameiri, Porat, Bar-Tal, & Halperin, 2016). It is still unclear how changing the method of dissemination would affect the impact of the intervention, and future work will be needed to examine these effects.

Group Malleability Combined with Contact

An immediate extension of our work is to think about our group-malleability intervention as a precursor to other interventions designed to improve conflict resolution. The basic rationale behind this approach is that changing perceptions of group malleability may enhance the impact of other well-known interventions as it would increase group members' hopefulness regarding a potential mutually beneficial outcome. One type of intervention that might especially benefit from group-malleability interventions is the contact-encounter intervention. Contact is perhaps the most used and well-researched approach to alleviate tension and reduce prejudice between groups (Paluck, Green, & Green, 2019; Tropp, 2015; Zhou, Page-Gould, Aron, Moyer, & Hewstone, 2018). The idea behind contact encounters is that by meeting members of the opposite side in a constructive environment, group members may be able to develop a better understanding of the other side, as well as acknowledge similarities between the two groups.

Since the contact approach was first suggested (Allport, 1954; Pettigrew, 1998; Pettigrew & Tropp, 2006; Williams, 1947), its popularity has increased substantially (Hewstone & Brown, 1986; Maoz & McCauley, 2008; Pettigrew & Tropp, 2006). In Israel, for example, a series of representative public opinion surveys conducted during 2002–2005 indicated that about 16% of the entire population of Israel had attended organized contact workshops (Maoz, 2011). However, alongside optimism regarding the potentially positive outcomes of contact, there have been some findings that suggest that contact may not be as useful in leading to real and long-term change as hoped, especially in intergroup conflicts (MacInnis & Page-Gould, 2015; Maoz, 2011; Paluck et al., 2019). One of the challenges that has been suggested in the literature is that during contact encounters, group members learn about the position of the other side, which makes them realize how challenging reconciliation will be for the two groups. It seems possible, therefore, that changing perceptions of group malleability may be useful to alleviate some of these concerns by making the possibility of group change more readily available.

We recently conducted an intervention that provides an initial investigation of the possibility of extending our intervention to the Palestinian population (Goldenberg et al., 2017). This intervention was designed with the intention of using a group-malleability manipulation as a way to improve a contact encounter between Jewish Israeli and Palestinian–Israeli adolescents. Both Jewish and Palestinian students were assigned to either a group-malleability or a coping intervention. Unlike the adult intervention that lasted 5 hours, the content of these workshops was divided into three separate meetings that were designed to prepare participants for a fourth contact encounter between those schools. During the contact encounter, participants played a few introduction games, as well as completed a set of tasks that measured their ability to cooperate with one another. Results suggested that participants' performance in the group-malleability condition was significantly better compared to the coping condition (Goldenberg et al., 2017). Although these findings cannot directly speak to the impact of the intervention on the Palestinian participants compared to the Israeli participants, the results are encouraging. Further work should be done to examine the specific effects of our intervention on Palestinian participants.

IMPLICATIONS FOR PSYCHOLOGICAL THEORY

One of the more influential insights from psychology is that we operate in the world on the basis of how we perceive the world to be (rather than how the world actually is). From a motivational perspective, our motivation to influence the world around us is determined in part by our estimation of whether we are actually able to impact the world or not (Bandura, 1997, 2006). Evidence for this insight can also be seen at the group level: groups are more likely to support a collective-action movement if they believe that it may change the reality and lead to the desired outcome (van Zomeren, Postmes, & Spears, 2008). The belief that reality can change increases the motivation to change it and forms a self-perpetuating cycle of change.

But the belief that one can influence the world is conditioned on a more basic belief that change and development are possible (Dweck, 2000, 2006). If a person does not believe that people can change in general, then it's likely that they won't believe that investing energy in a specific situation may lead to change. A similar rationale can be applied to the group context. If group members hold the belief that other groups cannot change their inherent nature, this is most likely to affect their belief regarding a specific group change. Our current intervention provides further evidence relevant to this theoretical background and to the fact that changing this belief can have important downstream implications.

FUTURE DIRECTIONS

The current intervention opens many interesting questions that call for further research. Here we present two main next steps that are currently planned. The first step involves further understanding of the active ingredient in our group-malleability manipulation. One important question that stems from our work is when participants are led to believe that groups can change, do they focus their attention on their own group or on the other group? Groups in conflicts often develop strong systems of moral justification for their behavior (Bar-Tal, 2007). It is therefore likely that group members think to themselves, "My group is completely OK, but now there is hope that the other side could change." We therefore hope to investigate this question and further examine whether convincing group members that their own group can also change may increase or decrease the impact of the intervention.

The second future direction involves the broader impacts of our intervention for those not directly targeted. The current work was done with a focus on just the individuals who took part in the interventions, ignoring their social networks. However, just like other behaviors, interventions may also spread (see, e.g., Centola, 2010). Participants in our intervention may share the content they learn with friends or family, and these people may either be influenced by the message, resist its effect, or even polarize their own opinion as a reaction to the message. Learning more about the potential impacts on others of the content of our intervention is key to leading a real change in the Israeli society. In a recent project, we began examining this question by creating predesigned social networks to manipulate and monitor real-time interactions among group members (Centola, 2010; Coman, Momennejad, Drach, & Geana, 2016). A certain portion of our network will go through our intervention, which allows us to examine its effects on their social network. Overall, the impact that our intervention has on influencing challenging intergroup relations motivates us to continue our research in this domain with the hope that it could be utilized for conflict resolution and also for real group change.

REFERENCES

Allport, G. W. (1954). *The nature of prejudice.* Cambridge, MA: Pegasus Books.

Bandura, A. (1997). *Self-efficacy: The exercise of control.* New York: Freeman.

Bandura, A. (2006). Toward a psychology of human agency. *Perspectives on Psychological Science, 1*(2), 164–180.

Bar-Tal, D. (2007). Sociopsychological foundations of intractable conflicts. *American Behavioral Scientist, 50*(11), 1430–1453.

Bar-Tal, D. (2013). *Intractable conflicts: Socio-psychological foundations and dynamics.* Cambridge, UK: Cambridge University Press.

Bar-Tal, D., & Halperin, E. (2011). Socio-psychological barriers to conflict resolution. In D. Bar-Tal (Ed.), *Intergroup conflicts and their resolution: A social psychological perspective* (pp. 217–239). New York: Psychology Press.

Bar-Tal, D., Halperin, E., & Pliskin, R. (2015). Why is it so difficult to resolve intractable conflicts peacefully?: A sociopsychological explanation. In G. Mauro (Ed.), *Handbook of international negotiation* (pp. 73–92). New York: Springer.

Bar-Tal, D., Oren, N., & Nets-Zehngut, R. (2014). Sociopsychological analysis of conflict-supporting narratives: A general framework. *Journal of Peace Research, 51*(5), 662–675.

Bass, B. M. (1985). *Leadership and performance beyond expectations.* New York: Free Press.

Batson, C. D., Chang, J., Orr, R., & Rowland, J. (2002). Empathy, attitudes, and action: Can feeling for a member of a stigmatized group motivate one to help the group? *Personality and Social Psychology Bulletin, 28*(12), 1656–1666.

Berg, J., Dickhaut, J., & McCabe, K. (1995). Trust, reciprocity, and social history. *Games and Economic Behavior, 10*(1), 122–142.

Bilali, R., & Vollhardt, J. R. (2013). Priming effects of a reconciliation radio drama on historical perspective-taking in the aftermath of mass violence in Rwanda. *Journal of Experimental Social Psychology, 49*(1), 144–151.

Bilewicz, M. (2009). Perspective taking and intergroup helping intentions: The moderating role of power relations. *Journal of Applied Social Psychology, 39*(12), 2779–2786.

Blackwell, L. S., Trzesniewski, K. H., & Dweck, C. S. (2007). Implicit theories of intelligence predict achievement across an adolescent transition: A longitudinal study and an intervention. *Child Development, 78*(1), 246–263.

Bolton, G. E., Katok, E., & Zwick, R. (1998). Dictator game giving: Rules of fairness versus acts of kindness. *International Journal of Game Theory, 27*(2), 269–299.

Brehm, J. W. (1966). *A theory of psychological reactance.* Oxford, UK: Academic Press.

Broockman, D., & Kalla, J. (2016). Durably reducing transphobia: A field experiment on door-to-door canvassing. *Science, 352*(6282), 220–224.

Caspit, B. (2014, October 23). Jerusalem's "silent intifada." *Al-Monitor.* Retrieved from *https://web.archive.org/web/20141030194410/http://www.al-monitor.com/pulse/originals/2014/10/israel-east-jerusalem-temple-mount-terror-attack-train.html.*

Centola, D. (2010). The spread of behavior in an online social network experiment. *Science, 329*(5996), 1194–1197.

Chiu, C., Dweck, C. S., Tong, J. Y., & Fu, J. H. (1997). Implicit theories and conceptions of morality. *Journal of Personality and Social Psychology, 73*(5), 923–940.

Chiu, C., Hong, Y., & Dweck, C. S. (1997). Lay dispositionism and implicit theories of personality. *Journal of Personality and Social Psychology, 73*(1), 19–30.

Cohen-Chen, S., Crisp, R. J., & Halperin, E. (2015). Perceptions of a changing world induce hope and promote peace in intractable conflicts. *Personality and Social Psychology Bulletin, 41*(4), 498–512.

Cohen-Chen, S., Crisp, R. J., & Halperin, E. (2016). A new appraisal-based framework underlying hope in conflict resolution. *Emotion Review, 9*(3), 208–220.

Cohen-Chen, S., Halperin, E., Crisp, R. J., & Gross, J. J. (2014). Hope in the Middle East: Malleability beliefs, hope, and the willingness to compromise for peace. *Social Psychological and Personality Science, 5*(1), 67–75.

Cohen-Chen, S., Halperin, E., Saguy, T., & van Zomeren, M. (2014). Beliefs about the malleability of immoral groups facilitate collective action. *Social Psychological and Personality Science,* *5*(2), 203–210.

Coman, A., Momennejad, I., Drach, R. D., & Geana, A. (2016). Mnemonic convergence in social networks: The emergent properties of cognition at a collective level. *Proceedings of the National Academy of Sciences of the USA, 113*(29), 8171–8176.

Dweck, C. S. (2000). *Self-theories: Their role in motivation, personality, and development.* Philadelphia: Psychology Press.

Dweck, C. S. (2006). *Mindset: The new psychology of success.* New York: Random House.

Dweck, C. S. (2012). Mindsets and human nature: Promoting change in the Middle East: The schoolyard, the racial divide, and willpower. *American Psychologist, 67*(8), 614–622.

Gaertner, S. L., Dovidio, J. F., Anastasio, P. A., Bachman, B. A., & Rust, M. C. (1993). The common ingroup identity model: Recategorization and the reduction of intergroup bias. *European Review of Social Psychology, 4*(1), 1–26.

Galinsky, A. D., & Moskowitz, G. B. (2000). Perspective-taking: Decreasing stereotype expression, stereotype accessibility, and in-group favoritism. *Journal of Personality and Social Psychology, 78*(4), 708–724.

Goldenberg, A. (2012, April 7). How convenient. *Haaretz.* Retrieved from *https://www.haaretz.co.il/opinions/1.1747338.*

Goldenberg, A., Endevelt, K., Ran, S., Dweck, C. S., Gross, J. J., & Halperin, E. (2017). Making intergroup contact more fruitful: Enhancing cooperation between Palestinian and Jewish–Israeli adolescents by fostering beliefs about group malleability. *Social Psychological and Personality Science, 8*(1), 1–8.

Graham, J., Haidt, J., & Nosek, B. A. (2009). Liberals and conservatives rely on different sets of moral foundations. *Journal of Personality and Social Psychology, 96*(5), 1029–1046.

Halperin, E. (2008). Group-based hatred in intractable conflict in Israel. *Journal of Conflict Resolution, 52*(5), 713–736.

Halperin, E., Cohen-Chen, S., & Goldenberg, A. (2014). Indirect emotion regulation in intractable conflicts: A new approach to conflict resolution. *European Review of Social Psychology, 25*(1), 1–31.

Halperin, E., Crisp, R. J., Husnu, S., Trzesniewski, K. H., Dweck, C. S., & Gross, J. J. (2012). Promoting intergroup contact by changing beliefs: Group malleability, intergroup anxiety, and contact motivation. *Emotion, 12*(6), 1192–1195.

Halperin, E., Russell, A. G., Trzesniewski, K. H., Gross, J. J., & Dweck, C. S. (2011). Promoting the Middle East peace process by changing beliefs about group malleability. *Science, 333*(6050), 1767–1769.

Hameiri, B., Porat, R., Bar-Tal, D., Bieler, A., & Halperin, E. (2014). Paradoxical thinking as a new avenue of intervention to promote peace. *Proceedings of the National Academy of Sciences of the USA, 111*(30), 10996–11001.

Hameiri, B., Porat, R., Bar-Tal, D., & Halperin, E. (2016). Moderating attitudes in times of violence through paradoxical thinking intervention. *Proceedings of the National Academy of Sciences of the USA, 113*(43), 12105–12110.

Hewstone, M., & Brown, R. (1986). Contact is not enough: An intergroup perspective on the 'contact hypothesis.' In M. Hewstone & R. Brown (Eds.), *Social psychology and society: Contact and conflict in intergroup encounters* (pp. 1–44). Cambridge, MA: Basil Blackwell.

Hilal, J. (Ed.). (2007). *Where now for Palestine?: The demise of the two state solution.* London: Zed Books.

Hong, Y., Chiu, C., Dweck, C. S., Lin, D. M.-S., & Wan, W. (1999). Implicit theories, attributions, and coping: A meaning system approach. *Journal of Personality and Social Psychology, 77*(3), 588–599.

Jost, J. T., Federico, C. M., & Napier, J. L. (2009). Political ideology: Its structure, functions, and elective affinities. *Annual Review of Psychology, 60*(1), 307–337.

Kahn, D. T., Reifen Tagar, M., Halperin, E., Bäckström, M., Vitriol, J. A., & Liberman, V. (2018). If they can't change, why support change?: Implicit theories about groups, social dominance orientation and political identity. *Journal of Social and Political Psychology, 6*(1), 151–173.

Kamins, M. L., & Dweck, C. S. (1999). Person versus process praise and criticism: Implications for contingent self-worth and coping. *Developmental Psychology, 35*(3), 835–847.

Kimel, S. Y., Huesmann, R., Kunst, J. R., & Halperin, E. (2016). Living in a genetic world: How learning about interethnic genetic similarities and differences affect peace and conflict. *Personality and Social Psychology Bulletin, 42*(5), 688–700.

MacInnis, C. C., & Page-Gould, E. (2015). How can intergroup interaction be bad if intergroup contact is good?: Exploring and reconciling an apparent paradox in the science of intergroup relations. *Perspectives on Psychological Science, 10*(3), 307–327.

Maoz, I. (2011). Does contact work in protracted asymmetrical conflict?: Appraising 20 years of reconciliation-aimed encounters between Israeli Jews and Palestinians. *Journal of Peace Research, 48*(1), 115–125.

Maoz, I., & McCauley C. (2008). Threat, dehumanization, and support for retaliatory aggressive policies in asymmetric conflict. *Journal of Conflict Resolution, 52*(1), 93–116.

Melander, E., Pettersson, T., & Themner, L. (2016). Organized violence, 1989–2015. *Journal of Peace Research, 53*(5), 727–742.

Norem, J. K., & Cantor, N. (1986). Defensive pessimism: Harnessing anxiety as motivation. *Journal of Personality and Social Psychology, 51*(6), 1208–1217.

Nussbaum, A. D., & Dweck, C. S. (2008). Defensiveness versus remediation: Self-theories and modes of self-esteem maintenance. *Personality and Social Psychology Bulletin, 34*(5), 599–612.

Paluck, E. L. (2009). Reducing intergroup prejudice and conflict using the media: A field experiment in Rwanda. *Journal of Personality and Social Psychology, 96*(3), 574–587.

Paluck, E. L., Green, S. A., & Green, D. P. (2019). The contact hypothesis re-evaluated. *Behavioral Public Policy, 3*(2), 129–158.

Paunesku, D., Walton, G. M., Romero, C., Smith, E. N., Yeager, D. S., & Dweck, C. S. (2015). Mind-set interventions are a scalable treatment for academic underachievement. *Psychological Science, 26*(6), 784–793.

Peterson, R. D. (2002). *Understanding ethnic violence: Fear, hatred, and resentment in twentieth-century Eastern Europe.* Cambridge, UK: Cambridge University Press.

Pettigrew, T. F. (1998). Intergroup contact theory. *Annual Review of Psychology, 49*(1), 65–85.

Pettigrew, T. F., & Tropp, L. R. (2006). A meta-analytic test of intergroup contact theory. *Journal of Personality and Social Psychology, 90*(5), 751–783.

Podolsky, P. (2012, July 1). Netanyahu intimates Shamir was right in wariness of Arabs. *Times of Israel.* Retrieved from *www.timesofisrael.com/netanyahu-shamir-was-right-in-criticism-of-arabs.*

Rivlin, R. (2015). Address to the 15th annual Herzliya Conference. Retrieved from *http://archive. president.gov.il/English/ThePresident/Speeches/Pages/news_070615_01.aspx.*

Ross, L., & Stittinger, C. (1991). Barriers to conflict resolution. *Negotiation Journal, 7*(4), 389–404.

Rydell, R. J., Hugenberg, K., Ray, D., & Mackie, D. M. (2007). Implicit theories about groups and stereotyping. *Personality and Social Psychology Bulletin, 33*(4), 549–558.

Sassenrath, C., Hodges, S. D., & Pfattheicher, S. (2016). Its all about the self: When perspective taking backfires. *Current Directions in Psychological Science, 25*(6), 405–410.

Schein, C., & Gray, K. (2015). The unifying moral dyad: Liberals and conservatives share the same harm-based moral template. *Personality and Social Psychology Bulletin, 41*(8), 1147–1163.

Tropp, L. R. (2015). Dismantling an ethos of conflict: Strategies for improving intergroup relations. In E. Halperin & K. Sharvit (Eds.), *The social psychology of intractable conflicts* (pp. 159–171). New York: Springer.

van Zomeren, M., Postmes, T., & Spears, R. (2008). Toward an integrative social identity model of collective action: A quantitative research synthesis of three socio-psychological perspectives. *Psychological Bulletin, 134*(4), 504–535.

Vorauer, J. D., & Sasaki, S. J. (2009). Helpful only in the abstract? *Psychological Science, 20*(2), 191–197.

Wang, C. S., Kenneth, T., Ku, G., & Galinsky, A. D. (2014). Perspective-taking increases willingness to engage in intergroup contact. *PLOS ONE, 9*(1), e85681.

Williams, R. M. (1947). *The reduction of intergroup tensions, Vol 57.* New York: Social Science Research Council.

Wohl, M. J. A., Cohen-Chen, S., Halperin, E., Caouette, J., Hayes, N., & Hornsey, M. J. (2015). Belief in the malleability of groups strengthens the tenuous link between a collective apology and intergroup forgiveness. *Personality and Social Psychology Bulletin, 41*(5), 714–725.

Yeager, D. S., Miu, A. S., Powers, J., & Dweck, C. S. (2013). Implicit theories of personality and attributions of hostile intent: A meta-analysis, an experiment, and a longitudinal intervention. *Child Development, 84*(5), 1651–1667.

Yeager, D. S., Trzesniewski, K. H., & Dweck, C. S. (2013). An implicit theories of personality intervention reduces adolescent aggression in response to victimization and exclusion. *Child Development, 84*(3), 970–988.

Yeager, D. S., Trzesniewski, K. H., Tirri, K., Nokelainen, P., & Dweck, C. S. (2011). Adolescents' implicit theories predict desire for vengeance after peer conflicts: Correlational and experimental evidence. *Developmental Psychology, 47*(4), 1090–1107.

Yeager, D. S., Walton, G. M., Brady, S. T., Akcinar, E. N., Paunesku, D., Keane, L., . . . Dweck, C. S. (2016). Teaching a lay theory before college narrows achievement gaps at scale. *Proceedings of the National Academy of Sciences of the United States of America, 113*(24), 3341–3348.

Zaki, J., & Cikara, M. (2015). Addressing empathic failures. *Current Directions in Psychological Science, 24*(6), 471–476.

Zhou, S., Page-Gould, E., Aron, A., Moyer, A., & Hewstone, M. (2018). The extended contact hypothesis: A meta-analysis on 20 years of research. *Personality and Social Psychology Review, 23*(2), 132–160.

CHAPTER 16

The Couples Activity for Reappraising Emotions Intervention

A 7-Minute Marital Conflict Intervention Benefits Relational and Individual Well-Being

Erica B. Slotter and Laura B. Luchies

Marital quality normatively declines over time, which is especially unfortunate given that it is a key contributor to overall life satisfaction. In an effort to preserve marital quality, we designed an intervention that uses emotional reappraisal to help spouses manage the negative emotions they experience during marital conflict. We tested the Couples Activity for Reappraising Emotions (CARE) intervention in a 2-year study of married couples ($N = 120$). Couples that spent 21 minutes over the course of a year engaging in exercises in which they viewed their marital conflicts from the perspective of a benevolent third party experienced stable marital quality, whereas those in a control group experienced a typical decline in marital quality. Moreover, couples in the CARE intervention group also reported better psychological health than those in the control group. In this chapter, we discuss procedures of the CARE intervention, processes that may underlie its effectiveness, predictions about couples for whom it may be less effective, and possibilities for scaling the intervention to make it available and easy for anyone to use. The success of the CARE intervention demonstrates that brief, inexpensive, theory-based social-psychological interventions can address ongoing, costly social problems, such as marital dissatisfaction.

BACKGROUND

Marital quality is one of the most crucial social factors in predicting people's health and well-being (e.g., Myers, 2000; Parker-Pope, 2010). Copious research has documented that lower-quality marriages come with health costs, whereas higher-quality marriages yield health benefits (e.g., Burman & Margolin, 1992; Carr & Springer, 2010; Kiecolt-Glaser & Newton, 2001; Proulx, Helms, & Buehler, 2007; Slatcher, 2010; Whisman, 2001). In terms of psychological health, greater marital quality is associated with greater feelings of general life satisfaction and well-being, with over half of people who report being "very happy" in their marriages also report high levels of general happiness. In contrast, only 10% of people who report being "pretty happy" in their marriages report similarly high levels of overall happiness. Indeed, the association of life satisfaction with marital quality is stronger than life satisfaction's ties to job satisfaction or overall health (Heller, Watson, & Hies, 2004). Low levels of marital happiness have been associated with an increased risk of negative mental health outcomes, including both subclinical and clinical levels of depression (e.g., Beach, 2014; Whisman, 2001).

Greater marital quality also confers benefits for physical health. For example, among patients who have had a coronary artery bypass graft, those who reported high rather than low marital satisfaction 1 year following the surgery were 3.2 times more likely to be alive 15 years after the surgery. This effect could not be explained by demographic, behavioral, or baseline health measures (King & Reis, 2012; see also Coyne et al., 2001). A recent meta-analysis demonstrated that the associations of marital quality with various health outcomes, ranging from cardiovascular events to chronic illness, had effect sizes similar in magnitude to the effects of diet and exercise on health outcomes (Robles, Slatcher, Trombello, & McGinn, 2014). The benefits of high-quality marriages and the tolls of strained marriages have been documented across adulthood, with analogous effects emerging among the newly married, those in midlife, and older adults (e.g., Beach, Katz, Kim, & Brody, 2003; Carr, Freedman, Cornman, & Schwarz, 2014).

Despite the fact that a strong marital bond is an important factor in determining health outcomes, marital quality normatively declines over time. Across couples, marital quality typically declines throughout the course of a marriage, with couples especially at risk for a drop in marital quality around the time they first become parents (e.g., Glenn, 1998; VanLaningham, Johnson, & Amato, 2001). Although the fact that marital quality tends to decline over time is well-known, exactly why this happens is not. Some contributing factors likely include a ceiling effect (i.e., couples typically start their marriages so happy that their satisfaction has nowhere to go but down), habituation (i.e., spouses simply get used to each other's positive traits and behaviors and take them for granted), and an accumulation of frustrations over time.

Given the unfortunate, almost paradoxical, effects wherein happy marriages are essential for well-being and yet marital happiness tends to decline, relationship scholars have sought to identify factors that predict marital quality. These factors may, in turn, be risk factors for negative psychological and physical health outcomes. Dozens of factors have been identified, including conflict dynamics within the marriage, social support provided by the marriage, and external factors placing stress on the marriage (e.g., Fincham & Beach, 1999; Neff & Karney, 2007; Reis, 2012). One recent theoretical model (Slatcher & Schoebi, 2017) categorized risk factors into three groups: external stressors, a lack of marital strengths, and marital strains. External stressors include factors outside of the marital dyad, such as financial pressures, parenting demands, or work concerns. Inadequate marital strengths include a lack of positive behaviors and interaction patterns, such as poor partner responsiveness, low levels of intimacy, or insufficient self-disclosure. Marital strains include negative behaviors and interaction patterns, such as hostility, demand/withdraw conflict patterns, or negative affect reciprocity. The effects of the factors within each category can be moderated by individual differences, such as attachment style or self-esteem.

Interventions designed to promote marital quality could target any of these categories. However, one marital strain has been shown to be an especially robust predictor of marital quality: *negative affect reciprocity*. Negative affect reciprocity is a chain of retaliatory negativity between spouses during marital conflict (Gottman, 1998). Negative affect reciprocity occurs during conflict when spouses counter their partner's complaint or criticism with an escalated complaint or criticism of their own. This pattern of interaction creates a destructive cycle in which behaviors become increasingly hostile as the conflict progresses. Negative affect reciprocity reliably distinguishes couples that are experiencing low marital quality and marital distress from higher-quality, nondistressed couples (e.g., Gottman, 1998; Fincham & Beach, 1999). One of the greatest challenges for couples locked into negative exchanges is to find an adaptive way to exit from such cycles (Weiss & Heyman, 1997). Moreover, the effects of negative affect reciprocity within a marriage are likely cumulative—the longer the pattern of behavior persists in the relationship, the less happy the relationship becomes. Thus, breaking the pattern of negative affect reciprocity should benefit couples at any stage in their relationship.

Scholars and practitioners have attempted to develop therapeutic interventions to interrupt cycles of negativity before they become all consuming (e.g., Baucom, Shoham, Mueser, Daiuto, & Stickle, 1998). For example, behavioral marital therapy uses social learning approaches to help spouses gain insight into problematic interaction patterns and learn to modify their behavior (e.g., Baucom & Epstein, 1990). Although traditional psychotherapy approaches can help spouses learn to manage their emotions and behavior more constructively, they come with drawbacks. They tend to require considerable investment of time and money on the part of the couple. Couples must have both the insight to know their relationship could be improved and the resources to seek and follow through with such treatment. Additionally, couples that are seeing a marital therapist may already be sufficiently distressed in their marriages that therapeutic interventions are rendered less effective than if they had been implemented sooner.

Inspired by research demonstrating that brief, theory-based, social-psychological interventions can yield remarkably enduring improvements in people's lives by fostering thoughts and behaviors that self-reinforce over time (see Walton & Wilson, 2018, for a review), we developed a brief intervention aimed at reducing conflict-based negative affect reciprocity. Given that marital happiness is strongly influenced by recursive, self-reinforcing dynamics, such as negative affect reciprocity, it represents a promising target for a social-psychological intervention. The relative ease and low cost of the intervention's implementation, together with its directed, theoretically driven approach, make it a promising way for couples to interrupt the cycle of negative affect reciprocity in the relationship. Alleviating this marital strain can help preserve marital quality over time, thereby allowing people to reap the psychological and physical health benefits of being in a satisfying marriage.

PSYCHOLOGICAL PROCESSES

Our intervention, called the Couples Activity for Reappraising Emotions (CARE) intervention, capitalized on the power of *emotional reappraisal*—reinterpreting the meaning of emotion-eliciting situations (Gross, 2002, 2015)—to help people manage negative emotions constructively. According to appraisal theories of emotion, it is the subjective interpretation of an event, rather than the event itself, that leads to specific emotional reactions (Folkman & Lazarus, 1985). Emotional reappraisal entails reframing an emotion-laden event in order to change one's emotional response to it, thus mitigating any associated distress (Gross, 1998, 2015; Ochsner & Gross, 2005).

At its core, emotional reappraisal involves construing emotion-eliciting occurrences in ways that alter their meaning with a focus on engaging in "cold" cognitive processing, rather than "hot" emotional processing (e.g., Gross, 2002; Lazarus & Alfert, 1964; Ochsner & Gross, 2005). Emotional reappraisal asks people to reconsider an emotion-eliciting event from the perspective of a person who is not involved in the event itself. The goal is to encourage people to distance themselves psychologically from an emotion-laden experience by considering the experience from an outsider's view. This psychological distance allows people to consider the event—its implications, consequences, and resolution—without becoming overwhelmed by high levels of affect (e.g., Kross, Ayduk, & Mischel, 2005; Richards, Butler, & Gross, 2003; Sbarra, Boals, Mason, Larson, & Mehl, 2013; Slotter & Ward, 2015). When applied to marital conflict, this psychological distance will reduce people's feelings of distress during disagreements with their spouse. Greater psychological distance and less distress will allow people to respond constructively, in a manner that promotes the health of their relationship, rather than react destructively, in a manner that escalates a cycle of negativity.

Research has demonstrated that reappraising a variety of negative emotional events improves subjective well-being, especially when contrasted with other emotional regulation strategies, such as suppressing emotions (e.g., John & Gross, 2004; Gross & John, 2003). For example, a 6-week intervention study of older adults experiencing depression and life challenges contrasted different types of cognitive therapies (Watt & Cappeliez, 2000). A key finding was that participants receiving "integrative therapy," in which they had completed emotional reappraisal exercises, exhibited reduced depressive symptomology over a 3-month time period compared to participants receiving "instrumental therapy," in which they had passively recalled positive coping strategies that could be applied to their current negative life conditions. These and other research findings (e.g., Gross, 1998, 2002; Slotter & Ward, 2015) show that emotional reappraisal can reduce emotional distress in response to negative life events.

The CARE intervention applied these theoretical principles to negative affect reciprocity in marital conflict. The intervention was adapted from a laboratory experiment in which participants were asked to (1) reconsider an interpersonal conflict from a third-party perspective, (2) ruminate about the conflict, or (3) were given no instructions (Ray, Wilhelm, & Gross, 2008; see also Kross et al., 2005). Participants in the reappraisal group experienced less anger and distress about the conflict than did participants in the rumination group. Conflict-related anger and distress dissipated more rapidly among people who completed emotional reappraisal exercises than among those who did not. Given the default tendency to view interpersonal conflict from a first-person perspective, helping people shift their perspective to that of a third party should provide psychological distance from emotion-laden events, such as interpersonal conflict, and thus reduce the negative emotional consequences of those events (e.g., Robinson & Swanson, 1993; Verduyn, Van Mechelen, Kross, Chezzi, & Van Bever, 2012).

Applied to marital quality, the same emotional reappraisal approach should help spouses view their disagreements from a more distanced, less emotionally "hot" perspective. In the CARE intervention, we did not ask participants to view conflicts with their spouse from the perspective of any third party. Instead, we asked them to adopt the perspective of a benevolent third party who "wants the best for all involved" and to consider how this person might "find the good that could come from" disagreements. With this distanced and benevolent perspective, spouses are prompted to see the bigger picture of their relationship and respond constructively instead of reacting destructively. Compared to destructive responses, which escalate conflict-related distress, constructive responses would reduce conflict-related distress; this dissipation represents a disruption in the cycle of negative affect reciprocity. Disrupting negative affect reciprocity helps preserve marital quality by reducing one type of marital strain that predicts declines in relational happiness. Furthermore, emotional reappraisal of marital conflict should be associated with better psychological well-being for the people in these happier marriages.

EMPIRICAL EVIDENCE

Outcomes

To test the effectiveness of the CARE intervention, we conducted a 2-year study of heterosexual married couples ($N = 120$; see Finkel, Slotter, Luchies, Walton, & Gross, 2013, for details). Both members of the couple participated in the study, although each individual completed study measures independently. At the beginning of the study and every 4 months thereafter, participants completed an online survey and reported on their marital quality, including feelings of trust, love, passion, intimacy, satisfaction, and commitment. At each follow-up survey, which occurred every 4 months for the remainder of the study, participants recalled and provided a brief, fact-based summary of the most significant conflict they had experienced in their marriage since the previous follow-up. They also reported on their feelings of postconflict distress as a proxy for negative affect reciprocity.

The first year of the 2-year study did not include the CARE intervention, and all participants underwent identical procedures. During the first year of the study, participants' reports showed decreases in marital quality, replicating the well-documented normative decline in marital quality (e.g., Glenn, 1998; VanLaningham et al., 2001). This decline was evident in all six aspects of marital quality, as well as in an overall composite measure of marital quality.

One year into the study, we randomly assigned half of the couples to the CARE intervention and the other half to a control group. During Year 2, all couples recalled and described a conflict they had experienced, just as they had in Year 1. Couples in the control group did not receive any additional instructions, whereas couples in the CARE intervention condition were instructed to engage in emotional reappraisal techniques after describing the conflict. They completed an additional writing task that involved three prompts and lasted approximately 7 minutes. In it, they were asked to take the perspective of a neutral third party who wants the best for everyone and consider how they could overcome barriers to adopting this perspective during future conflicts. Full details on the intervention and its implementation are available in the "Intervention Content and Implementation" section.

Participants in the control condition reported continued decreases in marital quality during Year 2, extending the trajectory they had experienced in Year 1. However, the decline in marital quality was stemmed among participants in the CARE intervention. In fact, the slope of marital quality in Year 2 among participants who completed the CARE intervention was statistically flat; the decline in marital quality disappeared for these participants in the second year of the study. Figure 16.1 illustrates the effect of the CARE intervention on the composite measure of marital quality.

We also examined how the CARE intervention might have impacted participants' psychological well-being. Whereas the effects on marital quality were published previously (Finkel et al., 2013), our examination of psychological well-being uses unpublished data from the same study, so we are including more details about it here. On the first and final surveys of the 2-year study, participants reported on three indicators of psychological distress: depressive symptomology (Radloff, 1977), psychological stress (Cohen, Kamarck, & Mermelstein, 1983), and life dissatisfaction (Diener, Emoons, Larsen, & Griffin, 1985). We used multilevel modeling analyses to predict each of the three indicators of psychological distress at the end of the study from participants' CARE intervention status (control = 0, reappraisal = 1), controlling for the same measure at the beginning of the study, 2 years earlier. As detailed in Table 16.1, CARE intervention participants exhibited significantly better end-of-study psychological outcomes than did control participants. Thus, the CARE intervention improves both relational and individual well-being.

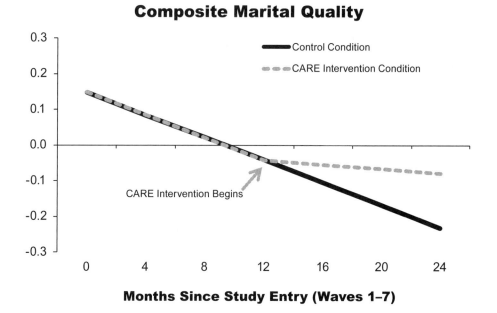

Notes T0 is a SEPARATE variable, intake is not part of this central analysis....T1 is the first followup wave
Overall Composite made by z-scoring composites and averaging them into 1

FIGURE 16.1. Trajectories of marital quality for participants in the CARE intervention condition and participants in the control condition. Reprinted with permission from Finkel, Slotter, Luchies, Walton, and Gross (2013).

TABLE 16.1. The CARE Intervention's Effects on Psychological Well-Being

Psychological distress variable	Parameter estimate	t value
End-of-study depressive symptomology		
Intake depressive symptomology	.66	12.99**
CARE intervention status	−.14	−2.23*
End-of-study stress		
Intake stress	.80	11.51**
CARE intervention status	−.11	−2.44*
End-of-study life dissatisfaction		
Intake life dissatisfaction	.78	12.67**
CARE intervention status	−.15	−2.41*

Note. Degrees of freedom ranged from 115 to 119; slight variations were due to missing data.
*$p < .05$; **$p < .001$.

Mechanism

We next sought to examine the mechanism by which the CARE intervention might be buffering participants against drops in marital quality over time. We tested two possible mechanisms. The first tested mechanism was the possibility that those in the CARE intervention condition experienced less severe marital conflicts than control participants. Results showed that this was not the case; there was no notable difference in how severe participants in the two conditions rated the conflicts they had experienced.

The second tested mechanism was the possibility that those in the CARE intervention experienced less distress related to their marital conflicts than control participants—even though the conflicts they had experienced were just as severe. Results provided evidence for this mechanism. CARE intervention participants experienced less distress about their marital conflicts over the course of the second year of the study, which was the same time they were engaging in the intervention. Additional mediation analyses showed that this reduction in conflict-related distress went on to predict more stable levels of marital quality. In sum, couples that participated in the CARE intervention experienced less conflict-related distress over time, and this led them to experience more stable marital quality over time.

Effects over Time

Because we have tested the CARE intervention in only one study to date, we have limited evidence about its long-term effects. However, from this study we do know that marital quality stabilized among couples that engaged in the CARE intervention, and that this stabilization lasted throughout the year that the intervention took place. On the other hand, marital quality continued a downward trajectory among control participants. We expect that both trends would continue, causing the gap in marital quality between those who engaged in the CARE intervention and those who did not to widen over time.

Learning, practicing, and mastering new skills takes much practice, repetition, and time. Yet, the CARE intervention took only 7 minutes at each of three occurrences, totaling just 21 minutes in a year's time. This small amount of time would not be enough for participants to learn, master, and implement a skill that would directly lead to better marital quality. Instead, we think that the CARE intervention instilled in participants a new mindset to use when facing marital conflicts. Unlike skills, new mindsets can be adopted quickly (Walton & Wilson, 2018). Once people adopt a new mindset about marital conflict, that mindset may remain, perhaps for the duration of their marriage. To the extent that this is true, continuing to complete reappraisal exercises may not yield additional benefits. However, to lessen the possibility of shifting back into the preintervention default tendency to see conflicts from an emotionally "hot" egocentric perspective, it may be helpful for people to continue to invest 21 minutes a year into their marriages by sustaining the CARE intervention over time. We do not foresee any downsides of continuing the intervention long term—doing so might help and would not hurt.

Heterogeneity

We tested whether the CARE intervention would be more or less effective among different groups of participants, including men versus women, younger versus older participants, or couples that had been married for shorter versus longer lengths of time. In our study, none of these factors affected the CARE intervention's effectiveness. We also examined six indicators of marital quality, including feelings of trust, love, passion, intimacy, satisfaction, and commitment. All six indicators yielded similar results.

However, it is important to note that all of our participants volunteered to take part in a study of romantic relationships. Couples whose relationships are very distressed are unlikely to want to participate in a study like this. We suspect that the CARE intervention would be less effective among clinically distressed couples living in a climate of contempt. Instead, this intervention presupposes that people who use it are living in a general climate of decency, believe their relationship is worth maintaining, and have a partner who warrants the benefit of the doubt. If a relationship is so troubled that wanting the best for all involved means that it may be best for the relationship to end, the CARE intervention is unlikely to work well, if at all. Moreover, it could give people living in a toxic relationship false hope for improvement, potentially putting them at risk if that relationship is abusive.

COUSINS

The CARE intervention is both similar to and different from several other social psychological interventions. Because marital conflicts are stressful, it is instructive to compare the CARE intervention to other interventions that have focused on people's views of stress and the implications of those views. For example, people can hold different appraisals about specific stressful situations. They can see stress arousal either as a useful tool that can be harnessed to help one rise to a challenge, or they can see stress arousal as a detriment to one's ability to address a threat (see, e.g., Jamieson & Hangen, Chapter 10, this volume; Jamieson, Nock, & Mendes, 2012). Interventions that induce people to see stress as indicating a challenge rather than a threat predict more optimal physiological responses and enhance one's performance. Other research has examined people's general mindsets about stress (see, e.g., Crum, Handley-Miner, & Smith, Chapter 9, this volume; Crum, Salovey, & Achor, 2013). Although people tend to see stress as negative, stress has enhancing as well as debilitating consequences. Inducing people to adopt a stress-is-enhancing mindset rather than a stress-is-debilitating mindset also predicts more optimal physiological responses and enhances one's performance. Both stress appraisal and stress-mindset interventions have focused on outcomes related to performance on specific, stressful tasks. In contrast, although marital conflicts are stressful, they are neither a task to be accomplished nor a challenge to be overcome. In fact, if spouses view marital conflicts as something to perform well on or "win," they may double down on their default egocentric view of the conflict—the opposite of the CARE intervention's goal. Therefore, we caution against broadly applying these other interventions to the stress of marital conflict.

A type of intervention that is more like the CARE intervention is one that uses self-distancing strategies (e.g., Kross et al., 2005; Ray et al., 2008). In a seminal study in this line of research, participants recalled an interpersonal situation in which they felt overwhelming anger and hostility (Kross et al., 2005). Then they were asked to view this experience in one of two ways. In the self-immersed condition, they viewed the situation through their own eyes all over again. In the self-distanced perspective, they viewed the situation as if they were a fly on the wall. In addition, half of the participants in both the immersed and distanced conditions were asked to think about *what* they were feeling, whereas the other half were asked to think about *why* they were feeling the way they were feeling. People who had adopted the self-distanced perspective and thought about the reasons underlying their emotions experienced less negative affect than those in the other conditions. These results showed that a self-distanced and abstract perspective allows people to think about negative experiences without eliciting high levels of negative emotions. The CARE intervention employed a self-distancing strategy for viewing marital conflicts. Yet, it went further than asking participants to view their marital conflict from the perspective of a fly on the wall. Instead, participants were asked to take the perspective of a third party who wants the best for all involved and to consider how this person might see the good that could come from the conflict. These instructions may have encouraged CARE intervention participants to adopt an abstract perspective, much like those in Kross et al.'s (2005) *why* condition.

Still other social psychological interventions have prompted mindset changes that have benefited dyadic relationships. For example, one intervention led teachers to adopt an empathic mindset about discipline, in which they were encouraged to understand and value their students' circumstances and perspectives (Okonofua, Paunesku, & Walton, 2016). Students in these teachers' classes were only half as likely to be suspended as those in a control group; they also perceived greater respect from their teachers. Another intervention was administered to mothers of medically at-risk infants during home visits (e.g., Bugental, Beaulieu, & Silbert-Beiger, 2010; Bugental et al., 2002). The intervention facilitated the mothers' own problem-solving and information search, whereas the control home visiting program provided mothers with ideas on how to solve problems and gave them information. It also discouraged mothers from holding pejorative views about themselves and their children, such as the belief that they are a bad mom or that their child is a bad baby. The intervention yielded several positive outcomes over time, including decreased use of corporal punishment, increased maternal investment of time in the child, and better child health. In both lines of research, the intervention targeted one member of a dyad, yet benefited both members. As currently designed, the CARE intervention targets both members of a married couple, but it could be adapted to involve only one spouse. We expect that the CARE intervention would be beneficial even if only one spouse participated in it, although its benefits are maximized when both spouses participate.

A final intervention is most similar to the CARE intervention in domain-romantic relationships—although it is quite different in the psychological process it seeks to change. People with low self-esteem often act in self-protective ways that ultimately harm their relationships, such as resisting compliments from their romantic partners (e.g., Murray, Holmes, Griffin, Bellavia, & Rose, 2001). An intervention sought to disrupt this self-fulfilling pattern of behavior. In it, people with low self-esteem were induced to take on a mindset in which they reframed their partners' compliments in an abstract way by explaining why their partner admired them (see, e.g., Marigold, Chapter 17, this volume; Marigold, Holmes, & Ross, 2007, 2010). Participants who completed this exercise felt better about the compliment, themselves, and their relationship. Moreover, this abstract reframing intervention (ARI) reduced low self-esteem individuals' negative behavior over a 2-week period as reported by their partners. There are several differences between the ARI and the CARE intervention. First, the ARI targets responses to and accentuates the meaning of a positive experience (i.e., a compliment), whereas the CARE intervention targets responses to and diminishes the meaning of a negative experience (i.e., marital conflict). Second, the ARI is designed to disrupt a process unique to people with low self-esteem in romantic contexts, whereas the CARE intervention is designed to disrupt a process that is widespread across romantic contexts (i.e., negative affect reciprocity). These differences highlight the importance of specifying the mechanism by which social-psychological interventions work. There is no universal intervention to fix problems in romantic relationships—instead, different interventions can address different problems that arise in romantic relationships.

INTERVENTION CONTENT AND IMPLEMENTATION

The CARE intervention was designed to be a brief, directed intervention to reduce negative conflict-related emotions, thus reducing negative affect reciprocity, with the aim of protecting marital quality in ongoing relationships. The study designed to test the CARE intervention was conducted largely online, with all procedures of the CARE intervention and its effects completed entirely online. As stated previously, participants in the study completed an intake session, as well as six follow-up waves, every 4 months over 2 years. Participants received e-mails when it was time to complete a follow-up wave with a link directing them to the assessment. They could complete the follow-up at their convenience within 2 weeks of receiving the e-mail. Each follow-up wave took an average of 20–30 minutes to complete.

Participants wrote about a recent conflict in their relationship at each wave of the study. They provided a "fact-based summary of the most significant disagreement" they had experienced with their spouse over the preceding 4 months, "focusing on behavior, not on thoughts or feelings." We asked them to "provide enough information that someone unfamiliar with the disagreement would be able to understand what happened." Participants were asked to respond to this prompt for about 2 minutes but could write as long as they liked.

During Year 2 (Waves 5–7), half of the couples were randomly assigned to the CARE intervention. The participants were asked to engage in an additional, approximately 7-minute writing task in which they were asked to emotionally reappraise the conflict they had written about from the perspective of a neutral third party who wanted the best outcome for all persons involved. Specifically, they were asked to respond to the following three prompts:

> "Think about the specific disagreement that you just wrote about having with your partner. Think about this disagreement with your partner from the perspective of a neutral third party who wants the best for all involved; a person who sees things from a neutral point of view. How might this person think about the disagreement? How might he or she find the good that could come from it? (Please write about this for 3 minutes.)"

> "Some people find it helpful to take this third-party perspective during their interactions with their romantic partner. However, almost everybody finds it challenging to take this third-party perspective at all times. In your relationship with your partner, what obstacles do you face in trying to take this third-party perspective, especially when you're having a disagreement with your partner? (Please write about this for 2 minutes.)"

> "Despite the obstacles to taking a third-party perspective, people can be successful in doing so. Over the next 4 months, please try your best to take this third-party perspective during interactions with your partner, especially during disagreements. How might you be most successful in taking this perspective in your interactions with your partner over the next 4 months? How might taking this perspective help you make the best of disagreements in your relationship? (Please write about this for 2 minutes.)"

Each prompt and a space for typing responses appeared on a separate page in the online survey. Participants clicked a button marked "Next" to proceed through the pages. For each prompt, participants were asked to consider the questions at hand and write about them for a set amount of time. They could take longer if they wished, but they could not advance the page until the base amount of time had passed. The CARE intervention occurred at the very end of the follow-up assessments before participants were thanked for their participation and dismissed.

Participants in the CARE intervention group also received reminder e-mails about the reappraisal task they had completed during their follow-up assessments. The e-mails were automatically sent 2 months after the completion of each wave in the second year of the study. The e-mail was designed to remind participants to engage in emotional reappraisal regarding conflict in their marriage. The e-mail text, slightly edited for space, was:

> Hello [name],
>> We're writing to check in. The next follow-up questionnaire isn't for another two months, but we wanted to thank you again for participating in the study.
>> When you completed your most recent questionnaire, you wrote about a specific disagreement with your partner. You thought about this disagreement from the perspective of a neutral third party who wants the best for all involved and about how this person might find the good that could come of the disagreement.
>> You then thought about obstacles you face in your own life that might interfere with your ability to take a neutral, third-party perspective regarding disagreements in your own relationship. Finally, you thought about specific ways that taking this third-party

perspective in your own relationship can help you make the most of disagreements with your partner.

As you go through your daily life, please keep in mind the benefits of adopting a third-party perspective regarding your relationship. Sometime today (now, if the timing works), please take a few moments to think about ways you can adopt this perspective about conflicts in your relationship, about ways to find the good that can come from them.

Thanks again for staying involved in the study. We'll check back with you in a couple of months. In the meantime, if you have any questions about the study, feel free to e-mail us.

Participants in the control group received e-mails in between their follow-up assessments in the second year of the study as well, but these e-mails simply thanked them for being involved in the study and told them that they would receive their next follow-up survey in 2 months.

The CARE intervention, as it was designed, has the advantage of being brief—it was completed in 7 minutes per wave, making participants' total investment in the intervention 21 minutes in a year—and yet, it was powerful enough to eliminate declines in couples' marital quality over a year. It is also easy and flexible to administer—participants in our study completed the intervention procedures online, largely at their convenience, in locations of their choosing. Overall, the design of the CARE intervention makes it an efficient, and yet powerfully effective, intervention to protect marital quality and psychological well-being.

NUANCES AND MISCONCEPTIONS

A dangerous misconception that some people may have about the CARE intervention is seeing it as a panacea that can replace marital therapy and fix troubled marriages. We tested the CARE intervention in couples that volunteered to participate in our study; few of them were likely to be highly distressed. In our view, the CARE intervention should be used by couples that want to maintain, not end, their relationship and in which partners have a foundation of care for each other and warrant the benefit of the doubt. If a relationship is so toxic that a reasonable third party could not see the good that could come from disagreements in it, the CARE intervention would not help. Instead, these spouses should consider whether their relationship should continue, and if so, they should seek professional counsel about how to improve it. Moreover, the CARE intervention stabilized marital quality, but it did not increase it. If the current level of marital quality in a relationship is not satisfying, the CARE intervention might be able to keep it from getting worse but probably won't improve it.

Another potentially important nuance about the CARE intervention is that we asked participants to take the perspective of a benevolent third party who wants the best for all involved. Participants were prompted to imagine how this person could see the good that could come from the disagreement and consider how they could make the best of future conflicts in the relationship. Although we did not compare this benevolent third-party perspective to a neutral one, we expect that it contributed to participants' ability to respond constructively to their marital conflicts, leading to less conflict-related distress. Other potential third-party perspectives, such as a friend's or family member's view, may not have been as effective, especially if people would choose to take the perspective of a person who might be on "their side" more than their spouse's side. It is also important to note that we did not ask participants to put themselves into their spouse's shoes and try to see things from their spouse's perspective. In the midst of marital conflict, people are likely to believe that their spouse's perspective is overblown, irrational, or just plain wrong. Trying to take a spouse's view is likely to heighten these beliefs and backfire by promoting the default egocentric and emotionally hot perspective, which would only make things worse.

A few other details of how we administered the CARE intervention may be critical to its effectiveness. First, both spouses participated in the CARE intervention. Although we do not think it is absolutely necessary for both spouses to complete the CARE intervention for it to yield some benefit, we expect that it is most powerful when both spouses take part because of the beneficial synergy that would occur. Second, participants completed the reappraisal exercises about specific conflicts in their own relationship, not interpersonal conflicts in general. We expect that reappraising concrete, personal conflicts was effectual because these are the conflicts about which participants can benefit from shifting from an emotionally hot, egocentric perspective to that of a distanced, rational, benevolent third party. Third, participants anticipated obstacles that they might encounter when adopting the benevolent third-party perspective during future marital conflicts and how they might overcome these obstacles. We expect that doing this helped participants push through challenges they might have encountered, rather than seeing them as evidence that taking the third-party perspective is too difficult. Fourth, participants were not forced to complete the intervention exercises or write in response to each prompt, although the survey did not allow them to move forward until the base amount of time had passed. Other social-psychological interventions have been shown to work best or only when people voluntarily take part in them (e.g., Bryan et al., 2016; Vansteenkiste, Simons, Lens, Sheldon, & Deci, 2004; Lyubomirsky, Dickerhoof, Boehm, & Sheldon, 2011; Silverman, Logel, & Cohen, 2013), and the CARE intervention might be less effective if it were a required activity.

Although these nuances may enhance or reduce the effectiveness of the CARE intervention, we do not anticipate ways in which it could backfire. We designed the CARE intervention to be straightforward, easily administered, conducted online, and scalable. Variations in the CARE intervention's procedures may render it less beneficial but are unlikely to make it harmful.

IMPLICATIONS FOR PRACTICE

Given the beneficial effects of the CARE intervention on marital quality and psychological health, it would be advantageous to make it available to couples on a larger scale. One way to roll out the CARE intervention to more people is through professionals and practitioners who work directly with couples. Although we have publicized our results in the popular media and are aware of practitioners who have adopted or adapted this intervention in their practice, there is much more opportunity to actively promote the intervention among those who work directly with couples. As previously discussed, the CARE intervention maintains, but does not improve, marital quality. We also caution its use among highly distressed couples. Therefore, it would be most helpful for practitioners who work with couples early in their relationships, such as those who provide premarital counseling or officiate weddings, to promote the CARE intervention.

A second and even more scalable way to roll out the CARE intervention to more couples is to build an application (app) that delivers the intervention to any person who would like to use it in his or her relationship. The app could lead users through the 7-minute intervention at regular intervals and send push notifications or e-mail reminders about adopting a third-party perspective during conflicts. As discussed in the "Nuances and Misconceptions" section, the CARE intervention was designed to be self-administered online, and we do not anticipate ways in which it could be harmful when used by people who are involved in average to high-quality relationships. The app could include an optional research component, perhaps varying the frequency of the intervention and reminder notifications. Users would report on their relationship quality periodically, creating a cost-effective way to test variations of the intervention while delivering the intervention to an unlimited number of couples at minimal cost.

IMPLICATIONS FOR PSYCHOLOGICAL THEORY

The CARE intervention's success has theoretical implications, informing researchers about the usefulness of emotional reappraisal to a new domain. Past research has shown that emotional reappraisal is useful to people navigating relationship dissolution (Slotter & Ward, 2015; Sbarra et al., 2013), smoking cessation (Fucito, Juliano, & Toll, 2010), anxiety disorders (Goldin et al., 2012), and suicidal ideation (Kiosses et al., 2018). Our work demonstrates that emotional reappraisal can be applied to the domain of close relationships as well, and especially to marital conflict. Furthermore, past research has shown that people tend to adopt a first-person perspective during interpersonal conflicts, often leading to a destructive pattern of negative affect reciprocity (e.g., Robinson & Swanson, 1993; Verduyn et al., 2012). This work indicates that this default pattern of behavior can be avoided—and quite easily.

As discussed in the "Effects over Time" section, the CARE intervention took only 7 minutes of participants' time at each of three occurrences over the course of a year. Twenty-one minutes in a year's time would not be enough for participants to learn and implement a skill—yet the CARE intervention had the power to maintain marital quality. Therefore, we see emotional reappraisal of marital conflicts as a shift in mindset or perspective (see Walton & Wilson, 2018). Such a shift can occur quickly and has the potential to yield long-term effects without additional iterations of the intervention that cultivated the changed mindset. Nonetheless, we do not foresee any reason why couples should not continue to invest 21 minutes a year into their marriage by continuing the CARE intervention exercises. Doing so could help keep people from sliding back into their previous, emotionally hot, egocentric view of marital conflicts.

FUTURE DIRECTIONS

Even though the intervention itself is inexpensive and easy to implement, conducting a standard study to test it is not. Recruiting a sufficient number of couples and tracking them for 2 years or more is expensive and time-consuming. To date, we have tested the intervention's outcomes only one time, and we are not aware of other studies that have replicated or extended our work. With that in mind, we outline six avenues for future empirical work.

First, as mentioned in the "Implications for Practice" section, future research could test the CARE intervention using an app that delivers the intervention to many users via their mobile devices. Doing so would be a cost-effective way to extend research on the CARE intervention.

Second, future research could test the CARE intervention with a more diverse sample of participants. Our participants varied in age and in the length of their marriages—however, they were predominantly White, of midrange socioeconomic status, and all of them were in heterosexual relationships. Given recent work showing that some of these factors can impact marital conflict and marital quality dynamics (e.g., Jackson et al., 2016), examining the effectiveness of the CARE intervention within a broader population is essential. One possibility would be to test the CARE intervention among newlyweds to determine whether it could help maintain the high level of marital quality that couples tend to experience in the so-called honeymoon phase. Another possibility would be to test the CARE intervention in couples undergoing the transition to parenthood, a time during which marital quality is especially likely to decline. It would also be informative to examine the CARE intervention across cultures. It is possible that the intervention would be less effective among couples living in interdependent cultures to the extent that their default perspective is less egocentric than it tends to be among people living in independent cultures (see Cohen & Gunz, 2002; Wu & Keysar, 2007).

Third, future research could follow up with the original participants some years after the original study period to gauge whether those who had been assigned to the CARE intervention condition have continued to reappraise conflicts in their relationships and/or have maintained higher levels of marital quality than those in the control condition. We expect that the CARE intervention brings about a mindset shift that yields recursive, self-perpetuating processes over time; these processes would continue to yield benefits even after the intervention ended. Nonetheless, it would be fruitful for future research to investigate the longer-term effects of the intervention, both with and without additional iterations of the intervention.

Fourth, future research could involve a study in which only one member of each couple completes the intervention to determine whether one or both members of the couple should participate to yield maximal benefits. As discussed in the "Nuances and Misconceptions" section, we think that having both members participate would create a synergy and make the intervention the most effective. However, it may yield some benefits if only one spouse engages in the intervention, especially because either partner can stop a cycle of negative affect reciprocity. Couples in which one spouse is truly behaving more negatively than the other are an interesting case. On the one hand, it would be most helpful to change the *behavior* of the spouse who is behaving most negatively. On the other hand, it may be the most helpful to change the *mindset* of the spouse who is on the receiving end of the negativity; doing so may avoid further instigating the spouse who is behaving most negatively. However, keep in mind our caution about using the CARE intervention while couples are highly distressed.

Fifth, future research could systematically vary aspects of the CARE intervention to determine the minimally necessary elements for the intervention to remain effective. This type of investigation would be similar to Marigold et al.'s (2007) work that isolated the core of an intervention to help people with low self-esteem to respond positively to a romantic partner's compliments. Furthermore, it would enable further refinement of the psychological processes that are at work in the CARE intervention. Relatedly, we used conflict-related distress as a proxy measure for negative affect reciprocity, the primary mechanism we targeted. A better measure that could be used in future research would be behavioral evidence of negative affect reciprocity, which could be captured in videotaped conflict discussions.

Sixth, future research could extend the scope of the CARE intervention's outcomes to include physical health. As reviewed at the beginning of this chapter, marital quality is an important predictor of physical health, but this finding is based on correlational and longitudinal studies. A future experiment of the CARE intervention's effectiveness on both marital quality and physical health could provide even stronger evidence of the causal effect of marital quality on physical health.

CONCLUSION

For decades, psychological researchers and practitioners have grappled with the paradox of marital quality: it is essential for people's psychological and physical well-being, and yet it declines over time within relationships. Fortunately, this decline is not inevitable. The CARE intervention, grounded in appraisal theories of emotion and capitalizing on people's ability to reinterpret their emotional experiences, interrupts the spiral of negative affect reciprocity that can occur during marital conflict. It both stops declines in marital quality and benefits psychological well-being. Compared to previous attempts to intervene in declining marital quality, the CARE intervention has the benefit of being brief (couples completed it in 7-minute sessions, three times during a year period), theory driven (it was developed out of a robust literature on the benefits of emotional reappraisal), and flexible (the current variant of the procedure was applied online but could be adapted to many other settings). Because of its effectiveness and ease of implementation, the CARE intervention represents a promising avenue for both researchers and practitioners to aid people in protecting and preserving their marital happiness.

REFERENCES

Baucom, D. H., & Epstein, N. (1990). *Cognitive-behavioral marital therapy.* New York: Brunner/ Mazel.

Baucom, D. H., Shoham, V., Mueser, K. T., Daiuto, A. D., & Stickle, T. R. (1998). Empirically supported couple and family interventions for marital distress and adult mental health problems. *Journal of Consulting and Clinical Psychology, 66*(1), 53–88.

Beach, S. R. H. (2014). The couple and family discord model of depression: Updates and future directions. In C. R. Agnew & S. C. South (Eds.), *Interpersonal relationships and health: Social and clinical psychological mechanisms* (pp. 133–155). New York: Oxford University Press.

Beach, S. R. H., Katz, J., Kim, S., & Brody, G. H. (2003). Prospective effects of marital satisfaction on depressive symptoms in established marriages: A dyadic model. *Journal of Social and Personal Relationships, 20*(3), 355–371.

Bryan, C. J., Yeager, D. S., Hinojosa, C. P., Chabot, A., Bergen, H., Kawamura, M., & Steubing,

F. (2016). Harnessing adolescent values to motivate healthier eating. *Proceedings of the National Academy of Sciences of the USA, 113,* 10830–10835.

Bugental, D. B., Beaulieu, D. A., & Silbert-Geiger, A. (2010). Increases in parental investment and child health as a result of an early intervention. *Journal of Experimental Child Psychology, 106*(1), 30–40.

Bugental, D. B., Ellerson, P. C., Lin, E. K., Rainey, B., Kokotovic, A., & O'Hara, N. (2002). A cognitive approach to child abuse prevention. *Journal of Family Psychology, 16*(3), 243–258.

Burman, B., & Margolin, G. (1992). Analysis of the association between marital relationships and health problems: An interactional perspective. *Psychological Bulletin, 112*(1), 39–63.

Carr, D., Freedman, V. A., Cornman, J. C., & Schwarz, N. (2014). Happy marriage, happy life?: Marital quality and subjective well-being in later life. *Journal of Marriage and the Family, 76*(5), 930–948.

Carr, D., & Springer, K. W. (2010). Advances in families and health research in the 21st century. *Journal of Marriage and Family, 72*(3), 743–761.

Cohen, D., & Gunz, A. (2002). As seen by the other . . . : Perspectives on the self in the memories and emotional perceptions of Easterners and Westerners. *Psychological Science, 13*(1), 55–59.

Cohen, S., Kamarck, T., & Mermelstein, R. (1983). A global measure of perceived stress. *Journal of Health and Social Behavior, 24*(4), 385–396.

Coyne, J. C., Rohrbaugh, M. J., Shoham, V., Sonnega, J. S., Nicklas, J. M., & Cranford, J. A. (2001). Prognostic importance of marital quality for survival of congestive heart failure. *American Journal of Cardiology, 88*(5), 526–529.

Crum, A. J., Salovey, P., & Achor, S. (2013). Rethinking stress: The role of mindsets in determining stress response. *Journal of Personality and Social Psychology, 104*(4), 716–733.

Diener, E., Emmons, R. A., Larsen, R. J., & Griffin, S. (1985). The Satisfaction with Life Scale. *Journal of Personality Assessment, 49*(1), 71–75.

Fincham, F. D., & Beach, S. R. H. (1999). Conflict in marriage: Implications for working with couples. *Annual Review of Psychology, 50*(1), 47–77.

Finkel, E. J., Slotter, E. B., Luchies, L. B., Walton, G. M., & Gross, J. J. (2013). A brief intervention to promote conflict reappraisal preserves marital quality over time. *Psychological Science, 24*(8), 1595–1601.

Folkman, S., & Lazarus, R. S. (1985). If it changes it must be a process: Study of emotion and coping during three stages of a college examination. *Journal of Personality and Social Psychology, 48*(1), 150–170.

Fucito, L. M., Juliano, L. M., & Toll, B. A. (2010). Cognitive reappraisal and expressive suppression emotion regulation strategies in cigarette smokers. *Nicotine and Tobacco Research, 12*(11), 1156–1161.

Glenn, N. D. (1998). The course of marital success and failure in five American 10-year marriage cohorts. *Journal of Marriage and Family, 60*(3), 569–576.

Goldin, P. R., Ziv, M., Jazaieri, H., Werner, K., Kraemer, H., Heimberg, R. G., & Gross, J. J. (2012). Cognitive reappraisal self-efficacy mediates the effects of individual cognitive-behavioral therapy for social anxiety disorder. *Journal of Consulting and Clinical Psychology, 80*(6), 1034–1040.

Gottman, J. M. (1998). Psychology and the study of marital processes. *Annual Review of Psychology, 49*(1), 169–197.

Gross, J. J. (1998). Antecedent- and response-focused emotion regulation: Divergent consequences for experience, expression, and physiology. *Journal of Personality and Social Psychology, 74*(1), 224–237.

Gross, J. J. (2002). Emotion regulation: Affective, cognitive, and social consequences. *Psychophysiology, 39*(3), 281–291.

Gross, J. J. (2015). Emotion regulation: Current status and future prospects. *Psychological Inquiry, 26*(1), 1–26.

Gross, J. J., & John, O. P. (2003). Individual differences in two emotion regulation processes: Implications for affect, relationships, and well-being. *Journal of Personality and Social Psychology, 85*(2), 348–362.

Heller, D., Watson, D., & Hies, R. (2004). The role of person versus situation in life satisfaction: A critical examination. *Psychological Bulletin, 130*(4), 574–600.

Jackson, G. L., Trail, T. E., Kennedy, D. P., Williamson, H. C., Bradbury, T. N., & Karney, B. R. (2016). The salience and severity of relationship problems among low-income couples. *Journal of Family Psychology, 30*(1), 2–11.

Jamieson, J. P., Nock, M. K., & Mendes, W. B. (2012). Mind over matter: Reappraising arousal improves cardiovascular and cognitive responses to stress. *Journal of Experimental Psychology, 141*(3), 417–422.

John, O. P., & Gross, J. J. (2004). Healthy and unhealthy emotion regulation: Personality processes, individual differences, and life span development. *Journal of Personality, 72*(6), 1301–1334.

Kiecolt-Glaser, J. K., & Newton, T. L. (2001). Marriage and health: His and hers. *Psychological Bulletin, 127*(4), 472–503.

King, K. B., & Reis, H. T. (2012). Marriage and long-term survival after coronary artery bypass grafting. *Health Psychology, 31*(1), 55–62.

Kiosses, D. N., Alexopoulos, G. S., Hajcak, G., Apfeldorf, W., Duberstein, P. R., Putrino, D., & Gross, J. J. (2018). Cognitive reappraisal intervention for suicide prevention (CRISP) for middle-aged and older adults hospitalized for suicidality. *American Journal of Geriatric Psychiatry, 26*(4), 494–503.

Kross, E., Ayduk, O., & Mischel, W. (2005). When asking "why" does not hurt: Distinguishing rumination from reflective processing of negative emotions. *Psychological Science, 16*(9), 709–715.

Lazarus, R. S., & Alfert, E. (1964). Short-circuiting of threat by experimentally altering cognitive appraisal. *Journal of Abnormal and Social Psychology, 69*(2), 195–205.

Lyubomirsky, S., Dickerhoof, R., Boehm, J. K., & Sheldon, K. M. (2011). Becoming happier takes both a will and a proper way: An experimental longitudinal intervention to boost well-being. *Emotion, 11*, 391–402.

Marigold, D. C., Holmes, J. G., & Ross, M. (2007). More than words: Reframing compliments from romantic partners fosters security in low self-esteem individuals. *Journal of Personality and Social Psychology, 92*, 232–248.

Marigold, D. C., Holmes, J. G., & Ross, M. (2010). Fostering relationship resilience: An intervention for low self-esteem individuals. *Journal of Experimental Social Psychology, 46*, 624–630.

Murray, S. L., Holmes, J. G., Griffin, D. W., Bellavia, G., & Rose, P. (2001). The mismeasure of love: How self-doubt contaminates relationship beliefs. *Personality and Social Psychology Bulletin, 27*(4), 423–436.

Myers, D. G. (2000). The funds, friends, and faith of happy people. *American Psychologist, 55*(1), 56–67.

Neff, L. A., & Karney, B. R. (2007). Stress crossover in newlywed marriage: A longitudinal and dyadic perspective. *Journal of Marriage and Family, 69*(3), 594–607.

Ochsner, K. N., & Gross, J. J. (2005). The cognitive control of emotion. *Trends in Cognitive Sciences, 9*(5), 242–249.

Okonofua, J. A., Paunesku, D., & Walton, G. M. (2016). Brief intervention to encourage empathic discipline cuts suspension rates in half among adolescents. *Proceedings of the National Academy of Sciences of the USA, 113*(19), 5221–5226.

Parker-Pope, T. (2010, April 14). Is marriage good for your health? *New York Times.* Retrieved from *www.nytimes.com/2010/04/18/magazine/18marriage-t.html.*

Proulx, C. M., Helms, H. M., & Buehler, C. (2007). Marital quality and personal well-being: A meta-analysis. *Journal of Marriage and Family, 69*(3), 576–593.

Radloff, L. S. (1977). The CES-D Scale: A self-report depression scale for research in the general population. *Applied Psychological Measurement, 1*(3), 385–401.

Ray, R. D., Wilhelm, F. H., & Gross, J. J. (2008). All in the mind's eye?: Anger rumination and reappraisal. *Journal of Personality and Social Psychology, 94*(1), 133–145.

Reis, H. T. (2012). Perceived partner responsiveness as an organizing theme for the study of relationships and well-being. In L. Campbell & T. J. Loving (Eds.), *Interdisciplinary research on close relationships* (pp. 27–52). Washington, DC: American Psychological Association.

Richards, J. M., Butler, E. A., & Gross, J. J. (2003). Emotion regulation in romantic relationships: The cognitive consequences of concealing feelings. *Journal of Social and Personal Relationships, 20*(5), 599–620.

Robinson, J. A., & Swanson, K. L. (1993). Field and observer modes of remembering. *Memory, 1*(3), 169–184.

Robles, T. F., Slatcher, R. B., Trombello, J. M., & McGinn, M. M. (2014). Marital quality and health: A meta-analytic review. *Psychological Bulletin, 140*(1), 140–187.

Sbarra, D. A., Boals, A., Mason, A. E., Larson, G. M., & Mehl, M. R. (2013). Expressive writing can impede emotional recovery following marital separation. *Clinical Psychological Science, 1*(2), 120–134.

Silverman, A. M., Logel, C., & Cohen, G. L. (2013). Self-affirmation as a deliberate coping strategy. *Journal of Experimental Social Psychology, 49*, 93–98.

Slatcher, R. B. (2010). Marital functioning and physical health: Implications for social and personality psychology. *Social and Personality Psychology Compass, 4*(7), 455–469.

Slatcher, R. B., & Schoebi, D. (2017). Protective processes underlying the links between marital quality and physical health. *Current Opinion in Psychology, 13*, 148–152.

Slotter, E. B., & Ward, D. E. (2015). Finding the silver lining: The relative roles of redemptive narratives and cognitive reappraisal in individuals' emotional distress after the end of a romantic relationship. *Journal of Social and Personal Relationships, 32*(6), 737–756.

VanLaningham, J., Johnson, D. R., & Amato, P. (2001). Marital happiness, marital duration, and the U-shaped curve: Evidence from a five-wave panel study. *Social Forces, 79*(4), 1313–1341.

Vansteenkiste, M., Simons, J., Lens, W., Sheldon, K. M., & Deci, E. L. (2004). Motivating learning, performance, and persistence: The synergistic effects of intrinsic goal contents autonomy-supportive contexts. *Journal of Personality and Social Psychology, 87*(2), 246–260.

Verduyn, P., Van Mechelen, I., Kross, E., Chezzi, C., & Van Bever, F. (2012). The relationship between self-distancing and the duration of negative and positive emotional experiences in daily life. *Emotion, 12*(6), 1248–1263.

Walton, G. M., & Wilson, T. D. (2018). Wise interventions: Psychological remedies for social and personal problems. *Psychological Review, 125*(5), 617–655.

Watt, L. M., & Cappeliez, P. (2000). Integrative and instrumental reminiscence therapies for depression in older adults: Intervention strategies and treatment effectiveness. *Aging and Mental Health, 4*(2), 166–177.

Weiss, R. L., & Heyman, R. E. (1997). A clinical-research overview of couples interactions. In W. K. Halford & H. J. Markman (Eds.), *Clinical handbook of marriage and couples interventions* (pp. 13–41). Hoboken, NJ: Wiley.

Whisman, M. A. (2001). The association between depression and marital dissatisfaction. In S. R. H. Beach (Ed.), *Marital and family processes in depression: A scientific foundation for clinical practice* (pp. 3–24). Washington, DC: American Psychological Association.

Wu, S., & Keysar, B. (2007). The effect of culture on perspective taking. *Psychological Science, 18*(7), 600–606.

CHAPTER 17

The Abstract Reframing Intervention
Helping Insecure Individuals Benefit
from Romantic Partners' Positive Feedback

Denise C. Marigold

Insecurity in romantic relationships can create a self-fulfilling prophecy, whereby people who doubt their partner's love and commitment consequently behave in ways that drive their partner away. Yet relational insecurity is difficult to overcome. Insecure individuals tend to ascribe considerable meaning to a partner's negative behavior but trivial meaning to their positive behavior. The intervention described in this chapter was designed to address the latter phenomenon. Participants recall an instance of receiving a compliment from their partner, then are encouraged to view this compliment more broadly as a meaningful and significant example of their partner's admiration for them. I have demonstrated in numerous studies that this abstract reframing intervention can foster a greater sense of relationship security and subsequent positive relationship behavior among individuals who are typically insecure in their relationships.

BACKGROUND

Romantic relationships have much potential to be rewarding and affirming. The confident belief that one is cared for and supported is hugely beneficial to both psychological and physical well-being (Myers, 2000), and relationship satisfaction is a strong contributor to overall life satisfaction (Gustavson, Røysamb, Borren, Torvik, & Karevold, 2016). Yet many such relationships are marred by conflict and doubt. Several of the factors that contribute to relationship troubles can be targets for intervention. For example, dyadic factors like poor communication can be addressed with training in problem-solving skills either through psychoeducational programs (Halford, Markman, & Stanley, 2008), conflict reappraisal exercises (Finkel, Slotter, Luchies, Walton, & Gross, 2013; see Slotter & Luchies, Chapter 16, this volume), or couple therapy (e.g., Sevier, Eldridge, Jones, Doss, & Christensen, 2008). Contextual factors like external stressors can fray relationships (Neff & Karney, 2004), so stress management strategies may be helpful for alleviating relationship troubles. The research reported in this chapter focuses on a psychological intervention designed to improve relationships for individuals with low self-esteem (LSEs) by addressing a social-cognitive factor: the tendency to interpret the meaning of partners' behavior in a maladaptive way.

Although there is little evidence that LSEs are any less attractive, intelligent, or capable than their high-self-esteem counterparts (HSEs), LSEs tend to view various aspects of their lives more negatively (Baumeister, Campbell, Krueger, & Vohs, 2003; Cameron & Granger, 2019; Orth, Robins, & Widman, 2012) and they are inclined to interpret positive information about the self in a relatively negative light (Danielsson & Bengtsson, 2016). In romantic relationships specifically, LSEs are generally less secure and satisfied (Fincham & Bradbury, 1993; Murray, Holmes, & Griffin, 1996) and they underestimate how much their partners love and value them (Murray, Holmes, & Griffin, 2000). These tendencies push LSEs in the direction of defensive self-protection; if they can keep a bit of distance from their partner, it won't be as painful when they eventually receive the rejection they expect is inevitable. Moreover, when feeling acutely threatened, such as when facing a partner's transgression, LSEs often become cold and critical toward their partner, again as a means of protecting themselves against hurt. Derogating their partner allows them to feel they are not losing anything of substantial value. In an unfortunate self-fulfilling prophecy, these defensive responses to perceived threats contribute to a decrease in partners' satisfaction over time (Murray, Bellavia, Rose, & Griffin, 2003).

There are at least two related psychological processes in which LSEs engage that serve to maintain their insecurities. One, they abstract from negative relationship events, reading broader meaning and significance into even minor, everyday kinds of slights (e.g., they might interpret a partner's bad mood as a sign of their partner's waning affection for them). Second, they fail to abstract from positive relationship events, often seeing them as little more than isolated incidents that do not signify anything of importance about their partner's feelings toward them. What's more, LSEs may even make a negative attribution about their partner's motivation for something like a compliment—perhaps their partner felt sorry for them, or was preparing to ask for a favor.

There is an extensive literature on the causes and consequences of partner attribution processes, but it has focused primarily on the meaning people make of their partner's negative or potentially threatening behavior, like during a conflict discussion (Pearce & Halford, 2008). Indeed, a number of individual difference variables linked to insecurity (low self-esteem, anxious attachment style, neuroticism, depression) predict the tendency to make distress-maintaining attributions for partners' transgressions (Bellavia & Murray, 2003; Collins, Ford, Guichard, & Allard, 2006; Karney, Bradbury, Fincham, & Sullivan, 1994; Pearce & Halford, 2008; Sümer & Cozzarelli, 2004; Uebelacker & Whisman, 2005). Critically, these attributions have long-term consequences for relationship well-being (Karney & Bradbury, 2000).

Far less research has focused on the kinds of attributions for positive partner behavior that may also serve to maintain insecurity. Theoretically, one should be less likely to attribute a partner's positive behavior to caring motives if that behavior is perceived to be facilitated by external factors, or to benefit the partner (e.g., the partner's act of kindness is public and makes a good impression on others; Kelley, 1973). Additionally, when people who are insecure believe their partner is aware of their insecurities, they are more likely to suspect that their partner's positive affirmations are not authentic (Lemay & Clark, 2008).

How can LSEs be made to see their value in their partner's eyes? Some attempts to boost LSEs' sense of security with positive feedback have actually backfired. For example, giving LSEs feedback that their questionnaire responses showed they were high in "considerateness" made them feel more insecure (compared to a no-feedback control condition; Murray, Holmes, MacDonald, & Ellsworth, 1998). Even prompting LSEs to affirm their own worth as a partner, by repeating "I am a lovable person," made LSEs feel more anxious (Wood, Perunovic, & Lee, 2009). More broadly, thinking about personal successes of various sorts can also increase LSEs' anxious feelings (Wood, Heimpel, Newby-Clark, & Ross, 2005). Such efforts are consistent with the "self-esteem movement" that aimed to increase self-esteem for the purpose of preventing associated social problems (Singal, 2017). Unfortunately, LSEs have defenses against such efforts. When positive feedback or self-statements are externally imposed, participants question whether they truly apply to themselves. HSEs are likely to conclude they do apply and then move on. LSEs, on the other hand, are also liable to be more equivocal, and search their memories for evidence that both supports and weakens that conclusion.

In designing the abstract reframing intervention (ARI), I considered how one might "fly under the radar" of LSEs' defenses. How could LSEs be affirmed without activating self-doubts and self-evaluation concerns? One key component was to have LSEs choose their own personal quality on which they were affirmed. False feedback from an experimenter may not be easily believed if there is clear evidence to the contrary. I expected that when LSEs had a chance to recall their own example of a compliment from their partner, they would likely recall one that they felt fairly confident about already. The second component was to have LSEs take their recalled compliment and subtly encourage them to ratchet up its meaning.

The intervention thus appears like this: On one page, participants are asked to "Think of a time when your current romantic partner told you how much he/she liked something about you. For example, a personal quality or ability you have that he/she thinks very highly of, or something you did that really impressed him/her." They are then asked to write down a few cue words that would identify that memory to them, note how long ago it occurred, and then turn to the next page to describe the compliment more fully. On the next page, the intervention instructions are as follows: "Explain why your partner admired you. Describe what it meant to you and its significance for your relationship." These instructions assume that the compliment reflected the partner's broader view of the participant (i.e., admired them), and that the compliment must have been meaningful and significant in some way.

The Linguistic Category Model (Semin & Fiedler, 1988; Semin & De Poot, 1997) was the primary inspiration for the wording of the ARI. This model makes the distinction between action verbs like *said* and state verbs like *admired,* with the state verb implying that the behavior has lasted for a longer period and is more likely to recur in the future. I expected that the use of a state verb would lead LSEs to perceive the compliments to be more broad and global in their implications about their value to their partner. Research in a number of other domains has supported the contention that subtle linguistic cues can indeed have significant effects on self-perceptions and behavior (e.g., *helping*: Bryan, Master, & Walton, 2014; *voting*: Bryan, Walton, Rogers, & Dweck, 2011).

One of the other conditions used for comparison instructed participants, after thinking of a compliment, to "Describe exactly what your partner said to you. Include any details you can recall about where you two were at the time, what you were doing, what you were both wearing, etc." Labeled as the "concrete" condition, this allowed us to test whether immersion in and elaboration on the incidence of positive feedback, which LSEs might typically avoid, was sufficient to yield beneficial outcomes. A control condition instructed participants to simply "Describe the event below." This condition allowed us to get a sense of self-esteem differences in spontaneous responses to compliments (see Appendix 17.1 for full materials).

PSYCHOLOGICAL PROCESSES

The participants in these intervention studies have been primarily young adults in dating relationships. The purpose of the ARI is to encourage them to consider the potential for broader meaning in their partner's feedback, and to consider the impact such affirmations may have on their relationship more globally. In doing so, there seems to be a corresponding move from primarily past-tense language to also include some present-tense language. The compliment becomes something their partner thinks or feels about them that is indicative of the kind of relationship they have, rather than something their partner simply said at one time. This is particularly important for LSEs, who are less inclined to reach this kind of broad conclusion naturally. Our research showed that when asked to describe compliments from their romantic partners with no further instructions (i.e., the control condition), LSEs tend to use more past-tense verbs than do HSEs (Marigold, Holmes, & Ross, 2007). What follows are two examples of participants in the control condition whose partner complimented them on their intelligence. The first is from a participant who scored low in self-esteem (over 1 standard deviation below the mean). Note the restriction to a single incident in the past.

> "I got the best score in a course in university. He took the course in the term after my course and the professor mentioned the best score for the previous term was exactly my score. So he told me afterwards that I was smart."

The second is from a participant who scored high in self-esteem (over 1 standard deviation above the mean). Note the description of the partner's ongoing positive view of the participant.

> "I get nervous about university, because I am in first year, and my boyfriend keeps reassuring me. He says I am very smart and that he is so proud of me. He is so loving and makes me feel like I can do anything."

How does the intervention affect how people reflect on a compliment? To see this, we compared the concrete condition and the ARI condition. In the concrete condition, participants are asked for further details about the time the compliment was given—where they were, who was there, what they were doing. Again, for the two examples that follow, the participants indicated that their partner complimented them on their intelligence. In the concrete condition, people stuck to what happened in the past. For example, one participant in this condition explained:

> "A week ago I won an award for being a top student at U of W. I told my boyfriend over the phone, on his way home from work. He said, 'That's awesome! I'm proud of you, you're so intelligent.' That same day he told everyone he knew that I was a top student at U of W."

In the abstract condition, people talked about how the past event indicated ongoing positive meaning for their relationship. For example, a different participant in the ARI condition went on to explain:

> "I had scored an [A] on my midterm. . . . He told me I was a very intelligent person. . . . It meant a lot to me that he sees me this way. It shows me how supportive he is of my school work and my goals for life. . . . We have a supportive relationship."

In another set of examples, two participants indicated that their partner complimented them on being caring. In the concrete condition, the participant went on to say:

> "In the conversation, he mentioned how he thinks I am a genuinely caring person."

In contrast, the participant in the ARI condition wrote:

> "He admired me because he was going through a tough time, and he realized he wasn't alone and that I cared about him. This was important to me because it meant that he knew my feelings for him and that I want to help him the best I can."

It is important to note that LSEs are not always less positive than HSEs about the exchange of compliments between romantic partners. I conducted one study (Hoplock, Stinson, Marigold, & Fisher, 2018) to compare LSEs' reactions to compliments directed at the self versus others, using hypothetical compliment scenarios. Would LSEs also minimize the meaning of compliments shared between other couples? Half of the participants were randomly assigned to read about a compliment one hypothetical person gave to their romantic partner. The other half of the participants were asked to imagine receiving the same compliment from their romantic partner. As expected, LSEs in the self-compliment condition were less enthusiastic about the compliment, and believed it was less sincere than did LSEs in the other-compliment condition. The simple effect of self-esteem was significant in the self-compliment condition but not in the other-compliment condition. LSEs did not differ from HSEs in their judgments about compliments exchanged between other people. These findings confirm that LSEs do have the capacity to see the potential for enjoyment and meaning in partners' praise; it's only when the compliment applies to themselves that they respond differently than HSEs, which can be taken as evidence of motivated thinking.

EMPIRICAL EVIDENCE

Outcomes

The first set of published studies established the basic effect of the ARI, both immediately after completing the intervention and in a follow-up 2 weeks later. In Study 2 of Marigold et al. (2007), all participants first thought of a time their partner said something nice to them. The control condition was simply asked to describe that event, with no further instructions. The concrete condition was asked to describe the concrete details surrounding what was said, where, who was there, and so forth. The ARI condition was asked to explain why their partner admired them, and describe what it meant to them and why it was significant to their relationship. There were a number of dependent variables that showed similar patterns. Among LSEs, those in the ARI condition reported greater positive feelings about the compliment, state self-esteem, felt security, and relationship valuing than did those in the control or concrete conditions. In fact, LSEs in the ARI condition reported outcomes that were just as high as HSEs (who did not differ between conditions). The typical pattern is illustrated in Figure 17.1.

Effects over Time

This effect persisted over time. In two studies, results of a follow-up questionnaire delivered 2–3 weeks later showed that LSEs who had been in the ARI condition at Time 1 continued to feel more secure than did LSEs in either the control or concrete conditions, mirroring the pattern of results from Time 1. LSEs who had been in the ARI condition

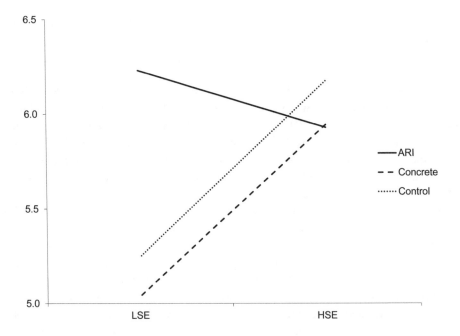

FIGURE 17.1. Self-reported felt security as a function of self-esteem and condition (Study 2 from Marigold, Holmes, & Ross, 2007).

also reported a greater frequency of positive partner behavior since Time 1. Although participants did not receive an explicit reminder of the compliment prior to making their ratings at Time 2, it is possible that receiving the follow-up questionnaire was sufficient to remind participants of their positive experience at Time 1. That may account for the increased felt security ratings and perceptions of partner positivity reported by LSEs in the ARI condition (i.e., they felt more secure when completing both Time 1 and Time 2 questionnaires but not in between). Another possibility is that receiving the ARI at Time 1 actually changed LSEs' experience, or the perception of their experience, in the intervening 2- to 3-week period (i.e., their felt security and perceptions of positive partner behavior remained high between Time 1 and Time 2). The next set of studies suggest some support for the latter explanation.

A study reported in a later paper employed partner reports to verify that the ARI had an effect beyond participants' perceptions, on their observable behavior (Marigold, Holmes, & Ross, 2010, Study 2). In this study, participants were randomly assigned to complete the ARI or a control condition with no instructions for describing the compliment (see Marigold et al., 2007). Findings on relationship ratings replicated previous research (Marigold et al., 2007) in that LSEs rated their relationships more positively in the ARI condition than in the control condition, as high as HSEs in either condition. Moreover, 2 weeks later, partners were contacted to report on the participants' behavior over the preceding 2 weeks. Results showed that LSE participants who had initially received the ARI had partners who reported lower frequency of critical, negative behavior from the participants in that time period (compared to LSEs who were in the control condition), as low as HSE participants in both conditions (see Figure 17.2).

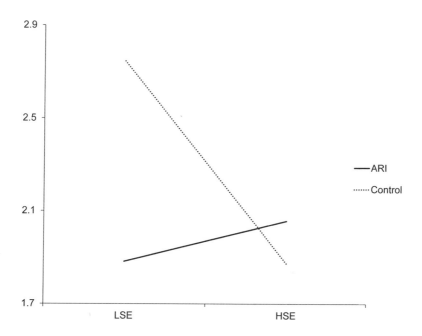

FIGURE 17.2. Partners' reports of participants' frequency of negative behavior in previous 2 weeks, as a function of participants' self-esteem and condition (Study 2 from Marigold, Holmes, & Ross, 2010). Reprinted with permission from Elsevier.

This finding is consistent with the notion that LSEs who have received the ARI are actually changing their behavior. In the previous set of studies (Marigold et al., 2007), when LSEs reported noticing more positive partner behavior in the weeks following the ARI, they may have actually been eliciting that positive behavior as a response to their own behavior changes.

Mechanism

In Marigold et al. (2007), the Linguistic Inquiry Word Count (LIWC; Pennebaker, Francis, & Booth, 2001) program was used to analyze the verb tense used in the narratives participants wrote to describe their compliment. These results showed that when participants were given no specific instructions on how to describe the compliment they recalled (simply, "Describe the event"), LSEs used more past-tense verbs than did HSEs. In the ARI condition, LSEs used fewer past-tense verbs and more present-tense verbs than did LSEs in the control or concrete conditions. HSEs did not differ in their verb use among the three conditions.

In addition to feeling more positively about the compliment in the ARI condition, LSEs also rated it as more sincere and thought they were more deserving of the compliment (Marigold et al., 2007). Thus, the abstraction seemed to lead them to a more internal attribution for the motivation behind their partner's praise, which mediated further effects on state self-esteem and relationship ratings. In unpublished data (Marigold, 2011), I found that LSEs who think of an "admired" quality compared to a "complimented" quality are more confident in their possession of that quality, which further supports the use of a state verb (*admired*) to connote a sense of endurance.

Process

Another study (Marigold et al., 2010, Study 1) provided evidence that the ARI could reduce LSEs' defensive reactions to relationship threats. The threat in Study 1 involved a "Secret Selves" exercise (Murray, Rose, Bellavia, Holmes, & Kusche, 2002) where participants were instructed to think about several aspects of themselves they try to keep hidden from their partner, knowing conflict could arise as a result. LSEs who completed this exercise rated their relationship significantly more negatively than LSEs who did not (HSEs were unaffected by the manipulation). It is thought that contemplating a negative evaluation from their partner prompts LSEs to become more negative and critical about their relationship as a means of self-protection. It is less painful to be rejected by a partner who is not all that great anyway. As described earlier, this kind of self-protective behavior in response to threat has important consequences in that it actually contributes to the demise of the relationship over time (Murray, Griffin, Rose, & Bellavia, 2003). Yet in our study, for LSEs who were asked to complete the ARI prior to the threat exercise, no such relationship derogation effect was found. These LSEs remained just as positive about their relationship as were those who were not threatened.

Furthering the evidence for behavioral effects of the ARI, another paper reported the effects of the ARI on a subsequent conflict discussion among romantic partners (Marigold & Anderson, 2016). In this study, partners' conflict history was the moderating variable. A history of difficult or destructive conflict interactions might function similarly to LSE in this context in that concerns about partners' care and responsiveness become activated. Indeed, partners with a higher conflict history had lower positive expectations of how a conflict discussion would go in the lab. However, the ARI increased positive expectations among couples with a stronger conflict history (those with less history of conflict were not affected by the manipulation). Subsequently, the increased positive expectations translated to less distress, more positive behavior (according to self- and partner reports), and better quality conflict discussions (according to coding by observers who were blind to both condition and conflict history).

It is worth noting that in all of these studies, coding by objective observers revealed that there was no association of self-esteem with the positivity of the compliments selected—that is, LSEs and HSEs recalled equally positive compliments; the difference lay in the way in which they naturally described them and the meaning they made of them. As Walton and Wilson (2018) point out, psychologically wise interventions assume that objective opportunities for enhancement may already be present, but the meaning people make of social information may limit them from taking advantage.

Heterogeneity

In one unpublished study (Marigold, 2010), I attempted to replicate the basic ARI effect with married couples, using self-esteem as a moderator, but the effect was not significant. Although one cannot make any firm conclusions based on this single sample, it seems reasonable that one incidence of praise has less potential to be consequential to partners who are seriously committed. It may take much larger or sustained gestures of affection to influence the felt security of long-term coupled or married LSEs. Further research can explore this notion more fully.

COUSINS

Self-affirmation is one intervention that bears some similarity to the ARI (see Sherman, Lokhande, Müller, & Cohen, Chapter 3, this volume). The self-affirmation exercise typically has participants choose their most cherished value from a list provided and describe how they have acted consistently with it in the past. This process seems to generate a more expansive view of the self and its resources, which buffers people from subsequent threats to the self. The similarity between the two interventions lies in the process of having participants generate their own affirmations, which may be particularly important for individuals who are chronically insecure, as discussed earlier in this chapter. Affirmations that are externally imposed are more likely to activate self-doubts and evaluative concerns.

Numerous positive outcomes of the self-affirmation intervention have been reported in relationships as well as in the domains of education and health (see Sherman et al., Chapter 3, this volume). In regard to relationships, for example, self-affirmation has been shown to improve relational security more broadly (i.e., with family, friends, and romantic partners), and facilitate more welcoming social behavior with a stranger (Stinson, Logel, Shepherd, & Zanna, 2011). In another study, self-affirmation increased adolescents' general prosocial feelings and behaviors over a 3-month period (Thomaes, Bushman, Orobio de Castro, & Reijntjes, 2012). Self-affirmation may not be as well suited to improving positive feelings and behavior in one's romantic relationship. The ARI is a more targeted intervention than self-affirmation in that it is person specific, resulting in more positive views of a particular partner and relationship.

INTERVENTION CONTENT AND IMPLEMENTATION

As described earlier, the ARI requires participants to "Think of a time when your current romantic partner told you how much he/she liked something about you. For example, a personal quality or ability you have that he/she thinks very highly of, or something you did that really impressed him/her." They are then asked to write down a few cue words that would identify that memory to them, note how long ago it occurred, and then turn to the next page to "Explain why your partner admired you. Describe what it meant to you and its significance for your relationship." (See Appendix 17.1 for full materials.) This intervention has been delivered both in person and online, with no apparent difference.

The intervention can be adapted to encourage abstraction of other positive partner behaviors. In one unpublished study (Marigold & Anderson, 2011), the manipulation was adapted to reflect on a partner's caring behavior rather than positive feedback. Specifically, participants were asked to "Think of a time when your romantic partner did something nice for you. For example, helped you with homework, brought you a present, put your preferences ahead of his or her own." In the abstract reframing condition, they were then asked to "Explain why your partner cared for you so much. Describe what it meant to you and its significance for your relationship." Participants in the control condition were simply asked to "Describe the event in the space below." Results showed that in the control condition, LSEs experienced less positive affect and made fewer positive attributions for the behavior than did HSEs. LSEs in the abstract condition reported more positive affect and attributions than did LSEs in the control condition, as high as HSEs in either condition.

A study published by Gaucher et al. (2012, Study 4) used the same ARI but substituted "close friend" for "partner." Participants were then asked to make a video that would ostensibly be shown to that friend in which they described a negative experience they had at their university. Results showed that LSEs were more expressive (according to both self-report and observer coding) in the ARI condition than in the control condition. The authors theorized that LSEs are generally reticent to share their true thoughts and feelings because that leaves them vulnerable to rejection, which may seem likely given their lower self-worth. Once LSEs' sense of perceived regard was increased by the ARI, they felt more comfortable expressing themselves authentically, which is critical to fostering closeness and intimacy.

In a completely different domain, Zunick, Fazio, and Vasey (2015) adapted the ARI for use with participants who hold relatively negative self-views to encourage them to generalize from success experiences in public speaking. They used a "directed abstraction" technique for which the ARI "was one of the primary inspirations" (Zunick et al., 2015, p. 4). After recalling a past public speaking success (Study 2) or having a public speaking success in the lab (Study 3), participants in the directed abstraction condition were asked to "Explain *why* you were able to achieve such a successful performance. Begin by completing the sentence stem below. 'I was able to achieve a successful performance because I am . . . ' " Participants in the control condition instead responded to the prompt "Describe *how* you performed as you did in this situation. What did you do?" Generalization from success was measured with a composite variable including participants' views of their overall public speaking abilities, expectations for future performance, and self-related affect. The directed abstraction led people with negative self-views to generalize more from a successful public speaking experience than they would have otherwise, leading to a greater likelihood of returning to the activity and more persistence in the face of difficulty.

NUANCES AND MISCONCEPTIONS

Without a strong understanding of the psychological process involved in low self-esteem, a well-intended intervention might easily be ineffective or even detrimental. There are at least two theoretically meaningful ways the effect of the ARI can be reduced or reversed. One is outlined in Marigold et al. (2007, Study 3). A very subtle rewording of the intervention instructions eliminated the boost for LSEs. Recall that the original instructions were to "Explain why your partner admired you. Describe what it meant to you and its significance for your relationship." In the modified version, the instructions were posed as thought-provoking questions: "Explain whether you think what your partner said indicated that he/she admired you. Consider whether it was meaningful to you and significant for your relationship." It was thought that the effectiveness of the ARI for LSEs was rooted in its subtlety. The original wording managed to assumptively imply that the compliment must have been meaningful and significant, and give participants the task of elaborating on an idea that is assumed to be true. This seemed to slip under the radar of LSEs' defenses and avoid activating their doubts. When LSEs were explicitly provided with an opportunity to question the broader meaning and significance of the feedback, their self-evaluative worries undermined their enjoyment of the compliment. For example, one LSE participant in this questioning condition, who had recalled a time her partner said she was smart, further remarked, "I don't think he admires this about me because I am really only smart at math/engineering. He is way smarter when it comes to real life stuff. It was not significant."

This study supports the idea that LSEs may do best with a gentle push toward the assumption that they are cared for and does not allow them to question this conclusion. There are other studies that have similarly shown that LSEs' self-doubts can be subtly and unexpectedly activated. For example, Wood et al. (2009) showed that encouraging LSEs to repeat positive self-statements (e.g., "I am a lovable person") made them more anxious than if they had repeated no statements. It was thought that this blanket positive conclusion led participants to search for evidence that may or may not support it, and LSEs were more focused, or could more easily access, evidence against that conclusion. In another line of research, when LSE children were praised for personal qualities, they felt especially ashamed after failure (Brummelman, Thomaes, Overbeek, et al., 2014). When they were given inflated praise, they were less likely to seek out challenging tasks (Brummelman, Thomaes, de Castro, Overbeek, & Bushman, 2014). In these studies, the authors theorized that positive feedback raised perceived expectations of others, which the LSE children doubted they could continue to meet.

A second way that shifting the original materials can undermine, and in this case, reverse the effects of the ARI involves applying it to the partner. In one study (Marigold, 2018), participants were asked to "Think of a time when you told your current romantic partner how much you liked something about him/her. For example, a personal quality or ability he/she has that you think very highly of, or something he/she did that really impressed you." The abstract condition was then asked to "Explain why you admired your partner. Describe what you think it meant to your partner and its significance for your relationship." The control condition was simply asked to "Describe the event in the space below." Essentially, the original wording of the ARI was taken and then shifted to focus on a compliment the participant gave to, rather than received from, their partner. Although writing abstractly about a compliment *received* from one's partner increases LSEs' felt security, in the modified version, writing abstractly about a compliment *given* to one's partner decreased LSEs' felt security. It is thought that this occurs because LSEs are particularly sensitive to feelings of inferiority in their relationship (Murray et al., 2005), and these feelings may be activated when considering their admiration for their partner.

It is also worth noting that giving participants false positive feedback is quite different from the ARI's approach of encouraging participants to generate their own affirmations, and in fact, the former can backfire. One example comes from Murray et al. (1998), where participants received feedback from the experimenter that a questionnaire they completed indicated they were high (or low) in considerateness. The positive feedback actually made LSEs feel more insecure (Murray et al., 1998). The ARI is clearly more effective than this type of approach.

IMPLICATIONS FOR PRACTICE

Therapists may use this research in either individual or couple therapy. With LSEs, therapists may challenge the notion that they are not well loved or will assuredly be rejected by partners by asking them to bring to mind evidence of their partner's love and care. However, if they stop there, it will be easy for the LSEs to dismiss past compliments or generous behaviors as isolated incidents, perhaps brought on by the partner's sense of obligation or pity for the LSE. Therapists can prevent this dismissal by prompting LSEs to describe the meaning and significance of these acts of admiration or care.

In couple therapy, therapists may encourage partners to express appreciation or admiration for each other (e.g., Gottman & Silver, 1999). Whether done in therapy or in everyday interactions, I believe there are three key considerations that can make or break the success of delivering compliments to LSEs. One is the particular quality chosen for the compliment. Recall that in the ARI, participants select their own quality on which they've been complimented, which they then go on to write about in an abstract way. This allows them to select a quality about which they are relatively confident, or view as important to their sense of self. Thus, people who are asked to express admiration to their partners should take care to choose a quality that their partner can easily embrace. It might intuitively seem more impactful to compliment partners on a quality about which they frequently express doubt, but this strategy could ultimately backfire if the complimenting further fuels the doubts (e.g., "Why is my partner saying this? Do they really mean it? Do they just feel bad for me?").

Second, given LSEs' suspicions about the authenticity of positive feedback (Lemay & Clark, 2008), partners should take care to reserve compliments for qualities that they truly appreciate in their partner, to be given in times in which they are feeling genuinely loving and affectionate. Given how readily LSEs attribute ulterior motives to their partner's expression of affection, it seems prudent to ensure those expressions are made without any ulterior motive that might be detected.

A third consideration is phrasing the compliment with some positive meaning for the relationship implied. For example, rather than saying, "You are really helpful," one might say, "I appreciate how willing you are to help when I need it. It makes me feel like we are a team." One might need to be careful to keep it simple and brief; going on too long about the partner's helpfulness and its significance for the relationship may eventually be perceived as manipulative.

Ultimately, these are speculations based on prior related research. More targeted research should be conducted on couples delivering compliments to each other, both in and out of a clinical setting. Further, therapists must use judgment to determine the context in which this activity may ultimately be helpful rather than harmful. If there is overwhelming evidence that the partner really does not care for the individual and treats them poorly, they may need to be coached to leave the relationship rather than increase an unwarranted sense of security and commitment.

Beyond therapeutic settings, people may benefit from the ARI by learning about it through literature in which it has been described. For example, in Eli Finkel's (2017) popular book *The All-or-Nothing Marriage,* the ARI is cited as one example of a "love hack," a strategy that involves "tweaking how we think about our partner and relationship" (p. 183). Love hacks on their own are not sufficient to rescue a failing relationship or even to make a stable relationship flourish. But they are relatively easy and accessible, they do not require much investment of time, and they do not rely on cooperation from the partner. The hope is that couples may benefit in at least some small way from using a variety of love hacks and even developing their own.

Presenting the ARI as one simple yet meaningful strategy, among others, for facilitating relationship well-being may be an effective way to reach a larger audience. However, no research has yet addressed whether awareness of the ARI and its intended effects may undermine its usefulness. Research on self-affirmation has shown that it is not awareness per se that can undermine its effect but rather the feeling of being manipulated or controlled (Silverman, Logel, & Cohen, 2013). This is an important distinction to make in future research investigating whether LSEs may still benefit from compliment abstraction once they know its intended effects; perhaps the answer is yes if they feel personally motivated to try the exercise themselves, but no if they feel someone is imposing it upon them.

Most of the previous research has focused on self-esteem as the moderator of the intervention's effect, but changing the context may change the moderator. At a conceptual level, the most appropriate moderator may be one that distinguishes reactions to the social information being conveyed in that particular context. Thus, self-esteem is most appropriate when considering reactions to feedback about the self; a measure of conflict history seems to be more appropriate when considering reactions to anticipated and actual conflict. Indeed, as discussed earlier in this chapter, a dyadic study of couples discussing a conflict in their relationship showed the ARI was particularly beneficial for couples with a stronger history of destructive conflict (Marigold & Anderson, 2016).

IMPLICATIONS FOR PSYCHOLOGICAL THEORY

These findings reinforce a long history of research showing that meaning matters (see Walton & Wilson, 2018, for a review). To the extent that people believe their partners' negative statements and behaviors signify a lack of care or concern for the self, they may become more insecure or dissatisfied. To the extent that people believe their partner's positive statements and behaviors *fail to signify* care and concern for the self, their security and satisfaction will not benefit. Insecurity and dissatisfaction further predispose people to make relationship-threatening attributions, and so the cycle continues (Bradbury & Fincham, 1990).

This research also tells us something about how relational insecurities operate. People's motivations shape their perceptions, such that those who are primarily motivated to protect themselves from hurt (e.g., LSEs) actually "see" things differently. Just as LSEs more readily identify acceptance cues directed at others than at themselves (Cameron, Stinson, Gaetz, & Balchen, 2010), they make more positive meaning of compliments directed toward others than to themselves (Hoplock et al., 2018). Thus there is little evidence to suggest that LSEs have some kind of perception deficit that prevents them from being able to accurately recognize cues of acceptance and positive regard—rather, they falter in these tasks only when their own sense of self and security are on the line. Understanding this phenomenon should be helpful to partners of individuals who are insecure, who often find that their behavior does not get interpreted as intended.

As with other "wise" interventions, the ARI research shows that we can target small changes that, with some reinforcement, can have larger, long-term effects. It also tells us that when we cannot change people's reality (e.g., by mandating the number or kind of compliments people pay their partners), there is still some utility in changing the way people think about their reality (e.g., seeing the potential for broader meaning in the compliments they do receive).

FUTURE DIRECTIONS

The highest priority next step for this research is to determine how partners of LSEs may deliver compliments more effectively, in a manner that prevents LSEs from dismissing them as genuine. People may naturally feel compelled to give their LSE partners feedback on qualities about which they know their partner is insecure in an effort to combat that insecurity. However, there is good evidence to suggest that approach may very well backfire (e.g., Brummelman, Thomaes, Overbeek, et al., 2014; Lemay & Clark, 2008). Instead, people may be better off giving LSE partners compliments on qualities about which they appear to be relatively confident—such qualities may lend themselves better to spontaneous abstracting by the LSEs. As discussed earlier in the chapter, people may also be able to give their partners compliments in a way that implies some meaning, though they must take care that those efforts to affirm are not too heavy-handed.

For the LSEs' part, ideally they would not continually require a researcher's gentle encouragement toward making meaning out of positive partner feedback. Over time, they can practice moving away from reflexively dismissing compliments outright and giving them further consideration. Of course not all compliments will be that meaningful, and sometimes their partner may actually be just trying to make them feel better or prepare them to be asked a favor. Another option would be to simply say "thank you" when they receive a compliment, allowing it to stand as is without any further consideration of whether the evidence actually backs it up. Perhaps this practice of acceptance would eventually extend beyond the moment.

Given the enormous potential of romantic relationships to be rewarding and affirming, and to benefit both psychological and physical well-being more broadly (Gustavson et al., 2016; Myers, 2000), the problem of LSEs' relationship insecurity is an important one. There is much opportunity to alleviate this problem when one understands the psychological processes involved in the experience of low self-esteem and of meaning making in relationships, and the "wise interventions" that are designed with this in mind.

REFERENCES

Baumeister, R. F., Campbell, J. D., Krueger, J. I., & Vohs, K. D. (2003). Does high self-esteem cause better performance, interpersonal success, happiness, or healthier lifestyles? *Psychological Science in the Public Interest, 4,* 1–44.

Bellavia, G., & Murray, S. (2003). Did I do that?: Self esteem-related differences in reactions to romantic partners' mood. *Personal Relationships, 10,* 77–95.

Bradbury, T. N., & Fincham, F. D. (1990). Attributions in marriage: Review and critique. *Psychological Bulletin, 107,* 3–33.

Brummelman, E., Thomaes, S., Orobio de Castro, B., Overbeek, G., & Bushman, B. J. (2014). "That's not just beautiful—that's incredibly beautiful!": The adverse impact of inflated praise on children with low self-esteem. *Psychological Science, 25,* 728–735.

Brummelman, E., Thomaes, S., Overbeek, G., Orobio de Castro, B., van den Hout, M. A., & Bushman, B. J. (2014). On feeding those hungry for praise: Person praise backfires in children with low self-esteem *Journal of Experimental Psychology: General, 143,* 9–14.

Bryan, C. J., Master, A., & Walton, G. M. (2014). "Helping" versus "being a helper": Invoking the self to increase helping in young children. *Child Development, 85,* 1836–1842.

Bryan, C. J., Walton, G. M., Rogers, T., & Dweck, C. S. (2011). Motivating voter turnout by invoking the self. *Proceedings of the National Academy of Sciences of the USA, 108,* 12653–12656.

Cameron, J. J., & Granger, S. (2019). Does self-esteem have an interpersonal imprint beyond self-reports?: A meta-analysis of self-esteem and objective interpersonal indicators. *Personality and Social Psychology Review, 23,* 73–102.

Cameron, J. J., Stinson, D. A., Gaetz, R., & Balchen, S. (2010). Acceptance is in the eye of the beholder: Self-esteem and motivated perceptions of acceptance from the opposite sex. *Journal of Personality and Social Psychology, 99,* 513–529.

Collins, N. L., Ford, M., Guichard, A. C., & Allard, L. M. (2006). Working models of attachment and attribution processes in intimate relationships. *Personality and Social Psychology Bulletin, 32,* 201–219.

Danielsson, M., & Bengtsson, H. (2016). Global self-esteem and the processing of positive information about the self. *Personality and Individual Differences, 99,* 325–330.

Fincham, F. D., & Bradbury, T. N. (1993). Marital satisfaction, depression, and attributions: A longitudinal analysis. *Journal of Personality and Social Psychology, 64,* 442–452.

Finkel, E. (2017). *The all-or-nothing marriage: How the best marriages work.* New York: Dutton.

Finkel, E. J., Slotter, E. B., Luchies, L. B., Walton, G. M., & Gross, J. J. (2013). A brief intervention to promote conflict reappraisal preservers marital quality over time. *Psychological Science, 24,* 1595–1601.

Gaucher, D., Wood, J. V., Stinson, D. A., Forest, A. L., Holmes, J. G., & Logel, C. (2012). Perceived regard explains self-esteem differences in expressivity. *Personality and Social Psychology Bulletin, 38,* 1144–1156.

Gottman, J., & Silver, N. (1999). *The seven principles for making marriage work.* New York: Harmony Books.

Gustavson, K., Røysamb, E., Borren, I., Torvik, F. A., & Karevold, E. (2016). Life satisfaction in close relationships: Findings from a longitudinal study. *Journal of Happiness Studies: An Interdisciplinary Forum on Subjective Well-Being, 17,* 1293–1311.

Halford, W. K., Markman, H. J., & Stanley, S. M. (2008). Strengthening couple relationships with education: Social policy and public health perspectives. *Journal of Family Psychology, 22,* 497–505.

Hoplock, L. B., Stinson, D. A., Marigold, D. C., & Fisher, A. N. (2018). Self-esteem, epistemic needs, and response to social feedback. *Self and Identity, 18*(5), 467–493.

Karney, B. R., & Bradbury, T. N. (2000). Attributions in marriage: State or trait?: A growth curve analysis. *Journal of Personality and Social Psychology, 78*(2), 295–309.

Karney, B. R., Bradbury, T. N., Fincham, F. D., & Sullivan, K. T. (1994). The role of negative affectivity in the association between attributions and marital satisfaction. *Journal of Personality and Social Psychology, 66,* 413–424.

Kelley, H. H. (1973). The processes of causal attribution. *American Psychologist, 28,* 107–128.

Lemay, E. P., Jr., & Clark, M. S. (2008). "Walking on eggshells": How expressing relationship insecurities perpetuates them. *Journal of Personality and Social Psychology, 95,* 420–441.

Marigold, D. C. (2010). [Replicating the ARI with married couples]. Unpublished raw data.

Marigold, D. C. (2011). *Responses to compliments.* Unpublished raw data.

Marigold, D. C. (2018). *Compliment reframing re-visited: The effect of positive feedback on low self-esteem individuals' relationship evaluations depends on relational self-construal.* Unpublished manuscript.

Marigold, D. C., & Anderson, J. E. (2011). [Modifying the ARI to reflect caring rather than complimenting]. Unpublished raw data.

Marigold, D. C., & Anderson, J. E. (2016). Shifting expectations of partners' responsiveness changes outcomes of conflict discussions. *Personal Relationships, 23,* 517–535.

Marigold, D. C., Holmes, J. G., & Ross, M. (2007). More than words: Reframing compliments from romantic partners fosters security in low self-esteem individuals. *Journal of Personality and Social Psychology, 92*(2), 232–248.

Marigold, D. C., Holmes, J. G., & Ross, M. (2010). Fostering relationship resilience: An intervention for low self-esteem individuals. *Journal of Experimental Social Psychology, 46,* 624–630.

Murray, S. L., Bellavia, G. M., Rose, P., & Griffin, D. W. (2003). Once hurt, twice hurtful: How perceived regard regulates daily marital interactions. *Journal of Personality and Social Psychology, 84,* 126–147.

Murray, S. L., Griffin, D. W., Rose, P., & Bellavia, G. (2003). Calibrating the sociometer: The relational contingencies of self-esteem. *Journal of Personality and Social Psychology, 85,* 63–84.

Murray, S. L., Holmes, J. G., & Griffin, D. W. (1996). The benefits of positive illusions: Idealization and the construction of satisfaction in close relationships. *Journal of Personality and Social Psychology, 70,* 79–98.

Murray, S. L., Holmes, J. G., & Griffin, D. W. (2000). Self-esteem and the quest for felt security: How perceived regard regulates attachment processes. *Journal of Personality and Social Psychology, 78,* 478–498.

Murray, S. L., Holmes, J. G., MacDonald, G., & Ellsworth, P. C. (1998). Through the looking glass darkly?: When self-doubts turn into relationship insecurities. *Journal of Personality and Social Psychology, 75,* 1459–1480.

Murray, S. L., Rose, P., Bellavia, G., Holmes, J. G., & Kusche, A. G. (2002). When rejection stings: How self-esteem constrains relationship-enhancement processes. *Journal of Personality and Social Psychology, 83, 556–573.*

Murray, S. L., Rose, P., Holmes, J. G., Derrick, J., Podchaski, E. J., Bellavia, G., & Griffin, D. W. (2005). Putting the partner within reach: A dyadic perspective on felt security in close relationships. *Journal of Personality and Social Psychology, 88, 327–347.*

Myers, D. G. (2000). The funds, friends, and faith of happy people. *American Psychologist, 55, 56–67.*

Neff, L. A., & Karney, B. R. (2004). How does context affect intimate relationships?: Linking external stress and cognitive processes within marriage. *Personality and Social Psychology Bulletin, 30, 134–148.*

Orth, U., Robins, R. W., & Widman, K. F. (2012). Life-span development of self-esteem and its effects on important life outcomes. *Journal of Personality and Social Psychology, 102, 1271–1288.*

Pearce, Z. J., & Halford, W. K. (2008). Do attributions mediate the association between attachment and negative couple communication? *Personal Relationships, 15, 155–170.*

Pennebaker, J. W., Francis, M. E., & Booth, R. J. (2001). *Linguistic inquiry and word count: LIWC 2001.* Mahwah, NJ: Erlbaum.

Semin, G. R., & De Poot, C. J. (1997). The question–answer paradigm: You might regret not noticing how a question is worded. *Journal of Personality and Social Psychology, 73, 472–480.*

Semin, G. R., & Fiedler, K. (1988). The cognitive functions of linguistic categories in describing persons: Social cognition and language. *Journal of Personality and Social Psychology, 54, 558–568.*

Sevier, M., Eldridge, K., Jones, J., Doss, B. D., & Christensen, A. (2008). Observed communication and associations with satisfaction during traditional and integrative behavioral couple therapy. *Behavior Therapy, 39, 137–150.*

Silverman, A., Logel, C., & Cohen, G. L. (2013). Self-affirmation as a deliberate coping strategy: The moderating role of choice. *Journal of Experimental Social Psychology, 49, 93–98.*

Singal, J. (2017, May). How the self-esteem craze took over America. *The Cut.* Retrieved from *www.thecut.com/2017/05/self-esteem-grit-do-they-really-help.html.*

Stinson, D. A., Logel, C., Shepherd, S., & Zanna, M. P. (2011). Rewriting the self-fulfilling prophecy of social rejection: Self-affirmation improves relational security and social behavior up to 2 months later. *Psychological Science, 22, 1145–1149.*

Sümer, N., & Cozzarelli, C. (2004). The impact of adult attachment on partner and self-attributions and relationship quality. *Personal Relationships, 11, 355–371.*

Thomaes, S., Bushman, B. J., Orobio de Castro, B., & Reijntjes, A. (2012). Arousing "gentle passions" in young adolescents: Sustained experimental effects of value-affirmations on prosocial feelings and behaviors. *Developmental Psychology, 48, 103–110.*

Uebelacker, L. A., & Whisman, M. A. (2005). Relationship beliefs, attributions, and partner behaviors among depressed married women. *Cognitive Therapy and Research, 29, 143–154.*

Walton, G. M., & Wilson, T. D. (2018). Wise interventions: Psychological remedies for social and personal problems. *Psychological Review, 125, 617–655.*

Wood, J. V., Heimpel, S. A., Newby-Clark, I. R., & Ross, M. (2005). Snatching defeat from the jaws of victory: Self-esteem differences in the experience and anticipation of success. *Journal of Personality and Social Psychology, 89, 764–780.*

Wood, J. V., Pernuovic, W. Q. E., & Lee, J. W. (2009). Positive self-statements: Power for some, peril for others. *Psychological Science, 20, 860–866.*

Zunick, P. V., Fazio, R. H., & Vasey, M. W. (2015). Directed abstraction: Encouraging broad, personal generalizations following a success experience. *Journal of Personality and Social Psychology, 109, 1–19.*

APPENDIX 17.1. Study Materials

Relationship Event

Think of a time when your current romantic partner told you how much he/she liked something about you. For example, a personal quality or ability you have that he/she thinks very highly of, or something you did that really impressed him/her. When you have thought of such an occurrence, please write a few cue words that will identify that memory to you (e.g., "said I was thoughtful"), then turn the page to describe the event more fully.

Cue words: _____

_____

_____

Please describe the event more fully:

ARI Condition

Explain why your partner admired you. Describe what it meant to you and its significance for your relationship.

Concrete Condition

Describe exactly what your partner said to you. Include any details you can recall about where you two were at the time, what you were doing, what you were both wearing, etc.

Control Condition

Describe the event in the space below.

PART IV

SUSTAINABILITY

CHAPTER 18

The Social Norms Approach
A Wise Intervention for Solving Social and Environmental Problems

Jessica M. Nolan, P. Wesley Schultz, Robert B. Cialdini, and Noah J. Goldstein

Social norms interventions work by communicating to a target audience that other people are engaging in the desired behavior, or will approve of you if you do the behavior (or conversely that other people are avoiding an undesired behavior, or will disapprove of you if you do it). Social norms interventions have been used to address a number of social and environmental problems with positive effects that have been documented to persist over time. Key considerations in social norms interventions are that they are believable, utilize credible sources, and reference meaningful groups. Importantly, social norms interventions are often most effective at changing the behavior of those who frequently engage in undesired behaviors (e.g., consuming electricity) or who infrequently engage in desired behaviors (e.g., recycling). This chapter includes sample messages and advice for successfully implementing a social norms intervention. The process by which social norms affect behavior and the implications for theory and practice are also discussed.

On a hillside in Italy, a large crowd has gathered to sing about how they would "like to buy the world a Coke" (*www.youtube.com/watch?v=C2406n8_rUw*). As the camera pans the crowd we see people with different skin colors and clothing presumably representing a multitude of countries and ethnicities from around the world. The crowd continues their heartfelt lip-syncing with "It's the real thing. Coke is what the world wants today." This commercial, released by Coca-Cola in 1971, went on to become one of its most famous (Andrews & Barbash, 2016). The theme of the ad is clear: People all over the world are drinking Coke and you should, too.

In this chapter, we describe how social norms can be harnessed as a wise intervention to influence behavior. As in the Coca-Cola commercial, social norms interventions provide "social proof" to the audience that other people engage in a desired behavior (or do not engage in an undesired behavior) in an attempt to leverage an individual's need to belong and the tendency to conform to the behavior of others. Because social norms interventions more frequently utilize descriptive social norms, that is the primary focus of this chapter. However, research on injunctive norms is included when it helps to clarify the differences between the two types of norms and their underlying mechanisms. We also focus primarily on research that utilizes explicit normative appeals and that attempts to impact behavior, rather than just attitudes or beliefs.

BACKGROUND

There are two origin stories to be told for social norms interventions: one for the academic discussion of social norms in social psychology, and the other for the development of social norms marketing to curb problematic drinking. We begin with the former. Many social norms interventions carried out today have been influenced by the work of Cialdini and colleagues in the early 1990s on the focus theory of normative conduct. This work was built on an understanding of social norms as "rules and standards that are understood by members of a group, and that guide and/or constrain social behavior without the force of laws" (Cialdini & Trost, 1998, p. 152). This definition allows social norms to exist at multiple levels, representing a shared understanding among members of a group that can be as small as a family unit or group of friends, or as large as a whole society. Cialdini and colleagues took this definition a step further by distinguishing between two types of social norms that can influence behavior: descriptive norms that describe what most people do, and injunctive norms that prescribe or proscribe what people think should or should not be done. Furthermore, more than a half-dozen experiments, many looking across real behavior in the field, provide substantial support for the focus theory of normative conduct.

The focus theory of normative conduct proposes that norms must be salient or activated to guide behavior. Both descriptive and injunctive norms can be activated, and a variety of manipulations can be used to bring a particular norm into focus. For example, in one of their early experiments, Cialdini, Reno, and Kallgren (1990) exposed participants to either a clean (antilittering descriptive norm) or littered (prolittering descriptive norm) parking garage and then had a confederate either walk by (low norm salience), drop a crumpled bag (high-descriptive norm salience), or pick up a crumpled bag (high-injunctive norm salience). Researchers recorded how many participants in each condition littered a large handbill that had been left on the windshield of their car. The results showed, first, that participants were more likely to litter the handbill when the environment was already littered versus when it was clean. Second (and more importantly), consistent with the prediction of focus theory (Cialdini et al., 1990) that salient norms will guide behavior, there was an interaction between the norm salience manipulation and the manipulation of the environment. In the high-descriptive norm salience condition, participants who saw the confederate drop the crumpled bag in an already littered parking garage were just as likely as those who saw the confederate walk by to litter the handbill. However, those who saw the confederate litter the crumpled bag into a clean environment were much *less* likely to litter compared to those who saw the confederate just walk by. When the confederate littered, they brought attention to the prevailing descriptive norm and made it more likely that the participant would use that norm to inform their own behavior. In the high-injunctive norm salience condition, participants littered less when the confederate picked up the crumpled bag versus just walked by, regardless of whether the environment was clean or littered (see Figure 18.1). Subsequent research showed that a salient piece of litter, like a watermelon rind, in an otherwise clean environment, could also activate the antilittering descriptive norm and that sweeping litter into a pile and using an antilittering message on the handbill left on the windshield could activate injunctive norms against littering with similar effects (Cialdini et al., 1990).

Let's turn now to the second origin story for social norms interventions. The development of social norms marketing began in the late 1980s with research at Hobart and William Smith Colleges. This early research on college drinking norms showed that college students frequently overestimated how much and how regularly their peers were consuming alcohol (Perkins & Berkowitz, 1986). Subsequent research found that exaggerated beliefs about the prevalence of alcohol use and abuse was widespread across college campuses of various sizes and in different regions of the country (Perkins, 2003). This discovery of exaggerated or "misperceived" norms, combined with correlational research showing that normative beliefs about the behavior of others are often a strong predictor of one's own behavior (e.g., Clapp & McDonnell, 2000), led to the development of the social norms marketing approach.

The social norms marketing approach provided an alternative to the traditional health promotion model. In the traditional model, problematic drinking was seen as a consequence of favorable attitudes toward drinking. As a result, interventions designed in the context of the traditional model focused on changing attitudes toward alcohol use as a way to promote responsible drinking behavior. Typically, these attitude-change interventions focused on educating the target audience about the dangers associated with the harmful effects of alcohol, whether they be health related or legal risks. The social

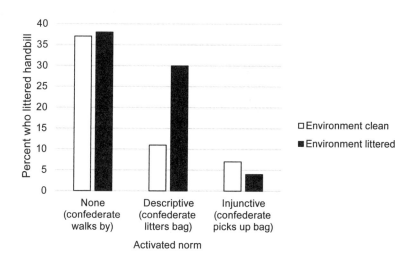

FIGURE 18.1. Percentage of people who littered a handbill based on which norm was activated and the state of the environment. Figure redrawn using data from Reno, Cialdini, and Kallgren (1993).

norms marketing approach acknowledged that problematic drinking behavior might also be caused by peer and social influences, real or imagined (see also Perkins, 2003, for a detailed history of the emergence of the social norms approach).

PSYCHOLOGICAL PROCESSES

How does the social norms approach achieve lasting effects? As a wise intervention, the social norms approach alters the way that people make sense of the world around them by providing answers to psychologically important questions, such as "How can I behave effectively in a given situation," or "How should I behave to avoid disapproval from important others?" The desire to find answers to these questions is driven by two of the fundamental motives that underlie meaning making: the need to understand and the need to belong (Walton & Wilson, 2018). Later in the chapter we discuss the details of three mechanisms that result from these fundamental needs:

1. A heuristic mechanism fueled by the need to understand and behave effectively—for example, a consumer shopping for a new washing machine chooses the one listed as "most popular" in a shopping guide.
2. A cognitive mechanism fueled by the need to belong—for example, a college student perceives that most of their peers are drinking alcohol and follows suit.
3. An internalization mechanism that is fueled by a combination of these two fundamental needs—for example, a homeowner may initially set out their recycling pail each week because the neighbors are doing it, but over time they may come to believe that it is the right thing to do.

We also discuss how the social norms approach engages recursive processes between an individual and their social environment that help to sustain changes into the future.

EMPIRICAL EVIDENCE

Outcomes

There is abundant evidence for the effectiveness of the social norms approach. Social norms interventions have been used successfully to promote a wide range of health, prosocial, and environmental behaviors. In the health domain, social norms interventions have increased vegetable consumption (Robinson, Thomas, Aveyard, & Higgs, 2014), hand washing (Lapinski, Maloney, Braz, & Shulman, 2013), and use of designated drivers (Perkins, Linkenbach, Lewis, & Neighbors, 2010), and decreased sedentary behavior (Priebe & Spink, 2015), binge drinking (Haines, 1998), pregame drinking (Burger, LaSalvia, Hendricks, Mehdipour, & Neudeck, 2011), drinking and driving (Perkins et al., 2010), and inappropriate antibiotic prescription by physicians (Linder et al., 2017). In the prosocial domain, social norms interventions have spurred signing petitions (Margetts, John, Escher, & Reissfelder, 2011), donating to charitable causes (Agerström, Carlsson, Nicklasson, & Guntell, 2016), and voting (Gerber & Rogers, 2009). As evidenced from this list, social norms interventions have broad generalizability across behaviors. In the environmental domain, social norms interventions have increased curbside recycling (Schultz, 1999), towel reuse among hotel guests (Goldstein, Cialdini, & Griskevicius, 2008), water conservation (Ferraro & Price, 2013), composting household organics (Phelps, Large, Schultz, & Ettlinger, 2017), and decreased energy consumption (Nolan, Schultz, Cialdini, Goldstein, & Griskevicius, 2008), littering (Cialdini et al., 1990), and theft of petrified wood at a national park (Cialdini et al., 2006).

In our own research on household energy conservation, we found that a message utilizing social norms outperformed more traditional approaches (Nolan et al., 2008). The research began with a survey of Californians to assess their energy-conservation behavior, normative beliefs, and beliefs about what motivated them to conserve. A majority of Californians reported engaging in many of the energy-conserving behaviors that we asked about, including using fans instead of air-conditioning at night and turning off unused lights. The results of this correlational study also showed that although respondents were most likely to attribute their motivation for conserving energy to a desire to protect the environment and future generations, in fact, the best predictor of their self-reported energy-conservation behavior was their descriptive normative beliefs about the energy-conserving behavior of others.

We followed up the statewide survey with a large-scale field experiment comparing the effectiveness of a social norms message inviting households to "join your neighbors" to more traditional appeals to "protect the environment," "do your part for future generations," and "save money." Door hangers were distributed to participating households for 4 weeks. Each week the door hanger promoted a different energy-saving behavior along with a motivational appeal specific to the type of message. Those in the environmental protection condition were told how much carbon dioxide emission they would prevent, those in the social responsibility condition were told how they could reduce demand for electricity, and those in the self-interest condition were told how performing the recommended behavior would save them money. In the social norms condition, we used information from the statewide survey to provide households with true information about the percentage of neighbors like them who were engaging in the recommended energy-saving behavior (see Figure 18.2 for a sample door hanger). We found that participants who received the social norms intervention used significantly less energy during the intervention compared to those in the other conditions. In addition to measuring home energy consumption, we also interviewed households to inquire about their perception of the effectiveness of the door hangers. Consistent with the results of the statewide survey, the results of the door-to-door survey revealed that the social norms message was rated as the least motivating, despite the fact that it had been most effective at reducing home energy consumption.

This and other related research (e.g., Schultz, Nolan, Cialdini, & Griskevicius, 2007) inspired companies such as Opower to adopt the social norms approach for large-scale application, providing customers with normative feedback on their home energy bills. Over a 10-year period, Opower reduced energy consumption by an average of 2–5% in more than 100 utility districts and reached nearly 60 million households (Allcott, 2011). The cumulative impact of this large-scale application is estimated to have reduced household energy costs by $1 billion and carbon dioxide emissions by 13 billion pounds (Schultz, Nolan, Cialdini, Goldstein, & Griskevicius, 2018).

FIGURE 18.2. Sample door hanger used in the study by Nolan, Schultz, Cialdini, Goldstein, and Griskevicius (2008).

Mechanism

Social Proof

There is evidence to suggest that conformity to social norms, and descriptive norms in particular, occurs through a heuristic process (Göckeritz et al., 2010; Jacobson, Mortensen, & Cialdini, 2011). Individuals, motivated by a need to understand how to behave effectively, use the behavior of others to quickly make decisions about their own behavior. Thus, activated social norms can serve as an efficient guide for the decision maker, providing "social proof" for the effectiveness of a particular behavior (Cialdini, 2001). This heuristic process is also consistent with evolutionary explanations of conformity. For example, in the domain of eating, adhering to descriptive norms may have provided an easy way to ensure the selection of safe foods and may have promoted food sharing in our environment of evolutionary adaptation (Higgs, 2015).

Support for the heuristic nature of this approach comes from research showing that social norms interventions can impact behavior, even when participants do not self-report greater intentions to engage in the behavior (Stok, Mollen, Verkooijen, & Renner, 2018). Furthermore, participants with *fewer* cognitive resources are *more* likely to conform to a descriptive norm message (Jacobson et al., 2011), and other research showing that individuals who are personally involved with the behavior being promoted (Göckeritz et al., 2010), or who are encouraged to elaborate on a message (Kredentser, Fabrigar, Smith, & Fulton, 2012), are *less* likely to conform to a descriptive norm message. In contrast, the reverse is true for social norms interventions that employ injunctive norms. Depleting cognitive resources makes injunctive norm messages *less* effective, while elaboration makes them *more* effective. These results support the notion that descriptive norms operate as a heuristic cue that help to achieve the goal of efficient and effective action with minimal cognitive resources, whereas injunctive norms are more focused on the maintenance of interpersonal interactions and thus require greater cognitive resources to process them.

Changing Normative Beliefs

The social norms approach can also be construed as an intervention that harnesses individuals' need to belong by linking belonging to beliefs about what constitutes desired behavior. In many cases, individuals overestimate the prevalence of undesirable behaviors and underestimate the prevalence of desirable behaviors. Social norms interventions correct these misperceptions of the norm by providing people with accurate information about what constitutes typical behavior in a valued social community. Norms and normative beliefs, though related, represent distinct constructs. Whereas the former speaks to the actual state of affairs regarding a target behavior's prevalence or acceptance, the latter encompasses individuals' perceptions of these actualities (Nolan, 2011). It is these normative beliefs that may become the proximate drivers of behavior (Morris, Hong, Chiu, & Liu, 2015).

Social norms marketing campaigns have been shown to be quite effective at correcting misperceptions of campus drinking norms (Clapp, Lange, Russel, Shillington, & Voas, 2003; Neighbors, Larimer, & Lewis, 2004). For example, a social norms marketing campaign was designed to reduce problematic drinking among young people from the United States crossing the border to go to the bars in Tijuana, Mexico (Johnson, 2012). The results showed that providing these young people with accurate information about how much alcohol previous border crossers had consumed succeeded in changing their normative beliefs about drinking and that this change in beliefs was negatively correlated with their blood alcohol levels as they crossed back into the United States. Other evidence for the role of normative beliefs comes from research showing that social norms interventions can be enhanced by first asking people to guess the norm before it is revealed (Bartke, Friedl, Gelhaar, & Reh, 2017). Importantly, asking people to guess the norm increased charitable giving only among people who perceived it to be less common than it actually was (i.e., those who underestimated the prevalence of the desired behavior). For those who overestimated the true descriptive norm, guessing only served to undermine their motivation as they learned that charitable giving was in fact less frequent than they had previously assumed.

Internalized Norms

A third way that social norms interventions may operate to change behavior (and maintain those changes) is via the internalization of social norms as personal norms—that is, a personal moral obligation to act in a certain way. It is accepted, and expected, that over time social norms will become internalized as personal norms (Schwartz, 1977; Sherif, 1966). According to Sherif, "Norms develop in man and become part of him as he develops in a social environment" (p. 46). Personal norms are internally sanctioned and backed by the anticipation of shame, guilt, and/or embarrassment when a personal norm has been violated (Horne, 2003; Kerr, Garst, Lewandowski, & Harris, 1997; Posner & Rasmusen, 1999; Rozin, Lowery, Haidt, & Imada, 1999) and as a "warm glow" when one has behaved consistently with their own personal standards (e.g., Andreoni, 1995). Thus, in addition to having short-term effects on behavior, social norms interventions may also be able to change behavior in the long term.

The long-term impact of social norms interventions is likely the result of a recursive process between the individual and their social environment. For example, someone who reduces their home energy consumption as a result of a social norms intervention may receive approval for this change from friends and colleagues or may be more likely to notice or associate with others who also conserve energy. These interactions reinforce the new pattern of behavior and help to maintain, or even strengthen, the energy-conservation norm, as well as to help the norm become internalized.

Effects over Time

Not only do social norms interventions have an immediate effect on behavior, they can continue to affect behavior for days, weeks, or even years later. The strongest effects seem to come from interventions that provide ongoing exposure to normative information or provide "boosters" on a semiregular basis. In the environmental domain, large-scale longitudinal research by Allcott and Rogers (2014) showed that the most dramatic decrease in energy consumption came immediately after the introduction of normative feedback. While these large reductions in energy usage were not sustained, households that continued to receive monthly or quarterly reports over the next 2 years did continue to conserve, just at a lower rate. In addition, these households continued to conserve energy over the next 2 years even after they stopped receiving regular home energy reports. It is possible that the continuation in energy conservation over time may, in part, be the result of households having implemented one-time behaviors, such as installing an energy-efficient appliance, that have a long-term impact on consumption. However, similar long-term effects have been found for social norms interventions designed to discourage overprescribing of antibiotics by physicians (e.g., Linder et al., 2017). In this problem space, behaviors must be repeated to be sustained, which suggests that these long-term effects cannot be attributed entirely to engaging in one-time behaviors with enduring effects. Instead, individuals must come to believe that these newly adopted behaviors are the correct and effective way to behave, and so continue to do so, even after the intervention has ended. On a smaller scale, college students continued to conserve water 3 weeks after a social norms sign encouraging them to do full loads of laundry was posted in their dorm laundry room (Sparkman & Walton, 2017). In this case, the sign remained present for the duration of the intervention. However, even one-shot treatments can persist over short periods of time. For example, participants exposed to a descriptive norm message for water conservation continued to use less water 1 week later, even with no new exposure to the message (Richetin, Perugini, Mondini, & Hurling, 2016). Nonetheless, one-shot treatments do tend to wane over longer periods of time (Ferraro & Price, 2013).

Another demonstrated way to prolong the effects of a social norms intervention is to couple it with commitment (Jaeger & Schultz, 2017). In a study of water conservation, households that received a social norms message and made a commitment to use water efficiently consumed less water 4 months later, compared to those that received a strong warning reminding them of the penalties associated with violating the water restrictions and that then made a commitment. The authors argue that these results are caused by cognitive dissonance resulting from an insufficient justification for making the commitment in the social norms condition. Because social norms interventions are minimally directive (Walton & Wilson, 2018), households that made a commitment after receiving the norms message perceived their behavior as freely chosen rather than attributing it to the coercive nature of the message. As a result, the behavior was more likely to become intrinsically motivated. In contrast, those in the strong warning condition could attribute their commitment to the coercive nature of the message and associated laws.

The goal of most interventions is to create long-term changes in behavior that are intrinsically motivated, and thus do not require external rewards, incentives, or reminders. The take-home message from these studies is that one-shot interventions are likely to have immediate effects on behavior but may not persist beyond a few days. This may be because normative beliefs are dynamic and constructed from a continuous flow of inputs that includes observing the behavior of others and communications about the behavior of others, as well as one's own behavior (Miller & Prentice, 1996). As time goes by, the information provided in a one-shot social norms intervention may be outweighed by other inputs suggesting that the behavior is less common than was suggested. In contrast, ongoing campaigns that last for several weeks, months, or years are more likely to persist far into the future. Like most wise interventions (Walton & Wilson, 2018), the key to success is to create a durable change in the way people make sense of themselves and/or the situation. For example, a student who previously saw binge drinking on campus as normal and expected may reconsider that view after being exposed to an ongoing social norms campaign. As we mentioned earlier, ongoing exposure to social norms, combined with repeated production of the behavior, may lead to internalization of those norms and the development of new habits. When new habits are formed and/or personal norms are developed, the intervention is no longer needed to spur behavior. Instead, behavior becomes internally motivated and free from external controls.

Heterogeneity

Like most persuasive efforts, social norms interventions can be more or less effective depending on important attributes of the message, the behavior, and the target audience.

Attributes of the Message

In order to be effective, messages must use credible sources and advertise social norms that are believable. Social norms marketing may be less effective, or ineffective, in situations in which the source of the message can be perceived to have a vested interest and stands to gain personally from participants conforming to the implied request of the message. For example, participants perceived a grocery store ad promoting natural products to be more deceptive when it included a descriptive norm (Raska, Nichols, & Shaw, 2015). While these ads did successfully change participants' perception of the norm, they were rated more negatively, and made participants less willing to purchase the advertised products. Likewise, descriptive norms must be believable to be effective. Smith, Atkin, Martell, Allen, and Hembroff (2006) found that normative messages vary in the extent to which the target audience accepts them as believable and propose that messages that utilize information that falls within the latitude of "noncommitment" will be most effective. Information that is too easily accepted may not provide a motivation to change, while information in the latitude of rejection may be dismissed as deceptive.

The most effective social norms interventions often use reference groups that are meaningful to the individual in some way. Messages that reference ingroups (Abrams, Wetherall, Cochrane, Hogg, & Turner, 1990) and proximal others (Agerström et al., 2016; Stok, de Vet, de Ridder, & de Wit, 2016) are more effective than those that reference outgroups and distal others. Similarly, identifying strongly with the reference group can increase the impact of social norms messages (Stok, de Ridder, de Vet, & de Wit, 2014), and in general, reference groups that are valued by the individual are better able to influence behavior. Social identity theory (Tajfel, 1974) predicts that people will be most inclined to follow the norms of groups that are important to them because they derive part of their sense of self (and self-esteem) from these social identities. Conforming to social norms provides a way to remain a member in good standing and to satisfy our fundamental need to belong.

Perhaps surprisingly, messages utilizing seemingly meaningless referents, such as "people who used this soap" (Richetin et al., 2016) and "guests in this room" (Goldstein et al., 2008; Reese, Loew, & Steffgen, 2014), can also be effective. Indeed, advertising that a majority of guests that had stayed in a particular hotel room reused their towels was more effective at motivating guests to reuse their towels than a traditional appeal to environmental protection or a patriotic social norms message that referenced citizens. Provincial norms are defined as "the norms of one's local setting and circumstances" (Goldstein et al., 2008, p. 476). Importantly, the results of this initial study showed that while the provincial norm had the biggest effect on behavior, it was rated as being the least important to participants' personal identity. Instead, Goldstein and colleagues speculate that adherence to these provincial norms is guided by a desire to behave effectively in one's immediate setting. These results are also consistent with predictions that would be made according to the logic-of-appropriateness framework (Weber, Kopelman, & Messick, 2004): "What does a person like me do in a situation like this?" If the guest assumes that they are similar to other guests that have stayed in that room, then the provincial norm provides clear guidance for what a person "like you" has done under similar circumstances.

Attributes of the Behavior

Two important aspects of the behavior that have been explored are the extent to which the behavior can be publicly observed and the level of uncertainty associated with what constitutes correct action in a given situation. Social norms interventions may be more effective at influencing publicly observable behaviors (Stok et al., 2016), but research has shown that they can also be used successfully to promote private or semiprivate behaviors, such as hand washing (Lapinski et al., 2013) and home energy consumption (Nolan et al., 2008). With respect to uncertainty or ambiguity about what constitutes correct action, the research clearly shows that social norms interventions are more likely to influence behavior when the situation is ambiguous. Because of our need to understand, when we are unsure about what constitutes safe, effective, or appropriate behavior we are more likely to rely on social norms (Gelfand & Harrington, 2015; Higgs, 2015; White & Simpson, 2013).

Attributes of the Target Audience

What you say in a message is important but so is understanding to whom you are saying it. In terms of demographic characteristics, social norms interventions tend to be more effective with younger people (Rivas & Sheeran, 2003), women (Higgs, 2015), and individuals from collectivistic cultures or those who have a more collectivistic orientation (Cialdini, Wosinska, Barrett, Butner, & Gornika-Durose, 1999). Younger people, and adolescents in particular, may be more susceptible to social norms associated with their peer groups because this is a developmental period that is heavily focused on identity development (Erikson, 1950). Women may be more likely to conform because of evolutionary factors that predispose men to conform *less* as part of a mating strategy to stand out, but only when nonconformity does not lead to behavior that is objectively less accurate (Griskevicius, Goldstein, Mortensen, Cialdini, & Kenrick, 2006). In collectivistic societies, there is greater societal pressure to conform to group norms and to elevate the needs of the group above self-interest (Triandis, 1995).

Whether it be energy or alcohol, social norms interventions designed to decrease undesirable levels of consumption are often more effective among high users. For example, high users of water accounted for the bulk of the savings achieved by providing comparative feedback indicating how an individual's household water consumption compared to their neighbor's average consumption (Ferraro & Price, 2013). High-use households may be more susceptible to social norms interventions for a few reasons. First, the personal behavior of high users is most discrepant from the advertised norm, which may produce stronger motivations to correct the deviant behavior. Second, it is easier for high-use households to identify easy ways to reduce their consumption. Third, high consumption of resources is often associated with greater wealth. These households tend to be less sensitive to prices, making the social norms approach even more important. Although the reasoning may be slightly different, a similar pattern has been found in the domain of alcohol use with heavy drinkers showing the largest reductions in consumption following exposure to personalized normative feedback (Prince, Reid, Carey, & Neighbors, 2014). Similarly, social norms interventions designed to increase desirable behaviors are often more effective among low users. For example, registered voters who had voted infrequently or only occasionally in the past were more likely than those who voted often or always to show greater intentions to vote when told that a majority of voters in the state had voted in the last election (Gerber & Rogers, 2009).

Highly empathic people and people with low self-esteem, or who are temporarily made to feel a lack of social acceptance, are more likely to imitate a confederate, and by extension may be more likely to conform to social norms (Robinson, Tobias, Shaw, Freeman, & Higgs, 2011). Similarly, Gelfand and Harrington (2015) argue that low-power or low-status individuals should be more likely to conform compared to their high-powered, high-status counterparts. The logic here is that those with high status or who have a lot of power or self-esteem are less susceptible to criticism for deviating from the group norms, and more immune to criticism even if it does occur.

Finally, individuals who are made to feel personally responsible for a behavior may be more susceptible to social norms targeting changes to that behavior. For example, bathroom users were more likely to turn off the light when leaving if they had to turn it on when they entered and thus felt more personally responsible for the behavior (Dwyer, Maki, & Rothman, 2015).

COUSINS

Of course, the social norms approach is not the only one that has been used to promote desirable behaviors. Two techniques that are similar to social norms and that have been used to target a similar range of behaviors are "modeling" and "feedback." Interventions that use modeling to change behavior are based on Bandura's (1977) social learning theory. According to social learning theory, individuals use the behavior of models to inform their own behavior and are more likely to imitate valued models and behaviors for which the models are rewarded. For children, these valued models are often parents and other caregivers, whereas for adolescents, valued models are more likely to be peers. Modeling can be an effective way to change behavior. For example, in the now classic study by Aronson and O'Leary (1982–1983), the number of college males who turned the water off while soaping up in a locker room shower more than doubled to 49% when a student confederate modeled this behavior, compared to when only a large sign was present. Compliance "jumped" further to 67% when two confederates modeled the water-saving behavior. At first glance, modeling and social norms might seem to be the same. Both approaches use the behavior of others as a guide to one's own behavior, so how are they different? While modeling has its effect by focusing on the behavior of a particular individual, social norms have their effect by conveying an impression of what most people do. Cialdini and colleagues (1990) conducted an experiment that nicely illustrates this distinction. Participants returning to their car in a hospital parking garage either encountered a confederate who littered a large handbill onto the ground or simply walked by in the opposite direction. Research on modeling would predict that those who saw the confederate litter the handbill should be more likely to litter as well. However, this was the case only when the ground was already littered. When participants saw the confederate litter the handbill in an otherwise clean garage, they were actually *less* likely to litter the handbill they found on their own vehicle, compared to when the confederate just walked by. Cialdini and colleagues argue that the confederate littering into the clean environment decreased littering because it made the descriptive antilittering norm salient. Thus, this example illustrates the importance of norm focus, but also the superior strength of social norms, compared to modeling by strangers. While both social norms and modeling can be used to resolve questions related to the need to understand and the need to belong, modeling may be effective only when the model is a valued other. In contrast, because social norms convey what most people approve or disapprove of, individuals can be more confident that conforming to social norms will lead to effective or socially rewarding behavior.

Social norms interventions, particularly those that utilize comparative or normative feedback, are similar to feedback interventions more generally. In everyday life we regularly receive feedback about our behavior. For example, the displays on an automobile dashboard tell you how fast you are driving, how far the car has traveled over its lifetime or on a particular trip, and in some cases, how efficiently your car is consuming gasoline. Feedback interventions refer to "actions taken by [an] external agent(s) to provide information regarding some aspect of one's task performance" (Kluger & DeNisi, 1996, p. 255). Personalized individual feedback can be an effective way to address many problematic behaviors, including home energy consumption (Faruqui, Sergici, & Sharif, 2010) and alcohol consumption among college students (Alfonso, 2015). Normative feedback is similar to personalized feedback in that both strategies provide feedback about individual or household behavior. They differ in that normative feedback provides additional information about how the individual's behavior compares to a specified group (e.g., Schultz, 1999).

INTERVENTION CONTENT AND IMPLEMENTATION

There are a variety of options available for implementing a social norms intervention that utilizes direct appeals to change behavior and that explicitly references a social norm. For example, descriptive social norms can be communicated several ways (see Table 18.1 for sample messages). Probably the most common approach is to advertise that a majority of people are engaging in the desired behavior, either by saying so directly or by providing an exact percentage (see Table 18.1, examples A–D). Variations on this approach might also use other numeric descriptors, such as "most" or "many" to quantify the extent to which the behavior is commonly done (see example E). A second option is to report that a specific (desired) frequency of the behavior is common, such as advertising that most college students have zero to five drinks when they party (see examples B and F). A third option is to report average usage, either alone, or more often in conjunction with personalized feedback (see example G).

As discussed previously, social norms messages can use proximal referents, such as neighbors or fellow students at a particular university (see example A), or provincial norms that reference a group that shares a connection to the location (see example D). There are also options for how to talk about the frequency of the behavior. Research suggests that using verbal quantifiers with positive polarity, such as "at least" and "a few" will be more effective at increasing a desired behavior compared to quantifiers with negative polarity, such as "at most" and "few" (Demarque, Charalambides, Hilton, & Waroquier, 2015; see example C). In all of these examples the goal of the message is to convince the reader that the recommended behavior is commonly done and therefore the right and correct thing to do.

NUANCES AND MISCONCEPTIONS

One of the most important points to remember when designing a social norms intervention is that people conform to social norms whether the advertised behavior is desirable or undesirable. This has two important implications for practice. First, the common tactic

TABLE 18.1. Sample Messages Used in Social Norms Interventions

	Reference	Message type	Behavior targeted	Message
A	Agerström, Carlsson, Nicklasson, & Guntell (2016)	Majority percentage Proximal referent	Donate to charity	"73% of Linnaeus University students who were asked for a contribution have donated 20 crowns to [Swedish] Golomolo."
B	Scribner et al. (2011)	Majority percentage Frequency of behavior	Binge drinking	"67% of university students have 4 or fewer drinks when they party."
C	Demarque, Charalambides, Hilton, & Waroquier (2015)	Majority percentage Positive polarity verbal quantifier	Green purchasing	"70% bought *at least one* ecological product."
D	Goldstein, Cialdini, & Griskevicius (2008)	Majority percentage Provincial norm	Towel reuse	"75% of the guests who stayed in this room [#*xx*] participated in our new resource savings program by using their towels more than once."
E	Perkins, Linkenbach, Lewis, & Neighbors (2010)	Majority descriptor	Drunk driving	"Most Montana young adults [4 out of 5] don't drink and drive."
F	Robinson, Thomas, Aveyard, & Higgs (2014)	Typical referent Frequency of behavior	Vegetable and fruit consumption	"A lot of people aren't aware that the typical student eats their five servings of fruits and vegetables each day."
G	Ferraro & Price (2013)	Comparative feedback	Water consumption	"Your total consumption June to October 2006: 50,000 gallons." "Your neighbors' average consumption June to October 2006: 35,000." "You consumed more water than 72% of your Cobb County neighbors."
H	Sparkman & Walton (2017)	Dynamic norm	Meat consumption	"Some people are starting to limit how much meat they eat. . . . Specifically, recent research has shown that, over the last 5 years, 30% of Americans have started to make an effort to limit their meat consumption. That means that, in recent years, 3 in 10 people have changed their behavior and begun to eat less meat than they otherwise would."
I	Mortensen et al. (2017)	Minority norm + trending norm	Water conservation	"48% of [university name] students engage in one or more of the following water conservation behaviors. . . . This has increased from 37% in [2 years previous]."

of health and environmental messages to advertise undesirable behaviors as "regrettably frequent" would be contraindicated by research and theorizing about social norms, and is not recommended (Cialdini et al., 2006). A typical message in this tradition focuses on how so many people are engaging in a dangerous, unhealthy, or polluting behavior. One of the most famous examples of advertising undesirable behavior as regrettably frequent is the "Iron Eyes Cody" public service announcement (PSA) produced by Keep America Beautiful in the 1970s. The ad showed an actor dressed in traditional American Indian clothing, paddling his canoe down a litter-filled river. When he brings the boat ashore he encounters more litter and a highway filled with car traffic. If it wasn't already clear, the high frequency of littering is further emphasized when a driver throws a bag full of trash out of the car window, landing at the feet of Iron Eyes Cody. To show that this high frequency of littering is "regrettable," the PSA ends by showing us a single tear rolling down the cheek of Iron Eyes Cody. We would do better to follow the example of the Coca-Cola ad described in the opening lines of the chapter and advertise the desired behavior as common and/or to focus the target audience on injunctive norms of approval for the desired behavior.

The second implication of this rule is the importance of baseline behavior, particularly when providing normative feedback about how an individual's behavior compares to the average or typical user. Social norms have the constructive power to decrease energy consumption among above-average users, but also the destructive power to increase consumption among below-average users (Schultz et al., 2007). One solution to this problem is to withhold normative feedback to below-average consumers if they can be identified in advance. Another option, suggested by our research, is to harness the reconstructive power of injunctive norms. Our results showed that incorporating an injunctive norm—a smiley face that expressed approval for consuming less than the average—buffered the tendency of low users to increase their consumption.

Another nuance that can be critical to the effectiveness of a social norms intervention is being aware of situational cues that might undermine the intervention message. People form beliefs about norms not only from explicit messages that assert the norm but also from inferences about the world around them. Environmental cues, such as the presence of litter or graffiti, can send a signal not just about the observed behavior, but also about the commonness and acceptability of related behaviors (Keizer, Lindenberg, & Steg, 2008). For example, when trash bags were placed in a prohibited location (signaling disorder), passersby were less likely to mail a lost letter or help a confederate pick up dropped items (Keizer, Lindenberg, & Steg, 2013). Most relevant to our discussion of social norms interventions is research showing that prohibition signs against litter *increased* the amount of littering when the environment was littered with trash or vandalized with graffiti (Keizer, Lindenberg, & Steg, 2011), and research showing that social norms marketing campaigns to reduce binge drinking are less effective on campuses with higher densities of onsite alcohol outlets (Scribner et al., 2011). In the case of the latter, the credibility of the social norms messages conveying that most students drink in moderation would be undermined by the plethora of bars and restaurants that serve alcohol, which presumably could not stay in business were they not well patronized.

Social norms interventions may simultaneously provide a heuristic cue for behavior and a communication input that is likely to alter normative beliefs. However, it may be difficult to capture these instantaneous changes in normative beliefs without altering the effects on behavior (e.g., Raska et al., 2015)—that is, while both effects occur simultaneously, inquiring about normative beliefs may call attention to the message in ways that undermine its effectiveness (Kredentser et al., 2012). Walton and Wilson (2018) argue that one of the features that makes interventions "wise" is that they are minimally directive—that is, it is possible that the covertness of the intervention is part of what makes it effective. People do not see social norms interventions as motivating, but asking questions about norms may draw attention to the influence attempt and increase resistance to the request. Taken together, the available research would suggest that while it is important to make the descriptive norm salient, it is also wise to discourage the target audience from thinking too much about the message.

IMPLICATIONS FOR PRACTICE

To effectively implement a social norms intervention in the field a series of steps should be followed. First, survey research should be used to determine the prevalence and/or frequency of the behavior(s) of interest and the prevailing normative beliefs about those behaviors among the target audience. Second, survey research can also be used to understand the target audience in terms of demographics and other variables deemed to be important, including those mentioned in this chapter. Third, structural barriers and opportunities should be identified. For example, it would not make sense to try to reduce heating among apartment dwellers who do not have control over their thermostats. The second and third steps are common to most community-based social marketing efforts (McKenzie-Mohr, Lee, Kotler, & Schultz, 2011). Fourth, a behavior should be selected that is performed by many people, but misperceived to be infrequent, and that has the potential to make a substantial impact in terms of units (e.g., pounds of greenhouse gases, number of students blacking out) deemed to be important by the community or organization.

Social norms interventions can be delivered effectively through various channels. In relatively small-scale applications, the intervention is typically delivered via posters, flyers (Robinson, Fleming, & Higgs, 2014), face-to-face discussion groups, or online via computer-mediated feedback (Prince et al., 2014). Small-scale applications might also manipulate the physical environment to convey social norms (Reese, Loeschinger, Hamann, & Neubert, 2013)—however, this approach typically requires time and resources that can make the intervention cost prohibitive. That said, there would be no harm, for example, in asking a computer lab manager with time on their hands to shut down unused monitors, knowing that it will make users more likely to turn them off themselves when they leave (Bator, Tabanico, Walton, & Schultz, 2014). In large-scale applications, the intervention is typically delivered via media campaigns that include print, television, and radio advertisements or PSAs (Cialdini, 2003; Perkins et al., 2010), or by collaborating with companies that already have direct access to customers (and consumption data), such as electricity, natural gas, and water utility companies (Allcott, 2011). Social norms can also be harnessed in online environments by advertising the number of times a post or video has been liked and/or shared. For example, participants who saw a description of a climate change video with a high number of views were more likely to perceive that climate change was an important issue for "most Americans" (Spartz, Su, Griffin, Brossard, & Dunwoody, 2017).

One of the questions we are frequently asked when presenting our research is "What happens when the behavior you want to promote is not performed by a majority of people?" and, sometimes, "Why promote behaviors that are already normative? After all, isn't it more important to increase the prevalence of unpopular but highly impactful behaviors?" Indeed, the usefulness of social norms interventions would be severely limited (although not altogether useless) if they could not be adapted to promote behaviors that are not descriptively normative. When we first started working on this research in the early 2000s there were really only two answers to this question: lie (a less than ideal option when working in field settings) or focus on injunctive norms. While focusing on injunctive norms is certainly a viable alternative when a behavior is not descriptively normative, we are happy to report that a flurry of activity in the last decade has produced additional options for using social norms marketing to promote behaviors that are not yet descriptively normative. One new option is to use positive polarity numeric qualifiers (Demarque et al., 2015). For example, a minority of people might be recycling paper, glass, and plastic each, but a majority of people may be recycling *at least* one type of recyclable item. This adaptation is most applicable in domains that consider a sphere of behaviors or instances of a behavior, rather than one unique behavior at one point in time. A second new option is to report dynamic or trending norms. Trending norms are "norms in which the number of people engaging in a behavior is increasing" (Mortensen et al., 2017; see also Sparkman, Chapter 19, this volume). Trending norms can be used successfully on their own (see example H in Table 18.1; Sparkman & Walton, 2017), or they can be added to a message that communicates the minority norm (see example I; Mortensen et al., 2017).

Like most interventions there is a tension between scaling up versus customizing social norms messages. This is especially true with respect to choosing a reference group for the message. Under ideal conditions, messages would be customized to refer to the group that is most meaningful for the target audience, for which there are data available. However, if customization is not possible, we would advise using a referent that has broad appeal among the target audience. If possible, we recommend pilot-testing messages prior to large-scale application to ensure that they are well received (though recall that they need not be perceived as motivational), ideally using a behavioral outcome measure.

The main challenge in conducting a social norms intervention is that it does require the practitioner to acquire normative information about the target behavior, and not everyone is in a position to conduct a survey, either due to limited time, money, or resources. The good news is that many of the behaviors targeted in social norms interventions are heavily studied by government agencies. For example, in the United States, information about transportation behavior can be found at *www.transportation.gov*, and about energy consumption at *www.energy.gov*. Public opinion polls can also be a good source of normative information about health and environmental behaviors.

Below is the story of how the social norms approach was used to reinvent home energy bills and save more energy than the Hoover Dam produces in a year:

Alex Laskey
Cofounder of Opower

In early 2007, my longtime friend Daniel Yates and I were introduced to the work of Professors Cialdini and Schultz by Rhea Suh of the Hewlett Foundation. Dan and I had recently decided to team up and work together to have a positive impact on the environment. At the time, we were exploring several novel ideas of projects—both for-profit and not-for-profit—to work on together. We met with Rhea because we were interested in the work

Hewlett was funding to protect temperate rain forests in British Columbia. Toward the end of our meeting, Rhea asked, "What else are the two of you thinking of working on?" It was at this point that we shared with her our preliminary idea to reinvent the electric utility bill. We had cooked up this idea while driving in my uncomfortable old Honda Civic, which we routinely chose to drive instead of Dan's relatively luxurious Nissan Pathfinder. We subjected ourselves—and our wives—to cramped rides in the Civic because we couldn't stomach the notion of unnecessarily wasting gasoline. At some point, we wondered out loud, "Wouldn't it be ironic if we were driving a Civic around town, but were returning home to Pathfinder apartments? And shouldn't everyone have a right to know whether their families were efficient or inefficient in their homes?"

We were aware that utilities were increasingly incentivized to help their customers save energy. And we were optimistic that if we helped utilities provide better information to their customers, we could change behaviors. When we shared this idea with Rhea, she said, "Surely you've read the research we've funded about the application of behavioral economics to conservation, right?" We responded, "No. And what is 'behavioral economics'?" She then introduced us to the work of Drs. Cialdini and Schultz, showing how normative information could reduce energy consumption in hotel guest rooms and suburban households. I remember very clearly the excitement Dan and I both felt after reading this research and learning more about the field of behavioral economics. After reading that the communication of social norms could significantly increase hotel visitors' likelihood to hang up their towels or motivate homeowners in the heat of summer to turn off their air conditioners and turn on their fans, we developed growing confidence that our idea to show homeowners how their energy use compared to their neighbors might actually make a difference.

Rhea soon connected us with Bob Cialdini. Although it's not easy to persuade a persuasion researcher, because of Bob's commitment to the environment, he agreed to serve as our chief scientist during the initial years of the company we formed, known as Opower. Bob worked closely with our communication team to design home energy reports sent to utility customers that communicated the energy use norms of their neighborhoods. Although Opower has since been purchased by Oracle, those energy reports, employed by over a hundred utilities worldwide, have now saved more than 35 billion pounds of CO_2 emissions and more than 23 trillion watts per hour of electricity. What's more, the energy reports are presently generating 5 trillion watts per hour per year in savings to utility customers. That works out to roughly $700 million in bill savings each year. The Hoover Dam, by comparison, produces only 4 trillion watts per hour of electricity. It's remarkable to me that our little behavioral science experiment is now roughly 20% bigger than the Hoover Dam!

IMPLICATIONS FOR PSYCHOLOGICAL THEORY

Research on social norms interventions reveals important qualities of our human nature, and also the nature of environmental problems. The research presented in this chapter supports the idea that, as human beings, we use the behavior of others as a guide for our own behavior. The evidence also suggests that people may not spend a great deal of time deliberating about daily choices, such as whether or not to recycle or turn the water off while brushing their teeth. Instead, people rely on heuristic cues, like descriptive norms, to satisfy their need to understand what is expected and to make these decisions about everyday behaviors.

There are several ways that the application of the social norms approach has affected our theoretical understanding of social norms and conformity. For example, while research does support original theorizing suggesting that individuals prefer to use the behavior of proximate, ingroup members to inform their own behavior, additional research shows that other referents can also be effective. Specifically, provincial or "situational" reference groups can also inform the behavior of targets. These results suggest that while meaningful ingroups may be more powerful than outgroups, conformity is not limited to those groups with which we identify. Instead, we use the behavior of others who are similar in some way—either by nature of their group membership or in having had contact with a particular product or location at different points in time.

Research on trending norms also forces us to reconsider our understanding of conformity to social norms. Original theorizing about descriptive social norms suggested that individuals will go along with what most people seem to be doing. However, research on trending norms shows that individuals will also conform to the behavior of a trending minority. This seems to be due in part to a belief that the behavior is moving toward majority status in the near future or that the changes described are expected to continue. Thus, conformity to social norms can occur when a behavior has already become normative, or when there is evidence that it is moving in that direction.

The social norms approach also reveals important qualities of environmental problems. Environmental problems possess the qualities of social dilemmas—situations in which the self-interest of the individual is at odds with the collective good. The costs of cooperating are immediate and accrue to the individual (e.g., the inconvenience of taking the bus vs. driving a personal automobile), while the benefits of cooperating are delayed and spread across society (e.g., benefits to air quality; see Rogers, Goldstein, & Fox, 2018, for a more general review of factors, including social norms interventions that mobilize individuals to cooperate in such situations). In addition, an individual cooperating alone cannot make much of an impact on large-scale problems such as global climate change. Individuals are understandably concerned that their efforts to conserve will be wasted if not enough others take action. One of the reasons why social norms interventions may be so effective at promoting environmental behaviors is that they assure the target that they will not be alone in their efforts.

FUTURE DIRECTIONS

As we have shown in this chapter, the social norms intervention has broad applicability across different domains of behavior and across populations. Companies like Opower have also shown that social norms interventions can be adapted for large-scale applications that benefit society and the environment. In addition, technologies such as smart thermostats provide yet another opportunity for harnessing the power of social norms. Indeed, some smart thermostat companies, such as Ecobee, have already incorporated comparative feedback that provides users with information about how their energy consumption compares to similar households as part of their "home IQ" interface. Future research should explore how these new technologies can be used to deliver social norms messages to optimize energy savings.

Going forward there are two key areas that should be explored in greater depth: boundary conditions of the intervention and the underlying mechanism. With few exceptions (e.g., Kormos, Gifford, & Brown, 2015), social norms research to date has focused primarily on relatively simple, everyday behaviors that must be enacted repeatedly to have a substantive impact. For example, in the environmental domain, application of the social norms intervention has focused primarily on reducing energy and water use via curtailment behaviors. These curtailment behaviors are often easy, inexpensive behaviors, such as taking shorter showers and doing full loads of laundry. Future research should explore whether the social norms intervention can be used to influence more difficult or expensive behaviors, such as purchasing a fuel-efficient vehicle or planting a rain garden.

There is also more to learn about the psychological mechanism that drives conformity to social norms. In particular, it would be interesting to explore whether measuring normative beliefs following exposure to a social norms intervention has the paradoxical effect of making the intervention less effective. This question could be tested by reviewing past research that has measured both beliefs and behavior, as well as with new research specifically designed to test the hypothesis. This prediction could be directly tested by exposing participants to the same message but asking some of them to report on their beliefs before versus after the behavior change opportunity is presented. In conducting the review of research, it would be important to distinguish between studies that measured behavioral intentions, self-reported past behavior, and actual behavior. Given the heuristic nature of social norms interventions, behavioral intentions are less likely to provide an accurate measure of the interventions' impact. Interference created by asking participants to think about the message may be common to other "minimally directive" techniques that rely on a heuristic mechanism.

REFERENCES

Abrams, D., Wetherall, M., Cochrane, S., Hogg, M. A., & Turner, J. C. (1990). Knowing what to think by knowing who you are: Self-categorization and the nature of norm formation, conformity, and group polarization. *British Journal of Social Psychology, 29,* 97–119.

Agerström, J., Carlsson, R., Nicklasson, L., & Guntell, L. (2016). Using descriptive social norms to increase charitable giving: The power of local norms. *Journal of Economic Psychology, 52,* 147–153.

Alfonso, J. (2015). The role of social norms in personalized alcohol feedback: A dismantling study with emerging adults. *Journal of Child and Adolescent Substance Abuse, 24*(6), 379–386.

Allcott, H. (2011). Social norms and energy conservation. *Journal of Public Economics, 95*(9–10), 1082–1095.

Allcott, H., & Rogers, T. (2014). The short-run and long-run effects of behavioral interventions: Experimental evidence from energy conservation. *American Economic Review, 104*(10), 3003–3037.

Andreoni, J. (1995). Warm-glow versus cold prickle: The effects of positive and negative framing on cooperation in experiments. *Quarterly Journal of Economics, 110,* 1–21.

Andrews, T. M., & Barbash, F. (2016). "I'd like to buy the world a Coke": The story behind the world's most famous ad, in memoriam its creator. Retrieved from *www.washingtonpost.com/news/morning-mix/wp/2016/05/17/id-like-to-buy-the-world-a-coke-the-story-behind-the-worlds-most-famous-ad-whose-creator-has-died-at-89.*

Aronson, E., & O'Leary, M. (1982). The relative effectiveness of models and prompts on energy conservation: A field experiment in a shower room. *Journal of Environmental Systems, 12*(3), 219–224.

Bandura, A. (1977). *Social learning theory.* Englewood Cliffs, NJ: Prentice-Hall.

Bartke, S., Friedl, A., Gelhaar, F., & Reh, L. (2017). Social comparison nudges—guessing the norm increases charitable giving. *Economics Letters, 152,* 73–75.

Bator, R. J., Tabanico, J. J., Walton, M. L., & Schultz, P. W. (2014). Promoting energy conservation with implied norms and explicit messages. *Social Influence, 9*(1), 69–82.

Burger, J. M., LaSalvia, C. T., Hendricks, L. A., Mehdipour, T., & Neudeck, E. M. (2011). Partying before the party gets started: The effects of descriptive norms on pre-gaming behavior. *Basic and Applied Social Psychology, 33,* 220–227.

Cialdini, R. B. (2001). *Influence: Science and practice.* Boston: Allyn & Bacon.

Cialdini, R. B. (2003). Crafting normative messages to protect the environment. *Current Directions in Psychological Science, 12*(4), 105–109.

Cialdini, R. B., Demaine, L. J., Sagarin, B. J., Barrett, D. W., Rhoads, K., & Winter, P. L. (2006). Managing social norms for persuasive impact. *Social Influence, 1*(1), 3–15.

Cialdini, R. B., Reno, R. R., & Kallgren, C. A. (1990). A focus theory of normative conduct: Recycling the concept of norms to reduce littering in public places. *Journal of Personality and Social Psychology, 58*(6), 1015–1026.

Cialdini, R. B., & Trost, M. R. (1998). Social influence: Social norms, conformity and compliance. In D. T. Gilbert, S. T. Fiske, & G. Lindzey (Eds.), *The handbook of social psychology* (4th ed., pp. 151–192). Boston: McGraw-Hill.

Cialdini, R. B., Wosinska, W., Barrett, D. W., Butner, J., & Gornik-Durose, M. (1999). Compliance with a request in two cultures: The differential influence of social proof and commitment/consistency on collectivists and individualists. *Personality and Social Psychology Bulletin, 25*(10), 1242–1253.

Clapp, J. D., Lange, J. E., Russel, C., Shillington, A., & Voas, R. B. (2003). A failed norms social marketing campaign. *Journal of Studies on Alcohol, 64,* 409–414.

Clapp, J. D., & McDonnell, A. L. (2000). The relationship of perceptions of alcohol promotion and peer drinking norms to alcohol problems reported by college students. *Journal of College Student Development, 41*(1), 19–26.

Demarque, C., Charalambides, L., Hilton, D. J., & Waroquier, L. (2015). Nudging sustainable consumption: The use of descriptive norms to promote a minority behavior in a realistic online shopping environment. *Journal of Environmental Psychology, 43,* 166–174.

Dwyer, P. C., Maki, A., & Rothman, A. J. (2015). Promoting energy conservation behavior in public settings: The influence of social norms and personal responsibility. *Journal of Environmental Psychology, 41,* 30–34.

Erikson, E. H. (1950). *Childhood and society.* New York: Norton.

Faruqui, A., Sergici, S., & Sharif, A. (2010). The impact of informational feedback on energy consumption—a survey of the experimental evidence. *Energy, 35*(4), 1598–1608.

Ferraro, P. J., & Price, M. K. (2013). Using nonpecuniary strategies to influence behavior: Evidence from a large-scale field experiment. *Review of Economics and Statistics, 95*(1), 64–73.

Gelfand, M. J., & Harrington, J. R. (2015). The motivational force of descriptive norms: For whom and when are descriptive norms most predictive of behavior? *Journal of Cross-Cultural Psychology, 46*(10), 1273–1278.

Gerber, A. S., & Rogers, T. (2009). Descriptive social norms and motivation to vote: Everybody's voting and so should you. *Journal of Politics, 71*(1), 178–191.

Göckeritz, S., Schultz, P. W., Rendón, T., Cialdini, R. B., Goldstein, N. J., & Griskevicius, V. (2010). Descriptive normative beliefs and conservation behavior: The moderating roles of personal involvement and injunctive normative beliefs. *European Journal of Social Psychology, 40*(3), 514–523.

Goldstein, N. J., Cialdini, R. B., & Griskevicius, V. (2008). A room with a viewpoint: Using social norms to motivate environmental conservation in hotels. *Journal of Consumer Research, 35*(3), 472–482.

Griskevicius, V., Goldstein, N. J., Mortensen, C. R., Cialdini, R. B., & Kenrick, D. T. (2006). Going along versus going alone: When fundamental motives facilitate strategic (non) conformity. *Journal of Personality and Social Psychology, 91*(2), 281–294.

Haines, M. P. (1998). Social norms: A wellness model for health promotion in higher education. *Wellness Management, 14*(4), 1–10.

Higgs, S. (2015). Social norms and their influence on eating behaviours. *Appetite, 86*, 38–44.

Horne, C. (2003). The internal enforcement of norms. *European Sociological Review, 19*(4), 335–343.

Jacobson, R. P., Mortensen, C. R., & Cialdini, R. B. (2011). Bodies obliged and unbound: Differentiated response tendencies for injunctive and descriptive social norms. *Journal of Personality and Social Psychology, 100*(3), 433–448.

Jaeger, C. M., & Schultz, P. W. (2017). Coupling social norms and commitments: Testing the underdetected nature of social influence. *Journal of Environmental Psychology, 51*, 199–208.

Johnson, M. B. (2012). Experimental test of social norms theory in a real-world drinking environment. *Journal of Studies on Alcohol and Drugs, 73*(5), 851–859.

Keizer, K., Lindenberg, S., & Steg, L. (2008). The spreading of disorder. *Science, 322*(5908), 1681–1685.

Keizer, K., Lindenberg, S., & Steg, L. (2011). The reversal effect of prohibition signs. *Group Processes and Intergroup Relations, 14*(5), 681–688.

Keizer, K., Lindenberg, S., & Steg, L. (2013). The importance of demonstratively restoring order. *PLOS ONE, 8*(6), e65137.

Kerr, N. L., Garst, J., Lewandowski, D. A., & Harris, S. E. (1997). That still, small voice: Commitment to cooperate as an internalized versus a social norm. *Personality and Social Psychology Bulletin, 23*(12), 1300–1311.

Kluger, A. N., & DeNisi, A. (1996). The effects of feedback interventions on performance: A historical review, a meta-analysis, and a preliminary feedback intervention theory. *Psychological Bulletin, 119*(2), 254–284.

Kormos, C., Gifford, R., & Brown, E. (2015). The influence of descriptive social norm information on sustainable transportation behavior: A field experiment. *Environment and Behavior, 47*(5), 479–501.

Kredentser, M. S., Fabrigar, L. R., Smith, S. M., & Fulton, K. (2012). Following what people think we should do versus what people actually do: Elaboration as a moderator of the impact of descriptive and injunctive norms. *Social Psychological and Personality Science, 3*(3), 341–347.

Lapinski, M. K., Maloney, E. K., Braz, M., & Shulman, H. C. (2013). Testing the effects of social norms and behavioral privacy on hand washing: A field experiment. *Human Communication Research, 39*(1), 21–46.

Linder, J. A., Meeker, D., Fox, C. R., Friedberg, M. W., Persell, S. D., Goldstein, N. J., & Doctor, J. N. (2017). Effects of behavioral interventions on inappropriate antibiotic prescribing in primary care 12 months after stopping interventions. *JAMA, 318*(14), 1391–1392.

Margetts, H., John, P., Escher, T., & Reissfelder, S. (2011). Social information and political participation on the Internet: An experiment. *European Political Science Review, 3*(3), 321–344.

McKenzie-Mohr, D., Lee, N. R., Kotler, P., & Schultz, P. W. (2011). *Social marketing to protect the environment: What works.* Newbury Park, CA: SAGE.

Miller, D. T., & Prentice, D. (1996). The construction of social norms and standards. In E. T. Higgins & A. W. Kruglanski (Eds.), *Social psychology: Handbook of basic principles* (pp. 799–829). New York: Guilford Press.

Morris, M. W., Hong, Y. Y., Chiu, C. Y., & Liu, Z. (2015). Normology: Integrating insights about social norms to understand cultural dynamics. *Organizational Behavior and Human Decision Processes, 129*, 1–13.

Mortensen, C. R., Neel, R., Cialdini, R. B., Jaeger, C. M., Jacobson, R. P., & Ringel, M. M. (2017). Trending norms: A lever for encouraging behaviors performed by the minority. *Social Psychological and Personality Science, 10*(2), 201–210.

Neighbors, C., Larimer, M. E., & Lewis, M. A. (2004). Targeting misperceptions of descriptive drinking norms: Efficacy of a computer-delivered personalized normative feedback intervention. *Journal of Consulting and Clinical Psychology, 72,* 434–447.

Nolan, J. M. (2011). The cognitive ripple of social norms communications. *Group Processes and Intergroup Relations, 14*(5), 689–702.

Nolan, J. M., Schultz, P. W., Cialdini, R. B., Goldstein, N. J., & Griskevicius, V. (2008). Normative social influence is underdetected. *Personality and Social Psychology Bulletin, 34,* 913–923.

Perkins, H. (Ed.). (2003). The emergence and evolution of the social norms approach to substance abuse prevention. In *The social norms approach to preventing school and college age substance abuse: A handbook for educators, counselors, and clinicians* (pp. 3–17). San Francisco: Jossey-Bass.

Perkins, H., & Berkowitz, A. D. (1986). Perceiving the community norms of alcohol use among students: Some research implications for campus alcohol education programming. *International Journal of the Addictions, 21*(9–10), 961–976.

Perkins, H., Linkenbach, J. W., Lewis, M. A., & Neighbors, C. (2010). Effectiveness of social norms media marketing in reducing drinking and driving: A statewide campaign. *Addictive Behaviors, 35*(10), 866–874.

Phelps, K., Large, L., Schultz, P. W., & Ettlinger, J. (2017). Keeping compostables out of the trash. *BioCycle, 58,* 16.

Posner, R. A., & Rasmusen, E. B. (1999). Creating and enforcing norms, with special reference to sanctions. *International Review of Law and Economics, 19,* 369–382.

Priebe, C. S., & Spink, K. S. (2015). Less sitting and more moving in the office: Using descriptive norm messages to decrease sedentary behavior and increase light physical activity at work. *Psychology of Sport and Exercise, 19,* 76–84.

Prince, M. A., Reid, A., Carey, K. B., & Neighbors, C. (2014). Effects of normative feedback for drinkers who consume less than the norm: Dodging the boomerang. *Psychology of Addictive Behaviors, 28*(2), 538–544.

Raska, D., Nichols, B. S., & Shaw, D. (2015). When descriptive norm cues fail as persuasion agents in green supermarket advertising. *Journal of Promotion Management, 21*(6), 721–738.

Reese, G., Loeschinger, D. C., Hamann, K., & Neubert, S. (2013). Sticker in the box!: Object–person distance and descriptive norms as means to reduce waste. *Ecopsychology, 5*(2), 146–148.

Reese, G., Loew, K., & Steffgen, G. (2014). A towel less: Social norms enhance pro-environmental behavior in hotels. *Journal of Social Psychology, 154*(2), 97–100.

Reno, R. R., Cialdini, R. B., & Kallgren, C. A. (1993). The transsituational influence of social norms. *Journal of Personality and Social Psychology, 64,* 104–112.

Richetin, J., Perugini, M., Mondini, D., & Hurling, R. (2016). Conserving water while washing hands: The immediate and durable impacts of descriptive norms. *Environment and Behavior, 48*(2), 343–364.

Rivas, A., & Sheeran, P. (2003). Social influences and the theory of planned behavior: Evidence for a direct relationship between prototypes and young people's exercise behavior. *Psychology and Health, 18*(5), 567–583.

Robinson, E., Fleming, A., & Higgs, S. (2014). Prompting healthier eating: Testing the use of health and social norm based messages. *Health Psychology, 33*(9), 1057–1064.

Robinson, E., Thomas, J., Aveyard, P., & Higgs, S. (2014). What everyone else is eating: A systematic review and meta-analysis of the effect of informational eating norms on eating behavior. *Journal of the Academy of Nutrition and Dietetics, 114*(3), 414–429.

Robinson, E., Tobias, T., Shaw, L., Freeman, E., & Higgs, S. (2011). Social matching of food intake and the need for social acceptance. *Appetite, 56*(3), 747–752.

Rogers, T., Goldstein, N. J., & Fox, C. R. (2018). Social mobilization. *Annual Review of Psychology, 69,* 357–381.

Rozin, P., Lowery, L., Haidt, J., & Imada, S. (1999). The CAD triad hypothesis: A mapping between three moral emotions (contempt, anger, disgust) and three moral codes (community, autonomy, divinity). *Journal of Personality and Social Psychology, 76,* 574–586.

Schultz, P. W. (1999). Changing behavior with normative feedback interventions: A field experiment on curbside recycling. *Basic and Applied Social Psychology, 21,* 25–36.

Schultz, P. W., Nolan, J. M., Cialdini, R. B., Goldstein, N. J., & Griskevicius, V. (2007). The constructive, destructive, and reconstructive power of social norms. *Psychological Science, 18,* 429–433.

Schultz, P. W., Nolan, J. M., Cialdini, R. B., Goldstein, N. J., & Griskevicius, V. (2018). The constructive, destructive, and reconstructive power of social norms: Reprise. *Perspectives on Psychological Science, 13*(2), 249–254.

Schwartz, S. H. (Ed.). (1977). *Normative influences on altruism.* New York: Academic Press.

Scribner, R. A., Theall, K. P., Mason, K., Simonsen, N., Schneider, S. K., Towvim, L. G., & Dejong, W. (2011). Alcohol prevention on college campuses: The moderating effect of the alcohol environment on the effectiveness of social norms marketing campaigns. *Journal of Studies on Alcohol and Drugs, 72*(2), 232–239.

Sherif, M. (1966). *The psychology of social norms.* New York: HarperCollins.

Smith, S. W., Atkin, C. K., Martell, D., Allen, R., & Hembroff, L. (2006). A social judgment theory approach to conducting formative research in a social norms campaign. *Communication Theory, 16*(1), 141–152.

Sparkman, G., & Walton, G. M. (2017). Dynamic norms promote sustainable behavior, even if it is counternormative. *Psychological Science, 28*(11), 1663–1674.

Spartz, J. T., Su, L. Y. F., Griffin, R., Brossard, D., & Dunwoody, S. (2017). YouTube, social norms and perceived salience of climate change in the American mind. *Environmental Communication, 11*(1), 1–16.

Stok, F. M., de Ridder, D. T., de Vet, E., & de Wit, J. B. (2014). Don't tell me what I should do, but what others do: The influence of descriptive and injunctive peer norms on fruit consumption in adolescents. *British Journal of Health Psychology, 19*(1), 52–64.

Stok, F. M., de Vet, E., de Ridder, D. T., & de Wit, J. B. (2016). The potential of peer social norms to shape food intake in adolescents and young adults: A systematic review of effects and moderators. *Health Psychology Review, 10*(3), 326–340.

Stok, F. M., Mollen, S., Verkooijen, K. T., & Renner, B. (2018). Unravelling social norm effects: How and when social norms affect eating behavior. *Frontiers in Psychology, 9,* 738.

Stok, F. M., Verkooijen, K. T., de Ridder, D. T., de Wit, J. B., & de Vet, E. (2014). How norms work: Self-identification, attitude, and self-efficacy mediate the relation between descriptive social norms and vegetable intake. *Applied Psychology: Health and Well-Being, 6*(2), 230–250.

Tajfel, H. (1974). Social identity and intergroup behaviour. *Social Science Information, 13,* 65–93.

Triandis, H. C. (1995). *Individualism and collectivism.* Boulder, CO: Westview.

Walton, G. M., & Wilson, T. D. (2018). Wise interventions: Psychological remedies for social and personal problems. *Psychological Review, 125*(5), 617–655.

Weber, J. M., Kopelman, S., & Messick, D. M. (2004). A conceptual review of decision making in social dilemmas: Applying a logic of appropriateness. *Personality and Social Psychology Review, 8*(3), 281–307.

White, K., & Simpson, B. (2013). When do (and don't) normative appeals influence sustainable consumer behaviors? *Journal of Marketing, 77*(2), 78–95.

CHAPTER 19

Dynamic Norm Interventions
How to Enable the Spread of Positive Change

Gregg Sparkman

Social problems where a majority of people contribute to the problem are especially difficult to solve. For example, how can we motivate people to live sustainably when many unsustainable behaviors are currently the norm? More generally, how can we dislodge problematic and widely endorsed norms? One answer is to focus people's attention on dynamic norm information: changes in others' behavior or attitudes over time. The research on dynamic norms reviewed here finds that drawing attention to positive changes in others can inspire observers to change their ways even when that change goes against the current norm. Further, dynamic norm interventions have a variety of strengths that may make them more effective than traditional norm interventions that focus solely on static information about the norms in the present moment. These findings substantially extend the contexts in which social norm interventions can be employed to those where current norms are problematic and give a clearer understanding of how social influence may perpetuate social problems, as well as solve them.

BACKGROUND

Social norms constitute one of the most reliable and powerful sources of influence on human behavior (Asch, 1952; Cialdini & Goldstein, 2004). Given their influence, social norms have been used in interventions across a wide range of contexts, including those related to health (Lewis & Neighbors, 2006), environmental sustainability (Goldstein, Cialdini, & Griskevicius, 2008; Schultz, Nolan, Cialdini, Goldstein, & Griskevicius, 2007), intergroup conflict (Paluck, 2009), civic action (Gerber & Rogers, 2009), and more (Tankard & Paluck, 2016; Miller & Prentice, 2016). Generally, these interventions operate by highlighting a positive norm—that others typically act in an appropriate way—in order to sway people to abandon counternormative behaviors or attitudes that

429

are problematic. For instance, one might send a letter to those who are late in paying their taxes that includes a statement that most people have already paid their taxes, and they are part of a very small minority of people who have not, in order to increase the payment rates of recipients (see Hallsworth, List, Metcalfe, & Vlaev, 2017).

But what can you do if the current norm is not "good"? In some cases, behaviors we hope to encourage may be done by the population very infrequently, done by only a small minority, or otherwise be counternormative. Similarly, current norms may be problematic or maladaptive, and do not reflect the desired outcome for those designing interventions. This is the case for many social problems. Indeed, severe social problems are, almost by definition, contexts where many or most people contribute to the problem. In such cases, conformity to existing norms can perpetuate the problem and forestall change. Fortunately, recent research on social influence has provided a possible solution: Learning that norms are changing over time and heading in a positive direction can help motivate people to abandon current norms to create positive social change (Sparkman & Walton, 2017). In other words, learning that others are changing can motivate people to follow suit, even if it means going against the current norm.

This form of intervention requires differentiating between *static* and *dynamic* norm information. Static norms refer to information about the behaviors and attitudes of others in the present moment (e.g., "Many people text while driving"). Dynamic norms refer to information about the trends in norms or changes in others' behavior and attitudes over time (e.g., "More and more people are starting to avoid texting while driving"). This conceptual distinction is fairly recent, and, upon reflection, nearly all past work in social influence and related interventions has focused on static norms. Prior research has shown that people conformed to whatever norm information their attention was focused on, whether it be about others' attitudes or behavior (Cialdini, Kallgren, & Reno, 1991). But until recently, it was unknown whether people also conformed to information that other people are changing.

This question was initially pursued in a behavioral context with substantial environmental and health impacts: high levels of meat consumption (see Gerber et al., 2013; Nijdam, Rood, & Westhoek, 2012). In countries like the United States, meat consumption is a salient and well-reinforced norm: People eat meat in social and public settings and the norm is echoed by default options at almost all restaurants. However, there was a substantial multiyear decline in meat consumption per capita in the United States starting in the late 2000s (Bittman, 2012). Would drawing people's attention to this dynamic norm increase their interest in eating less meat, even though that behavior was counternormative? A series of studies compared the effects of static and dynamic norms by randomizing participants to either learn about the static norm that some people make an effort to limit how much meat they eat, or learn about the dynamic norm that, in recent years, some people had changed and started to make an effort to eat less meat (Sparkman & Walton, 2017). We found that learning about the dynamic norm—that others were changing over time—was more influential and piqued people's interest in eating less meat, even though only a minority of people currently did so. In other words, the actions of a minority were more influential when people knew it was a growing minority (see also Mortensen et al., 2017).

These findings show that a growing minority can help entice people to abandon problematic norms. More generally, they showed that people were sensitive to information about others changing over time. This raised another possibility: In cases where the current norms are already desirable, would learning about a growing majority be more influential than learning about a static majority? Further research, discussed below, suggests this is the case. Thus, the broad implications of dynamic norms for interventions are twofold: first, dynamic norm interventions can help create change that goes against the grain of current norms; second, in contexts where current norms already reflect desirable outcomes, dynamic norm interventions can strengthen traditional norm interventions by adding information about positive changes in others' behavior over time.

PSYCHOLOGICAL PROCESSES

Dynamic norms are influential for many of the same reasons that past research has found static norm information to be influential. When we witness a majority of people behaving a certain way, we are likely to infer that this behavior is effective, efficient, or wise. We may also suspect that most people disapprove of those who act in a counternormative way. Therefore, norms are said to possess both "informational influence" and "normative influence" (Deutsch & Gerard, 1955). Essentially, we may be persuaded to conform to a norm we see because we assume there is good reason it is the norm (informational influence), and because we may fear the reputational costs of going against the grain (normative influence). Indeed, motives to be accurate and to be liked by others drive conformity to norms across a wide range of contexts (Cialdini & Goldstein, 2004; Cialdini & Trost, 1998). Just as someone may infer that something is the norm for a good reason, they may also infer that widespread changes are happening for a good reason. And just as someone may be worried that acting against the group will lead to social rejection, they may also worry that if they do not keep up with trends, they will be "left behind" and fall out of favor with others.

Although there are some similarities in how static and dynamic norms function, there are also unique inferences people may draw from dynamic norms that make them especially suited to encourage people to change. For instance, when we learn that something is becoming more popular, we may infer that a larger number of people will act that way in the future (Mortensen et al., 2017). In the aforementioned work on meat consumption, participants who read a dynamic norm message were more likely to assume that a larger number of people would make some effort to eat less meat in the coming years as well (Sparkman & Walton, 2017). Further, believing that more people would be cutting back on meat in the future increased people's interest in reducing one's own meat consumption. More generally, seeing people change *now* invites us to consider a future world where those trends have continued and where the norms may be different. Then we may conform to those anticipated changes as if they were a current reality. This process is referred to as "preconformity," and enables dynamic norms to encourage conformity to future norms that have not yet arrived. Consistent with this theory, we found in a follow-up study that when people were told about the recent decline in meat consumption, but then told that the trend was not expected to continue, this information was no longer influential.

Further, dynamic norms may be especially well equipped to address a variety of potential concerns about change. Consider the wide variety of psychological barriers that could stand in the way of change: people may doubt that change is possible, that change is important enough to pursue, that change is "for people like me," or have other identity-related concerns. Imagine you shared these concerns, but then witnessed many people changing: Would it still seem like change wasn't possible if many people were doing it? Would it still feel unimportant if people, en masse, put in the effort to alter their habits and make changes? If the people changing are people who, like you, did not do it before, would it still seem incompatible with the kind of person you are? Broadly, dynamic norms convey that others have changed despite whatever reasons were anticipated to stand in the way. By providing social proof that contradicts our expectations, dynamic norms invite us to reconsider these common psychological barriers to change.

Further, the barriers that loom largest in a context are the ones that should be called into question when we learn that other people are changing. This would suggest that dynamic norms operate by resolving whichever barriers people anticipate in a given context. A series of experiments explored this idea (Sparkman & Walton, 2019). One study examined the context of quitting smoking, where doubts of being able to quit often prevent people from trying. Here, we found that learning that others were successful in their attempts to change led participants to believe they could succeed in changing, too.

Another study examined a very different context, where identity-related barriers are present: men identifying as feminist and supporting feminist legislation. Here, we found that learning that some men were changing and starting to identify as feminist helped men see feminism as more compatible with their own identity, increased self-identification as feminist, and increased policy support for the Paycheck Fairness Act. In these and other contexts, dynamic norms signal that others overcame expected barriers to change, or that the barriers they imagined were perhaps not barriers at all (see Table 19.1). Moreover, across all of these studies, static norms alone did not help resolve these barriers, or did so significantly less than dynamic norms. Thus, it appears that dynamic norms have a unique ability to challenge these barriers in contexts where they loom large.

In a follow-up study designed to experimentally assess whether dynamic norms help resolve barriers that are more salient or loom large, participants read about late-night screen use, including an op-ed that discussed how it can disrupt one's quality of sleep (Sparkman & Walton, 2019, Experiment 5). Participants saw one of four versions of this op-ed, each written to highlight a different barrier that made it hard to avoid late-night screen use. One version, for example, was written to raise concerns that participants might lack the ability to change this habit. In it, participants read about how experts thought late-night screen use was similar to an addiction. It also included testimonies

TABLE 19.1. Dynamic Norm Effects on Different Psychological Barriers to Change

Psychological barrier (and example context)	Effects of dynamic norms
"Change is not possible" (e.g., quitting smoking).	Increased belief that change is possible
"Change is not important enough to pursue" (e.g., late-night screen use).	Increased belief that others feel change is important enough to pursue
"Change is not for people like me" (e.g., men identifying as feminist).	Increased belief that a change would be consistent with one's sense of identity

Note. In each context, dynamic norms help whichever barrier looms large within these contexts.

from people who had tried to quit late-night screen use but had repeatedly failed to do so despite its negative impacts on their lives. In a different version of the op-ed designed to highlight identity-related concerns, participants read about how experts thought that late-night screen use had become a normal part of people's lives and identities. It also gave testimonies from people who remarked that the only people they knew who did not look at screens at night were people they did not identify with, such as Luddites or older adults. Next, half of the participants read a dynamic norm statement about how many people had recently changed and started to avoid late-night screen use. Those who only saw the op-ed, but did not learn that people had changed, were more likely to be concerned about whichever psychological barrier that had been discussed in the op-ed (e.g., if they read that people had struggled to quit, they were less likely to believe they could quit, too). But those who read about these concerns in the op-ed, and then read about the dynamic norm, no longer showed concern over the barrier that had been discussed in the op-ed. Notably, dynamic norms helped improve perceptions only about whichever barrier had been discussed in the op-ed, and did not help with the barriers that seemed irrelevant. This study helps confirm that dynamic norms operate by calling into question whichever barriers loom largest for people. More generally, these findings highlight how dynamic norms can help resolve a variety of different psychological barriers that stand in the way of change and may be helpful across a wide range of contexts.

EMPIRICAL EVIDENCE

Dynamic norm interventions have been developed in a variety of domains. In one field experiment aimed at encouraging people to act against current meat-eating norms, participants waiting in line to order lunch at a café were given a survey in exchange for a discount on lunch. Surveys were randomized to include either static or dynamic norm information about meat consumption, or information about something irrelevant to meat consumption as the control group. Those in the static norm read that "Recent research has shown that 30% of Americans make an effort to limit their meat consumption. That means that 3 in 10 people eat less meat than they otherwise would." Those in the dynamic norm read "Recent research has shown that, over the last 5 years, 30% of Americans have started to make an effort to limit their meat consumption. That means that, in recent years, 3 in 10 people have changed their behavior and begun to eat less meat than they otherwise would." In the control survey, participants read about a decline in Facebook use. When the survey was complete, participants were given a coupon for a discount on lunch. Unbeknown to participants, each coupon could be used to identify their experimental condition and track their food-ordering behavior later. Orders among the static norm and control conditions were roughly similar—about one in six persons bought a meatless lunch. But these numbers doubled in the dynamic norm condition, with one in three persons buying a meatless lunch (Sparkman & Walton, 2017).

Dynamic norms research conducted independently by Mortensen and colleagues (2017) has examined the effects of being told about a growing minority, but in this case in the domain of conserving water. In one study, they found that people were more likely to conserve water in the laboratory when they learned that a *growing* minority had done so than when simply learning about a static norm that a minority had done so. In a second study, they found that participants were more likely to donate their time to an environmental charity when they had learned that a growing minority of people had done so, as compared to both a neutral control, and that a (static) minority had done so. These studies examined contexts of "trending norms" in which the minority was on the precipice of becoming a majority (48%, specifically).

This work has found that a dynamic norm message about a growing minority was more influential than a static norm about a minority.[1] But what about in contexts where the desired behavior is already the norm and done by a majority? Is there some benefit of adding dynamic norm information here as well? In other words, can a growing majority be more influential than a static one? One study examined whether dynamic norms would help encourage water conservation during a drought by encouraging university residents to use full loads of laundry (Sparkman & Walton, 2017). In this randomized controlled trial, residential buildings were either assigned to a static norm, dynamic norm, or control condition. In the static and dynamic norm conditions, signs were hung in the laundry facilities with conservation messages. The static norm signs highlighted that most residents used full loads of laundry, while the dynamic norm signs highlighted that *residents were changing and now most used full loads of laundry*. The static norm messages led to a (nonstatistically significant) 10% reduction in water use over the 3-week intervention period, while the dynamic norm messages led to a (significant) 29% reduction in usage. This work demonstrates that dynamic norms can strengthen traditional norm intervention approaches.

MECHANISM

How are dynamic norms able to achieve these behavioral outcomes? As discussed, research has found that dynamic norms can impact several psychological factors that are important to behavior change. In the context of meat consumption, for instance, research finds that learning that others are changing and eating less meat leads them to infer that others must have put in some effort to make this change because they felt it was of substantial importance (Sparkman & Walton, 2017). Therefore, dynamic norms can help shift perceptions of prescriptive norms that others care about this behavior change enough to pursue it. As mentioned, "preconformity" was also a source of influence in this context: It was found that information about others eating less meat also led participants to infer that the norm in the future would be different (i.e., that the trend of eating less meat would continue), which increased their motivation to eat less meat. Further, expectations of future norm levels were also shown to be a driving factor in motivating participants to conserve water in the laboratory research conducted by Mortensen and colleagues (2017). However, given that dynamic norms can impact a variety of important psychological processes, depending in part on which barriers loom largest, it is important to note that different mechanisms are likely to drive conformity to dynamic norms in different contexts.

---

[1] Since these original findings others have conducted conceptual replications and found similar results. For instance, one intervention found that posting signs in a café that contained a dynamic norm message about an increase in people choosing to use a reusable coffee mug (something done only by a minority) led to more people choosing to use a reusable mug and reduced the number of disposable cups used (Loschelder, Siepelmeyer, Fischer, & Rubel, 2019).

EFFECTS OVER TIME

Prior research finds that social norms are a prevalent factor in our decision making (Ajzen, 1985; Terry, Hogg, & White, 1999). However, this literature also emphasizes that norms have to be salient in order to have effects (Cialdini et al., 1991). This would suggest that norm interventions will have direct influence over others over time to the extent they maintain salience in people's minds. For instance, research on home energy interventions where households are sent monthly reports comparing their home energy use to their neighbors finds positive effects persist over the course of years so long as the reports continue to be sent (Allcott, 2011). Work on dynamic norms specifically has mostly examined effects on immediate behaviors. In one notable exception, the research on water conservation in laundry usage assessed repeated behavior over a course of 2–3 weeks and did not find any attenuation of effects during that time (Sparkman & Walton, 2017). More generally, the pattern of effects for dynamic norms over time could be similar to the broader body of norms research, which finds that repeated exposure can generate longitudinal effects.

Given that dynamic norms deal with contemporary trends and changes in behavior, those designing interventions need to consider how to give "booster shots" of the intervention that still feel contemporary. For instance, consider the aforementioned intervention where signs were hung in residential laundry facilities that mentioned that many people had changed and now most used full loads to reduce water consumption. If those signs were still up 6 months or a year later, should we assume that residents will look at a dusty sign and still believe this trend is continuing? Would people even notice the signs if they became a long-term part of the landscape? Perhaps not. In this case, new signs with updated norm content could need to be put up from time to time both to increase salience of the signs, and to help the perception that the trends being reported are, in fact, credible and contemporary ones. The general takeaway here is that the content of dynamic norm messages, especially if that content discusses "recent" or "current" changes in others, or responses of others to current events, may need to be edited over time to ensure it is still perceived to be true and relevant at the time it is being seen.

In some cases, we are able to intervene only once in a given population. To what extent can we expect a onetime norm intervention to permanently change behavior? Prior research suggests this is by no means guaranteed, as brief norm messages may be later forgotten and lose impact. But a few general approaches may be considered to extend the duration of a onetime dynamic norm intervention where booster shots are not feasible. First, one may try to incorporate the perception of dynamic norms into people's general day-to-day experiences and meaning-making process. One way to do this would be to create a reminder of the dynamic norm perception that is reinforced every time the behavior in question is observed. For instance, in the context of meat consumption intervention materials one could say, "Every time you see someone eating a meatless dish or see vegetarian dishes listed at a restaurant, remember that's the direction things are heading," or similarly, "Every time you see someone who eats large amounts of meat for every meal and refuses to try a vegetarian dish from time to time, remember that you are seeing something that is quickly becoming 'old-fashioned.'" There are certainly cases where people look at some behavior and think, "Oh, I have noticed more and more people doing that," or cases where people see something and think, "Wow, how out of touch!" To the extent that dynamic norms interventions can manipulate these beliefs, they may have long-term effects. Much like work on "goal priming" and "goal-relevant cues" (Papies, 2016), the idea here is to help create cues or help people recognize existing cues in their environment that lead them to think about the dynamic norm at or before the point of decision making, so effects persist over time.

One method to achieve long-term outcomes may be to use dynamic norms to change beliefs that underlie important goals, such as goals related to one's well-being or one's identity. For example, as previously noted, dynamic norms about many people success-fully quitting smoking can lead smokers to believe that quitting smoking is easier than they imagined (Sparkman & Walton, 2019). So even while the trend of people quitting may lose salience over time or even be forgotten, the belief that they may be able to quit smoking may persist, which could help smokers attempt to quit. Similarly, men who learned that other men are changing and starting to identify as feminist can come to believe that being a feminist is not at odds with who they are. And while the trend may quickly decline in salience, the notion that being a feminist is "for people like me" could persist. This may lead them to be more open or feel more comfortable engaging when issues pertaining to gender inequality come up, like discussions in the classroom or work-place. More generally, the duration of dynamic norm effects will likely depend on how long lasting the dynamic norm's impact is on beliefs that are of major consequence to the behaviors one is trying to intervene on.

Another approach used by many interventions is to operate as a "foot in the door" for a lengthier commitment that comes next. For instance, one could first offer partici-pants a dynamic norm about meat consumption, and then once their interest in eating less meat is piqued, get them to sign up for a weekly e-mail letter that gives tips on how to cook more vegetarian dishes and highlights local restaurants that have well-reviewed plant-based options. In the laundry context, one could imagine first using the dynamic norm message, and then once residents are motivated to conserve water, offer them a larger laundry bin that has a "full" line indicating when they have enough laundry to do a load. Here, dynamic norms may be especially effective as the first step in a two-part intervention that is followed by an "implementation-intention intervention" (see Leven-thal, Singer, & Jones, 1965, for an example). This would work by using dynamic norms to motivate people to create an intention to change their behavior, and then intervening to channel those intentions into a concrete plan that makes it simple to follow through on their actions in the long haul.

Finally, it is worth noting that in many cases, onetime behaviors have long-term ben-efits. Deciding to install solar panels or water-saving shower heads, or persuading voters to pass a ballot measure, may only require an appeal to succeed once. Dynamic norm interventions, such as those in the existing literature, can be readily translated to these kinds of structural or political decision-making contexts without as much concern over how to maintain the longevity of the desired effects.

HETEROGENEITY

In what contexts should dynamic norms be effective, and when will they be less helpful? One obvious context where dynamic norms should not be effective are cases where key barriers to personal change are structural or otherwise not psychological. For instance, if an intervention sought to increase the use of mass transit in a city, but the city's mass transit system was inaccessible to the target audience, dynamic norms about an increase in people using mass transit would not be likely to help. Generally, dynamic norms are unlikely to enable change or challenge salient barriers if people have no real affordance to change.

Even where change is technically possible, the effectiveness of dynamic norms may still depend on contextual factors. Existing research on dynamic norms shows they are effective largely because they signal inferences that can help encourage personal change, such as altering perceptions of future norms, self-efficacy beliefs, identity-related beliefs, and so on. While this work suggests dynamic norms should be effective against a variety of psychological barriers in a variety of contexts, it is also possible that certain contextual factors will impede these change-promoting inferences and impact the effectiveness of dynamic norm interventions. In particular, existing narratives about change in a given behavioral context (such as beliefs about why or how a change is happening) are likely to have a dramatic impact on the inferences people draw from dynamic norms. For instance, a smoker who learns that others are succeeding in quitting smoking may doubt that they too can quit *if* a common narrative conveys that only a privileged few can quit smoking, such as those who are wealthy enough to purchase helpful resources, or who live less stress-filled lives because of relative high status. Generally, we have to interpret the changes we see, and as we attempt to make sense of change, we are likely to reach for existing narratives to help us explain that change. In behavioral contexts with narratives that steer people away from inferences that encourage personal change, we should not expect dynamic norms to be effective.

Just as behavioral contexts vary in their existing narratives for change, so too do individuals vary in their personal narratives and existing understandings of what a particular change may mean. For example, if some men have an existing narrative that the only reason other men are starting to identify as feminist is because they feel pressured to do so, they may not find it compatible with their identity to follow suit. Generally, we should expect dynamic norms to be more effective for subpopulations that do not possess narratives that hamper change-promoting inferences.

However, dynamic norm interventions dealing with behavioral contexts or individuals who have problematic existing narratives of change are not a lost cause. Those designing an intervention could hone the dynamic norm content to actively resist such narratives. Using the prior smoking example, one could highlight that many of the people who quit were, in fact, low income. In the feminism example, one could highlight that a lot of men began to identify as feminist not because they felt pressured to do so but because they were finally willing to stand up for their beliefs *despite being pressured not to do so*. In any event, successful dynamic norm interventions will have to be aware of the existing narratives of change for the behavioral context and across individuals in order to better understand how the dynamic norm will be understood, and whether that understanding will help promote change.

Some may wonder whether dynamic norms are more effective for those thought to be more favorable to any kind of social change, such as those who are politically liberal or young in age. Thus far, dynamic norms examined in the contexts of meat consumption, quitting smoking, avoiding late-night screen use, avoiding sugary beverages, and endorsing feminist politics have not found any moderation by political orientation, age, or gender. In all of these contexts, dynamic norm effects on interest in personal change were found to have similar effect sizes across these demographic dimensions. However, for a given behavioral context, if a particular demographic is more likely to have an interpretation of change that does not promote personal change, we should expect weaker effects for that group.

Further, in some contexts, it may be easier or harder to manipulate the salience of the dynamic norm as desired. Even when a dynamic norm is stated directly, it does not guarantee a rise in salience (e.g., see Sparkman, Weitz, Robinson, Malhotra, & Walton, 2020, Studies 5–7). In some contexts, dynamic norm information may already be highly salient, in which case the intervention is effectively redundant with naturally occurring norm observations. In such cases, the salience of a dynamic norm may effectively be at ceiling level and unable to be raised. Alternatively, discussing the rise of an unfamiliar behavior that is highly unusual may, ironically, lead people to fixate on the counternormative status of that behavior (the static norm), instead of the information about change. For instance, consider the dynamic norm statement "More and more people are installing composting toilets in their home." This behavior is so deviant from the present norm that people may not even process this as information about norms changing over time, or many individuals changing, but simply get stuck thinking about how strange or unusual composting toilets may be. Therefore, raising the salience of dynamic norms may prove difficult for behavior changes that are either *already salient,* or *completely unknown.* Conceptually, dynamic norm interventions aim not just to provide information about change but to make the fact that others are changing stand out more than it otherwise would.

COUSINS

Dynamic norm interventions are an extension of prior norm interventions research. The core features of these interventions are similar as they both utilize information about others to instigate personal change. But what makes dynamic norms unique is that, at their core, they deal with representations of others' change. As such, they can serve as a psychological road map of how to get from point A to point B. This provides some advantages over traditional static norm interventions. Specifically, three benefits have thus far been mentioned. First, one can use dynamic norm interventions in cases where the desired behavior is obviously counternormative, so long as there is improvement over time. Second, in contexts where the desired behavior is already normative, learning about a growing majority may be more influential than just a static one. And third, that information about others changing can convey inferences helpful for others considering change (e.g., that change is possible; that others feel that something is important enough to change for; and that it is normal for "people like me," who have never done something before to change, to start changing).

A fourth potential benefit is that dynamic norm interventions may be able to avoid condemning those who have not yet changed and thereby may avoid making people feel defensive. Consider the basic conceptual appeal (implicit or explicit) of a typical static norm message hoping to change someone's behavior: "Most people do this, and if you are in the minority of people who do not do this, you are wrong and should change." This may be problematic as people often struggle to accept negative information about themselves or their current behavior (Sherman & Cohen, 2006; Sherman, Nelson, & Steele, 2000) that can prevent people from being inspired by others' actions (Minson & Monin,

2012; Sparkman & Attari, 2020) and hamper positive behavior change (Armitage, Harris, & Arden, 2011; Epton & Harris, 2008). In fact, norm messaging that leads people to feel overly pressured can, ironically, be less effective (Howe, Carr, & Walton, 2020). By contrast, dynamic norm appeals essentially convey that "others are changing, and you should, too." So, while static norms convey that one is outside of the majority and ought to change to conform to it, dynamic norms convey that people like you are currently changing and thereby avoid the implication that you were foolish for not having changed yet. Dynamic norms are therefore unique as they can still apply social pressure to change, but without positioning the target of the intervention as a member of a mistaken minority. In contexts where people are likely to be defensive, dynamic norms may allow for an approach to get people to consider change that is more sympathetic to their current state.

However, there may also be some drawbacks of using a dynamic norm intervention rather than a static norm intervention. For instance, if a problematic behavior is done by a growing minority of people, highlighting this negative change could yield ironic effects. Instead, one should use a static norm intervention to motivate conformity to the present norm and curb the negative changes. Additionally, in some cases, the rapid adaptation of a behavior can serve as a sign that it is a fad and will soon pass; such is the case with the rapid rise in popularity of specific baby names (Berger & Le Mens, 2009). In cases where existing beliefs about change strongly suggest something is a fad, a static norm may be more persuasive.

INTERVENTION CONTENT AND IMPLEMENTATION

How was information about dynamic norms constructed and delivered in past interventions? As mentioned in the café study, participants encountered the dynamic norm materials in a survey where they were paid to closely examine it and respond to it shortly before they chose something for themselves for lunch. Participants therefore had a high level of engagement with the materials, which they experienced immediately before the point of decision making in order to maximize impact. The full dynamic norm statement, as it was presented, read:

> Some people are <u>starting to limit</u> how much meat they eat. This is true both nationally and here at Stanford.
>
> Specifically, recent research has shown that, over the last 5 years, 30% of Americans have started to make an effort to limit their meat consumption.
>
> That means that, in recent years, 3 in 10 people have *changed their behavior* and begun to eat less meat than they otherwise would.

Each sentence directly indicates that people are changing or have changed. The first statement is meant to help participants recognize that the change is large in magnitude to emphasize the importance of the matter ("nationally"), while still pertaining to a relevant ingroup ("and here at Stanford"), which has been shown to strengthen norm statements (Rimal & Real, 2005). Subsequent statements add detail that clarify that these changes are due to people who have *intentionally* altered their behavior, which was chosen to convey that others believe this is something worth changing for. Participants were then asked, "Why do you think this is?" in order to guide them in elaborating the reasons why one would change. In doing so, we are inviting participants to articulate reasons they find to be compelling to change and eat less meat.

In the study targeting full loads of laundry, participants in the dynamic norm condition read the following message on signs hung in laundry facilities: STANFORD RESIDENTS ARE CHANGING: NOW MOST USE FULL LOADS! accompanied by an illustration of a laundry machine with a "full" line indicated, and HELP STANFORD CONSERVE WATER! Similar to the café study, the first line clearly articulates that a relevant ingroup is making intentional changes in their behavior, and this change is portrayed as substantial (such that with these changes, those who use full loads now constitute a majority). The signs were hung on the wall behind the laundry machines so that seeing them would occur naturally as one was about to do laundry. Thus, the information was available immediately before deciding whether to combine different types of clothing into a full load, or divide up one's clothing into many smaller loads (lights, darks, delicates, etc.). In the section below, I further articulate the logic behind these choices and how to create effective dynamic norm interventions.

NUANCES AND MISCONCEPTIONS

In designing the content to be used in a dynamic norm intervention, one must make decisions about how to represent social change. For instance, should one simply give a qualitative description of the trend? "More and more people are doing this." Or would a detailed quantitative representation be more effective? "In the past 5 years, 20% of people have started doing this." Or would a visual representation of the change, such as a line graph over time, be better yet? Further, one needs to decide exactly which dynamic norm information to include: simply the direction of change? The direction, duration, and pace of change? Who is changing and who is not? How are people making this change? Are people successful or not in making this change? Are they making this change intentionally or not? Should it be said or implied that the change is intrinsically motivated (e.g., people really care about this), or extrinsically motivated (e.g., people are responding to a financial incentive or legal punishment)? Additionally, one must decide whether and how to present peripheral information, such as the source of the information, who the messenger is, and what their motives are. Aside from the content of the dynamic norm, there is also a choice of medium (Posters hung in public places? Letters sent to homes? E-mails?) and a variety of aesthetic choices. The answer to all of these questions likely depends in large part upon the population one is working with, the behavioral context, and practical limitations, such as the project budget. However, there are some general guidelines in designing successful dynamic norm interventions that are discussed below, including having the message be believable, easily noticed, personally elaborated (by the target audience), signaling intentionality, and being delivered at relevant times for the decision-making process. While these guidelines are informed by prior research in other domains, it is important to note that they remain a prospect for future research to better ascertain how important each is for dynamic norm interventions.

The intervention materials should be *believable*. When people feel they are asked to change something substantial, the credibility and quality of the message is a key factor in their decision making (Langer, Blank, & Chanowitz, 1978; Petty, Cacioppo, &

Goldman, 1981). If the information provided seems unbelievable to the target audience, it is very possible that it will simply be dismissed. In some cases, providing supporting evidence may be necessary. For example, someone reading the statement "More men are starting to consider themselves feminist" may wonder what exactly they were just told: Is this supposed to be the author voicing their opinion? Is it grounded in some truth? And if it is true, how did the author come to know this information? It is not simply visible by looking around a public space. Further, is the change due to cohort differences (younger men identify as feminist more than older ones)? Or is it that specific men have actually changed? Readers may better understand that the message contains dynamic norm information and have fewer lingering questions if they read "More men are starting to identify as feminist. Specifically, a recent poll finds that many men, who did not consider themselves feminist before, have changed and now do." While no quantitative numbers were introduced, and no specific sources were listed (or a specific time frame or population, for that matter), the information presented does give a simple and complete narrative regarding what kind of social change has occurred and how we know about it. Of course, skeptics may still want to know details, such as what the actual percentage of change was, in what population, who conducted the poll, when it was conducted, how "feminist" was defined in the poll, and so on. But in cases where the population will take the information that is presented at face value, a short and coherent message is likely best.

The intervention materials should be *noticed* and, ideally, *contemplated*. People conform to norm information more when it is salient to them (Cialdini et al., 1991). However, getting people to open a letter that was mailed to them, or read a sign in public, is not easy to do. It is harder yet to get people to take their time and actively engage with intervention materials so that they understand the social change being conveyed and arrive at specific inferences that will induce personal change. In a survey context, one can explicitly ask respondents to discuss why they think a change is happening or what that change means in order to ensure they give it adequate attention and time. But in the context of a sign hung in a hallway, or a billboard along a roadway, there is no captive audience—the content has to be visually interesting and sufficiently brief to engage the observer. In some contexts where people are so busy that contemplation is unlikely, like a billboard next to a freeway, it may be ideal to explicitly state the important inferences alongside the dynamic norm: MANY PEOPLE ARE QUITTING SMOKING, *and You Can Too*. The advantage being that we do not need to gamble on whether busy drivers reach the important inference on their own. But, this does come at a cost: had they made the inference on their own that they could quit, they might more strongly believe it to be true, as discussed below.

The intervention materials should lead *observers to generate a persuasive argument to change on their own, rather than explicate the full argument for them*. In many cases, when people are directly told what to do, they may rebel in order to maintain a sense of freedom and personal choice (Brehm, 1966). Imagine you read a billboard that said STOP LOOKING AT ELECTRONIC DEVICES BEFORE GOING TO BED, IT'S BAD FOR YOUR SLEEP! This might invite someone to think, "C'mon, how bad could it really be?" Or perhaps they'll think, "Thanks, *Mom*," and reject the nagging tone of the message. To avoid such a reaction, interventions should gently guide people to a point where they draw conclusions that are favorable to change *on their own* so that they engage in "self-persuasion" (see Aronson, 1999). Dynamic norms can enable this process: others' change often garners our attention, and may lead us to wonder how or why are people changing as we try to make sense of the world around us. Those designing interventions should capitalize on people's intrigue with change, and use it to get the audience to create persuasive reasons for why others are changing. Consider the following message: "More and more people are choosing to avoid looking at their electronic devices at night before going to bed." After reading this, people are likely to automatically start trying to explain why many people would do this, and try to recall whether they have heard anything about the detriments of looking at electronic screens late at night. They might recall an article they once saw saying it disrupted sleep, or maybe they think about their own late-night device use, and how it often keeps them up later than they want to be. If so, they are more likely to internalize the idea that it may not be such a good idea to spend hours at night looking at a screen before bed.

Importantly, some dynamic norm messages may be better than others at leading people to identify reasons to change behavior. For instance, imagine you read that "Time spent using electronic devices late at night has declined in recent years." Compared to the prior dynamic norm message on screen use, this one does not remark on decision making or *intentionality* of others, and is generally distant from the psychological experience of people choosing to change their behavior. People reading this may wonder whether others are losing interest in smartphones and tablets given their waning novelty, or whether other late-night activities have become more popular. Critically, it does not lead the reader to envision strong reasons to avoid or change this behavior. Further, in cases where one learns about a decline in smoking, it may be ambiguous whether that decline is due to smokers actually quitting, or simply to younger generations not smoking as much as prior ones. The latter interpretation would not lead one to believe in others' or their own ability to quit. Generally, in order for dynamic norms to lead to helpful inferences about personal change, they should be written to clearly convey that social changes are due to many people intentionally making changes in their lives.

The intervention materials should be delivered *in a place and time that facilitate change*. In many cases, it is ideal to deliver information about others' changes just before the point of decision making. Consider the café study mentioned earlier where we gave people dynamic norm information as they waited in line before reaching the café's menu stand. Had the message come much earlier, such as on a billboard they read that morning, people may simply have forgotten about the dynamic norm information, and any positive shifts in opinion they had may have faded away before they had the opportunity to act. If we had given them the message after they reached the menu stand and already made a selection for lunch, then the task of encouraging change would have been much harder: We would no longer be trying to persuade someone that it is a good idea to order a meatless dish, but instead we would have to persuade participants to abandon their existing preference, even though they were already anticipating eating that dish. Generally, dynamic norm interventions should review when and where people are making decisions in order to find the proper moment to interject information about others' change.

Taken together, one should think carefully about how to deliver the dynamic norm information in a way that attracts attention and succeeds in getting people to engage with the content. That content should ring true to observers, and lead them to think about why change would be suitable for themselves. This process should occur in a time and a place shortly before important junctions in their decision making for that behavior.

IMPLICATIONS FOR PRACTICE

As mentioned, it may be wise to combine dynamic norm interventions with implementation-intention interventions to create longer-lasting effects. However, this point is also important in interventions that target immediate behavior. Designing a successful intervention will require making sure other basic prerequisites to change behavior are met: Even if sufficiently motivated by the dynamic norm content, people must also be *informed and knowledgeable about how to change behavior*, and *capable of changing behavior*. This means likely having to assess the gaps in people's knowledge about how to change their behavior, and provide information to remove any ambiguity. For example, in the intervention targeting water conservation through using full loads of laundry, talking to residents led us to discover that many were unsure of how full a "full load" was supposed to be. Many also thought that loads that were near full were actually "overfilled," such that the clothing would not get cleaned. This meant that some people thought a "full load" was actually about half or two-thirds full, when in actuality it was about seven-eighths full, very near the top. Therefore, in addition to hanging highly visible signs with dynamic norm information, we also placed stickers directly on the machines in both norm conditions that indicated when a load was full, and another sticker indicating that the load was not full roughly near the half-full line. While perhaps seeming obvious, these stickers helped ensure that people were sufficiently informed about how to do a full load. Had we hung the signs without adding the stickers, it is possible that people would have been motivated to do full loads, but may not have reliably translated that motivation into behavior change. They could look at a three-quarter-filled load or even a half-filled load and think, "I guess that's full enough." When in doubt, make things foolproof by providing people with enough information so that the desired behavior is clear and how to enact it is obvious.

While I have largely discussed how to use text to display dynamic norm information, other mediums may be just as, or more, effective. In some cases, having people physically model the desired changes in behavior in the real world may be more effective than simply presenting written statements telling people that others are changing (see Dorn & Stöckli, 2018, for an example). We might imagine, for example, that reading signs saying that more grocery store customers are beginning to use reusable bags may be influential, but seeing each person in front of you in line purchase a reusable bag when given the option may be a stronger signal. Physical manifestations of norm information may also be highly noticeable, and if they are naturalistic, they may be highly influential as well (e.g., Keizer, Lindenberg, & Steg, 2008). Seeing many homes in your neighborhood install bars on the windows, for instance, may be a strong signal that your neighborhood is becoming more dangerous. While it may be hard to envision how an intervention would be able to manipulate such mediums without a massive undertaking, it is possible to shift the salience of a dynamic norm without physically changing the context dramatically. For example, imagine that solar installers targeted and prioritized installations for highly salient homes at visible intersections because it would lead people to believe that more and more people in their neighborhood were getting solar power. Shifting perceptions of norms through changes in the physical environment, media, or institutional signals rather than actual norm levels is employed in a variety of norm interventions (see Tankard & Paluck, 2016, for a review) and can be done for dynamic norm interventions as well.

IMPLICATIONS FOR PSYCHOLOGICAL THEORY

What do dynamic norms teach us about how people think and how to solve social problems? We have long known that people are highly attentive to others and often conform to how they act, and what they believe. It has been argued that our interest and conformity to others is driven by a fundamental psychological need to share common ground with others in understanding and purpose (Asch, 1952; Hardin & Higgins, 1996). We feel compelled to see things the way others do, and for them to see things the way that we do. People therefore converge on a common shared reality from which any divergence is acting against the grain. But research on dynamic norms suggests that this is not the whole story. It demonstrates that social influence is an evolving process—one where people are particularly sensitive to information about other people changing in ways that can drive people to alter how they see the world and how they decide to act. Therefore, social influence is not only a force of greater convergence on current norms, it is also a force that can be harnessed for social change. Indeed, looking at wide-scale social changes that have taken place historically, large numbers of people often change rapidly, abandoning prior norms and converging on new ones.

It is notable that dynamic norms can help resolve diverse barriers to change in a variety of contexts, and do so by helping resolve the barriers that loom largest for people. Thus, dynamic norms interventions may be a particularly flexible and resilient way to create change, and those designing interventions may not need to identify the specific barriers to change in a given context, so long as they seem more surmountable when others change.

FUTURE DIRECTIONS

Many important areas for future research on dynamic norm interventions have already been discussed, including the need to design and assess interventions aimed at longitudinal outcomes, and systematically test which presentations of dynamic norm information are the most effective. In addition, further research can help clarify how to translate dynamic norm effects into highly scalable formats, how understanding dynamic norm effects can help curb undesirable behaviors that are becoming more popular over time, and whether dynamic norm interventions can improve the effectiveness of current interventions that typically rely on static norms.

Scaling up dynamic norm interventions presents a number of questions to be further explored. In the context of reducing meat consumption, for instance, it may be possible to incorporate dynamic norm information about the rise in popularity of meatless dishes into restaurant menus. While highly scalable, and delivered very near the point of decision making, such an intervention would no longer be able to ensure that people notice or actively engage customers. Generally, more research is needed to better understand how dynamic norm messages can be translated to passive reading contexts and still manage to actively engage the target audience to elucidate psychological inferences that have been shown to drive effects.

Dynamic norms may hold the answer to another kind of important intervention context besides those investigated here: What should one do when undesirable behaviors are becoming more popular over time? Understanding how the direction of change influences others may hold the key to stopping problematic changes before they spread. The current research suggests that making novel problematic behaviors less salient should help. It also suggests that it may be worth assessing whether portraying changes as likely to be short-lived ("a fad"), or done for reasons that go against the target audience's broader values, would be helpful. However, research has not yet assessed a dynamic norm intervention aiming to intervene on existing norm changes to halt them. Further, more research is needed to understand whether regressive changes spread via the same psychological mechanisms as those discussed here or because of novel processes.

Further, there are a number of places where static norm interventions are presently used that might be strengthened by using dynamic norm information instead. Many utility companies, for instance, provide static social norm feedback to their customers that compares their home's energy use to their neighbors' energy use in order to encourage users to decrease their monthly usage. If results are similar to those examined in the studies here, providing dynamic norm information about the positive changes in one's neighbors' energy savings over time may improve the effects of such interventions. Given how widely social norm interventions are used, there are many areas where comparing the effectiveness of dynamic and static norm interventions may highlight areas for improvement.

REFERENCES

Ajzen, I. (1985). From intentions to actions: A theory of planned behavior. In J. Kuhl & J. Beckmann (Eds.), *Action control* (pp. 11–39). Berlin: Springer-Verlag.

Allcott, H. (2011). Social norms and energy conservation. *Journal of Public Economics, 95*(9–10), 1082–1095.

Armitage, C. J., Harris, P. R., & Arden, M. A. (2011). Evidence that self-affirmation reduces alcohol consumption: Randomized exploratory trial with a new, brief means of self-affirming. *Health Psychology, 30*(5), 633–641.

Aronson, E. (1999). The power of self-persuasion. *American Psychologist, 54*(11), 875.

Asch, S. E. (1952). Group forces in the modification and distortion of judgments. In *Social psychology* (pp. 450–501). Englewood Cliffs, NJ: Prentice-Hall.

Berger, J., & Le Mens, G. (2009). How adoption speed affects the abandonment of cultural tastes. *Proceedings of the National Academy of Sciences of the USA, 106*(20), 8146–8150.

Bittman, M. (2012, January). We're eating less meat: Why? Retrieved February 1, 2019, from *https://opinionator.blogs.nytimes.com/2012/01/10/were-eating-less-meat-why*.

Brehm, J. W. (1966). *A theory of psychological reactance.* Oxford, UK: Academic Press.

Cialdini, R. B., & Goldstein, N. J. (2004). Social influence: Compliance and conformity. *Annual Review of Psychology, 55*(1), 591–621.

Cialdini, R. B., Kallgren, C. A., & Reno, R. R. (1991). A focus theory of normative conduct: A theoretical refinement and reevaluation of the role of norms in human behavior. *Advances in Experimental Social Psychology, 24*(20), 201–243.

Cialdini, R. B., & Trost, M. R. (1998). Social influence: Social norms, conformity and compliance. In D. T. Gilbert, S. T. Fiske, & G. Lindzey (Eds.), *The handbook of social psychology* (4th ed., Vol. 1, pp. 151–192). New York: McGraw-Hill.

Deutsch, M., & Gerard, H. B. (1955). A study of normative and informational social influences upon individual judgment. *Journal of Abnormal and Social Psychology, 51*(3), 629–636.

Dorn, M., & Stöckli, S. (2018). Social influence fosters the use of a reusable takeaway box. *Waste Management, 79,* 296–301.

Epton, T., & Harris, P. R. (2008). Self-affirmation promotes health behavior change. *Health Psychology, 27*(6), 746–752.

Gerber, A. S., & Rogers, T. (2009). Descriptive social norms and motivation to vote: Everybody's voting and so should you. *Journal of Politics, 71*(1), 178–191.

Gerber, P. J., Steinfeld, H., Henderson, B., Mottet, A., Opio, C., Dijkman, J., & Tempio, G. (2013). *Tackling climate change through livestock: A global assessment of emissions and mitigation opportunities.* Rome: Food and Agriculture Organization of the United Nations.

Goldstein, N. J., Cialdini, R. B., & Griskevicius, V. (2008). A room with a viewpoint: Using social norms to motivate environmental conservation in hotels. *Journal of Consumer Research, 35*(3), 472–482.

Hallsworth, M., List, J. A., Metcalfe, R. D., & Vlaev, I. (2017). The behavioralist as tax collector: Using natural field experiments to enhance tax compliance. *Journal of Public Economics, 148,* 14–31.

Hardin, C. D., & Higgins, E. T. (1996). Shared reality: How social verification makes the subjective objective. In E. T. Higgins & R. M. Sorrentino (Eds.), *Handbook of motivation and cognition: Vol.3. The interpersonal context* (pp. 28–84). New York: Guilford Press.

Howe, L., Carr, P., & Walton G. M. (2020). *Normative appeals are more effective when they invite people to work together toward a common cause.* Manuscript under review.

Keizer, K., Lindenberg, S., & Steg, L. (2008). The spreading of disorder. *Science, 322*(5908), 1681–1685.

Langer, E. J., Blank, A., & Chanowitz, B. (1978). The mindlessness of ostensibly thoughtful action: The role of "placebic" information in interpersonal interaction. *Journal of Personality and Social Psychology, 36*(6), 635–642.

Leventhal, H., Singer, R., & Jones, S. (1965). Effects of fear and specificity of recommendation upon attitudes and behavior. *Journal of Personality and Social Psychology, 2*(1), 20.

Lewis, M. A., & Neighbors, C. (2006). Social norms approaches using descriptive drinking norms education: A review of the research on personalized normative feedback. *Journal of American College Health, 54*(4), 213–218.

Loschelder, D. D., Siepelmeyer, H., Fischer, D., & Rubel, J. A. (2019). Dynamic norms drive sustainable consumption: Norm-based nudging helps café customers to avoid disposable to-go-cups. *Journal of Economic Psychology, 75*(A).

Miller, D. T., & Prentice, D. A. (2016). Changing norms to change behavior. *Annual Review of Psychology, 67,* 339–361.

Minson, J. A., & Monin, B. (2012). Do-gooder derogation: Disparaging morally motivated minorities to defuse anticipated reproach. *Social Psychological and Personality Science, 3*(2), 200–207.

Mortensen, C. R., Neel, R., Cialdini, R. B., Jaeger, C. M., Jacobson, R. P., & Ringel, M. M. (2017). Trending norms: A lever for encouraging behaviors performed by the minority. *Social Psychological and Personality Science, 10*(2), 201–210.

Nijdam, D., Rood, T., & Westhoek, H. (2012). The price of protein: Review of land use and carbon footprints from life cycle assessments of animal food products and their substitutes. *Food Policy, 37*(6), 760–770.

Paluck, E. L. (2009). Reducing intergroup prejudice and conflict using the media: A field experiment in Rwanda. *Journal of Personality and Social Psychology, 96,* 574–587.

Papies, E. K. (2016). Health goal priming as a situated intervention tool: How to benefit from nonconscious motivational routes to health behaviour. *Health Psychology Review, 10*(4), 408–424.

Petty, R. E., Cacioppo, J. T., & Goldman, R. (1981). Personal involvement as a determinant of argument-based persuasion. *Journal of Personality and Social Psychology, 41*(5), 847–855.

Rimal, R. N., & Real, K. (2005). How behaviors are influenced by perceived norms: A test of the theory of normative social behavior. *Communication Research, 32*(3), 389–414.

Schultz, P. W., Nolan, J. M., Cialdini, R. B., Goldstein, N. J., & Griskevicius, V. (2007). The constructive, destructive, and reconstructive power of social norms. *Psychological Science, 18*(5), 429–434.

Sherman, D., & Cohen, G. L. (2006). The psychology of self-defense: Self-affirmation theory. *Advances in Experimental Social Psychology, 38,* 183–242.

Sherman, D., Nelson, L. D., & Steele, C. M. (2000). Do messages about health risks threaten the self?: Increasing the acceptance of threatening health messages via self-affirmation. *Personality and Social Psychology Bulletin, 26*(9), 1046–1058.

Sparkman, G., & Attari, S. Z. (2020). Credibility, communication, and climate change: How lifestyle inconsistency and do-gooder derogation impact decarbonization advocacy. *Energy Research and Social Science, 59,* 101290.

Sparkman, G., & Walton, G. M. (2017). Dynamic norms promote sustainable behavior, even if it is counternormative. *Psychological Science, 28*(11), 1663–1674.

Sparkman, G., & Walton, G. M. (2019). Witnessing change: Dynamic norms help resolve diverse barriers to personal change. *Journal of Experimental Social Psychology, 82,* 238–252.

Sparkman, G., Weitz, E., Robinson, T. N., Malhotra, N., & Walton, G. M. (2020). Developing a scalable dynamic norm menu-based intervention to reduce meat consumption. *Sustainability, 12*(6), 2453.

Tankard, M. E., & Paluck, E. L. (2016). Norm perception as a vehicle for social change. *Social Issues and Policy Review, 10*(1), 181–211.

Terry, D. J., Hogg, M. A., & White, K. M. (1999). The theory of planned behaviour: Self-identity, social identity and group norms. *British Journal of Social Psychology, 38*(3), 225–244.

Author Index

Subject Index

Note. *f, n,* or *t* following a page number indicates a figure, note, or a table.